9/99

W9-BZC-936

W9-BZC-936

REVOLUTIONARY AMERICA
1763 to 1800

REVOLUTIONARY AMERICA
1763 to 1800

Thomas L. Purvis

Richard Balkin
General Editor

Facts On File, Inc.

Revolutionary America, 1763 to 1800

Facts On File, Inc.
11 Penn Plaza
New York NY 10001

Library of Congress Cataloging-in-Publication Data
Purvis, Thomas L., 1949–
     Revolutionary America, 1763–1800 / Thomas L. Purvis.
          p.   cm. — (Almanacs of American life)
     Includes bibliographical references (p.) and index.
     ISBN 0-8160-2528-2
     1. United States—Civilization—To 1783—Miscellanea. 2. United
     States—Civilization—To 1783—Statistics. 3. United States—
     Civilization—1783–1865—Miscellanea. 4. United States—
     Civilization—1783–1865—Statistics. 5. United States—History—
     Revolution, 1775–1783—Social aspects—Miscellanea. 6. United
     States—History—Revolution, 1775–1783—Social aspects—Statistics.
     I. Title. II. Series.
     E162.P86   1994
     973—dc20   93-38382

Facts On File books are available at special discounts when purchased in
bulk quantities for businesses, associations, institutions, or sales promotions.
Please call our Special Sales Department in New York at 212/967-8800
or 800/322-8755.

You can find Facts On File on the World Wide Web at http://www.factsonfile.com

Text and jacket design by Fred Pusterla
Maps on pages 6, 9, 12, 15, 18, and 23 by Marc Greene

Printed in the United States of America

VB VC 10 9 8 7 6 5 4 3 2

This book is printed on acid-free paper.

To

Joseph Lee Purvis

"A young gentleman of great expectations."

Note on Photos

Many of the illustrations and photographs used in this book are old, historical images. The quality of the prints is not always up to modern standards, as in many cases the originals are from glass negatives or the originals are damaged. The content of the illustrations, however, made their inclusion important despite problems in reproduction.

Contents

List of Maps

Acknowledgments

Contributing to this volume's completion were numerous persons whose help deserves recognition and my thanks. The staff of the Campbell County, Kentucky, Library at Newport processed what must have seemed like an endless chain of Inter-Library Loan requests for esoteric books and articles. Dr. Conard "Sandy" Carroll aided me in using services at Northern Kentucky University's Steely Library.

Very much of the credit for the high-quality illustrations that grace this volume is due to dedicated curators and idealistic administrators who helped me locate appropriate artwork and avoid unnecessary delays. I wish in particular to acknowledge Wayne Furman's exceptional consideration in making available nineteen prints from the New York Public Library's Office of Special Collections. Special thanks are also due Mary Ison and Jennifer Brathovde for their assistance in expediting a very difficult order for nine illustrations from the Library of Congress's Prints and Photographs Division.

I profited greatly from excellent suggestions on suitable artwork from Nancy Heywood of the Peabody & Essex Museum, Alan Gowans of the National Images of North American Living's Research and Archival Center, Harry Hunter and Barbara Clark Smith of the Smithsonian Institution, and Dennis Moyer of the Schwenkfelder Library.

For offering helpful assistance and special considerations in a variety of ways, I also wish to thank Michael Averdick of the Kenton County, Kentucky, Library, James Addington of the Ohio Bureau of Environmental Services, Jennifer Code of the American Antiquarian Society, Janet Deranian of the Historical Society of York County, Pennsylvania, Martha Harrison and Hildegard Stephens of the American Philosophical Society, Elizabeth McLaughlin of the Delaware Art Museum, and Arlene Shy of the Clements Library.

I would finally like to recognize the valuable improvements that resulted from series editor Richard Balkin's suggestions and the hard work by Nicole Bowen and Christa Sidman at Facts On File.

Preface

Because so many books have been written about the American Revolution, most people would assume that information regarding that period is readily accessible. In fact, although a wealth of data exists concerning the years from 1763 to 1800, it remains scattered among such a wide variety of government publications, scholarly monographs, and journal articles that few libraries have collections large enough to conduct research in depth on more than a few of this era's topics. Historians have produced many source books on the Revolution, but nearly all either are documentary collections of narratives written by politicians and soldiers, or are narrowly defined studies of particular subjects.

The full extent of the difficulty in finding quick answers to questions about Revolutionary America can be illustrated through the book that currently stands as the best reference source on United States history, the U.S. Census Bureau's two-volume *Historical Statistics of the United States: Colonial Times to 1970* (Washington, D.C., 1975). Out of 1,200 pages, the *Historical Statistics* devotes just 33 pages to data for the entire period from 1607 to 1789. This work includes no information for the 1790s on health, the labor force, working conditions, consumer expenditure patterns, education, crime, or housing, and next to nothing on agriculture, incomes, banking, manufacturing, immigration, slavery, and most other topics. Even when topics are covered for the Revolutionary era in the *Historical Statistics*—such as the federal budget, international trade, and the first two national censuses—they are reprinted in far less detail than is available in the original sources.

Revolutionary America, 1763–1800 provides libraries with a compendium of basic quantitative data from the most important government sources and scholarly studies. It includes more than 425 statistical tables. It places these tables in scholarly perspective with brief sketches or extended essays (as are appropriate) summarizing current ideas on the broadest range of topics about early American society and culture. To enhance the reader's appreciation of this period, the text includes nearly one hundred illustrations and maps.

Whenever possible, information has been selected or essays added that give insight into everyday life. It should be understood that many experiences that are universal in the twentieth century were less common in the eighteenth, and vice versa. In the most pure sense, a book about everyday life in the 1700s would focus heavily on the work rhythms of white farm families, who made up the great majority of the population. Most small farmers (as opposed to highly literate, wealthy planters) who left diaries recorded little outside of the weather and crop prices. This work has set more ambitious goals for itself and attempts to provide insight into numerous circumstances affecting the widest range of people, not just the majority who were white agriculturalists.

The closer one examines Revolutionary America, the more questions seem to arise about how ordinary people were affected by larger social, cultural, and political developments. How did war disrupt the lives of men and women? How much of their income was siphoned off by taxes and inflation? What was education like, and what types of reading material were available to adults? How did the economic cycle affect a family's financial well-being? How likely was an average person to run for office? What sort of employment opportunities existed as alternatives to farming? Did the character of the general population shift due to changing demographic patterns? How were people affected by living in different cities or states? In all these regards, everyday life was affected quite directly by larger political or economic trends.

Certain considerations governed the presentation of tables and other descriptive information. Although perhaps most scholars of early America have arranged statistical tables in descending order from the earliest date to the most recent, this book presents columns of numbers in ascending order. In doing so, it follows the example of the Census Bureau's previously mentioned *Historical Statistics of the United States,* which has the best claim to serve as a model for standardizing the organization of quantitative materials.

As a reference work, this volume incorporates phraseology that is two centuries old. Some terms of that age, especially those concerning race or ethnicity, have become dated, either because they carried disparaging connotations or simply because newer words have become fashionable. As a rule, this work retains original labels when reprinting tables or quotations; it does so not in order to endorse "politically incorrect" or dated language, but only to ensure a historically correct context. Otherwise, this volume uses interchangeably the terms *Anglo-American* and *white, African American* and *black,* and *Native American* and *Indian.*

In any conventional historical almanac, one would expect to find reprints of such political documents as the Declaration of Independence, the Constitution, the Bill of Rights, and many others such as the Virginia and Kentucky Resolutions. The editors and I reluctantly decided to exclude them for two reasons. First, no shortage exists of source books that reprint these materials, and everyone could readily find them among any library's reference shelves. Second, these documents are so lengthy that they could not be included without cutting much other material that is far less accessible and more relevant to everyday life. In their place is substituted a group of autobiographical memoirs that reveal the lives of four ordinary Americans: a Pennsylvania woman captured and adopted by Indians, a Continental private from Connecticut, a Rhode Island slave who served the army as a teamster, and a lad who grew up on a frontier farm in Kentucky. As the final chapter, they form the most appropriate conclusion for a book on everyday life in that era.

Thomas Purvis
Associate Editor
American National Biography

REVOLUTIONARY AMERICA
1763 to 1800

CHAPTER 1 Climate, Natural History, and Historical Geography

Climate

Systematic weather data was first collected within the United States during the eighteenth century. Reliable meteorological instruments had come into use by 1700, and observations based on them date from 1715 in North America. Climatic record-keeping nevertheless depended on a small number of amateur scientists who could seldom coordinate their activities, and consequently they left an incomplete and haphazard body of statistics. Because surviving tables of temperature are rare, and measurements of precipitation are almost nonexistent before 1800, the handful of remaining records merits special scrutiny as the sole source of documentation about atmospheric conditions in Revolutionary times.

Temperature in the late eighteenth century had changed greatly since 1700. After the so-called Little Ice-Age (which was most intense 1550–1700), the Northern Hemisphere experienced a warming trend that moderated winters and lengthened the growing season. This change occurred rapidly, for Thomas Jefferson noted that even middle-aged Americans had noticed that the climate had become much more temperate during their lifetimes by 1780. By then, at least south of New England, snow rarely covered the ground for all of winter, and rivers seldom froze over. Jefferson noted how the vicinity of Monticello, Virginia went 28 years without losing any fruit to frost prior to 1770.

Late-eighteenth-century weather conditions were very similar to those of the twentieth century. Mean temperatures were slightly lower at that time, but the variance equaled less than one degree Fahrenheit. An unusually complete table of atmospheric warmth has been reconstructed for Philadelphia from 1763 to 1800, and in comparison with temperatures from the twentieth century it shows that mean annual temperatures had risen only 0.3 degree by 1980. Comparison with a less complete series of data compiled by Thomas Jefferson reveals that average temperatures at Williamsburg, Virginia were just 0.4 degree higher by 1980 than they had been in the 1770s. The amount of precipitation at Philadelphia remained constant at 41.4 inches over the same two centuries, while rainfall at Williamsburg barely increased over the 47.038 inches measured by Jefferson in the 1770s to 47.57 inches between 1950 and 1980.

Because approximately 25% of Americans lived within 125 miles of Philadelphia in 1775, that city's meteorological records provide the best indication of weather's impact on agriculture. The chance of losing crops to early or late frosts seems to have been slight, since only four of the 38 springs from 1763 to 1800 are known to have averaged less than 50 degrees (compared to a mean of 53.6) and the coldest autumn was just 54.7 (compared to a mean of 56.1). The probability of ground being too wet at planting time was minor, for winter and spring's combined precipitation exceeded the mean of 18.36 inches by more than 2.5 inches only twice from 1763 to 1800. The likelihood of crops being spoiled before harvest by excessive rain was also slim, since total precipitation in summer and autumn surpassed the average of 21.7 inches by over 2.5 inches just twice during the same period. Aside from a few brief periods, farmers enjoyed optimal conditions for maximizing output and stood minimal risk of losing a year's crop.

TABLE 1.1 SEASONAL AND ANNUAL PRECIPITATION (INCHES) AT PHILADELPHIA, PA., 1763–1800

	Winter[a]	Spring[b]	Summer[c]	Autumn[d]	Year
1800	8.39	11.89	11.61	9.61	41.61
1799	8.11	10.39	13.11	9.21	42.72
1798	8.31	10.91	12.01	9.21	41.22
1797	8.51	11.18	12.60	9.21	42.01
1796	8.51	9.80	11.50	9.02	40.91
1795	7.40	11.69	13.82	9.49	43.58
1794	8.00	7.72	11.42	8.31	39.41
1793	7.72	10.20	9.09	8.82	39.61
1792	. . .	10.31	9.80	9.41	39.29
1791	9.09	10.39	13.58	10.12	44.41
1790	8.82	10.20	10.98	9.49	39.68
1789	8.90	10.12	12.01	9.69	40.71
1788	9.21	10.59	11.89	9.69	42.09
1787	9.29	10.12	11.85	10.20	42.91
1786	8.82	11.69	11.85	9.02	41.89
1785	9.80	11.89	12.72	10.98	44.21
1784	8.70	11.18	14.29	10.91	44.21
1783	8.51	7.72	15.51	10.79	42.48
1782	. . .	11.30	11.61	9.29	40.98
1781	. . .	. . .	. . .	. . .	. . .
1780	. . .	. . .	. . .	. . .	. . .
1779	7.91	. . .	. . .	. . .	. . .
1778	7.79	8.70	13.19	. . .	40.39
1777	7.40	9.02	12.60	. . .	40.12
1776	. . .	. . .	. . .	8.58	. . .
1775	7.01	. . .	. . .	9.41	. . .
1774	8.31	9.61	11.69	9.41	40.51
1773	7.72	8.58	10.59	8.70	39.68
1772	8.00	9.49	13.39	10.79	42.40
1771	8.58	12.28	11.42	9.02	41.81
1770	8.00	8.19	14.02	9.49	41.10
1769	8.00	9.21	10.00	9.41	39.49
1768	8.19	7.40	12.80	9.09	40.39
1767	7.40	10.51	11.69	9.69	41.30
1766	7.28	10.39	13.39	8.90	40.51
1765	8.39	10.51	12.48	9.21	42.20
1764	8.31	10.31	12.60	9.41	42.01
1763	8.31	9.88	12.28	9.21	40.51
Mean	8.26	10.10	12.22	9.48	41.40

[a] Dec.–Feb.
[b] Mar.–May
[c] Jun.–Aug.
[d] Sep.–Nov.
Note: Data includes snow's equivalent in rainfall. During 1951–1980, precipitation in this area averaged 9.44 inches in winter, 10.51 inches in spring, 11.90 inches in summer, 9.57 inches in autumn, and 41.42 inches annually.
Source: H. H. Lamb, *Climate: Present, Past, and Future,* vol. 2, *Climatic History and the Future* (1977), 625, 626.

TABLE 1.2 COMPARISON OF AVERAGE MONTHLY TEMPERATURES ALONG ATLANTIC COAST, 1763–1800, WITH AVERAGE MONTHLY TEMPERATURES IN 1951–1980

	Cambridge, Mass.[a]			Salem, Mass.[b]		Albany, N.Y.	
	1780–1783	1784–1788	1951–1980	1786–1792	1951–1980	1795–1796	1951–1980
Jan.	28.00	22.50	29.6	24.8	27.8	25.00	21.1
Feb.	30.70	23.90	30.7	25.1	28.5	26.00	23.4
Mar.	36.50	32.90	38.4	36.1	35.8	34.00	33.6
Apr.	48.50	45.10	48.7	45.1	45.2	48.50	46.6
May	58.50	54.40	56.5	56.9	54.8	59.25	57.5
Jun.	68.50	66.10	68.0	67.2	63.9	66.25	66.7
Jul.	73.70	69.60	73.5	69.8	69.6	73.50	71.4
Aug.	72.50	69.40	71.9	69.7	68.4	71.50	69.2
Sep.	64.00	60.00	64.6	61.6	61.5	62.50	61.2
Oct.	50.70	50.10	54.8	49.8	52.2	49.75	50.5
Nov.	37.00	40.20	45.2	40.1	42.7	38.16	39.3
Dec.	31.50	29.04	33.2	27.8	32.1	27.00	26.5
Year	50.01	46.94	51.5	47.9	48.5	48.45	47.3

	New York, N.Y.		Philadelphia, Pa.		Williamsburg, Va.	
	1782–1784	1951–1980	1798–1804	1951–1980	1760–1778	1951–1980
Jan.	25.25	31.8	33.3	31.2	41.43	38.4
Feb.	27.27	33.4	33.4	33.1	43.68	40.2
Mar.	38.75	41.4	41.2	41.8	47.88	47.9
Apr.	49.32	52.4	52.9	52.9	57.59	58.1
May	65.97	62.5	62.1	62.8	64.00	66.3
Jun.	80.37	71.4	71.9	71.6	72.48	73.4
Jul.	81.05	76.7	76.4	76.5	76.49	77.5
Aug.	80.82	75.4	75.6	75.3	75.26	76.7
Sep.	67.10	68.3	68.1	68.2	68.72	70.9
Oct.	54.27	57.7	57.1	56.5	59.41	59.8
Nov.	40.10	47.2	43.7	45.8	47.28	50.4
Dec.	36.50	36.2	34.9	35.5	42.65	41.6
Year	53.90	54.5	54.2	54.3	58.07	58.4

[a] 1951–1980 data from Boston.
[b] 1951–1980 data from Rockport.
Sources: Charles A. Schott, *Tabulation of Resulting Mean Temperatures from Observations Extending Over a Series of Years, . . . for Stations in North America* (1874), 38, 39, 54–55, 60–61, 74–75, 86–87. Edward A. Holyoke, "An Estimate of the Heat and Cold of the American Atmosphere Beyond the European, in the Same Parallel of Latitude," *Memoirs of the American Academy of Arts and Sciences* 2 (1793), 89–92. James A. Ruffner, ed., *Climates of the States* (1985 ed.), 519, 521, 784, 785, 957, 1162.

TABLE 1.3 COMPARISON OF AVERAGE SEASONAL TEMPERATURES RECORDED ALONG ATLANTIC SEABOARD DURING 1763–1800 AND 1951–1980

	Cambridge, Mass.[a]			Salem, Mass.[b]		Albany, N.Y.	
	1780–1783	1784–1788	1951–1980	1786–1792	1951–1980	1795–1796	1951–1980
Spring	47.91	47.83	47.9	46.0	45.3	47.25	45.9
Summer	70.36	71.57	71.1	68.9	67.3	70.42	69.1
Autumn	51.57	50.57	54.9	50.5	52.1	50.14	50.3
Winter	30.36	30.07	31.2	25.9	29.5	26.00	23.7
Yearly	50.05	50.01	51.5	47.9	48.5	48.45	47.3

	New York, N.Y.		Philadelphia, Pa.		Williamsburg, Va.	
	1782–1784	1951–1980	1763–1800	1951–1980	1760–1778	1951–1980
Spring	51.35	52.1	53.6	52.5	56.49	57.4
Summer	80.75	74.5	74.2	74.5	74.74	75.9
Autumn	53.82	57.7	56.1	56.8	58.47	60.4
Winter	29.67	33.8	34.2	33.3	42.59	40.1
Yearly	53.90	54.5	54.0	54.3	58.07	58.4

[a] 1951–1980 data from Boston.
[b] 1951–1980 data from Rockport.
Note: Data was collected from Jan. to Dec. for all columns except Cambridge (Jul. 1780–Dec. 1783), New York (May 1782–Jun. 1784), and Williamsburg (Jan. 1760–Aug. 1778). Seasonal divisions were as follows: Spring (Mar., Apr., May), Summer (Jun., Jul., Aug.), Autumn (Sep., Oct., Nov.), Winter (Dec., Jan., Feb.).
Sources: Charles A. Schott, *Tabulation of Resulting Mean Temperatures from Observations Extending Over a Series of Years, . . . for Stations in North America* (1874), 38, 39, 54–55, 60–61, 74–75, 86–87. Edward A. Holyoke, "An Estimate of the Heat and Cold of the American Atmosphere Beyond the European, in the Same Parallel of Latitude," *Memoirs of the American Academy of Arts and Sciences* 2 (1793), 89–92. H. H. Lamb, *Climate: Present, Past, and Future,* vol. 2, *Climatic History and the Future* (1977), 577, 579. James A. Ruffner, ed., *Climates of the States* (1985 ed.), 519, 521, 784, 785, 957, 1162.

TABLE 1.4 AVERAGE SEASONAL AND ANNUAL TEMPERATURES (FAHRENHEIT) AT PHILADELPHIA, PA., 1763–1800

	Winter [a]	Spring [b]	Summer [c]	Autumn [d]	Year
1800	33.1	53.4	76.1	57.0	54.9
1799	32.0	51.6	75.7	57.0	54.3
1798	31.8	54.1	76.3	57.0	54.9
1797	32.7	52.5	75.2	55.4	54.1
1796	36.7	52.5	75.2	56.3	54.0
1795	35.6	54.3	75.7	58.1	55.8
1794	33.6	53.2	75.4	57.0	55.9
1793	34.5	54.9	76.3	57.4	55.9
1792	31.1	54.9	74.1	56.8	54.9
1791	29.8	55.0	75.6	56.1	54.9
1790	35.1	51.0	74.8	56.8	54.1
1789	30.6	51.6	75.4	55.8	54.0
1788	31.1	52.9	75.4	58.6	54.5
1787	28.8	52.9	73.0	55.9	54.0
1786	30.0	52.3	73.9	55.0	52.9
1785	28.2	48.2	74.7	54.9	52.2
1784	25.2	51.4	74.7	55.8	51.6
1783	36.7	54.7	75.7	55.2	55.0
1782	33.4	54.0	75.6	56.3	54.7
1781	36.7	53.8	75.7	55.2	55.6
1780	. . .	51.4	76.3	56.7	. . .
1779	. . .	. . .	. . .	. . .	. . .
1778	. . .	. . .	. . .	. . .	. . .
1777	. . .	49.8	. . .	. . .	51.1
1776	. . .	51.1	. . .	. . .	53.4
1775	36.5	53.4	72.7	56.7	54.3
1774	37.2	52.5	72.3	56.7	53.8
1773	37.8	53.1	72.9	56.3	54.7
1772	36.0	47.8	72.0	55.8	53.2
1771	37.8	52.2	72.7	56.1	53.1
1770	36.0	50.0	72.9	55.4	53.1
1769	37.4	50.5	72.7	54.9	52.9
1768	37.9	49.6	72.1	55.0	52.7
1767	37.0	51.6	73.8	55.4	53.8
1766	37.9	52.7	73.0	56.3	54.7
1765	36.5	54.0	72.1	55.8	54.3
1764	37.8	. . .	71.4	54.7	. . .
1763	36.0	51.6	71.6	54.9	53.4

[a] December–February
[b] March–May
[c] June–August
[d] September–November
Note: See Table 1.3 for averages during 1951–1980.
Source: H. H. Lamb, *Climate: Present, Past, and Future,* vol. 2, *Climatic History and the Future* (1977), 577.

TABLE 1.5 AVERAGE ANNUAL TEMPERATURES IN EASTERN MASSACHUSETTS, 1772–1800

Year	Salem	Cambridge	Andover	Bedford
1800	49.16	48.52	48.87	. . .
1799	48.63	46.76	47.97	. . .
1798	48.64	47.85	48.87	. . .
1797	47.30	46.82	. . .	. . .
1796	47.84	47.01	. . .	. . .
1795	49.34	49.79	. . .	. . .
1794	49.93	51.53	. . .	. . .
1793	50.13	50.67	. . .	. . .
1792	47.71	48.01	. . .	. . .
1791	48.04	49.71	. . .	. . .
1790	45.97	48.72	. . .	. . .
1789	46.83	. . .	. . .	. . .
1788	47.01	. . .	. . .	. . .
1787	47.02	. . .	. . .	. . .
1786	47.70	. . .	. . .	. . .
1783	. . .	50.00	. . .	. . .
1781	. . .	49.81	. . .	. . .
1772	. . .	. . .	. . .	48.88

Note: See Table 1.3 for averages during 1951–1980.
Source: Charles A. Schott, *Tabulation of Resulting Mean Temperatures from Observations Extending Over a Series of Years, . . . for Stations in North America* (1874), 257.

TABLE 1.6 DAILY EXTREMES OF TEMPERATURE (FAHRENHEIT) RECORDED AT SALEM, MASS. (1786–1792) AND WILLIAMSBURG, VA. (1772–1777)

	Salem, Mass.			Williamsburg, Va.	
	8:00 A.M.	Noon	Sunset	8:00 A.M.	4:00 P.M.
Jan.	22.1	29.4	25.3	38.5	44.0
Feb.	22.1	30.9	25.2	41.0	47.5
Mar.	35.0	41.4	35.5	48.0	54.5
Apr.	44.3	52.0	45.3	56.0	62.5
May	57.3	63.3	55.7	63.0	70.5
Jun.	67.6	74.6	64.7	71.5	78.25
Jul.	71.0	78.8	69.5	77.0	82.5
Aug.	69.1	76.6	68.8	76.25	81.0
Sep.	59.4	68.3	61.2	69.5	74.25
Oct.	47.6	56.3	49.3	61.25	66.5
Nov.	37.6	45.0	41.7	47.75	53.5
Dec.	24.8	32.3	28.8	43.0	48.75

Note: Salem, Mass. yearly averaged 38 days above 80, and another 5 above 90; it averaged 109 days below 32, and another 4 below 0. Its hottest day was July 13, 1791, at 96, and its coldest days were Jan. 17, 1786 and Jan. 23, 1792, both at −11.
Sources: Edward A. Holyoke, "An Estimate of the Heat and Cold of the American Atmosphere Beyond the European, in the Same Parallel of Latitude," *Memoirs of the American Academy of Arts and Sciences* 2 (1793), 89–92. Thomas Jefferson, *Notes on the State of Virginia* (ed. William Peden, 1955), 74.

Natural History

Environmental Change

The most significant environmental development in the late eighteenth century was the removal of tree cover from large areas of the Atlantic seaboard. Prior to 1760 (when total population in the thirteen colonies stood at about 1,600,000), deforestation had proceeded gradually and primarily affected land within seventy-five miles of the coastline. The speed of clearing wilderness thereafter accelerated rapidly, with the inevitable consequence that wildlife suffered a concomitant decline in variety and density.

The easiest manner of denuding forest was to set large tracts on fire, but this method was often impractical and seems to have been seldom used. If a settler prepared agricultural land through clear cutting—felling every tree in a single season and then hauling away the downed logs—he could open up barely twelve acres per year, even if he left stumps in the ground and plowed around them. Clear cutting was the usual manner of bringing land under cultivation in New England, but other Americans preferred to kill trees by cutting

Frontier farms often presented eerie landscapes like the one shown here, where leafless trees slowly died over a decade from girdling (in which deep rings were gashed into their trunks). When the trees finally fell over, the trunks might be used for fuel or burned to make potash. [engraved by W. J. Bennett, N.A., from the original painting by G. Harvey, A.N.A.] (I. N. Phelps Stokes Collection, Miriam & Ira D. Wallach Div. of Arts, Prints and Photographs. Courtesy The New York Public Library. Astor, Lenox and Tilden Foundations.)

deep rings at their base and waiting for them to fall of their own weight after dying, a process called girdling. (The landowner meanwhile let his livestock forage among the trees or planted crops around the trunks once leaves no longer blocked the sunlight.) Stumps usually did not rot out before seven to ten years, unless they were cut up for fuel in the meantime, and so the transformation from woodland to improved agricultural fields often took a decade to complete.

Many Americans unwittingly contributed to soil erosion by clearing ground that sloped ahead of level terrain. Even though flat fields were easier to sow and harvest, hilly areas had less vegetation and took less effort to open, besides having the advantage of not requiring drainage. Eager to alleviate the heavy labor of hacking away raw wilderness, farmers often cleared sloped fields and in the process produced an unnecessary loss of valuable topsoil.

Rapid deforestation also resulted from the many industries that needed timber. By the 1790s, over 240,000 barrels or hogsheads were required every year to package American exports of tobacco and rice. In 1799, it is estimated that the country's sawmills annually produced 300,000,000 board feet of planks for domestic use or for export. Fences also consumed enormous amounts of wood. The most commonly used style, the Virginia or zigzag design, employed about 4,000 rails just to enclose 40 acres, and even if a straight-line fence

were built using upright posts, the same area could not be surrounded with fewer than 2,200 rails.

The greatest demands on woodland arose from the population's rising need for fuel. Because Americans heated their homes by open chimneys, which were so inefficient that they wasted 80% of all warmth produced, every year the average family burned perhaps 30 cords of wood, which would have equaled an acre of trees. Since the iron industry relied on charcoal rather than coal, it also required enormous amounts of fuel, equal to 750 acres for every hundred tons of pig iron manufactured. Average iron production of 30,000 tons denuded approximately 225,000 acres every year after 1761. (New Jersey's Union Furnace exhausted 20,000 acres of virgin wilderness in no more than fifteen years.) A conservative estimate of the amount of land deforested to provide firewood or charcoal in the late 1700s is given below. The total woodland consumed equaled 28,366,655 acres, or 4.3% of the 657,000,000 acres that are believed to have been forested east of the Great Plains about 1600. In just forty years, Americans burned enough trees to cover an area roughly the size of Pennsylvania.

The reduction in forest eliminated the natural habitat for many animals, fowl, and reptiles. As the frontier expanded, farmers invariably distorted the ecological balance to an even greater degree through widespread destruction of snakes, wolves, wildcats, foxes,

TABLE 1.7 WOODLAND CONSUMED TO PROVIDE FUEL IN UNITED STATES, 1760–1799

Decade	Cords Consumed[a] for Heating Family Homes	Cords Consumed[b] for Iron Production	Acres of[a] Woodland Required
1760–1769	100,000,000	67,500,000	5,583,333
1770–1779	125,000,000	67,500,000	6,416,666
1780–1789	155,000,000	67,500,000	7,416,666
1790–1799	201,000,000	67,500,000	8,950,000
Totals	581,000,000	270,000,000	28,366,665

[a] Final estimate assumes an acre could yield 30 cords.
[b] 300 bushels (225 cords of wood) yielded a ton of iron. Annual output averaged 30,000 tons in the late 1700s.
Source: Michael Williams, *Americans and Their Forests: A Historical Geography* (1989), 77–81, 104–109.

and panthers, either to protect their own barnyard animals or to supplement their income by selling the furs. By eliminating these predators, settlers inadvertently removed the natural limit on the population of smaller rodents like rabbits, mice, and moles, which multiplied in great numbers to become a major nuisance by wreaking havoc on family vegetable gardens.

Destruction of wildlife sometimes proceeded on a massive scale through "big hunts," in which a concentric ring of hunters would drive animals inward and then shoot all that could not escape. During one such "circle drive" across the Susquehanna Valley in 1760, 200 Pennsylvanians under "Black Jack" Schwartz slaughtered 198 deer, 114 bobcats, 112 foxes, 111 bison, 109 wolves, 98 deer, 41 mountain lions, 18 bear, 2 elk, and more than 500 smaller animals.

Overhunting eliminated entire species from areas within a generation or two of settlement. Bison, which had roamed as far east as Pennsylvania and South Carolina, disappeared from those states soon after 1760. Even in Kentucky, a territory where the population density was less than two persons per square mile in 1790, buffalo and elk (which had earlier ranged in enormous herds) had virtually disappeared just twenty years after the first Anglo-Americans had arrived in 1775. Shooting or trapping on such a scale reduced the density of major game animals so far below normal levels, that Indians sometimes complained of hunting being spoiled in areas a hundred miles beyond the edge of white habitation.

Natural Disasters

The greatest danger to life posed by nature came from storms or other hazards at sea. Relatively few major catastrophes can be attributed to the weather, as opposed to poor seamanship, from 1763 to 1800, however, and fewer than 200 fatalities resulted from them. A far greater number of fishermen doubtless perished when caught in small boats too far from land by sudden storms, but no one has ever tallied these losses.

The eastern United States was a far more active earthquake zone during the eighteenth century than in the twentieth. In the thirty-eight years after 1762, Americans experienced eight minor tremors and three major earthquakes. The most powerful quake was centered at East Haddam, Connecticut, on May 18, 1791. Two heavy shocks collapsed stone walls and chimneys, threw open latched doors, moved rocks weighing several tons, and opened a crevasse almost fifty feet long in the ground. Boston and Philadelphia both felt reverberations of this quake, which produced 130 aftershocks within a

TABLE 1.8   NATURAL DISASTERS IN THE UNITED STATES, 1763–1800

Date	Event	Lives Lost
May 27, 1771	Floods swept all rivers in Virginia east of Appalachians. Worst inundation was near Richmond on James River.	. . .
Sep. 1–3, 1772	Hurricane drove fifteen ships onto North Carolina coast near Edenton.	50
Aug. 14, 1773	Violent storm raged across Massachusetts and caught many small vessels at sea.	dozens
Summer 1776	Earthquake reported along Muskingum River in Ohio, in which ground rumbled and furniture was overthrown.	none
1779	Earthquake reported in northern Kentucky and probably felt in Ohio and Indiana.	none
Jan. 1780	Beginning of Kentucky's "hard winter," so cold that game froze in the forest and there was great loss of cattle.	. . .
Winter 1779–80	Severe storms dropped over five feet of snow near Niagara upon homeless Iroquois refugees whose villages and food stocks had been destroyed by Continental forces.	hundreds
May 19, 1780	Smoke from forest fires on "Black Friday" blocked out the sun over Connecticut so densely that candles were needed at mid-day and birds went silent.	. . .
Nov. 29, 1783	An earthquake shook area from New Hampshire to Pennsylvania. New York felt three shocks at 9:00 P.M., 11:00 P.M., and then 2:00 A.M. Philadelphia felt the first and last. Shocks were moderate at Boston and in New England.	none
May 8, 1784	Violent hailstorms struck Winnsborough, S.C. Large hailstones killed some slaves, plus large numbers of sheep, poultry, wild birds, and small animals.	several
May 18, 1791	Earthquake centered on East Haddam, Conn. did much structural damage to houses and stone walls. Fish jumped out of water at Killingworth. Shock extended to Boston and Philadelphia. About 100 aftershocks felt that day and another 30 that night.	none
Spring 1791	Earthquake reported in eastern and northern Kentucky at 7:00 A.M.	none
Aug. 28, 1792	Mild earthquake felt at East Haddam, Conn.	none
Jan. 11, 1793	Mild earthquake felt at East Haddam, Conn.	none
Mar. 6, 1794	Two earth shocks felt at East Haddam, Conn.	none

Date	Event	Lives Lost
Sep. 1, 1794	Southern Louisiana swept by hurricane. Most livestock in lower Mississippi valley were drowned.	unknown
Jan. 8, 1795	An earthquake struck Kaskaskia, Ill. and western Kentucky; it lasted 90 seconds and caused subterranean noise.	none
Aug. 2, 1795	Ship carrying immigrants foundered in a gale off Cape Charles, Virginia.	100
Nov. 17–21, 1798	New England buried by snowstorms so deep that tunnels had to be dug to rescue families trapped in their homes.	dozens
Mar. 17, 1800	Philadelphia struck by an earthquake described as a severe shock.	none
Nov. 29, 1800	Mild earthquake felt at Philadelphia.	none

Sources: Jay R. Nash, *Darkest Hours: A Narrative Encyclopedia of Worldwide Disasters from Ancient Times to the Present* (1976), 665–750. U.S. Coast and Geodetic Survey, *Earthquake History of the United States* (rev. ed., 1965), 6, 11, 19, 29, 31, 41. James Cornell, *Great International Disaster Book* (1982), 267. Stephen J. Pyne, *Fire in America: A Cultural History of Woodland and Rural Fire* (1982), 56.

day. This quake probably would have registered close to 6.0 on the Richter scale.

The United States was fortunate in being spared from any severe natural disasters during the late eighteenth century. The greatest loss of life occurred as an unforeseen consequence of an American military campaign that drove thousands of Iroquois, shelterless and without food, from central New York into the wilderness around Niagara, where several hundred died from malnutrition or exposure to the elements during the unusually harsh winter of 1779–1780.

Historical Geography

Exploration

The French had already completed the initial exploration of territory east of the Mississippi River and published reasonably accurate maps when Britain acquired France's trans-Appalachian territory in 1763. Anglo-Americans made surprisingly few important discoveries during the Revolutionary era. Geographical knowledge expanded, but it grew far more in depth than it did in breadth.

John and William Bartram have been almost entirely forgotten over the last two centuries, but no one traveled more extensively or contributed more information about the American interior during the mid- and late 1700s than they did. A Philadelphia Quaker and self-taught scientist, John Bartram (1699–1777) gained appointment as botanist to the king in 1765. Although sixty-six years old, John used his £50 salary to finance a ten-month journey from Cape Fear in North Carolina to St. Johns River in Florida during 1765–1766, on which he was accompanied by his son William. The expedition catalogued an enormous variety of flora and fauna, much of which had not been previously known to non-Indians, and its journals were printed in London in 1766.

Financed by a wealthy English patron, William Bartram (1739–1823) returned to the Southeast in April 1773 for more extensive scientific investigations. He spent the next forty-three months traveling by horse or canoe—and often alone—from Cape Fear to northern Florida, to North Carolina's mountains, and across central Georgia, central Alabama, and southern Mississippi to the delta of lower Louisiana. An excellent artist, gifted writer, and attentive observer of Indian life, Bartram authored the most detailed account of the southern woodlands prior to their being settled by Anglo-Americans. The printed version of his travels appeared in several editions, and it made him one of the first Americans to win acclaim abroad for scientific accomplishments.

The single explorer of Revolutionary times whose reputation remains familiar to modern Americans is Daniel Boone (1734–1820). Although commonly thought of as the first Anglo-American to find his way to Kentucky, Boone only extended a route through Cumber-

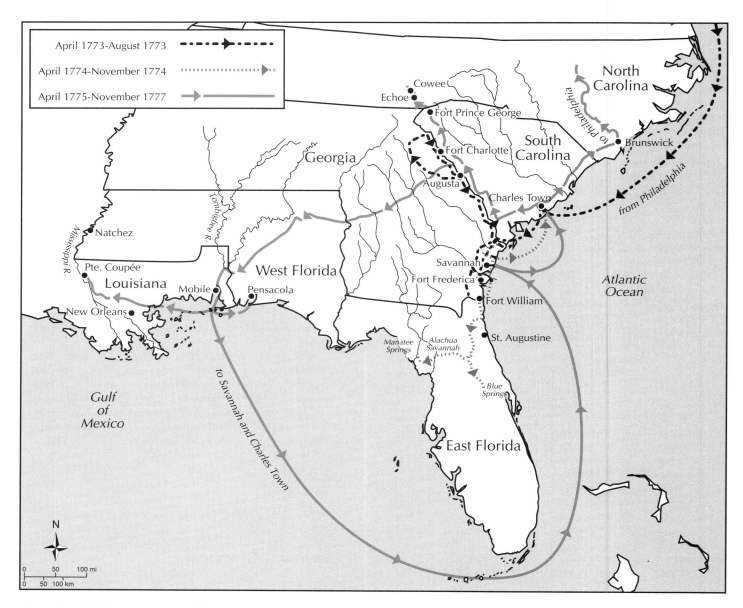

Travels of William Bartram, 1773–1777

No American traveler covered such large tracts of wilderness in such a short period as did the naturalist William Bartram. In less than four years, he rode or canoed from northern Florida to North Carolina's mountains, and then crossed the territory between the Savannah and Mississippi rivers, before returning to Philadelphia overland from Charles Town. Bartram did most of his field work in Indian lands.

land Gap that had first been identified in 1750 by a Virginia doctor, Thomas Walker. Walker never escaped the mountain barrier, but beginning with Christopher Gist in 1750, several wandering hunters had preceded Boone to central Kentucky's fertile meadows. Boone did not see the bluegrass region until 1769, on his second trip across the mountains.

Daniel Boone's true importance as an explorer lay in making a thorough reconnaissance of Kentucky's interior and identifying the best sites for occupation. After spending two years, mostly alone, in Kentucky during 1769–1771, he provided critical information that interested wealthy land speculators in promoting migration to the area. After Richard Henderson purchased title to the area from the Cherokee in 1775, it was Boone who judged the easiest route for wagons to follow from Cumberland Gap to central Kentucky and who blazed the Wilderness Road, which became the primary overland route to the Ohio Valley. During the Revolutionary War, he played a major role in holding the West for the Continental Congress. Now a mythic figure in American history, Daniel Boone played a heroic part in opening the West, but other, less known, men shared in discovering and exploring Kentucky.

Few truly original or important discoveries were made about geography during the late eighteenth century, and all of these events occurred outside the areas then possessed by the United States. Long concealed to passing ships by its thick fog, San Francisco Bay was first sighted by Captain Gaspar de Portola in 1769. Captain Robert Gray of Boston first located the Columbia River in May 1792 while on a voyage to acquire furs from the Indians of the Pacific Northwest for sale in China. By 1800, the territory east of the Mississippi held few secrets, and not until after the Louisiana Purchase of 1803 would the challenge of exploration again loom large for adventurous Americans.

Expansion of Settlement

As the victor of the Seven Years' War, Britain acquired all of its former enemies' territories east of the Mississippi, including Florida. Almost immediately the Royal Army confronted a major Indian uprising (Pontiac's War of 1763–1764) in the Ohio Valley. Pontiac's War convinced the British leaders that avoiding future conflicts required an orderly process of frontier expansion that eliminated Indian grievances by negotiating mutually agreeable treaties for selling land to whites. On October 7, 1763, George III defined the Appalachian crest as the boundary between whites and Indians, ordered settlers beyond there to leave, and required royal permission to buy land from Indians.

The Proclamation of 1763 found many whites already living beyond the Appalachian divide along Virginia's New River and many others streaming west to buy land along the Monongahela River below Pittsburgh. The Iroquois, Cherokee, and Creek furthermore held large areas east of the designated boundary. The proclamation line thus did not serve as a realistic limit for the frontier, and the Crown came under immediate pressure to modify its policies. The Crown also found the Iroquois and Cherokee quite ready to sell claims over the Ohio Valley, in part to obtain trade goods but also to deflect white expansion away from their own heartland and toward tribes with whom they were hostile. Between 1768 and 1772, British authorities approved several treaties that opened all territory below the Ohio River, as far west as the Kentucky River, to white occupation. The Anglo-American presence in western Pennsylvania and southwestern Virginia multiplied rapidly, and in 1769 whites began entering the mountain valleys of northeastern Tennessee. Despite the Proclamation of 1763, settlers steadily took up the best lands in the Appalachian highlands, although they would not break free of of the mountain barrier until 1775.

East of the proclamation line, the frontier surged forward following Britain's victory in the Seven Years' War. Once Maine, Vermont, and central New Hampshire were no longer threatened by France's former Indian allies, Yankees flooded into those areas. From 1763 to 1775, New Englanders founded forty-three new towns in Vermont, sixty-one in New Hampshire, twenty-seven in western Massachusetts, and fifteen in Maine. The Mohawk's willingness to sell or lease their lands allowed New Yorkers to extend their settlements well west and north of Albany, until the Mohawk found themselves entirely encircled by whites. The frontier grew at such a rapid pace in the lower south, which contained vast tracts of sparsely populated land east of Indian territory, that the number of inhabitants in the Carolinas and Georgia more than doubled in the fifteen years after 1760.

By 1772, knowledgeable whites realized that all of modern Kentucky and about half of central Tennessee contained no Indian inhabitants aside from transient parties of hunters or trappers. The Iroquois and Cherokee voluntarily renounced their titles to this area by 1775; and the Shawnee abandoned their claim in 1774 to end Lord Dunmore's War, a brief—but bloody—conflict that escalated from a series of murders and revenge killings near Wheeling, Virginia, and ended with the Treaty of Camp Charlotte. The first per-

Few Americans realize that the most violent period of frontier expansion occurred during the Revolutionary era. Horatio Greenough's statue *The Rescue* portrays the nineteenth century's idealized image of an Anglo-Saxon pioneer (in this case Daniel Boone, who seems to be wearing a helmet). The statue's romantic pose belies the brutal and horrific nature of that warfare. (Once located on the Capitol's east-front staircase, *The Rescue* is now in storage.) (United States Capitol Art Collection, courtesy Architect of the Capitol, Washington.)

manent settlement beyond the Appalachians took place in 1775, when Virginians founded Harrodsburgh, Kentucky. That same year, Richard Henderson, a North Carolina land speculator, sought to engross all the land between the Cumberland and Ohio rivers into a private colony named Transylvania; he employed Daniel Boone to cut the Wilderness Road from Cumberland Gap and build a fort on the Kentucky River. Henderson's land schemes ultimately failed, but they were instrumental in stimulating a significant migration to Kentucky within a few years.

The Revolution greatly slowed the pace of westward migration. The British enjoyed almost universal support from the Indians, who ravaged the frontier incessantly. A steady stream of land-hungry pioneers nevertheless continued to cross the mountains. Tennessee's earliest settlement in the transmontane plateau took place in 1779, when John Donelson founded Nashboro (now Nashville), which became the nucleus for many satellite forts along the Cumberland River. Stockades proliferated even more rapidly in Kentucky, whose militia was primarily responsible for ending British military authority south of the Great Lakes and enabling the United States to retain 410,450 square miles of western territory when the Revolution ended in 1783. By that date, the combined population of Kentucky and Tennessee was probably 20,000.

Having reluctantly surrendered the area north of the Ohio River because of military necessity, Britain encouraged Indians to repel further American expansion. If the Indians could prevent U.S. citizens from gaining footholds north of the Ohio, Britain hoped they might create an autonomous client-state closely allied with itself. Spain, which had regained Florida in 1783, promoted Indian harassment of the southwestern frontier (i.e., Tennessee and Georgia) for similar reasons. Following a brief pause from 1783 to 1785, when Indians reevaluated their options in light of Britain's defeat, the frontier once again became engulfed in bitter warfare.

Despite relentless Indian opposition, Anglo-Americans flooded into Kentucky and Tennessee, whose combined population exceeded 100,000 by 1790. Beginning with Marietta in 1787, a small number of U.S. outposts also began appearing north of the Ohio River. Not until 1794, when General Anthony Wayne decisively defeated the northwestern Indians (a loose confederacy of tribes, including Miami, Shawnee, Ojibway, Delaware, Potawatomi, and Ottawa Indians) at Fallen Timbers, near Ft. Miami on the Maumee River in northwestern Ohio, was the backbone of Indian resistance broken. Britain and Spain thereafter abandoned their territorial ambitions and left the Indians without essential foreign support.

Once Indian warfare had been suppressed, frontier migration proceeded at a rapid pace. Well over 200,000 pioneers crossed the mountains to Kentucky, Tennessee, western Virginia, or Ohio in the five years after 1794. By 1800, more than 400,000 persons, 7.5% of all inhabitants of the country, lived beyond the Appalachian crest. Settlement in western New York, which had also been inhibited by uncertainty over British ambitions along the Great Lakes, proceeded rapidly after 1795 as well. Georgia, whose frontier had been contained by fierce resistance from Creek warriors, saw its line of settlement advance very slowly in the 1790s. By 1800, parts of the West such as Kentucky's bluegrass plateau were as densely populated as districts east of the Appalachians and could no longer be classed as frontiers. As the nineteenth century dawned, the true frontier had shifted to Georgia and the territories of Mississippi and Indiana.

The most impressive index of frontier expansion is the grand total of counties and towns (or townships) organized in the late 1700s. Some new communities arose from rising population density in long-settled areas, which led to the incorporation of outlying towns as independent entities, but the great majority resulted from a need to provide government in areas previously uninhabited. New England is not often described as a frontier region during the Revolutionary era, but migration into Maine, New Hampshire, and Vermont produced 340 new towns from 1763 to 1800. New York and New Jersey added 235 townships during those years. In all of the United States, 269 new counties had to be created to accommodate the needs of a migratory population, including 150 in areas that had been uninhabited by whites in 1763.

TABLE 1.9 FOUNDING OF NEW COUNTIES, TOWNS, AND TOWNSHIPS, 1763–1800

	1763–1775		1776–1790		1791–1800	
	New Towns	New Counties	New Towns	New Counties	New Towns	New Counties
Maine	15	...	35	2	55	1
N.H.	61	5	10	...	14	...
Vt.	43	...	88	7	19	4
Mass.	41	...	40	...	13	1
Conn.	4	...	28	2	6	...
R.I.	2	...	1	...	...	...
N.Y.	19[a]	2	50[a]	3	136[a]	15
N.J.	13[a]	...	3[a]	...	14[a]	...
Pa.	...	3	...	10	...	14
Del.	...	...	...	...	...	...
Md.	...	2	...	2	...	1
Va.	...	6	...	23	...	7
N.C.	...	6	...	22	...	6
S.C.	...	...	...	28	...	...
Ga.	...	...	...	13	...	11
Tenn.	...	...	...	6	...	12
Ky.	...	...	9	9	13	34
Ohio	...	...	...	2	...	7
Ill.	...	...	...	...	...	2
Miss.	...	...	...	...	...	1

[a] Townships

Sources: Joseph N. Kane, *The American Counties* (3d ed., 1972). Alice Eicholz, ed., *Ancestry's Redbook: American State, County, and Town Sources* (1989).

The National Domain and Statehood

The Revolution ended royal interference over the disposition of western lands and consequently forced Americans to confront the question of how government would be extended beyond the mountains. The parent states of Kentucky and Tennessee, respectively Virginia and North Carolina, immediately organized counties that enjoyed full representation in their legislatures. This practical solution could not be applied universally, however, because several states had overlapping claims to lands north of the Ohio River.

Alarmed that a few states would dominate national politics if allowed to retain control over large areas of the West, states with no land claims proposed to end overlapping jurisdictions by ceding all unsettled territories to Congress, which would then manage them in the common interest. Maryland delayed the ratification of the Articles of Confederation until 1781 by refusing to sign until it was generally agreed that the West should be amalgamated into a national domain (excepting Kentucky and Tennessee). Because several states made conditional cessions that Congress initially rejected, the territory northwest of the Ohio did not become national domain until 1784, and Georgia's western claims did not pass to federal control until 1802.

Congress established the land policy that would govern all future territorial development in the Land Ordinance of 1785. This law prescribed a system of surveying by uniform grids in which the basic unit would be a township measuring six miles by six miles. All public land would be auctioned publicly as described below.

Land Ordinance of 1785

1 township equalled 36 sq. mi. (23,040 acres)
1 township equalled 36 sections of 1 sq. mi. (640 acres) each
1 section equalled 4 quarter-sections of .25 sq. mi. (160 acres) each
Rent or sale of Section No. 16 reserved for school expenses
Surveyor fees of $36 per township to be paid by purchasers
Minimum unit of sale was 1 section (640 acres)
Minimum price accepted at public auction was $1.00 per acre.

The Land Ordinance provided an efficient means of organizing the national domain prior to open auctions, but it also priced land beyond the reach of most ordinary citizens, who could not raise $640 for an entire section and would presumably have to wait for a speculator to divide the land into eighty acres, the unit most appropriate for a family farm. The Land Act of 1796 increased the difficulty of buying public land by doubling the cost per acre and demanding payment in a year. Just 48,566 acres were sold in the next four years. Congress consequently liberalized the terms of sale in its Land Act of 1800 (Harrison Act), which kept the price at $2.00 per acre, but lowered the minimum purchase to a half-section of 320 acres, allowed payment in four years, and gave a discount of 8% for cash payments. Although these terms remained unrealistic for the average family, the act greatly stimulated land sales, which totalled 398,466 acres from April 1800 to November 1, 1801.

Congress specified the procedures for extending government to the West in the Northwest Ordinance of 1787 (which applied neither to Vermont's admission in 1791 nor Kentucky's in 1792). This

TABLE 1.10 TERRITORIAL DEVELOPMENT OF THE UNITED STATES, 1776–1802

Feb. 1, 1780 New York ceded all land claims in the Ohio Valley

Oct. 10, 1780 Connecticut ceded all land claims in Ohio Valley but its Western Reserve of 3,000,000 acres in Ohio.

Dec. 30, 1782 Congressional arbitrators gave Pennsylvania title to lands claimed by Connecticut in Wyoming Valley.

Mar. 1, 1784 Congress accepted Virginia's cession of land claims north of Ohio River (two prior cessions rejected).

Aug. 23, 1784 Settlers in east Tennessee petitioned for admission to Union as the state of Franklin but were rejected and reverted to control of North Carolina in 1787.

May 20, 1785 Congress passed the Land Ordinance of 1785, which set procedures for surveying the territories.

Jul. 13, 1787 Congress passed the Northwest Ordinance of 1787, which established procedures for admitting states.

Mar. 8, 1787 South Carolina ceded its western lands.

Apr. 2, 1790 Congress accepted North Carolina's cession of Tennessee (an earlier offer was withdrawn in 1787).

May 4, 1791 Vermont admitted as the fourteenth state.

Jun. 1, 1792 Kentucky admitted as first state beyond Appalachians.

Mar. 18, 1796 Congress passed the Land Act of 1796, which set terms for sale of public land that were favorable to large speculators rather than small farmers.

Jun. 1, 1796 Tennessee admitted as the sixteenth state.

Apr. 7, 1798 Mississippi Territory organized.

May 7, 1800 Indiana Territory organized.

(continued)

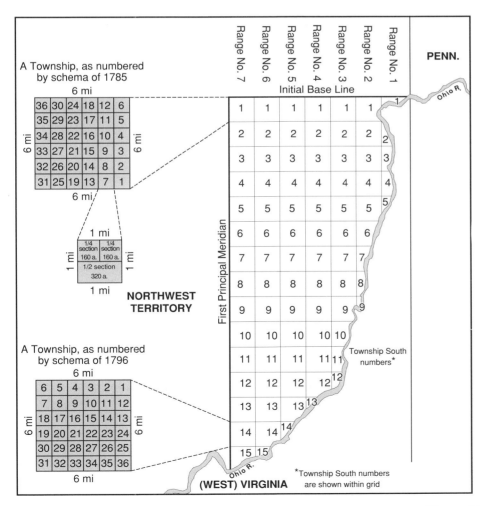

Public Domain Survey as Set by Ordinance of 1785

The first base line, the foundation of all later land divisions, was surveyed in 1785 by Thomas Hutchins. The first seven ranges laid out in Ohio established a uniform system of identifying boundaries based on townships, which were numbered consecutively north and south of the base line. The system's only significant modification came in 1796, when the numbering schema for a township's sections was changed to its present form.

TABLE 1.10 (continued)

May 10, 1800	Congress passed the Land Act of 1800, which set more liberal terms for buying public land.
Jul. 10, 1800	The Western Reserve, which the Connecticut Land Co. had bought from Connecticut in 1795, came under the jurisdiction of Ohio Territory as Trumbull County.
Jun. 16, 1802	Georgia ceded all its western lands.

Source: Richard B. Morris, ed., *Encyclopedia of American History* (rev. ed., 1961), 440–42, 461.

law stipulated three stages for admitting new states to the Union. Once it bestowed territorial status upon an area, Congress would appoint a governor, executive secretary, and three judges to keep the law. When the population reached 5,000 free adult males (about 20,000 persons) its voters could govern themselves through a territorial legislature, although Congress's designated governor could veto their laws. When all free inhabitants numbered 60,000 (the size of the Union's smallest state in 1787), they could draft a state constitution and be entitled to full statehood, provided Congress approved their constitution. Although originally applicable only to the Northwest Territory, this ordinance established the basic procedure for certifying statehood into the twentieth century. Tennessee, although not a part of the Northwest Territory, was the first territory to enter the Union under the Northwest Ordinance's procedures in 1796 as the sixteenth state.

Population Density

Population density varied enormously across the landscape of late-eighteenth-century America. By 1800, there were 12.6 people (slightly more than two families) per square mile, after excluding Indian territory; in districts settled for at least twenty-five years, population density ranged from 3.4 in Virginia's mountain counties to 81.4 in southeastern Pennsylvania. New England was the most compactly populated area, while people were most thinly distributed in the Carolinas and Georgia.

The older coastal regions in general had remained more thickly settled than interior counties, but this pattern varied by locale and had exceptions. The population in the seaboard counties of Massachusetts was two and a half times as crowded as in Virginia's tidewater by 1800, despite the fact that both had been colonized simultaneously. Though it had scarcely been occupied before 1760, southwestern Pennsylvania contained a far greater concentration of people in 1800 than the coastal plain of North and South Carolina, which had been settled since the late 1600s. Kentucky's bluegrass region had filled up so rapidly by 1800, that there were fewer acres available for agricultural use per free family than in the settled districts of Virginia or the Carolinas.

Contemporary observers attributed western migration to a shortage of agricultural land in the seaboard states, but any such scarcity was relative rather than absolute. By 1790, no state except Rhode Island had approached the upper limit of farmers that its territory could sustain. In Virginia and Maryland, which both experienced heavy outmigration after 1790, the rural population would eventually double before a peak was reached in the number of people directly or indirectly dependent on agriculture. In most states east of the Appalachians, the land was capable of supporting three to six times as many people in the countryside as lived there in 1790. Even in thickly settled Massachusetts and Connecticut, the population in rural communities stood at less than 70% of the maximum level reached in the next century. People migrated en masse to the frontier less because of land scarcity than to enjoy the economic advantages of buying fertile western land for far less than its equivalent cost in the East.

Compared to European standards, even the most heavily inhabited districts of the East Coast were lightly peopled. There were 157

TABLE 1.11 POPULATION DENSITY (PER SQ. MI.) AND NUMBER OF ACRES PER FREE, RURAL FAMILY IN UNITED STATES, 1775–1800

State	1775		1790		1800	
	Pop. Dens.[a]	Acres/ Family[b]	Pop. Dens.[a]	Acres/ Family[b]	Pop. Dens.[a]	Acres/ Family[b]
Maine	1.5	3,600	3.2	1,166	4.9	745
Settled area of 8,129 sq. mi.	5.9	946	11.9	306	18.7	195
N.H.	9.0	420	15.8	239	20.4	185
Vt.	1.0	3,300	9.3	396	16.7	219
Mass.	37.2	105[c]	47.1	80[c]	54.0	72[c]
Seacoast counties	56.0	72[c]	66.9	59[c]	73.6	56[c]
Interior counties	22.2	166	33.7	115	38.5	95
R.I.	55.2	93[d]	63.1	60[d]	65.5	58[d]
Conn.	40.6	93	49.1	76	51.5	71
N.Y.	4.1	1,100[e]	7.1	620[e]	12.4	340[e]
N.Y.–Long Island	31.3	228[e]	41.6	175[e]	60.2	154[e]
Hudson Valley	10.7	367	18.2	223	25.4	143
Former Iroquois lands	. . .	. . .	1.0	3,800	4.7	860
N.J.	16.3	244	24.7	160	28.3	139

State	1775 Pop. Dens.[a]	1775 Acres/Family[b]	1790 Pop. Dens.[a]	1790 Acres/Family[b]	1800 Pop. Dens.[a]	1800 Acres/Family[b]
Pa.	6.0	696[f]	9.6	420[f]	13.4	298[f]
Southeast counties[g]	43.5	120[f]	64.1	77[f]	81.4	59[f]
Northeast-central[h]	13.2	287	18.4	202	21.3	174
Southwest counties[i]	6.8	555	13.4	281	20.2	186
Indian lands of 1775	. . .	. . .	0.9	4,260	2.6	1,394
Del.	19.3	214	30.2	150	33.3	130
Md.	25.9	213[j]	32.2	182[j]	36.1	160[j]
Tidewater[m]	31.4	187[j]	38.3	167[j]	42.8	144[j]
Piedmont[m]	12.4	319	18.1	238	19.9	221
Va.	7.9	823	11.5	539	13.8	455
Tidewater[m]	23.2	327	30.6	254	29.4	266
Piedmont[m]	14.0	479	20.0	327	24.4	284
Shenandoah Valley	5.7	805	11.7	420	15.3	296
Mountain counties	1.0	4,130	2.2	1,920	3.4	1,270
N.C.	5.0	1,010	8.1	594	9.8	508
Coastal Plain[m]	8.8	628	10.5	518	11.7	503
Piedmont[m]	2.2	1,900	6.2	669	8.4	510
S.C.	5.6	1,520[k]	8.3	805[k]	11.4	540[k]
Lowcountry[m]	8.7	1,950[k]	10.1	1,477[k]	11.8	1,335[k]
Upcountry[m]	3.9	1,355	6.8	645	11.2	408
Ga. (present area)	0.6	11,100	1.4	3,765	2.8	1,948
Minus Indian lands	1.9	3,400	4.6	1,157	9.0	600
Ky.	. . .	. . .	1.9	2,321	5.6	787
Bluegrass Plain of 3,000 sq. mi.	. . .	. . .	15.0	273	25.0	205
Remaining territory	. . .	. . .	0.6	6,005	4.0	1,025
Tenn.	. . .	. . .	0.9	4,570	2.6	1,600
Settled area of 21,932 sq. mi.	. . .	. . .	1.7	2,435	4.8	851
United States	3.1	895	4.8	529	6.6	388
Settled area only[l]	6.0	455	9.4	269	12.6	197

[a] Persons per sq. mi.
[b] Acres per free, rural family.
[c] Minus Boston.
[d] Minus Newport and Providence.
[e] Minus New York City.
[f] Minus Philadelphia.
[g] Bucks, Chester, Philadelphia.
[h] Northampton, Lancaster, Berks, York.
[i] Bedford, Cumberland, Westmoreland.
[j] Minus Baltimore.
[k] Minus Charleston.
[l] 417,170 sq. mi.
[m] See Sutherland, 202, 219–220.

Sources: Stella H. Sutherland, *Population Distribution in Colonial America* (1936), xii, 34, 174, 175, 231, 240. Bureau of the Census, *A Century of Population Growth, 1790–1900* (1909), 54–56, 58–59, 96.

persons per square mile in England and Wales in 1801, but only 81 in the most thickly settled part of North America, southeastern Pennsylvania. Ireland, with approximately 150 persons per square mile, was twice as densely populated as eastern Massachusetts, which had the next greatest concentration of residents. The third most crowded state, Rhode Island, still contained 73 acres for every rural family as late as 1800, but in Germany's Hesse-Cassell district, the supply of land equaled only 30 acres per family and much of the soil was poor. As late as 1800, there still remained nearly a quarter of a square mile (154 acres) for every rural family—including non-farmers—in the highly urbanized area of New York County, Long Island, and Staten Island. Nowhere in Europe was there such access to agricultural land as existed even in the most populous districts of the United States.

TABLE 1.12 MEASUREMENTS OF LAND UTILIZATION, BY STATE, 1790–1798

	Percent[a] of State Settled 1790	Total Acres in State 1798	Acres Surveyed 1798	Percent Surveyed[b] 1798
N.H.	52%	5,755,520	3,749,961	65%
Vt.	. . .	5,934,720	4,918,722	83%
Mass.[c]	66%	24,844,160	7,831,028	32%
R.I.	83%	675,200	565,844	84%
Conn.	63%	3,118,080	2,649,149	85%
N.Y.	13%	30,321,280	16,414,510	54%
N.J.	33%	4,779,520	2,788,282	58%
Pa.	14%	28,728,320	11,959,865	42%
Del.	. . .	1,236,480	1,074,105	87%
Md.	48%	6,295,680	5,444,272	86%
Va.[d]	42%	40,846,720	40,458,644	99%
N.C.	19%	31,259,520	20,956,467	67%
S.C.	17%	19,329,920	9,772,587	51%
Ga.	4%	37,155,840	13,534,159	36%
Ky.	. . .	25,388,160	17,674,634	70%
Tenn.	. . .	26,339,200	3,651,357	14%
U.S.	. . .	525,041,280	163,746,686	31%

[a]Measured as a percentage of the maximum number of persons living in rural areas when each state's nonurban population initially peaked.
[b]Much surveyed land was unimproved or unoccupied. Some 36,100,000 acres were improved (including 9,600,000 acres in meadow and 9,900,000 in tillage or orchards) by 1798. Samuel Blodgett, *Economica: A Statistical Manual of the United States of America* (1806), 60.
[c]Includes Maine.
[d]Includes West Virginia.
Sources: Timothy Pitkin, *A Statistical View of the Commerce of the United States of America* (1835), 335. Lee J. Alston and Morton Owen Shapiro, "Inheritance Laws Across Colonies: Causes and Consequences," *Journal of Economic History*, 44 (1984), 286.

Population Density in the United States, 1790

Population density increased from south to north. Excluding recently settled frontier areas, Georgia had the fewest people per square mile, while the seacoast counties of Massachusetts had the greatest number. For further information, see Table 1.11.

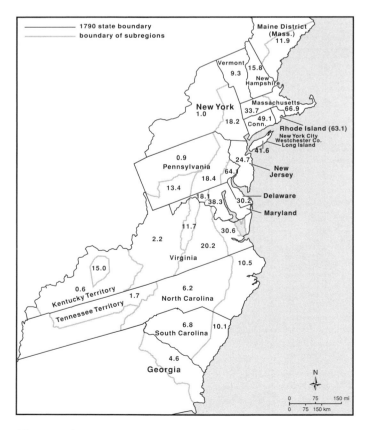

CHAPTER 2 Native American Life

Indian–White Relations

The year 1763 became a pivotal time in Native American history. Before then, the French and Spanish reinforced Indian resistance that kept Anglo-American settlements contained east of the Appalachian crest. After France and Spain ceded their colonies east of the Mississippi to Great Britain in 1763, their former allies faced the prospect that British forts in the newly won territory would become the nuclei for a rapid expansion of white settlements in the Ohio Valley. To counter this threat, a loose confederacy of tribes inspired by the Ottawa Pontiac destroyed every British garrison in the Ohio Valley watershed except Ft. Pitt and Ft. Detroit. Britain moved to restore peace with the Proclamation of 1763, which limited the frontier's future advance to the crest of the eastern continental divide.

The Proclamation of 1763 did less to stem the surge of whites westward than did the prospect of violent resistance by the Indians themselves. In 1768 the Iroquois approved moving the "proclamation line" westward to include mountainous regions that were unoccupied by themselves or other Indians and were unlikely to attract many white settlers. Native Americans also sold the Monongahela Valley in Pennsylvania but refused to permit settlement more than a few miles beyond Pittsburgh. Pontiac's War consequently deflected frontier expansion away from the Ohio Valley and into the Carolina backcountry, where the Cherokee and the Muskogee (Creek) would enjoy less success in stopping incursions on their land.

The point at which the Indians were most vulnerable in trying to contain whites at the Appalachian barrier lay between the Ohio and Tennessee rivers. This area, comprising all of Kentucky and most of Tennessee, was then uninhabited by Native Americans, who used it primarily as a hunting reserve. The Iroquois and Cherokee sold their titles to that region between 1768 and 1775, and the Shawnee, whose claims were strongest, relinquished possession to it in 1774 after being defeated in Lord Dunmore's War. The tide of frontier settlement shifted rapidly to the meadows south of the Ohio, and by 1780 the white population in Kentucky and Tennessee had become too numerous for the Indians to dislodge. Having failed to prevent Anglo-Americans from breaking through the Appalachian Mountains, the Indians faced increased difficulty in preserving the large amounts of territory necessary for maintaining their traditional economy based on agriculture and extensive hunting.

The Revolutionary War offered Native Americans the opportunity to forestall further white expansion by fighting on the side of the British. Virtually every Indian nation, including many in the upper midwest who were unthreatened by any immediate danger of white encroachment, raided the frontier as British allies. Continental forces retaliated in expeditions that dispossessed almost every hostile Indian from central New York, western Pennsylvania, South Carolina, and North Carolina. Indians in the Ohio Valley also lost many villages burned by vengeful militia, and the tribes of southern Ohio, who were most exposed to attacks from Pennsylvania and Kentucky, gradually relocated northwest for safety. When the war ended in 1783, Indians had forfeited most of their lands east of the Appalachians and were under enormous pressure to cede much of modern Ohio and Georgia.

Despite suffering severe losses of population and land during the Revolution, Native Americans remained formidable opponents of westward expansion. They benefited greatly from support provided at forts occupied by British and Spanish garrisons within American territory. Credit for the Indians' success nevertheless derived from the leadership provided by two gifted leaders, Little Turtle of the Miami and Alexander McGillivray of the Muskogee. Little Turtle united the nations of the Northwest Territory to establish the Ohio River as a firm boundary separating Indians from whites. In 1790 his forces inflicted substantial losses on an American army led by Josiah Harmar, and in 1791 he dealt forces under Arthur St. Clair the worst defeat ever suffered by the U.S. military against Indians. A shrewd strategist and diplomat, McGillivray had orchestrated a lightning campaign in 1786 to retake lands in Georgia that the Muskogee had been forced to surrender three years earlier. He then exploited fears of a Muskogee-Spanish alliance to negotiate treaties with the United States that frustrated efforts by Georgia to confiscate large amounts of Creek territory.

The Indians' cause suffered a severe setback in 1793 when McGillivray died prematurely at age forty-five. Two years later, the Spanish, who held Louisiana and the lands west of the Mississippi, signed Pinckney's Treaty and agreed to cease fomenting Indian resistance to Anglo-American expansion in the southwest. An uneasy peace eventually took hold along the borders of Georgia and Tennessee, and within a few years whites were able to obtain significant land cessions from the Muskogee and Cherokee.

In 1794, Little Turtle's War ended when Anthony Wayne routed the Indian warriors (now led by Turkey Foot) decisively at Fallen Timbers. Convinced that it could no longer maintain military garrisons upon U.S. soil, Britain quickly agreed to evacuate them when it signed Jay's Treaty later that year. Bereft of their only foreign ally and demoralized by defeat, the northwestern Indians accepted the terms of peace dictated to them, abandoned their claims to two-thirds of modern Ohio in the Treaty of Greenville (1795), and lost the Ohio River as an effective barrier to white settlement. Perhaps 200,000 Anglo-Americans flooded west in the five years after 1795, and this mass migration doomed the efforts of Native Americans to preserve their way of life east of the Mississippi.

The fortunes of war dealt severe blows to the majority of Native Americans during the Revolutionary era, but the actual experience of living through this period varied widely according to each nation's proximity to the white frontier. Those groups living farthest from the Appalachian Mountains suffered minimal disruption in their way of life, while others, like the Iroquois and Cherokee, sustained extreme losses of population and territory. The following summaries describe the central events in the histories of the most important tribes living in the Northeast and Southeast culture areas.

Indians of the Northeast Culture Area

Abnaki   During the Seven Years' War, most Abnaki from northern New England had supported the French and relocated to Canada, where many of their kinsfolk had been living for several generations. They reoccupied their homeland in the region from Lake Champlain to the Androscoggin River after 1763. Emboldened by France's defeat and lacking sympathy for former enemies who had recently been raiding their own neighbors, Yankee frontiersmen also began clearing farms in Abnaki territory. Armed resistance was not a realistic alternative for the Indians, and so they had no choice but to coexist peacefully, if somewhat tensely, with the whites.

The Abnaki responded ambivalently to American independence, and few ever fought for the Continental Congress. By 1783, most of the tribe had once again departed New England for Canada; there, some stayed neutral but many supported the British military effort, although with little apparent enthusiasm. A few Abnaki families returned to the United States after peace resumed, but most of the refugees joined their fellow tribespeople who lived along the Saint-François River in Quebec. The Abnaki migration eliminated the last major group of unacculturated Indians from New Hampshire and Vermont, but by 1800 perhaps 200 still lived in eastern Maine. The Abnaki did not entirely cut their ties with the United States, however, for they provided half the students educated in Dartmouth College's Indian missionary curriculum until about 1850.

Cayuga The Cayuga included about 10% of all Iroquois when the colonial period ended. Their villages clustered around New York's Cayuga Lake, east of the Seneca. During Pontiac's War, they debated joining their Seneca neighbors in attacks on British garrisons, but wisely remained neutral. They avoided taking sides in the Revolution until 1777, when they helped besiege Ft. Stanwix, near present-day Rome, New York, and fought a bloody drawn-out battle with New York militia at Oriskany Creek. In reprisal for Indian raids on the frontiers, General John Sullivan's Continentals marched into western New York in 1779, forced the Cayuga and other Iroquois into headlong flight, and burned their villages to the ground.

The Cayuga population dropped during the Revolution, but it did not experience the staggering declines suffered by other Iroquois nations. The Cayuga Nation had perhaps 1,040 members in 1771, and incomplete counts indicate that it still contained 860 people about 1790. Well over a third of all Cayugas had relocated to Canada by 1785. A large band of Iroquois moved to Ohio's Sandusky River about 1790 and was known as the Sandusky Seneca but seems to have been about half Cayuga in composition. By 1789, the Cayuga had sold all their claims in New York except for 100 square miles, and by 1795 their landholdings had dwindled to four square miles. The Cayuga joined the Seneca at various reservations in western New York, but did not relinquish their own sense of tribal identity.

Delaware The Delaware left Pennsylvania for southeastern Ohio after the Seven Years' War. Their new position lay squarely in the path of Anglo-American expansion. During the Revolution, the United States attempted to keep them neutral with promises that white settlements would be restricted east of the Ohio River, and the fledgling country's first Indian treaty was signed with the Delaware in 1778.

The Delaware included neutral, pro-British, and pro-American factions, but the majority supported the British out of self-interest, the accumulated weight of grievances against Anglo-Americans, and a wish to avenge several unprovoked attacks upon neutral kinsfolk assumed by Pennsylvania militia to be pro-British. To lessen their vulnerability to attacks across the Ohio River, the Delaware moved their towns into northeast Ohio and even Indiana. Delawares fought with Little Turtle's followers to keep the Ohio River as a barrier against white expansion, and they had to forfeit a large amount of their lands at the Treaty of Greenville in 1795. Most withdrew into Indiana to avoid white influence, but some migrated to Missouri and a few joined with Seneca who settled in Canada.

Miami The Miami primarily occupied Ohio west of the Scioto River. Their villages also extended through much of eastern Indiana, where they lived near the closely related Wea and Piankeshaw nations. As allies of Pontiac, they Miami slaughtered Ft. Miami's British garrison in 1763, except for one soldier whom they adopted.

The Miami fought for Britain during the Revolution and became a scourge for Kentucky's pioneers. Miami belligerency continued after 1783, and by 1790 the tribe's greatest leader, Little Turtle, had emerged as the outstanding battle commander for a loose Indian alliance fighting to block white expansion north of the Ohio River. Little Turtle's forces bested U.S. armies in 1790 and 1791, but they nevertheless retired their towns from southern Ohio to northeast

Indiana to escape retaliatory raids from Kentucky. Little Turtle's followers (then under Turkey Foot) suffered a decisive defeat at the Battle of Fallen Timbers in 1794. At the Treaty of Greenville, in 1795, the Miami ceded most of their holdings in Ohio. The tribe sold much of their remaining lands over the next fifteen years.

Mohawk The Mohawk were the easternmost and smallest nation of the Iroquois League. In 1770 they numbered about 400 living in two major villages about two days' ride west of Schenectady, New York. By 1770, they had sold off most of the eastern Mohawk Valley and lived in close contact with whites. Mohawk society consequently had incorporated more elements of white culture than other Iroquois had. The Mohawk also proved highly receptive to Protestant missionaries.

The Mohawk were the most pro-English of all Iroquois. This policy stemmed in large part from the close personal relationship they established with Sir William Johnson, Britain's superintendent of Indian affairs for the northern colonies, who married two Mohawk women. In Pontiac's War, the Mohawk not only spurned invitations to join the onslaught against the British, but also destroyed four towns of Pontiac's supporters on the Susquehanna River.

After Johnson died in 1774, leadership of the tribe fell upon Joseph Brant, a nephew of Johnson's second Indian wife. Brant was unreservedly pro-English and fled to Canada in 1775 to avoid arrest by rebel authorities. Brant enlisted all the Iroquois but the Oneida and Tuscarora as British allies, and by 1777 he had won recognition as the preeminent Iroquois war leader. Because they were closest to American lines, the Mohawk became the first Iroquois to suffer for their loyalty to the Crown when, in 1777, New York militia and Oneida plundered their villages. The Mohawk abandoned their homeland in New York and migrated to Canada, where in 1784 they received two large tracts of land in Ontario.

Oneida The Oneida numbered over 1,000 members about 1760. Their main villages sat on the western shore of Oneida Lake in New York, but a few lay on the upper Susquehanna River. The Oneida shared close ties with their neighbors, the Tuscarora.

The Oneida had long been strongly pro-British. When Pontiac's War erupted in 1763, they helped Mohawks attack four towns of Pontiac's supporters on the Allegheny River. Once a Presbyterian Mission was established among the Oneida, in 1767, many young adults became Christian. The Presbyterian missionaries, New Englanders who supported American independence, undermined the tribe's English allegiance and gained its support for the Continental Congress.

The Oneida did not hesitate for long to shed the blood of their brethren who remained loyal to the crown. They first fought other members of the Six Nations (the Iroquois League) at Oriskany Creek in 1777. In 1779, they aided Continental forces in destroying all hostile Iroquois villages. The Oneida paid dearly for this policy the next year, when Joseph Brant's warriors burned their towns and forced them to endure a long exile of hunger and privation in the white settlements.

The shattered tribe returned to Oneida Lake in 1783. Although entitled to more than 9,000 square miles by the Treaty of Ft. Stanwix in 1784, the Oneida sold large tracts to white land speculators after 1785. Having lost the resources necessary to live in their homeland by their traditional mix of trapping, hunting, and farming, many tribal members moved. In 1838 one group purchased land in Wisconsin; others settled in Ontario. A few remained near Utica, New York.

Onondaga Less than 10% of all Iroquois were Onondaga. Their villages lay near modern Syracuse, New York. They remained pro-British in Pontiac's War only after intense lobbying by Sir William

Northeastern Indian Nations, 1775

In 1775, about 51,000 Indians inhabited the area south of the Great Lakes, where population dispersion equaled 17 people for every 100 square miles (about four families in an area ten miles by ten miles). These Indians were soon flanked by whites pouring into the unoccupied zone below the Ohio River. In the 1780s, many Indians relocated northward toward Canada to escape the reach of pioneers whose settlements they raided as British allies in the Revolution.

Johnson, himself an adopted Iroquois. During the Revolution, the Onondaga shared the pro-British sympathies of most Iroquois. They paid heavily for this alliance in 1779, when a Continental army under John Sullivan methodically burned every Onondaga longhouse, uprooted their crops, and drove them panic-stricken to British Ft. Niagara.

By 1783, the number of Onondaga had declined by perhaps 150 from the 800 said to be living in 1771. About 225 relocated in Canada on land provided by the British government, and in 1790 there were approximately 400 remaining in New York. The tribe gave up all its lands in 1788 except for 100 square miles lying south of modern-day Syracuse, and five years later they sold all but about twenty-five square miles. The Onondaga gradually sold off parts of their reservation over the next three decades until it had been reduced to an area three miles square.

Ottawa Although the Ottawas' homeland surrounding Lake Michigan lay far distant from European settlements, they had integrated their economy closely with the fur trade and eagerly fought as French allies against Britain. When the Seven Years' War ended, the Ottawa were recovering from a severe smallpox epidemic brought home by warriors infected while serving with French troops

in New York. By 1763, the nation probably included 4,000 to 6,000 persons.

By 1763, British troops had assumed control over the French garrisons along the Great Lakes. The Great Lakes Indians had much difficulty establishing rapport with the British and distrusted the motives of their former enemies. The Ottawa leader Pontiac assumed the leading role in a general alliance of Native Americans to extinguish the British military presence west of the Appalachians. Pontiac's War erupted in 1763, and his forces destroyed every garrison of redcoats except Ft. Detroit and Ft. Pitt. At Ft. Pitt, defenders had the advantage of a strongly fortified position and held out until British reinforcements arrived after the Battle of Bushy Run. The siege of Ft. Detroit continued from the summer of 1763 until late October when Pontiac called it off. Because the Indians could not capture these two critical positions without taking unusually heavy losses, and the British dreaded the expense of waging a massive campaign of conquest across thousands of miles of wilderness, the fighting petered out during early 1764 and both sides made peace in 1766.

The Ottawa never again played so prominent a role in Native American affairs. Many Ottawa dispersed away from Lake Michigan, although the group's largest concentration stayed near Michigan's Grand River. Various bands encroached on Potawatomi and Chippewa territory by drifting south to the Sandusky and Maumee rivers or west to the Minnesota River.

Hundreds of Ottawa fought for Britain in the Revolution. They primarily raided settlements south and east of the Ohio River, even though this area lay well outside their homeland. The Ottawa continued plundering the frontier after 1783 until the decisive U.S. victory at Fallen Timbers in northwestern Ohio in 1794. The Ottawa signed the Treaty of Greenville in 1795 and ceded some Ohio hunting lands. Some of the tribe's bands migrated to Ontario.

Piankeshaw The Piankeshaw occupied the lower Wabash River valley near Vincennes. They began the Revolution as enemies of the United States but switched allegiance after George Rogers Clark captured the British garrison at Vincennes. The Americans, however, could not reward them with trade goods equal to those given Britain's Indian allies, so the Piankeshaw slowly drifted away from the American side. Many took up arms with their kinsman, the Miami Little Turtle, after sixty frontiersmen attacked a group of peaceful Piankeshaw at Vincennes in late 1788. The tribe helped Little Turtle inflict defeats on U.S. armies in 1790 and 1791 but later shared in the crushing defeat at Fallen Timbers in 1794. By the Treaty of Greenville in 1795, the Piankeshaw ceded some lands in Indiana. The tribe soon ceased to be ranked as an important Indian nation as it declined in population and sold off much of the land it needed for a hunting and trapping preserve.

Potawatomi The Potawatomi had close ties with the Ottawa and assisted that tribe in Pontiac's War by sacking Ft. Saint Joseph and helping besiege Ft. Detroit in 1763. Many Potawatomi relocated from their traditional home on Lake Michigan's eastern shore to nearby parts of Indiana, Illinois, and Wisconsin. This migration produced much violence with the Illinois tribe, upon whose lands they encroached.

The Potawatomi became British allies in the Revolution. The British principally used them to harass the frontier from Kentucky to western Pennsylvania, although the Potawatomi had no land claims in this area. The tribe continued raiding western settlements after the Revolution ended, and supported Little Turtle's War to block U.S. expansion north of the Ohio River. Defeated at the Battle of Fallen Timbers in 1794, the tribe made peace the next year through the Treaty of Greenville. At the same time, the easternmost bands began relocating to the Wabash River, where they encroached upon territory of the Miami.

Seneca The Seneca were the largest Iroquois tribe and included almost half the 9,000 members of the Six Nations in 1775. They primarily lived in western New York between Seneca Lake and Niagara, but some dwelled along the Allegheny River in Pennsylvania. They also comprised most of the Iroquois migrants to the Ohio Valley known as Mingo.

The western Seneca and Mingo had not shared the traditional pro-English sympathies of other Iroquois. Most Seneca supported Pontiac's War in 1763. The tribe's warriors played key roles in battles at Ft. Venango, Ft. Le Boeuf, Ft. Presqu' Isle, Ft. Pitt, Devil's Hole, and Bushy Run.

The Seneca showed initial reluctance to assist Britain in the Revolution. Persuaded to join forces under Colonel Barry St. Leger during the 1777 campaign, they participated in the siege of Ft. Stanwix and the battle of Oriskany Creek. Continental forces led by General John Sullivan devastated the Seneca territory in 1779. The demoralized survivors fled west to Niagara, and many later resettled in Canada. Spurred by an intense desire for revenge, Senecas terrorized the frontiers of New York and Pennsylvania until peace was declared.

The Revolution left the Seneca devastated. Of 4,000 who had inhabited New York in 1775, only 1,800 remained in 1797. From 1784 to 1797, the Seneca sold nearly all their lands in New York and Pennsylvania, besides renouncing all claims to territory in the Ohio Valley. By 1800, the nation's vast empire, which had formerly included all of New York west of modern Elmira, had shrunk to ten reservations totalling a mere 310 square miles, an area smaller than all but a few of that state's counties.

Shawnee The Shawnee had left Pennsylvania and reestablished themselves in southern Ohio by the 1770s. They claimed Kentucky and Tennessee as hunting grounds (as did the Cherokee), but had no permanent towns there. They fought the British during Pontiac's War of 1763.

In 1774, some Shawnee helped Mingos avenge the murder of thirteen Indians by whites near Wheeling. This bloodshed unleashed Lord Dunmore's War, in which two expeditions of Virginia militia invaded Shawnee territory. One force inflicted a stinging defeat on the Shawnee at Point Pleasant, on the Ohio River, while the other crossed the Ohio and threatened to burn their villages. The Shawnee sued for peace and renounced their claims to Kentucky in the Treaty of Camp Charlotte.

Defeat in Lord Dunmore's War made the Shawnee hesitate to take the British side in the Revolution, and some migrated across the Mississippi to avoid further conflict. The British finally won over the Shawnee in 1777, after which they waged unrelenting warfare against settlers south of the Ohio. The tribe suffered the loss of many towns by Kentucky militia and tried to escape Anglo-American retribution by migrating northward into Ohio. Shawnees continued in arms against the United States until Anthony Wayne's victory over Little Turtle's confederacy at Fallen Timbers in 1794.

The tribe ceded most of the area it formerly had occupied in Ohio at the Treaty of Greenville in 1795. A majority of its members relocated to the Auglaize, Maumee, and Wabash rivers of Ohio and Indiana, and a few removed to Ontario. Factions of the Shawnee soon after began selling large amounts of land to speculators, and the tribe found itself running out of sufficient land to maintain its traditional economy after 1800.

Tuscarora The Tuscarora comprised about 10% of all Iroquois in 1771. They had two villages east of modern Syracuse and five others along the upper Susquehanna River. Tuscarora welcomed Protestant missionaries in the 1760s and many converted to Christianity.

Living within easy striking distance of rebel militia and influenced toward the Continental cause by the American missionaries among them, most Tuscarora were pro-American. In 1779, however, when General John Sullivan laid waste to all villages among the Six Nations that had taken up arms against the United States, he burned three Tuscarora towns known to be pro-British. The pro-American faction earned the enmity of other Iroquois for assisting Sullivan, and in 1780 Joseph Brant destroyed their villages and winter food caches. A small trickle of Tuscarora thereafter deserted to the British cause. When the war ended, approximately every fifth Tuscarora joined the Iroquois exodus to Canada.

Half the tribe may have perished during the Revolution. In 1789, 340 Tuscarora reportedly lived in New York and probably 130 were in Canada. Some others had migrated to the Sandusky River in Ohio. Those remaining in New York eventually resettled north of Niagara Falls on a reservation of ten square miles. Because the British military garrison at Niagara deterred Americans from migrating to that part of New York, the reservation remained isolated and the tribe enjoyed good hunting, fishing, and trapping. When the British abandoned Ft. Niagara in 1795 according to Jay's Treaty, the Tuscarora economy became primarily dependent upon agriculture.

Wea The Wea were closely related to the Miami; they lived east and south of the Wabash in central Indiana. They joined Pontiac's War in 1763 and negotiated the peaceful surrender of Ft. Ouiatanon; they treated the surrendered redcoats well until they were exchanged at the end of hostilities. The Wea launched many raids against the Kentucky frontier on behalf of the British during the Revolution. During the 1780s, they continued attacking settlements south of the Ohio, but many of their villages were plundered by retaliatory expeditions of Kentuckians between 1789 and 1791. The Wea helped their Miami kinsman Little Turtle repel invasions by U.S. armies in 1790 and 1791, but they shared in the Indian rout at Fallen Timbers in 1794. As their penalty for defeat, they ceded a small amount of land by the Treaty of Greenville in 1795.

Wyandot (Huron) Numerous Wyandot from eastern Michigan settled after 1750 in northeastern Ohio, where they lay directly in the path of Anglo-American expansion. In 1763 they joined Pontiac's uprising, burned Ft. Sandusky, and helped besiege Ft. Pitt. The Wyandot allied with the British in the Revolution to block white settlers from the Ohio Valley. In 1782, Wyandot and Delaware routed a Pennsylvania militia force of nearly 500 that was marching to burn their villages in the Sandusky Valley.

The United States pressured the Wyandot into surrendering large tracts of land under the Treaty of Ft. McIntosh (1785), which they repudiated. The Wyandot assisted in Little Turtle's War to hold the Ohio River as a barrier to white settlement until the Indian defeat at Fallen Timbers in 1794. The Wyandot then made peace at the Treaty of Greenville and surrendered their claims in the Sandusky Valley. They ceded most of their other Ohio lands ten years later and migrated farther west.

Indians of the Southeast Culture Area

Catawba Formerly the most powerful Indian group in South Carolina's piedmont, the Catawba survived a devastating smallpox epidemic in 1759 as a mere shadow of themselves. By 1763, the nation had likely declined from about 1,500 to little more than 500, and it stabilized at that level for the next four decades. Because the weakened tribe could muster little more than 100 warriors, down from over 300 previously, the attitude of colonial officials soon changed from respect to condescension, and finally to neglect.

In July 1760, the Catawba abandoned their claims to an area of approximately 940 square miles for a reservation of 225 square miles, which would be protected by a fort built at the colony's expense. The Catawba voluntarily requested reservation status as the most realistic strategy for survival. Their original claim was too vague to be enforced against the growing number of whites squatting on their territory, but an officially surveyed reservation gave them legal authority to expel trespassers.

The tribe began renting its land near Rock Hill to whites before 1770, and by 1791 they had given leases to more than 300 white farmers. Within a decade, the Catawba had rented almost all the reservation's acreage not needed by themselves to outsiders. Many tribespeople supplemented this source of income by selling their own handcrafts, such as deerskin clothing, pottery, and baskets or other utensils woven from reeds. Few Catawba engaged in commercial agriculture (although virtually all were subsistence farmers), and their failure to produce a marketable surplus left them with living standards lower than their white tenants who grew cotton or grains.

Surrounded by Anglo-Americans who mostly favored independence, the Catawba prudently supported the Continental Congress. In 1776 the Catawba had the satisfaction of helping Carolina militia burn numerous villages of their old enemies, the Cherokee. The tribe's military contributions to the American cause were minor, but they paid a heavy price for their loyalty in 1781 when British troops burned their homes and commandeered all their livestock. Their sacrifices earned them not only financial compensation from South Carolina's legislature, but also grudging respect from frontiersmen who swarmed around their reservation, and so endowed them with a moral claim to remain in their homeland that enabled them to avoid being dispossessed like other Native Americans.

Cherokee Numbering perhaps 16,000, the Cherokee were the second largest Native American group east of the Mississippi about 1763. Despite having been recently at war with British Carolinians, the Cherokee took Britain's side during Pontiac's War and sent war parties to attack the Ohio Valley Indians and the French traders who armed them. Hoping to deflect the tide of white settlement north and west of their territory, the Cherokee sold title to large tracts along the New, Clinch, Holston, and Powell river valleys of Virginia and eastern Tennessee. By 1775, they had also relinquished claims to West Virginia, Kentucky, and much of central Tennessee. Despite these concessions, whites continued to pour into the Carolina backcountry and threaten their homeland.

The Revolution offered the Cherokee the chance to exploit white divisions by attacking the southeastern frontier as British allies. In July 1776, they launched a massive assault against settlements from northern Georgia to southwest Virginia. Many of the most exposed white communities were abandoned after suffering heavy casualties, but the pioneers had held out long enough for eastern militia to launch counterattacks into the Cherokee's own country. The result was a debacle for the Cherokees, who lost dozens of towns and had to surrender more territory to obtain peace than had formerly been disputed with the whites.

A virulently anti-American faction known as the Chickamauga Cherokee resettled along the upper Tennessee River, where they fought bitterly to drive whites out of the mountain valleys. Exasperated by continued Cherokee hostility, frontier militia carried out punitive expeditions that burned dozens of towns from 1780 to 1782. These attacks often drove even more Cherokee to arms because they destroyed towns inhabited by the peace party as well as the war faction. Warfare, ruthlessly pursued by both sides, continued long after the Revolution. Weakened by combat and a major smallpox epidemic in 1780, the Cherokee sought peace in 1785 by ceding the territory between the Cumberland and Tennessee rivers at the Treaty of Hopewell. They sold off many other large tracts in eastern Tennessee, Georgia, and the Carolinas over the next six years. By the time the protracted Cherokee wars ended in 1796, the Cherokee Nation's population had dropped from about 16,000 (1776) to 10,000. Despite these setbacks, the Cherokee rebuilt their lives, adopted new methods of farming, and went on to write their own constitution. Some Cherokee fought the Creek in 1813, but they were a minority.

Chickasaw The Chickasaw lived west and south of the Tennessee River. Traditionally hostile to the French, friendly toward the English, and antagonistic toward their Indian neighbors, they aided the British during the Revolution and raided Anglo-Americans in central Tennessee. After Spain declared war on Britain, the tribe raided colonists in Spanish Louisiana from New Orleans to St. Louis. The Chickasaw's most notable wartime achievement was their intermittent, yearlong harassment of Ft. Jefferson, Kentucky, near the mouth of the Ohio River; they did not capture the Virginia garrison but did force its abandonment in 1781.

In 1783, the treaties ending the Revolution left the Chickasaw bereft of British support and living in territory granted to their enemy Spain. The tribe slowly modified its former hostility toward the United States and in 1786 signed a peace treaty that confirmed it in possession of all lands it had claimed in 1776. Chickasaws fought against Little Turtle's Indians north of the Ohio as part of armies led by Arthur St. Clair in 1791 and Anthony Wayne in 1794. The United States rewarded them with 500 muskets and large amounts of ammunition, which the Chickasaw used to settle old grudges against the Creek. Peace gradually returned, and in 1800 the Chickasaw still retained possession of the territory they had physically occupied in 1760, although part of the hunting grounds they claimed in central Tennessee were inhabited by whites.

Choctaw About 14,000 Choctaw inhabited southern Mississippi and Alabama. They engaged in small-scale hostilities with the neighboring Chickasaw, Creek, and Cherokee. Although far distant from the Anglo-American frontier, they fought in the American Revolution as British allies. They harried Spanish outposts in the lower Mississippi Valley and sent several hundred warriors to assist British garrisons on the Gulf of Mexico under attack by Spanish forces. The British found the Choctaw to be lukewarm supporters, however, and blamed their loss of Mobile in 1780 on several hundred Choctaw who deserted the post as it awaited Spanish attack. After 1783, the Choctaw tried to play off the United States against Spain, both of which claimed to own the tribe's homeland. In 1786, the United States recognized Choctaw claims to all lands held in 1776. The tribe's relations with the United States stayed fairly amicable, in

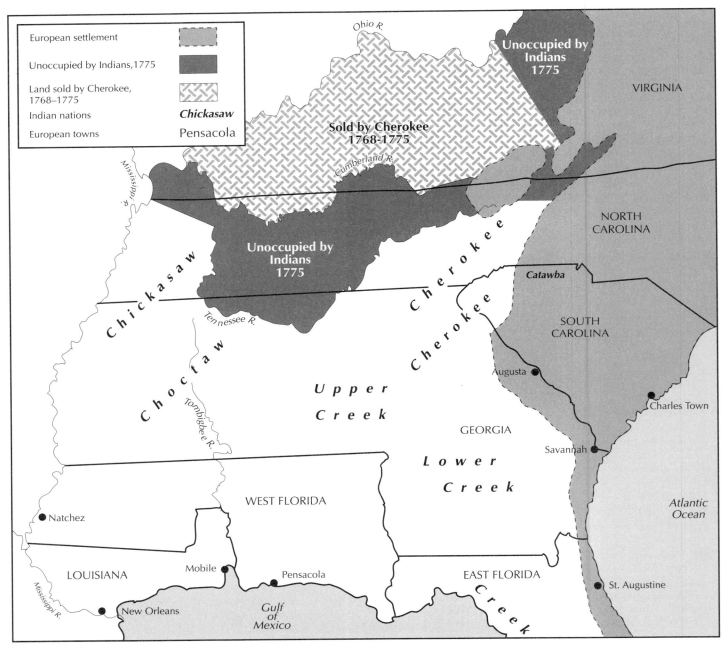

Southeastern Indian Nations, 1775

In 1775, about 52,000 Indians inhabited the region from the Carolinas to the Mississippi River. Their population dispersion equaled 33 people per 100 square miles (approximately eight families in an area ten miles by ten miles). These Indians were soon encircled to the north by Anglo-Americans, who first settled areas sold by the Cherokees and soon entered the unoccupied zone between the Cumberland and Tennessee rivers.

large part because their lands remained distant from the areas into which white settlers migrated before 1800.

Creek The Creek, or Muskogee, were the largest Indian nation east of the Mississippi. Their 20,000 members could field 5,500 fighting men, but internal rivalries among the nation—whose people spoke six different dialects—left them so divided that rarely could more than 1,000 warriors be roused to fight a common enemy. They occupied most of Georgia, Alabama, and the Florida panhandle.

The Creek economy was closely connected with the deerskin trade, and most households owned a wide variety of European-made goods. About 300 white men, mostly traders, lived among the nation and were raising children by Creek wives about 1780. The Creek valued mixed-blood members who could defend their interests against whites, and one such Creek, Alexander McGillivray (son of a Scottish trader), became their most effective leader.

The Creek launched many raids against the backcountry of Georgia and South Carolina as British allies during the Revolution. When peace returned, Georgia extracted a heavy price for having supported the losing side by pressuring a minority faction of the nation to cede large tracts east of the Oconee River through the treaties of Augusta (1783) and Galphintown (1785). McGillivray and his faction waged a brief and relatively bloodless war that drove whites from the disputed areas in 1786.

The Creek won greater success by diplomacy than warfare. Although his people were disunited and reacted fatalistically to setbacks, McGillivray convinced both the United States and Spain that his nation held the balance of power that would decide which country controlled the Southwest. McGillivray obtained large stocks of arms and ammunition through secret treaties with Spain. He then used the prospect of a Creek-Spanish alliance to win concessions from the United States in the Treaty of New York (1790), which allowed whites to stay in areas where they were too strong to be repelled but secured the national government's recognition that large grants of Creek territory sold by Georgia to land speculators in the Yazoo land controversy were invalid. McGillivray continued to fish in troubled waters, however, and on July 6, 1792 he signed a secret treaty with the Spanish, who recognized his right to wage war on the United States until Creek borders were restored to those of 1776.

McGillivray ultimately intended to convince his people to abandon each town's traditional autonomy in favor of a central authority that could resist white encroachments with the full force of all their warriors, who outnumbered the U.S. Army for most of the early national period. When McGillivray died in 1793, no one of equal stature succeeded him and the Creek remained disunited. The Creek's ability to resist Anglo-American land encroachments seriously deteriorated and in 1802 the nation surrendered large amounts of land at the Treaty of Ft. Wilkinson.

TABLE 2.1 CHRONOLOGY OF THE INDIAN WARS, 1763–1800

May 7, 1763 Pontiac's War began when his Ottawas initiated a five-month siege of Ft. Detroit.

May 16, 1763 Wyandots burned Ft. Sandusky (near Sandusky, Ohio) and killed all but one of its defenders.

May 25, 1763 Potawatomis destroyed Ft. Saint Joseph (near Niles, Mich.) and killed or captured its 14 troops.

May 27, 1763 Ft. Miami (Ft. Wayne, Ind.) surrendered to the Miami.

Jun. 1, 1763 Ft. Ouiatonon (near Lafayette, Ind.) surrendered to Weas, who spared the defenders' lives.

Jun. 4, 1763 Chippewa and Sauk Indians captured Ft. Mackinac (Mackinaw City, Mich.).

Jun. 16, 1763 Senecas burned Ft. Venango (Franklin, Pa.).

Jun. 18, 1763 Indians captured Ft. Presqu'Isle (Erie, Pa.) and its 27 defenders after a three-day siege.

Jun. 19, 1763 Indians burned Ft. Le Boeuf (Waterford, Pa.), but the garrison escaped under fire to Ft. Pitt.

Jun. 21, 1763 British troops abandoned Ft. La Baye (Green Bay, Wis.) peacefully by permission of local Indians.

Jun. 22, 1763 Indians began a forty-nine-day siege of Ft. Pitt.

Jul. 29, 1763 British troops reinforced Ft. Detroit. On Jul. 31, the garrison took heavy losses when it attacked Pontiac's camp. Pontiac continued the siege until Oct..

Aug. 5–6, 1763 Col. Henry Bouquet's Highlanders and Royal Americans defeated Indians at Bushy Run, Pa., and broke Ft. Pitt's siege on Aug. 10.

Sep. 13, 1763 Senecas destroyed a British supply train and killed 70 troops at Devil's Hole, near Ft. Niagara, N.Y.

Dec. 14–27, 1763 Residents of Paxton Township murdered 20 Christian Indians at Conestoga, Pa.

Feb. 1764 Mohawks and Oneidas destroyed four villages of Pontiac's supporters on the upper Susquehanna River and took 41 prisoners.

Aug. 1764 Col. John Bradstreet led redcoats and colonials against Pontiac's supporters on the Great Lakes and negotiated a truce on Aug. 12.

Nov. 1764 Col. Henry Bouquet marched to Ohio's Muskingum River and forced Indians to sign a truce and release white captives on Nov. 9–12.

Apr. 1774 Settlers murdered 13 Mingos near Wheeling, W. Va. Logan and other Mingos then killed settlers on the Ohio and Holston rivers.

Aug. 1774 Maj. Angus McDonald's 400 Virginia militia burned five Shawnee villages on Muskingum River in Ohio.

Oct. 10, 1774 Colonial Andrew Lewis's 900 Virginia militia defeated Cornstalk's 800 Shawnee at Point Pleasant, W. Va.

Oct. 1774 Lord Dunmore led 1,200 Virginia militia against Shawnee and Mingo villages on Scioto River; he negotiated Treaty of Camp Charlotte on Oct. 30.

Jul.–Nov. 1776 Cherokees launched massive attacks on frontiers of Carolinas, Virginia, and Georgia.

Jul. 1776 Capt. Samuel Jack and 200 Georgia militia repulsed the Cherokee and burned two Indian towns.

Aug. 1776 Gen. Griffith Rutherford's 2,400 North Carolina militia drove the Cherokee into east Tennessee.

Aug. 1776 Gen. Andrew Williamson's 1,100 South Carolina militia counterattacked the Cherokee and burned many of their villages.

Oct. 1776 Col. William Christian's 1,800 Virginia militia retaliated for Cherokee raids by burning five towns.

Dec. 1776 McClelland's Fort, Ky., survived a long siege.

Aug. 16, 1777 Joseph Brant's 600 Iroquois and Tories ambushed Col. Nicholas Herkimer's 800 New York militia at Oriskany Creek but withdrew after sustaining about 100 casualties (to about 150 for the New Yorkers).

Aug. 31, 1777 Ft. Henry, W. Va., withstood attack by 400 Indians.

Summer 1777 Ft. Donnally, W. Va., withstood siege by Indians.

Feb. 1778 In the "Squaw Campaign," Gen. Edward Hand's 500 Pennsylvania militia killed five women, but only one warrior, attacking the Delaware on the Beaver River.

Feb. 1778 100 Shawnees raided Kentucky and captured 27 men boiling salt on the Licking River.

May–Jun. 1778 Joseph Brant's Iroquois ravaged the Mohawk Valley.

Jul. 3, 1778 Iroquois and Tories devastated Wyoming Valley, Pa., and killed 340 militia.

Sep. 7–16, 1778 400 Shawnees and 50 Canadian militia failed to capture Boonesborough, Ky., defended by 60 men and boys.

Sep. 1778 Col. Thomas Hartley's Continentals attacked two Munsee towns on Susquehanna River near Tioga, N.Y.

Oct. 1778 Col. William Butler's Continentals burned three Iroquois towns on the Susquehanna in New York.

Nov. 11, 1778 Iroquois killed or captured 110 settlers at Cherry Valley, N.Y.

Mar. 1779 George Rogers Clark attacked Delaware towns on Indiana's White River.

Apr. 1779 Col. Goose Van Schaick's 500 New York militia burned three Onondaga villages.

May 1779 Col. John Bowman's 300 Kentucky militia attacked the Shawnee at Chillicothe on the Little Miami River.

Aug. 1779 Gen. John Sullivan and Gen. James Clinton's 5,000 Continentals burned 41 Iroquois towns in New York and drove their occupants to Canada.

Aug.–Sep. 1779 Col. Daniel Brodhead's 605 troops destroyed 11 Seneca and Mingo towns on the Allegheny River.

Jun. 1780 Col. John Montgomery led 300 Spanish and Virginia troops against Indians harassing Spanish forts at St. Louis and Cahokia; they destroyed a Sauk-Mesquakie town at Rock Island, Ill.

(continued)

TABLE 2.1 (continued)

Jun. 1780 Several hundred Indians and Tories under Col. Henry Bird, with two small cannon, raided Kentucky and captured Ruddle's and Martin's stations.

Aug. 7–8, 1780 George Rogers Clark's 1,100 Kentucky militia burned Shawnee villages of Chillicothe and Piqua in Ohio, and inflicted 70 Indian casualties.

Nov. 1780 Col. Augustin de la Balme's 90 French *habitants* and Indian allies raided the Wabash Valley but were defeated and captured by Miami Indians.

Dec. 1780 J. B. Hamelin's 16 militia from Cahokia destroyed Ft. Saint Joseph, next to a Potawatomi village, but were then pursued and defeated by British troops.

Dec. 1780 Arthur Campbell and John Sevier's 700 Tennessee militia burned all major Cherokee towns on the Little Tennessee and Hiawasee rivers.

1781 Chickasaw harassed militia at Ft. Jefferson, Ky., until the post was abandoned.

Jan. 11, 1781 Freeland's Station, Tenn., repulsed Indian attack.

Feb. 1781 Sixty-five Spanish militia from St. Louis invaded Potawatomi territory and captured Ft. Saint Joseph.

Mar. 1781 Col. John Sevier's Tennessee militia destroyed 15 towns of the middle Cherokee settlements.

Apr. 1781 Col. Daniel Brodhead's 300 troops burned Delaware towns of Coshocton and Lichtenau on Ohio's Tuscarawas River.

May 1781 Wyandots killed 22 Kentucky militia near Estill's Station, Ky.

Aug. 1781 500 Indians and Tories invaded Kentucky, unsuccessfully besieged Bryan's Station on Aug. 16–17, and inflicted 97 casualties on 180 militia at Blue Licks on Aug. 19.

Aug. 24, 1781 Joseph Brant's Indians wiped out a force of 105 Pennsylvania militia near modern Aurora, Ind.

Oct. 1781 Col. David Williamson's Pennsylvania militia attacked Delawares on the Tuscarawas and Muskingum rivers.

Nov. 1–10, 1782 Kentucky militia burned Chillicothe and five other Indian towns in Ohio, and killed 20 warriors.

Mar. 7, 1782 Col. David Williamson's 100 Pennsylvania militia executed 90 Christian Indians at Gnadenhutten, Ohio.

Jun. 4, 1782 Delawares and Wyandots killed one-tenth of Col. William Crawford's 488 Pennsylvania militia on Ohio's Sandusky River and later burned Crawford alive.

Sep. 1782 John Sevier's 250 Tennessee militia defeated the Cherokee at Lookout Mountain, burned their towns in the Chickamauga country, and burned another four Cherokee towns on the Coosa River in Georgia.

Sep. 11–13, 1782 300 Indians and Tories unsuccessfully attacked Ft. Henry, W. Va.

Nov. 1782 1,050 Kentucky militia under George Rogers Clark and Benjamin Logan burned three Shawnee villages on the Great Miami River and one on Lorimie Creek in Ohio.

Sep. 1786 George Rogers Clark led 1,200 Kentucky militia against the Miami on the Wabash River, but lack of supplies led the force to turn back before engaging the enemy.

Oct. 1786 Col. Benjamin Logan's 800 Kentucky militia burned seven Shawnee towns on the Mad River in Ohio.

Apr. 1787 Col. James Robertson's 130 Tennessee militia attacked Coldwater, where French traders sold ammunition and arms to Indians, and killed 20 Cherokees and Creeks.

Sep. 1787 Kentucky militia burned the Shawnee town of Old Chillicothe in Ohio.

Jun. 1788 John Sevier's Tennessee militia made retaliatory raids on Cherokee villages on Little Tennessee River.

Aug. 1788 Gen. Joseph Martin's 500 Tennessee militia attacked Cherokee near Lookout Mountain but withdrew after minor skirmishing.

Summer 1788 100 Cherokees killed 31 settlers near Houston's Fort, Tenn., but failed to capture the stockade.

Aug. 1788 John Sevier's 172 Tennessee militia burned two Cherokee towns on the Hiwassee River.

Aug. 1788 Patrick Brown and 60 men attacked the Piankashaw, then at peace with whites, near Vincennes.

Oct. 13, 1788 300 Cherokees burned Gillespie's Fort, Tenn., killed 17 defenders, and took 28 prisoners.

Jan. 1789 John Sevier's Tennessee militia killed 145 Cherokees near Jonesboro at a loss of only five men.

Aug. 1789 Maj. John Hardin's 250 Kentucky militia attacked Wea villages on the Wabash River.

Oct. 1790 Gen. Josiah Harmar's 1,433 militia and regulars burned five towns of Miami, Shawnee, and Delaware along Indiana's Maumee River but withdrew after losing 183 dead in two skirmishes that resulted in few Indian dead.

Winter 1790 Indians killed 36 settlers at Big Bottom, Ohio, 30 miles north of Marietta.

May 1791 Gen. Charles Scott's 1,000 Kentucky militia burned three Wea and two Kickapoo towns on the Wabash.

Aug. 1791 Gen. James Wilkinson's 500 Kentucky militia drove Indians from the Miami towns on the Eel River and from the Wea villages on the Wabash.

Nov. 4, 1791 Little Turtle's Indians inflicted 915 casualties on Gen. Arthur St. Clair's 1,400 troops 90 miles north of Ft. Washington at a loss of 60 warriors.

Oct. 1793 Gen. Anthony Wayne's Legion of the Ohio began operations against Little Turtle's Indians by fortifying Camp Greenville 70 miles north of Ft. Washington.

Apr. 1794 Elijah Clarke led a volunteer force west of Oconee River in Georgia to reoccupy lands from which whites had been driven in 1786.

Jun. 29, 1794 150 soldiers defeated 1,000 Indians attacking Ft. Recovery, Ohio, under Little Turtle and Blue Jacket.

Aug. 20, 1794 Gen. Anthony Wayne's 1,500 regulars and 1,500 Kentucky militia defeated Little Turtle's confederacy at the Battle of Fallen Timbers, and then devastated nine Indian villages along the Maumee River.

Sep. 1794 Tennessee and Kentucky militia destroyed the towns of the Chickamauga Cherokee.

Nov. 11, 1794 40 Cherokees attacked Valentine Sevier's blockhouse near the Tennessee River and scalped seven.

Sources: Helen Hornbeck Tanner, ed., *Atlas of Great Lakes Indian History* (1987), 71–73. Dale Van Every, *A Company of Heroes: The American Frontier, 1775–1783* (1962), passim, and *Ark of Empire: The American Frontier, 1784–1803* (1963), passim.

Treaties and Land Cessions

During the Revolutionary era, Native Americans entered into forty-two treaties with white governments. Prior to independence, the Indians most often signed treaties with the separate colonies, rather than with the British government itself. Under the Articles of Confederation, only the United States could negotiate treaties with Indians and any agreements arranged between the states and Indians lacked formal treaty status. The U.S. government's monopoly over Indian diplomacy did not include land sales until 1790, when Congress required purchasers to obtain its approval.

The four decades after 1760 witnessed a rapid acceleration in the pace of Indian land cessions. Prior to the Revolution, most surrenders of territory were done voluntarily. The Iroquois and Cherokee gave up huge areas from 1768 to 1775 that were marginal to their own needs; both groups followed a strategy of trying to steer whites away from their own territory by letting them settle in areas that would channel the flow of whites into modern West Virginia and Kentucky, both of which then had no permanent Indian inhabitants. From 1763 to 1798, Native Americans relinquished their claim to approximately 175,000 square miles, of which about one-third had been lost either by the Iroquois or Cherokee. The United States gained territory greater in size than all the states north of Maryland, and the total area of 112,000,000 acres was far greater than all improved land then under cultivation (estimated at 20,800,000 acres in 1774 and 36,800,000 acres in 1800 by Samuel Blodget in *Economica: A Statistical Manual of the United States* [1806], 60).

In 1795, the Treaty of Greenville, Ohio ended two decades of warfare in which the Indians of the Northwest Territory attempted to prevent whites from settling the Ohio Valley. The treaty gave up two-thirds of Ohio, and it marked the first of many land transfers by which the Indians sold their birthright north of the Ohio River. [Howard Chandler Christy, *Signing the Treaty of Greene Ville*] (Courtesy Ohio Historical Society, Columbus, Ohio.)

TABLE 2.2 TREATIES SIGNED BY NATIVE AMERICAN NATIONS, 1763–1800

Date	Indian Parties	White Parties	Provisions
Nov. 5, 1763	Cherokee, Creek,[a] Choctaw, Chickasaw	Great Britain	Boundary defined, peace, land ceded
Apr. 3, 1764	Seneca	Great Britain	Peace, land ceded
Jul. 18, 1764	Huron	Great Britain	Peace, alliance
Mar. 26, 1765	Choctaw, Chickasaw	Great Britain	Boundary defined, land ceded
May 8, 1765	Delaware	Great Britain	Peace
May 28, 1765	Creek[a]	Great Britain	Boundary defined
Jul. 13, 1765	Shawnee, Mingo	Great Britain	Peace
Nov. 18, 1765	Creek[a]	Great Britain	Boundary defined
Jul. 23–31, 1766	Ottawa, Ojibwa, Six Nations, Huron, Potawatomi	Great Britain	Peace
Jun. 2, 1767	Cherokee	Great Britain	Boundary lines

Date	Indian Parties	White Parties	Provisions
Jun. 5, 1767	Creek[a]	Great Britain	Trade regulations
Jun. 22, 1768	Nanticoke	Maryland	Land ceded
Oct. 14, 1768	Cherokee	Great Britain	Land ceded
Nov. 5, 1768	Six Nations	Great Britain	Boundary defined, land ceded
Oct. 18, 1770	Cherokee	Great Britain	Land ceded
1771	Cherokee	John Donnelson	Land ceded
Jun. 3, 1773	Cherokee, Creek[a]	Great Britain	Land ceded
Oct. 2, 1774	Creek[a]	Georgia	Peace, trade
Oct. 30, 1774	Shawnee, Mingo	Virginia	Peace, land ceded
Jun. 29–Jul. 6, 1775	Shawnee, Mingo	Virginia	Boundary, return of hostages
May 20, 1777	Cherokee	South Carolina	Land ceded
Jul. 20, 1777	Cherokee	Virginia, North Carolina	Land ceded

(continued)

TABLE 2.2 (continued)

Date	Indian Parties	White Parties	Provisions
Sep. 17, 1778	Delaware	United States	Peace, alliance
Oct. 22, 1784	Six Nations	United States	Western boundary
Jan. 21, 1785	Wyandot, Delaware, Chippewa, Ottawa	United States	Land ceded
Nov. 28, 1785	Cherokee	United States	Land ceded
Jan. 3, 1786	Choctaw	United States	Boundary defined
Jan. 10, 1786	Chickasaw	United States	Boundary defined
Jan. 31, 1786	Shawnee	United States	Peace, boundary
Jan. 9, 1789	Wyandot, Delaware, Ottawa, Chippewa, Potawatomi, Sauk	United States	Peace, treaty of 1785 confirmed
Jan. 9, 1789	Six Nations	United States	Confirmed Treaty of 1784
Aug. 7, 1790	Creek[a]	United States	Peace, land ceded
Jul. 2, 1791[b]	Cherokee	United States	Treaty of 1785 confirmed
Jul. 6, 1792	Creek[a]	Spain	Secret alliance
Jun. 26, 1794	Cherokee	United States	Treaty of 1791 confirmed
Nov. 11, 1794	Six Nations	United States	Boundaries
Dec. 2, 1794	Tuscarora, Oneida, Stockbridge	United States	Compensation for military service
Aug. 3, 1795	Wyandot, Delaware, Shawnee, Ottawa, Chippewa, Miami, Wea, Potawatomi, Eel River, Kickapoo, Piankeshaw, Kaskaskia	United States	Peace, land ceded
May 31, 1796	Seven Nations of Canada	United States	Annuity for lands relinquished
Jun. 29, 1796	Creek[a]	United States	Treaty of 1790 confirmed
Mar. 29, 1797	Mohawk	United States	Annuity for land relinquished
Oct. 2, 1798	Cherokee	United States	Land ceded

[a]Muskogee
[b]Amendments added Jul. 2, 1791 and Feb. 17, 1792
Sources: Wilcomb E. Washburn, ed., *History of Indian–White Relations* (1988), 194. Richard Peters, ed., *The Public Statutes at Large of the United States of America, from 1789 to Mar. 3, 1845: Treaties Between the United States and the Indian Tribes* (1856), 13–64.

Native American Population

Population estimates for Indian nations are very conjectural. Eighteenth-century government officials were primarily interested in how many Indians could go to war, and they seldom tried to find out how many women, children, and elderly belonged to the tribes. Except for a few Indian groups, such as the Iroquois or Catawba, that had close contact with Anglo-Americans, most of the surviving

TABLE 2.3 MAJOR CESSIONS OF LAND BY NATIVE AMERICANS, 1763–1800

Date	Place	Indian Parties	White Parties	Location	Square Miles
Nov. 5, 1763	Augusta, Ga.	Creek, Cherokee	Ga.	Ga.	3,700
May 28, 1765	. . .	Creek	Ga.	Ga.	30
Oct. 14, 1768	Hard Labor Creek, S.C.	Cherokee	Va.	Va., W.Va.	2,700
Nov. 5, 1768	Ft. Stanwix, N.Y.	Iroquois	Great Britain	Pa., W.Va.	20,000
Oct. 18, 1770	Lachaber, S.C.	Cherokee	Va.	Va., W.Va.	7,300
1771	. . .	Cherokee	Va.[a]	W.Va., Va., Ky.	14,000
Jun. 3, 1773	Augusta, Ga.	Creek, Cherokee	Ga.	Ga.	3,300
Oct. 30, 1774	Camp Charlotte, Ohio	Shawnee	Va.	Ky., Tenn.	40,000
Mar. 17, 1775	Sycamore Shoals, Tenn.	Cherokee	Richard Henderson	Ky., Tenn.	29,500
May 20, 1777	DeWitt's Corner, S.C.	Cherokee	S.C.	S.C.	2,000
Jul. 20, 1777	Long Island, Tenn.	Cherokee	Va., N.C.	Va., N.C.	6,800
Nov. 1, 1783	Augusta, Ga.	Cherokee	Ga.	Ga.	2,200
Oct. 22, 1784	Ft. Stanwix, N.Y.	Iroquois	U.S.	N.Y., Pa.	2,900
Oct. 23, 1784	Ft. Stanwix, N.Y.	Iroquois	Pa.	Pa.	18,000
Jun. 28, 1785	Ft. Herkimer, N.Y.	Oneida, Tuscarora	N.Y.	N.Y.	2,100
Jan. 21, 1785	Ft. McIntosh, Pa.[b]	Western Indians	U.S.	Ohio	24,500
Nov. 12, 1785	Galphintown, Ga.[c]	Creek	Ga.	Ga.	2,200
Nov. 28, 1785	Hopewell Plantation, S.C.	Cherokee	U.S.	Tenn., N.C., Ky.	7,000
Jul. 1788	Buffalo Creek, N.Y.	Seneca	Phelps & Gorham Co.	N.Y.	4,400
Sep. 1788	Ft. Schuyler, N.Y.	Onondaga	N.Y.	N.Y.	2,200
Sep. 1788	Ft. Schuyler, N.Y.	Oneida	N.Y.	N.Y.	2,700
Feb. 25, 1789	Albany, N.Y.	Cayuga	N.Y.	N.Y.	1,100
Aug. 7, 1790	New York, N.Y.	Creek	U.S.	Ga.	6,500
Jul. 2, 1791	Holston River, Tenn.	Cherokee	U.S.	Tenn., N.C.	3,200
Mar. 11, 1793	. . .	Onondaga	N.Y.	N.Y.	75
Jul. 27, 1795	. . .	Cayuga	N.Y.	N.Y.	98
Aug. 3, 1795	Greenville, Ohio	Western Indians	U.S.	Ohio,	28,000

(continued)

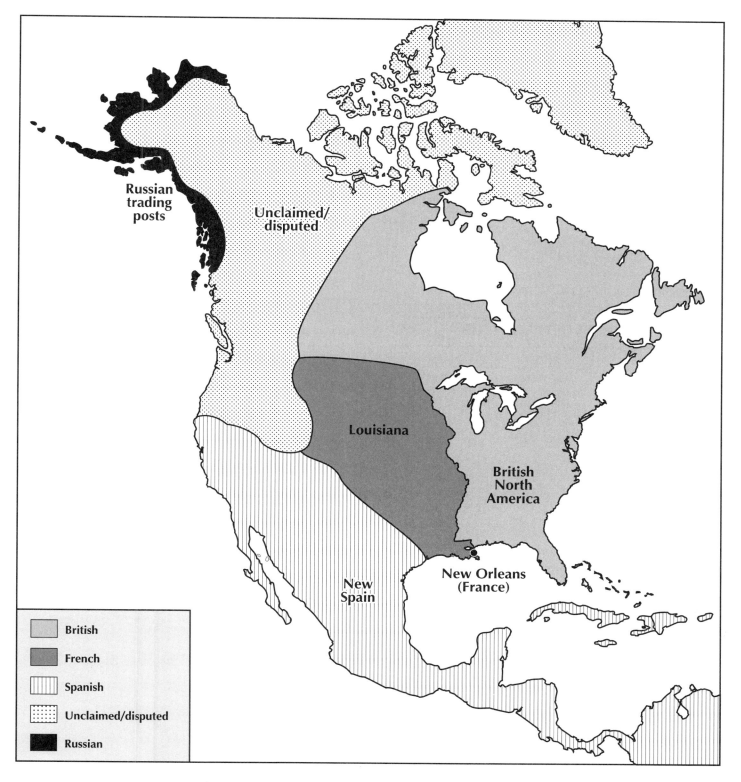

British

French

Spanish

Unclaimed/disputed

Russian

Russian
trading
posts

Unclaimed/
disputed

Louisiana

British
North
America

New
Spain

New Orleans
(France)

European Influence in North America after 1763

Various Native American groups were subject to influence from, and often domination by, different European powers depending upon where they lived.

TABLE 2.3 (continued)

Date	Place	Indian Parties	White Parties	Location	Square Miles
Mar. 29, 1797	Albany, N.Y.	Mohawk	U.S.	N.Y.[d]	2,000
Sep. 15, 1797	Genesee, N.Y.	Seneca	Holland Land Co.	N.Y.	4,400
Oct. 2, 1798	Tellico River, Tenn.	Cherokee	U.S.	Tenn., N.C.	1,200

[a] Negotiated by John Donnelson.
[b] Repudiated by Indians and ceded again in Treaty of Greenville, 1795.
[c] Repudiated by Indians and returned to them by Treaty of N.Y., 1790.
[d] Relinquished tribal lands without specifying exact area claimed.
Sources: Charles C. Royce, *Indian Land Cessions in the U.S.* (1900), passim. Lester J. Cappon, ed., *Atlas of Early American History: The Revolutionary Era, 1760–1790* (1976), 61.

counts of warriors were couched in round figures and represented little more than intelligent guesses by traders or soldiers. When knowledgeable people reported on population shifts, whether over short or long periods, they made general observations rather than providing specific details about the impact of epidemics, war, or migration. The federal census likewise made no enumeration of Native Americans unless they lived among whites in settled areas.

Because so little information exists concerning the division of Native American society according to age and sex, scholars still differ about the ratio of warriors to total population. Historians generally agree that for each warrior there were at least 3.5 other members, and no more than 6 additional persons. The most commonly used estimate is that there was one warrior for every six Indians, or a ratio of 1:5. Using a conservative figure of 22,000 warriors east of the Mississippi in about 1770, the total number of Indians outside the settlements would have ranged from 110,000 (based on a ratio of 1:5) to 132,000 (based on a ratio of 1:6). If the actual number of warriors was 25,000 or more, then the total population may have been 150,000 in about 1770, after which the Indian population may have declined by 10% to 15% as a result of the Revolution.

TABLE 2.4 ESTIMATED POPULATION OF INDIAN TRIBES EAST OF MISSISSIPPI RIVER, 1768

Indian Nation	Locale	Total
Abnaki	Maine, Vt., N.H.	200
Catawba	S.C.	500
Cherokee	Carolinas, Ga.	16,000
Chickasaw	Miss., Tenn.	4,000
Choctaw	Miss., Ala.	14,000
Creek	Ga., Ala., Fla.	20,000
Dakota	Minn.	6,000[a]
Delaware-Munsee	Pa.–Ohio	3,500
Illinois	Ill.	2,200[a]
Iroquois	N.Y.–Pa.	7,500
Refugees with Iroquois[b]	N.Y.	800
Kickapoo-Mascouten	Ill.	2,000
Mahican[c]	Ohio	300
Menominee	Wis.	800
Mesquakie (Fox)	Wis.	1,500[a]
Miami, Wea, Piankeshaw	Ind.–Ohio	4,000
Mingo	Ohio	600
Missisaga (Chippewa)	Mich.–Ohio	2,200
Ojibwa	Minn., Mich., Wis.	5,000[a]
Ottawa	Mich.–Ohio	5,000
Potawatomi	Wis., Ill., Ind.	3,000
Sauk	Ill., Wis.	2,000[a]
Shawnee	Ohio, Pa.	1,800
Winnebago	Wis.	1,500
Wyandot	Ohio	1,000
Subtotal	Northern Indians	50,900
Subtotal	Southern Indians	52,500
Total	. . .	105,400

Note: Not counted are Indians living among whites and in Florida.
[a] Includes unknown number on west bank of Mississippi.
[b] Nanticoke, Conoy, Tutelo, Saponi
[c] Primarily with Wyandot
Sources: Helen Hornbeck Tanner, ed., *Atlas of Great Lakes Indian History* (1987), 66. See also Evarts B. Greene and Virginia D. Harrington, *American Population Before the Federal Census of 1790* (1932), 196–206, for southern nations.

TABLE 2.5 ESTIMATED INDIAN POPULATION LIVING WITHIN WHITE JURISDICTION, 1790

State, Tribal Group	Population	Location
Maine		
Passamaquoddy	. . .	Near Passamaquoddy Bay
Penobscot	400	On Penobscot River, northward from head of tidewater
Mass. [a]		
Herring Pond	120	Sandwich, on Cape Cod
Wampanoag	. . .	Troy, in Bristol County
Wampanoag	280[b]	Mashpee, on Cape Cod
Wampanoag	400	Martha's Vineyard Island
R.I.		
Narraganset	500	Charlestown, in Washington County
Conn.		
Mohegan and others	. . .	At Stonington and Groton, between Norwich and New London
N.Y.		
Montauk	. . .	Montauk Point, on Long Island
Cayuga	500	Reservation on Cayuga Lake
Tuscarora	400	On Tuscarora or Oneida Creek
Mohawk	1 family	Ft. Hunter, on Mohawk River
Oneida	700	Oneida Reservation
Onondaga	500	Reservation on Onondaga Lake
Seneca	2,000	Chiefly on Genesee River, also a town on Buffalo Creek and 2 small towns on Allegheny River
Pa.		
Delaware, Munsee, Saponi	1,300	North branch of Susquehanna River
Va.		
Mattaponi, Nottoway, Pamunkey	100	Southampton County
Seneca	150	Two towns on French Creek
S.C.		
Catawba	450	At Catawba, in York County

[a] Half of mixed blood
[b] Only 40 or 50 were pure Indian
Source: U.S. Bureau of the Census, *A Century of Population Growth, 1790–1900* (1909), 39.

TABLE 2.6 NUMBER OF WARRIORS EAST OF MISSISSIPPI RIVER, 1763–1768

Nations	Warriors	Nations	Warriors
In the West		**Iroquois**	
Delaware	750	Mohawk	160
Munsee	150	Oneida	300
Mahican	100	Tuscarora	200
Wyandot	250	Onondaga	260
Shawnee	300	Cayuga	200
Mingo	300	Seneca	1,000
Miami	350		2,120
Wea	300		
Piankeshaw	300	**Refugees with Iroquois**	
Potawatomi	300	Oka	150
Kickapoo	300	Nanticoke	100
Mascoutens	500	Conoy	30
Kaskaskia	300	Saponi	30
Peoria	300		310
Sauk	a		
Iowa	b	**In the Southeast**	
Mesquakie (Fox)	750		
Chippewa	5,800	Alabama	600
Wisconsin	550	Catawba	150
Ottawa	a	Cherokee	4,000
	11,600	Chickasaw	750
		Choctaw	4,500
		Creek	4,000
		Natchez	200
			14,200

ªCounted with Chippewa, perhaps 500.
ᵇCounted with Chippewa, perhaps 300.
Source: Evarts B. Greene and Virginia D. Harrington, *American Population Before the Federal Census of 1790* (1932), 196–206.

CHAPTER 3 Chronology, 1763–1800

The four decades following 1763 were the most momentous in U.S. history. The thirteen colonies not only achieved independence but also confounded foreign predictions that self-determination would lead only to political chaos, economic decline, and either civil strife or subservience to more powerful countries. Americans instead created a remarkably stable system of federal power-sharing that outlived every European government of that time except Great Britain's. They also rapidly expanded over the Appalachian Mountains, quelled Indian hostilities on the frontier, successfully resisted foreign attempts to detach large amounts of American territory, rebuilt the merchant marine, regained much of their lost overseas commerce, and financed the country's first stock exchange and investment banks. These results were not foreordained, however, and had the United States not been endowed with strong leadership, its independence might have generated the sort of post-revolutionary disintegration and economic problems experienced in Latin America after the Spanish Empire fell.

February 10, 1763 The Treaty of Paris ended the Seven Years' War. Britain gained Canada, all of French Louisiana east of the Mississippi River, and Spanish Florida. Spain acquired New Orleans and French Louisiana west of the Mississippi.

May 7, 1763 Pontiac's War began when Ottawa Indians initiated a five-month siege of the British garrison of Ft. Detroit.

May 1763 Pontiac's supporters captured Ft. Sandusky, Ohio, Ft. Saint Joseph, Mich., and Ft. Miami, Ind.

June 22, 1763 Pontiac's followers began besieging Ft. Pitt, Pa.

June 1763 Pontiac's followers gained control of Ft. Venango, Pa., Ft. Mackinac, Mich., Ft. Presqu'Isle, Pa., Ft. Le Boeuf, Pa., and Ft. La Baye, Wis.

August 5–6, 1763 Col. Henry Bouquet's Highlanders and Royal Americans decisively defeated Indians at Bushy Run, Pa., and then relieved Ft. Pitt on Aug. 10.

October 7, 1763 George III issued the Proclamation of 1763, which temporarily forbade English settlement west of the Appalachians' crest. (On April 17, 1766, Britain's attorney general declared that the proclamation did not void land grants already held by 1763.)

December 14–27, 1763 In retaliation for Indian raids, residents of Paxton, Pa. murdered 20 peaceful Conestoga Indians. Despite the offer of high rewards for the killers, no arrests were ever made.

1763 Henry Williams built the first prototype of a steam-powered boat at Lancaster, Pa., but could not make it function properly.

January 24, 1764 Several hundred armed Pennsylvania frontiersmen assembled outside Philadelphia and threatened to burn it because the government had failed to protect them from Indian attacks. They left after Benjamin Franklin, acting in a private capacity, reasoned with them.

February 16, 1764 Auguste Chouteau and 30 Frenchmen founded St. Louis, Mo., which Pierre Laclède named that April.

April 5, 1764 Britain replaced the Molasses Act of 1733 with the Sugar Act, the first British external (i.e., maritime) tax designed to raise treasury revenue from the colonies. The law also violated traditional civil rights by denying jury trials to persons charged with smuggling and requiring the accused to prove his or her innocence.

April 19, 1764 George III signed the Currency Act, which forbade the colonies to alleviate their shortage of hard money by issuing paper currency without the royal Privy Council's permission.

August 12, 1764 Most Great Lakes Indian tribes abandoned Pontiac and signed a peace treaty with Col. John Bradstreet.

November 9–14, 1764 At the Muskingum River in Ohio, Col. Henry Bouquet negotiated a truce with Pontiac's local Indian allies and obtained the release of white prisoners captured since 1763.

March 22, 1765 George III signed the Stamp Act, effective as of November 1, the first internal (i.e., nonmaritime) tax imposed on the colonies. Prime Minister George Grenville hoped the tax would raise £60,000 from a wide range of legal and business transactions.

May 15, 1765 George III signed the Quartering Act, the first measure to tax the colonies indirectly by requiring certain legislatures to provide inexpensive barracks supplies for the army.

May 30, 1765 The Virginia House of Burgesses adopted Patrick Henry's resolutions opposing the Stamp Act as taxation without representation. Most other colonies soon took similar positions.

August 15, 1765 The Massachusetts collector of stamp taxes, Andrew Oliver, resigned following an attack on his home in Boston by an enraged crowd the night before.

August 28, 1765 Rhode Island's Stamp Tax collector resigned after the "Sons of Liberty" wrecked his Newport home the previous day.

September–November 1765 All Stamp Tax commissioners (except Georgia's, who was in England) resigned, so that no revenue could be collected.

October 19, 1765 Meeting at New York, representatives of nine colonies at the Stamp Act Congress adopted resolutions demanding the Stamp Act's repeal and denying that Parliament could tax them.

October 31, 1765 New York merchants initiated the nonimportation movement by agreeing to boycott British goods, as a way of pressuring Parliament to repeal the Stamp Act. Nonimportation soon spread to other ports and sharply reduced British exports.

1765 The first chocolate milled in British North America was made by John Harmon at Dorchester, Mass.

1765 The first college literary club, the Well Meaning Society (later the Cliosophic Society) began meeting at Princeton, N.J.

March 18, 1766 George III signed both the Stamp Act's repeal and the Declaratory Act, which denied that the colonists were exempt from any Parliamentary taxes or laws.

July 23–31, 1766 Sir William Johnson negotiated a treaty at Ft. Oswego, N.Y. that formally ended Pontiac's Indian War.

July 30, 1766 William Pitt, a strong opponent of the Stamp Act, became Britain's prime minister as Lord Privy Seal.

November 1, 1766 To overcome the problems of taxing foreign molasses entering the colonies, Parliament cut the Sugar Act's rates by 50%.

November 10, 1766 New Jersey chartered Queen's College, a Dutch Reformed institution that became Rutgers College in 1825.

1766 The first Western, the play *Ponteach, or the Savages of America* by Robert Rogers of New Hampshire, was published in London.

March 1767 Charles ("Champagne Charley") Townshend, chancellor of the Exchequer, assumed leadership of Parliament from the pro-American prime minister William Pitt who had fallen severely ill.

April 24, 1767 Philadelphia's longstanding hostility to plays failed to prevent the city's first permanent theater, the Southwick on

South Street, from opening with Thomas Godfrey's *Prince of Parthia.*

June 29, 1767 George III signed Charles Townshend's Revenue Act, which attempted to raise £37,000 in taxes upon various imports entering North America; he also signed the American Board of Customs Act, which would tighten the enforcement of import duties.

July 2, 1767 George III signed the New York Suspending Act, which threatened to deny New York's right to pass laws for itself if it did not comply with the Quartering Act of 1765 by October 1. New York had already done so on June 6, and the law was not implemented.

October 28, 1767 Boston's Town Meeting voted to boycott British imports until the Townshend taxes were repealed. Not until early 1768, however, did other major ports begin to follow Boston's lead.

November 5, 1767 The *Pennsylvania Chronicle* published the first of John Dickinson's "Letters from a Farmer in Pennsylvania," which were critical in galvanizing opposition to the Townshend laws.

February 11, 1768 The Massachusetts Assembly denounced the Townshend duties in a letter to all other colonies. When Lord Hillsborough demanded in April that Americans repudiate the circular letter, his effort backfired and generated strong support for Massachusetts.

April 5, 1768 Merchants formed the New York Chamber of Commerce, the forerunner of modern American business organizations.

July 1768 New Smyrna, Fla., was settled by 1,300 Greek, Armenian, and Italian refugees. Disease killed half of them by 1770, the town was abandoned in 1777, and by 1783 only 291 still survived at nearby Saint Augustine.

Fall 1768 Dr. Bodo Otto of Bethlehem, Pa., extracted the first domestically produced cottonseed oil.

June 10, 1768 Following the seizure of John Hancock's ship *Liberty* by customs officials, rioting erupted at Boston's docks. Customs officers fled the city, and on June 15 the royal governor requested British troops be sent to protect the customs service.

October 1, 1768 Seventeen hundred British soldiers landed at Boston to protect customs officers.

January 1769 Tennessee's first permanent white inhabitants settled on the Watauga River in the mountains. The earliest known resident, William Bean, fathered the first white child born in Tennessee.

June 7, 1769 Daniel Boone first saw Kentucky's bluegrass plateau from Pilot Knob in the Appalachians. Boone and his companions entertained themselves nightly by reading *Gulliver's Travels* aloud.

July 22, 1769 Charles Town, S.C., became the last major port to adopt a nonimportation agreement to protest Parliament's taxes. Alarmed by a 40% drop in exports to North America by late 1769, British merchants began lobbying Parliament to repeal the tax.

1769 The earliest known water closet in British America was designed for Whitehall, a mansion in Anne Arundel County, Maryland.

January 19, 1770 Many injuries, but no deaths, resulted when 40 British troops with drawn bayonets brawled with New Yorkers armed with clubs in a hard-fought clash called the Battle of Golden Hill, caused by the soldiers' recent destruction of a "Liberty Pole."

March 5, 1770 British soldiers guarding the customs house fired upon a riotous crowd threatening them; they killed five civilians and wounded six others in the Boston Massacre. On Oct. 30, a Boston jury declared all of the soldiers innocent, except two found guilty of manslaughter—who were then discharged on a technicality.

April 12, 1770 The government of Lord North, prime minister since January, repealed all Townshend taxes except the tea duty, which had been projected to raise over half of all revenue under the law. North's compromise undermined the colonial nonimportation policy, and most cities replaced it with a selective boycott of tea.

May 1, 1770 Harvard College ceased ranking its entering students according to the social prominence of their fathers.

May 16, 1771 Gov. William Tryon and 1,300 North Carolina militia, mostly easterners, defeated 2,500 Regulators (westerners opposing corrupt officials) at the Battle of Alamance near Hillsboro. About 300 casualties resulted and seven Regulators were later executed.

June 10, 1772 The British revenue cutter *Gaspee,* whose crew were widely despised for abusing their authority to plunder local ship cargoes, was boarded and burned near Providence, R.I.

October 28, 1772 Boston's Town Meeting issued a call for all towns in Massachusetts to form committees of correspondence. These committees, which later spread elsewhere in New England, became the primary means of mobilizing popular opposition against Britain.

1772 Wheeling, W. Va., was first settled. The city's name came from the Indian word *Weeling* (Place of Skulls), which described the decapitated heads of several white travelers left on poles by Indians as a warning for other whites to stay away.

March 12, 1773 Virginia requested all colonial assemblies to form committees of correspondence. By February 1774, all but North Carolina and Pennsylvania had done so, and for the first time since 1767 an intercolonial network was operating to defend American rights.

April 27, 1773 To prevent the East India Company's bankruptcy and to undermine American resistance to buying taxed tea, Parliament passed the Tea Act, which reduced taxes on East India tea, which could then undersell any tea smuggled in as competition.

December 16, 1773 Boston citizens threw a tea party by heaving 45 tons of East India tea into the harbor to prevent the government from collecting taxes on the proceeds of its sale.

1773 The first volume of verse written by an African American to be published was Phillis Wheatley's *Poems on Various Subjects.*

March 31, 1774 George III signed the Boston Port Bill, which ordered that the city's harbor be closed on June 1 if Bostonians had not by that date made compensation for the tea destroyed on Dec. 16, 1773. This measure along with the Administration of Justice Act, the Massachusetts Government Act, the Quebec Act, and the Quartering Act became known in the colonies as the Intolerable Acts.

May 17, 1774 Rhode Island made the earliest recommendation that the first intercolonial meeting called since the Stamp Act Congress of 1766 be held to consider a response to the Boston Port Bill.

May 20, 1774 George III signed the Administration of Justice Act, which allowed that in cases like that of the soldiers charged with the Boston Massacre, the trial could be held in any colony or even in Britain. Colonists termed this law the Murder Act.

May 20, 1774 George III signed the Massachusetts Government Act, which ended the practice of electing jurymen and members of the legislature's upper house. It also required that every town get the governor's permission to hold more than one town meeting annually.

May 20, 1774 George III signed the Quebec Act, which annexed western lands claimed by several colonies to Quebec; it also alarmed Anglo-Americans by dispensing with both legislative government and English civil law in the French colony.

June 2, 1774 George III signed the Quartering Act, which allowed governors to send troops to the scene of riots and quarter them in private buildings, provided they were unoccupied by civilians.

September 1, 1774 Fighting was narrowly averted during the "Powder Alarm," when hundreds of armed colonists confronted redcoats seizing arms and ammunition from a Cambridge, Mass. militia depot.

September 5, 1774 The First Continental Congress convened at Philadelphia with 56 delegates from all colonies but Georgia. Peyton Randolph of Virginia took office as president.

September 17, 1774 Congress adopted the Suffolk Resolves, which declared the newly formed Massachusetts government to be illegal and authorized passive resistance by the citizens there.

October 10, 1774 During Lord Dunmore's War, Andrew Lewis's 900 Virginians defeated 800 Shawnees under Cornstalk at Point Pleasant, W. Va. on October 30, near Chillicothe, Ohio, Shawnees and Governor Dunmore signed the Treaty of Camp Charlotte that allowed whites to settle Kentucky.

October 14, 1774 Congress passed a Declaration and Resolves naming thirteen Parliamentary acts as unconstitutional, and it pledged to use an economic boycott to press for their repeal.

October 18, 1774 Congress established the Continental Association, which prescribed procedures for terminating commerce between the thirteen colonies and all other parts of the British Empire.

October 24, 1774 The Continental Congress recommended that local governments ban plays and other public entertainments as frivolous distractions from the political crisis. (Congress repeated this resolution on Oct. 12, 1778.) During the Revolution, most theater companies went to other colonies, such as Jamaica, or to Britain.

October 26, 1774 The Continental Congress adjourned until May 1775.

December 14, 1774 New Hampshire militia took possession of the first British military post to fall into American hands when they removed ammunition from a royal gunpowder magazine at Portsmouth.

January 11, 1775 Francis Salvador, the first Jewish citizen to win public office, was elected to South Carolina's Provincial Congress. Captain Salvador died fighting Cherokee Indians on July 31, 1776.

February 9, 1775 Parliament declared Massachusetts to be in rebellion.

February 22, 1775 The first U.S. industrial company capitalized by the sale of stock began selling its shares for £10 to finance the American Manufactory of Woolens, Linens, and Cottons at Philadelphia.

March 6, 1775 The first African American initiated as a Mason, Prince Hall, was initiated into the British army's lodge (no. 441) at Castle William in Boston. Hall would organize African Lodge No. 1 on July 3, 1776, which white American Masons did not recognize.

March 15, 1775 Kentucky's permanent white settlement began when Ft. Harrodsburg (begun in 1774) was reoccupied after Dunmore's War.

March 17, 1775 The Cherokee sold Kentucky and north-central Tennessee to Richard Henderson's Transylvania Company for £10,000, an amount equivalent to a suit of clothes for each Cherokee. Daniel Boone and thirty axemen then blazed the Wilderness Trail and on April 6 founded Boonesborough, Kentucky's second oldest white settlement.

March 23, 1775 Patrick Henry delivered his "Give me liberty or give me death" speech at the Virginia House of Burgesses.

April 14, 1775 Philadelphians organized America's earliest abolitionist organization, the Society for the Relief of Free Negroes Unlawfully Held in Bondage.

April 19, 1775 Armed hostilities began with skirmishes between minutemen and redcoats at Lexington and Concord, Mass., followed by a running battle along the sixteen-mile road to Boston. There were 286 casualties among the British and 88 among the Yankees.

May 1775 On May 12, Ethan Allen, with Benedict Arnold and 83 Vermonters, took Ft. Ticonderoga, N.Y., "in the name of the great Jehovah and the Continental Congress." Allen's men seized Ft. Crown Point on May 12 and Arnold occupied St. John's, Canada on May 16.

May 10, 1775 The Second Continental Congress convened at Philadelphia, with Georgia still unrepresented. President Peyton Randolph withdrew on the 24th and John Hancock replaced him.

June 12, 1775 The Revolution's first naval engagement occurred

Bostonians enjoyed the best seats possible to watch the battle for Bunker Hill (largely fought over preliminary positions on Breed's Hill) of June 17, 1775. The fight was the Revolution's first major, set-piece battle conducted along European rules of combat. The British finally took the position, but only after the Yankees ran out of ammunition and withdrew in good order. [From *Harper's Magazine,* October 1901] (Howard Pyle Collection, courtesy Delaware Art Museum, Wilmington, Delaware)

at Machias, Me., when the Massachusetts ships *Diligent* and *Machias Liberty* captured HMS *Margaretta*.

June 14, 1775 Congress resolved to establish the Continental Army.

June 15, 1775 Congress named George Washington commander of the Continental Army, and he accepted the next day.

June 17, 1775 Outnumbered New Englanders stubbornly resisted British regulars attacking Breed's Hill (near Bunker Hill) before withdrawing. The British lost 1,054 men and the Yankees lost 441.

June 22, 1775 Congress printed the first U.S. paper money.

July 5, 1775 Congress made its last offer of conciliation in John Dickinson's Olive Branch Petition, which demanded a cease-fire at Boston, repeal of the Intolerable Acts, and peace negotiations. On the next day Congress affirmed its willingness to wage war in a "Declaration of the Causes and Necessities of Taking up Arms."

July 26, 1775 Congress established a post office department with Benjamin Franklin as first postmaster general.

August 23, 1775 Having already refused the Olive Branch Petition, George III proclaimed the thirteen colonies to be in rebellion.

October 13, 1775 Congress authorized the creation of the Continental Navy, with an initial authorization of two ships of ten guns each. The navy commissioned its first warship, the *Hannah,* on September 2. Esek Hopkins became its first commander-in-chief on December 22.

November 10, 1775 Congress established the Marine Corps, at an initial strength of two battalions (about 1,000 men). The Marines first saw battle at Ft. Nassau, in the Bahamas, on March 4, 1776.

November 17, 1775 Governor Dunmore of Virginia promised freedom to all slaves who helped him uphold royal authority. About 800 slaves ran away to become soldiers under Dunmore and were defeated by Whig militia at the Battle of Great Bridge, Va., on Dec. 11, 1775.

December 3, 1775 The first raising of an official U.S. flag occurred on the USS *Alfred* in the Delaware River. This Grand Union Flag flew Britain's Union Jack on a blue field superimposed on thirteen red and white stripes. It was first saluted over land on Jan. 1, 1776, at Washington's headquarters at Somerville, Mass.

December 31, 1775 Generals Richard Montgomery and Benedict Arnold launched a futile attack against Quebec. Montgomery was killed and Arnold wounded, along with 400 others lost. Continental forces retreated from Canada in summer 1776.

1775 The first woman postmaster, Mary Katherine Goddard, took over the mail in Baltimore, Md.; she served until Nov. 14, 1789.

January 15, 1776 The first edition of Thomas Paine's *Common Sense* was printed. The pamphlet, which sold perhaps 100,000 copies in three months, decisively cracked the lingering allegiance felt to George III and so ended the last emotional barrier to independence among the majority of colonists.

January 26, 1776 The Continental Army appointed its first Catholic chaplain, Fr. Louis Eustace Lotbinière, to serve French Canadians who enlisted in Col. James Livingston's regiment.

February 27, 1776 North Carolina revolutionaries decisively defeated a large force of Scottish Tories at Moore's Creek Bridge.

March 17, 1776 His position made hopeless by U.S. siege artillery dragged from Ticonderoga by Henry Knox, Gen. Gage evacuated Boston.

March 19, 1776 Congress authorized civilians to go privateering against British merchant ships. U.S. privateers would capture more than 2,000 merchant vessels and 16,000 crewmen during the war.

April 12, 1776 North Carolina became the first colony to authorize its delegates at the Continental Congress to vote for independence.

May 2, 1776 Louis XVI of France ordered arms and ammunition worth a million livres to be sent secretly to the Continental Army. Through 1777, France supplied about 80% of the rebels' arms and ammunition.

May 4, 1776 Rhode Island declared itself independent of Britain.

June 12, 1776 Virginia adopted the first bill of rights, drafted by George Mason.

June 28, 1776 South Carolina militia under Gen. Charles Lee repulsed a British amphibious assault on Charles Town.

July 2, 1776 The first state constitution that did not exclude women from voting was adopted by New Jersey. Few women voted until a 1790 voting law specifically used "his and her" in referring to electors. The Democratic legislature disfranchised women in 1807.

July 2, 1776 Congress passed Richard Henry Lee's resolution establishing the thirteen colonies as an independent nation.

July 4, 1776 Congress approved Thomas Jefferson's Declaration of Independence as a preamble to the Lee resolution adopted July 2. Except for President Hancock, the delegates did not sign until August 2, and Mathew Thornton of New Hampshire did not sign until November.

August 27, 1776 British forces attacked Continental troops on Long Island, N.Y. At a loss of about 400, the British inflicted 1,300 American casualties, including two generals captured. Washington saved 9,500 survivors from annihilation with a night evacuation to New York City on August 29–30.

September 6, 1776 David Bushnell's underwater vessel *Turtle* launched the first submarine attack against British admiral Lord Howe's flagship off New York City but failed to sink its target.

September 9, 1776 Congress belatedly ordered that the nation be referred to as the United States rather than the United Colonies.

September 15, 1776 The British drove American forces from Kip's Bay and then entered New York City.

September 21, 1776 Fire destroyed about 300 buildings in New York.

September 22, 1776 The British hung Capt. Nathan Hale of Connecticut as a spy. Hale's dying words, that he regretted having "but one life to lose for [his] country," made him a national hero.

November 16, 1776 At a cost of 458 casualties, the British took Ft. Washington, N.Y. and killed or captured 2,818 American defenders.

November 18, 1776 After American forces evacuated Ft. Lee, N.J., across the Hudson from Ft. Washington, the Continental Army left New York to the British and began retreating across New Jersey, from which it entered Pennsylvania on December 11.

December 5, 1776 The earliest college fraternity, Phi Beta Kappa, was inaugurated at the College of William and Mary.

December 25, 1776 Washington took Trenton, N.J., and captured 918 Hessians and suffered just 4 casualties (including future president James Monroe, who was wounded).

January 3, 1777 Washington inflicted 400 casualties on British forces at Princeton, N.J., while losing only 40 men himself.

May 20, 1777 In the Treaty of DeWitt's Corner, the Cherokee surrendered all their claims to territory in South Carolina.

June 14, 1777 Congress adopted the flag's modern design: "thirteen stripes alternate red and white, that the Union be thirteen stars white in a blue field."

June 17, 1777 Gen. John Burgoyne launched an invasion of New York with 8,300 British troops; he took Ft. Ticonderoga on July 30.

July 2, 1777 Vermont adopted the first constitution to forbid slavery and allow all adult men to vote without regard to property.

July 20, 1777 In the Treaty of Long Island (Tennessee), the Cherokee surrendered most of their claims to territory in North Carolina.

July 31, 1777 The Marquis de Lafayette, a French aristocrat, received rank as a major general in the Continental Army.

August 16, 1777 John Stark's Vermont militia destroyed a foraging party of 900 Hessians from Burgoyne's army at Bennington, Vt.

August 16, 1777 Iroquois and Tories ambushed 800 militia under Nicholas Herkimer at Oriskany, N.Y. The New Yorkers lost about 150 men but held their ground until the Indians and Tories withdrew.

August 22, 1777 The American garrison of Ft. Stanwix, N.Y. forced Col. Barry St. Leger to abandon his siege and prevented him from reinforcing Gen. John Burgoyne's British troops as planned.

September 1, 1777 Maj. Samuel McCulluck escaped an Indian war party near Wheeling, W. Va., by forcing his horse over an almost perpendicular, 150-foot cliff. He and the horse survived unhurt. When Indians finally killed McCulluck on July 30, 1782, they respectfully ate his heart to gain some of his courage.

September 11, 1777 The British under General William Howe inflicted a major defeat on Washington's army at Brandywine Creek, Pa. The Americans had about 1,000 casualties, compared to 544 for the British.

September 26, 1777 British forces occupied Philadelphia, from which Congress had fled on the 19th.

October 4, 1777 Washington's army suffered defeat in an attack on British troops at Germantown, Pa. American casualties totaled about 1,090, while British losses numbered around 550 men.

October 17, 1777 After two battles near Saratoga, N.Y. (September 19 and October 7), Gen. John Burgoyne surrendered his 5,800 British troops to Gen. Horatio Gates.

November 15, 1777 Congress approved John Dickinson's constitution, the Articles of Confederation, and asked the states to ratify it.

December 17, 1777 Washington's army took up winter quarters at Valley Forge, Pa., where one quarter of these battle-worn troops would die from disease or malnutrition by the next spring.

January 11, 1778 Commanding a keelboat he whimsically christened the USS *Rattletrap,* Navy captain James Willing left Pittsburgh to raid Tories on the lower Mississippi. Part patriot and part pirate, Willing plundered Natchez, Miss., on February 19; sacked Manchac, La., on February 23; and then captured and sold four British merchant ships.

February 6, 1778 Foreign recognition of U.S. independence first came when French diplomats signed a treaty of friendship, which Congress ratified on May 4, but France otherwise remained neutral in the war until June.

February 23, 1778 Prussian officer Friedrich von Steuben arrived at Valley Forge. Von Steuben's organizational genius and practical training techniques turned the amateur Continental soldiers into a professional army with standards roughly equal to those of the British army by mid-1778.

April 27, 1778 John Paul Jones fought the Revolution's only land battle fought on English soil when his sailors and marines captured Whitehaven, Cumberland, and destroyed the artillery protecting its harbor.

June 17, 1778 A British naval attack on French ships resulted in France immediately entering the war against Great Britain.

June 1778 The earliest U.S. espionage agency was organized as the Headquarters Secret Service and headed by Aaron Burr.

June 18, 1778 British general Henry Clinton evacuated Philadelphia.

June 28, 1778 Washington's army attacked Clinton's forces at Monmouth Court House, N.J. Clinton withdrew that evening and left Washington holding the battlefield. British losses were at least 385, compared to 267 American casualties. About one-third of the 106 U.S. dead were victims of heat stroke on that torrid day.

December 29, 1778 Guided by slaves who showed them where the town's defenses were weakest, British troops seized Savannah, Ga., which fell with the loss of 94 Americans killed and wounded and another 453 captured. The British lost just 7 killed and 19 wounded.

December 1778 Americans first employed mine warfare against ships supplying British-held Philadelphia by sending David Bushnell's floating explosives down the Delaware River. The first casualties resulted when a mine killed four bargemen on Jan. 5, 1779.

1778 The earliest organization to pool African-American financial resources, the Free African Society, began serving as a rudimentary insurance company among Philadelphia blacks. The society used its capital to assist the poor, treat the sick, and pay for burials.

February 25, 1779 Though lacking any artillery, George Rogers Clark and 170 riflemen took Vincennes, Ind., a post with twelve cannons, from the British, who had just recaptured it on Dec. 17, 1778. His victory solidified U.S. control over the Ohio Valley.

March 3, 1779 Lt. Col. James Prevost's 900 British troops surprised and defeated 1,700 Carolinians and Georgians at Briar Creek, Ga. The British inflicted 377 casualties at a loss of only 8 men.

June 21, 1779 Spain declared war on Great Britain, but as an ally of France and without recognizing U.S. independence.

July 16, 1779 Carrying unloaded muskets and attacking only with bayonets, 1,200 Virginians and Pennsylvanians under Anthony Wayne inflicted 134 casualties and took 442 prisoners at Stony Point, N.Y., at a cost of 100 American dead and wounded.

August 29, 1779 Gen. John Sullivan defeated Iroquois Indians under Joseph Brant near Elmira, N.Y. Sullivan's forces then destroyed 41 Iroquois villages and drove the Indians into Canada.

September 22–Oct. 9, 1779 U.S. and French forces suffered 1,094 casualties while besieging Savannah, Ga. The outnumbered British garrison lost only 40 killed and 62 wounded.

September 23, 1779 John Paul Jones uttered the famous words "I have not yet begun to fight" while his *Bonhomme Richard* battled the British ship *Serapis.* Jones won, but his ship sank a day later.

September 1779 Gov. Bernardo Polinar de Galvez led Spanish troops from New Orleans, La., and took Britain's outposts at Baton Rouge, La., and Natchez, Miss.

December 4, 1779 The College of William and Mary named America's first professor of law, George Wythe.

March 1, 1780 Pennsylvania became the first of the thirteen original states (not counting Vermont) to emancipate slaves by declaring free all children born of slaves after that date.

May 12, 1780 Gen. Henry Clinton captured Charles Town, S.C., its 3,371 American troops, and four U.S. warships.

May 25, 1780 Continental troops at Morristown, N.J., briefly mutinied to protest cuts in rations and five months without pay.

May 29, 1780 Banistre Tarleton's Tory dragoons massacred more than 100 Virginia Continentals as they tried to surrender at Waxhaw Creek, S.C., in one of the war's worst atrocities.

May 1780 Transylvania Academy, the oldest institution of higher learning west of the Appalachians, was chartered at Lexington, Ky.; it became a university on Dec. 22, 1798.

August 16, 1780 Lord Cornwallis's British army lost just 324 men but inflicted 1,000 U.S. casualties at the Battle of Camden, S.C.

September 25, 1780   Gen. Benedict Arnold fled to safety upon learning that his treasonous contacts with the British had been discovered.

October 7, 1780   Virginia and Tennessee militia annihilated 1,100 Tories at King's Mountain, S.C., but lost only 90 men themselves.

December 20, 1780   The Netherlands entered the war against Britain.

January 1, 1781   Pennsylvania Continentals marched on Congress at Philadelphia to demand their back pay, but they returned peacefully to duty on January 7. New Jersey troops mutinied on January 20 and were suppressed on January 27, after which two leaders were hung.

January 17, 1781   Gen. Daniel Morgan inflicted 637 casualties on Tarleton's Tory dragoons at Cowpens, S.C., at a loss of 72 men.

January 1781   Spanish forces under Don Eugenio Pourre captured the British post of Ft. Saint Joseph, near modern Niles, Mich.

March 1, 1781   The first constitution of the United States, the Articles of Confederation, went into effect when Maryland ratified it.

March 15, 1781   Lord Cornwallis drove Gen. Greene's Continentals from Guilford Courthouse, N.C., but lost 600 men, a quarter of his force, while the Americans had 261 casualties.

April 19, 1781   Lord Rawdon, with only 900 British, drove 1,500 Americans under Gen. Greene from Hobkirk's Hill, S.C. Rawdon lost 258 men, a quarter of his force, while Greene lost 264.

April 22, 1781   The Spanish garrison of Ft. Panmure at Natchez, Miss. surrendered to 200 Tories and Indians.

May 9, 1781   Ft. George's 1,600 British defenders at Pensacola, Fla. surrendered to 5,000 Spanish troops after the post gunpowder magazine exploded. The siege cost the Spanish 298 men.

September 8, 1781   After losing control of his Americans, who had begun looting the British camp, Gen. Greene retreated from Eutaw Springs, S.C. Greene suffered 554 casualties, but the British lost 693 men.

October 19, 1781   Following a three-week siege, Lord Cornwallis's army of 8,081 British troops was surrendered to Washington at Yorktown, Va.

December 31, 1781   Congress chartered the country's first investment bank, the Bank of North America, to help service the national debt. The bank commenced business on Jan. 7, 1782.

March 5, 1782   The House of Commons authorized George III to make peace with the United States. Prime Minister Lord North resigned on March 20.

August 2, 1782   George Washington instituted the U.S. Army's first medal, the Badge of Military Merit (nicknamed the Purple Heart).

September 16, 1782   The Great Seal of the United States was first used to authorize Gen. Washington to negotiate prisoner

The British army's surrender at Yorktown, Va. on Oct. 19, 1781 is here depicted by John Trumbull. The British commander, Lord Cornwallis, snubbed the ceremony, and his adjutant, Brig. Gen. Charles O'Hara, tried to hand over his sword to the French army's commander, who would not take it. Washington refused to treat with a lower ranking officer, so O'Hara capitulated to Maj. Gen. Benjamin Lincoln, who himself had surrendered a Continental garrison at Charles Town in 1780. (United States Capitol Art Collection, courtesy Architect of the Capitol, Washington.)

exchanges. The design formally became the nation's official seal on Sept. 13, 1789.

October 15, 1782 Maryland chartered its first college, Washington College at Chestertown; its first commencement was on May 14, 1783.

March 21, 1783 The Revolution's last naval action occurred when a Maryland ship under Capt. John Lynn captured several British supply barges at Devil's Island, Chesapeake Bay.

April 17–24, 1783 The Revolution's last land battle occurred when Capt. Raymondo Du Breuil's 40 Spanish troops held Ft. Carlos, Ark., against a siege by James Colbert's 100 Tories and 40 Indians.

May 13, 1783 The first U.S. veterans' organization, the Society of the Cincinnati, was founded by Continental Army officers.

May 30, 1783 The first daily newspaper in the United States, the *Pennsylvania Evening Post,* began publication in Philadelphia.

July 2, 1783 Britain forbade U.S. ships to land foodstuffs at its West Indian colonies, which were one of the most important markets for American farm produce.

July 8, 1783 The Massachusetts Supreme Court declared slavery a violation of the state constitution.

August 30, 1783 The first American ship to reach China, Capt. John Greene's *Empress of China,* arrived at Canton.

September 3, 1783 The Treaty of Paris ended the Revolutionary War.

September 22, 1783 The first African-American Congregational minister, Lemuel Haynes, received ordination in Litchfield County, Conn. Haynes ministered to white parishes in Connecticut, Vermont, and New York.

November 3, 1783 Congress ordered all Continental soldiers discharged except for a small force waiting for the British to leave New York.

November 25, 1783 Gen. Clinton's British troops evacuated New York.

December 23, 1783 George Washington resigned as commander-in-chief at Annapolis, Md.

1783 The first African American to become a licensed physician, Dr. James Durham, bought his freedom for 500 pesos from Dr. Robert Dow, who had provided his medical training, and began practicing medicine in New Orleans, La.

April 8, 1784 Britain violated the Treaty of Paris by ordering Canada's governor not to withdraw six military garrisons from U.S. soil. These forts provided arms and encouragement for Indian raids in the Ohio Valley over the next decade.

Summer 1784 Glutted markets for goods, a credit shortage, and a rising number of suits for unpaid debts dragged the seaport cities into a commercial depression that lasted for several years.

June 24, 1784 The first balloon flight in the United States lifted Edward Warren, age 13, airborne at Baltimore, Md.

June 26, 1784 Contrary to the Treaty of Paris, Spain prohibited Americans from shipping exports to world markets via New Orleans.

August 24, 1784 Congress refused to grant statehood to Franklin, a group of Tennessee counties that had seceded from North Carolina.

November 14, 1784 The first American Protestant bishop, Samuel Seabury, was consecrated as head of the Protestant Episcopal Church in Edinburgh, Scotland; he had been elected in the United States in 1783.

December 24, 1784 Congress voted to move the U.S. capital from Trenton, N.J., to New York City.

January 27, 1785 Georgia chartered the Franklin College of Arts and Sciences, now the University of Georgia, the first state-supported college in the United States.

May 20, 1785 Congress passed the Land Ordinance of 1785, which set the basic unit of settling the Northwest Territory as a township six miles square, divided into thirty-six equal sections.

September 10, 1785 The United States completed its first treaty with a German state when John Adams signed a commercial agreement with Prussia.

January 16, 1786 Virginia adopted Thomas Jefferson's Statute for Religious Freedom, a model for the later U.S. First Amendment.

June 8, 1786 The earliest mass-produced ice cream was advertised for sale by Mr. Hall in New York City.

July 29, 1786 The *Pittsburgh Gazette,* the first newspaper printed west of the Appalachians, began publication.

August 8, 1786 Congress ordered the U.S. currency, then denominated in British pounds, shillings, and pence, to be replaced with a system resembling Spanish dollars, with dimes and pennies as small coins.

August 29, 1786 Congress rejected Jay's Treaty with Spain because it abandoned U.S. rights to ship exports via the Mississippi River.

September 14, 1786 Delegates to the Annapolis, Md., conference on interstate commerce called for a convention to consider ways to strengthen the national government, to meet at Philadelphia in May 1787. Congress endorsed the proposal on Feb. 21, 1787.

1786 New Jersey minted the first coin to use the motto *E Pluribus Unum* ("One From Many"). The United States adopted the motto on April 2, 1792.

January 25, 1787 Dissatisfaction with heavy state taxes climaxed in violence when Daniel Shays and 1,200 followers were repulsed by Massachusetts militia while trying to take the Springfield armory. Shays's forces were finally dispersed at Petersham on February 4.

February 21, 1787 Congress endorsed the calling of a convention to consider amendments to the Articles of Confederation.

April 17, 1787 The first comedy to be both written and professionally acted in the United States, Royall Tyler's *The Contrast,* opened in New York.

May 25, 1787 A convention to consider amending the Articles of Confederation convened at Philadelphia under George Washington.

July 13, 1787 The Ordinance of 1787 established official U.S. practices for organizing unsettled territories into states.

August 22, 1787 The first successful public operation of a steam-powered boat (45 feet long) was demonstrated by John Fitch on the Delaware River at Philadelphia, but it proved to be a commercial failure.

September 17, 1787 The Philadelphia Convention approved a draft Constitution to replace the Articles of Confederation.

December 7, 1787 Delaware became the first state to ratify the Federal Constitution.

March 24, 1788 Rhode Island's voters rejected the Constitution 2,708 to 237. Rhode Island remained outside the Federal Union until May 29, 1790, when a convention voted to ratify by 34 to 32.

April 7, 1788 The first white settlers in Ohio landed at Marietta after sailing down the Ohio River in a bullet-proof barge named the *Mayflower,* which carried a few descendants of the Pilgrims of 1620.

April 13–14, 1788 Outrage that grave robbers were selling corpses to New York's College of Medicine for dissection classes produced riots at the offending hospital that left three men dead.

June 21, 1788 The Federal Constitution secured the nine states necessary for ratification when New Hampshire approved it.

August 2, 1788 North Carolina's ratifying convention voted to reject the Constitution 184 to 84. The state stayed outside the Union until Nov. 21, 1789, when a convention ratified 195 to 77.

October 10, 1788 The Congress at New York transacted its last day of business under the Articles of Confederation.

December 1, 1788 Spain opened up the port of New Orleans to U.S. exports but imposed a 15% duty on American goods.

January 23, 1789 U.S. Catholics founded their first college at Georgetown, Md.

February 4, 1789 The Electoral College conducted the first presidential election and unanimously chose George Washington.

March 4, 1789 Neither house of the First Congress was able to conduct business on the day set for its opening session because each lacked a quorum. Congress convened a month late in April.

April 30, 1789 Because no Supreme Court existed, New York chancellor Robert R. Livingston gave George Washington his oath as president. John Adams was sworn in as vice president nine days before Washington so that he could begin presiding over Senate debates.

May 12, 1789 New York's Society of St. Tammany, which had been organized in 1786, was chartered. Aaron Burr soon transformed this fraternal club into the city's Democratic Party organization.

September 25, 1789 Having sifted through 210 proposed constitutional amendments, Congress recommended 12 to the states for ratification. New Jersey was the first state to ratify them on November 20. (Two amendments, concerning Congressional apportionment and salaries, failed ratification and did not become part of the Bill of Rights.)

September 24, 1789 The Judiciary Act formed a Supreme Court of five associate justices and one chief justice; it also created three circuit courts and thirteen district courts.

January 4, 1790 Treasurer Alexander Hamilton issued his first report on the national debt. A second report on debt, taxation, and a national bank followed on December 13. Hamilton's program established U.S. national finances on a firm basis but became the catalyst for the swift rise of the Federalist and Democratic-Republican parties.

April 4, 1790 The U.S. Coast Guard, then called the Revenue Marine Service, was established by Congress.

April 17, 1790 The first American crew to sail around the world returned home to Boston, whence they had left in September 1787 under Capt. Robert Gray in the *Columbia*.

July 10, 1790 Congress voted to fix the capital at the District of Columbia. Philadelphia became temporary capital until 1800.

July 31, 1790 The United States awarded its first patent to Samuel Hopkins of Vermont for an improved method of making potash and pearl ash.

August 1, 1790 The United States completed its first census. The United States was the second nation to conduct regular censuses (Sweden was first), and it preceded Great Britain in taking censuses by a half century.

August 15, 1790 The first native-born American to become a Catholic bishop, John Carroll of Maryland, was consecrated to head Baltimore Diocese (created April 6, 1789), which included the entire United States.

September–October 1790 Gen. Josiah Harmar and some 1,400 troops floundered along Indiana's Maumee River trying to engage Indians in a decisive battle but withdrew after losing 200 casualties in skirmishes.

December 21, 1790 The first water-powered textile factory to spin cotton using Arkwright's patented English spindles began operating under Samuel Slater at Pawtucket, R.I.

1790 The Walnut Street Prison in Philadelphia was the first penitentiary constructed with individual cells.

February 25, 1791 President Washington signed Congress's charter for the (First) Bank of the United States. The Bank's main office opened at Philadelphia on Dec. 12, 1791.

March 4, 1791 Vermont became the first state to enter the Union after the original thirteen colonies.

June 24, 1791 Grandmaster Prince Hall organized the first black Masonic Grand Lodge at Boston.

September 13, 1791 John Green, a Boston sailor on the *Atrevida*, became the first known U.S. citizen to set foot in California when he went ashore to seek medical aid at Monterey, where he immediately died.

November 4, 1791 The U.S. Army's worst defeat by Indians occurred when Little Turtle's warriors killed 632 troops and wounded 283 others under Gen. Arthur St. Clair at modern Ft. Recovery, Ohio.

December 5, 1791 Treasurer Alexander Hamilton issued his report on manufactures. Congress rejected his call to stimulate industry with tariffs, but it later passed incentives for the merchant marine.

December 15, 1791 The Bill of Rights became part of the Constitution when Virginia's legislature ratified the first ten amendments.

1792 The first issue of the *Farmer's Almanac* appeared at Boston.

May 11, 1792 Capt. Robert Gray of Boston discovered the Columbia River and named it for his ship.

May 17, 1792 Merchant-brokers founded the nation's first stock market, which evolved into the New York Stock Exchange.

June 1, 1792 Kentucky entered the Union as the first state west of the Appalachians.

December 5, 1792 The first attempt to operate a theater in Boston failed when its manager, Joseph Harper, was arrested for violating a state law against performing plays dating from 1755.

ca. December 8, 1792 The first cremation in the United States consumed Henry Laurens at Charleston, S.C., shortly after his death on December 8.

February 12, 1793 The first Fugitive Slave Law was enacted; though never declared unconstitutional, it violated the Bill of Rights by denying free black citizens who had been wrongly arrested as runaway slaves the protection of the Fifth and Sixth Amendments.

March 21, 1793 Cherokees killed Thomas Ross, the first U.S. mail carrier to be scalped, on the Wilderness Trail to Kentucky.

April 8, 1793 French ambassador Edmond Genêt landed at Charleston, S.C. and began enlisting Americans as privateers to attack British shipping. By mid-1793, a dozen U.S. ships carrying a thousand American sailors were part of the French naval war against England.

April 22, 1793 Washington issued a Proclamation of Neutrality urging citizens to avoid involvement in French-British hostilities. Not until the Neutrality Act of June 5, 1794 would it be illegal for U.S. citizens to perform military service for foreign nations.

May 25, 1793 The first Catholic priest ordained in the United States, Fr. Stephen Badin, received holy orders at Baltimore, Md.

August 2, 1793 Washington's cabinet voted to demand Citizen Genêt's recall as French ambassador for violating U.S. neutrality.

August–October 1793 The nation's most deadly Yellow Fever epidemic struck Philadelphia and took about 5,000 lives, 10% of the city's population. The federal government fled the city, and Secretary of the Treasury Alexander Hamilton almost died of the disease.

October 28, 1793 Eli Whitney perfected the cotton gin at Mulberry Grove Plantation, Ga.

November 6, 1793 Britain's Privy Council issued secret Orders in Council forbidding neutral ships to trade with the French Caribbean islands. Without warning, the Royal Navy seized more than 250 U.S. ships by early 1794 and confiscated their cargoes.

December 31, 1793 Frustrated by Federalist and Hamiltonian dominance of the president, Thomas Jefferson resigned as secretary of state.

February 17, 1794 The British established Ft. Miami on U.S. soil (near modern Toledo, Ohio) to encourage Indian belligerence.

July 15, 1794 Large-scale violence against enforcement of the U.S. whiskey tax erupted near Pittsburgh. On August 7, Washington called for 15,000 militia to suppress the tax rebels. The troops quelled the disorders by arresting 150 insurgents, of whom 20 were tried for treason. Washington pardoned two men who had been sentenced to death.

July 29, 1794 Richard Allen and other African Americans in Philadelphia dedicated the first black Methodist congregation, from which the African Methodist Episcopal Church emerged in 1816.

August 20, 1794 Gen. Anthony Wayne decisively defeated 2,000 Indians at the Battle of Fallen Timbers (near Toledo, Ohio). This victory ended Indian warfare in the Ohio Valley until 1811.

September 10, 1794 Tennessee's first college, Blount College in Knoxville, received its charter.

December 14, 1794 Boston's town meeting ended its opposition to stage plays and petitioned the legislature to repeal a 1755 statute prohibiting their performance within Massachusetts. Shortly after, Charles Stuart Powell opened Boston's first theater.

1794 The Philadelphia–Lancaster turnpike, the nation's first major toll road and its earliest asphalt highway, was completed. The first segment of its 61-mile length had opened in 1791.

January 31, 1795 Secretary of the Treasury Alexander Hamilton resigned to resume his law practice.

May 15, 1795 The first African-American missionary among the Indians, Rev. John Morront, was ordained a Methodist minister in London, England; he preached successfully among the Cherokee.

June 24, 1795 The Senate ratified Jay's Treaty (signed by Jay on Nov. 19, 1794) with Britain. The British refused to repudiate the practice of impressing U.S. sailors, but they agreed to withdraw all troops from U.S. soil and to repay Americans for cargoes seized by the Royal Navy. Though the United States gained few trade concessions, Jay's Treaty improved relations with Britain and led to a 300% rise in American exports to the British Empire within five years.

August 3, 1795 Twelve Indian nations agreed to surrender two-thirds of Ohio and parts of Indiana in the Treaty of Greenville, Ohio.

March 15, 1796 The Senate ratified the Treaty of San Lorenzo with Spain (signed by Thomas Pinckney in Madrid on Oct. 27, 1795). Spain gave up its territorial claims in the southwestern United States and opened the port of New Orleans to American exports for three years.

April 13, 1796 The first elephant seen in the United States came to New York.

June 1, 1796 Tennessee became the sixteenth state.

July 2, 1796 Outraged over Jay's Treaty, France declared all U.S. ships sailing to British ports liable to searches by its warships. By Mar. 1797, French privateers had confiscated 316 U.S. ships.

1796 James Finley built the first substantial suspension bridge, a span of 70 feet over Jacob's Creek in Westmoreland County, Pa.

March 28, 1797 Nathaniel Briggs patented the first model of a washing machine.

May 10, 1797 The *United States,* the first warship commissioned since the navy had been demobilized in 1783, was launched.

June 26, 1797 Charles Newbold of New Jersey patented the first cast-iron plow. This plow's ability to slice through thick-rooted prairie grass would be essential in settling the midwestern frontier.

January 30, 1798 Representatives Roger Griswold of Connecti-

Ft. Washington, Ohio, was the primary supply base and headquarters for the U.S. Army's Legion of the Ohio while it defended settlers against Indians in the Northwest Territory. In 1791, Maj. Jonathan Heart, a regular officer stationed there, sketched this picture of the fort, which was located at Cincinnati. (Henry Ford, *History of Cincinnati, Ohio* [1881].)

cut and Mathew Lyon of Vermont fought the first brawl on the floor of Congress. Lyon spit at Griswold, who tried to hit him with a metal bar.

April 3, 1798 The Senate received documents of the XYZ Affair, when French agents tried to extort bribes from U.S. diplomats. American public opinion rallied around South Carolina Congressman Harper's toast: "Millions for defense, but not one cent for tribute."

April 7, 1798 Congress established Mississippi Territory.

May 3, 1798 The Navy Department received cabinet status.

May 9, 1798 President John Adams proclaimed a day of fasting and prayer to protect the United States from the "horror of French atheism."

June–July 1798 The following Alien and Sedition Acts became law: Naturalization Act (June 18), Alien Friends Act (June 25), Alien Enemies Act (July 6), and Sedition Act (July 14). Except for the Alien Enemies Act, the laws' Federalist authors intended to use them to harass Thomas Jefferson's party in the next election.

July 11, 1798 Congress reestablished the Marine Corps, which had been demobilized with the Navy since 1783.

July 16, 1798 The forerunner of the U.S. Public Health Service, the Marine Hospital Service, became a federal agency.

August 28, 1798 The first successful Anglo-American vineyard was established at Lexington, Ky.

November 16, 1798 The Kentucky Resolutions were passed by the state assembly to declare the Alien and Sedition Acts unconstitutional. A similar set of Virginia Resolutions was passed on December 24.

November 20, 1798 An undeclared naval war with France commenced when the USS *Retaliation* was taken by the French near Guadaloupe. This loss was the last suffered by the U.S. Navy, which captured 93 French warships in the next two years.

1798 Eli Whitney developed the first system of mass-producing interchangeable parts while designing his New Haven, Conn. factory for manufacturing muskets.

March 6, 1799 Eighteen men landed in jail at Bethlehem, Pa. for harassing U.S. tax collectors, but were soon released by a crowd led by John Fries. Federal troops quelled "Fries's Rebellion" without bloodshed and arrested Fries, who was sentenced to hang but was pardoned by President John Adams on May 21.

March 29, 1799 New York enacted a gradual abolition law granting freedom to children thereafter born to its 20,903 slaves, but only when females became 25 (in 1824) and males became 28 (in 1827).

July 17–21, 1799 Aroused by the murder of a man last seen at a bawdyhouse on Murray and Greenwich streets in New York City, crowds up to 1,000 tried to wreck the house of pleasure, which had to be protected by armed militia. There were many injuries and 45 arrests.

September–December 18, 1799 The *Franklin* under Capt. Deveraux became the first U.S. ship to land in Japan by claiming to be Dutch, and therefore entitled to trading rights. Deveraux stayed for four months in Japan.

November 22, 1799 The first declaration that states were empowered to nullify federal laws was made in the Second Kentucky Resolutions.

February 9, 1800 Napoleon I ordered the French army to observe ten days of mourning in memory of George Washington, who had died December 13.

February 17, 1800 The House of Representatives broke the Electoral Congress's only tie vote for president, between Thomas Jefferson and his running mate Aaron Burr, by electing Jefferson president, but only after casting 35 stalemated ballots over six days.

April 4, 1800 The first federal Bankruptcy Law was enacted, in part to let former U.S. treasurer Robert Morris leave debtor's prison.

April 24, 1800 The Library of Congress was authorized.

May 7, 1800 Indiana became a territory.

August 30, 1800 Gabriel Prosser's conspiracy, in which 1,000 slaves planned to seize Richmond, Va., failed when heavy rains kept them from rendezvousing as planned. Betrayed by three fellow slaves but aided by a white ship captain opposed to slavery, Prosser was later captured and hanged, as were about 35 of his followers.

October 1, 1800 Spain transferred Louisiana to France in the secret Treaty of San Ildefonso.

November 17, 1800 Congress met for the first time in Washington, D.C.

CHAPTER 4 The Economy

Much more is known about the American economy during the years 1763–1800 than for the preceding colonial period, but the data is far from complete. The Revolutionary War disrupted the normal recording of economic statistics, and even after hostilities ended in 1783, the bureaucracy of the Articles of Confederation lacked both the authority and inclination to measure commerce, personal wealth, or various components of domestic output. Not until 1790 did federal authorities resume compiling systematic information on the country's manufactures, trade, and finances. Even during the 1790s, however, many important elements of domestic production (especially concerning agriculture) were never documented, and virtually no effort was made to compute aggregate levels of personal or national income.

This era's major event, the War for Independence, dramatically affected the American economy in three major ways. By sharply limiting the country's ability to export agricultural commodities, the war curtailed farm income, although this reduction was partly offset by diverting labor toward the provision of goods needed for military purposes and other domestic consumption. By disrupting overseas trade, the war also forced the economy to become more self-sufficient through the substitution of home-manufactures for necessary imports excluded by the British blockade; when peace returned, however, the least efficient of these nascent industries quickly collapsed when abundant supplies of less expensive European goods became available. As a final consequence, the country's first private, commercial banks were founded to meet the increased needs of the government and the business community for capital.

The reestablishment of peace imposed serious disabilities upon U.S. overseas commerce. The U.S. merchant marine was excluded from the West Indies, formerly its best market for foodstuffs and timber, and the nation's fishing fleet was barred from taking catches at many favored banks offshore of Canada. Although some new trade was won in other foreign countries, America's merchant marine and most port cities fell into serious economic decline for seven years after 1783, but they finally recovered in the 1790s after the government negotiated several favorable commercial agreements, in particular Jay's Treaty with Great Britain in 1794, which eased former restrictions on trade with imperial ports. Rising overseas demand for foodstuffs likewise lifted farm income in the United States at the same time.

This chapter's data is first organized according to type of economic activity (agriculture, maritime pursuits, etc.). Because of extensive governmental regulation over oceanic trade—by both British and U.S. agencies—far more is known about the production of export goods than about the economy's purely domestic functions, which absorbed perhaps nine-tenths of labor resources. The later sections of the chapter provide information on such general topics as gross measures of economic transactions, levels of wealth, price indices, and usage of unfree or contract labor.

A Note on Monetary Values

Until the U.S. Treasury recoined the country's currency in the 1790s, Spanish coins earned in overseas trade formed the main stock of circulating money. The prime coin was Spain's silver dollar, which was often cut into eight equal pieces—or bits—for making change (hence the designation of a quarter as "two bits"). A Spanish dollar equaled four shillings, six pence (4s, 6d) in British sterling and was the usual price of a buckskin, so the term *buck* came to mean a dollar. North Americans translated the value of Spanish dollars into equivalent units of the British pound, which divided into twenty

shillings, each of twelve pence. Since silver and gold were relatively scarce, Spanish coins were valued at a premium—called the proclamation rate—to British sterling. When American governments issued their own paper monies, they also set exchange values by this proclamation rate. About 1770, the following exchange rates prevailed in the thirteen colonies:

When the United States denominated its currency in dollars, it set them at the approximate parity of a Spanish dollar to British sterling:

Colonial Currency of 1770		British Sterling of 1770		U.S. Dollars of 1791		Equivalent Value of U.S. Dollars in 1991
£1 Mass.	=	15s, 3d	=	$3.40	=	$56.65
£1 N.Y.	=	11s, 3d	=	$2.55	=	$42.50
£1 Pa.	=	12s, 5d	=	$2.75	=	$46.00
£1 Md.	=	15s, 7d	=	$2.75	=	$46.30
£1 Va.	=	17s, 10d	=	$3.60	=	$60.20
£1 S.C.	=	4s, 6d	=	$0.65	=	$10.70

$1.00 = 4s, 4d. For more detailed information, see "Currency and Money Supply," page 104, and Table 4.200, page 107.)

Agriculture

The Revolutionary era brought minor changes to American farming, and in general the agricultural practices of colonial times lasted into the early nineteenth century. The elimination of Parliamentary bounties led to the rapid demise of silk and indigo cultivation in the lower southern states, while cotton, which had previously been a minor crop, quickly emerged as a major staple in that region during the 1790s. Chesapeake farmers increasingly cut back on tobacco acreage to plant wheat, corn, and hemp, but tobacco output nevertheless held steady because production expanded into the South Carolina, Georgia, and Kentucky frontiers. Southern agriculture became less dependent upon the fortunes of tobacco and rice, and like northern farming, it derived an increasing share of its income from the sale of grains and livestock. Northern agriculture experienced no significant changes in the late 1700s, but it did benefit substantially from the growth of domestic demand, due to increasing urbanization, and from a rise in overseas demand, due to famine and warfare in Europe during the 1790s.

The most common statistics covering this period's agriculture concern exports and price fluctuations. Because relatively few first-hand accounts of farm management survive, except for records kept by large planters untypical of the average farmer, it has so far been difficult to determine how most farms operated. The following section first provides information regarding farms in general, and then presents data on exports and prices of the major commodities produced.

The Farm

While it is recognized that late-eighteenth-century agriculture experienced enormous disruption and change, there are still no precise measurements of the short-term damage done to farm incomes and production by the Revolution, nor any quantitative studies of how far recovery had proceeded through 1800. Probate records and tax lists contain a wealth of information about the rural economy, but no study has yet attempted to compile the data needed for a comprehensive profile of farming. At a minimum, such a study would describe what percentage of the population was primarily engaged in farming, and provide figures on median farm sizes and livestock holdings, the average return as a percent of land and fixed improvements, and the division of output between home consumption and surplus for sale.

Most detailed information about farms comes from local studies of a few communities, and the data is often not presented in a manner that allows for easy comparison. Until historians adopt broader research agendas and address one another's findings in a more direct fashion, the state of knowledge about farming in the Revolutionary era will remain sketchy. The materials in this section nevertheless provide some indication of the typical range of land utilization, livestock holdings, the equipment needed for an average farm, crop yields, and work schedules.

TABLE 4.1   AVERAGE LAND AND LIVESTOCK OWNED BY COLONIAL FARMERS, 1765–1771

	Conn. 1765–1769	Anne Arundel Co., Md., 1760–1769	Southeast Pa., 1772
Average acres	60	204	125
Average cattle	13	12	9
Average horses	3	4	4
Average sheep	16	11	15
Average swine	7	19	7

Sources: Jackson Turner Main, *Society and Economy in Colonial Connecticut* (1985), 234–38. Carville V. Earle, *The Evolution of a Tidewater Settlement System: All Hallow's Parish, Maryland, 1650–1783* (1975), 124, 203. James T. Lemon, *The Best Poor Man's Country: A Geographical Study of Southeastern Pennsylvania* (1976 ed.), 152, 162.

George Washington is here shown inspecting work in his fields at Mt. Vernon. Washington paid close attention to his plantation's management and read widely on agricultural topics. He experimented with new crops and livestock that might help diversify the southern economy; he also set an example as a progressive farmer by adopting practices designed to conserve the soil's fertility. [Engraving made after Junius Brutus Stearns, *Washington as a Farmer at Mount Vernon*] (Courtesy Library of Congress)

TABLE 4.2 UTILIZATION OF FARM LAND IN CONNECTICUT, 1796, AND MASSACHUSETTS, 1801

Counties	All Taxable Acreage	% Used for Tillage	% of Mowed Upland	% of Unmowed Meadow	% of Unimproved Meadow	% of Waste or Woodland
Connecticut						
Hartford	303,737	17.7%	18.0%	4.0%	26.2%	34.1%
New Haven	235,915	13.1%	26.0%	8.5%	33.6%	18.8%
New London	246,526	8.7%	27.1%	4.3%	39.4%	20.5%
Fairfield	231,473	21.7%	18.9%	10.2%	28.6%	20.6%
Windham	288,886	8.8%	19.3%	4.4%	29.3%	34.3%
Litchfield	283,011	11.9%	19.3%	8.4%	20.3%	44.1%
Middlesex	140,875	9.3%	25.0%	5.7%	33.8%	26.2%
Tolland	158,247	8.9%	21.6%	4.6%	29.9%	35.0%
(Summary)	1,888,670 [a]	12.8%	21.4%	6.2%	29.1%	30.5%
Massachusetts						
Hampshire	920,647	6.4%	5.1%	3.5%	17.0%	68.0%
Berkshire	475,147	6.0%	6.0%	2.2%	18.3%	67.5%
Worcester	811,122	3.9%	5.9%	6.6%	23.3%	60.3%
Middlesex	433,766	6.3%	7.1%	9.3%	25.9%	51.4%
Norfolk	217,800	4.4%	10.1%	8.9%	26.0%	50.6%
Essex	241,133	6.0%	9.5%	13.3%	44.2%	27.0%
(Summary)	3,099,615	5.5%	6.4%	6.1%	22.8%	59.2%

[a] Error in original source, which gave total as 1,988,688.
Note: Meadow included all mowing acreage except upland, plus salt marsh in Massachusetts. Unmowed pasture included improved commons land in Massachusetts and boggy lands now mowed. Woodland or waste included unenclosed land in Connecticut and unimprovable commons land in Massachusetts.
Source: Percy W. Bidwell and John I. Falconer, *History of Agriculture in the Northern United States, 1620–1860* (1925), 119–120.

TABLE 4.3 EXPENSE OF BUILDING A RICE AND INDIGO PLANTATION WITHIN 40 MILES OF CHARLES TOWN, S.C., ABOUT 1775

	£	s.	d.
To 1,000 acres of land (one third of which ought to be good swamp, the rest oak and hickory, with some pine barren) at 11s. 5d.	575	0	0
To a dwelling house, barn, stable, overseer's house, negro huts, &c.	142	15	0
To two valuable negroes (a cooper and a carpenter) at 71£. 7s. 6d.	142	15	0
To 26 other negroes (two thirds men and one-third women) at 35£. 10s.	927	10	0
To two ordinary old negroes to look after the poultry, kine, hogs, &c.	57	0	0
To a waiting boy	28	10	0
To a house-wench	40	15	0
To 20 head of oxen, cows, &c. at 1£. 8s.	28	0	0
To 2 stallions and 4 breeding mares, at 5£. 14s.	11	8	0
To hogs, sheep, and poultry	21	8	0
To plantation tools, a cart, plough, &c.	21	8	0
To 2 riding horses, for yourself, family, overseer, bridles, saddles, &c.	28	0	0
To clothes, provisions, &c. for negroes, seed, vats, &c. for the first year	35	15	0
To contingencies, nails, oil, &c.	15	15	0
	2,075	19	0

Source: Harry J. Carman, ed., *American Husbandry* (1939 ed. of 1775 imprint), 285.

TABLE 4.4 ESTIMATED PROFIT OF A RICE AND INDIGO PLANTATION IN SOUTH CAROLINA, ABOUT 1775

The plantation per annum after the first year. N.B. This calculation is for good years, and exclusive of accidents

	£	s.	d.
To the overseer's wages, and allowance for rum, &c.	35	15	0
To 32 pairs of shoes for negroes, at 2s. 6d.	3	0	0
To 160 yards of white plains (5 yards each negro) at 1s. 5d.	11	6	8
To thread, buttons, &c.	50	1	8
To one third of 32 blankets given every third year	3	17	0
To physic for each negro, as per agreement with the doctor	4	14	6
To Osnaburg cloth, lime, oil, nails, and iron ware	8	13	6
To freight and cooperage of 50 barrels of rice, at 2s. 10d.	7	1	8
To ditto of 6 of indigo, at 3s. 2d.	0	19	0
To tax and quitrent of 1,000 acres of land	2	2	6
To tax of 32 slaves, about	4	4	0
To purchase of two slaves annually, to keep up the original stock, which it is judged this and their increase may do	71	5	0
To wear and tear	14	10	0
	168	3	1
By the produce of 60 acres of indigo at 50 lb. per acre, at 2s. 10d. per lb. or 7£. 1s. 8d. per acre	425	0	0
By 50 barrels of rice, on 25 acres, each barrel 500 lb. net, at 6s. per cwt.	66	18	0
By 50 barrels	3	13	6
Total,	495	11	6
Expences	168	3	1
Balance, planter's profit	327	8	5

Source: Harry J. Carman, ed., *American Husbandry* (1939 ed. of 1775 imprint), 286.

TABLE 4.5 MODEL ORGANIZATION AND YIELDS OF A 150-ACRE NORTHERN FARM, CA. 1799

I. *Recommended Organization of Fields*
 1. General Division: 10 a. for home, barnyard, and garden plot
  51–60 a. for grains
  81–90 a. for meadow or fodder plants

 2. Field Division:

	5-Year Cycle	7-Year Cycle
(1 field to be	20 a. wheat	17 a. maize
manured yearly)	20 a. rye	17 a. wheat
	20 a. barley	17 a. rye or barley
	40 a. clover	17 a. roots (for 2 years)
	20 a. fallow	34 a. clover
		17 a. fallow

II. *Estimated production and value of crops*

maize	to yield 20 bu. per acre @ $ .50 per bu.
wheat	to yield 12 bu. per acre @ $1.00 per bu.
buckwheat	to yield 12 bu. per acre @ $ .50 per bu.
rye, barley	to yield 15 bu. per acre @ $ .60 per bu.
hay	to yield 2 tons per acre @ $1.00 per ton
potatoes	to yield 200 bu. per acre @ $ .10 per bu.
turnips	to yield 400 bu. per acre (not marketable)

III. *Fodder requirements for livestock*
 2 horses 3½ a. for hay (7 tons) and 1 a. for summer grass
 8 swine ½ a. for potatoes (100 bu.) and 150 bu. of corn
 9 sheep 1¼ a. for hay (2½ tons) and odd summer grass
 7 cattle 9 a. for straw (from grains) or 1 a. for turnips [or alternately, allocate for each cow either 2 a. of common pasture or ¼ a. carefully mowed hay] To fatten two cattle are needed 3½ tons of hay, ¼ a. of turnips, and 25 bu. of corn or other grain meal.

IV. *Estimated produce and value of livestock*
 Each cow to produce 80 lb. of butter yearly @ $ .20 per lb.
 A fattened cow or ox to sell for $22.75.
 Fattened swine to average of 161 lb. @ $6.00 per 100 lb.
 Each sheep to yield 3.4 lb. wool @ $ .25 per lb.
Note: Annual expenses estimated at 40% of value of farm output.

Source: John B. Bordley, *Essays and Notes on Husbandry and Rural Affairs* (Philadelphia, 1799), 57, 69, 72, 78, 175.

TABLE 4.6 PROPERTY NEEDED TO WORK A FARM OF AVERAGE SIZE: ESTATE INVENTORY OF ROBERT EVANS, HILLTOWN TWSP., BUCKS COUNTY, PA.

Inventory dated June 16, 1774.

	£	s	d
Wearing apparel	12	—	—
Riding mare, saddle & bridle	23	10	—
Mare & colts 20£ A Black Mare £10	30	—	—
A sorrel filly £10 An old sorrel horse £20	30	—	—
A pale red cow £4/15 a dark red do. £4/15	9	10	—
A red cow £4/5, a red & white do. £3	7	5	—
a black do. £3/15 a red heifer £2/15	6	10	—
A bull £4 a yearling calf £1/15 2 spring do. 49/	7	17	—
19 sheep £7:2:6 Swine £4/10	11	12	6
Winter grain £24 Indian Corn in the ground 40/	26	—	—
Oats & flax in the ground £2/10 flax in the sheaf 10/	3	—	—
A wagon Cart Body etc. £9 gears £3/5 a sled 3/	12	8	—
2 plows, Harrows, Swingletrees, etc.	2	12	6
wind mill 37/6 10 cow chains 26/	3	2	6
Walnut boards 45/ Oak shingles £4/10	6	15	—
Hay in the barn 15/ Pitch forks, Dung fork & hook 6/6	1	1	6
Broad ax and other axes 14/ a grubbing hoe & weeding do.	1	2	—
Handsaws auger, chisels hammer & anvil	—	9	6
Shovel & spade 7/ Maul & wedges 3/6	—	10	6
Scythes, sickles, rakes etc. 10/9, Iron bar 10/	1	—	9

[Inventory table — Alice Hanson Jones]

	£	s	d
Hogsheads, barrels, kegs, tubs, etc. 20/ grindstone 3/	1	3	—
2 beds & all the appurtenances thereto belonging	18	—	—
a case & drawers	2	—	—
2 chaff beds & appurtenances	2	—	6
10 tow sheets 50/ 5 blankets & coverlid 24/6	3	14	6
6 napkins, 7 pillowcases, 3 table cloths 38/6	1	18	6
Striped & check linen 22/6, flaxen linen 24½ yd. 55/1½	3	17	7½
flaxen linen 17 yd. 42/6, do. 25 yd. 50/	4	12	6
tow linen 18 yd. 27/, do. 15 yd. 18/9, flaxen do. 3 yd. 6/	2	11	9
16 bags 32/, 2 table cloths & a clothesline 4/	1	16	—
wool 30 lb. 40/, cords 5/, 2 Hackles 8/	2	13	—
11 bu. Buckwheat 24/9, leather 22/6, some Indian Corn & bag 3/6	2	10	9
Pewter 24/ Iron pots, gridiron etc. 64/	3	4	—
Delph & teaware 9/ Earthern ware 7/ Cedar ware 12/	1	8	—
Tea kettle 18/ a tea table 15/	1	13	—
Tables & Dough trough 20/ frying pan Ladle etc. 5/6	1	5	6
Bottles & glasses 5/ Some books 28/	1	13	—
8 Chairs 19/, a chest 10/, a half bushel 2/	1	11	—
Bake iron & hanger 7/6, fire shovel & tongs 5/	—	12	6
Gun & powder horn etc. 30/ a watering pot 2/6	1	12	6
Meal & Malt 22/6, Meat 35/	2	17	6
Old Chest, Cradle & some lumber upstairs	1	—	—
Cloth 90/ 72/, a great wheel, little do. & reel 18/	4	10	—
a drawing knife & some lumber in the loft	—	5	6
Nails, 30 lb., 22/6, Butter boxes 2/, Old Iron 3/	1	7	6
Cheese & Cheese hoops 8/, Candles & tallow 5/	—	13	—
a side saddle 40/, do. 3/6	2	3	6
Pocket book, spectacles & inkhorn 5/ Razer & hone 5/	—	10	—
Box iron & heaters 4/, Knives & forks 2/	—	6	—
Pottery 7/6, Book debt 2/6	—	10	—
Cash & Book	4	6	6
horse lock	—	3	6
	264	19	0½

Source: Alice Hanson Jones, *American Colonial Wealth: Documents and Methods* (1978), 227–28.

TABLE 4.7 ESTIMATED LAND USE AND OUTPUT FOR AN AVERAGE CONNECTICUT FARM, 1771

Land Usage	Crop Tillage	English & Upland Mowing	Fresh Meadow	Other Pasturage	Total Improved
Land taxed	12.93 a.	3.89 a.	5.90 a.	3.40 a.	26.12 a.

Farm Output		Grain	Hay	Cider
Average output per farm		82.5 bu	8.8 tons	4.3 barrels
Average output per family		69.3 bu.	7.4 tons	3.6 barrels

Note: 81% of farms had barns.
Source: Tax lists from Hadley, South Hadley, Granby, and Amherst, Conn., analyzed in Max G. Schumacher, *The Northern Farmer and His Markets During the Late Colonial Period* (1975), 31–32.

TABLE 4.8 PERCENT OF AVERAGE WHOLESALE PRICE OF FLOUR, WHEAT, AND CORN ABSORBED BY WATER TRANSPORT COSTS ON UPPER DELAWARE RIVER, 1769

Commodity (Unit)	Distance to Philadelphia	Freight Rate[d]	Price at Philadelphia[d]	% of Transport Costs
Flour (barrel)	70 mi.[a]	2s.	15.04s.	13.3%
Flour (barrel)	127 mi.[b]	2.50s.	15.04s.	16.6%
Flour (barrel)	170 mi.[c]	3s.	15.04s.	20.0%
Wheat (bushel)	70 mi.[a]	7d.	5.48s.	10.7%
Wheat (bushel)	127 mi.[b]	9d.	5.48s.	13.7%
Wheat (bushel)	170 mi.[c]	12d.	5.48s.	18.3%
Corn (bushel)	70 mi.[a]	7d.	2.80s.	20.8%
Corn (bushel)	127 mi.[b]	9d.	2.80s.	26.8%
Corn (bushel)	170 mi.[c]	12d.	2.80s.	35.7%

[a] From Marshall's Island
[b] From Easton
[c] From Minisinks
[d] Rates are given in shillings (s) and pence (d).
Source: Max G. Schumacher, *The Northern Farmer and His Markets During the Late Colonial Period* (1975), 59.

TABLE 4.9 MAXIMUM DISTANCE FROM PHILADELPHIA AT WHICH GRAINS COULD BE HARVESTED AND TRANSPORTED TO MARKET PROFITABLY, 1755–1772

Commodity	Distance at which land transport exceeded 50% of wholesale price at Philadelphia in given year — 1755[a]	— 1772[b]
corn	47 mi. @ 6.05s. per cwt.	62 mi. @ 10.33s. per cwt.
wheat	64 mi. @ 4.49s. per bu.	86 mi. @ 7.74s. per bu.
flour	106 mi. @ 13.76s. per cwt.	122 mi. @ 20.26s. per cwt.

Note: See introductory note on monetary values.
[a] 1 cwt. (hundredweight) carried at .78d. (pence) per mi.
[b] 1 cwt. (hundredweight) carried at 1d. (pence) per mi.
Source: Max G. Schumacher, *The Northern Farmer and His Markets During the Late Colonial Period* (1975), 63–64.

TABLE 4.10 COMPARATIVE VALUE, PER TON, OF AMERICAN FARM PRODUCTS ABOUT 1775

Commodity	Price per Ton (Sterling)[a]
Hemp	£21.0.0
Tobacco	£16.0.0
Wheat @ 30s./quarter	£7.10.0
Indigo @ 2½s./lb	£280.0.0
Ditto @ 5s./lb.	£560.0.0
Silk @ 20s./lb	£2,240.0.0
Wine	£20.0.0
Maize, barley, peas, and beans @ 16s./quarter	£4.8.0

[a] See introductory note on monetary values.
Source: Harry J. Carman, ed., *American Husbandry* (1939 ed. of 1775 imprint), 185.

TABLE 4.11 FARM YIELDS PER ACRE FOR UNITED STATES AGRICULTURE, ABOUT 1791

Districts	Wheat	Rye	Barley	Oats	Indian Corn	Buckwheat	Potatoes	Turnips
New England good crop	30	35	40	45	45	30	400	450
common crop	11	15	20	30	30	15	150	200
N.Y. good crop	32	35	40	45	45	35	300	350
common crop	10	12	14	25	25	16	90	100
Pa. good crop,	35	35	40	45	45	35	300	350
common crop	10	12	13	15	15	16	65	75
N.J. good crop	30	30	35	35	35	30	250	250
common crop	9	11	12	14	14	15	60	65
Del. good crop	35	35	34	56	36	30	250	250
common crop	10	12	13	15	15	16	65	65
Va. good crop	30	35	35	45	45	30	150	150
common crop	7	9	9	25	25	15	60	75
Carolina good crop	25	20	25	45	45	20	60	75
common crop	6	10	8	23	20	15	50	50
West. Terr. good crop	40	45	45	45	50	35	350	400
common crop	25	25	36	37	30	40	200	300

Source: Samuel Blodget, *Economica: A Statistical Manual for the United States of America* (1806), 97.

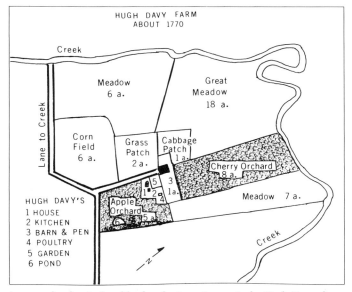

An example of agricultural land under intensive use is the Hugh Davey farm on Hollander Creek, near Philadelphia, about 1770. Although Davey held just 55 acres, half of his land was pasture, the most valuable type of real estate. He also had 6 acres in plowland and 1 acre for his garden. Davey must have also derived a significant income by using fruit from his two orchards, covering perhaps 15 acres, to brew cider. (Drafted by author from James T. Lemon, *The Best Poor Man's Country: A Geographical Study of Early Southeastern Pennsylvania* [1976], 194.)

TABLE 4.12   ESTIMATED OUTPUT OF UNITED STATES LAND UNDER CULTIVATION, 1800

Crops	Output (bu. or lb.)	Yield per Acre	Land in Crops
Wheat	25,850,000 bu.	10.0 bu.	2,590,000 a.
Rye	5,260,000 bu.	12.7 bu.	410,000 a.
Barley	1,290,000 bu.	14.4 bu.	90,000 a.
Oats	35,710,000 bu.	24.6 bu.	1,450,000 a.
Buckwheat	2,030,000 bu.	17.1 bu.	120,000 a.
Irish Potatoes	20,240,000 bu.	92.3 bu.	220,000 a.
Sweet Potatoes	13,300,000 bu.	92.3 bu.	140,000 a.
Indian Corn	135,440,000 bu.	24.0 bu.	5,640,000 a.
Rice	1,680,000 bu.	25.0 bu.	70,000 a.
Cotton	30,100,000 lb.	132.0 lb.	230,000 a.
Hemp	300,000 lb.	700.0 lb.	ca. 500 a.
Flax	2,300,000 lb.	100.0 lb.	20,000 a.
Peas and Beans	2,120,000 bu.	. . .	[acreage of garden crops and tobacco estimated at 400,000 a.]
Truck Crops	worth $1,100,000	. . .	
Fruits	10,600,000 bu.	. . .	
Hops	580,000 lb.	. . .	
Tobacco	114,800,000 lb.	. . .	
		Total Acreage	11,380,500 a.

Source: Robert E. Gallman, "Changes in Total U.S. Agricultural Factor Productivity in the Nineteenth Century," Agricultural History XLVI (1972), 199.

TABLE 4.13   GROSS FARM OUTPUT AND GROSS FARM PRODUCT OF UNITED STATES IN 1800

I. *Gross Output of Sales and Home Consumption of Farm Products*	
Livestock slaughtered	$194,000,000.
Crops harvested	$113,000,000.
Increase in herds of livestock	$13,000,000.
Gross rent from farm dwellings	$23,000,000.
Total gross output	$343,000,000.
II. *Gross Farm Product, Including Improvements and Manufactures*	
Farm gross output	$343,000,000.
Improvements to farms	$21,000,000.
Value of home manufactures	$8,000,000.
[minus home consumption of	$10,000,000.]
Gross farm product	$362,000,000.

Note: Most values were extrapolated from data known for later periods according to population ratios. Monetary values represent U.S. dollars of 1800.
Source: M. W. Towne and W. E. Rasmussen, "Farm Gross Product and Gross Investment During the 19th Century," in National Bureau of Economic Research, Studies in Income and Wealth XXIV (1960), 265–266.

TABLE 4.14   DAYS PER LABORER EXPENDED TO PRODUCE 10,000 TOBACCO PLANTS AND 5,445 CORN STALKS WHEN PLANTING IS DONE WITH PLOWS, ABOUT 1775

	Working Days in Period	Tobacco Hills Days	Tobacco Hills Tasks	Corn Hills Days	Corn Hills Tasks	Days Left
Jan.–Feb.	50	5.5	make beds	0		43.9
		0.6	tend beds			
Mar.	26	1.1	tend beds	9.1	hill	10.2
Apr.	26	1.1	plow	4.5	plow	0
		14.3	hill	3.0	hill	
		2.7	tend beds	4.1	plant	
May	26	1.9	plow			0
		6.0	hill	10.0	weed (1)	
		3.9	tend beds	5.0	weed (2)	
Jun.	26	1.1	transplant			1.9
		1.9	hill	5.0	weed (2)	
		1.7	tend beds	10.0	weed (3)	
		3.3	transplant			
		2.2	weed			
Jul.–Aug.	54	43.3	weed, top, sucker, worm	4.5	sucker	6.2
Sep.	26	3.3	sucker, worm	9.0	top	1.5
		12.2	cut, house			
Oct.	27	5.5	cut, house	5.0	gather, house	10.9
		5.5	strip			
Nov.	25	16.6	strip, pack	2.0	gather, house	6.4
Dec.	26	0		3.9	gather, house	22.1
Total	312	133.7		75.1		103.1

Note: Calculations are based on 10,000 tobacco plants on about 3 acres and 5,445 corn hills on 4.5 acres. Subsistence output per hand required 3,630 hills on three acres, and required about 52 days. Hilling is calculated at 450 hills per man per day. Time for plowing is estimated at an acre per day.
Source: Lois G. Carr and Russell R. Menard, "Land, Labor, and Economies of Scale in Early Maryland: Some Limits to Growth in the Chesapeake System of Husbandry," Journal of Economic History XLIX (1989), 416.

Cattle

During the last half of the eighteenth century, American farmers began abandoning traditional practices of raising cattle in favor of more efficient techniques to grow fodder and increase body weight. Customary practices of grazing cattle on fields of natural grass resulted in the animals devouring the leaves before the soil could be reseeded. Pastures consequently soon wore out and could not provide the nutrition needed for proper fattening or for substantial milkings. Although quite healthy and remarkably resistant to diseases, such cattle were small by modern standards; when dressed they yielded only 300 to 500 pounds of meat (700 to 800 if fattened on grain), and cows on average gave only one quart of milk daily and were dry about three months while calving.

Farmers increasingly refrained from pasturing their cattle exclusively on summer grass or allowing them to forage through unfenced woodlands. Americans slowly adopted the European custom of tilled upland cultivation, which created artificial meadows of clover or timothy grass, rather than allowing their livestock to graze freely in woods. These plants were more nutritious than field grass and helped preserve the soil's fertility, and—since they could be mowed three times a season—they provided more ample supplies of winter hay. The practice of sheltering cattle in barns during winter, which reduced weight loss by conserving the animals' energy, also became more widespread. These changes enabled American cattle to become more efficient producers of meat and milk.

Beyond the more densely populated areas of the eastern seaboard, however, cattle husbandry in the backcountry from Pennsylvania to South Carolina continued to follow traditional methods. Frontier farmers left their animals to roam at large for food and organized cattle drives to markets such as Philadelphia or Charleston. Once

Pictured here is an elaborate New England barn from Peabody, Massachusetts. Because winters were so cold, New England barns were often segmented into compartments that served as insulation to keep the interior warmer than the single-bay style used by Americans in other regions. Many New Englanders built barns adjacent to their homes in order to conserve even more heat in winter. (For interior, see photo p. 50.) (James Duncan Phillips Library collections, courtesy, Peabody & Essex Museum, Salem, Massachusetts)

they were sold at the seacoast, the cattle were stall-fed and slaughtered when they had regained the weight lost en route to market.

By 1760, a commercial dairy industry had developed to supply cheese and butter for export to the West Indies. Since cows gave relatively little milk, yields remained small as late as 1800, when the average annual production of dairy cattle in Massachusetts was estimated to be 70 to 100 pounds of butter and 50 to 150 pounds of skim-milk cheese. While American cheese enjoyed a good reputation, butter was reportedly of low quality and had to be heavily salted. Significant centers of commercial dairying emerged in Rhode Island, Connecticut, and the Delaware Valley, but the industry was largely absent from the South.

TABLE 4.15   RATIO OF HORNED CATTLE TO POPULATION IN NEW JERSEY, MASSACHUSETTS, AND MAINE, 1784

	Horned Cattle	Population	People/Cattle
Maine	49,006	50,493	1.0/1
Mass.	237,993	307,018	1.3/1
N.J.	102,221	149,435	1.5/1

Sources: Jedidiah Morse, *American Geography* (1792), 172, 284. U.S. Bureau of the Census, *Historical Statistics of the United States: Colonial Times to 1970* (1975), 1169–70.

TABLE 4.16   CATTLE PRICES (IN LOCAL CURRENCY) IN THREE COLONIES, 1774

	Essex Co., Mass.	Northampton Co., Pa.	Orange Co., N.C.
ox	£5.0.0	£5.0.0	. . .
young ox	£4.0.0	. . .	. . .
steer (3 years)	£4.4.0	. . .	. . .
steer (2 years)	£2.0.0	. . .	. . .
steer (1 year)	£2.0.0	. . .	12½ s.–15 s.*

	Essex Co., Mass.	Northampton Co., Pa.	Orange Co., N.C.
steer	. . .	£3.0.0	£1.7.4–£2.15.0
bull	£2.4.0	. . .	£1.5.3–£2.5.0
"heifer bull"	. . .	£2.0.0	. . .
bull (2 years)	£1.10.0	. . .	. . .
fattened cow	£4.0.0	. . .	. . .
cow	£3.0.0	£3.0.0–£4.0.0	£2.10.6–£4.0.0
"young cattle"	. . .	£2.0.0	. . .
heifer (3 years)	£2.14.0	. . .	. . .
heifer (2 years)	£2.13.0	. . .	. . .
heifer (1 year)	£1.16.0	£1.5.0	. . .
heifer	. . .	. . .	12½ s.–£1.2.6
calf	15 s.	3 s.	7½ s.
milk calf	. . .	7½ s.	. . .
calf (6 months)	. . .	6 s.	. . .

*"s" stand for shillings; see introductory note on monetary values.
Source: Alice Hanson Jones, *American Colonial Wealth: Documents and Methods* (1977), 69–105, 607–799, 1443–71.

TABLE 4.17   PRICE OF BARREL OF BEEF (31.5 GAL., CA. 225 LB.) AT PHILADELPHIA, 1761–1800 (IN LOCAL CURRENCY AND U.S. DOLLARS)

1800	$14.22	1790	48.50 s.	1780	9,917. s.	1770	51.39 s.
1799	$11.75	1789	58. s.	1779	1,965. s.	1769	55.21 s.
1798	$13.04	1788	78. s.	1778	226. s.	1768	52.41 s.
1797	$15.45	1787	81. s.	1777	169. s.	1767	55.35 s.
1796	$17.25	1786	92. s.	1776	94.10 s.	1766	55.21 s.
1795	$5.17	1785	86. s.	1775	57.00 s.	1765	58.75 s.
1794	$8.46	1784	90. s.	1774	54.31 s.	1764	60.00 s.
1793	$11.17	1783	84.80 s.	1773	54.58 s.	1763	60.29 s.
1992	$7.62	1782	73.50 s.	1772	57.05 s.	1762	58.04 s.
1791	56.50 s.	1781	555. s.	1771	51.48 s.	1761	54.91 s.

Sources: Arthur H. Cole, *Wholesale Commodity Prices in the United States, 1700–1861* (1938), 5–124. Anne Bezanson, *Prices and Inflation During the American Revolution: Pennsylvania, 1770–1790* (1951), 335–38.

TABLE 4.18 **AVERAGE ANNUAL EXPORTS OF BUTTER AND CHEESE FROM BRITISH NORTH AMERICA, 1768–1772**

	Butter lb.	Cheese lb.	Both[a] lb.
Maine	166	1,395	1,524
Mass.	18,700	15,269	43,514
N.H.	717	988	248
R.I.	67,243	196,354	145,096
Conn.	11,805	94,115	123,676
N.Y.	31,900	15,865	13,726
N.J.	1,206	140	1,345
Pa.	16,893	53,037	32,770
Del.	. . .	377	377
Md.	891	38,770	61,864
Va.	18,911	35,835	24,175
N.C.	1,327	26,346	29,096
S.C.	35,394	28,964	8,272
Ga.	4,689	6,748	8,307

[a]Butter and cheese reported as one category.
Source: Max G. Schumacher, *The Northern Farmer and His Markets During the Late Colonial Period* (1975), 162–66.

TABLE 4.19 NUMBER AND VALUE (STERLING) OF LIVE CATTLE EXPORTED TO THE WEST INDIES FROM BRITISH MAINLAND COLONIES, 1768–1772

Year	From New England No.	(£ Ster.)	From Mid-Atlantic No.	(£ Ster.)	From Upper South No.	(£ Ster.)	From Lower South No.	(£ Ster.)
1768	3,561	(£21,366)	111	(£666)		. . .	37	(£222)
1769	2,683	(£16,098)	162	(£972)		. . .	42	(£252)
1770	3,038	(£18,228)	67	(£402)		. . .	79	(£474)
1771	3,287	(£19,722)	1	(£6)		. . .	97	(£582)
1772	3,719	(£22,314)	65	(£390)		. . .	217	(£1,302)

Source: James F. Shepherd and Gary M. Walton, *Shipping, Maritime Trade, and the Economic Development of Colonial North America* (1972), 212–27.

Table 4.20 EXPORTS OF U.S. BEEF, CHEESE, BUTTER, AND LIVE CATTLE, 1790–1800

Year Ending Sep. 30	Beef Barrels	Cheese Pounds	Butter Firkins and Pounds	Horned Cattle Number
1790	44,662	144,734	8,379 f.	5,406
1791	62,371	120,901	16,670 f.	4,627
1792	74,338	125,925	11,761 f.	4,551
1793	74,980	146,269	9,130 f.	3,690
1794	100,886	601,954	38,772 f.	3,495
1795	96,149	2,343,093	28,389 f.	2,510
1796	92,521	1,794,536	2,544,885 lb.	4,625
1797	51,812	1,256,109	1,255,435 lb.	3,827
1798	89,421	1,183,234	1,313,563 lb.	4,283
1799	91,321	1,164,590	1,314,502 lb.	5,304
1800	75,045	913,843	1,822,341 lb.	9,824

Note: Barrels of beef equaled 31.5 gallons (about 200–225 lb.) and firkins equaled a quarter barrel or about 8 gallons.
Source: U.S. Congress, *American State Papers: Commerce and Navigation* (1832), VII, 30–452.

TABLE 4.21 DESTINATION OF PICKLED BEEF EXPORTED FROM UNITED STATES, 1790–1800

Purchaser	1790 Barrels	Percent	1800 Barrels	Percent
British West Indies	47	.1%	30,944	44.2%
Spanish West Indies	816	1.8%	10,472	15.0%
French West Indies	34,765	77.8%	7,876	11.2%
Danish West Indies	1,352	3.0%	5,789	8.3%
Dutch West Indies	906	2.0%	5,440	7.8%
Swedish West Indies	59	.1%	4,132	5.9%
Canadian Provinces	1,131	2.5%	1,243	1.8%
Spain	961	2.2%	1,231	1.7%
Madeira	1,439	3.2%	1,006	1.4%
Africa	240	.5%	950	1.3%
Other	2,946	6.8%	960	1.4%
Total	44,662	100%	70,043	100%

Source: Timothy Pitkin, *A Statistical View of the Commerce of the United States of America* (1835), 125.

Corn

Corn was not only equally nourishing for both humans and animals, but also hardy and resistant to pests because of its protective husk. Because corn required minimal care after mid-season and almost never experienced a crop failure unless stunted by a severe drought, planting just eight acres was normally sufficient to guarantee a year's supply of grain for a family, plus a substantial stock of winter straw. Since it ripened before the first frost of even the northernmost colonies, corn was ubiquitous and became the most common farm crop in America.

Because an adequate harvest was most often gathered with minimal effort, colonial farmers had customarily grown corn in a haphazard manner by using hoes to place seeds in individual hills and to cut undergrowth. By the late eighteenth century, however, it was

TABLE 4.22 PRICE OF A BUSHEL OF CORN AT PHILADELPHIA (IN SHILLINGS OF LOCAL CURRENCY AND U.S. DOLLARS), 1761–1800

Year	Price	Year	Price
1800	$ .65	1780	274.00 s.
1799	$ .53	1779	109.00 s.
1798	$ .50	1778	14.20 s.
1797	$ .75	1777	7.60 s.
1796	$ .90	1776	3.40 s.
1795	$4.95	1775	2.90 s.
1794	$4.60	1774	2.83 s.
1793	$ .58	1773	3.14 s.
1792	$ .46	1772	3.69 s.
1791	3.10 s.	1771	3.50 s.
1790	4.10 s.	1770	3.60 s.
1789	3.10 s.	1769	2.80 s.
1788	2.60 s.	1768	2.57 s.
1787	3.20 s.	1767	2.93 s.
1786	4.30 s.	1766	3.29 s.
1785	4.20 s.	1765	3.01 s.
1784	4.70 s.	1764	2.74 s.
1783	5.20 s.	1763	3.75 s.
1782	4.50 s.	1762	3.48 s.
1781	112.00 s.	1761	2.42 s.

Sources: Arthur H. Cole, *Wholesale Commodity Prices in the United States, 1700–1861* (1938), 1–124. Anne Bezanson, *Prices and Inflation During the American Revolution: Pennsylvania, 1770–1790* (1951), 335–38.

TABLE 4.23   PRICE OF CORN, PER BARREL IN PENCE OF LOCAL CURRENCY, IN TALBOT AND KENT COUNTIES, MD., 1763–1774

Year	Kent Co.	Talbot Co.
1774	111	. . .
1773	117	. . .
1772	112	138
1771	117	120
1770	123	126
1769	112	111
1768	99	102
1767	121	115
1766	113	116
1765	115	97
1764	100	106
1763	114	113

Source: Paul G. E. Clemens, *The Atlantic Economy and Colonial Maryland's Eastern Shore: From Tobacco to Grain* (1980), 227.

TABLE 4.24   ESTIMATED ANNUAL AVERAGE OF HARVEST AND EXPORTS OF CORN, 1768–1772

Colonies	Harvest (Value in £ sterling)	Exports (Value)
Va.	5,484,000 bu. (£422,000)	567,000 bu. (£43,631)
N.Y., N.J., Pa., Del.	1,450,800 bu. (£111,600)	150,000 bu. (£11,500)

Source: David C. Klingaman, "The Significance of Grain in the Development of the Tobacco Colonies," *Journal of Economic History* XXIX (1969), 270–274 and n. 22, p. 273.

TABLE 4.25   VOLUME (BU.) AND VALUE (£ STERLING) OF CORN EXPORTS FROM THE BRITISH MAINLAND COLONIES, 1768–1772

	To Britain and Ireland		To Southern Europe		To West Indies	
	bu.	£ ster.	bu.	£ ster.	bu.	£ ster.
From New England						
1768	140	£11	7,773	£598	12,690	£977
1769	100	. . .	4,379	£388	9,846	£872
1770	9	. . .	13,561	£1,587	11,174	£1,308
1771	. . .	. . .	7,466	£788	14,437	£1,523
1772	. . .	. . .	3,018	£345	5,995	£686
From Mid-Atlantic						
1768	5,619	£433	118,608	£9,133	59,756	£4,601
1769	294	£26	119,458	£10,572	36,170	£3,201
1770	. . .	. . .	83,356	£9,753	61,363	£7,180
1771	35	£4	109,453	£11,458	110,611	£11,669
1772	45	£5	127,378	£14,585	63,382	£7,257
From Upper South						
1768	96,136	£7,402	217,293	£16,732	454,707	£35,013
1769	. . .	. . .	152,797	£13,523	447,939	£39,643
1770	150	£18	71,314	£8,344	275,809	£32,270
1771	8,500	£897	93,389	£9,852	419,431	£44,250
1772	. . .	. . .	117,439	£13,447	396,650	£45,417

	To Britain and Ireland		To Southern Europe		To West Indies	
	bu.	£ ster.	bu.	£ ster.	bu.	£ ster.
From Lower South						
1768	8,361	£732	7,897	£691	95,141	£8,326
1769	. . .	. . .	16,850	£1,669	85,044	£8,419
1770	. . .	. . .	6,989	£734	88,505	£9,293
1771	. . .	. . .	3,865	£483	60,053	£7,507
1772	4,355	£662	7,942	£1,207	73,907	£11,233

Source: James F. Shepherd and Gary M. Walton, *Shipping, Maritime Trade, and the Economic Development of Colonial North America* (1972), 211–27.

more typical for farmers to plow before planting seeds and to cross-plow between hills, and these practices reduced the time needed to put in a crop and keep a field clean of weeds. An increasing number of farmers also began to increase yields by manuring their corn stalks after several weeks' growth and by abandoning the practice of topping the stalks prematurely for animal fodder. As these techniques became more common, corn cultivation required fewer man-hours and began producing greater yields per acre.

The greatest part of each year's corn harvest was consumed in the domestic market, most of it on the very farms where it was grown. Perhaps 10% to 20% of the crop was also sent overseas, and corn ranked as the eighth most valuable commodity exported from British mainland America in the years 1768–1772. During the period 1790–1792, the United States was selling twice as much corn overseas as it had prior to independence; corn then ranked as the fifth most valuable American export and accounted for 5% of all Americans goods marketed abroad.

TABLE 4.26   EXPORTS OF CORN AND CORN MEAL FROM THE UNITED STATES, 1791–1800

Year	Corn (bu.)	Corn Meal (barrels)
1800	1,694,327	338,108
1799	1,200,492	231,226
1798	1,218,231	211,694
1797	804,922	254,799
1796	1,173,552	540,286
1795	1,935,345	512,445
1794	1,505,977	241,570
1793	1,233,768	189,715
1792	1,964,973	263,405
1791	1,713,241	351,695

Source: Timothy Pitkin, *A Statistical View of the Commerce of the United States of America* (1835), 102.

TABLE 4.27   CORN YIELDS (BARRELS) PER LABORER IN THE CHESAPEAKE, 1764–1799

	Lower Western Shore of Md.	Upper Eastern Shore of Md.	York River Basin, Va.	James River Piedmont, Va.
1764–69	15.3	17.3	19.4	22.5
1770–74	13.8	20.5	19.6	22.0
1775–81	14.3	31.7	18.9	44.4
1782–89	9.3	30.2	17.6	26.5
1790–99	12.5	22.5	19.5	24.3

Note: Source does not specify size of barrels.
Source: Lorena S. Walsh, "Plantation Management in the Chesapeake, 1620–1820," *Journal of Economic History* IXL (1989), 398

TABLE 4.28 HOURS OF LABOR ESTIMATED TO PRODUCE 100 BUSHELS OF CORN, 1800

Total hours per acre	86
Before harvest	56
In the harvest	30
Average yield per acre	25 bu.
Hours per 100 bushels	344

Source: U.S. Bureau of the Census, *Historical Statistics of the United States: Colonial Times to 1957* (1960), 281.

Cotton

Cotton remained a minor crop through the colonial period because it commanded virtually no overseas demand. Since it requires more than 100 frost-free days for a successful harvest, cotton was inappropriate for farmers north of south-central Virginia. Most colonial cotton seems to have been consumed domestically for household spinning, although it was probably less often used for this purpose than flax, which was more widely grown.

Large-scale cotton cultivation began in the mid-1780s with the introduction of the Sea Island variety offshore of South Carolina and Georgia. This species had a long fiber that combed away from its seeds with relative ease; it exceeded all other types in strength, fineness, and softness, and so commanded high prices as material for delicate laces and cloth with a silky luster. Sea Island cotton remained a specialty crop produced in small quantities since its demand was minor and it grew poorly on the mainland.

Rising demand for cotton by British textile manufacturers sparked renewed interest in the crop during the 1790s. The variety suited to mainland cultivation, short-staple, nevertheless was expensive to prepare for market due to the exceptional difficulty of removing seeds from lint. Eli Whitney's development of a more efficient gin, which cleaned about 50 pounds of fiber per day, burst this bottleneck in 1793 and stimulated an enormous rise in production. By 1804 cotton output had grown eightfold over the previous decade.

TABLE 4.29 PRICE OF COTTON, PER POUND (IN SHILLINGS OF LOCAL CURRENCY) AT PHILADELPHIA, 1763–1774

1774	1.48 s.	1768	1.71 s.
1773	1.44 s.	1767	1.93 s
1772	1.27 s.	1766	. . .
1771	1.24 s.	1765	. . .
1770	1.32 s.	1764	. . .
1769	1.37 s.	1763	1.87 s.

Source: Anne Bezanson, et al., *Prices in Colonial Pennsylvania* (1935), 422–24.

TABLE 4.31 PRICES FOR MIDDLING UPLANDS COTTON, PER POUND, AT CHARLESTON, S.C.; NEW YORK; AND LIVERPOOL, ENGLAND 1790–1800

	Charleston (cents)	New York (cents)	Liverpool (pence)
1790	. . .	14.5	. . .
1791	. . .	26.0	13–30
1792	. . .	29.0	20–30
1793	. . .	32.0	13–22
1794	. . .	33.0	12–18
1795	. . .	36.0	15–27
1796	31.8	36.5	12–29
1797	25.1	34.5	12–37
1798	29.8	39.0	22–45
1799	30.9	44.0	17–60
1800	24.9	24.0	16–36

Sources: George R. Taylor, "Wholesale Commodity Prices at Charleston, South Carolina, 1796–1861," *Journal of Economic and Business History* IV (1932), 870. Stuart W. Bruchey, *Cotton and the Growth of the American Economy, 1790–1860* (1967), 15.

This cotton gin is the original patent model of Eli Whitney's invention of 1793. Little cotton had formerly been grown in the United States, but Whitney's machine encouraged a massive shift to the crop south of Virginia, where the climate provided the hundred days of frost-free cultivation necessary for cotton to ripen. Whitney failed to prevent others from pirating his idea and made little money from his epochal discovery. (Negative 73-11289, courtesy Smithsonian Institution)

TABLE 4.30 AMOUNT (POUNDS) AND VALUE (STERLING) OF COTTON EXPORTED TO GREAT BRITAIN AND IRELAND FROM BRITAIN'S MAINLAND COLONIES, 1768–1772

Year	From New England		From Mid-Atlantic		From Upper South		From Lower South	
	lb.	£ ster.	lb.	£ ster.	lb.	£ ster.	lb.	£ ster.
1768	17,072	£851	11,100	£572	43,350	£2,233	3,300	£170
1769	500	£22	6,480	£282	2,950	£128	554	£25
1770	. . .	. . .	6,097	£262	1,727	£74	2,444	£105
1771	300	£13	9,600	£360	1,400	£53	2,615	£98
1772	19,930	£917	14,093	£557	2,484	£98	1,128	£45

Source: James F. Shepherd and Gary M. Walton, *Shipping, Maritime Trade, and the Economic Development of Colonial North America* (1972), 211–27.

Although cotton became associated with wealthy planters, it served as the primary mainstay of small farmers. Planted in hills or holes and raised in patches, cotton needed no expensive draft animals for plowing and so could be cultivated with a simple hoe and still produce respectable yields as high as 300 pounds per acre. Prices remained much above the level necessary to support a family during the 1790s, and even after dropping by more than half in the years 1800–1801, cotton still offered a good profit for a year's work. Cotton soon became the dominant crop in the lower south, and by 1840 it accounted for more than half the value of all the country's exports.

TABLE 4.32 PRODUCTION AND EXPORTS OF UNITED STATES COTTON, 1784–1800

Year	Production		Exports		Percent of Crop Exported
	Bales	Pounds	Bales	Pounds	
1784	. . .	. . .	10	1,000	. . .
1785	. . .	. . .	10	2,000	. . .
1786	. . .	. . .	10	1,000	. . .
1787	. . .	. . .	110	16,000	. . .
1788	. . .	. . .	390	58,000	. . .
1789	. . .	1,000,000	840	126,000	12.6%
1790	. . .	1,500,000	80	12,000	.8%
1791	9,000	2,000,000	890	189,316	9.5%
1792	13,000	3,000,000	630	138,328	4.6%
1793	22,000	5,000,000	2,000	487,600	9.6%
1794	35,000	8,000,000	7,000	1,601,760	20.0%
1795	36,000	8,000,000	28,000	6,276,300	78.5%
1796	44,000	10,000,000	27,000	6,106,729	61.1%
1797	49,000	11,000,000	17,000	3,788,429	34.4%
1798	67,000	15,000,000	42,000	9,360,005	62.4%
1799	89,000	20,000,000	42,000	9,532,263	47.7%
1800	156,000	35,000,000	79,000	17,789,803	55.1%

Notes: Production and export data are for years beginning Oct. 1 and ending Sept. 30. Great Britain received over 99% of all exports in every year but 1800, when it purchased 71,000 bales weighing 16,180,000 lb. (91% of total exports).
Sources: Stuart W. Bruchey, Cotton and the Growth of the American Economy, 1790–1860 (1967), 14–15. Timothy Pitkin, A Statistical View of the Commerce of the United States of America (1835), 111.

TABLE 4.33 EXPORTS OF SEA ISLAND COTTON FROM SOUTH CAROLINA, 1789–1801

	Pounds	Bags
Oct. 1, 1789 to Sep. 30, 1790	9,840	30
Oct. 1, 1790 to Sep. 30, 1791	54,075	164
Oct. 1, 1791 to Sep. 30, 1792	76,710	232
Oct. 1, 1792 to Sep. 30, 1793	93,540	284
Oct. 1, 1793 to Sep. 30, 1794	159,040	482
Oct. 1, 1794 to Sep. 30, 1795	1,109,653	3,363
Oct. 1, 1795 to Sep. 30, 1796	912,600	2,765
Oct. 1, 1796 to Sep. 30, 1797	1,008,511	3,056
Oct. 1, 1797 to Sep. 30, 1798	2,476,431	7,504
Oct. 1, 1798 to Sep. 30, 1799	2,801,996	8,491
Oct. 1, 1799 to Sep. 30, 1800	6,425,863	19,472
Oct. 1, 1800 to Sep. 30, 1801	8,301,907	25,157

Source: Lewis C. Gray, History of Agriculture in the Southern United States to 1860 (1933), 679.

TABLE 4.34 UNITED STATES COTTON OUTPUT COMPARED TO WORLD PRODUCTION, 1791–1801

Area	1791		1801	
	Output in Pounds	% of World Production	Output in Pounds	% of World Production
Africa	45,000,000	9.6%	46,000,000	8.8%
Brazil	22,000,000	4.7%	26,000,000	5.0%
India	130,000,000	27.7%	160,000,000	30.7%
Other Asia	190,000,000	40.5%	160,000,000	30.7%
Spanish America	68,000,000	14.5%	56,000,000	10.7%
West Indies	12,000,000	2.6%	10,000,000	2.0%
Other areas	. . .	. . .	15,000,000	2.9%
United States	2,000,000	.4%	48,000,000	9.2%
[Ga.]	[500,000]	[.1%]	[10,000,000]	[1.9%]
[N.C.]	. . .		[4,000,000]	[.8%]
[S.C.]	[1,500,000]	[.3%]	[20,000,000]	[3.8%]
[Tenn.]	. . .		[1,000,000]	[.2%]
[others]	. . .		[13,000,000]	[2.5%]
Total	469,000,000	100%	521,000,000	100%

Note: Those figures given in brackets are not from source but were calculated by author.
Source: Stuart W. Bruchey, Cotton and the Growth of the American Economy, 1790–1860 (1967), 7.

TABLE 4.35   ESTIMATED HOURS OF LABOR USED TO PRODUCE COTTON IN 1800

Hours per acre	185
Before harvest	135
In the harvest	50
Yield of lint per acre	147 lb.
Hours per 500-lb. bale	601

Source: U.S. Bureau of the Census, *Historical Statistics of the United States: Colonial Times to 1957* (1960), 281.

Flax

Flax produced both fibers for linen thread and seeds that could be crushed into linseed oil. Although cultivated throughout America, its center of production was the mid-Atlantic region. The plant's tissue could be spun for home manufactures but only after a long, hard, and dirty process of rotting the stems, separating the fibers by breaking and swinging, and combing out the threads. Seeds furnished the primary cash product. A bushel of seed yielded six quarts of linseed oil, and the resulting residue of oil cake could be sold to fatten hogs or cattle.

Parliament encouraged flax production with a bounty of £8 per ton in 1764 (reduced to £6 in 1771). Ireland constituted the main overseas market, and by the 1770s it imported virtually all its flax from the mainland colonies. Disrupted by the Revolution, the trade resumed to its former levels in the 1780s. The value of flax sold overseas seems to have remained constant at about 1.5% of Anglo-American exports from 1768 to 1792.

TABLE 4.36   PRICE OF FLAXSEED, PER BUSHEL (IN SHILLINGS OF LOCAL CURRENCY) AT PHILADELPHIA, 1763–1775

1775	10.64
1774	8.32
1773	9.39
1772	8.67
1771	6.37
1770	4.90
1769	4.03
1768	5.75
1767	5.96
1766	5.17
1765	8.79
1764	8.21
1763	9.08

Source: Anne Bezanson, et al., *Prices in Colonial Pennsylvania* (1935), 416.

TABLE 4.37   VOLUME (BU.) AND VALUE (£ STERLING) OF FLAXSEED EXPORTS FROM THE BRITISH MAINLAND COLONIES, 1768–1772

	To Ireland		To Great Britain	
	bushels	£ ster.	bushels	£ ster.
From New England				
1768	. . .	. . .	5,256	£870
1769	16,233	£2,069	6,370	£812
1770	5,743	£962	4,407	£738
1771	2,500	£490	7,190	£1,409
1772	5,745	£1,569	9,014	£2,461
From Mid-Atlantic				
1768	240,295	£39,769	7,692	£1,273
1769	165,516	£21,104	4,305	£549
1770	256,948	£43,039	2,142	£359
1771	147,517	£28,914	3,821	£749
1772	157,874	£43,100	3,383	£923
From Upper South				
1768	15,685	£2,596	5,636	£933
1769	13,821	£1,763	434	£55
1770	30,101	£5,042	140	£23
1771	9,191	£1,801	2,514	£493
1772	20,243	£5,526	48	£13
From Lower South				
1768	1,734	£287	133	£22
1769	4,347	£554	702	£90
1770	. . .	. . .	92	£15
1771	5,143	£1,008	854	£167
1772	2,554	£697	. . .	. . .

Source: James F. Shepherd and Gary M. Walton, *Shipping, Maritime Trade, and the Economic Development of Colonial North America* (1972), 211–27.

TABLE 4.38   EXPORTS AND PRICE OF FLAXSEED FROM BRITISH NORTH AMERICA TO IRELAND (PER HOGSHEADS, IN SHILLINGS OF £ STERLING), 1763–1784

Year	Hogsheads	Price/hhd.	% of Flax Imported
1784	21,185	60 s.	. . .
1783	170	60 s.	. . .
1782	869	60 s.	. . .
1781	23,641	60 s.	. . .
1780	1,776	60 s.	9.1%
1779	3,836	50 s.	. . .
1778	2,110	50 s.	. . .
1777	4,512	50 s.	. . .
1776	12,441	50 s.	. . .
1775	38,806	40 s.	96.5%
1774	24,728	40 s.	. . .
1773	39,344	30 s.	. . .
1772	22,772	30 s.	. . .
1771	42,023	30 s.	. . .
1770	19,433	30 s.	99.1%
1769	49,331	30 s.	. . .
1768	17,150	30 s.	. . .
1767	41,339	30 s.	. . .
1766	27,969	30 s.	. . .
1765	20,446	30 s.	73.6%
1764	25,422	30 s.	. . .
1763	19,745	30 s.	. . .

Source: Thomas M. Truxes, *Irish-American Trade, 1660–1783* (1988), 284.

TABLE 4.39 PERCENT OF FLAXSEED EXPORTED BY STATES, OCT. 1, 1791–SEPT. 30, 1792

State	Casks	% of Exports
N.H.	691	1.3%
Mass.	4,047	7.7%
R.I.	4,595	8.8%
Conn.	2,249	4.3%
N.Y. & East Jersey	24,687	47.1%
Pa., Del., West Jersey	10,150	19.4%
Md.	2,464	4.7%
Va.	721	1.4%
N.C.	2,739	5.2%
S.C.	38	.1%
Total	52,381	100%

Source: U.S. Congress, *American State Papers: Commerce and Navigation* (1832), 157.

tidewater. Output was greatest in Virginia, which in 1768 sent overseas 388 tons, about 81% of that year's exports, and in 1775 produced about 5,000 tons, worth approximately £208,000. A laborer could tend up to 4 acres of hemp per season, and yields were estimated to range from highs of 900 to 1,400 pounds per acre to lows of 500 pounds per acre. The labor entailed in cutting the stalks and rotting the fibers off the trunk was heavy, and this factor discouraged widespread cultivation in spite of Parliament's bounty. Hemp cultivation experienced a revival during the 1790s, especially in Virginia, but it had difficulty competing with foreign imports because of their superior reputation for quality and the high cost of domestic labor. After supplying the domestic market for cables and rope, little hemp was available for export in either its raw state or as cordage. As early as 1790 planters began raising the crop in central Kentucky, which replaced Virginia as the center of hemp production in the early 1800s.

TABLE 4.40 EXPORTS OF FLAX, FLAXSEED, AND LINSEED OIL FROM THE U.S., 1790–1800

Year Ending Sep. 30	Flaxseed bushels or casks	Percent to Ireland	Flax pounds	Largest Market	Linseed Oil gallons	Largest Market
1800	289,684 bu.	. . .	2,488	. . .	18,857	. . .
1799	350,857 bu.	94%	6,304	Canada	24,227	French West Indies
1798	224,473 bu.	93%	. . .	. . .	17,016	Dutch West Indies
1797	222,269 bu.	87%	4,274	Canada	19,759	West Indies
1796	256,200 bu.	91%	16,594	Portugal	34,721	France
1795	58,752 c.	85%	90,460	Canada	48,995	France
1794	38,620 c.	67%	8,665	Portugal	6,997	Spanish West Indies
1793	51,708 c.	91%	1,474	Canada	1,183	British West Indies
1792	52,381 c.	95%	10,400	Portugal	199	British West Indies
1791	58,492 c.	72%	18,600	Portugal	90	Canada
1790	40,019 c.	. . .	21,970	. . .	[119 bbl.]	. . .

Source: U.S. Congress, *American State Papers: Commerce and Navigation* (1832), VII, 24–452.

Hemp

Hemp was a minor crop prior to the mid-eighteenth century, despite the efforts of several colonies to promote its output through bounties. In order to reduce British dependence upon Baltic and Russian cordage needed for ship rigging, Parliament encouraged production with a bounty of £8 per ton in 1764 (it had been £6 in 1771). This financial incentive led to an upswing in colonial cultivation of hemp during the next decade.

The southern provinces became the primary suppliers of the crop, which grew best in the low-lying, moist soils of that region's

TABLE 4.41 PRICE OF A POUND OF HEMP (IN PENCE OF LOCAL CURRENCY) AT PHILADELPHIA, 1761–1775

1775	5.0	1767	5.0
1774	5.0	1766	5.7
1773	5.3	1765	6.1
1772	6.0	1764	6.2
1771	5.8	1763	7.4
1770	5.8	1762	6.7
1769	4.9	1761	4.8
1768	4.5		

Source: Anne Bezanson, et al., *Prices in Colonial Pennsylvania* (1935), 417.

TABLE 4.42 TONS AND VALUE (STERLING) OF HEMP EXPORTED TO GREAT BRITAIN AND IRELAND FROM THE BRITISH MAINLAND COLONIES, 1768–1772

	From Upper South		From Lower South	
	Tons	£ Ster.	Tons	£ Ster.
1768	398.41	£10,187	9.27	£237
1769	124.77	£3,645	101.35	£2,961
1770	. . .	. . .	4.31	£151
1771	. . .	. . .	6.28	£207
1772	. . .	. . .	1.10	£38

Source: James F. Shepherd and Gary M. Walton, *Shipping, Maritime Trade, and the Economic Development of Colonial North America* (1972), 214–27.

TABLE 4.43 EXPORTS OF HEMP AND CORDAGE FROM THE UNITED STATES, 1790–1800

Year Ending Sep. 30	Hemp (tons)	Major Market	Cordage (cwt.)	Major Market
1800	86	. . .	12,406	. . .
1799	2	Spanish West Indies (100%)	5,766	Spanish America (47%)

(continued)

TABLE 4.43 (continued)

Year Ending Sep. 30	Hemp (tons)	Major Market	Cordage (cwt.)	Major Market
1798	none	. . .	9,434	Spanish America (48%)
1797	none	. . .	7,872	Spanish America (56%)
1796	117	Britain (98%)	8,707	Asia 73%
1795	110	France (100%)	2,664	France (27%)
1794	none	. . .	1,790	Asia (41%)
1793	none	. . .	9,383	French West Indies (51%)
1792	1	Britain (100%)	4,517	Asia (64%)
1791	1	France (43%)	3,533	. . .
1790	none	. . .	5,739	Wine Islands (49%)

Source: U.S. Congress, *American State Papers: Commerce and Navigation* (1832), VII, 24–452.

Horses

By the Revolutionary era, Americans' traditional preference for oxen as draft animals was declining in favor of horses. More scrutiny was given to controlled breeding for the development of sturdy animals. The most notable stocks were the Conestoga horses from Pennsylvania and Vermont's Morgans, whose bloodline originated in

TABLE 4.44 NUMBER AND VALUE (STERLING) OF HORSES EXPORTED TO THE WEST INDIES FROM THE BRITISH MAINLAND COLONIES, 1768–1772

Year	From New England No.	From New England £ Ster.	From Mid-Atlantic No.	From Mid-Atlantic £ Ster.	From Upper South No.	From Upper South £ Ster.	From Lower South No.	From Lower South £ Ster.
1768	16	£160	139	£1,390	2	£20	322	£3,220
1769	99	£990	199	£1,990	3	£30	581	£5,810
1770	17	£170	250	£2,500	5	£50	488	£4,880
1771	54	£540	272	£2,720	8	£80	365	£3,650
1772	. . .	. . .	151	£1,510	5	£50	505	£5,050

Source: James F. Shepherd and Gary M. Walton, *Shipping, Maritime Trade, and the Economic Development of Colonial North America* (1972), 212–27.

TABLE 4.45 HORSE PRICES (IN PROCLAMATION MONEY) IN THREE COLONIES, 1774

	Essex Co., Mass.	Northampton Co., Pa.	Orange Co., N.C.
colt	. . .	£2.0.0	£1.10.0
yearling colt	. . .	. . .	£3.0.0
mare (2 years)	£6.0.0	. . .	. . .
"young mare"	. . .	£6.0.0	. . .
"young horse"	£6.10.0	. . .	. . .
mare	£7.4.0	£10 to £20	£3 to £11
colt (3 years)	£10.0.0	. . .	. . .
horse	£8 to £9	. . .	£7.10.0 to £12.4.0
saddle horse	. . .	£14 to £17	. . .
stallion	. . .	. . .	£26.11.0
"old mare"	£2.0.0	. . .	. . .

Note: See introductory note on monetary values.
Source: Alice Hanson Jones, *American Colonial Wealth: Documents and Methods* (1978), 69–105, 607–799, 1443–71.

the 1790s. Greater efforts to enforce laws against allowing stallions to run at large and a careful attention to the selection of mating partners were more characteristic of the Revolutionary period than the colonial era; as a result the country's farm horses gradually acquired more strength and became less subject to disabling accidents.

TABLE 4.46 EXPORT OF U.S. HORSES AND MULES, BY STATE, 1791–1792

State	No. of Horses	%	No. of Mules	%
N.H.	62	1.1%	. . .	. . .
Mass.	400	7.1%	200	18.2%
R.I.	213	3.8%	393	35.7%
Conn.	4,349	76.9%	498	45.2%
N.Y.	445	7.9%	10	.9%
Pa.	12	.2%	. . .	. . .
Va.	17	.3%	. . .	. . .
N.C.	18	.3%	. . .	. . .
S.C.	31	.5%	. . .	. . .
Ga.	109	1.9%	. . .	. . .
Total	5,656	100%	1,101	100%

Source: U.S. Congress, *American State Papers: Commerce and Navigation* (1832), 24–452.

This interior of a barn at Peabody, Massachusetts (see photo p. 43) shows the construction style and use of space in Yankee outbuildings. A characteristic element of New England barns was an exterior ramp that allowed wagons to be driven onto a floor built above the ground level. (James Duncan Phillips Library collections, courtesy, Peabody & Essex Museum, Salem, Massachusetts)

TABLE 4.47 EXPORTS OF HORSES AND MULES FROM THE UNITED STATES, 1790–1800

Year Ending Sep. 30	Horses Number	Exports to		Mules Number	Exports to	
		British West Indies	French West Indies		British West Indies	Dutch West Indies
1800	4,406	. . .	. . .	151	. . .	. . .
1799	6,290	4,980	291	707	543	106
1798	2,132	1,143	16	993	493	285
1797	1,177	359	34	1,064	357	433
1796	4,283	2,040	663	1,718	555	822
1795	2,626	971	361	1,426	471	583
1794	1,828	510	218	1,617	527	406
1793	4,613	1,177	2,387	1,105	247	578
1792	5,656	1,394	3,583	1,101	191	792
1791	6,975	. . .	. . .	444	. . .	. . .
1790	8,628	932	6,970	237	8	207

Source: U.S. Congress, *American State Papers; Commerce and Navigation* (1832), VII, 24–452.

Mules began appearing in significant numbers after the Revolution. Mules quickly became popular because, as the German traveler Johann Schoepf observed, "they are so perfectly adapted to the American economy, thriving with scant attention and bad feed." During the 1790s, the United States annually exported more than a thousand mules to the West Indies.

Indigo

Indigo's cultivation was well established in the Lower South by the 1760s, in large part due to a six-pence bounty offered by Parliament in 1748. (The bounty was reduced to four pence in 1763, but again set at six pence in 1770.) South Carolina and Georgia produced essentially all of the crop, with the remainder coming from North Carolina, which exported just 647 pounds from 1768 to 1772. Production continued strong until the War of Independence sharply curtailed exports. Although mainland indigo was considered inferior in quality to Caribbean varieties, and yielded fewer plants per acre than on West Indian islands, exports of the plant steadily revived in the 1780s. Even without the incentive of Parliamentary bounties, indigo exports had risen by 1792 to 839,666 pounds, a level 10% higher than their former high of 759,800 pounds in 1772.

Indigo was nevertheless an industry destined for eventual extinction in the South. Great Britain encouraged production in the East Indies, and the resulting rise in output depressed world prices and made the crop less attractive to Americans, who rapidly abandoned it in favor of cotton. Exports of indigo fell sharply after 1800, and the crop was thereafter grown in small quantities for domestic use, primarily around Orangeburg, South Carolina.

TABLE 4.48 PRICE OF INDIGO, PER POUND (IN SHILLINGS OF LOCAL CURRENCY), AT CHARLESTON, S.C., 1761–1800

1800	2.7	1780	2.9
1799	2.6	1779	. . .
1798	3.5	1778	. . .
1797	2.8	1777	. . .
1796	2.6	1776	. . .
1795	4.0	1775	32.8
1794	3.1	1774	33.0
1793	3.8	1773	30.1
1792	5.2	1772	37.5
1791	4.5	1771	33.9
1790	4.5	1770	26.2
1789	4.3	1769	26.3
1788	4.8	1768	21.9
1787	5.1	1767	20.8
1786	5.1	1766	21.9
1785	4.8	1765	23.3
1784	4.7	1764	24.6
1783	5.0	1763	28.9
1782	4.6	1762	26.9
1781	3.3	1761	22.5

Note: Numbers following the decimals are fractions of a shilling, not pence.
Source: Arthur H. Cole, *Wholesale Commodity Prices in the United States, 1700–1861* (1938), 28–123.

TABLE 4.49 PRICE RANGE FOR CAROLINA INDIGO AND FOREIGN COMPETITORS, CA. 1770

Origin of Indigo	Price Range
French Blue [West Indies]	9s. to 9½s. sterling
South Carolina	2½s. to 6½s. sterling
Florida	3s. to 8s. sterling
Mississippi	3s. to 6½s. sterling
Spanish Flora	
1st quality	13s. to 13s., 9d. sterling
2nd quality	12s. to 12s., 9d. sterling
3rd quality	8s., 9d. to 9½s. sterling

Source: Lewis C. Gray, *History of Agriculture in the Southern United States to 1860* (1933), 293.

TABLE 4.50 QUANTITY AND VALUE (STERLING) OF INDIGO EXPORTED TO GREAT BRITAIN FROM THE BRITISH MAINLAND COLONIES, 1768–1772

Year	From New England		From Mid-Atlantic		From Upper South		From Lower South	
	lb.	£ ster.	lb.	£ ster.	lb.	£ ster.	lb.	£ ster.
1768	1,790	£270	1,487	£224	2,700	£408	517,301	£78,113
1769	. . .	. . .	380	£69	7,087	£1,283	416,436	£75,375
1770	. . .	. . .	. . .	. . .	2,741	£495	573,017	£103,430
1771	. . .	. . .	. . .	. . .	. . .	. . .	454,207	£106,285
1772	. . .	. . .	. . .	. . .	2,423	£626	758,677	£196,118

Source: James F. Shepherd and Gary M. Walton, *Shipping, Maritime Trade, and the Economic Development of Colonial North America* (1972), 212–27.

TABLE 4.51   BRITISH BOUNTIES PAID TO AMERICAN INDIGO PLANTERS, 1763–1777

1777	£939
1776	£3,769
1775	£20,039
1774	£14,137
1773	£14,575
1772	£9,445
1771	£9,108
1770	£8,732
1769	£6,995
1768	£6,520
1767	£8,840
1766	£6,808
1765	£7,484
1764	£9,026
1763	£7,695

Source: Oliver M. Dickerson, *The Navigation Acts and the American Revolution* (1951), 28.

TABLE 4.52   EXPORTS OF INDIGO FROM THE UNITED STATES, 1790–1800

Year Ending Sep. 30	Pounds	Year Ending Sep. 30	Pounds	Casks
1800	572,999	1795	666,926	2,097
1799	312,133	1794	283,928	4,250
1798	311,457	1793	690,989	338
1797	269,639	1792	371,442	1
1796	915,635	1791	497,720	"sundry"
		1790	612,119	. . .

Source: U.S. Congress, *American State Papers: Commerce and Navigation* (1832), VII, 24–452.

Pork

American swine were a mongrel breed descended of various stocks carried from either Great Britain or the West Indies. Their rapid multiplication since the early colonial period and the widespread practice of allowing them to forage through the woods greatly inhibited attempts to improve bloodlines. Although these swine were low in weight, they were extremely hardy, resistant to disease, and reasonably safe from wolves.

An English traveler in the late 1790s, Richard Parkinson, wrote of the stock as follows. "The real American hog is what is termed the wood hog; they are long in the leg, narrow on the back, short in the body, flat on the sides, with a long snout, very rough in their hairs, in make more like the fish called a perch than any thing I can describe. You may as well think of stopping a crow as those hogs. They will go to a distance from a fence, take a run, and leap through the rails three or four feet from the ground, turning themselves sidewise. These hogs suffer such hardships as no other animal could endure."

The earliest improvements in breeding American swine occurred in the late eighteenth century when they were crossed with imported varieties. The first major strain introduced was the Woburn or Bedford hog, which was brought from England sometime before 1800. The Woburns had small bones, short legs, a rounded barrel body, and an early maturity that dressed at 400 to 700 pounds after twelve to eighteen months. Such yields gave twice or more meat than American razorbacks, and encouraged experimentation with other imported breeds like the China, Guinea, Berkshire, and Wiltshire stocks.

TABLE 4.53   PRICES OF SWINE (IN LOCAL CURRENCY) IN THREE COLONIES, 1774

	Essex Co., Mass.	Northampton Co., Pa.	Orange Co., N.C.
shoat	10s.	5s.	. . .
pig	8s.–£1.4.0	3s.	. . .
sow	18s.	13s.	13½s.–19s.
large sow	. . .	. . .	16s., 5d.
small hog	. . .	7½s.	. . .
fattening hog	. . .	12s., 3d.–15s.	. . .
hog	£1.5.0	£2.5.0–£3	5s.–9s.
large hog	£2.7.0	. . .	. . .
old hog	. . .	10s.	. . .

Source: Alice Hanson Jones, *American Colonial Wealth: Documents and Methods* (1978), 69–105, 607–799, 1443–71.

TABLE 4.54   PRICE OF A BARREL (31.5 GAL.) OF PORK AT PHILADELPHIA (IN SHILLINGS OF LOCAL CURRENCY AND U.S. DOLLARS), 1761–1800

1800	$14.81	1780	10,391s.
1799	$14.62	1779	2,009s.
1798	$17.50	1778	246s.
1797	$18.88	1777	224s.
1796	$18.91	1776	109s.
1795	121s.	1775	64.88s.
1794	$14.22	1774	69.50s.
1793	$13.64	1773	83.97s.
1792	$11.04	1772	93.46s.
1791	87s.	1771	80.31s.
1790	75s.	1770	77.04
1789	67s.	1769	80.29
1788	75s.	1768	73.43
1787	89s.	1767	71.76
1786	96s.	1766	76.88
1785	109s.	1765	74.36
1784	102s.	1764	98.26
1783	103s.	1763	86.95
1782	118s.	1762	85.63
1781	6,316s.	1761	73.92

Source: Arthur H. Cole, *Wholesale Commodity Prices in the United States, 1700–1861* (1938), 67–124. Anne Bezanson, et al., *Prices and Inflation During the American Revolution: Pennsylvania, 1770–1790* (1951), 335–38.

TABLE 4.55   EXPORTS OF U.S. PORK (IN BARRELS OF 31.5 GAL.), 1791–1800

Year	Barrels
1800	55,167
1799	52,268
1798	33,115
1797	40,125
1796	73,881
1795	88,193
1794	49,442
1793	38,563
1792	38,098
1791	27,781

Source: Timothy Pitkin, *A Statistical View of the Commerce of the United States of America* (1835), 105.

British customs records did not distinguish between exports of pickled beef and salted pork, both of which found strong markets in the West Indies. By the early 1790s, annual shipments of pork from the United States averaged 29,741 barrels (about 3,000 tons), an amount equal to 1.5% of American exports. Exports of pork almost doubled during the 1790s and prices in 1800 were 25% higher than they had been in 1792.

TABLE 4.56 DESTINATION OF SALTED PORK EXPORTED FROM THE UNITED STATES, 1790 AND 1800

Purchaser	1790 Barrels	1790 Percentage	1800 Barrels	1800 Percentage
British West Indies	823	3.3%	19,282	37.5%
French West Indies	9,589	39.2%	12,700	24.7%
Danish West Indies	796	3.3%	5,493	10.7%
Spanish West Indies	558	2.3%	4,081	8.0%
Dutch West Indies	8,676	35.5%	3,193	6.2%
Canadian Provinces	1,131	4.6%	2,155	4.2%
Swedish West Indies	213	.8%	1,725	3.4%
Spain	779	3.2%	696	1.4%
Azores, Madeira	785	3.2%	476	1.0%
Great Britain	32	.1%	619	1.2%
Others	1,080	4.5%	899	1.7%
Total	24,462	100%	51,319	100%

Source: Timothy Pitkin, *A Statistical View of the Commerce of the United States of America* (1835), 128.

Rice

Prior to 1760, rice primarily had been cultivated on inland swamps, but thereafter planters in South Carolina and Georgia succeeded in extending production along the banks of the coast's tidal rivers. Exploitation of the tidal systems allowed Georgia to expand its rice exports eightfold from 1761 to 1775. Rising demand offset this increase in production, and prices generally advanced through the period until peaking in 1772.

The Revolutionary War severely disrupted the rice industry. Congress embargoed the crop as a war measure, although some foreign sales were permitted to the French Caribbean. Rice production was greatly disorganized when British forces occupied the tidewater of South Carolina and Georgia because many slaves ran away and necessary maintenance of irrigation dikes was neglected. Exports from 1782 to 1787 averaged only half of pre-war levels. Overseas sales finally resumed the levels of the 1770s after 1790, when bad harvests in Europe stimulated demand and once again brought high prices to the planters.

TABLE 4.57 PRICES OF 100 LB. OF RICE AT CHARLESTON, S.C., 1761–1800

1800	$3.85	1780	11.4s.
1799	$1.95	1779	. . .
1798	$1.75	1778	. . .
1797	$2.28	1777	. . .
1796	$4.16	1776	. . .
1795	$3.59	1775	7.1s.
1794	$2.71	1774	7.4s.
1793	$2.68	1773	9.4s.
1792	. . .	1772	11.7s.
1791	10.4s.	1771	7.9s.
1790	11.8s.	1770	6.9s.
1789	10.9s.	1769	8.6s.
1788	12.8s.	1768	9.3s.
1787	14.2s.	1767	8.0s.
1786	14.2s.	1766	8.2s.
1785	12.5s.	1765	6.4s.
1784	15.4s.	1764	6.2s.
1783	13.2s.	1763	6.5s.
1782	20.3s.	1762	4.8s.
1781	14.0s.	1761	5.5s.

Note: Prices given in sterling until 1775 and then in local currency until 1793, when quotes are in U.S. dollars. Numerals after decimals of shillings represent fractions of a shilling, not pence.
Sources: George R. Taylor, "Wholesale Commodity Prices at Charleston, South Carolina, 1732–1791," *Journal of Economic and Business History*, IV (May 1932), 372, and his "Wholesale Commodity Prices at Charleston, South Carolina, 1796–1861," *Ibid.*, IV (August 1932), 870.

This sketch by Basil Hall shows an arrangement of rice fields dating from the late eighteenth century. A series of irrigation canals and dikes served to keep the fields' water from becoming stagnant. An adult male slave could cultivate between three and four acres during a season, and his daily task would usually entail weeding and clearing a quarter-acre. (Courtesy Library of Congress)

TABLE 4.58 VOLUME (BARRELS) AND VALUE (£ STERLING) OF RICE EXPORTS FROM THE BRITISH MAINLAND COLONIES, 1768–1772

	To Britain & Ireland		To Southern Europe		To West Indies	
	barrels	£ ster.	barrels	£ ster.	barrels	£ ster.
From Northern Ports						
1768	481	£1,202	4	£10	63	£157
1769	137	£360	322	£844	363	£952
1770	960	£1,110	579	£1,434	1,444	£3,580
1771	3,800	£9,067	662	£1,579	884	£2,109
1772	1,288	£4,378	278	£945	342	£1,163
From Southern Ports						
1768	91,680	£214,908	30,027	£70,387	16,070	£37,675
1769	79,692	£173,838	[27,000]	£63,217	21,620	£47,161
1770	73,625	£128,907	35,718	£62,538	39,488	£69,139
1771	95,531	£191,581	78,797	£30,100	30,601	£61,378
1772	96,085	£283,750	9,708	£28,669	21,876	£64,606

Source: James F. Shepherd and Gary M. Walton, *Shipping, Maritime Trade, and the Economic Development of Colonial North America* (1972), 211–25.

TABLE 4.59 RICE EXPORTS FROM THE CAROLINAS AND GEORGIA, 1763–1775

Year	Charles Town, S.C. (Barrels)	Georgetown & Beaufort, S.C. (Barrels)	Savannah, Ga. (Barrels)	North Carolina (Barrels)	Total Barrels	Total Pounds
1775	. . .	. . .	. . .	418	418	219,450
1774	118,482	6,594	20,192	. . .	145,268	76,265,700
1773	126,940	6,681	21,572	. . .	155,193	81,476,325
1772	104,821	4,076	22,948	76	131,921	69,258,525
1771	125,151	5,209	25,364	629	156,353	82,085,325
1770	131,805	5,568	22,072	495	159,940	83,968,500
1769	115,582	6,900	16,716	75	139,273	73,118,325
1768	125,538	7,045	14,625	84	147,292	77,328,300
1767	104,125	5,480	11,281	. . .	120,886	63,465,150
1766	74,031	3,896	14,257	. . .	92,184	48,396,600
1765	107,292	5,647	12,224	. . .	125,163	65,710,575
1764	91,960	4,840	9,690	. . .	106,490	55,907,250
1763	104,800	5,516	7,702	. . .	118,018	61,959,450

Sources: Data of Lawrence A. Harper, in U.S. Bureau of the Census, *Historical Statistics of the United States: Colonial Times to 1957* (1960), 767. Harry R. Merrens, *Colonial North Carolina in the Eighteenth Century: A Study in Historical Geography* (1964), 126.

TABLE 4.60 RICE EXPORTED FROM THE UNITED STATES, 1782–1800

Year	Pounds	Tierces [a]
1800	56,920,000	112,056
1799	67,234,000	110,599
1798	66,359,000	125,243
1797	75,146,000	60,111
1796	36,067,000	131,039
1795	78,623,000	138,526
1794	83,116,000	116,486
1793	69,892,000	134,611
1792	80,767,000	141,762
1791	85,057,000	96,980

Year	Pounds	Tierces [a]
1790	74,136,000	
1789	60,507,000	
1788	50,000,000	
1787	. . .	
1786	32,598,000	
1785	32,929,000	
1784	31,857,000	
1783	30,987,000	
1782	12,112,000	

[a] A tierce equalled 4.51 bu., or approximately 525 lb. of rice.

Sources: Lewis C. Gray, *History of Agriculture in the Southern United States to 1860* (1933), 1030. Timothy Pitkin, *A Statistical View of the Commerce of the United States of America* (1835), 101.

TABLE 4.61 REPORTED YIELDS OF RICE PER ACRE IN SOUTH CAROLINA

Period	Yield per Acre
ca. 1775	25 bu. (1,625 lb.)
ca. 1791	2.5 to 3 barrels (1,500 to 1,800 lb.)
ca. 1795	20 to 40 bu. (1,250 to 2,500 lb.)

Source: Lewis C. Gray, *History of Agriculture in the Southern United States to 1860* (1933), 283–4, 730.

TABLE 4.62 DESTINATION OF RICE EXPORTED FROM THE UNITED STATES, 1790–1800

Purchaser	1790		1800	
	Tierces[a]	Percentage	Tierces[a]	Percentage
Great Britain	36,930	36.6%	28,634	29.0%
France	9,964	9.9%	. . .	. . .
French West Indies	10,129	10.0%	. . .	. . .
Sweden	50	. . .	20,648	20.9%
Portugal	627	.6%	12,173	12.3%
Spanish Colonies	556	.6%	9,076	9.2%
Madeira	352	.4%	6,989	7.1%
Spain	3,875	3.8%	6,493	6.6%
Swedish West Indies	. . .	. . .	3,888	3.9%
British West Indies	11,705	11.6%	2,796	2.8%
Netherlands	10,315	10.2%	2,413	2.4%
Germany	14,711	14.6%	1,333	1.3%
Others	1,631	1.7%	4,493	4.5%
Total	100,845	100%	98,926	100%

[a] A tierce equalled 4.51 bu., or approximately 525 lb. of rice.
Sources: Timothy Pitkin, *A Statistical View of the Commerce of the United States of America* (1835), 122. U.S. Congress, *American State Papers: Commerce and Navigation* (1832), VII, 32–33.

Sheep

The sheep industry was a marginal enterprise in eighteenth-century America, even though most farmers owned a few of the animals. The domestic and foreign market for mutton was small, and there was little demand for wool after the needs of small-scale home manufacturers were met. Sheep were difficult to protect from wolves in newly settled areas and they fared poorly in northern winters, so wool production centered in the more temperate regions and densely populated seaboard regions, especially on the islands of Narragansett Bay, on Martha's Vineyard, and on Nantucket Island.

TABLE 4.63 PRICES OF SHEEP AND WOOL IN BRITISH MAINLAND COLONIES, 1772–1774

Conn.	Orange Co., N.C.
sheep 5s., 3d.	sheep 7½s. to 13s.

Essex Co., Mass.	Northampton Co., Pa.
lamb 6s., 4d.	lamb 7½s.
sheep 6s. to 12s., 6d.	sheep 6s. to 15s.
wool 3½s. per lb.	wool 2s. per lb.

Note: Connecticut's prices are from 1772 and the others are from 1774. Prices are in local currency, shillings (s) and pence (d).
Sources: Alice Hanson Jones, *American Colonial Wealth: Documents and Methods* (1978), 69–105, 607–799, 1443–71. Jackson Turner Main, *Society and Economy in Colonial Connecticut* (1985), 57.

Because no efforts were made to improve the stock through breeding, American sheep produced wool much shorter than, and in general far inferior to, European varieties. Commercial sheep raising only developed during the era of the French Revolution, when disruptions in overseas trade stimulated a demand for raw wool to supply domestically produced textiles. This opportunity induced Americans to cross their own sheep with the imported Merino breed, which contributed to a significant improvement in the quantity and quality of wool yielded by American flocks after 1800.

A herd of sheep is here shown being driven west for sale in newly settled regions. Commercial production of wool remained in its infancy by 1800, but sheep were nevertheless a near-universal feature of late-eighteenth-century farm life. Sheep provided an inexpensive source of fiber for making clothes and some food, although mutton was the least favorite meat of early Americans. [*An Old Wayside Tavern on the Old National Pike*] (*Harper's Magazine*, November 1879)

TABLE 4.64 EXPORTS OF LIVE SHEEP FROM THE UNITED STATES, 1790–1800

Year Ending Sep. 30	Sheep Number	To British West Indies	To French West Indies	To Dutch West Indies
1800	9,445	. . .	. . .	. . .
1799	9,733	7,675	753	566
1798	4,808	2,651	794	355
1797	3,291	506	795	418
1796	6,140	2,547	1,216	335
1795	6,494	1,909	1,226	439
1794	9,577	3,895	2,213	392
1793	11,858	2,158	6,119	1,238
1792	12,153	1,700	7,735	1,180
1791	10,377	. . .	. . .	. . .
1790	10,058	2,741	8,502	748

Source: U.S. Congress, *American State Papers: Commerce and Navigation* (1832), VII, 24–542.

Silk

Established against great odds during Georgia's first three decades of settlement, silk was an expensive undertaking that proved profitable only because Parliament paid a bounty of 3 shillings per pound

<u>TABLE 4.65</u> **SILK PRODUCTION AND EXPORTS IN GA., 1763–1772**

Year Starting Jan. 5	Output of Cocoons	Silk Exported	Value of Exports
1763	15,248 lb.	953 lb.	£142.19.0
1764	14,368 lb.	898 lb.	£134.14.0
1765	11,376 lb.	711 lb.	£106.13.0
1766	17,344 lb.	1,084 lb.	£162.12.0
1767	10,736 lb.	671 lb.	£100.13.0
1768	8,656 lb.	541 lb.	£81.03.0
1769	5,312 lb.	332 lb.	£24.18.0
1770	4,640 lb.	290 lb.	£21.15.0
1771	7,008 lb.	438 lb.	£32.17.0
1772	7,760 lb.	485 lb.	£36.07.6

Note: Production of cocoons was calculated at sixteen times each pound of silk exported. Value of exports was calculated on the basis of a fixed price per pound of 3s. before 1769 and 1s., 6d. after then. Prices in sterling.
Source: Lewis C. Gray, *History of Agriculture in the Southern United States to 1860* (1933), 187.

through 1765. Not only did white mulberry trees have to be imported from abroad (because the leaves of native black varieties were too bitter for the worms' taste), but the skilled labor entailed in reeling a pound of silk from sixteen pounds of cocoons was also very expensive. Parliament reduced the fixed price to 1 s., 6 d. in 1766, the same year that exports peaked at 1,084 pounds; in 1769, the government bounty was raised to 25% of the accustomed price. The reduction of the traditional 3-shilling bounty hastened the silk industry's collapse, and no sizeable shipments were sold overseas after 1772. Small amounts of raw silk were nevertheless registered as U.S. exports during the 1790s.

<u>TABLE 4.66</u> **EXPORTS OF RAW SILK FROM THE UNITED STATES, 1790–1798**

Year Ending Sep. 30	Raw Silk lb. or chests	To Great Britain	To France	To Holland	To Spain
1798	47 lb.	47 lb.	. . .	. . .	. . .
1797	33 lb.	33 lb.	. . .	. . .	. . .
1794–96	. . .	. . .	. . .	. . .	. . .
1793	104 lb.	104 lb.	. . .	. . .	. . .
1792	14 chests	. . .	. . .	14 chests	. . .
1791	153 lb.	118 lb.	. . .	. . .	35 lb.
1790	177 lb.	93 lb.	84 lb.	. . .	. . .

Source: U.S. Congress, *American State Papers: Commerce and Navigation* (1832), VII, 24–452.

Tobacco

Tobacco was the most valuable commodity produced during the colonial era, and by the eve of independence it accounted for more than 25% of all exports. The disruption of usual marketing arrangements drastically reduced tobacco output during the Revolution, but after peace returned American producers benefited from competition between British and French merchants to monopolize the trade for themselves. Output rose quickly from 1783 to 1786, but poor weather conditions limited crop sizes for the next three years.

<u>TABLE 4.67</u> **PRICES OF TOBACCO (IN PENCE) IN MD., 1762–1775**

Year	Sterling Low	Sterling High	Sterling Mean	Local Money
1775	1.20	2.43	1.67	2.23
1774	.90	2.52	1.41	1.88
1773	1.13	2.93	1.64	2.19
1772	1.08	2.40	1.64	2.18
1771	.90	2.70	1.90	2.53
1770	1.13	2.52	2.06	2.75
1769	1.35	3.00	2.23	2.98
1768	1.13	3.00	1.81	2.41
1767	.72	2.16	1.63	2.18
1766	1.17	1.80	1.45	1.93
1765	.90	1.62	1.33	1.77
1764	1.04	1.50	1.26	1.68
1763	.88	1.44	1.10	1.65
1762	. . .	3.00	1.39	2.08

Note: The specified exchange rate was £133⅓ local to £100 sterling from 1764 to 1775, and £150 to £100 in 1762 and 1763.
Source: Carville V. Earle, *The Evolution of a Tidewater Settlement System: All Hallow's Parish, Maryland, 1650–1783* (1973), 228–29.

<u>TABLE 4.68</u> **TOBACCO PRICES (IN GUILDERS PER DUTCH LB.) AT AMSTERDAM, 1763–1792**

Year	Imported from Va.	Other Imports to Amsterdam
1792	.20	.19
1791	.19	.17
1790	.25	.19
1789	.22	.20
1788	.25	.20
1787	.26	.20
1786	.23	.20
1785	.27	.20
1784	.33	.19
1783	.33	.16
1782	.74	.21
1781	.70	.24
1780	.51	.23
1779	.51	.34
1778	.61	.35
1777	.50	.25
1776	.34	.17
1775	.26	.15
1774	.22	.14
1773	.19	.16
1772	.20	.16
1771	.21	.14
1770	.21	.16
1769	.21	.16
1768	.21	.15
1767	.19	.13
1766	.19	.15
1765	.17	.11
1764	.16	.11
1763	.18	.11

Source: Jacob M. Price, *France and the Chesapeake: A History of the French Tobacco Monopoly, 1674–1791, and of Its Relationship to the British and American Tobacco Trades* (1973), 852.

TABLE 4.69   EXPORTS OF AMERICAN TOBACCO (IN POUNDS), BY ORIGIN AND DESTINATION, 1768–1772

	Great Britain	West Indies	Coastal Trade	Southern Europe and Africa	Total Exports
1772					
Northern Ports	. . .	9,300	89,600	27,500	126,400
Md.	33,902,000	2,500	4,700	. . .	33,909,200
Va.	70,449,400	147,000	35,900	. . .	70,632,300
N.C.	1,573,400	11,800	19,600	. . .	1,604,800
S.C.	479,000	7,400	35,700	5,500	527,600
Ga.	170,200	. . .	8,900	. . .	179,100
Total	106,574,000	178,000	194,400	33,000	106,979,400
1771					
Northern Ports	. . .	3,900	102,200	25,300	131,400
Md.	38,931,400	15,300	16,300	. . .	38,963,000
Va.	71,268,700	160,500	39,500	. . .	71,468,700
N.C.	1,872,200	2,000	12,400	. . .	1,886,600
S.C.	401,400	. . .	27,100	8,100	436,600
Ga.	34,900	. . .	. . .	. . .	34,900
Total	112,508,600	181,700	197,500	33,400	112,921,200
1770					
Northern Ports	. . .	14,200	56,100	9,300	79,600
Md.	27,266,800	3.100	2,100	. . .	27,272,000
Va.	60,811,100	145,600	91,800	. . .	61,048,500
N.C.	1,084,700	2,400	10,200	. . .	1,097,300
S.C.	145,500	. . .	87,700	. . .	233,200
Ga.	13,300	100	. . .	. . .	13,400
Florida	. . .	. . .	300	. . .	300
Total	89,321,400	165,400	248,200	9,300	89,744,300
1769					
Northern Ports	. . .	17,800	79,300	3,900	101,000
Md.	25,781,800	1,200	7,800	. . .	25,790,800
Va.	57,337,800	78,200	29,200	. . .	57,445,200
N.C.	549,600	3,400	1,000	700	554,700
S.C.	275,400	100	34,900	. . .	310,400
Ga.	600	1,600	3,000	. . .	5,200
Total	83,945,200	102,300	155,200	4,600	84,207,300
1768					
Northern Ports	. . .	25,600	13,200	4,300	43,100
Md.	24,382,300	. . .	. . .	. . .	24,382,300
Va.	44,769,700	107,200	. . .	. . .	44,876,900
N.C.	367,100	6,400	7,300	. . .	380,800
S.C.	. . .	. . .	. . .	. . .	. . .
Total	69,519,100	139,200	20,500	4,300	69,683,100

Source: Data compiled by Lawrence A. Harper in U.S. Bureau of the Census, *Historical Statistics of the U.S.* (1960), 767.

TABLE 4.70   TOTAL IMPORTS OF TOBACCO (IN POUNDS) TO GREAT BRITAIN, 1763–1792, INCLUDING AMOUNT PURCHASED FROM AREA OF THE MODERN UNITED STATES

Year	To England	To Scotland	Total Britain	From Modern U.S.
1792	. . .	. . .	44,143,000	44,058,000
1791	38,169,000	14,417,000	52,587,000	52,461,000
1790	46,991,000	10,616,000	57,606,000	57,570,000
1789	47,600,000	11,555,000	59,156,000	59,117,000
1788	39,065,000	9,796,000	48,860,000	48,824,000
1787	31,790,000	7,829,000	39,619,000	39,520,000
1786	37,656,000	7,765,000	45,420,000	45,299,000
1785	34,101,000	9,159,000	43,260,000	43,091,000
1784	39,991,000	3,530,000	43,520,000	43,407,000
1783	15,619,000	2,260,000	17,879,000	14,687,000

(continued)

TABLE 4.70 (continued)

Year	To England	To Scotland	Total Britain	From Modern U.S.
1782	7,203,000	2,625,000	9,828,000	1,082,000
1781	11,387,000	1,952,000	13,339,000	1,873,000
1780	12,299,000	5,126,000	17,425,000	985,000
1779	14,017,000	3,138,000	17,156,000	3,321,000
1778	9,077,000	2,884,000	11,962,000	1,693,000
1777	2,146,000	295,000	2,441,000	361,000
1776	7,275,000	7,423,000	14,698,000	14,698,000
1775	55,969,000	45,863,000	101,832,000	101,322,000
1774	56,057,000	41,348,000	97,405,000	97,395,000
1773	55,936,000	44,543,000	100,478,000	100,472,000
1772	51,502,000	45,260,000	96,762,000	. . .
1771	58,093,000	47,269,000	105,362,000	. . .
1770	39,188,000	38,709,000	77,897,000	. . .
1769	33,797,000	36,303,000	70,100,000	. . .
1768	35,555,000	33,237,000	68,792,000	. . .
1767	39,145,000	28,938,000	68,082,000	. . .
1766	43,318,000	29,344,000	72,663,000	. . .
1765	48,320,000	33,160,000	81,479,000	. . .
1764	54,443,000	26,347,000	80,790,000	. . .
1763	65,179,000	32,839,000	98,018,000	. . .

Note: English imports for 1777–1782 include a large amount of tobacco captured from enemy vessels during the Revolution.
Source: Jacob M. Price, *France and the Chesapeake: A History of the French Tobacco Monopoly, 1674–1791, and of Its Relationship to the British and American Tobacco Trades* (1973), 844.

TABLE 4.71 IMPORTS OF U.S. TOBACCO (IN POUNDS) TO FRANCE, 1778–1789

Year Ending Sep. 30	Imports from U.S.	Total Imports
1789	13,458,000	22,747,000
1788	3,939,000	16,849,000
1787	32,043,000	40,878,000
1786	24,708,000	. . .
1785	. . .	. . .
1784	6,424,000	. . .
1783	6,293,000	. . .
1782	6,032,000	11,455,000
1781	. . .	. . .
1780	2,142,000	13,778,000
1779	2,385,000	10,047,000
1778	1,976,000	9,838,000

Source: Jacob M. Price, *France and the Chesapeake: A History of the French Tobacco Monopoly, 1674–1791, and of Its Relationship to the British and American Tobacco Trades* (1973), 723, 737.

Although many farmers in the Chesapeake were cutting back on tobacco production to grow more grains, this decline in output was offset by an expansion of the industry into Kentucky, the Carolina backcountry, and Georgia. By the years 1790–1792, shipments of U.S. tobacco abroad had surpassed the previous export peaks of the early 1770s, but they now ranked behind wheat products as the country's second most valuable staple marketed overseas. Per capita tobacco production had also fallen significantly during the previous two decades. During the 1790s, overseas shipments of unprocessed tobacco fell, but this reduction was offset by a large rise in the export of snuff and other manufactured leaf products.

TABLE 4.72 VIRGINIA TOBACCO EXPORTS, 1770–1792 (YEARS ENDING SEP. 30)

Period	Hogsheads
1791–1792	61,203
1790–1791	56,288
1788–1789	58,673
1787–1788	58,544
1786–1787	60,041
1785–1786	60,380
1784–1785	55,624
1783–1784	49,497
1770–1773	67,247 (annual average)

Source: Jacob M. Price, *France and the Chesapeake: A History of the French Tobacco Monopoly, 1674–1791, and of Its Relationship to the British and American Tobacco Trades* (1973), 729.

TABLE 4.73 SOUTH CAROLINA TOBACCO PRODUCTION AND EXPORTS, 1782–1788

Year and Production		Exported from State	
1787	5,019 hogsheads	[1788]	62,095 quintals
1786	5,493 hogsheads	[1787]	. . .
1785	3,929 hogsheads	[1786]	2,975 hogsheads
1784	2,302 hogsheads	[1785]	357 hogsheads
1783	2,680 hogsheads	[1784]	29,414 quintals
1782	643 hogsheads	[1783]	7,073 quintals

Note: One year's crop is the next year's exports, which include shipments to other states.
Source: Jacob M. Price, *France and the Chesapeake: A History of the French Tobacco Monopoly, 1674–1791, and of Its Relationship to the British and American Tobacco Trades* (1973), 730.

Tobacco was the most valuable North American commodity during most of the Revolutionary era. Tobacco composed about 27% of all American exports around 1770. Tobacco was nevertheless declining in importance, and by 1791, the crop's share of U.S. exports had fallen to 20%. Tobacco production primarily centered in Virginia, North Carolina, and Kentucky, all states where the climatic conditions were unfavorable for cotton. (Courtesy Library of Congress)

TABLE 4.74 EXPORTS OF U.S. LEAF TOBACCO (HOGSHEADS) BY STATE, 1790–1792

	Oct. 1790–Sep. 1791 hhd.	Oct. 1791–Sep. 1792 hhd.
N.H.	7	3
Mass.	1,190	1,221
R.I.	743	1,429
Conn.	499	105
N.Y.	1,290	1,952
N.J.	7	5
Pa.	1,928	3,203
Del.	—	8
Md.	25,019	28,992
Va.	56,288	61,203
N.C.	4,772	3,546
S.C.	3,708	5,290
Ga.	5,821	5,471
Total	101,272	112,428

Source: Jacob M. Price, *France and the Chesapeake: A History of the French Tobacco Monopoly, 1674–1791, and of Its Relationship to the British and American Tobacco Trades* (1973), 730.

TABLE 4.75 EXPORTS OF UNMANUFACTURED (LEAF) TOBACCO AND OF SNUFF AND OTHER MANUFACTURED TOBACCO FROM THE UNITED STATES, 1790–1800

Year	Unmanufactured	Manufactured		
		Snuff	Other Manufactured	Total
	hogsheads	pounds	pounds	pounds
1790	118,460	15,350	. . .	15,350
1791	101,272	15,689	81,122	96,811
1792	112,428	10,042	117,874	127,916
1793	59,947	35,559	137,784	173,343
1794	72,958	37,415	19,370	56,785
1795	61,050	129,436	20,263	149,699
1796	69,018	267,046	29,181	296,227
1797	58,167	65,703	12,805	78,508
1798	68,567	114,151	142,269	256,420
1799	96,070	109,682	416,076	525,758
1800	78,680	41,453	457,713	499,166

Source: Lewis C. Gray, *History of Agriculture in the Southern United States to 1860* (1933), 1035.

TABLE 4.76 DESTINATION OF U.S. TOBACCO EXPORTS (BY HOGSHEADS), 1790–1800

Country	1790	1793	1795	1798	1800
Low Countries	23,448	7,290	11,015	10,832	6,087
Austrian Neth.		3,238			
Great Britain	73,708	30,206	43,702	21,579	37,798
England		24,700	32,769	16,980	. . .
Scotland		2,394	3,982	2,194	. . .
Ireland		3,112	6,951	2,405	. . .
Germany	5,612	3,427	10,138	13,711	16,885
France	10,876	8,897	2,070	4,881	143
Spain	568	1,541	629		7,555
Total all countries	118,460	59,341	72,958	58,167	75,716

Source: Edward C. Papenfuse, In Pursuit of Profit: The Annapolis Merchants in the Era of the American Revolution, 1763–1805 (1975), 220.

TABLE 4.77 POUNDS OF TOBACCO PRODUCED PER LABORER IN THE CHESAPEAKE, 1764–1799

	Lower Western Shore of Md.	Upper Eastern Shore of Md.	York River Basin of Va.	James River Piedmont, Va.
1764–69	774	665	795	1,025
1770–74	839	732	914	835
1775–81	747	631	384	574
1782–89	792	1,072	557	1,338
1790–99	732	832	585	740

Source: Lorena S. Walsh, "Plantation Management in the Chesapeake, 1620–1820," Journal of Economic History IXL (1989), 395.

Wheat

Wheat was the primary export staple of northern agriculture. The production of this grain became even more widely distributed during the late eighteenth century, when its cultivation spread in Maryland, Virginia's tidewater counties, and the Shenendoah Valley. By the Revolutionary era, output had been significantly curtailed in New England from the persistence of black stem-rust, which was

TABLE 4.78 PRICE OF WHEAT PER BUSHEL, IN PENCE OF LOCAL CURRENCY, IN KENT AND TALBOT COUNTIES, MARYLAND, 1763–1774

Year	Kent Co.	Talbot Co.
1774	63	. . .
1773	65	. . .
1772	61	48
1771	53	48
1770	47	44
1769	47	44
1768	50	44
1767	50	46
1766	45	44
1765	39	42
1764	43	45
1763	49	46

Source: Paul G. E. Clemens, The Atlantic Economy and Colonial Maryland's Eastern Shore: From Tobacco to Grain (1980), 227.

TABLE 4.79 AVERAGE PRICE OF WHEAT, BREAD, AND FLOUR (IN SHILLINGS OF LOCAL CURRENCY AND U.S. DOLLARS) AT PHILADELPHIA, 1763–1800

	Wheat Bushels	Flour cwt. of 112 lb.	Ship Bread cwt. of 112 lb.
1800	$6.43	$5.73	$4.00
1799	$5.85	$5.51	$4.00
1798	$1.30	$4.66	$3.63
1797	$1.40	$5.08	$5.76
1796	$1.95	$1.16	$5.85
1795	$12.51	45.3s.	31.3s.
1794	$6.67	30.0s.	$3.11
1793	$1.12	26.4s.	16.4s.
1792	$.96	21.6s.	14.4s.
1791	7.4s.	22.4s.	16.5s.
1790	10.1s.	27.7s.	22.0s.
1789	6.9s.	19.9s.	14.7s.
1788	5.9s.	17.3s.	14.6s.
1787	6.7s.	19.2s.	18.3s.
1786	7.4s.	20.5s.	19.4s.
1785	8.0s.	21.8s.	22.7s.
1784	7.7s.	23.1s.	22.2s.
1783	6.8s.	21.5s.	21.0s.
1782	6.5s.	16.1s.	17.5s.
1781	334.2s.	925.6s.	671.3s.
1780	487.2s.	1,800.5s.	2,427.7s.
1779	150.2s.	581.1s.	776.8s.
1778	17.6s.	56.6s.	96.0s.
1777	8.5s.	24.0s.	30.3s.
1776	5.0s.	14.8s.	14.0s.
1775	5.68s.	15.36s.	. . .
1774	6.93s.	18.12s.	14.57s.
1773	7.42s.	18.92s.	17.30s.
1772	7.74s.	20.26s.	19.95s.
1771	6.78s.	17.50s.	15.68s.
1770	5.92s.	15.71s.	14.11s.
1769	5.48s.	15.04s.	13.65s.
1768	6.31s.	16.89s.	15.91s.
1767	6.25s.	17.16s.	16.80s.
1766	5.73s.	14.81s.	15.44s.
1765	4.70s.	13.50s.	13.88s.
1764	4.60s.	12.81s.	12.95s.
1763	6.06s.	16.94s.	17.82s.

Note: Numerals behind decimal places of local currency represent fractions of a shilling, not pence.
Sources: Arthur H. Cole, Wholesale Commodity Prices in the United States, 1700–1861 (1938), 77–124. Anne Bezanson, et al., Prices and Inflation During the Revolution: Pennsylvania, 1770–1790 (1951), 335–38.

particularly virulent in that region but sometimes infected crops in the middle-Atlantic region. This parasite drove many farmers out of wheat and into rye cultivation, especially in the older seaboard communities. By the late 1700s, however, farmers recognized that losses could be largely eliminated by substituting for spring wheat an early crop of winter wheat, which ripened before the fungus matured to its most destructive extent.

A second major threat confronted wheat cultivators during the Revolution, when the Hessian fly began its first infestations in New York. Large damage occurred in 1785 and 1786, after which the insect's depredations spread to the Delaware Valley. It was first reported west of the Appalachians in 1797. The fly induced a small shift from wheat to rye, but the most common defense was to delay planting spring wheat long enough for the crop to ripen after most

TABLE 4.80 ESTIMATED AVERAGE ANNUAL HARVEST AND EXPORTS OF WHEAT, 1768–1772

Colonies	Annual Output and Value		Annual Exports and Value	
Va.	2,325,000 bu.	£442,000	403,000 bu.	£76,613
N.Y. & East Jersey	3,058,000 bu.	£582,000	530,000 bu.	£100,800
Penn., Del., & West Jersey	8,654,000 bu.	£1,646,000	1,500,000 bu.	£285,200

Note: Monetary values are in sterling.
Source: David C. Klingaman, "The Significance of Grain in the Development of the Tobacco Colonies," *Journal of Economic History* XXIX (1969), 272–74 and n. 22, 273.

of the insects had died in the early fall. This solution was not applicable to winter wheat, however, and so the fly continued to ravage New England, where that variety was dominant. The Hessian fly remained a serious threat until after 1830, when farmers adopted new strains of spring wheat, especially the Black Sea variety, that ripened before the insect could reach full maturity.

Wheat, flour, and bread comprised almost one-fifth the value of all exports from the British mainland colonies about 1770, when they ranked as the second most important item of trade (behind

TABLE 4.81 AN ANALYSIS OF THE OVERHEAD AND PROFIT OF EXPORTING NORTH AMERICAN WHEAT TO THE LONDON MARKET IN 1775

	£	s.	d.
Gross sales 200 quarters of wheat at £2 10s. 0d. per qtr.	500	0	0
417½ quarters of wheat at £2 8s. 0d. per qtr.	990	6	0
79 barrels of flour at 16s. per cwt.	128	5	10
Total gross sales	1,618	11	10
Freight on wheat	247	0	0
Freight on flour	19	15	0
Primage	5	5	0
Duty on 617½ qtrs. of wheat at 6d. per qtr.	15	8	9
Entry and fees	1	15	6
Meters bill into lighter on wheat	10	13	7
Lighterage, screening, turning and delivery on wheat	10	4	2
Duty on flour	1	7	0
Entry and officers landing and attendance	0	10	6
Lighterage, lading, weighing and delivery of flour	3	12	5
Cooper bill paid	0	5	6
Brokerage on wheat	30	12	6
Brokerage on flour	3	4	0
Commission on gross sales at 2½%	40	9	4
Total charges	390	3	3
Net proceeds	1,228	8	7

Source: James F. Shepherd and Gary M. Walton, *Shipping, Maritime Trade, and the Economic Development of Colonial North America* (1972), 56.

TABLE 4.82 VOLUME (BU.) AND VALUE (£ STERLING) OF WHEAT EXPORTS FROM THE BRITISH MAINLAND COLONIES, 1768–1772

	To Britain and Ireland		To Southern Europe		To West Indies	
	bu.	£ ster.	bu.	£ ster.	bu.	£ ster.
From New England						
1768	. . .	. . .	200	£45	. . .	. . .
1769	. . .	. . .	3,311	£654	. . .	. . .
1770	. . .	. . .	1,078	£218	. . .	. . .
1771	. . .	. . .	16,476	£3,756	. . .	. . .
1772	. . .	. . .	. . .	. . .	16	£4
From Mid-Atlantic						
1768	39,421	£7,470	191,255	£36,243	. . .	. . .
1769	50,678	£8,767	248,880	£43,056	. . .	. . .
1770	10,216	£1,961	173,590	£33,329	755	£145
1771	14,358	£2,937	92,938	£19,006	28	£6
1772	1,644	£395	127,942	£30,706	144	£35
From Upper South						
1768	86,496	£16,391	214,772	£40,699	. . .	. . .
1769	110,145	£19,055	609,033	£105,363	. . .	. . .
1770	147,969	£28,409	381,499	£73,248	. . .	. . .
1771	112,326	£22,971	158,627	£32,440	. . .	. . .
1772	26,465	£6,352	165,635	£39,752	. . .	. . .
From Lower South						
1768	. . .	. . .	940	£178	. . .	. . .
1769	. . .	. . .	1,700	£294	. . .	. . .
1770	4,290	£824	2,810	£540	. . .	. . .
1771	. . .	. . .	. . .	. . .	. . .	. . .
1772	. . .	. . .	. . .	. . .	. . .	. . .

Source: James F. Shepherd and Gary M. Walton, *Shipping, Maritime Trade, and the Economic Development of Colonial North America* (1972), 211–27.

tobacco). Twenty years later, wheat products were the country's leading export and made up 28% of all commodities sold abroad. The amount of wheat purchased for domestic consumption, or consumed on the farms where it was grown, has been estimated as five to ten times greater than these exports. Average per capita consumption of wheat may have been as high as 6.43 bushels in about 1770.

In 1780, the *Columbian Magazine* published this illustration of farm laborers reaping wheat. Wheat products briefly emerged as the leading U.S. export during the 1790s due to crop failures in Europe and wars spawned by the French Revolution. By 1791, flour, bread, and unmilled wheat accounted for 28% of all U.S. commodities shipped overseas, whereas they had comprised just 19% of all American exports two decades earlier. (Courtesy Library of Congress)

TABLE 4.83 VOLUME (TONS) AND VALUE (£ STERLING) OF BREAD AND FLOUR EXPORTED FROM THE BRITISH MAINLAND COLONIES, 1768–1772

	To Britain and Ireland		To Southern Europe		To West Indies	
	tons	£ ster.	tons	£ ster.	tons	£ ster.
From New England						
1768	8	£84	186	£1,889	768	£7,799
1769	11	£104	526	£4,994	1,625	£15,440
1770	1	£11	71	£728	1,967	£20,061
1771	1	£6	197	£2,081	1,462	£15,455
1772	. . .	. . .	79	£997	972	£12,223
From Mid-Atlantic						
1768	3,407	£34,583	5,112	£51,886	10,394	£105,498
1769	3,286	£31,222	17,278	£164,145	15,593	£148,135
1770	1,202	£12,260	15,369	£156,763	17,360	£177,078
1771	792	£8,353	10,124	£107,014	16,721	£176,740
1772	130	£1,625	14,661	£184,291	19,711	£247,770
From Upper South						
1768	449	£4,557	1,176	£11,942	1,576	£15,996
1769	1,249	£11,862	3,212	£30,515	2,811	£26,703
1770	2,576	£26,274	3,031	£30,921	3,610	£36,824
1771	1,646	£17,405	1,978	£20,905	3,181	£33,632
1772	335	£4,204	3,177	£39,931	2,710	£34,068
From Lower South						
1768	11	£112	14	£146	133	£1,346
1769	43	£407	36	£342	297	£2,821
1770	66	£678	30	£304	320	£3,264
1771	64	£679	2	£26	293	£3,093
1772	5	£69	. . .	. . .	118	£1,485

Source: James F. Shepherd and Gary M. Walton, *Shipping, Maritime Trade, and the Economic Development of Colonial North America* (1972), 211–27.

TABLE 4.84 ESTIMATED PERCENTAGE OF U.S. WHEAT PRODUCTION EXPORTED, 1770–1800

Year	Total Production	Domestic Consumption (%)	Wheat Exports (%)
1770	11,830,000 bu.	9,240,000 bu. (78%)	2,590,000 bu. (22%)
1790	20,960,000 bu.	16,900,000 bu. (81%)	4,060,000 bu. (19%)
1800	25,790,000 bu.	22,830,000 bu. (88%)	2,960,000 bu. (12%)

Source: Geoffrey N. Gilbert, "The Role of Breadstuffs in American Trade, 1770–1790," *Explorations in Economic History* XIV (1977), 385.

TABLE 4.85 DESTINATION OF FLOUR EXPORTS FROM THE UNITED STATES, 1768–1800

Export Market	1768–1772 barrels (%)	1790–1792 barrels (%)	1800 barrels (%)
West Indies	233,000 (53%)	400,000 (60%)	313,692 (50%)
Southern Europe	174,000 (39%)	160,000 (24%)	118,980 (19%)
Other Europe and Canada	35,000 (8%)	102,000 (15%)	199,287 (31%)

Sources: Geoffrey N. Gilbert, "The Role of Breadstuffs in American Trade, 1770–1790," *Explorations in Economic History* XIV (1977), 384. Timothy Pitkin, *A Statistical View of the Commerce of the United States of America* (1835), 119.

TABLE 4.86 EXPORTS OF WHEAT, FLOUR AND BREAD FROM THE UNITED STATES, 1790–1800

Year	Wheat (bushels)	Flour (barrels)	Bread (barrels)
1800	26,853	653,052	81,199
1799	10,056	519,265	47,340
1798	15,021	567,558	52,793
1797	15,655	515,633	84,679
1796	31,226	725,194	181,065
1795	141,273	687,369	71,331
1794	698,797	846,010	69,907
1793	1,450,575	1,074,639	76,405
1792	853,790	824,464	80,986
1791	1,018,339	619,681	100,279
1790	1,124,458	724,623	75,667

Source: Timothy Pitkin, *A Statistical View of the Commerce of the United States of America* (1835), 96. U.S. Congress, *American State Papers: Commerce and Navigation* (1832) VII, 24–452.

TABLE 4.87 WHEAT OUTPUT (BU.) PER LABORER IN THE CHESAPEAKE, 1764–1799

	Lower Western Shore of Md.	Upper Eastern Shore of Md.	Potomac River Basin of Va.	York River Basin of Va.
1764–69	55.9	43.0	64.7	15.0
1770–74	18.0	34.6	61.2	14.2
1775–81	8.3	36.3	28.1	7.2
1782–89	16.2	73.5	13.5	11.3
1790–99	22.4	71.0	26.6	28.3

Source: Lorena S. Walsh, "Plantation Management in the Chesapeake, 1620–1820," *Journal of Economic History* IXL (1989), 399.

TABLE 4.88 HOURS OF LABOR ESTIMATED TO PRODUCE 100 BUSHELS OF WHEAT IN 1800

Total hours per acre	56
Before harvest	16
In the harvest	40
Average yield per acre	15 bu.
Hours per 100 bushels	373

Source: U.S. Bureau of the Census, *Historical Statistics of the United States: Colonial Times to 1957* (1960), 281.

The Maritime Industries

The Fisheries

The fisheries were almost exclusively a New England industry during the late eighteenth century. By 1763, New Englanders were taking an annual catch of about 240,000,000 pounds, largely composed of cod and mackerel. The most marketable fish were sold to be consumed during days of religious abstinence observed by southern European Catholics, who bought about 40% of the catch, while the inferior part of the catch was disposed of at lower prices as rations for slaves in the West Indies. From 1768 to 1772, foreign markets annually purchased fish worth an average £287,000. Fish comprised two-thirds of the value of New England's exports and ranked as the fourth most valuable commodity shipped from British North America (behind tobacco, flour, and rice).

The Revolutionary War severely disrupted New England's fisheries, which lost many of their former markets in the West Indies and Mediterranean to British competitors. With a return to peace in 1783, the British government excluded U.S. fish from its markets and even France erected tariff barriers against American fish. Britain's government also offered bounties to encourage the development of its own fishing fleet, which then could undersell American competitors in many markets; Britain also attempted to entice American fishermen to relocate in Canada or in its other dominions. Finding themselves legally excluded from many former markets and forced

TABLE 4.89 PRICE OF 100 LB. OF JAMAICA COD AT BOSTON, MASS., IN SHILLINGS OF LOCAL CURRENCY, 1763–1795

1795	19.20	1778	. . .
1794	14.40	1777	. . .
1793	17.00	1776	. . .
1792	14.90	1775	11.50
1791	14.60	1774	9.80
1790	12.30	1773	11.20
1789	10.80	1772	13.20
1788	11.30	1771	13.30
1787	13.50	1770	13.60
1786	15.70	1769	13.20
1785	18.00	1768	12.70
1784	20.20	1767	11.90
1783	. . .	1766	13.50
1782	. . .	1765	13.10
1781	. . .	1764	13.10
1780	. . .	1763	13.70
1779	. . .		

Source: Arthur H. Cole, *Wholesale Commodity Prices in the United States, 1700–1861* (1938), 50–121.

TABLE 4.90 PRICE OF WHALE OIL (IN LOCAL SHILLINGS AND DOLLARS) AT NEW YORK AND PHILADELPHIA, 1784–1800

Philadelphia (per gallon)		New York (per barrel)	
1800	$.44	1800	$.40
1799	$.27	1799	$.32
1798	$.43	1798	$.34
1797	$.38	1797	$.34
1796	$.42	1796	. . .
1795	3.00s.	1795	87s.
1794	$.29	1794	53s.
1793	2.10s.	1793	60s.
1792	1.90s.	1792	. . .
1791	2.00s.	1791	53s.
1790	2.00s.	1790	53s.
1789	2.00s.	1789	65s.
1788	2.60s.	1788	72.5s.
1787	2.70s.	1787	70s.
1786	2.40s.	1786	66s.
1785	2.70s.	1785	. . .
1784	3.00s.	1784	. . .

Source: Arthur H. Cole, *Wholesale Commodity Prices in the United States, 1700–1861* (1938), 78–123.

to dispose of catches at prices that were barely profitable, many fishermen withdrew their vessels from the industry during the 1780s. From 1775 to 1790, Massachusetts alone experienced a reduction of almost 20% in its fishing fleet and a decline of 25% in the number of seamen employed.

	Spermaceti Candles					
	To Great Britain		To Southern Europe		To West Indies	
	Pounds	Value	Pounds	Value	Pounds	Value
1772	. . .	. . .	8,760	£623	220,066	£15,625
1771	. . .	. . .	5,850	£384	346,170	£22,674
1770	. . .	. . .	10,867	£723	324,650	£21,589
1769	. . .	. . .	19,093	£1,289	239,745	£16,182
1768	. . .	. . .	5,316	£359	225,210	£15,202

Source: James F. Shepherd and Gary M. Walton, *Shipping, Maritime Trade, and the Economic Development of Colonial North America* (1972), 211–24.

TABLE 4.92 TONNAGE OF THE U.S. FISHING INDUSTRY, OCT. 1789–SEP. 1790

State	Tonnage	Percent
N.H.	473	1.8%
Mass.	24,826	94.6%
R.I.	838	3.2%
Md.	60	.2%
Va.	55	.2%
Total	26,252	100.0%

Source: U.S. Congress, *American State Papers: Commerce and Navigation* (1832), VII, 7.

TABLE 4.91 VOLUME AND VALUE OF NEW ENGLAND EXPORTS OF WHALE OIL, SPERMACETI CANDLES, AND DRIED FISH, 1768–1772

	Dried Fish					
	To Great Britain		To Southern Europe		To West Indies	
	Quintals	Value	Quintals	Value	Quintals	Value
1772	7	£4	105,364	£52,840	251,720	£126,238
1771	2,000	£1,018	131,200	£66,781	193,194	£98,336
1770	4	£2	104,695	£53,499	179,258	£91,600
1769	10	£5	116,176	£57,623	168,860	£83,754
1768	. . .	. . .	116,273	£55,230	155,455	£73,841

	Whale Oil					
	To Great Britain		To Southern Europe		To West Indies	
	Tons	Value	Tons	Value	Tons	Value
1772	2,536	£30,438	1	£11	170	£2,043
1771	2,838	£34,064	7	£86	106	£1,272
1770	4,011	£48,137	2	£29	190	£2,278
1769	3,870	£46,446	21	£253	243	£2,912
1768	3,594	£43,130	22	£262	192	£2,303

The whaling industry, which accounted for 53% of New England's exports to Great Britain from 1768 to 1772, suffered a similar decline after 1776. On the eve of independence, New Englanders manned more than 250 whaling vessels, 183 of which sailed out of Massachusetts. By 1789, Massachusetts's whaling fleet had declined by a third and the number of crewmen had dropped by 60%; its exports of oil also decreased by more than half in that period. Britain and France both offered financial incentives for whalers to emigrate from the United States and succeeded in luring small groups of whalers to Dartmouth in Nova Scotia, Milford Haven in Wales, and Dunkirk in France.

Beginning in 1785, when Massachusetts voted to pay bounties on whale oil, the state and national governments devised policies to encourage recovery in the fisheries. New England states reduced the tax burden borne by the industry, and the United States enacted subsidies in 1792. The national government also strove to negotiate diplomatic agreements with Britain and Spain favorable to the maritime industries. The outbreak of war between Britain and France in 1793 also benefited America's fishing and whaling industries because of the damage inflicted upon the fleets of their competitors in Britain and France. By the late 1790s, the United States was exporting approximately 400,000,000 pounds of dried fish annually, far above pre-Revolutionary levels, and was once again the major supplier of whale oil for Europeans, with annual sales exceeding 400,000 gallons by 1800.

TABLE 4.93 DECLINE OF THE WHALING INDUSTRY IN MASS., 1771–1789

State of the Whale Fishery in Massachusetts, from 1771 to 1775, inclusive.

Ports From Which the Equipments Were Made	The Number of Vessels Fitted Out Annually for the Northern Fishery	Their Tonnage	The Number of Vessels Fitted Out Annually for the Southern Fishery	Their Tonnage	The Number of Seamen Employed	Barrels of Spermaceti Oil Taken Anually	Barrels of Whale Oil Taken Annually
Nantucket	65	4,875	85	10,200	2,025	26,000	4,000
Wellfleet	20	1,600	10	1,000	420	2,250	2,250
Dartmouth	60	4,500	20	2,000	1,040	7,200	1,400
Lynn	1	75	1	120	28	200	100
Martha's Vineyard	12	720	. . .	. . .	156	900	300
Barnstable	2	150	. . .	. . .	26	240	. . .
Boston	15	1,300	5	700	260	1,800	600
Falmouth, county of Barnstable	4	300	. . .	. . .	52	400	. . .
Swanzey	4	300	. . .	. . .	52	400	. . .
Total	183	13,820	121	14,020	4,059	39,390	8,650

State of the Whale Fishery, from 1787 to 1789, both inclusive.

Ports From Which the Equipments Were Made	The Number of Vessels Fitted Out Annually for the Northern Fishery	Their Tonnage	The Number of Vessels Fitted Out Annually for the Southern Fishery	Their Tonnage	The Number of Seamen Employed	Barrels of Spermaceti Oil Taken Annually	Barrels of Whale Oil Taken Annually
Nantucket	18	1,350	18	2,700	487	3,800	8,260
Wellfleet, and other ports at Cape Cod	12	720	4	400	212	. . .	1,920
Dartmouth	45	2,700	5	750	650	2,700	1,750
Cape Ann	. . .	. . .	2	350	28	. . .	1,200
Plymouth	1	60	. . .	. . .	13	100	. . .
Martha's Vineyard	2	120	1	100	39	220	. . .
Boston	6	450	. . .	. . .	78	360	. . .
Dorchester and Wareham	7	420	1	90	104	800	. . .
Total	91	5,820	31	4,390	1,611	7,980	13,130

Source: Timothy Pitkin, *A Statistical View of the Commerce of the United States of America* (1835), 89.

TABLE 4.94 DECLINE OF THE COD FISHERY IN MASS., 1765–1790

	State of the Cod Fishery of Mass., from 1765 to 1775					From 1786 to 1790 inclusive				
Towns	Vessels Annually	Tonnage	Seamen	Quintals to Europe a 3.5 Dolls	Quintals to West Indies a 2.6 Dolls	Vessels Annually	Tonnage	Seamen	Quintals to Europe a 3 Dolls	Quintals to West Indies a 2 Dolls
Marblehead	150	7,500	1,200	80,000	40,000	90	5,400	720	50,000	25,000
Gloucester	146	5,530	888	35,000	42,500	160	3,600	680	19,500	28,000
Manchester	25	1,500	200	10,000	10,000	15	900	120	3,000	7,500
Beverly	15	750	120	6,000	6,000	19	1,235	157	5,200	10,000
Salem	30	1,500	240	12,000	12,000	20	1,300	160	6,000	10,000
Newburyport	10	400	60	2,000	2,000	10	460	80	1,000	5,000
Ipswich	50	900	190	8,000	5,500	56	860	248	3,000	6,000
Plymouth	60	2,400	420	8,000	16,000	36	1,440	252	6,000	12,000
Cohasset	6	240	42	800	1,600	5	200	35	1,000	1,500
Hingham	6	240	42	800	1,600	4	180	32	800	1,200
Scituate	10	400	70	1,000	3,000	2	90	16	400	600
Duxborough	4	160	28	400	1,200	9	360	72	1,500	3,000
Kingston	6	240	42	800	1,600	4	160	28	700	1,300
Yarmouth	30	900	180	3,000	6,000	30	900	180	2,000	10,000
Wellfleet	3	90	21	300	600	. . .	. . .	. . .	. . .	. . .

(continued)

TABLE 4.94 (continued)

Towns	State of the Cod Fishery of Mass., from 1765 to 1775					From 1786 to 1790 inclusive				
	Vessels Annually	Tonnage	Seamen	Quintals to Europe a 3.5 Dolls	Quintals to West Indies a 2.6 Dolls	Vessels Annually	Tonnage	Seamen	Quintals to Europe a 3 Dolls	Quintals to West Indies a 2 Dolls
Truro	10	400	80	1,000	3,000	. . .	. . .	. . .	. . .	. . .
Provincetown	4	160	32	500	1,100	11	550	88	3,000	5,200
Chatham	30	900	240	4,000	8,000	30	900	240	3,000	9,000
Nantucket	8	320	64	1,000	2,200	5	200	40	500	1,500
Maine	60	1,000	230	4,000	8,000	30	300	120	1,000	3,500
Weymouth	2	100	16	200	600	3	150	24	1,000	1,250
Total	665	25,630	4,405	178,800	172,500	539	19,185	3,278	108,600	142,050

Source: Timothy Pitkin, *A Statistical View of the Commerce of the United States of America* (1835), 84.

TABLE 4.95 EXPORTS OF U.S. FISHERIES FROM AUG. 20, 1789 TO SEP. 30, 1790

	Fish Dried.		Fish Pickled.		Oil Whale.		Oil Spermaceti.		Whale-Bone.		Candles, Sperm.		Total Value
	Quant.	Value	Quant.	Value	Quant.	Value	Quant.	Value	Quant.	Value	Quant.	Value	
	Quin's.	Dollars.	Barrels.	Dollars.	Barrels.	Dollars.	Barrels.	Dollars.	Pounds.	Dollars.	Pounds.	Dollars.	Dollars.
France	543	1,086	12	20	9,914	73,767	1,403	17,523	108,807	17,917	1,200	480 }	749,497
French West Indies	251,116	518,288	29,294	90,818	1,756	13,685	80	1,029	. . .	. . .	38,754	14,884 }	749,497
Amount of 1st Class	251,659	519,374	29,306	90,838	11,670	87,452	1,483	18,552	108,807	17,917	39,954	15,364	749,497
Spain	72,300	194,457	280	813	593	4,147	. . .	. . .	. . .	. . .	2,896	1,256 }	203,276
Spanish West Indies and Florida	824	978	300	886	5	38	. . .	. . .	. . .	. . .	1,685	674 }	203,276
Great Britain	5	10	. . .	. . .	1,738	21,048	3,840	60,000	1,075	215	. . .	. . . }	89,000
British West Indies	1,970	4,114	795	3,075	15	124	. . .	. . .	. . .	. . .	756	353 }	89,000
Nova Scotia	. . .	. . .	13	40	1	10	100	870	. . .	. . .	. . .	. . .	
Holland	. . .	. . .	15	45	807	5,683	. . .	. . .	5,220	1,050	. . .	. . . }	79,404
Dutch West Indies	23,822	48,631	4,778	13,404	179	1,317	. . .	. . .	. . .	. . .	23,162	9,274 }	79,404
Portugal	18,594	41,306	69	242	4	60	. . .	. . .	. . .	. . .	. . .	. . . }	55,137
Portuguese Islands	5,432	11,307	292	801	139	1,243	8	120	. . .	. . .	148	58 }	55,137
Germany	. . .	. . .	. . .	. . .	470	2,990	. . .	. . .	6,150	1,230	. . .	. . .	4,220
Danish West Indies	1,180	2,386	803	2,421	3	27	. . .	. . .	. . .	. . .	. . .	. . .	4,834
African Islands and Continent of Africa	613	1,324	147	564	6	42	. . .	. . .	. . .	. . .	165	66	1,996
Mediterranean	2,314	4,628	6	36	135	700	. . .	. . .	29	5	238	150	5,519
Sweden	8	16	. . .	. . .	. . .	. . .	. . .	. . .	. . .	. . .	. . .	. . .	16
East Indies	. . .	. . .	. . .	. . .	. . .	. . .	. . .	. . .	. . .	. . .	1,285	529	529
Amount of 2d Class	127,062	309,157	7,498	22,337	4,095	27,456	3,948	60,990	12,474	2,500	30,425	12,360	444,790
Amount of both Classes	378,721	828,531	36,804	113,165	15,765	124,908	5,431	79,542	121,281	20,417	70,379	27,724	1,194,287

Source: Timothy Pitkin, *A Statistical View of the Commerce of the United States of America* (1835), 85.

TABLE 4.96 EXPORTS AND TONNAGE OF UNITED STATES FISHERIES, 1791–1800

	Exports of Dried and Pickled Fish			Tonnage of		Bounties Paid on Exports	Number of Sailors
	Quintals	Barrels	Kegs	Cod Fishery	Whaling Industry		
1800	392,726	50,388	12,403	25,787	652	$18,325	3,841
1799	428,495	63,542	15,993	31,003	529	$20,769	. . .
1798	411,175	66,827	6,220	40,964	763	$19,220	. . .
1797	406,016	69,782	7,351	40,423	1,104	$12,399	. . .
1796	377,713	84,558	5,256	36,556	2,364	$16,999	. . .
1795	400,818	55,999	. . .	30,939	3,163	$14,855	. . .
1794	436,907	36,929	. . .	23,121	4,129	$13,768	. . .
1793	372,825	45,440	. . .	38,177	. . .	$16,731	. . .
1792	364,898	48,277	. . .	32,062	. . .	$44,772	. . .
1791	383,237	57,426	. . .	32,542	. . .	$27,787	. . .

Source: U.S. Congress, *American State Papers: Commerce and Navigation* (1832) I, 511.

TABLE 4.97 MAJOR MARKETS FOR DRIED FISH EXPORTED FROM UNITED STATES, 1790–1800

Quintals Exported in Fiscal Years Ending Sep. 30

	British West Indies	French West Indies	Other West Indies	France	Spain	Italy and Portugal	Total Exports
1800	141,420	36,703	66,240	. . .	110,184	34,309	392,726
1799	141,977	24,104	97,538	. . .	128,546	27,770	428,495
1798	42,567	117,383	139,118	17,384	63,781	28,881	411,175
1797	15,297	131,627	140,251	21,860	83,036	12,035	406,016
1796	51,285	89,269	169,276	1,580	55,628	6,392	377,713
1795	26,177	53,801	161,480	36,709	80,388	35,782	400,818
1794	51,751	115,011	150,449	1,717	83,585	11,036	416,711
1793	2,635	186,404	84,245	3,462	61,810	32,407	372,805
1792	795	180,617	99,348	73	53,859	26,191	364,898
1791	265	252,171	60,019	. . .	59,167	10,136	383,237
1790	1,970	251,116	25,826	543	72,300	20,908	378,721

Sources: U.S. Congress, American State Papers: Commerce and Navigation (1832), VII, 27–426. Timothy Pitkin, A Statistical View of the Commerce of the United States of America (1835), 86.

Joseph Sansom sketched this view of Sherburne (modern Nantucket town), on Nantucket Island, Massachusetts. Nantucket was the leading center of international whaling by 1800. To the left of the harbor, the engraving depicts homes and whaling-related industries, including large power-supplying windmills that stand out against the skyline. (I. N. Phelps Stokes Collection, Miriam & Ira Wallach Div. of Arts, Prints and Photographs. Courtesy The New York Public Library. Astor, Lenox and Tilden Foundations.)

TABLE 4.98 WHALING SHIPS AND OIL PRODUCED FROM NANTUCKET, MASS., 1763–1789

Period	Number of Ships	Average Tonnage	Barrels of Oil	Value (Sterling)
1787–89	36	113	. . .	£12,060
1785	15		a	a
1784	28		5,400	£14,500
1783	19		2,260	£16,280
1772–75	150	90–180	30,000	£167,000
1772	98		7,825	. . .
1771	115		12,754	. . .
1770	125	75–110	14,331	. . .
1769	119		19,140	. . .
1768	125	75	15,439	. . .
1767	108		16,561	. . .
1766	118		11,969	. . .
1765	101		11,512	. . .
1764	72		11,983	. . .
1763	60	75	9,238	. . .

a Ships at sea when reports made.
Sources: Obed Macy, The History of Nantucket (1835), 232–33. U.S. Congress, American State Papers: Commerce and Navigation (1832), I, 16.

TABLE 4.99 EXPORTS OF OIL AND OTHER PRODUCTS OF WHALING INDUSTRY, 1790–1800

Year Ending Sep. 30	Whale Oil (gallons)	Spermaceti Oil (gallons)	Spermaceti Candles (boxes)	Whalebone (pounds)
1800	204,468	221,762	181,321 a	32,636
1799	420,949	114,264	240,301 a	89,552
1798	700,040	128,758	144,149 a	149,774
1797	582,425	27,556	130,438 a	452,127
1796	1,176,650	164,045	221,903 a	308,314
1795	810,524	80,856	5,998	410,664
1794	1,000,208	82,493	5,271	354,617
1793	505,460	140,056	5,874	202,620
1792	436,423	63,383	3,938	154,407
1791	447,323	134,595	4,560	124,829
1790	15,765 b	5,431 b	70,379 b	121,281

a Measured in pounds.
b Measured in barrels.
Source: U.S. Congress, American State Papers: Commerce and Navigation (1832), VII, 27–426.

The Merchant Marine

By 1763, Britain's North American colonies possessed a sizeable merchant marine, which contemporary observers estimated to include about one-third of the empire's vessels. Despite the importance of shipping to the Anglo-American economy, historians have still not ascertained the number of ships, crewmen, or carrying capacity registered in the thirteen colonies during the Revolutionary era. Based upon very inexact information provided by royal governors to the royal officials, the colonial merchant marine may have included 2,500 vessels in 1775, with an average carrying capacity ranging from 80 to 160 tons. Provincial shippers dominated the overseas commerce of the northern colonies and the provision trade with the West Indies, but seaborne transportation between the southern colonies and England remained largely in British hands.

The merchant marine loomed unusually large in the colonial economy by enlarging the stock of capital available for investment with cash and credits earned in foreign markets. By 1770, the carrying and distributional services provided by Anglo-American shippers had reached an annual value of £600,000 sterling, an amount that exceeded the value of any commodity exported from the thirteen colonies except tobacco (for which overseas sales then averaged £766,000). Profits from the merchant marine were a critical source of foreign currency that enabled the colonies to avoid a deficit in their overseas trade balance. Overseas earnings were particularly important for New England, which exported fewer commodities per capita than any other region but received more than 54% of the income that accrued from colonial shipping.

Overseas trade plummeted during the Revolutionary War. Unable to continue serving their normal markets, captains increasingly converted their merchantmen into privateers. The bulk of America's naval forces came from the 1,697 merchant ships, newly armed with 14,872 guns, that Congress commissioned as privateers, rather than from the U.S. Navy, which outfitted only 57 vessels and carried just 1,192 cannon. American privateers wreaked havoc upon Britain's merchant marine and took 2,208 ships (not counting 879 other prizes that were regained at sea by the Royal Navy), besides capturing 89 British privateers. The United States lost 1,108 merchant vessels (excluding 27 retaken by American forces) and 216 privateers.

Independence burdened the U.S. merchant marine with major disadvantages that required more than a decade to surmount. No longer protected by the British navy, Yankee ships trading with the Mediterranean became subject to attack by pirates from North Africa. Defined as aliens by Britain's navigation laws, American vessels faced exclusion from the commerce of their country's most important trading partner. Although freed from former restrictions on transporting certain commodities, such as tobacco and naval stores, directly to markets in Europe or Latin America, American shippers still faced discriminatory duties or exclusionary rules favoring local traders that prevented them from establishing profitable relations with numerous countries.

Spain and Portugal generally treated U.S. vessels on an equal basis with their own ships, although neither gave foreign merchantmen entry to its colonial markets. The Dutch, Danes, and Swedes discouraged imports of various American products to their home ports with discriminatory regulations, but they generally admitted U.S. goods to their Caribbean colonies. France initially permitted trade on liberal terms but by 1793 had placed a prohibitory duty on any tobacco carried in American bottoms and enacted high tariffs on New England fish.

Britain allowed U.S. ships to carry commodities of value to its own economy—such as tobacco, naval stores, flaxseed, indigo, and forestry products—but injected a high element of risk into this trade by making these privileges subject to immediate cancellation. American vessels paid the same duties as British ships at London but received additional charges of 1s., 9d. at other domestic ports. Britain purposefully attempted to cripple the U.S. merchant marine by excluding Americans from all traffic with its Canadian and Caribbean colonies. This prohibition deprived American shippers of an especially profitable market and threatened to force a long-term reduction in the U.S. maritime economy. In the meantime, however, Yankee captains retained a significant portion of the large Caribbean trade through smuggling and other illegal subterfuges.

Congress and several state legislatures enacted preferential duties on goods carried in American holds, and the Washington administration worked strenuously to win trading concessions from Britain. Although Jay's Treaty failed to open up West Indian ports when ratified in 1795, the resulting relaxation in Anglo-American relations gave Caribbean officials a pretext for opening their harbors to U.S. ships in the late 1790s. This change in policy, and concessions concerning the transport of merchandise from India, were largely re-

Warfare disrupted American commerce, not only in the Revolution, but also during the 1790s, when the United States had great difficulty persuading the British and French to respect its merchant marine as a neutral carrier. Hundreds of American captains also retaliated against foreign seizures by recommissioning their vessels as privateers and preying on hostile merchant vessels. This illustration shows the plundering of a British ship by an armed Pennsylvania sloop commissioned as a French privateer during the 1790s. [from *Harper's Magazine,* October 1908] (Howard Pyle Collection, courtesy Delaware Art Museum, Wilmington, Delaware.)

TABLE 4.100 SHIPPING EARNINGS (POUNDS STERLING) OF THIRTEEN COLONIES, 1768–1772

	To Britain and Ireland		To Southern Europe		To West Indies	
	Freight Charges	Other[a] Earnings	Freight Charges	Other[a] Earnings	Freight Charges	Other[a] Earnings
From New England[b]						
1772	£60,000	£17,000	£48,000	£16,000	£235,000	£80,000
1771	£60,000	£18,000	£55,000	£21,000	£225,000	£70,000
1770	£66,000	£16,000	£42,000	£13,000	£205,000	£71,000
1769	£62,000	£16,000	£46,000	£14,000	£195,000	£67,000
1768	£55,000	£15,000	£39,000	£12,000	£193,000	£55,000
From Mid-Atlantic						
1772	£55,000	£8,000	£40,000	£24,000	£83,000	£60,000
1771	£66,000	£9,000	£36,000	£15,000	£69,000	£41,000
1770	£59,000	£10,000	£51,000	£23,000	£75,000	£51,000
1769	£57,000	£9,000	£52,000	£23,000	£64,000	£44,000
1768	£61,000	£11,000	£39,000	£12,000	£62,000	£30,000
From South						
1772	£28,000	£13,000	£20,000	£11,000	£44,000	£27,000
1771	£30,000	£11,000	£16,000	£7,000	£40,000	£24,000
1770	£25,000	£9,000	£28,000	£12,000	£39,000	£21,000
1769	£27,000	£10,000	£43,000	£17,000	£37,000	£20,000
1768	£27,000	£9,000	£28,000	£8,000	£36,000	£16,000
Totals						
1772	£143,000	£38,000	£108,000	£51,000	£362,000	£167,000
1771	£156,000	£38,000	£107,000	£43,000	£334,000	£135,000
1770	£150,000	£35,000	£121,000	£48,000	£319,000	£143,000
1769	£146,000	£35,000	£141,000	£54,000	£296,000	£131,000
1768	£143,000	£35,000	£106,000	£32,000	£291,000	£101,000

[a] Includes insurance, interest on credit, merchants' profits.
[b] From the African trade, New England earned £3,000 in 1768, £4,000 in 1769, £4,000 in 1770, £2,000 in 1771, and £5,000 in 1772.
Source: James F. Walton and Gary M. Shepherd, *Shipping, Maritime Trade, and the Economic Development of Colonial North America* (1972), 128.

sponsible for an expansion in merchant shipping during the late 1790s, despite a decline in commerce with France, which viewed Jay's Treaty as a hostile action. The 1790s consequently saw a sharp drop in the tonnage of U.S. trade carried in British holds, from 115,176 tons in 1790 to 41,525 in 1800, accompanied by a corresponding rise in freight handled by the American merchant marine, from 84,675 tons in 1790 to 236,611 tons in 1800. By 1800, American shipping had recovered from the aftermath of the Revolution and was once again a major participant in the transatlantic carrying trade.

TABLE 4.101 OWNERSHIP OF MERCHANT VESSELS ENGAGED IN TRADE BETWEEN BRITISH PORTS AND BRITAIN'S NORTH AMERICAN COLONIES, 1770

Colony from which Vessels Cleared	Residence of Vessels' Owners			Total Residing in the Colonies
	Residents of Great Britain	British Merchants Temporarily in Colonies	Permanent Residents of the Colonies	
New England	12.5%	12.5%	75.0%	87.5%
N.Y.	37.5%	37.5%	25.0%	62.5%
Pa.	25.0%	37.5%	37.5%	75.0%
Md. and Va.	75.0%	12.5%	12.5%	25.0%
N.C.	62.5%	25.0%	12.5%	37.5%
S.C. and Ga.	62.5%	25.0%	12.5%	37.5%

Source: John J. McCusker and Russell R. Menard, *The Economy of British America, 1607–1789* (1985), 192.

During the late 1790s, the merchant marine faced an especially difficult time maintaining its neutral status while trading with the belligerents in European wars. Although few American ships were seized by Britain's navy after Jay's Treaty was ratified in 1795, the French captured 450 vessels from 1796 to 1799 and only ceased this

TABLE 4.102 Tonnage of Merchant Marine Registered in United States, 1789–1800

Year Ending Dec. 31st	Tonnage of the United States			
	Registered in Foreign Trade	Enrolled and Licensed		Total
		In Coasting Trade	In the Fisheries	
1789	123,893	68,607	9,062	201,562
1790	346,254	103,775	28,348	478,377
1791	363,110	106,494	32,542	502,146
1792	411,438	120,957	32,062	564,457
1793	367,734	114,853	38,177	520,764
1794	438,863	162,579	27,176	628,618
1795	529,471	184,398	34,096	747,965
1796	576,733	217,840	37,326	831,899
1797	597,777	237,403	41,733	876,913
1798	603,376	251,443	43,509	898,328
1799	662,197	246,641	30,571	939,409
1800	669,921	272,492	30,079	972,492

Source: Timothy Pitkin, *A Statistical View of the Commerce of the United States of America* (1835), 361.

TABLE 4.103 TONNAGE OF FOREIGN MERCHANT VESSELS ENTERING U.S. PORTS, 1789–1800

Years Ending Dec. 31st	National Character of the Tonnage													Total
	British	French	Span-ish	Portu-guese	Ital-ian	Dutch	Aus-trian	Hanse-atic	Dan-ish	Swe-dish	Prus-sian	Rus-sian	All Other	
1789	94,410	4,223	2,761	1,168	. . .	2,275	342	816	659	. . .	. . .	. . .	. . .	106,654
1790	216,914	12,059	7,381	3,777	. . .	6,136	459	1,978	1,113	535	394	. . .	. . .	250,746
1791	210,618	8,988	4,337	4,766	. . .	3,751	2,326	2,989	2,092	361	. . .	320	. . .	240,448
1792	206,065	24,343	2,692	2,341	. . .	3,557	. . .	3,214	1,159	907	. . .	. . .	. . .	244,278
1793	100,180	45,287	3,090	3,153	458	577	4,972	1,166	2,364	2,319	. . .	. . .	. . .	163,566
1794	37,058	11,249	2,230	6,044	192	417	978	4,373	9,390	11,043	. . .	. . .	. . .	82,974
1795	27,097	7,425	1,999	738	409	1,128	1,007	4,006	8,637	4,316	. . .	. . .	. . .	56,832
1796	19,669	2,055	2,449	637	758	301	. . .	4,987	10,430	5,560	. . .	. . .	. . .	46,846
1797	33,168	1,336	571	554	1,460	451	. . .	11,996	16,726	6,064	431	. . .	. . .	72,757
1798	40,773	1,519	542	. . .	1,057	973	. . .	18,773	19,148	4,149	721	. . .	105	87,760
1799	54,087	1,330	1,122	374	257	135	. . .	22,070	22,110	5,513	585	. . .	. . .	107,583
1800	71,689	1,007	1,432	55	173	. . .	. . .	15,365	23,978	7,724	705	. . .	275	121,403

Source: Timothy Pitkin, *A Statistical View of the Commerce of the United States of America* (1835), 364.

TABLE 4.104 FOREIGN AND DOMESTIC MERCHANT TONNAGE ENGAGED IN THE SEABORNE COMMERCE OF THE UNITED STATES, 1789–1800

Year Ending Dec. 31	Tonnage Employed in Foreign Trade			
	American Vessels	Foreign Vessels	Total	Proportion of Foreign to Total Amount Employed
1789	127,329	106,654	233,983	45.6 to 100
1790	355,079	250,746	603,825	41.4 "
1791	363,854	240,548	604,402	39.8 "
1792	414,679	244,278	658,957	37.0 "
1793	447,754	163,566	611,320	26.7 "
1794	525,649	82,974	608,623	15.8 "
1795	580,277	56,832	637,109	8.9 "
1796	675,046	46,846	721,892	6.2 "
1797	605,078	72,757	680,835	10.7 "
1798	522,245	87,760	610,005	14.4 "
1799	626,495	107,583	734,078	14.6 "
1800	682,871	123,882	806,753	15.4 "

Source: Timothy Pitkin, *A Statistical View of the Commerce of the United States of America* (1835), 363.

TABLE 4.105 NET SHIPPING EARNINGS OF UNITED STATES MERCHANT MARINE, 1790–1800

Fiscal Year	Registered Tons of Shipping	Estimated Gross Freight Earnings	Foreign Port Charges	Net Earnings
1800	557,000	$32,800,000	$6,600,000	$26,200,000
1799	557,000	$30,200,000	$6,000,000	$24,200,000
1798	513,000	$20,800,000	$4,200,000	$16,600,000
1797	518,000	$21,400,000	$4,300,000	$17,100,000
1796	507,000	$27,000,000	$5,400,000	$21,600,000
1795	469,000	$23,900,000	$4,800,000	$19,000,000
1794	389,000	$19,400,000	$3,900,000	$15,500,000
1793	328,000	$14,900,000	$3,000,000	$11,900,000
1792	381,000	$9,200,000	$1,800,000	$7,400,000
1791	343,000	$7,800,000	$1,600,000	$6,200,000
1790	336,000	$7,400,000	$1,500,000	$5,900,000

Source: Douglass C. North, "The United States Balance of Payments, 1790–1860," in National Bureau of Economic Research, *Trends in the American Economy in the Nineteenth Century* (1960), 595.

TABLE 4.106 U.S. MERCHANT VESSELS CAPTURED BY HOSTILE POWERS, 1793–1800

Period	Ships Captured	By Whom
Sep. 1793–Mar. 1794	250	Great Britain
May 1796–Mar. 1797	316	France
Mar. 1797–Aug. 1799	134	France
Oct. 1796–Feb. 1799	55	Spain
Sep. 1796–May 1797	9	Great Britain
May 1799–Dec. 1800	16	Great Britain

Source: U.S. Congress, *American State Papers: Foreign Relations* (1832), I, 28–29, 345–46, 446–52, 453–55; II, 57–61, 429.

aggression after their privateers began suffering heavy losses at the hands of a newly recommissioned U.S. Navy. Spain likewise impounded many American merchantmen trading in the Mediterranean after 1796, and attacks by North African pirates sparked an undeclared naval war soon after 1800. The problems of carrying on commerce among hostile powers became even more acute during the Napoleonic Wars. Although the U.S. government declared temporary or selective cessations of trade in 1807 and 1809 to avoid being drawn into armed conflict, violations of the American merchant marine's neutrality led to war in 1812.

Forestry Products

The three major sectors of the forestry industry were lumber (sawn or split), naval stores (tar, pitch, and turpentine), and potash, an alkali compound made from burnt trees. Earnings from wood products sold overseas comprised about 8% of the thirteen colonies' exports by the 1760s and 7% of U.S. exports by the early 1790s. Although exports of forestry products declined relative to other commodities during the Revolutionary era, with the exception of potash, there was probably an offsetting rise in demand for construction supplies as the country rebuilt structures damaged during wartime, expanded the housing stock to accommodate rapid urbanization, and added ships to the merchant marine. The various forestry enterprises almost certainly comprised early America's third largest sector of gross domestic product, after agriculture and the maritime trades, but no research has yet made a comprehensive estimate of this industry's total output and value.

Lumber

The business of providing construction materials and firewood was highly decentralized. Relatively little lumber production resulted from companies that bought tracts of forest and hired laborers to cut the trees, although some commercial lumbering was carried on in New Hampshire and Maine. Most timber was felled by agriculturalists clearing fields for cultivation or exploiting nearby tracts of unsettled forest. These individuals either dragged logs to nearby sawmills for sale, or spent their winter months splitting logs into shingles, staves, fence rails, posts, or firewood. Southern planters also found that cutting lumber was a profitable way of employing their slaves after the autumn harvest of tobacco or rice.

TABLE 4.107 WHOLESALE PRICES (IN LOCAL CURRENCY) OF STAVES AND BOARDS AT PHILADELPHIA, 1763–1800

Year	Hogshead Staves (per 1,200)	Boards (1000 ft.)	Year	Barrel Staves (per 1,200)	Hogshead Staves (per 1,200)	Pipe Staves (per 1,200)
1800	$40.00	$28.00		[no data for 1775–1783]		
1799	$35.85	$36.00	1774	72.54s.	6.85s.	10.51s.
1798	$35.00	$46.00	1773	63.49s.	5.97s.	9.88s.
1797	$40.33	$29.29	1772	71.85s.	6.72s.	10.05s.
1796	$43.63	$28.53	1771	75.15s.	6.77s.	10.09s.
1795	£14.17	£9.50	1770	68.68s.	6.17s.	9.09s.
1794	$20.30	$22.00	1769	61.32s.	5.02s.	9.17s.
1793	£12.43	£12.58	1768	65.47s.	5.39s.	10.01s.
1792	£7.83	$23.30	1767	79.60s.	7.06s.	9.88s.
1791	£7.29	£7.54	1766	67.71s.	6.56s.	9.31s.
1790	£7.29	£6.00	1765	70.63s.	6.84s.	11.19s.
1789	£7.29	£6.00	1764	64.90s.	5.40s.	9.18s.
1788	£6.43	£6.00	1763	66.04s.	6.82s.	12.79s.
1787	£7.20	£6.00				
1786	£7.67	£6.00				
1785	£8.41	£6.75				
1784	£9.27	£7.14				

Note: Barrel staves measured 28 to 32 in. × 3.5 in. Pipe staves measured 56 in. × 4 in. Hogshead staves measured 42 in. × 3.5 in.
Sources: Anne Bezanson, et al., eds., *Prices in Colonial Pennsylvania* (1935), 424. Arthur C. Cole, *Wholesale Commodity Prices in the United States, 1700–1861* (1938), 78–123.

TABLE 4.108 PRICES OF PINE BOARDS (PER 1,000 FT., IN LOCAL CURRENCY) AT CHARLESTON, S.C., 1749–1791

Year	Boards (per 1000 ft.)
1791	£3.00
1790	£2.75
1789	£2.96
1788	£3.00
1787	£3.30
1786	£3.72
1785	£4.40
1784	£4.66
[no data 1782–83]	
1781	£9.37
1780	£6.96
[no data 1776–79]	
1775	£25.00
1774	£25.00
1773	£24.06
1772	£22.50
1771	£21.88
1770	£21.88
1769	£20.00
1768	£20.31
1767	£20.00
[no data 1755–66]	
1754	£17.50
[no data 1751–53]	
1750	£17.50
1749	£21.25

Source: Arthur H. Cole, *Wholesale Commodity Prices in the United States, 1700–1861* (1938), 30–97.

Most statistical information about the business of cutting lumber concerns exports. New England provided almost 45% of the sawn timber sold overseas prior to independence, and in the 1790s it exported over 70% of all boards and planks, though only about a quarter of all staves and shingles. Because the Caribbean sugar islands had become largely deforested, they became the principal market for Anglo-American timber, with most of the remainder going to Spanish colonies bordering the Gulf of Mexico.

Lumber declined as a source of overseas earnings from 4.8% of exports about 1770 to 3.5% in the early 1790s, and overseas timber shipments grew little by 1800. Prices for cut wood nevertheless rose noticeably during this period, and so it seems probable that increased domestic demand was diverting lumber from export sales. By the late colonial era, many of the older, more densely populated coastal areas were already experiencing local timber shortages for construction and fuel. Wood remained the overwhelming preference for housing material, because brick structures were far more expensive, and the need for lumber increased steadily with rapid urbanization, frontier expansion, and the growth of timber-intensive industries such as shipbuilding. By 1799, it is estimated that the United States was producing 300,000,000 board feet of lumber (263,000,000 in softwoods and 37,000,000 hardwoods), of which less than 20% was exported as boards and plank, at least 14% was used for shipbuilding (42,500,400 board feet, at 400–500 feet used per ton), and two-thirds were used for general construction.

TABLE 4.109 VOLUME (FT.) AND VALUE (£ STERLING) OF PINE BOARDS EXPORTED FROM THE BRITISH MAINLAND COLONIES, 1768–1772

	To Britain and Ireland		To Southern Europe		To West Indies	
	Feet	£ Ster.	Feet	£ Ster.	Feet	£ Ster.
From New England						
1768	1,638,000	£2,212	687,000	£927	24,291,000	£32,794
1769	2,518,000	£3,399	262,000	£354	23,854,000	£32,204
1770	3,303,000	£5,286	292,000	£467	25,716,000	£41,145
1771	1,596,000	£2,552	424,000	£679	27,992,000	£44,789
1772	1,435,000	£2,440	237,000	£404	28,167,000	£47,883
From Mid-Atlantic						
1768	191,000	£332	67,000	£106	1,217,000	£2,077
1769	282,000	£530	114,000	£157	1,428,000	£2,330
1770	588,000	£1,161	52,000	£102	2,198,000	£4,170
1771	280,000	£502	47,000	£75	2,400,000	£4,429
1772	132,000	£294	106,000	£183	6,089,000	£12,959
From Upper South						
1768	207,000	£415	117,000	£234	721,000	£1,442
1769	175,000	£351	63,000	£125	700,000	£1,399
1770	671,000	£1,510	20,000	£45	649,000	£1,459
1771	98,000	£222	. . .	. . .	2,031,000	£4,570
1772	34,000	£81	50,000	£119	2,545,000	£5,981
From Lower South						
1768	267,000	£744	2,000	£6	5,355,000	£14,942
1769	141,000	£388	26,000	£71	5,257,000	£14,510
1770	236,000	£703	. . .	. . .	5,417,000	£16,143
1771	203,000	£611	. . .	. . .	5,723,000	£17,225
1772	105,000	£325	2,000	£6	6,536,000	£20,262

Source: James F. Shepherd and Gary M. Walton, *Shipping, Maritime Trade, and the Economic Development of Colonial North America* (1972), 211–27.

TABLE 4.110 VOLUME (NUMBER) AND VALUE (£ STERLING) OF STAVES AND HEADINGS EXPORTED FROM THE BRITISH MAINLAND COLONIES, 1768–1772

	To Britain and Ireland		To Southern Europe		To West Indies	
	Number	£ Ster.	Number	£ Ster.	Number	£ Ster.
From New England						
1768	922,000	£2,528	409,000	£1,119	4,009,000	£10,992
1769	806,000	£2,150	322,000	£859	3,399,000	£9,065
1770	1,011,000	£3,100	145,000	£444	3,448,000	£10,572
1771	976,000	£3,057	274,000	£858	3,861,000	£12,098
1772	1,270,000	£4,031	203,000	£647	4,382,000	£13,912
From Mid-Atlantic						
1768	955,000	£2,617	1,513,000	£4,146	3,886,000	£10,653
1769	817,000	£2,181	956,000	£2,549	3,013,000	£8,033
1770	1,513,000	£4,638	1,037,000	£3,180	3,848,000	£11,802
1771	2,004,000	£6,278	878,000	£2,753	4,410,000	£13,817
1772	1,638,000	£5,200	635,000	£2,015	6,278,000	£19,930
From Upper South						
1768	2,541,000	£6,967	814,000	£2,231	1,874,000	£5,137
1769	3,164,000	£8,439	263,000	£702	1,222,000	£3,257
1770	3,407,000	£10,447	102,000	£314	2,096,000	£6,426
1771	4,353,000	£13,640	303,000	£949	2,773,000	£8,691
1772	4,348,000	£13,803	267,000	£849	3,449,000	£10,952

	To Britain and Ireland		To Southern Europe		To West Indies	
	Number	£ Ster.	Number	£ Ster.	Number	£ Ster.
From Lower South						
1768	738,000	£2,289	505,000	£1,563	701,000	£2,173
1769	897,000	£2,848	500,000	£1,587	1,663,000	£5,280
1770	578,000	£1,835	404,000	£1,284	1,684,000	£5,345
1771	714,000	£2,428	364,000	£1,241	1,876,000	£6,380
1772	468,000	£1,568	365,000	£1,223	2,019,000	£6,764

Source: James F. Shepherd and Gary M. Walton, *Shipping, Maritime Trade, and the Economic Development of Colonial North America* (1972), 211–27.

TABLE 4.111 EXPORTS OF LUMBER FROM N.C., S.C., AND GA., 1763–1774

Year	Colony	Boards (Feet)	Shingles (Number)	Staves (Number)
1774	S.C.[a]	119,923	858,100	27,400
1773	S.C.[b]	528,637	1,313,500	79,875
1772	S.C.[b]	647,047	1,392,075	207,280
	N.C.	4,118,377	6,216,170	3,119,697
	Ga.	2,163,582	3,525,930	988,791
1771	S.C.	675,000	709,000	101,228
	N.C.	3,811,654	5,687,610	3,711,941
	Ga.	2,159,072	2,247,598	403,253
1770	S.C.	697,393	1,305,625	117,860
	N.C.	3,460,866	5,653,050	2,744,479
	Ga.	1,805,992	2,896,991	466,276
1769	S.C.	592,026	2,072,947	282,180
	N.C.	2,923,846	7,703,220	2,778,125
	Ga.	1,634,331	3,474,588	747,903
1768	S.C.[c]	760,125	2,131,000	182,940
	N.C.	3,168,508	6,006,137	1,741,617
	Ga.	1,787,258	3,669,477	806,609

Year	Colony	Boards (Feet)	Shingles (Number)	Staves (Number)
1767	S.C.[c]	450,118	1,717,800	240,813
	Ga.	1,767,199	2,570,725	748,166
1766	S.C.	. . .	. . .	. . .
	Ga.	2,101,466	2,036,947	737,898
1765	S.C.[b]	697,648	. . .	186,375
	Ga.	1,879,454	3,722,050	661,416
1764	S.C.	948,121	1,553,365	228,015
	Ga.	1,043,535	2,061,151	423,251
1763	S.C.	647,112	1,225,160	362,065
	Ga.	917,384	1,470,120	594,356

[a]Data for four months.
[b]Data for seven months.
[c]Data for ten months.
Sources: Charles J. Gayle, "The Nature and Volume of Exports from Charleston, 1724–1774," in *Proceedings of South Carolina Historical Association* (1937), 31. G. Melvin Herndon, "Forest Products of Colonial Georgia," *Journal of Forest History* XXIII (1979), 134. Harry Roy Merrens, *Colonial North Carolina in the Eighteenth Century: A Study in Historical Geography* (1964), 94–96.

TABLE 4.112 EXPORTS OF U.S. LUMBER, BY STATE, OCT. 1, 1791–SEP. 30, 1792

	Boards and Plank[a] (ft.)	Scantling and Timber[b] (ft.)	Staves and Heading (ft.)	Shingles (no.)	Hoops and Poles (no.)
N.H.	7,798,550	. . .	1,250,100	1,209,000	36,150
Mass.	28,730,324	778,993	5,257,475	14,386,700	1,232,481
R.I.	281,676	35,840	277,950	110,000	314,813
Conn.	595,935	69,000	1,124,842	325,800	573,605
N.Y.	3,477,160	286,020	5,565,590	2,200,700	144,550
N.J.	89,000	18,000	48,412	1,210,000	16,125
Pa.	1,604,342	51,814	2,814,634	2,789,173	84,460
Del.	3,385	. . .	37,250	228,000	. . .
Md.	500,679	399,737	1,731,067	2,629,550	88,525
Va.	829,126	362,928	7,419,823	11,873,935	27,340
N.C.	4,303,468	1,663,949	2,291,089	27,456,801	42,844
S.C.	717,210	499,814	512,550	2,573,500	2,500
Ga.	3,525,142	4,024,959	866,527	4,644,704	. . .
Totals	52,455,907	8,190,954	29,197,309	71,637,863	2,563,393

[a]Boards and plank averaged 97.8% pine, 1.6% oak, and .6% other.
[b]Average division was 71.6% scantling and 28.4% timber.
Source: U.S. Congress, *American State Papers: Commerce and Navigation* (1832), VII, 161–62.

TABLE 4.113   EXPORTS OF LUMBER FROM THE UNITED STATES, 1790–1800

Year Ending Sep. 30	Boards and Plank[a] (ft.)	Scantling and Timber (ft.)	Staves and Heading (no.)	Shingles (no.)	Hoops and Poles (no.)
1800	68,825,280[a]	. . .	19,375,625	76,027,827	2,121,189
1799	56,647,098[a]	. . .	34,008,285	58,510,460	2,914,089
1798	52,404,392[a]	. . .	28,073,279	50,915,427	2,328,027
1797	43,220,969[a]	. . .	33,073,521	51,604,896	3,956,340
1796	53,871,476[a]	. . .	34,588,904	47,307,112	3,711,062
1795	40,735,561[a]	. . .	30,012,759	38,938,814	3,423,609
1794	35,154,544[a]	. . .	27,000,400	28,869,117	2,654,845
1793	65,784,524[a]	. . .	29,703,532	80,627,357	2,304,353
1792	52,455,907	8,190,954	29,197,309	71,637,863	2,563,393
1791	41,716,423	8,417,633[b]	29,061,590	74,205,976	1,425,605
1790	46,747,730	8,719,638[c]	36,402,301	67,331,115	1,908,310

[a] Includes scantling and timber during 1793–1800.
[b] 74% scantling and 26% timber.
[c] Scantling only.
Source: U.S. Congress, *American State Papers: Commerce and Navigation* (1832), VII, 29, 132, 135, 243–45, 291, 292, 310, 311, 316, 342, 361, 383, 416, 430, 452.

TABLE 4.114   PERCENT OF U.S. LUMBER EXPORTED TO WEST INDIES, 1791–1799

Year Ending Sep. 30	Boards and Plank[a]	Staves and Heading	Shingles	Hoops and Poles
1799				
To British West Indies	66.4%	51.0%	72.2%	32.9%
To other West Indies	29.7%	10.5%	24.5%	36.9%
1797				
To British West Indies	14.9%	19.4%	22.9%	9.3%
To other West Indies	57.9%	29.8%	67.3%	80.0%
1795				
To British West Indies	46.3%	32.0%	53.0%	18.3%
To other West Indies	32.2%	14.8%	37.2%	54.2%
1793				
To British West Indies	31.8%	24.2%	36.3%	4.4%
To other West Indies	53.6%	25.5%	60.8%	88.1%
1791				
To British West Indies	31.4%	32.6%	45.4%	7.8%
To other West Indies	41.4%	20.8%	51.3%	90.0%

[a] Includes scantling and timber.
Source: U.S. Congress, *American State Papers: Commerce and Navigation* (1832), VII, 132–35, 291, 292, 342, 383, 430.

Naval Stores and Masts

After Great Britain emerged as Europe's greatest maritime power during the 1700s, it promoted colonial enterprises to supply naval stores (turpentine, resin, tar, and pitch), along with masts, spars, bowsprits, and yardarms, all of which had to be imported from foreign countries. New England became the birthplace for these industries, and it dominated the mast trade through the 1790s, but output of naval stores rose rapidly in the Carolina pine forests when Parliament offered bounties for their production. By the late 1760s, about 60% of naval stores exported from the colonies came from the Carolinas or Georgia, principally from the tributaries of North Carolina's Cape Fear River. Significant amounts of turpentine and tar also went overseas from Virginia, but an unknown part of these exports were also made by North Carolina "Tarheels." By the 1760s, New England could not supply its own shipbuilders with tar, pitch, and turpentine, and had to import naval stores from the southern colonies.

During the twenty years after 1772, the amount of naval stores sold abroad declined from 1.7% of exports to 1.1% (shipments of tar and pitch fell, while turpentine rose). Exports of naval stores peaked about 1796 and generally sank in the next four years. The fact that prices for naval stores rose in the late 1780s as exports were faltering nevertheless suggests that increased demand by domestic shipbuilders was reducing the amount of turpentine, pitch, and tar available for overseas markets, and that the industry did not suffer an economic decline.

The mast industry also underwent major changes. New Hampshire was the earliest center of mast cutting, but by 1750 its own timber stock had become very depleted and it was supplanted by Maine. After a massive forest fire scorched vast areas from New Hampshire to Maine's Casco Bay in the summer of 1761, the collection of masts shifted eastward past the Kennebec River in Maine.

This view of a frontier sawmill in New England suggests the great volume of lumber produced by Anglo-Americans in the late eighteenth century. The United States not only produced for its own needs, which included a substantial ship-building industry, but also provided much of the boards and planks needed for construction in the West Indies. By the 1760s, areas near some of the larger American cities had begun to experience shortages of available wood. (Courtesy Library of Congress)

Mast exports reached 788 (including 603 great masts) in 1760, largely due to the British navy's expansion in the Seven Years' War, but the United States shipped an average of just 364 masts abroad in 1791–1792, and the Customs Bureau ceased itemizing their ex-port after 1795. As in the case of naval stores, it seems likely that exports slumped because the domestic economy absorbed an increased number of masts to outfit the rapidly expanding merchant marine in the 1790s.

TABLE 4.115 WHOLESALE PRICES OF NAVAL STORES (IN LOCAL CURRENCY, PER BARREL OF 31.5 GAL.) AT PHILADELPHIA, 1763–1790

Year	Tar[a] (barrels)	Turpentine[b] (barrels)	Year	Pitch[a] (barrels)	Tar (barrels)	Turpentine (barrels)
1790	14.94s.	17.96s.	1775	. . .	. . .	. . .
1789	11.29s.	13.24s.	1774	15.13s.	13.81s.	19.17s.
1788	10.22s.	12.23s.	1773	14.70s.	13.79s.	18.29s.
1787	10.33s.	11.00s.	1772	14.54s.	14.32s.	16.69s.
1786	9.67s.	13.79s.	1771	12.19s.	12.41s.	14.31s.
1785	13.79s.	21.54s.	1770	11.54s.	11.33s.	13.83s.
1784	18.69s.	29.88s.	1769	11.93s.	10.17s.	14.65s.
1783	26.10s.	28.10s.	1768	14.34s.	11.01s.	15.86s.
1782	36.30s.	72.40s.	1767	16.16s.	11.69s.	18.97s.
1781	542.60s.	90.00s.	1766	17.25s.	11.90s.	20.73s.
1780	1,501.20s.	1,844.00s.	1765	17.33s.	12.40s.	17.55s.
1779	266.00s.	365.30s.	1764	15.28s.	12.36s.	16.75s.
1778	143.70s.	140.90s.	1763	14.93s.	12.30s.	13.56s.
1777	26.40s.	35.50s.				
1776	18.30s.	36.25s.				

[a]To weigh 321 lb. per barrel.
[b]To weigh 460 lb. per barrel.
Sources: Anne Bezanson, et al., eds., *Prices in Colonial Pennsylvania* (1935), 424. Anne Bezanson, *Prices and Inflation During the American Revolution: Pennsylvania, 1770–1790* (1951), 335–42. Arthur H. Cole, *Wholesale Commodity Prices in the United States, 1700–1861* (1938), 78–123.

TABLE 4.116 BRITISH BOUNTIES PAID FOR COLONIAL NAVAL STORES, 1763–1776

Year	Bounties
1776	£8,574
1775	£45,866
1774	£37,292
1773	£35,203
1772	£34,534
1771	£34,702
1770	£29,803
1769	£30,119
1768	£34,700
1767	£38,909
1766	£41,100
1765	£35,579
1764	£29,516
1763	£18,753
Total	£454,650

Source: Robert G. Albion, *Forests and Sea Power: The Timber Problem of the Royal Navy, 1652–1862* (1926), 418.

TABLE 4.117 VOLUME (BARRELS) AND VALUE (£ STERLING) OF COLONIAL NAVAL STORES EXPORTED TO GREAT BRITAIN, 1768–1772

	Pitch		Tar		Turpentine	
	Barrels	£ Ster.	Barrels	£ Ster.	Barrels	£ Ster.
From New England						
1768	1,646	£709	8,506	£2,815	2,615	£1,246
1769	473	£178	5,041	£1,618	2,883	£1,334
1770	240	£90	3,413	£1,256	1,813	£814
1771	51	£18	11,303	£4,239	1,055	£456
1772	12	£5	11,317	£5,025	215	112
From Mid-Atlantic						
1768	613	£264	5,309	£1,758	6,676	£3,181
1769	462	£174	1,423	£457	4,047	£1,871
1770	221	£83	1,794	£660	2,910	£1,307
1771	51	£19	3,007	£1,128	141	£61
1772	572	£258	6,987	£3,102	1,134	£587
From Upper South						
1768	7,916	£3,412	14,978	£4,958	472	£225
1769	564	£213	17,004	£5,458	10,317	£4,772
1770	. . .	. . .	12,792	£4,707	1,605	£721
1771	949	£349	17,993	£6,747	4,053	£1,750
1772	12	£5	21,006	£9,327	1,411	£730

(continued)

TABLE 4.117 (continued)

	Pitch		Tar		Turpentine	
	Barrels	£ Ster.	Barrels	£ Ster.	Barrels	£ Ster.
	From Lower South					
1768	11,489	£4,951	59,155	£19,581	14,373	£6,849
1769	12,293	£4,635	59,466	£19,089	19,745	£9,132
1770	7,666	£2,871	60,012	£22,084	8,697	£3,905
1771	6,330	£2,329	71,575	£26,841	8,947	£3,865
1772	5,362	£2,419	60,280	£26,764	6,240	£3,229

Note: Not reflected in above figures are average annual imports of 20,555 barrels of pitch and tar by northern ports from the southern colonies. Joseph J. Malone, *Pine Trees and Politics: Naval Stores and Forest Policy in Colonial New England, 1691–1775* (1964), 36–37.
Source: James F. Shepherd and Gary M. Walton, *Shipping, Maritime Trade, and the Economic Development of Colonial North America* (1972), 212–15.

TABLE 4.118 EXPORTS OF NAVAL STORES FROM N.C., S.C., AND GA., 1763–1774

Year	Colony	Turpentine (barrels)	Pitch (barrels)	Tar (barrels)	Green Tar (barrels)
1774	S.C.[a]	1,394	870	1,176	. . .
1773	S.C.[b]	1,043	821	1,236	396
1772	S.C.[c]	864	4,125	2,728	2,995
	N.C.	5,336	873	54,259	. . .
	Ga.	40	364	298	. . .
1771	S.C.	1,353	7,429	2,259	1,142
	N.C.	7,549	. . .	68,072	. . .
	Ga.	45	193	102	. . .
1770	S.C.	1,335	4,133	827	2,111
	N.C.	7,259	3,453	56,969	. . .
	Ga.	103	80	105	. . .
1769	S.C.	3,201	5,256	1,278	3,849
	N.C.	16,476	6,545	54,201	. . .
	Ga.	68	492	138	. . .
1768	S.C.[c]	5,761	6,948	1,454	822
	N.C.	8,410	4,045	56,712	. . .
	Ga.	202	496	167	. . .
1767	S.C.[c]	3,787	12,339	2,232	. . .
	Ga.	88	627	387	. . .
1766	S.C.	. . .	. . .	. . .	. . .
	Ga.	82	506	723	. . .
1765	S.C.[b]	653	8,751	2,183	392
	Ga.	. . .	. . .	486	. . .
1764	S.C.	1,643	7,459	3,093	65
	Ga.	19	. . .	359	. . .
1763	S.C.[d]	3,042	6,087	1,265	411
	Ga.	8	23	175	. . .

[a] Data for four months.
[b] Data for seven months.
[c] Data for ten months.
[d] Data for eleven months.
Sources: Charles J. Gayle, "The Nature and Volume of Exports from Charleston, 1724–1774," in *Proceedings of South Carolina Historical Association* (1937), 31. G. Melvin Herndon, "Forest Products of Colonial Georgia," *Journal of Forest History* XXIII (1979), 134. North Carolina data for 1768–1772 derived from Table 4.117 minus preceding figures for South Carolina and Georgia.

TABLE 4.119 EXPORTS OF U.S. NAVAL STORES, BY STATE, OCT. 1, 1791–SEP. 30, 1792

State	Pitch (barrels)	Tar (barrels)	Rosin (barrels)	Turpentine (barrels)	Turpentine Spirits (barrels)
N.H.	. . .	780	. . .	119	. . .
Mass.	623	3,998	88	4,348	. . .
R.I.	20	600	. . .	122	. . .
Conn.	2	85	. . .	. . .	. . .
N.Y.	1,953	9,377	539	11,531	. . .
N.J.	. . .	8	. . .	. . .	. . .
Pa.	462	5,889	106	7,140	. . .
Del.	. . .	29	. . .	17	. . .
Md.	196	2,900	334	1,481	. . .
Va.	202	19,017	41	17,620	. . .
N.C.	4,490	21,395	214	13,589	960
S.C.	795	2,509	15	11,102	68
Ga.	402	2,692	. . .	79	. . .
Totals	9,145	69,279	1,337	67,148	1,028

Source: U.S. Congress, *American State Papers: Commerce and Navigation* (1832), VII, 159–60.

TABLE 4.120 EXPORTS OF UNITED STATES NAVAL STORES, 1790–1800

Year Ending Sep. 30	Pitch (barrels)	Tar (barrels)	Rosin (barrels)	Turpentine (barrels)	Turpentine Spirits (gallons)
1800	1,881	59,410	3,075	33,129	4,900
1799	2,592	58,254	16,396	40,382	33,899
1798	5,192	33,898	8,364	40,188	31,603
1797	7,979	47,397	7,015	53,291	54,151
1796	18,083	64,600	14,183	41,490	28,628
1795[a]	. . .	. . .	. . .	. . .	. . .
1794	2,824	46,650	2,480	20,598	75[b]
1793	8,338	67,911	1,715	36,907	91[b]
1792	9,145	69,279	1,337	67,148	1,028
1791	3,818	51,044	228	58,107	1,172
1790	8,875	85,067	316	28,326	193

[a] Not itemized. Total naval stores exports reported as 132,866 gal.
[b] Casks.
Source: U.S. Congress, *American State Papers: Commerce and Navigation* (1832), VII, 31, 33, 121, 233, 282, 307, 338, 359, 360, 381, 382, 414, 415, 428, 429, 452.

TABLE 4.121 PERCENT OF U.S. TAR AND TURPENTINE EXPORTED TO BRITISH EMPIRE

Year Ending Sep. 30		To Britain and Ireland	To British West Indies	To Canada	To Gibraltar	Total
1799	Tar	59.2%	9.7%	5.5%	1.0%	75.4%
	Turpentine	88.8%	3.9%	1.1%	. . .	93.8%
1797	Tar	73.3%	1.6%	2.9%	. . .	77.8%
	Turpentine	77.8%	.5%	.3%	. . .	78.6%
1796	Tar	66.2%	4.2%	1.9%	1.1%	73.4%
	Turpentine	67.6%	3.3%	1.7%	.7%	73.3%
1793	Tar	69.3%	9.1%	.6%	. . .	79.0%
	Turpentine	90.1%	3.1%	.2%	. . .	93.4%
1791	Tar	65.1%	10.7%	.7%	. . .	76.5%
	Turpentine	94.4%	2.0%	.2%	. . .	96.6%

Source: U.S. Congress, *American State Papers: Commerce and Navigation* (1832), VII, 121, 282, 360, 415, 429.

TABLE 4.122 EXPORTS OF U.S. MASTS, BY STATE, OCT. 1, 1791 TO SEP. 30, 1792

State	Masts	Bowsprits	Spars
Mass.	210	21	2,565
N.H.	79	2	11
Conn.	. . .	. . .	12
R.I.	. . .	. . .	790
N.Y.	11	. . .	222
Pa.	. . .	. . .	9
Md.	. . .	. . .	17
Va.	11	. . .	. . .
N.C.	4	. . .	6
Ga.	8	. . .	125
Totals	323	23	3,757

Source: U.S. Congress, American State Papers: Commerce and Navigation (1832), VII, 162.

TABLE 4.123 EXPORTS OF MASTS AND SPARS FROM UNITED STATES, 1791–1795

Year Ending Sep. 30	Masts	Spars	Masts and Spars	% Exported to British Empire		
				of Masts	of Spars	of Both
1795	. . .	. . .	4,056	. . .	. . .	52%
1794	. . .	. . .	1,296	. . .	. . .	41%
1793	. . .	. . .	5,012	. . .	. . .	38%
1792 [a]	323	3,757	4,080	64%	41%	43%
1791 [b]	405	4,983	5,388	85%	42%	46%

[a] 23 bowsprits exported.
[b] 42 bowsprits and 74 booms exported.
Source: U.S. Congress, American State Papers: Commerce and Navigation (1832), VII, 133, 245, 292, 311, 342.

Potash

Significant amounts of potash (an alkaline compound leached from wood ash that was used by a wide variety of British industrialists) first began to be manufactured in the thirteen colonies after Parliament exempted the commodity from British import duties in 1751. The initial phase of its production was dominated by the construction of relatively large-scale and costly factories that refined wood ash bought from local farmers. Although these early ventures did not attain their founders' financial objectives and were largely defunct by 1761, the mistakes learned in these pioneering enterprises made it possible for the industry to be reorganized along profitable lies by 1765.

The most elemental problem plaguing potash partnerships in the 1750s had been difficulty in identifying trees with the proper chemical composition to produce an alkaline residue from ash. The largest factories had been located in Pennsylvania and Virginia, where the timber stock yielded insufficient potash to justify high investment costs. By the mid 1760s, it was recognized that the highest yields came from regions where there were few pines but many maples and elms, and that areas as far south as Pennsylvania offered no better than marginal returns. Production rapidly shifted to New York and New England, where the proper hardwood mix existed.

By the 1760s, it was also understood that centralized refining of ashes at expensive factories with special vats and kilns imposed unnecessary overhead costs that made it difficult to profit given current prices in Britain. After a decade of practical experience making potash, North Americans learned to streamline the process of treating ashes so that ordinary farmers or lumbermen could leach an alkaline residue with simple kettles and pans. The simplified techniques of making potash were easily mastered and became widely disseminated through the northeastern provinces. By the early 1770s, potash production had become a widespread activity among farmers seeking remunerative pursuits during the winter.

Americans rapidly became the dominant source of potash for Britain's manufacturers. In the dozen years following 1763, colonial potash exports rose from 50 tons, just 3% of British imports, to 1,429 tons, 66% of imports. Although the Revolution temporarily cut off this trade, American exports of potash rose more than fourfold from 1775 to 1800, by which date the Untied States probably sold 6,100 tons of potash to Britain, or two-thirds of its total imports. Britain usually purchased 90% of U.S. exports of this commodity.

TABLE 4.124 PRICES OF POTASH (IN LOCAL CURRENCY) AT BOSTON, 1763–1775, AND PHILADELPHIA, 1784–1800

Philadelphia		Boston	
Price per ton of 2,240 lb.		Price per cwt. of 112 lb.	
1800	$167.33	1775	29.50s.
1799	$178.15	1774	26.02s.
1798	$144.48	1773	27.70s.
1797	$143.96	1772	30.92s.
1796	$175.00	1771	40.85s.
1795	£53.33	1770	36.85s.
1794	$120.000	1769	29.25s.
1793	$117.08	1768	29.22s.
1792	$95.67	1767	28.69s.
1791	£38.73	1766	36.22s.
1790	£36.58	1765	37.90s.
1789	£39.58	1764	. . .
1788	£39.06	1763	25.35s.
1787	£38.33		
1786	£40.00		
1785	£50.00		
1784	£41.25		

Source: Arthur H. Cole, Wholesale Commodity Prices in the United States, 1700–1861 (1938), 51–85.

TABLE 4.125 EXPORTS OF POTASH BY STATE, OCT. 1, 1791 TO SEP. 30, 1792

State	Tons Exported	% of Total
N.H.	90	2%
Mass.	691	15%
R.I.	52	1%
Conn.	23	1%
N.Y.	3,550	79%
Pa.	50	1%
Md.	15	1%

Source: U.S. Congress, American State Papers: Commerce and Navigation VII (1832), 157.

TABLE 4.126 TONS OF NORTH AMERICAN POTASH IMPORTED BY GREAT BRITAIN, 1760–1800

	North American Potash (tons)	Total British Imports (tons)	% of Imports from 13 Colonies or U.S.
1800[a]	6,100[a]	9,028	67%[a]
1799[b]	4,190	. . .	. . .
1798[b]	4,965	. . .	. . .
1797[b]	1,723	. . .	. . .
1796[b]	3,231	. . .	. . .
1795[b]	2,289	. . .	. . .
1794[b]	1,767	. . .	. . .
1793[b]	3,532	. . .	. . .
1792[b]	3,630	6,444	56%
1791[b]	2,670	. . .	. . .
1790[b]	6,315	. . .	. . .
1780[c]	2	1,839	1%
1775[c]	1,429	2,159	66%
1772[c]	1,581	. . .	. . .
1771[c]	1,632	. . .	. . .
1770[c]	1,132	2,826	40%
1769[c]	1,204	. . .	. . .
1768[c]	1,344	. . .	. . .
1767[d]	1,286	. . .	. . .
1766[d]	1,225	. . .	. . .
1765[d]	596	1,624	37%
1764[d]	127	. . .	. . .
1763[d]	50	1,727	3%
1760[d]	10	2,424	0.5%

[a] In year ending Sep. 30, 1800, the United States exported 6,760 tons, and probably 6,100 went to Britain. Total British potash imports from North America were 7,504 tons for year ending Dec. 25.
[b] For year ending Sep. 30; includes only imports from United States.
[c] For year ending Dec. 25; includes only imports from 13 colonies.
[d] For year ending Dec. 25; includes imports from Canada.
Sources: William I. Roberts III, "American Potash Manufacture Before the American Revolution," American Philosophical Society, *Proceedings* CXVI (1972), 389–90. U.S. Congress, *American State Papers: Commerce and Navigation* VII (1832), 24, 104, 219, 268, 302, 334, 355, 377, 410, 424, 452. James F. Shepherd and Gary M. Walton, *Shipping, Maritime Trade, and the Economic Development of Colonial North America* (1972), 211–27.

The Fur Trade

Beaver and Peltries

In 1764, Sir William Johnson estimated that 10,000 Indians annually hunted furs throughout the watershed of the Great Lakes and the upper Mississippi River to exchange for British manufactures. Numerous small parties left for thinly populated wilderness areas, some as far as a thousand miles from their own villages, in the early autumn to search for territories that had not been depleted of game. They spent the winter obtaining skins of all types, but especially beaver, which commanded high prices and were a simple prey.

Indians forced beaver into the open by draining their artificial ponds or driving them from their lodges by way of air holes that served as passageways through the ice. Hunters usually killed them with hatchets, sometimes with firearms, but by the 1760s they had begun using metal traps baited with mating scent. Wooden cages or nets were set to snare small game such as martens, foxes, and minks. Indians hunted bigger animals such as moose or bear with guns.

The long journey back began in late winter and required weeks of dragging sleds across ice until the spring thaw allowed travel by canoes, some of which reached forty feet in length and held six thousand pounds. Once home, the Indians either convoyed the skins to a trading post or waited for white merchants to arrive at their village, depending on where prices seemed highest. The fur trade enabled Indians to buy vast amounts of wares that revolutionized their material culture: guns, ammunition, metal utensils, rum, plus strouds (coarse woolen cloth) and other clothing textiles such as blankets made of duffel (coarse woolen material with a thick nap).

Sir William Johnson in 1764 estimated that northern merchants annually bartered about £180,000 sterling in manufactured goods for pelts, upon which a shrewd trader stood to profit as much as 100%. An unknown, but undoubtedly large, portion of the beavers were bought by American hatters, who supplied most of the mainland market and sent surplus headware to the West Indies. Following Great Britain's acquisition of Canada and the Ohio Valley during the Seven Years' War, the exchange of furs for trade goods shifted west to British outposts on the Great Lakes, especially to Fort Detroit. By 1775, Canadian merchants had engrossed almost four-fifths of all furs exported from North America (excluding deer). French fur traders from Missouri, then in Spanish Louisiana, also siphoned off a large share of skins for sale at New Orleans.

The Revolution further disrupted the flow of skins to New York and Pennsylvania, and it allowed merchants from Canada and Spanish Louisiana to control virtually the entire western fur trade. After peace returned in 1783, Americans never succeeded in regaining any significant portion of the traffic in Indian pelts, although about half of Canada's fur exports after the Revolution were trapped in territories south of the Great Lakes lying well within the United States. By 1793, fur exports had declined to such low levels that the Customs Bureau ceased itemizing them by type of animal and grouped all overseas shipments of pelts together with deerskins, which comprised the bulk of these goods. The fur trade remained essentially moribund in the United States until it revived during the 1820s, when renewed demand for beaver skins in Europe led to an orgy of overtrapping by mountain men in the Rockies.

TABLE 4.127 VALUE OF FURS (IN POUNDS STERLING) IMPORTED BY ENGLAND, 1760–1775

From	1775	1770	1765	1760
Canada	£34,486	£28,433	£24,512	£1,930
Hudson Bay	£5,640	£9,213	£9,770	£8,321
Newfoundland	£1,913	£403	£648	£470
Nova Scotia	£210	£132	£78	£24
New England	£1,642	£2,453	£2,811	£946
N.Y.	£3,939	£2,340	£5,565	£1,023
Pa.	£2,866	£1,148	£1,927	£1,879
Md. and Va.	£63	£169	£70	£21
Carolina	£128	£26	£491	£20
Ga.	£63	£9	£53	£3
Fla.	£108	£68	. . .	. . .
Total North America	£51,058	£44,394	£45,925	£14,637
Other Imports	£2,651	£3,364	£3,368	£5,348
Total Imports	£53,709	£47,758	£49,293	£19,985

Source: Murray G. Lawson, *Fur: A Study in English Mercantilism, 1700–1775* (1943), 108–09.

TABLE 4.128 EXPORTS OF BEAVER AND OTHER FURS FROM NORTH AMERICA, 1760–1775

	1775	1770	1765	1760
Beaver[a]				
Number	129,229	136,392	160,466	44,172
Value	£22,654	£23,895	£28,116	£7,958
Bear				
Number	13,767	15,136	11,390	4,868
Value	£4,485	£4,927	£3,363	£1,235
Fox				
Number	23,606	16,803	16,728	15,841
Value	£1,475	£1,050	£1,046	£990
Marten				
Number	83,948	92,827	59,236	29,641
Value	£3,205	£3,094	£1,975	£988
Mink				
Number	40,198	20,840	24,294	9,612
Value	£3,517	£1,870	£2,188	£841
Muskrat				
Number	141,441	55,677	65,164	2,837
Value	£3,540	£1,392	£1,650	£71
Otter				
Number	27,312	21,929	24,198	6,301
Value	£4,782	£3,685	£4,034	£947
Raccoon				
Number	198,148	69,986	74,830	6,776
Value	£1,750	£1,871	£5,004	£169
Wildcat				
Number	21,823	13,625	10,198	8,220
Value	£212	£115	£100	£78
Wolf				
Number	7,608	6,581	4,195	3,705
Value	£1,902	£1,645	£1,049	£926

[a]Value includes skins, wombs, and wool.
Source: Murray G. Lawson, *Fur: A Study in English Mercantilism, 1700–1775* (1943), 87–102.

TABLE 4.129 EXPORTS OF U.S. PELTRY BY STATE, OCT. 1, 1791–SEP. 30, 1792

Skins	N.H.	Mass.	N.Y.	Pa.	Va.	N.C.	S.C.	Ga.
Elk (no.)	. . .	79	. . .	. . .	. . .	. . .	. . .	. . .
Bear (no.)	. . .	. . .	270	. . .	. . .	3	16	62
Seal (no.)	. . .	. . .	4,800	14,536	. . .	. . .	. . .	. . .
Beaver (lb.)	4,000	. . .	. . .	. . .	700	. . .	. . .	. . .
Otter (no.)	. . .	. . .	500	. . .	. . .	25	. . .	85
Sable (no.)	. . .	22	. . .	. . .	. . .	. . .	. . .	. . .
Wildcat, fox, and mink (no.)	. . .	12	. . .	. . .	. . .	390	. . .	6
Misc. boxes	. . .	84	104	337	6	. . .	376	. . .

Source: U.S. Congress, *American State Papers: Commerce and Navigation* (1832), VII, 161.

TABLE 4.130 EXPORTS OF PELTRY FROM UNITED STATES, 1790–1792

Year Ending Sep. 30	Elk and Moose (no.)	Seal[a] (no.)	Bear, Wolf, etc. (no.)	Beaver (lb.)	Otter (no.)	Misc.[b] Skins and Furs (boxes)	Total Value ($)
1792	79[c]	19,336	781[d]	4,700	610	929	. . .
1791	1,063	2,672	37	. . .	100[e]	889	$146,147[f]
1790	. . .	. . .	. . .	. . .	. . .	. . .	$60,515

[a]Seals obtained from trade with Columbia River Indians.
[b]Dimensions of boxes not specified.
[c]Elk.
[d]351 bear, 22 sable, 408 wildcats or foxes.
[e]Includes beaver.
[f]May include deerskins under category of "skins and furs unknown."
Source: U.S. Congress, *American State Papers: Commerce and Navigation* (1832), VII, 25, 145, 240, 241.

The Deerskin Trade

The deerskin trade grew steadily during the eighteenth century and peaked during the decade prior to the Revolution. From 1768 to 1772, Britain received an annual average of 721,558 pounds of deerskins from its North American possessions situated south of Canada. All but 20,289 pounds (3%) came from southern colonies, with 53% originating from either Georgia or the Carolinas and 23% from Florida, a British territory since 1763. Annual shipments of deer hides averaged £69,443 sterling, or about 2.5% of the thirteen colonies' exports, and contributed more to their trade balance than did overseas sales of iron, naval stores, or whale oil.

Colonial merchants obtained virtually all their skins from Indians. To collect the vast amount of hides being bartered about 1770, hunters would build two long fences that converged at an apex and then drive entire herds into the enclosure, where, once caught in the trap, they were easily slaughtered with guns. Overhunting seriously depleted the stock of deer within the Carolinas and Georgia and forced hunters to range farther afield in Alabama and Mississippi to kill sufficient numbers of animals.

TABLE 4.131 DEERSKIN PRICES IN FLORIDA, PER POUND OF UNDRESSED SKIN, 1768–1778

Date	French Sols	Sterling
Sep. 1778	40 sols	2s., 4d.
Jan. 1778	30 sols	1s., 9d.
Jan. 1777	40 sols	2s., 4d.
Aug. 1775	40 sols	2s., 4d.
Jun. 1775	35 sols	2s., ½d.
Jan. 1775	37 sols	2s., 2d.
Jun. 1774	35 sols	2s., ½d.
Jun. 1771	48 sols	2s., 10d.
Aug. 1769	35 sols	2s., ½d.
Jul. 1769	37 sols	2s., 2d.
Jun. 1769	33 sols	2s., 11d.
Apr. 1769	40 sols	2s., 4d.
Sep. 1768	35 sols	2s., ½d.
Aug. 1768	45 sols	2s., 8d.

Note: Source gives prices in sols, which equaled ¹/₈₀ of a Spanish dollar, for which sterling usually traded at 4s., 8d (pence).
Source: Robin F. A. Fabel, *The Economy of British West Florida, 1763–1783* (1988), 212.

By interrupting the deer trade, the Revolution allowed the southeastern herds to replenish themselves. When peace returned in 1783, however, citizens of the United States found it difficult to acquire skins from the Indians, most of whom had been allies of the British. The Indians preferred to exchange their hides with merchants residing in Florida or along the Gulf Coast, territories that Britain had just restored to Spain. Spain purposefully sowed disaffection among the Indians against Americans, and consequently Pensacola and Mobile replaced Charleston and Savannah as the major markets for the southern fur trade.

American deerskin exports, which averaged 552,714 pounds from the thirteen colonies between 1768 and 1772, fell to an annual level of just 103,198 pounds in 1791 and 1792. By 1800 the deerhide trade nevertheless had rebounded far more than the market for beavers and other pelts. Exports of deerskins had decisively eclipsed those of beaver and other pelts during the 1760s, and even as the peltry business dwindled to insignificance in the 1790s, they emerged as the only viable, albeit diminished, sector of the domestic fur industry to survive the eighteenth century.

TABLE 4.132 VOLUME (LB.) AND VALUE (£ STERLING) OF DEERSKIN EXPORTS TO GREAT BRITAIN FROM BRITISH MAINLAND COLONIES, 1769–1772

From Middle Atlantic		
	(lb.)	(£ ster.)
1772	19,802	£1,726
1771	22,330	£2,271
1770	31,775	£2,927
1769	7,250	£752
From Lower South		
	(lb.)	(£ ster.)
1772	359,482	£34,563
1771	438,344	£42,241
1770	328,832	£31,731
1769	392,739	£39,838
From Upper South		
	(lb.)	(£ ster.)
1772	197,592	£16,304
1771	168,263	£13,724
1770	175,260	£14,282
1769	69,188	£5,972
From British Florida		
	(lb.)	(£ ster.)
1772	204,530	£21,185
1771	248,947	£25,696
1770	117,932	£12,358
1769	103,969	£12,200

Note: New England exported 1,800 lb. worth £225 in 1772.
Source: James F. Shepherd and Gary M. Walton, Shipping, Maritime Trade, and the Economic Development of Colonial North America (1972), 211–16.

TABLE 4.133 EXPORTS OF U.S. DEERSKINS BY STATE, OCT. 1, 1791–SEP. 30, 1792

	Mass.	R.I.	N.Y.	Pa.	Va.	N.C.	S.C.	Ga.
Pounds	318	. . .	. . .	4,881	12,858	54,867	34,675	50,765
Packages[a]	156	7	. . .	162	25	. . .	479	. . .
Number	. . .	. . .	444			. . .	. . .	. . .

[a]Dimensions of packages not specified.
Source: U.S. Congress, American State Papers: Commerce and Navigation (1832), VII, 161.

TABLE 4.134 EXPORTS OF DEERSKINS FROM THE UNITED STATES, 1790–1792

Deerskins Exported in Years Ending Sep. 30

Destination	1792 (Quantity)	1791 (Quantity)	1790 (Value)
England	112,625 lb.	32,247 lb.	$25,642
Scotland	1,548 lb.	2,462 lb.	not given
Ireland	37,660 lb.	8,283 lb.	not given
France	1,650 lb.	3,456 lb.	$307
Spain	. . .	675 lb.	. . .
Holland	. . .	. . .	$7,060
Germany	4,881 lb.	. . .	. . .
Denmark	. . .	908 lb.	. . .
Totals	158,364 lb.	48,031 lb.	$33,009

Source: U.S. Congress, American State Papers: Commerce and Navigation (1832), VII, 24, 25, 129. 240.

TABLE 4.135 EXPORTS OF SKINS AND FURS FROM UNITED STATES, 1793–1800

Year Ending Sep. 30	Pounds	Packages[a]	Number	Value
1800	. . .	. . .	. . .	$308,262
1799	. . .	. . .	. . .	$493,724
1798	. . .	. . .	. . .	$355,487
1797	. . .	. . .	. . .	$288,591
1796	. . .	. . .	. . .	$273,201
1795	24,903	1,196	79,296	. . .
1794	8,463	2,061	43,768	. . .
1793	368,618	1,123	27,446	. . .

[a]Dimensions of packages not specified.
Note: Source did not distinguish between furs and deerskins.
Source: U.S., Congress, American State Papers: Commerce and Navigation (1832), VII, 288–452.

Manufacturing, Handicrafts, and Mining

Manufacturing and mining experienced uneven growth during the Revolutionary era. The economy continued to diversify as new enterprises proliferated in fields such as textile fabrication, papermaking, coal extraction, and lead mining. The output of shipbuilding evidently suffered a short-term decline, iron smelting sank into a long-term decline in productivity, and copper mining became essentially moribund.

By ending the flow of imported manufactures from Britain, the Revolution provided incentives for entrepreneurs to establish fledgling factories and find new supplies of natural resources. Although the war generated greater economic self-sufficiency in manufacturing, this rise in production largely constituted an inefficient and temporary attempt at import substitution. Military hostilities interrupted many industries by making labor more expensive and scarce, by cutting off the finished materials from overseas needed by various

American industries (such as tackle and blocking required by ship-builders to outfit vessels), and by the random destruction or disruption of industrial facilities. When peace resumed in 1783, many small, war-inspired manufacturing institutions collapsed, particularly textiles it seems, because they could not compete with the resumed trade in finished goods from Britain. A financial depression also gripped most of the United States during the 1780s, and it brought stagnation to much of the industrial sector, especially ironmaking and shipbuilding.

As the U.S. economy strengthened, capital began to flow into factories and mining ventures. The Society for the Encouragement of Useful Manufactures was founded in 1791 by investors who built Paterson, New Jersey, as the country's earliest planned center for mass-production in North America. A similar group, organized in 1787 as the Pennsylvania Society for the Encouragement of Manufactures and the Useful Arts, sought to finance technological improve-ments to make American factories more competitive with those in Europe. This latter group sponsored the emigration of English mill-wright Samuel Slater, who constructed the earliest water-powered textile factory in America to use advanced machinery at Pawtucket, Rhode Island, in 1790. The Pawtucket factory was a milestone in economic history, for despite the uneven course of industrial devel-opment over the next half century, the financial success enjoyed by Slater's textile works presaged the United States' later emergence as a major manufacturing power.

Alcohol Distilling

Large-scale distilling primarily involved rum production in the late colonial era. Dependent upon imported West Indian molasses, rum manufacturing suffered severe disruptions during the Revolution and then recovered slowly because of postwar restrictions limiting trade with Britain's Caribbean colonies. Output of domestic rum

TABLE 4.136 DOMESTIC RUM PRODUCTION AND CONSUMPTION IN THIRTEEN COLONIES, 1770

Colony	Domestic Production (gal.)	Coastwise Imports (gal.)	Overseas Exports (gal.)	Coastwise Exports (gal.)	Consumed at Home (gal.)
N.H.	120,000	11,000	80,000	2,000	48,000
Mass.	2,059,000	24,000	584,000	328,000	1,170,000
R.I.	814,000	3,000	183,000	247,000	388,000
Conn.	200,000	28,000	1,000	13,000	213,000
N.Y.	699,000	58,000	47,000	135,000	575,000
N.J.	1,000	13,000	. . .	1,000	12,000
Pa.	584,000	166,000	7,000	97,000	645,000
Md.	160,000	174,000	. . .	1,000	333,000
Va.	40,000	146,000	. . .	4,000	181,000
N.C.	40,000	49,000	1,000	3,000	86,000
S.C.	89,000	126,000	30,000	. . .	186,000
Ga.	1,000	34,000	1,000	. . .	34,000
Total Gallons	4,807,000	831,000	935,000	831,000	3,871,000
Total Value	£270,394	£46,744	£52,639	£46,744	£217,755

Note: Value of rum calculated at 1.125s., sterling, per gallon.
Source: John J. McCusker, *Rum and the American Revolution: The Rum Trade and the Balance of Payments of the Thirteen Continental Colonies* (1989), 474–75, 531.

TABLE 4.137 QUANTITY AND VALUE OF RUM EXPORTS FROM THIRTEEN COLONIES, 1770

	West Indian Rum		North American Rum	
	Gallons	£ Ster.	Gallons	£ Ster.
Africa	3,000	£300	313,000	£17,600
Newfoundland	40,000	£4,300	234,000	£13,200
Quebec	15,000	£1,600	231,000	£13,000
Nova Scotia[a]	21,000	£2,300	58,000	£3,200
Bahamas, Bermuda[b]	28,000	£3,000	19,000	£1,100
Great Britain	12,000	£1,300	8,000	£400
Ireland	10,000	£1,100	4,000	£200
West Indies	1,000	£100	5,000	£300
Southern Europe[c]	4,000	£400	34,000	£1,900
Fur Trade	. . .	. . .	30,000	£1,700
Totals	133,000	£14,400	935,000	£52,600

[a]Includes 1,000 gal. of North American rum to Prince Edward Island.
[b]Includes Florida.
[c]Includes exports to Atlantic wine islands.
Source: John J. McCusker, *Rum and the American Revolution: The Rum Trade and the Balance of Payments of the Thirteen Continental Colonies* (1989), 481, 482, 529, 531.

TABLE 4.138 WHOLESALE PRICE OF AMERICAN RUM (IN STERLING PER GAL.), 1770–1775

Year	Boston[a]	New York[a]	Philadelphia[b]	Charles Town[a]
1775	1.20s.	1.49s.	1.34s.	1.48s.
1774	1.08s.	1.36s.	1.29s.	1.44s.
1773	.99s.	1.46s.	1.33s.	1.46s.
1772	.89s.	1.47s.	1.37s.	1.88s.
1771	1.06s.	1.35s.	1.32s.	1.61s.
1770	1.13s.	1.49s.	1.44s.	1.54s.

[a]New England rum.
[b]Pennsylvania rum.
Source: John J. McCusker, *Rum and the American Revolution: The Rum Trade and the Balance of Payments of the Thirteen Continental Colonies* (1989), 1133, 1134.

slumped from 4,800,000 to 4,200,000 gallons between 1770 and 1792; by the 1790s, annual exports of U.S. rum had fallen to about 550,000 gallons, 40% lower than overseas shipments from the thirteen colonies in 1770.

The Revolution marked an important transition period in U.S. distilling. As rum output contracted due to the problems of obtaining molasses, Americans began producing more spirits fermented from local supplies of grain. By the early 1800s, this process had led to the near eclipse of rum in favor of rye, various grain-based whiskeys, and a corn derivative called bourbon whose output rose rapidly after it first appeared in Kentucky in 1784.

TABLE 4.139 RUM DISTILLERIES IN THE THIRTEEN COLONIES, CA. 1770

Colony and Total		City and Distilleries	
N.H.	1	Portsmouth	1
Mass.	64	Boston	36
		Salem	5
		Haverhill	2
		Ipswich	1
		Lanesboro	1
		Plymouth	1
		Newburyport	10
		Medford	4
		Watertown	2
		Marblehead	1
		Dartmouth	1
R.I.	26	Newport	22
		Bristol	1
		Providence	3
Conn.	5	Hartford	1
		New Haven	1
		Salem	1
		Middletown	1
		Norwich	1
N.Y.	18	N.Y.	12
		Albany	1
		Manhattan Island	4
		Oyster Bay	1
N.J.	3	Newark	1
		Bordentown	1
		Princeton	1
Pa.	14	Philadelphia	14
Del.	1	New Castle County	1
Md.	3	Annapolis	1
		Charlestown	1
		Baltimore	1
Va.	4	Alexandria	2
		Norfolk	2
N.C.	1	Wilmington	1
S.C.	3	Charles Town	3

Source: Lester J. Cappon, ed., Atlas of Early American History: The Revolutionary Era, 1760–1790 (1976), 26.

TABLE 4.140 NUMBER AND OUTPUT OF ALCOHOLIC STILLS IN UNITED STATES, 1792

State	Rum Stills	Output (Gallons)	Grain Stills	Output (Gallons)	Total Output (Gallons)
N.H.	3	47,874	5	230	48,104
Mass.	156	2,581,443	13	375,300	2,956,743
R.I.	29	771,400	5	228,541	999,941
Conn.	22	166,449	104	21,505	187,954
Vt.	1	4,177	16	2,297	6,474

State	Rum Stills	Output (Gallons)	Grain Stills	Output (Gallons)	Total Output (Gallons)
N.Y.	33	415,326	42	53,049	468,375
N.J.	3	2,221	201	28,000	30,221
Pa.	21	67,764	831[b]	182,616[b]	250,380
Del.	2	. . .[a]	151	15,026	15,026
Md.	2	76,800	559	41,118	117,917
Va.	. . .[a]	9,687	. . .[a]	440[b]	. . .[a]
N.C.	. . .[a]	9,065	. . .[a]	. . .[a]	. . .[a]
S.C.	18[b]	59,540[b]	130[b]	2,496[b]	62,037[b]
Ga.	0	0	120	3,393	3,393
Totals	290	4,211,746	2,177	934,819	5,146,565

[a]No returns made by revenue supervisors.
[b]Surveys incomplete.
Source: U.S. Congress, American State Papers: Finance (1832), V, 250, 251.

TABLE 4.141 EXPORTS OF ALCOHOLIC SPIRITS FROM THE UNITED STATES, 1790–1800

Year Ending Sep. 30	Beer, Cider, Porter[a] (gal.)	(bottles)	Rum[a] (gal.)	Whiskey[a] (gal.)
1800	74,763	20,652	481,569	27,801
1799	110,340	151,464	494,365	16,979
1798	76,991	86,400	305,010	6,233
1797	48,664	153,528	373,328	43,692
1796	328,883	168,024	963,325	. . .
1795	224,075	14,148	685,167	. . .
1794	83,881	6,828	276,137	5,970[b]
1793	135,993	9,312	665,522	10,731[b]
1792	93,386	12,756	948,115	. . .
1791	44,526	8,628	513,234	10,252
1790	. . .	. . .	370,331	. . .

[a]Domestically distilled spirits only.
[b]Gin, measured in cases.
Source: U.S. Congress, American State Papers: Commerce and Navigation (1832), VII, 24–453.

Shipbuilding

Abundant timber supplies and strong demand from a rapidly expanding merchant marine turned colonial shipbuilding into a major area of industrial activity by 1763. Because Americans enjoyed lower construction costs than English shipyards, they produced numerous craft for British buyers. By 1776, the thirteen colonies annually earned £143,000 sterling by sending British purchasers an average of 117 vessels, with carrying capacity of almost 19,000 tons. About half the ship tonnage constructed in America went to foreign owners, so that merchant vessels sold overseas stood fifth in value among colonial exports, just behind the fish trade and slightly ahead of lumber shipments.

The Revolution severely disrupted this industry. British forces occupied every major center of shipbuilding during all or part of the war, except for Salem, Massachusetts, and Baltimore, Maryland. Shipyards sometimes ground to a halt because the fighting disrupted supplies of planks and masts from the frontier. Shipwrights also found it extremely difficult to outfit completed hulls with the necessary blocking and tackling, which they had customarily bought from England before 1775, because of the wartime blockade. Even without these problems, ship construction would have declined precipitously, for the war cut off Americans from their best customers, who were British merchants.

Shipbuilding was slow to recover when peace returned in 1783. British trade restrictions exacted a heavy price upon the country's merchant marine and fishing fleet, which shrank considerably and ordered few replacements for its aging craft. A commercial depression engulfed the nation for much of the mid-1780s and brought more hardship to the industry. As American trade revived during the Washington administration, particularly after Jay's Treaty of 1795,

shipbuilding's fortunes also rose. The volume of ship construction increased substantially after 1797, when U.S. shipyards outfitted approximately 730 vessels, with a combined carrying capacity of 56,679 tons; and in 1800 their output had reached 995 ships that totalled 106,261 tons. By about 1800, shipbuilding had recovered from the Revolution and was producing more than twice as much merchant tonnage as before the war.

This painting by George Ropes shows the merchant ship *Fame* being launched at Salem, Massachusetts. The sale of ships to English merchants became a major American enterprise because proximity to sources of hardwood and masts allowed Americans to build vessels less expensively than could be done in Britain, which was largely deforested. American shipbuilders were nevertheless largely dependent on European manufacturers to provide cables, sails, tackle, and blocking to make their vessels seaworthy. (James Duncan Phillips Library collections, courtesy Peabody & Essex Museum, Salem, Massachusetts.)

TABLE 4.142　SHIPS AND TONNAGE BUILT IN THE THIRTEEN COLONIES, 1769–1772

1772	New England				N.Y.	N.J.	Pa.	Md.	Southern Colonies				Total
Ships, snows, and brigs	123				15	1	18	8	17				182
Total tons	18,149				1,640	80	2,897	1,626	2,152				26,544

1771	N.H.	Mass.	R.I.	Conn.	N.Y.	N.J.	Pa.	Md.	Va.	N.C.	S.C.	Ga.	Total
Ships, snows, and brigs	15	42	15	7	9	0	15	10	10	0	3	2	128
Sloops, schooners	40	83	60	39	28	2	6	8	9	8	4	4	291
Total tons	4,991	7,704	2,148	1,483	1,698	70	1,307	1,645	1,678	241	560	543	24,068

1770	N.H.	Mass.	R.I.	Conn.	N.Y.	N.J.	Pa.	Md.	Va.	N.C.	S.C.	Ga.	Total
Ships, snows, brigs	27	31	16	5	8	0	18	7	6	0	0	0	118
Sloops, schooners	20	118	49	41	10	0	8	10	15	5	3	3	282
Total tons	3,581	7,274	2,035	1,522	960	0	2,354	1,545	1,105	125	52	57	20,610

1769	N.H.	Mass.	R.I.	Conn.	N.Y.	N.J.	Pa.	Md.	Va.	N.C.	S.C.	Ga.	Total
Ships, snows, and brigs	16	40	8	7	5	1	14	9	6	3	4	0	113
Sloops, schooners	29	97	31	43	14	3	8	11	21	9	8	2	276
Total tonnage	2,452	8,013	1,428	1,542	955	83	1,469	1,344	1,269	607	789	50	20,001

Source: Jacob M. Price, "A Note on the Value of Colonial Exports of Shipping," *Journal of Economic History* XXXVI (1976), 707.

TABLE 4.143 TONNAGE AND COST OF VESSELS BUILT IN THIRTEEN COLONIES, 1775–1784

Measured Tonnage		Shipbuilding Costs Region (Year)	(Sterling) Cost per Ton
Vessel	Average Size		
Ship	223.0 tons	New England (1775)	£6.16.6
Snow	148.6 tons	Other Colonies (1775)	£8.10.0
Brig	127.3 tons	All Colonies (1775)	£7.11.10
Sloop	70.0 tons	New England (1784)	£7.10.0
Schooner	72.3 tons	Other Colonies (1784)	£7.3.6
All above	160.9 tons	All Colonies (1784)	£7.6.9

Note: Building costs include full rigging and accessories.
Source: Jacob M. Price, "A Note on the Value of Colonial Exports of Shipping," *Journal of Economic History* XXXVI (1976), 707–21.

TABLE 4.144 OVERSEAS SALES OF COLONIAL VESSELS TO BRITISH MERCHANTS, CA. 1775

Domestic Output	New England	Other Colonies	Total
Vessels Built	140	115	255
Total Tonnage[a]	22,600	17,300	39,900
Value (Sterling)	£154,100[a]	£151,400[b]	£305,500
Overseas Sales			
Vessels Sold	64	53	117
Total Tonnage[a]	10,400	8,200	18,600
Value (Sterling)	£70,900[b]	£72,100[c]	£143,000

[a] Adjusted from registered tons to measured tons in source by increasing average tonnage from table 4.143 by one third. Registered tonnage was official carrying capacity. Measured tonnage was actual carrying capacity.
[b] At about £6.16.6 per ton.
[c] At about £8.10.0 per ton.
Sources: John J. McCusker, "The Rise of the Shipping Industry in Colonial America," in Robert A. Kilmarx, ed., *America's Maritime Legacy: A History of the U.S. Merchant Marine and Shipbuilding Industry Since Colonial Times* (1979), 21. Jacob M. Price, "A Note on the Value of Colonial Exports of Shipping," *Journal of Economic History* XXXVI (1976), 721.

TABLE 4.145 SHIPBUILDING IN PHILADELPHIA, MD., VA., 1763–1796

Year	Philadelphia		Md.		Va.	
	Vessels Built	Total Tons	Vessels Built	Total Tons	Vessels Built	Total Tons
1796	22	3,907	. . .	. . .	. . .	. . .
1795	31	5,506	. . .	. . .	. . .	. . .
1794	23	4,118	. . .	. . .	. . .	. . .
1793	46	8,145	. . .	. . .	. . .	. . .
1789	19	2,966	. . .	. . .	. . .	. . .
1787	16	2,740	. . .	. . .	. . .	. . .
1786	13	1,508	. . .	. . .	. . .	. . .
1785	20	4,020	. . .	. . .	. . .	. . .
1784	44	8,838	. . .	. . .	. . .	. . .
1783	40	7,412	55	4,183	68	3,155
1782	22	3,577	73	5,817	119	3,951
1781	7	1,867	25	3,348	37	1,330
1780	. . .	. . .	50	4,003	44	2,033
1779	. . .	. . .	20	945	20	599
1778	. . .	. . .	5	321	15	470
1777	. . .	. . .	4	107	11	155
1776	. . .	. . .	1	18	7	124
1775	19	2,910	7	. . .	. . .	. . .
1774	29	3,397	16	ca. 1,360	7	475
1773	31	3,438	20	ca. 1,700	30	1,797
1772	21	2,220	7	ca. 595	26	1,419
1771	20	1,913	21	ca. 1,785	37	2,454
1770	18	1,880	20	ca. 1,700	20	1,050
1769	18	1,335	19	ca. 1,615	26	1,480
1768	17	1,096	14	ca. 1,190	27	2,280
1767	21	1,810	22	ca. 1,870	33	2,474
1766	21	1,555	12	ca. 1,020	37	3,515
1765	31	2,114	18	ca. 1,530	47	3,880
1764	. . .	. . .	16	ca. 1,360	39	2,852
1763	. . .	. . .	27	ca. 2,295	31	2,785

Sources: Billy G. Smith, The *"Lower Sort:" Philadelphia's Laboring People, 1750–1800* (1900), 223. William M. Kelso, "Shipbuilding in Virginia, 1763–1774," Columbia Historical Society, *Records* XLVIII (1971), 3. Arthur P. Middleton, "Ships and Shipping in the Chesapeake and Tributaries," in Ernest P. Eller, ed., *Chesapeake Bay in the American Revolution* (1981), 132. Paul H. Giddens, "Trade and Industry in Colonial Maryland, 1753–1769," *Journal of Economic and Business History* IV (1932), 535.

TABLE 4.146 MERCHANT VESSELS BUILT IN THE UNITED STATES, 1797–1801

Year	Number of Vessels	Gross Tons	Average Tons
1801	1,168	124,755	106.8
1800	995	106,261	106.8
1799	767	77,921	101.6
1798	635	49,435	77.8
1797	728	56,679	77.8

Source: Treasury Department and Bureau of Marine Inspection and Navigation sources compiled in Bureau of Census, *Historical Statistics of the United States: Colonial Times to 1957* (1960), 448.

Ironmaking

The eighteenth-century iron industry reached its peak period of production during the decade before 1775. Since they consumed vast quantities of wood for charcoal, most ironworks occupied remote sites in dense forests, and by necessity these enclaves were largely self-sufficient. English investors transformed one such wilderness outpost, a tract of 50,000 acres around Ringwood, New Jersey, into the colonies' largest manufacturing complex. Between 1764 and 1768, the American Iron Company's supervisor, Peter Hasenclever, cleared 10 miles of roads, built 10 bridges, dammed 13 millponds, transported 535 ironworkers from Germany, and erected 7 forges and 4 iron furnaces, besides building a gristmill, more than 100 houses, stables for 122 horses, and barns for 51 cattle and 214 oxen.

By 1775, the thirteen colonies contained more than 250 operational ironworks, including 82 blast furnaces smelting iron and six others for making steel. The industry's greatest center of production lay in Pennsylvania and western New Jersey, which accounted for one-third to half of all colonial output. At its height, ironmaking employed as many as 30,000 laborers and required the annual cutting of 15,000 to 20,000 acres of forest to provide 500,000 cords of wood for charcoal.

So vigorously had colonial iron smelting expanded in the half century after 1720, that more furnaces and forges operated in the thirteen colonies than in England and Wales. American productivity was moreover no less efficient than in Britain, so colonial output certainly exceeded the mother country's on the eve of independence. At their peak level of 30,000 tons per year, the colonies ranked as the world's third greatest center of ironmaking (behind Sweden and Russia) and manufactured about 15% of its iron supply.

The Revolutionary War initiated a period of decline followed by decades of stagnation. The fighting destroyed some ironworks, slowed production by creating a labor scarcity that drove up wages—which comprised 70% of pig iron's production expenses—and cut off the immigration of valuable skilled workers from Europe. An economic depression put pressure on iron prices and made investment capital difficult to obtain in the 1780s. The country briefly lost its self-sufficiency in iron and increased its imports from foreign sources. The iron industry started reviving in the early 1790s and even expanded to the frontiers of Kentucky and Tennessee.

TABLE 4.147   WHOLESALE PRICE OF A TON OF IRON AT PHILADELPHIA, 1763–1800

Year	Bar Iron	Pig Iron
1800	$107.19	$35.11
1799	$101.01	$39.33
1798	$103.54	$36.65
1797	$110.25	$33.35
1796	$111.35	$31.25
1795	£34.96	$11.00
1794	£31.00	$25.21
1793	$85.80	$24.33
1792	£32.79	$25.30
1791	£30.00	£9.60
1790	£28.25	£8.66
1789	£26.46	£8.50
1788	£26.32	£8.50
1787	£25.37	£8.50
1786	£26.50	£8.83
1785	£31.83	£9.60
1784	£39.26	£10.40
1783	£37.30	. . .
1782	£45.10	. . .
1781	£1,143.30	. . .
1780	£2,601.10	. . .
1779	£895.10	. . .
1778	£202.39	. . .
1777	£87.32	. . .
1776	£29.27	. . .
1775	£24.26	. . .
1774	£26.12	£8.42
1773	£26.43	£8.35
1772	£27.07	£8.15
1771	£24.07	£8.00
1770	£23.17	£7.77
1769	£23.35	£7.92
1768	£23.71	£8.20
1767	£24.06	£9.20
1766	£25.83	. . .
1765	£26.42	. . .
1764	£25.50	£7.75
1763	£26.25	£9.33

Note: Ton equals 2,240 lb. Prices in local money or U.S. dollars.
Sources: Arthur H. Cole, *Wholesale Commodity Prices in the United States, 1700–1861* (1938), 78–123. Anne Bezanson, ed., *Prices and Inflation During the American Revolution: Pennsylvania, 1770–1790* (1951), 334–39.

Despite a significant rise in output, the United States fell increasingly behind foreign competitors in technology. The British tripled their average furnace's output to 900 tons between 1770 and 1800 by replacing water-driven bellows with steam engines and by experimenting with a process of coke smelting. American ironmasters failed to achieve any productivity gains and their average furnace continued yielding 300 tons after 1800. Although it had led the world in per capita iron production in 1775, the United States steadily regressed and fell far behind global standards until a new wave of innovation modernized the industry after 1840.

TABLE 4.148   WORKFORCE OF STERLING IRONWORKS IN ORANGE CO., N.Y., 1776
182 Laborers Needed for Iron Furnace, Forge, and Steel Works

Supervisory Staff (10)	Charcoal Operations (126)
3 operations managers	55 woodcutters
3 operations blacksmiths	10 master coalers
3 operations carpenters	5 charcoal stokers
1 clerk	16 charcoal carters
Furnace Operations (6)	40 laborers
2 filler men	**Ore Loading Operations (9)**
1 gutter man	3 ore raisers
2 founders	2 ore burners
1 banking man	2 mine powderers
Steel Works (11)	2 ore carters
6 steel makers	**Forge Operations (20)**
4 forge men	10 at anchor forge
1 carter	10 ordinary laborers

Source: Charles S. Boyer, *Early Forges and Furnaces in New Jersey* (1931), 225, 226.

Table 4.149   COST OF PENNSYLVANIA BAR IRON ARISING FROM FREIGHT CHARGES, 1768

Charge per Ton-Mile	Distance Carried	Charge per Ton	Freight as % of Price per Ton
£0.04	15 mi.	£0.60	2.5% of £23.71
£0.05	30 mi.	£1.50	6.3% of £23.71
£0.04	39 mi.	£1.60	6.7% of £23.71
£0.04	75 mi.	£3.10	13.1% of £23.71

Source: Paul F. Paskoff, *Industrial Evolution: Organization, Structure, and Growth of the Pennsylvania Iron Industry, 1750–1860* (1983), 55.

TABLE 4.150   WAGE AND LABOR COSTS PER TON OF PENNSYLVANIA BAR IRON, 1768–1773

	Woodcutter[a]	Collier[b]	Finer[c]	Chafer	Price of Ton of Bar Iron (Pa. £)
	Wages for 3.75 days	Wages for 2.06 days	Wages for 1 day	Wages for 1 day	
1773	£1.12	£1.73	£2.00	£2.00	£26.43
1772	£1.12	. . .	£1.35	£1.35	£27.07
1769	£1.25	£1.88	£1.63	£1.63	£23.25
1768	£1.24	. . .	£1.25	£1.25	£23.71

[a] Cut 3 cords daily.
[b] Made 210 bu. daily.
[c] Finished 1 ton daily.
Source: Paul F. Paskoff, *Industrial Evolution: Organization, Structure, and Growth of the Pennsylvania Iron Industry, 1750–1860* (1983), 13–14.

TABLE 4.151 LABOR OUTPUT AND FUEL USAGE AT HOPEWELL FORGE, PA., 1769–1774

Year	Inactive[a] Time	Tons of[c] Anconies	Tons per Man	Man-days per Ton	Char-coal[b] Burned	Char-coal[b] per Ton
1774	23%	157.36	9.68	24.90	571.50 cbu.	3.63 cbu.
1773	19%	148.88	9.65	26.05	606.75 cbu.	4.08 cbu.
1772	15%	106.22	7.24	36.74	476.25 cbu.	4.48 cbu.
1771	21%	169.71	11.77	25.84	713.74 cbu.	4.21 cbu.
1770	22%	175.73	9.72	25.12	762.00 cbu.	4.34 cbu.
1769	24%	193.18	8.65	27.55	726.44 cbu.	3.67 cbu.

[a]Percent of maximum possible man-days worked.
[b]Cubic bushels.
[c]A dumbell-shaped ingot of wrought iron.
Source: Paul F. Paskoff, Industrial Evolution: Organization, Structure, and Growth of the Pennsylvania Iron Industry, 1750–1860 (1983), 28.

TABLE 4.152 IRONWORKS OPERATIONAL IN THIRTEEN COLONIES ABOUT 1770

Date	Colony	Iron Furnaces	Forges	Steel Furnaces	Slitting Mills	Plating Mills
1774	N.H.	. . .	4	. . .	. . .	. . .
1758	Mass.	14	41	0	4	2
1768	R.I.	2	10	. . .	. . .	. . .
1766	Conn.	1	8	1	. . .	8
1757	N.Y.	3	. . .	1	. . .	1
1770	N.J.	8	42	1	4	1
1775	Pa.	20	45	2	1	1
1775	Md.	17	18	. . .	. . .	. . .
1776	Va.	14	. . .	. . .	. . .	. . .
1771	N.C.	3	. . .	. . .	. . .	. . .
1770	S.C.	. . .	. . .	. . .	. . .	. . .
	Total	82	175	5	9	13

Source: Arthur C. Bining, British Regulation of the Colonial Iron Industry (1933), 14–30, 91.

TABLE 4.153 IRON PRODUCTION IN THIRTEEN COLONIES AND ENGLAND, ABOUT 1775

	Thirteen Colonies		England and Wales	
	Number	Output	Number	Output
Furnaces	82	24,600 tons	77	23,100 tons
Forges	175	26,250 tons	135	20,250 tons
Total	257	50,850 tons	212	43,350 tons
Per Capita	. . .	.020 tons	. . .	.006 tons

Source: Arthur C. Bining, British Regulation of the Colonial Iron Industry (1933), 30.

TABLE 4.154 PRODUCTION OF IRON IN THIRTEEN COLONIES/STATES AND WORLD, 1700–1800

Year	World Output	U.S. Output	Percent Colonial or U.S.
1800	400,000 tons	45,000 tons	11.25%
1790	325,000 tons	38,000 tons	11.69%
1775	210,000 tons	30,000 tons	14.28%
1750	150,000 tons	10,000 tons	6.66%
1700	100,000 tons	1,500 tons	1.5%

Note: On p. 30, source gives colonial output in 1775 as 50,800 tons.
Source: Arthur C. Bining, British Regulation of the Colonial Iron Industry (1933), 134.

TABLE 4.155 VOLUME (TONS) AND VALUE (£ STERLING) OF IRON EXPORTS FROM THE BRITISH MAINLAND COLONIES, 1768–1772

	To Britain and Ireland				To West Indies	
	Bar Iron		Pig Iron		Bar Iron	
	Tons	£ Ster.	Tons	£ Ster.	Tons	£ Ster.
From New England						
1772	. . .	. . .	119	£601	4	£71
1771	1	£17	179	£863	6	£90
1770	7	£126	236	£1,191	13	£235
1769	11	£163	183	£918	6	£81
1768	40	£721	145	£714	8	£31
From Middle Atlantic						
1772	542	£9,092	1,221	£6,180	200	£3,363
1771	1,217	£17,688	2,014	£9,729	157	£2,276
1770	1,442	£21,708	2,645	£13,358	211	£3,183
1769	1,114	£16,428	1,832	£9,159	202	£2,977
1768	729	£10,394	2,029	£10,005	197	£2,807
From Upper South						
1772	461	£7,738	2,376	£12,022	27	£454
1771	923	£13,427	2,873	£13,876	31	£456
1770	738	£11,111	2,866	£14,475	41	£623
1769	1,108	£16,349	2,678	£13,390	34	£500
1768	2,569	£36,609	944	£4,653	19	£272

Note: Source did not record exports of pig iron to West Indies. Total exports of iron from Lower South were 19 tons.
Source: James F. Shepherd and Gary M. Walton, Shipping, Maritime Trade, and the Economic Development of Colonial North America (1972), 211–27.

TABLE 4.156 ANNUAL AVERAGE OF TONS OF AMERICAN-SMELTED IRON TRANSSHIPPED WITHIN THE THIRTEEN COLONIES VIA THE COASTAL TRADE, 1768–1772

	Bar Iron		Pig Iron		Cast Iron	
	Exports	Imports	Exports	Imports	Exports	Imports
N.H.	. . .	149	. . .	. . .	1	7
Mass.	50	549	9	182	86	5
R.I.	42	93	176	199	87	4
Conn.	12	82	. . .	54	6	63
N.Y.	222	22	297	127	6	34
N.J.	6	1	. . .	. . .	. . .	1
Pa.	847	28	30	131	13	20
Md.	238	2	354	5	27	26
Va.	26	106	4	245	2	12
N.C.	. . .	83	. . .	1	. . .	37
S.C.	. . .	142	. . .	3	2	11
Ga.	. . .	19	. . .	. . .	. . .	3
Fla.	. . .	6	. . .	. . .	. . .	1
Total	1,450[a]	1,282	866	947	230	224

[a]Includes total of 7 tons from New Hampshire, North Carolina, South Carolina, Georgia, and Florida.
Note: Years end January 4 of following year. Ton equals 2,240 lb.
Source: Research of Lawrence A. Harper in Bureau of the Census, Historical Statistics of the United States: Colonial Times to 1957 (1960), 763–64.

Typical of cold-blast charcoal furnaces was the Hecla Iron Company's operations in Centre Co., Pennsylvania. The photograph highlights the predominantly rural character of eighteenth-century heavy industry. Energy-intensive technologies such as iron production had to be located in rural areas so they would have access to abundant, inexpensive supplies of wood for charcoal. (Bining Collection, courtesy Pennsylvania Historical and Museum Commission)

TABLE 4.157   PERCENT OF BRITISH IRON IMPORTS SUPPLIED BY COLONIES, 1761–1776

Year	Tons[a] from Europe[b] Bar Iron	Tons[a] from 13 Colonies Bar Iron	Pig Iron	Percent from 13 Colonies
1776	49,828	28	316	.7%
1775	40,771	916	2,996	8.8%
1773	45,541	837	2,937	7.6%
1771	43,614	2,222	5,303	14.7%
1769	46,848	1,779	3,401	10.0%
1765	50,294	1,078	3,264	7.9%
1761	42,328	39	2,766	6.2%

[a] Ton equals 2,240 lb.
[b] No pig iron was imported from Europe.
Source: Arthur C. Bining, *British Regulation of the Colonial Iron Industry* (1933), 85.

TABLE 4.158   EXPORTS OF IRON AND STEEL FROM THE UNITED STATES, 1790–1800

Year Ending Sep. 30	Pig Iron (Tons)	Bar Iron (Tons)	Iron Hoops (Tons)	Iron Castings[a] ($)	Manufactured Iron & Steel[b] ($)
1800	190	531	. . .	$11,174	$372,261
1799	140	614	. . .	$16,573	$271,575
1798	120	793	. . .	$29,861	$173,074
1797	597	204	. . .	$22,001	$135,594
1796	502	843	. . .	$453	$160,094
1795	1,046	2,444	216	. . .	. . .
1794	2,037	893	50	. . .	. . .
1793	2,089	763	27	. . .	. . .
1792	3,267	351	15	. . .	. . .
1791	4,178	357	16	$1,967	$28,152
1790	3,555	200	. . .	$7,878	$4,004[c]

[a] Includes anvils, cambooses, cannon, shot, pots, and kettles.
[b] Includes nails, axes, saws, hoes, knives, muskets, shovels, scythes, anchors, grapnels, locks, bolts, ladles, swords.
[c] 10 tons of bombshells and 15,537 muskets only.
Source: U.S. Congress, *American State Papers: Commerce and Navigation* (1832), VII, 24–452.

Glassmaking

In 1763, there were only three centers of glassmaking in the thirteen colonies: at Alloway Creek in Salem County, New Jersey, at New York City, and at New Windsor in Ulster County, New York. These furnaces, like most of their predecessors, produced inexpensive green glass for bottles and windows. Clear glass, decorative wares, and other pieces of high value had to be imported from Great Britain.

American craftspeople began producing glass equal to European standards shortly before the Revolution. The earliest manufacturer to achieve distinction in this regard was Henry William Stiegel; from 1763 to 1769, he built three furnaces near Heidelberg and Manheim, Pennsylvania, which he operated with skilled artisans from England and Germany. Until his creditors pushed him into bankruptcy in

TABLE 4.159   GLASSHOUSES ESTABLISHED IN THE UNITED STATES, 1763–1800

Dates	Proprietors and Location	Products
1763–1765?	William Henry Steigel Lancaster Co., Pa.	Windows, bottles, hollow ware
1765–1774[a]	William Henry Steigel Manheim, Lancaster Co., Pa.	Molded tableware, bottles, hollow ware
1769–?	Barge, Morgan, White, and Reno Philadelphia, Pa.	Flint glass
1771–1900+	Robert Towars and Joseph Leacock Kensington (Philadelphia), Pa.	Green and flint glass, windows, tablewares
1780–1782?	Robert Hewes (of Boston) Temple, N.H.	Crown window glass, probably bottles

(continued)

TABLE 4.159 (continued)

Dates	Proprietors and Location	Products
1781?–1824+	Stanger Brothers Glassboro, N.J.	Bottles
1783–1830?	William and Elisha Pitkin East Manchester, Conn.	Bottles, hollow ware
1784–1796?[b]	John Frederick Amelung Frederick, Md.	Windows, fine tableware
1784?–1823+	Robert Morris and John Nicholson Philadelphia, Pa.	Probably windows and possibly tablewares
1786?–1820?	DeNeufville, Heffke, and Walfahrt Downesborough (Hamilton), N.Y.	Windows, demijohns, snuff jars, bottles
1788–?	David Goff and Co., Madison, Conn.	Windows
1790?–?	John Brown, Providence, R.I.	Unknown
1791–1825	Thomas and Benjamin Johnson (Aetna Glass Works) Frederick, Md.	Possibly windows and bottles
1793–1829	Boston Crown Glass Co. (Robert Hewes) Boston, Mass.	Windows, hollow ware
1797–1847	Albert Gallatin New Geneva, Fayette Co., Pa.	Windows, bottles, possible tableware
1798–1841+	Isaac Craig and James O'Hara Pittsburgh, Pa.	Windows, bottles, hollow ware

[a]Second furnace added 1769.
[b]Second furnace added by 1790.
Source: George S. McKearin and Helen McKearin, American Glass (1941), 585–86.

1774, Stiegel imitated European glasswares so successfully that his products were almost indistinguishable from them.

Eleven glasshouses were established from 1781 to 1800. Among the most noteworthy furnaces were those of John Frederick Amelung, who produced items of superior quality at Frederick and Baltimore, Maryland. Several glasshouses revived or opened in Philadelphia after the Revolution, and Glassboro, New Jersey, became a significant center of production for several decades after 1781. By 1798, glassmaking had become established across the Appalachian crest at Pittsburgh, which had begun its rise to become one of the country's greatest centers of this industry. Virtually all glass was produced for domestic consumption. The value of all exports in 1790 and 1791 (the only years in which glass products were enumerated) was just $1,990 and $1,004, respectively.

Gunmaking

Prior to the Revolution, arms making had been a handicraft carried on by numerous artisans rather than an enterprise marked by factory production. Because most American gunsmiths made hunting rifles that were unsuited as infantry weapons, war with Britain found the United States poorly disposed to provide muskets for the Continental army. Although several states established arms factories, and Congress exempted their employees from military duty, it proved impossible to acquire sufficient domestic firearms to equip Washing-

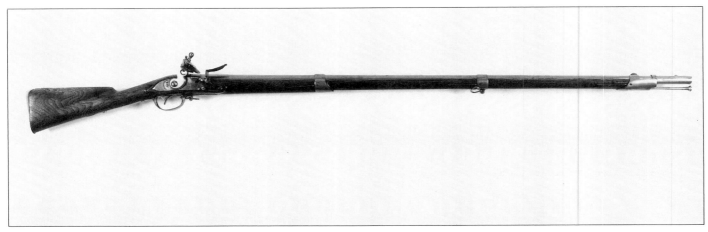

This Model 1795 Springfield, Massachusetts, flintlock musket was the first truly standardized and official model of a musket made for the U.S. government; it was the first whose production was supervised by a federal arsenal. This basic model was produced until 1814, by which time the Springfield Armory had completed approximately 80,000 to 85,000 stands. (Negative 77-3310, courtesy Smithsonian Institution)

TABLE 4.160 ANNUAL MUSKET PRODUCTION AT SPRINGFIELD, MASS., ARMORY, 1795–1800

Year	Muskets	Contract Price	Army Estimate of Musket Cost	Cost of Producing Musket to Armory
1800	4,862	. . .	$12.06	$13.42
1799	4,595	. . .	$9.29	$17.82
1798	1,044	$13.40	. . .	$16.28
1797	1,028	. . .	. . .	. . .
1796	838	. . .	. . .	. . .
1795	245	. . .	. . .	. . .

Source: Felicia Johnson Deyrup, Arms Making in the Connecticut Valley: A Regional Study in the Economic Development of the Small Arms Industry, 1798–1870 (1970), 229, 233.

ton's troops. Only by purchasing more than 80,000 French muskets was Congress able to field a well-armed military force.

With a huge inventory of surplus French military weapons on hand when the Revolution ended, there was little incentive for an American arms industry to develop in the 1780s. In 1794, Congress decided that proper military preparedness required a domestic gunmaking industry, and it authorized the building of a federal armory capable of producing 4,200 muskets annually with seventy workmen assisted by thirty apprentices. Rather than place the arsenal in Pennsylvania, the nation's long-established center of weapons manufacture, the government built it at Springfield, Massachusetts, which seemed relatively safe from foreign invasion and also contained a sizeable concentration of gunsmiths. The Springfield armory's establishment marked the beginning of a long-term trend that saw arms making shift from Pennsylvania to the Connecticut Valley, which became the center of this enterprise by the 1860s. Beginning in 1798, when it gave contracts to private businessmen for 40,200 stands of small arms, the government served to stimulate a domestic weapons industry by providing entrepreneurs with a rising demand for large-scale manufacture of guns. Federal contracts led to the proliferation of private arms factories that would supplement the Springfield arsenal's output, and consequently were critical in the rapid rise of arms production as a major industrial activity.

Home and Building Construction

No systematic survey of the country's housing took place until 1798, when 576,800 homes were assessed for taxation, and statistics on construction starts and costs only begin with 1868. The study of

concentrated around Philadelphia and Boston. Papermaking expanded rapidly after then, and by independence thirty-one mills had gone into operation. Demand for newsprint soared after the Revolution's end, especially during the 1790s, when the number of papers multiplied from 92 to 242.

Eighteenth-century papermaking underwent few technological changes, except for the gradual acceptance of "hollanders," which were Dutch machines that pulverized rotted cloth to pulp in oval tubs more efficiently than older pounding and shredding devices. Since rags and linen, rather than wood pulp, served as the major source of fiber for printing or writing materials, early American paper had little acidic content and remained durable for centuries. During the Revolutionary era, papermaking remained a labor-intensive enterprise that relied heavily on human brawn and required employees to work in wet, damp, and often chilly buildings, just as it had in the Middle Ages.

TABLE 4.161   VALUE OF ESTIMATED HOUSE CONSTRUCTION IN UNITED STATES, 1761–1800

Years	Population	Increase	Dwellings Built	Annual Average	Value of New Homes
1800	5,281,588	153,823	35,000	. . .	$9,170,000
1799	5,127,756	149,352	30,000	. . .	$7,860,000
1798	4,978,404	145,002	25,000	. . .	$6,550,000
1797	4,833,402	140,776	25,000	. . .	$6,550,000
1796	4,692,624	136,678	30,000	. . .	$7,860,000
1795	4,555,946	132,697	30,000	. . .	$7,860,000
1794	4,423,249	128,632	32,000	. . .	$8,384,000
1793	4,292,417	125,180	29,000	. . .	$7,598,000
1792	4,169,337	121,337	19,000	. . .	$4,978,000
1791	4,047,900	117,900	25,000	. . .	$6,550,000
1785–90	3,930,000	680,000	145,000	24,000	$62,880,000
1775–84	3,250,000	764,000	160,000	16,000	$41,920,000
1771–74	2,486,000	337,924	70,770	17,700	$46,373,000
1761–70	2,148,076	554,451	116,100	11,600	$30,392,000

Note: Average home's value in 1798 was $262; see Soltow in sources.
Sources: Samuel Blodget, Economica: A Statistical Manual of the United States of America (1806), 58. Lee J. Soltow, Distribution of Wealth and Income in the United States in 1798 (1989), 50.

early American housing has largely focused upon how changing public tastes led to the popularization of new architectural styles. Economic historians have essentially ignored other aspects of the home construction industry, such as units built per year, the rate at which the pre-existing housing stock was replaced, the consumption of raw materials, labor expended by various craftsmen, total employment in the construction industry, the value of new housing added yearly, building starts for barns or minor shelters, and supplementary economic activities stimulated by home building such as the demand created for furniture or other domestic furnishings. Only the crudest of estimates presently provide any indication of the volume of building activity, and no studies give any indication of construction's total contribution toward the gross national product. Until such elemental work is undertaken, scholars will remain entirely ignorant of the volume of building activity created by population growth, wartime destruction, and migration to the frontier.

Papermaking

Papermaking expanded slowly after the first colonial mill was built near Philadelphia in 1690. By 1763, there were no paperworks in eleven of the continental colonies and the industry was essentially

By 1800, papermaking had become established in every state but South Carolina, Georgia, and Tennessee. The business grew rapidly in New England, especially in eastern Massachusetts. As the nation's oldest center of blank-sheet production, Pennsylvania emerged as the true center of paper manufacture by 1790, when it was the site of half of all the industry's mills.

TABLE 4.162   EXPANSION OF PAPER MILLS IN THE UNITED STATES, 1770 TO 1790

Mills Operational About 1770	Mills Operational About 1790
Colony Location and Number	State Location and Number
Pa. (18)	Pa. (30)
Philadelphia County (8)	Berks County (8)
Chester County (4)	Philadelphia County (7)
Berks County (4)	Chester County (5)
Lancaster County (1)	Delaware County (5)
Bucks County (1)	Montgomery County (3)
	Bucks County (1)
	Cumberland County (1)

(continued)

TABLE 4.162 (continued)

Mills Operational About 1770	Mills Operational About 1790
Colony Location and Number	State Location and Number
Mass. (5) Suffolk County (4) Middlesex County (1)	Mass. (9) Suffolk County (4) Middlesex County (1) Essex County (1) Worcester County (1) Hampshire County (2)
Conn. (3) Hartford County (2) New London County (1)	Conn. (7) Hartford County (3) New London County (2) New Haven County (2)
R.I. (1) Providence County (1)	R.I. (1) Providence County (1)
N.Y. (3) New York City (1) Queens County (1) Orange County (1)	N.Y. (3) New York City (1) Queens County (1) Orange County (1)
Md. (2) Baltimore County (2)	Md. (2) Baltimore County (2)
	N.J. (5) Burlington County (2) Hunterdon County (1) Middlesex County (1) Monmouth County (1) Vt. (1) Cheshire County (1) N.C. (1) Orange County (1)

Source: Lester J. Cappon, ed., *Atlas of Early American History: The Revolutionary Era, 1760–1790* (1976), 28, 30.

Pottery

For much of the colonial era, British merchants supplied the bulk of pottery used by Americans and provided all pieces of high quality. American potters, many of whom followed this profession part-time when not pressed by farming, primarily operated small-scale workshops to supply neighbors with inexpensive jugs, pots, stoneware, mugs, plates, and platters. By the 1760s, however, an increasing number of pot-houses operated several kilns year-round and organized their employees into rudimentary factories.

Fine earthenware was expensive to make and could often be undersold by British imports, so American potters concentrated on redware (brick clay colored naturally by iron oxide). Of thirty-four kilns known to be operating about 1770, twenty-seven fired only redware, as did forty-five of the sixty known potteries known to exist about 1790. Potters slowly shifted output to stoneware fired from silica-based clays, which could be heated to a harder consistency. At least five potters produced stoneware about 1770, and twelve did so about 1790.

Large-scale production of pottery was rare in the South, but two major areas of specialization developed in the North. Potteries proliferated around Boston and probably sold most of their output to other Americans, especially southerners, in the coastal trade. The geographic center of potterymaking was the Delaware Valley, especially near Philadelphia. American potters evidently acquired a

greater share of the domestic market at the expense of British imports, but they exported virtually none of their own earthen or stone ware. Americans sold just $1,984 of pottery abroad in 1791, and customs officials ceased itemizing pottery exports by 1796.

TABLE 4.163 EXPANSION OF POTTERIES IN THE UNITED STATES, 1760–1790

Potteries Operating About 1770	Potteries Operating About 1790
Colony Location and Number	State Location and Number
Mass. (9) Boston, Braintree, Danvers (3), Newbury, Newburyport, Salem, Weston	Mass. (16) Beverly, Cambridge, Danvers (7), Newbury, Newburyport, Salem, Weston, Whately, Gorham (Me.), Wicasset (Me.)
R.I. (1) Providence	N.H. (1) Lyndeborough
Conn. (1) Greenwich	Conn. (7) Goshen, Greenwich, Hartford (2), Norwalk, Norwich (2)
N.Y. (5) N.Y. (4), Huntington	N.Y. (6) N.Y. (4), Huntington, Poughkeepsie
	N.J. (2) South Amboy, Bedminster
Pa. (14) Bucksville, East Caln, Ephrata, Gardenville, Haycock, Philadelphia (5), Reading, Rockland, Tulpehocken, Wrightstown	Pa. (21) Bucksville, Dryville, East Caln, Ephrata, Gardenville, Newmanstown, Nockamixon (2), Reading (3), Philadelphia (7), Souderton, Womelsdorf, Wrightstown
	Md. (2) Cumberland, Elk Ridge Landing
	Va. (1) Morgantown (W. Va.)
N.C. (3) Bethabara, Salem, Steeds	N.C. (2) Bethabara, Salem
S.C. (1) Charles Town	S.C. (1) Camden

Note: Perhaps only 30% of American potteries have been identified.
Source: Lester J. Cappon, ed., *Atlas of Revolutionary American History: The Revolutionary Era, 1760–1790* (1976), 28, 30.

Shoemaking

Shoemaking expanded dramatically during the Revolutionary era. By the 1760s, the American footwear industry centered around the Massachusetts towns of Braintree, Bridgewater, Brookfield, and Lynn. Production was highest at Lynn, where the attainment of high standards of quality is thought to have dated to about 1750, with the emigration of a Welsh cobbler, John Adam Dagyr, whose superior craftsmanship forced competing cordwainers to produce better shoes to keep their customers. Lynn's footwear apparently enjoyed a high reputation, for on October 21, 1764, the *Boston Gazette* reported: "It is certain that women's shoes made at Lynn do now exceed those usually imported, in strength and beauty, but not in price." By 1768, it was believed that annual shoe production had reached 80,000 pairs at Lynn.

The Revolution increased the demand for domestically made shoes by cutting off British imports, and by 1783 shoe manufacturing at Lynn had reached 400,000 pairs annually. Peace was followed by intense competition as foreign merchants sold footwear at steep discounts. In response to declining domestic production, Congress enacted import duties of 7.5% on shoes and fifty cents on boots in 1789, when the United States was a net importer of approximately 75,000 pairs annually. Massachusetts cordwainers began winning an increasing share of the southern shoe market, and they found significant export markets in the West Indies, where traditional imports of footwear were disrupted by European wars. After 1794, the United States exported an average of more than 140,000 pairs of shoes and boots each year, versus imports of approximately 103,000 pairs.

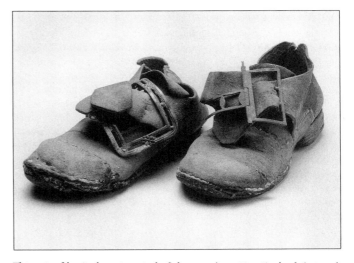

This pair of boy's shoes is typical of those made in New England during the late 1700s, when the United States became largely self-sufficient in footwear production. The sharp rise in output resulted from an expansion of the workforce, not the use of machines, since manufacture by hand remained the only way of producing shoes. (James Duncan Phillips Library Collections, courtesy Peabody & Essex Museum, Salem, Massachusetts.)

TABLE 4.164 UNITED STATES EXPORTS AND IMPORTS OF SHOES AND BOOTS, 1790–1800

Year Ending Sep. 30	Exports (pairs)	Percent Exported to West Indies	Imports (pairs)	Percent Imported from Britain
1800	75,195	. . .	97,869	88%
1799	148,478	94%	103,806	86%
1798	159,088	97%	79,121	80%
1797	112,551	92%	135,611	85%
1796	220,724	94%	131,215	63%
1795	147,537	75%	71,687	78%
1794	99,009	79%	. . .	. . .
1793	16,269	68%	. . .	. . .
1792	9,251	79%	. . .	. . .
1791	7,528[a]	74%	77,190	94%[c]
1790	5,862[b]	71%	87,470	95%

[a]Valued at $9,233.
[b]Valued at $5,741.
[c]Valued at $65,368.
Source: U.S. Congress, *American State Papers: Commerce and Navigation* (1832), VII, 32–452.

TABLE 4.165 PRICES CHARGED FOR A PAIR OF SHOES, 1763–1799

1763	Women's calico shoes	£1.6.0	(Massachusetts)
1766	Women's "everlasting" shoes	£2.0.0	"
1766	Men's leather shoes	£1.10.0	"
1768	Women's shoes	£2.0.0	"
1768	Deerskin shoes	£7.18.0	"
1768	Men's shoes	£2.15.0	"
1768	Stuff shoes	5s	"
1792	Custom-made shoes	4s.6d [$.76]	(Philadelphia)
1794	Custom-made shoes	6s [$1.02]	"
1795–99	Custom-made shoes	$1.00	"

Sources: Blanche E. Hazard, *The Organization of the Boot and Shoe Industry in Massachusetts Before 1875* (1921), 38, 185. Paul G. Faler, *Mechanics and Manufacturers in the Early Industrial Revolution: Lynn, Massachusetts, 1780–1860* (1981), 85.

TABLE 4.166 COSTS AND INCOMES OF PHILADELPHIA JOURNEYMAN SHOEMAKERS, 1762–1800

Year	Sales Price of Shoes (per Pair)	Cost of Shoe Materials	Net Gain After Paying 1s. to Master Shoemaker	Annual Income (for 312 Pairs of Shoes)
1800	14s.,2d.	7s.	6s.,2d.	£96
1799	12s.,11d.	6s.,11d.	5s.	£78
1798	15s.,6d.	6s.,8d.	6s.,10d.	£107
1797	16s.,8d.	5s.,7d.	10s.,1d.	£157
1796	13s.,4d.	6s.	6s.,4d.	£99
1795	17s.,3d.	7s.,10d.	8s.,5d.	£130
1794	13s.,1d.	7s.,2d.	3s.,11d.	£61
1793	17s.,1d.	6s.,11d.	9s.,2d.	£142
1792	10s.,5d.	6s.,11d.	2s.,6d.	£39
1791	10s.,3d.	7s.,2d.	2s.,1d.	£33
1790	10s.,2d.	7s.,4d.	1s.,10d.	£29
1789	10s.	6s.,7d.	2s.,5d.	£38
1788	10s.,2d.	6s.,5d.	2s.,9d.	£43
1787	9s.,11d.	6s.,8d.	2s.,3d.	£35
1786	10s.,5d.	7s.,4d.	2s.,1d.	£33
1785	10s.,9d.	6s.,8d.	3s.,1d.	£49
1784	11s.,5d.	7s.,2d.	3s.,3d.	£51
1783	11s.,9d.	7s.,4d.	3s.,5d.	£53
1776	12s.,5d.	8s.,8d.	2s.,9d.	£43
1775	10s.,9d.	6s.,4d.	3s.,5d.	£53
1774	11s.	6s.,3d.	3s.,9d.	£59
1773	. . .		. . .	
1772	11s.,1d.	5s.,10d.	4s.,3d.	£66
1771	11s.	5s.,10d.	4s.,2d.	£65
1770	10s.,5d.	5s.,10d.	3s.,7d.	£56
1762	11s.,5d.	6s.,6d.	3s.,11d.	£61

Source; Billy G. Smith, *The "Lower Sort:" Philadelphia's Laboring People, 1750–1800* (1990), 116–17.

Sugar Refining

In the course of purchasing molasses for rum distilling, the continental colonists also had opportunity to buy large amounts of sugar from the West Indies. Due to steady rises in their standard of living, Anglo-Americans were increasingly able to afford cutting the bitter taste of that period's coffee and tea with white sugar instead of cheaper unprocessed varieties; by 1770, they were consuming about 3,400,000 pounds of refined sugar annually, or about 3.5 pounds per free adult. Britain's sugar industry benefited greatly from Parliamentary subsidies on exports to America, but Yankee merchants, who owned most of the refineries, remained dominant in their home market. Despite a serious challenge from their British competitors, domestic manufacturers met about 75% of local demand from the twenty-six refineries in the thirteen colonies.

TABLE 4.167   SUGAR REFINERIES IN THE THIRTEEN COLONIES, 1770

Colony	Location	Refineries
Mass. (8)	Boston	1
	Charlestown	7
R.I. (5)	Newport	4
	Providence	1
N.Y. (4)	New York City	4
Pa. (7)	Philadelphia	7
S.C. (2)	Charles Town	2

Source: John J. McCusker and Russell R. Menard, *The Economy of British America, 1607–1789* (1985), 292.

Textiles

Domestic textile production received a sudden stimulus from the non-importation and non-consumption movements used to force the repeal of Parliamentary taxation in the 1760s. William Molineux, for example, taught basic skills at his Spinning School in 1769 to 300 Boston women who agreed to weave cloth in their homes for his factory's ten looms. Home-produced fabrics nevertheless failed to displace British imports before independence because the latter were more competitive in both quality and price. The Revolution induced a temporary surge in American-made clothing, but output collapsed after 1783 when trade with Britain resumed.

From 1783 to 1800, the groundwork was laid for cloth manufacture to emerge as a significant element of the U.S. economy. "Spinning Jennys and carding machines from the English models are in great use and well made in Mass. Bay and in other parts of New England," wrote British Consul Phineas Bond in 1789; "[i]n Hertford, [Connecticut]," he added, "a considerable fund has been raised, as the poor people take away flax, hemp and wool, they pay the price of it and when they return it spun they are allowed a reasonable equivalent for their labor. If they are destitute of utensils they are provided with them by the societies upon securities (or depositing the price of the utensils) to restore them at a given time or when required." The earliest textile operations utilized this system of "putting out" and collected workers at factories only for the final stages of cutting patterns and stitching clothes together.

The domestic textile industry received important encouragement from private organizations founded to promote manufacturing. The first such group to appear was the New York Society for the Promotion of Arts, Agriculture, and Economy, which supported a linen mill after its founding in 1764. At least nine other societies appeared by 1790 to encourage manufacturing, including the nation's two ear-

In 1791, at Pawtucket, Rhode Island, Samuel Slater reproduced this complex Arkwright spinning frame from memory based on his experience as a millwright in English factories. Slater's feat of industrial espionage in replicating the latest British textile machinery is generally considered to be the beginning of the U.S. industrial revolution. (Negative 41, 151, courtesy Smithsonian Institution)

liest chambers of commerce at New York City and Charles Town, South Carolina.

Completed sometime before January 1789, the Beverly, Massachusetts, Cotton Manufactory was the first textile mill organized along lines of a modern factory. The Beverly plant combined all operations of cloth making under one roof, divided its workers by specialized skills, and organized production by departments. In 1791, the country's most advanced textile factory began production under Samuel Slater at Pawtucket, Rhode Island; harnessing water power to drive spinning frames designed according to Richard Arkwright's patent, this mill was the technological equal of English textile factories.

Americans founded approximately two dozen textile establishments from 1783 to 1800. In many cases, the best known being that of Samuel Slater, English emigrants familiar with advanced technology provided critical skills in building and supervising these mills. Following a burst of investment and increased cloth production from about 1788 to 1794, the industry faced increasing pressure from British competitors, who increased annual exports to the United States from £1,488,000 in 1790–92 to £2,368,000 in 1797–98. Crippled by expensive start-up costs, interest on borrowed capital, and higher wages than prevailed in England, numerous American textile factories were unable to sell their goods at a profit and went bankrupt in the late 1790s.

During this period, fabric production shifted gradually from lin-

ens and woolens, which had predominated before independence, to cotton. By 1800, about 2,000 spindles on Arkwright Spinning Jennys spun 50,000 to 100,000 pounds of cotton in the United States, but in the short span of four years from then to 1804, the number of spindles and their output would double. Textiles remained a struggling industry until after 1820, when domestic producers truly became competitive with foreign suppliers.

Copper Mining

Copper mining had been a minor industry before 1763, but major centers of production flourished near Hackensack, New Jersey, and Simsbury, Connecticut. Upon acquiring New France in 1763, Britain gained large copper deposits in modern Michigan, which had long been known to the French but never developed. In 1769, the partnership of Bostwick, Baxter, and Henry formed to dig mines near Ft. Michilimackinac. Work began in late 1771 when several miners tunneled a forty-foot shaft along the Ontonagon River, but they abandoned it in early 1772 when warm weather caused the clay walls to collapse. The partners moved operations to Lake Superior's north shore a year later, but they found no ore and ended the project in 1774. Not until the next century would Michigan's copper deposits, the richest east of the Mississippi, be exploited.

By 1763, colonial copperworks were experiencing increased difficulty in maintaining production. The large mine, smelter, and refinery at Simsbury, Connecticut, had been used since 1709 and its veins were severely depleted; about 1773 it was sold to Connecticut and converted into Newgate Prison. Persistent flooding and several ruinous fires led the Schuyler family to close America's biggest mine near Hackensack, New Jersey, in 1773. Shortly after they began exporting ore to London, William Buntin's two copper pits at Topsfield, Massachusetts, were abandoned in 1772 when Buntin died on a business trip to England. American copper mining declined sharply in the 1770s and was moribund when the Revolution started.

TABLE 4.168 TEXTILE ESTABLISHMENTS BUILT IN UNITED STATES, 1764–1799

Location	1764–1775	1776–1783	1783–1789	1790–1799
N.H.	. . .	. . .	2	. . .
Mass.	2	. . .	5	4
Conn.	. . .	. . .	5	6
R.I.	. . .	. . .	. . .	3
N.Y.	2	. . .	1	1
N.J.	. . .	. . .	. . .	1
Pa.	5	. . .	. . .	3
Md.	. . .	3	1	2
Total	9	3	14	20

Source: William G. Bagnall, The Textile Industries of the United States (1893), 49–279.

TABLE 4.169 OUTPUT OF BENJAMIN SHEPHERD'S COTTON MILL, WRENTHAM, MASS., 1796

Dimensions		
Length	Width	Stories
50 ft.	20 ft.	2

Machines					
Carding Machines	Spinning Jennys	Roping Jenny	Hand Looms	Horse-powered Callendar	Coloring Vats
1[a]	2	1	4	1	several

Output of Cotton		
Carding	Spinning	Weaving
100 lb. weekly (5,200 lb. annually)	72–120 lb. weekly (3,700–6,200 lb. annually)	120 yards weekly (6,200 yards annually)

[a]Water powered.
Source: William G. Bagnall, The Textile Industries of the United States (1893), 175.

TABLE 4.170 WHOLESALE PRICE OF COPPER SHEET (PER LB. IN LOCAL CURRENCY) AT PHILADELPHIA, 1785–1800

1800	$ .53	1792	. . .
1799	$ .50	1791	1.88s.
1798	$ .43	1790	1.88s.
1797	$ .38	1789	1.88s.
1796	$ .36	1788	1.88s.
1795	$ .37	1787	1.92s.
1794	. . .	1786	1.88s.
1793	. . .	1785	1.91s.

Source: Arthur C. Cole, Wholesale Commodity Prices in the United States, 1700–1861 (1938), 81–124.

TABLE 4.171 PROJECTED YIELD OF SCHUYLER COPPER MINE, BELLEVILLE, N.J., 1800

Metal	Yield per 100 lb. of Ore	Annual Production	Value
Copper	15 lb.	50 imperial tons	$50,000
Silver	4 to 7 oz.	6,160 oz.	$6,160

Note: Production assumes 100 workers and steam pumping engine.
Source: Benjamin H. Latrobe, American Copper Mines (1800), 6–7.

TABLE 4.172 EXPORTS OF COPPER FROM UNITED STATES, 1796–1800

Year Ending Sep. 30	Value	Year Ending Sep. 30	Pack-ages	Manufac-tured (lb.)	Ore (lb.)	Sheet (lb.)
1800	$50,608[a]	1795	263	. . .	. . .	. . .
1799	$56,655[a]	1794	. . .	9,895	. . .	. . .
1798	$20,532[a]	1793	146	. . .	. . .	. . .
1797	$17,676[a]	1792	. . .	3,500	28	3,000
1796	$3,273[a]	1791[b]	. . .	1,480	2,240	33,152

[a]Value of both copper and brass manufactures.
[b]Also 24,192 lb. of pig copper.
Source: U.S. Congress, *American State Papers: Commerce and Navigation* (1832), VII, 143–425.

The return of peace in 1783 further discouraged American copper production because English merchants unloaded large inventories of copper goods at bargain rates. The industry began reviving in the 1790s as prices rose to meet a growing demand for ship sheathing at home and abroad. All copper exports came from Massachusetts in 1792. Some abandoned mines reopened, and the New Jersey Copper Mine Association launched an ambitious effort to resume ore extraction in 1793 at the Schuyler mine and several nearby sites. Substantial investments were made to rehabilitate these works and hire skilled labor from Europe, but the New Jersey company produced little ore by 1800 and it eventually converted its steam engines, foundry, and machine shops to manufacturing. Even after Britain restricted copper exports in 1798 to ensure its navy adequate supplies of sheathing, uncertainty about copper's future profitability deterred investors from risking their capital. So wary of the industry's prospects had Americans become, that a rich copper vein located at Bristol, Connecticut, about 1800 remained unexploited until 1836.

Coal Mining

Significant deposits of coal were first discovered about 1701 west of the James River's falls in modern Powhatan County, Virginia, but this industry did not emerge as a significant commercial enterprise until just before the Revolution. The ready availability of wood minimized the demand for coal in warming homes. The robust iron industry could not utilize coke blasting since its technology relied on the heating and oxidizing properties of charcoal into the 1840s. Until the 1750s, colonial blacksmiths, glassblowers, and other manufacturers could obtain ample and inexpensive supplies of this fuel whenever coal stored as ballast was offloaded to allow British ships to take on American cargoes.

Aside from Nova Scotia, Virginia was the only British colony to develop this resource commercially. Coal was not excavated from underground shafts, but rather was dug out of pits until the surface veins became exhausted. All but the smallest collieries depended on slave labor. A few pits operated north of the James River as early as the 1740s, but their output was minimal.

Virginians were sending small shipments of coal through the coastal trade by 1758. Coal from Henrico County's Deep Run Pits sold for 12 pence a bushel at Richmond in 1767, and was declared to be "equal to Newcastle coal." Production along the James River Valley expanded to satisfy Philadelphia's growing use of coal after 1770, and it increased further when the Revolution disrupted supplies from Nova Scotia and Britain.

The largest carboniferous deposits in Virginia's piedmont lay south of the James River, and they began to be exploited in 1788, when the Heth Pits opened in Chesterfield County. Veins in the Heth Pits averaged from 25 to 50 feet thick, and sometimes ranged

TABLE 4.173 TONS OF COAL EXPORTED FROM JAMES RIVER OF VA., 1758–1765

Destination	1765	1763	1762	1761	1760	1758
Salem, Mass.	161	112	. . .	. . .	. . .	. . .
Boston, Mass.	60	232	288	. . .	. . .	. . .
Nantucket, Mass.	. . .	34	. . .	. . .	. . .	. . .
R.I.	256	136	156	. . .	. . .	. . .
N.Y.	. . .	247	40	136	182	24
Piscataqua, N.H.	214	168	. . .	. . .	. . .	. . .
Philadelphia	21	102	47	60	. . .	. . .
Newcastle, Del.	. . .	24	. . .	. . .	. . .	. . .
Lower James, Va.	. . .	. . .	. . .	. . .	. . .	8
West Indies, Bermuda	. . .	21	. . .	15	12	. . .
Totals	712	1,076	531	211	194	32

Note: Measured in net tons of 2,000 lb.
Source: Howard N. Eavenson, *The First Century and a Quarter of the American Coal Industry* (1942), 32–34.

TABLE 4.174 TONS OF COAL IMPORTED BY AMERICAN COLONIES, 1769–1772

Imported to	From 13 Colonies				From Great Britain		
	1772	1771	1770	1768	1771	1770	1769
N.H.	. . .	50	. . .	130	89	158	293
Boston, Mass.	204	174	. . .	153	527	989	1,894
Marblehead, Salem, and Falmouth, Mass.	83	183	23	101	. . .	165	42
R.I.	. . .	13	76	. . .	206	208	159
Conn.	. . .	37	. . .	. . .	. . .	69	37
N.Y.	. . .	226	. . .	. . .	2,248	337	1,537
Philadelphia	. . .	122	69	86	. . .	1,119	1,507
Md.	. . .	. . .	40	. . .	555	65	172
Va.	. . .	. . .	. . .	. . .	661	432	1,021
N.C.	. . .	. . .	. . .	. . .	65	. . .	3
Charles Town	. . .	244	. . .	. . .	774	901	1,819
Ga.	. . .	4	. . .	. . .	93	84	74
St. Augustine	. . .	3	. . .	. . .	23	. . .	. . .
Totals	287	1,056	208	470	5,241	4,527	8,558

Note: Measured in net tons of 2,000 lb.
Source: Customs records published in Department of the Census, *Historical Statistics of the United States: Colonial Times to 1957* (1960), 761.

TABLE 4.175 WHOLESALE PRICES OF COAL (PER BU. IN LOCAL MONEY) AT PHILADELPHIA, 1785–1800

1800	$ .31	1792	.21d.
1799	$ .31	1791	.18d.
1798	$ .33	1790	.16d.
1797	$ .32	1789	.15d.
1796	$ .39	1788	.14d.
1795	.28d.	1787	.17d.
1794	$ .31	1786	.17d.
1793	.22d.	1785	.17d.

Note: A bushel of coal equaled .0357% of a ton.
Source: Arthur H. Cole, *Wholesale Commodity Prices in the United States, 1700–1861* (1938), 81–124.

TABLE 4.176   BUSHELS OF COAL EXPORTED FROM UNITED STATES, 1791–1800

Year Ending Sep. 30	Coal (bu.)
1800	8,406
1799	49,275
1798	512
1797	11,432
1796	9,536
1795	3,749
1794	2,397
1793	14,719
1792	13,023
1791	3,788

Note: A bushel of coal equaled .0357% of a ton.
Source: U.S. Congress, *American State Papers: Commerce and Navigation* (1832), VII, 107–452.

to 60 feet, while those north of the James averaged 7 to 25 feet. Collieries proliferated through the Appomattox River counties of Cumberland, Buckingham, Powhatan, and Prince Edward. Virginia's rising output ended U.S. dependence on foreign coal by 1791 and made the country a net exporter of this resource.

Lead Mining

Lead mining developed slowly in the thirteen colonies because England had abundant supplies of the metal and produced regular surpluses for export. Excess English lead often arrived in America as ship ballast and became available at inexpensive prices. Imports easily met American demand for bullets, fishing sinkers, and reinforced glass panes.

For most of the colonial period, Americans were motivated to extract lead less for its own sake than because small amounts of silver could often be separated from it. A lead mine operated intermittently at Southampton, Massachusetts, for a century after 1689, but primarily for the sake of its silver content. Lead production first began in New York when Frederick Phillipse began digging ore at Westchester County in 1768, but his lease described the site as a silver mine.

TABLE 4.177   EXPORTS OF LEAD AND SHOT FROM UNITED STATES, 1790–1800

Year Ending Sep. 30	Pounds of Lead
1800	420,000
1799	6,985
1798	24,662
1797	306,189
1796	1,199,439
1795	32,911
1794	25,302
1793	2,952[a]
1792	28,756
1791	39,473[b]
1790	12,000

[a] Plus 241 pigs of lead.
[b] Plus 45 sheets of lead.
Source: U.S. Congress, *American State Papers: Commerce and Navigation* (1832), VII, 29–452.

The most productive lead mine in early America opened in 1759 on the Great Kanawha River at Montgomery County, Virginia. This mine yielded approximately 60 pounds of pure metal per 100 pounds of washed ore, but its silver content was negligible. The owners imported skilled miners from Wales and also utilized many slaves as laborers. Workers extracted ore by digging horizontal tunnels into hillsides up to a hundred yards underground. The complex also had a furnace, stamping mill, and shot tower; its output sometimes reached sixty tons of metal, but about 1782 its thirty workers were producing only half of that amount.

Many modest veins of lead were tapped during the Revolution to supply the Continental forces with bullets. Lead was briefly mined at Sturbridge, Massachusetts, (1767–ca. 1783), Middletown, Connecticut, (ca. 1776–1778), Dutchess County, New York, (ca. 1777), and Sinking Springs Valley, Pennsylvania, (ca. 1780). When peace returned, most American mines ceased operations because they were too marginal to compete with inexpensive English lead imports, although the Kanawha River mines continued making bullets and roof sheeting. The United States reverted to its former status as a net importer of lead through the 1790s and annually bought an average of 2,000,000 pounds of English pig and sheet lead, as well as large supplies of white lead for paint.

Occupations and Income

Occupational Structure

Sources abound for a comprehensive examination of the late eighteenth century's workforce, but there are few detailed studies of that period's occupational structure. This general failure to investigate the division of labor evidently stems from the erroneous assumption that because the national economy centered upon farming, non-agricultural workers comprised a numerically insignificant group. Artisans and professionals nevertheless were a large part of the rural popula-

TABLE 4.178   OCCUPATIONAL STRUCTURE OF PENNSYLVANIA ECONOMY, 1800

Occupation	Number	Percent
Farmer-yeoman	20,347	43.9%
Miscellaneous trades	6,142	13.2%
Laborer	4,301	9.3%
Carpenter	2,154	4.6%
Tailor, hatter, clothing maker	2,002	4.3%
Weaver	1,797	3.9%
Blacksmith	1,652	3.6%
Merchandising	1,457	3.1%
Miller	1,170	2.5%
Cooper	769	1.7%
Ropemaker	769	1.7%
Bricklayer, mason	707	1.5%
Innkeeper-tavernkeeper	677	1.5%
Shoemaker	671	1.4%
Metalworker	525	1.1%
Distiller, brewer	445	1.0%
Doctor, dentist	394	.9%
Wheel-wagonmaker	363	.8%

Source: Lee Soltow and Kenneth Keller, "Rural Pennsylvania in 1800: A Portrait from the Septennial Census," *Pennsylvania History* IXL (1982), 34–37.

TABLE 4.179 CRAFTSMEN AND ARTISANS IN THREE PENNSYLVANIA TOWNS, 1773–1779

Occupations	Lancaster, 1773 Number	(%)	Germantown, 1774 Number	(%)	York, 1779 Number	(%)
Shoemakers	31	(6.7%)	14	(2.9%)	17	(4.4%)
Carpenters/joiners	28	(6.1%)	7	(1.5%)	15	(3.9%)
Masons/brickmen	22	(4.8%)	4	(.8%)	6	(1.6%)
Tailors	19	(4.1%)	6	(1.2%)	17	(4.4%)
Weavers	16	(3.5%)	9	(1.9%)	9	(2.3%)
Coopers	15	(3.3%)	14	(2.9%)	6	(1.6%)
Butchers	14	(3.0%)	6	(1.2%)	9	(2.3%)
Blacksmiths	13	(2.8%)	4	(.8%)	11	(2.3%)
Tanners	10	(2.2%)	9	(1.9%)	11	(2.8%)
Potter/turner/ glaziers	10	(2.2%)	2	(.4%)	9	(2.3%)
Sadlers	9	(2.0%)	5	(1.0%)	16	(4.1%)
Bakers	9	(2.0%)	. . .	. . .	4	(1.0%)
Tabacconists	8	(1.7%)	1	(.2%)	6	(1.6%)
Hatters	7	(1.5%)	4	(.8%)	9	(2.3%)
Stockingmakers	7	(1.5%)	. . .	. . .	7	(1.8%)
Skinners/curriers	5	(1.1%)	4	(.8%)	2	(.5%)
Wheelwrights	5	(1.1%)	3	(.6%)	1	(.3%)
Wagoners	5	(1.1%)	. . .	. . .	7	(1.8%)
Distillers/brewers	5	(1.1%)	. . .	. . .	4	(1.0%)
Gunsmiths	4	(.9%)	. . .	. . .	6	(1.6%)
Miscellaneous crafts	28	(6.1%)	12	(2.5%)	30	(7.8%)
Laborers	39	(8.5%)	3	(.6%)	10	(2.6%)
All Taxpayers	461	(100%)	481	(100%)	385	(100%)

Source: William H. Egle, et al., eds., *Pennsylvania Archives,* 3d ser., 30 vols. (1897–1899), XIV, 334–45; XVII, 454–65; XXI, 3–11.

TABLE 4.180 OCCUPATIONAL STRUCTURE OF PHILADELPHIA TAXPAYERS, 1772–1798

Occupational Group	1772	1774	1780	1789	1798
Government	1.1%	1.3%	2.4%	.5%	1.7%
Services	49.6%	48.2%	54.3%	59.4%	53.3%
Professional	3.6%	2.9%	2.6%	3.9%	5.0%
Retail and local wholesale	6.0%	6.8%	10.3%	11.8%	10.9%
Retail crafts	17.0%	17.4%	23.4%	23.1%	17.9%
Building crafts	11.2%	9.7%	7.1%	9.7%	11.3%
Travel and transport	10.0%	10.3%	9.4%	8.2%	6.0%
Other services	1.8%	1.1%	1.4%	2.7%	2.2%
Industrial	15.8%	17.0%	17.8%	16.4%	12.7%
Textile	1.3%	2.5%	2.4%	1.2%	.2%
Leather and fur working	1.9%	2.6%	3.2%	2.6%	1.8%
Food and drink processing	1.3%	1.3%	1.2%	1.7%	.9%
Shipbuilding and fitting	4.1%	4.2%	1.9%	1.1%	1.6%
Metal crafts	2.9%	2.3%	4.0%	3.6%	3.4%
Furniture making	1.4%	.8%	1.6%	1.5%	1.8%
Other crafts	3.0%	3.2%	3.4%	4.8%	3.0%
Commerce	25.9%	20.0%	18.1%	16.7%	27.1%
Mariners	10.6%	7.5%	5.1%	2.0%	5.2%
Merchants and clerks	15.3%	12.0%	13.0%	14.7%	21.9%
Laborers	7.6%	13.9%	7.4%	7.0%	5.1%

Source: Billy G. Smith, *The "Lower Sort": Philadelphia's Laboring People, 1750–1800* (1990), 214.

tion; they probably equaled a fifth of all inhabitants in the northern countryside, while in some districts, such as Lancaster and Chester counties in Pennsylvania, 30% of adult males had non-agricultural skills. The diversity of trades was likewise impressive, with some areas of the hinterland, such as Chester County, Pennsylvania, furnishing a market for sixty-five different occupations or professions. By 1790, for example, Kentucky frontiersmen were carrying on a greater number of industries than had been pursued in New York City in the 1760s.

More is known about the division of labor within Revolutionary cities, but even so the occupational structures of relatively few urban communities have been examined in depth. The workforces in these cities, virtually all of which were seaports, were predominantly engaged in foreign trade, construction, and various service businesses, rather than manufacturing. The number and type of crafts pursued in larger towns grew progressively varied and sophisticated, as economic growth permitted an increasing number of people to acquire luxuries such as musical instruments, watches, books for light reading, candies, and various metalwares.

Incomes

Most Anglo-Americans earned high incomes by eighteenth-century standards. Median annual incomes, on a per capita basis, have been estimated at a minimum of £10 sterling for the 1770s. According to calculations by Edwin Perkins in *The Economy of Colonial America,* a yearly cash flow of £10, combined with exceptionally low tax rates, would have supported a standard of living perhaps 10% higher than that enjoyed by residents of Great Britain itself, where incomes seem to have been double those earned in the majority of countries at that time.

TABLE 4.181 ESTIMATED INCOMES FOR 300 DAYS' WORK IN UNITED STATES, 1765–1775

	Local Money	Sterling
Rice planter with 40 slaves	£1,155	£700
Tobacco planter with 20 slaves	£330	£200
Anglican minister, Va.	£160–£200	£97–£121
Professor, private academy	£135	£81
Minister, New England, with house	£70	£42
Carpenter (with victuals provided)	£74	£45
(providing own victuals)	£122	£60
Merchant's clerk	£66–£82	£40–£50
Average craftsman (with victuals provided)	£41–£62	£25–£30
(providing own victuals)	£66–£74	£40–£45
Tutor, Va. plantation, with bed and board	£60	£35
Farmer in Chesapeake	£50	£30
Grammar-school teacher	£40	£24
Country schoolteacher	£20–£70	£12–£42
Storekeeper, hired with victuals and board	£25–£40	£15–£24
Urban unskilled laborer (food provided)	£25	£15
Farm laborer, New England (with food)	£18	£13.10.0
South (with food)	£16	£10
Pennsylvania (with food)	£17–£25	£10–£16
Farmer in middle colonies, cash earned	£16–£24	£10–£15
Tenant in N.Y., cash earned	£16	£10
Mass. farmer, cash earned	£16	£10

Note: When both currencies are not given in source, local currency has been calculated at £165 to £100 sterling.
Source: Jackson T. Main, *The Social Structure of Revolutionary America* (1965), 68–114.

TABLE 4.182 AVERAGE ANNUAL WAGES (LOCAL CURRENCY) IN PHILADELPHIA, 1762–1800

Year	Seaman	Ship's Mate	Laborer	Journeyman Shoemaker	Tailor
1800	£101.12	£139.3	£95.16	£96.	£83.7
1799	£75.7	£165.7	£116.10	£78.	£63.9
1798	£119.11	£139.3	£116.10	£107.	£68.8
1797	£88.9	£145.8	£105.6	£157.	£62.4
1796	£128.6	£130.8	£100.13	£99.	£69.13
1795	£105.19	£134.16	£102.18	£130.	£56.
1794	£123.18	. . .	£84.12	£64.	£76.10
1793	£58.16	£78.	£61.10	£142.	£51.
1792	£46.3	£59.6	£70.8	£39.	£67.16
1791	£37.8	£58	£50.17	£33.	£51.
1790	£37.8	£58	£52.1	£29.	£62.4
1789	. . .	. . .	£69.4	£38.	£49.3
1788	. . .	. . .	£61.10	£43.	£52.5
1787	£38.18	£58.	£71.	£35.	£48.10
1786	£39.17	£69.18	£74.10	£33.	£51.

Year	Seaman	Ship's Mate	Laborer	Journeyman Shoemaker	Tailor
1785	£39.17	£81.2	£65.1	£49.	£52.5
1784	£52.19	£86.15	£73.19	£59.	£77.3
1783	. . .	. . .	. . .	£53.	£82.2
1776	. . .	. . .	£55.	£43.	£64.14
1775	. . .	. . .	£43.15	£53.	£62.4
1774	. . .	. . .	£46.14	£59.	£59.14
1773	. . .	. . .	£40.4	. . .	£61.12
1772	. . .	. . .	£48.10	£63.	£60.19
1771	. . .	. . .	£51.9	£65.	£60.19
1770	£36.19	£53.13	£52.13	£56.	£60.7
1769	. . .	. . .	£49.14	. . .	£60.7
1768	£39.7	£58.	£59.14	. . .	£61.12
1767	£39.17	£58.	£62.2	. . .	£61.12
1766	£38.8	£58.	£62.2	. . .	£60.19
1765	£38.8	£58.	£54.8	. . .	£60.19
1764	£40.7	£56.16	£50.17	. . .	£61.12
1763	£32.13	£58.	£53.4	. . .	£62.4
1762	£48.12	£62.8	£59.3	£61.	£62.4

Note: Incomes are maximum amount likely to be earned from full-time work for a year.
Source: Adapted from indexed wages in Billy G. Smith, *The "Lower Sort:" Philadelphia's Laboring People, 1750–1800* (1990), 101–21.

When converted into modern monetary values, median, per capita annual income for white Americans in the Revolutionary era approximated $900, compared to a median income of $11,700 for the white population in 1985. Slaves then probably received food, shelter, garments, and medical attention worth about £7, or $630, each,

TABLE 4.183 DAILY WAGE RATES (IN DOLLARS) IN PHILADELPHIA, 1790–1800

Year	Laborer	House Carpenter	Ship Carpenter	Joiner	Rigger	Ship Captain	Seaman
1800	$1.00	$1.41	$2.00	$1.66	$1.50	$1.67	$.73
1799	$1.00	$1.33	$2.00	$1.66	$1.50	$1.67	$.57
1798	$1.00	. . .	$2.00	$1.66	$1.50	$1.67	$.90
1797	$1.00	. . .	$2.00	$1.66	. . .	$1.67	$.67
1796	$1.00	$1.44	$2.13	$1.66	. . .	$1.67	$.97
1795	$1.00	. . .	$2.00	$1.66	$1.33	. . .	$.80
1794	$1.00	$1.06	$1.86	$1.50	$1.13	. . .	$.93
1793	$.80	. . .	$1.50	$1.25	$1.00	. . .	. . .
1792	$.66	. . .	$1.20	. . .	$.80	. . .	. . .
1791	$.53	. . .	$1.16	$1.00	$1.00	. . .	. . .
1790	$.50	$1.06	$1.06	$1.00	$1.00	. . .	. . .

Source: Donald R. Adams, Jr., *Wage Rates in Philadelphia, 1790–1830* (1975), 202–204, 213.

compared to median income of $6,900 for African Americans in 1985. Although such comparisons make eighteenth-century incomes seem tiny relative to modern times by distorting changes in living standards and consumer prices, it is significant that per capita American income about 1775 already stood at a higher level than currently prevails in most nations in the late twentieth century, when average incomes outside of Europe generally fall between $500 and $900 per head. Americans, including African Americans, were already affluent by world standards in the late 1700s, and their incomes have risen almost thirteen times over since then.

TABLE 4.184 WAGES OF AGRICULTURAL LABORERS IN THE UNITED STATES, 1800

	N.Y.	New England	N.J. and Pa.
By the Month			
Summer	1s., 5d.	2s.	2s.
Winter	1s., 1d.	1s., 1d.	1s., 9½d.
By the Day	2s.	2s., 7d.	2s., 3d.
Foreman's Pay, per Year	£14	£18.15s.	£24

Source: William Strickland, *Observations on the Agriculture of the United States of America* (1801), 28.

TABLE 4.185 WAGES OF AGRICULTURAL LABORERS IN MD., 1760–1800

	Male Laborers		Female Laborers		Monthly Value of Room & Board
	Daily	Monthly	Daily	Monthly	
1800	. . .	. . .	. . .	. . .	$6.00
1799	. . .	. . .	. . .	. . .	. . .
1798	. . .	. . .	. . .	. . .	. . .
1797	. . .	. . .	. . .	. . .	. . .
1796	$.50–66	$14.00–16.00	. . .	. . .	$8.00
1795	$.77	. . .	. . .	. . .	$7.00
1794	$.50–66	. . .	. . .	. . .	. . .
1793	$.47	. . .	. . .	. . .	. . .
1792	$.47	. . .	. . .	. . .	$11.80
1791	$.40–50	. . .	. . .	. . .	$9.90
1790	. . .	. . .	. . .	. . .	$12.00
1789	. . .	. . .	. . .	. . .	. . .
1788	. . .	. . .	. . .	. . .	. . .
1787	. . .	. . .	. . .	$4.00	. . .
1786	. . .	. . .	. . .	$4.00	. . .
1785	. . .	. . .	. . .	$4.00	. . .
1784	. . .	$5.33	. . .	$3.33	. . .
1783	. . .	$4.66–6.66	. . .	$3.33	. . .
1782	. . .	$4.00–5.35	. . .	$3.33	. . .
1781	. . .	$4.00–5.33	. . .	$3.33	. . .
1780	. . .	$5.33	. . .	$3.33	. . .
1779	$.67	$5.33	. . .	$3.33	. . .
1778	. . .	$5.33	. . .	$3.33	. . .
1777	$.50	$5.33–8.00	. . .	$3.33	. . .
1776	. . .	$5.33–6.66	. . .	$3.33	. . .
1775	. . .	$5.33	. . .	$3.33	. . .
1774	. . .	$5.33	. . .	$3.33	. . .
1773	$.27–40	$4.44–5.33	. . .	$3.33	. . .
1772	$.27	$4.66–6.66	. . .	$3.33	. . .
1771	$.27–67	$4.66–8.88	. . .	$3.33	$1.31
1770	$.27–40	$4.00–4.44	. . .	$3.33	$1.31
1769	$.27–47	$4.00–9.33	. . .	$3.33	$3.55
1768	. . .	$5.55–6.66	. . .	. . .	$3.10
1767	$.27–53	$5.33–8.00	. . .	$3.33	$3.55
1766	$.53	. . .	. . .	. . .	$.98
1765	$.27–40	. . .	$.20	. . .	$.98
1764	$.33–43	$5.33–10.66	$.20	. . .	$2.66
1763	$.33–40	$8.00–10.63	$.20	. . .	. . .
1762	$.33–40	$8.66	$.17–20	. . .	. . .
1761	$.40	$5.33–9.66	. . .	. . .	. . .
1760	$.33	$6.66–10.00	. . .	. . .	. . .

Source: Donald R. Adams, Jr., "One Hundred Years of Prices and Wages: Maryland, 1750–1850," *Working Papers of the Regional Economic History Research Center* V (1982), 97, 98, 106, 107.

TABLE 4.186 ANNUAL SALARIES OF FEDERAL EMPLOYEES, 1789–1800

President	$25,000
Vice President	$5,000
Secretaries of State and Treasury	$3,500 through 1798, $5,000 after 1799
Secretaries of War and Navy	$3,000 through 1798, $4,500 after 1799
Attorney General	$1,500 in 1789
	$1,900 from 1791 through 1794
	$2,400 from 1795 through 1798
	$3,000 after 1799
Postmaster General	$1,500 from 1789 to 1791
	$2,000 from 1792 through 1793
	$2,400 from 1794 through 1798
	$3,000 in 1799
Chief Justice	$4,000 through 1819
Associate Justices	$3,500 through 1819
District Judges	$1,000 through 1819
Congressmen	$6 per day
Senators	$6 per day 1789–1794, 1796–1816 (temporarily raised to $7 in 1795)
Territorial Governor	$2,000 in 1790
Governor's Secretary	$750 in 1790
Chief Clerk, Cabinet Officer	$600 in 1790
Clerk, Cabinet Officer	$500 in 1790
Lieutenant Colonel, Army	$600 in 1790
Captain, Army	$420 in 1790
Surgeon, Army	$540 in 1790
Sergeant, Army	$72 in 1790, plus $43.80 in rations
Private, Army	$48 in 1790, plus $43.80 in rations

Source: Erik W. Austin, *Political Facts of the United States Since 1789* (1986), 58, 59. U.S. Congress, *American State Papers: Finance* (1834), I, 33–35.

The most salient aspect of American trade was the recurring surplus of imports over exports. The thirteen colonies purchased 30% more goods from abroad than they sent overseas, and imports to the United States averaged about 25% higher than exports during the 1790s. The net balance of payments (or current account of financial

At locations like the docks by Philadelphia's Arch Street Ferry, as sketched above in 1800, American commodities flowed to world markets and helped equalize the country's balance of trade. The United States was the only former European colony that achieved true economic independence by developing a merchant marine capable of carrying on its own foreign trade. (I. N. Phelps Stokes Collection, Miriam & Ira Wallach Div. of Arts, Prints and Photographs. Courtesy The New York Public Library. Astor, Lenox and Tilden Foundations.)

International Trade and the Balance of Payments

International trade constituted about 15% of gross national product for the thirteen colonies by 1770. Official statistics for oceanic commerce are very uneven for the last dozen years of colonial rule and almost nonexistent for the period of the Articles of Confederation, but they become reasonably accurate with the inception of the federal government, in particular after 1795. As a result, it is only for the years 1768–1772 and 1790–1800 that sufficient data exists, or has been reconstructed, to calculate the volume of overseas trade and the net international balance of payments.

TABLE 4.187 AVERAGE YEARLY BALANCE OF TRADE AND FINANCIAL TRANSACTIONS FOR THE THIRTEEN COLONIES, IN POUNDS STERLING, 1768–1772

	Debit	Credit
Merchandise Trade		
Exports[a]	. . .	£2,800,000
Imports[b]	£3,920,000	. . .
Sales of ships	. . .	£140,000
Slave purchases	£200,000	. . .
Indentured servants	£80,000	. . .
Earnings on Foreign Trade		
Shipping earnings	. . .	£600,000
Fees, risk, insurance	. . .	£220,000
British Government Expenditures		
Taxes and duties	£40,000	. . .
Civil service salaries	. . .	£40,000
Army expenditures	. . .	£230,000
Navy expenditures	. . .	£170,000
Total debit	£4,240,000	. . .
Total credit	. . .	£4,200,000
Net imbalance (short-term loans)	£40,000	. . .

[a]Value exclusive of shipping, insurance, and merchandising costs.
[b]Value includes cost of oceanic shipping and insurance.
Source: Gary M. Walton and James F. Shepherd. *The Economic Rise of Early America* (1979), 101.

transactions) was nevertheless much more narrow because of credits earned by the merchant community and the shipping industry. These "invisible earnings" (so called because they went unrecorded by customs officials) offset most of the deficit in the merchandise trade account, and under normal circumstances they kept the inflow and outflow of financial credits from seaborne commerce in rough equilibrium.

During the late colonial era, the American balance of payments seems to have registered very small deficits that were met through short-term loans borrowed from British merchants. Because the American merchant marine experienced a sharp reduction in the Revolution and lost its former trading privileges within the British Empire, the U.S. balance of payments swung into a deep deficit in the 1780s when the country could no longer offset import purchases with shipping and other invisible earnings. As American commerce revived after 1789, especially after Jay's Treaty of 1795 led to increasing trade with the British Empire, shipping earnings rose steadily and reduced the deficit in the balance of payments.

By the late 1790s, invisible earnings were again compensating for the surplus of imports over exports. The nation's overall balance of payments nevertheless remained slightly in deficit because Europeans held a substantial part of the national debt, and the treasury was obliged to pay them a yearly average of more than $5 million in interest from 1796 to 1800. Had $50.3 million in interest not been deposited in European coffers, the net balance of payments for the United States would have registered an inflow of $20.5 million in currency credits from 1790 to 1800. By 1800, therefore, the United States earned slightly more than it spent from overseas commerce and would have experienced a net balance of international payments except for the large amounts of interest owed to European owners of U.S. bonds.

TABLE 4.188 FOREIGN TRADE OF THIRTEEN COLONIES (IN POUNDS STERLING), 1768–1772

	With Britain and Ireland		With Southern Europe		With West Indies	
	Imports	Exports	Imports	Exports	Imports	Exports
From New England						
1772	£912,000	£78,000	£20,000	£59,000	£403,000	£347,000
1771	£1,446,000	£88,000	£15,000	£78,000	£322,000	£319,000
1770	£457,000	£96,000	£14,000	£62,000	£350,000	£318,000
1769	£228,000	£90,000	£26,000	£70,000	£362,000	£281,000
1768	£441,000	£89,000	£15,000	£62,000	£258,000	£252,000
From Mid-Atlantic						
1772	£979,000	£105,000	£32,000	£237,000	£321,000	£344,000
1771	£1,551,000	£127,000	£22,000	£146,000	£185,000	£253,000
1770	£717,000	£139,000	£43,000	£214,000	£307,000	£255,000
1769	£325,000	£120,000	£30,000	£225,000	£290,000	£207,000
1768	£1,005,000	£155,000	£35,000	£103,000	£169,000	£162,000
From Upper South						
1772	£1,100,000	£1,003,000	£10,000	£96,000	£134,000	£120,000
1771	£1,339,000	£1,081,000	£10,000	£65,000	£115,000	£110,000
1770	£1,117,000	£951,000	£5,000	£116,000	£112,000	£102,000
1769	£774,000	£990,000	£14,000	£153,000	£104,000	£95,000
1768	£728,000	£784,000	£15,000	£72,000	£82,000	£73,000
From Lower South						
1772	£635,000	£637,000	£9,000	£32,000	£83,000	£129,000
1771	£572,000	£446,000	£7,000	£32,000	£53,000	£115,000
1770	£261,000	£340,000	£7,000	£67,000	£94,000	£127,000
1769	£429,000	£379,000	£5,000	£69,000	£64,000	£103,000
1768	£399,000	£380,000	£6,000	£73,000	£47,000	£85,000

(continued)

TABLE 4.188   (continued)

	With Britain and Ireland		With Southern Europe		With West Indies	
	Imports	Exports	Imports	Exports	Imports	Exports
	Total					
1772	£3,626,000	£1,823,000	£71,000	£424,000	£941,000	£940,000
1771	£4,908,000	£1,742,000	£54,000	£321,000	£675,000	£797,000
1770	£2,552,000	£1,526,000	£69,000	£459,000	£863,000	£802,000
1769	£1,756,000	£1,579,000	£75,000	£517,000	£820,000	£686,000
1768	£2,573,000	£1,408,000	£71,000	£310,000	£556,000	£572,000

Source: James F. Shepherd and Gary M. Walton, *Shipping, Maritime Trade, and the Economic Development of Colonial North America* (1972), 115.

TABLE 4.189   TRADE OF THE UNITED STATES WITH ENGLAND AND SCOTLAND, 1776–1791

Year	New England	Mid-Atlantic Colonies	Va., Md.	Carolinas and Ga.	Total
1791					
Imports	£588,739	£1,528,900	£1,548,220	£557,590	£4,223,449
Exports	£79,214	£218,647	£572,274	£324,044	£1,194,179
1790					
Imports	£339,973	£1,263,949	£1,389,257	£438,601	£3,431,780
Exports	£100,864	£171,702	£566,774	£351,731	£1,191,071
1789					
Imports	£350,118	£784,657	£912,468	£448,179	£2,495,422
Exports	£90,392	£135,849	£539,355	£284,594	£1,050,190
1788					
Imports	£233,690	£543,178	£766,282	£343,002	£1,886,152
Exports	£67,146	£144,655	£504,672	£307,316	£1,023,789
1787					
Imports	£201,375	£570,726	£905,764	£336,247	£2,014,112
Exports	£67,696	£121,956	£423,335	£280,648	£893,635
1786					
Imports	£126,833	£437,885	£824,821	£213,927	£1,603,466
Exports	£45,392	£98,127	£451,671	£247,930	£843,120
1785					
Imports	£163,349	£774,979	£1,015,103	£354,595	£2,308,026
Exports	£56,648	£119,378	£443,581	£273,990	£893,597
1784					
Imports	£526,561	£1,399,039	£1,272,346	£540,065	£3,738,011
Exports	£51,079	£117,566	£390,251	£190,434	£749,330
1783					
Imports	£202,556	£848,410	£219,834	£273,065	£1,543,865
Exports	£26,526	£133,633	£105,063	£83,506	£348,728
1782					
Imports	. . .	£230,566	. . .	£70,083	£300,649
Exports	. . .	£114,517	. . .	£20,986	£135,503
1781					
Imports	. . .	£604,196	. . .	£391,255	£995,941
Exports	£2,068	£35,771	. . .	£106,318	£144,157
1780					
Imports	. . .	£570,307	. . .	£426,441	£996,748
Exports	£2,232	£76,539	£15,296	£4,180	£98,247
1779					
Imports	. . .	£412,217	. . .	£206	£412,423
Exports	£808	£49,247	. . .	£4,339	£54,394

Year	New England	Mid-Atlantic Colonies	Va., Md.	Carolinas and Ga.	Total
1778					
Imports	. . .	£69,196	. . .	. . .	£69,196
Exports	£372	£37,551	£1,177	£3,428	£42,528
1777					
Imports	. . .	£92,848	. . .	. . .	£92,848
Exports	£1,880	£11,608	£888	£2,234	£16,610
1776					
Imports	£55,955	£365	. . .	. . .	£56,320
Exports	£762	£3,739	£155,004	£26,311	£185,816

Note: Data is in official sterling values as arbitrarily assigned by Customs Service, not market valuation of merchandise.
Source: Jacob M. Price, "New Time Series for Scotland's and Britain's Trade with the Thirteen Colonies and States, 1740–1791," *William and Mary Quarterly* XXXII (1975), 322–25.

TABLE 4.190   UNITED STATES TRADE WITH FRANCE (IN LIVRES), 1775–1794

Year	Imports	Exports	Balance to U.S.
1794	6,735,000 liv.	94,454,789 liv.	+ 87,719,789 liv.
1793	4,732,000 liv.	55,985,330 liv.	+ 51,253,330 liv.
1792[b]	5,622,000 liv.	25,098,000 liv.	+ 19,476,000 liv.[a]
1791	1,476,000 liv.	23,643,000 liv.	+ 22,167,000 liv.[a]
1790	1,937,000 liv.	9,842,000 liv.	+ 7,905,000 liv.
1789	1,719,000 liv.	9,653,000 liv.	+ 7,934,000 liv.
1788	1,888,000 liv.	9,705,000 liv.	+ 7,817,000 liv.
1787	1,815,000 liv.	9,595,000 liv.	+ 7,780,000 liv.
1786	1,781,000 liv.	9,476,000 liv.	+ 7,695,000 liv.
1785	1,778,000 liv.	9,211,000 liv.	+ 7,433,000 liv.
1784[b]	1,678,000 liv.	9,110,000 liv.	+ 7,432,000 liv.
1783	11,723,000 liv.	3,615,000 liv.	− 8,108,000 liv.
1782	11,520,000 liv.	3,498,000 liv.	− 8,022,000 liv.
1781	11,197,000 liv.	3,369,000 liv.	− 7,828,000 liv.
1780	3,371,000 liv.	2,640,000 liv.	− 731,000 liv.
1779	3,152,000 liv.	2,427,000 liv.	− 725,000 liv.
1778	3,080,000 liv.	2,310,000 liv.	− 770,000 liv.
1777	5,394,000 liv.	3,432,000 liv.	− 1,862,000 liv.
1776	5,362,000 liv.	3,370,000 liv.	− 1,992,000 liv.
1775	5,250,000 liv.	3,145,000 liv.	− 2,105,000 liv.

[a] In 1791 and 1792, $1.00 equaled 5.5 livres.
[b] From 1784 to 1792, U.S. exports to the French West Indies totaled 11,362,387 livres, while U.S. imports from there equaled 4,987,684 livres.
Source: Edmond Buron, "Statistics on Franco-American Trade, 1778–1806," *Journal of Economic and Business History* IV (1932), 579.

TABLE 4.191 ANNUAL AVERAGE EXPORTS OF MAJOR COMMODITIES FROM THE THIRTEEN COLONIES, 1768–1772, AND UNITED STATES, 1790–1792

Commodity	Quantity	% of all Exports	Value in Sterling of 1768–72	Value in U.S. Dollars of 1790–92
Beef and Pork[a]	(barrels)			
1768–72	26,036	1.8%	£51,000	[$209,000]
1790–92	90,198	3.3%	[£159,000]	$652,000
Bread and Flour[b]	(tons)			
1768–72	38,634	14.6%	£410,000	[$2,534,000]
1790–92	67,079	22.6%	[£712,000]	$4,399,000
Live Cattle	(number)			
1768–72	3,433	0.75%	£21,000	[$63,000]
1790–92	4,861	0.5%	[£29,000]	$89,000
Corn	(bushels)			
1768–72	·839,314	3.0%	£83,000	[$424,000]
1790–92	1,926,784	5.0%	[£191,000]	$974,000
Cotton	(pounds)			
1768–72	29,425	0.04%	£1,000	[$7,000]
1790–92	163,822	2.0%	[£8,000]	$41,000
Dried Fish	(quintals)			
1768–72	308,993	5.5%	£154,000	[$740,000]
1790–92	375,619	4.6%	[£187,000]	$900,000
Flaxseed	(bushels)			
1768–72	233,065	1.5%	£42,000	[$189,000]
1790–92	352,079	1.5%	[£64,000]	$268,000
Horses	(number)			
1768–72	6,0488	2.1%	£60,000	[$240,000]
1790–92	7,086	1.5%	[£71,000]	$282,000
Indigo	(pounds)			
1768–72	547,649	4.0%	£113,000	[$567,000]
1790–92	493,760	2.6%	[£101,000]	$511,000
Bar Iron	(tons)			
1768–72	2,416	1.3%	£36,000	[$195,000]
1790–92	300	0.1%	[£4,000]	$24,000
Pig Iron	(tons)			
1768–72	4,468	0.8%	£22,000	[$116,000]
1790–92	3,667	0.5%	[£18,000]	$95,000
Pitch	(barrels)			
1768–72	11,384	0.2%	£5,000	[$21,000]
1790–92	7,279	0.1%	[£3,000]	$13,000

Commodity	Quantity	% of all Exports	Value in Sterling of 1768–72	Value in U.S. Dollars of 1790–92
Potash	(tons)			
1768–72	1,381	1.2%	£35,000	[$134,000]
1790–92	4,872	2.4%	[£123,000]	$472,000
Pine Boards	(feet)			
1768–72	38,991,000	2.5%	£70,000	[$228,000]
1790–92	45,118,000	1.4%	[£81,000]	$264,000
Rice	(barrels)			
1768–72	140,254	11.0%	£311,000	[$1,971,000]
1790–92	129,367	9.0%	[£287,000]	$1,818,000
Rum	(gallons)			
1768–72	935,000	1.9%	£52,600	[$315,600]
1790–92	441,782	0.9%	[£28,000]	$170,000
Staves, Headings	(number)			
1768–72	21,585,000	2.3%	£65,000	[$275,000]
1790–92	31,554,000	2.1%	[£95,000]	$401,000
Tar	(barrels)			
1768–72	90,472	1.2%	£34,000	[$135,000]
1790–92	68,463	0.5%	[£25,000]	$102,000
Tobacco	(hogsheads)			
1768–72	87,986	27.0%	£766,000	[$3,093,000]
1790–92	110,687	20.0%	[£964,000]	$3,891,000
Turpentine	(barrels)			
1768–72	19,870	0.3%	£9,000	[$42,000]
1790–92	51,194	0.6%	[£24,000]	$108,000
Whale Oil	(tons)			
1768–72	3,841	1.6%	£46,000	[$212,000]
1790–92	1,826	0.5%	[£22,000]	$101,000
Wheat	(bushels)			
1768–72	599,127	4.1%	£115,000	[$654,000]
1790–92	998,862	5.6%	[£192,000]	$1,090,000
Total, Above Commodities				
1768–72	. . .	88.2%	£2,471,000	[$12,181,000]
1790–92	. . .	85.7%	[£3,388,000]	$16,683,000
All Exports				
1768–72	. . .	100.0%	£2,802,000	. . .
1790–92	. . .	100.0%	. . .	$19,465,000

[a] Not differentiated for 1768–72. Exports for 1790–92 included 60,457 bbl. of beef ($367,000) and 29,741 bbl. of pork ($285,000).
[b] Not differentiated for 1768–72. Exports for 1790–92 included 3,823 tons of bread ($221,000) and 63,256 tons of flour ($4,178,000).
Source: Gary M. Walton and James F. Shepherd, *The Economic Rise of Early America* (1979), 194.

TABLE 4.192 VALUE AND DESTINATION OF UNITED STATES EXPORTS, 1790–1800

	1800	1799	1798	1797	1796	1795	1794	1793	1792	1791	1790
England	$15,879,196	$15,120,622	$9,479,137	$5,022,568	$15,244,460	$5,045,296	$4,481,912	$5,171,014	$4,110,156	$4,425,316	$6,888,979
Scotland	$1,688,600	$2,125,534	$1,550,320	$562,611	$459,118	$173,786	$148,315	$180,837	$258,538	$520,080	. . .
Ireland	$1,517,867	$1,684,372	$949,413	$1,052,044	$1,449,735	$1,104,984	$723,679	$895,573	$1,070,642	$961,052	. . .
British West Indies	$6,404,785	$6,285,254	$4,283,940	$2,149,025	$5,446,559	$2,634,664	$2,048,388	$1,855,307	$2,144,638	$1,723,266	$2,077,757
Canada and Fisheries	$694,446	$612,198	$623,572	$404,896	$422,496	$259,810	$72,059	$202,043	$243,429	$297,745	$279,826
British East Indies	$130,461	$7,296	$39,075	$21,325	$66,316	. . .	$21,192	. . .	$31,043	. . .	. . .
Gibraltar	$865,957	$528,142	$225,067	$1,866[a]	$85,861[a]	. . .	$10,940	$53,178	$23,465	$25,959	. . .
Cape of Good Hope	$128,977	$183,569	$33,823	. . .	. . .	. . .	. . .	. . .	. . .	. . .	. . .
Total British Empire	$27,310,289	$26,546,987	$17,184,347	$9,214,335	$23,174,545	$9,218,540	$7,506,485	$8,357,952	$7,881,911	$7,953,418	$9,246,562
France	$40,400	. . .	$1,476,588	$3,825,231	$3,171,759	$7,698,683	$1,138,866	$1,934,395	$1,500,561	$806,882	$1,384,246
French West Indies	$5,123,433	$2,776,604	$5,344,690	$8,565,053	$8,408,936	$4,954,952	$3,607,934	$5,058,485	$3,705,918	$3,465,694	$3,284,656
Bourbon and Mauritius	. . .	$3,900	$147,718	$58,792	$42,609[a]	. . .[a]	. . .	. . .	. . .	. . .	. . .
French Fisheries	. . .	. . .	. . .	. . .	. . .	. . .	$6,000	$7,987	$37,064	$26,186	$4,668,902
Total French Empire	$5,163,833	$2,780,504	$6,968,996	$12,449,076	$11,623,304	$12,653,635	$4,752,800	$7,000,867	$5,243,543	$4,298,762	$4,668,902

(continued)

TABLE 4.192 (continued)

	1800	1799	1798	1797	1796	1795	1794	1793	1792	1791	1790
Spain	$4,743,678	$4,237,954	$2,274,223	$1,812,558	$1,324,060	$2,253,754	$2,648,464	$1,859,489	$1,602,258	$1,172,563	$1,841,614
Spanish Wine Islands	$303,630	$154,517	$96,486	$50,208	$29,202	$8,128	$8,504	$1,664	$54,149	$38,276	. . .
Spanish West Indies	$8,270,400	$8,993,401	$5,082,127	$3,595,519	$1,821,347	$1,389,219	$872,616	$159,426	$112,493	$65,221	$147,807
Florida and Louisiana	$2,035,789	$3,504,092	$1,074,947	$1,044,367	$475,992	$1,113,763	$222,811	$164,475	$36,544	$25,227	. . .
Other Spanish Colonies	$307,109	$531,438	$218,116	$129,700	$77	. . .	. . .	. . .	. . .	. . .	. . .
Total Spanish Empire	$15,660,606	$17,421,402	$8,745,899	$6,632,352	$3,650,678	$4,764,864	$3,752,395	$2,185,054	$1,805,444	$1,301,287	$1,989,421
Portugal	$448,548	$538,662	$286,781	$229,750	$142,567	$549,801	$661,890	$744,182	$724,654	$581,711	$1,051,830
Portuguese Wine Islands	$817,296	$319,069	$443,108	$244,264	$416,881	$214,474	$143,567	$250,528	$252,500	$457,985	$231,632
Total Portuguese Empire	$1,265,844	$857,731	$729,889	$474,014	$559,448	$764,275[a]	$805,457	$994,710	$977,154	$1,039,696	$1,283,462
Dutch West Indies	$1,296,052	$5,154,535	$2,720,969	$1,903,638	$1,758,548	$962,705	$1,111,386	$1,073,555	$955,141	$697,948	$649,395
Swedish West Indies	$471,343	$629,526	$631,805	$922,673	$1,078,787	$871,288	$368,945	$248,715	$5,130	$6,995	$4,259
Danish West Indies	$1,757,589	$3,397,262	$1,513,104	$2,453,606	$2,553,810	$1,659,306	$811,562	$545,650	$194,126	$198,782	$209,444
West Indies, generally	$115,631	$92,020	$248,121	$1,534,734	$3,367,942	$1,543,348	$823,219	$399,559	$295,102	$59,434	. . .
Total	$3,640,615	$9,273,343	$5,113,999	$6,814,651	$8,759,087	$5,036,647	$3,115,112	$2,267,479	$1,449,499	$963,159	$863,098
Russia	. . .	$46,330	$60,030	$3,450	$47,381	$69,221	$90,388	$5,769	. . .	$3,570	. . .
German Ports	$8,068,877	$17,867,093	$14,605,069	$11,953,017	$9,507,457	$9,655,524	$4,498,992	$1,805,884	$646,117	$426,270	$492,348
Sweden, Denmark, Norway	$448,195	$1,055,648	$1,501,915	$183,703	$439,399	$326,519	$418,138	$354,605	$300,103	$93,363	$57,953
Netherlands	$4,372,964	$696,968	$4,713,976	$7,713,976	$6,083,491	$1,917,336	$4,048,544	$1,953,751	$1,600,595	$915,762	$1,276,585
Italy	$2,689,968	$1,157,212	$1,334,036	$767,064	$1,100,522	$1,223,150	$145,673	$214,840	$94,124	$31,727	$41,298
Europe, generally	$35,389	$11,818	$74,858	$207,077	$481,725	$684,127	. . .	. . .	. . .	. . .	. . .
Total Europe	$15,615,393	$20,835,069	$22,289,884	$20,828,287	$17,659,975	$13,875,877	$9,201,735	$4,334,849	$2,640,939	$1,470,692	$1,868,184
Africa, generally	$440,067	$282,596	$152,071	$269,292	$537,355	$470,027	$180,428	$261,172	$233,354	$172,138	$139,984
Dutch East Indies	. . .	. . .	. . .	. . .	$33,325	$4,376	. . .	$91,531	$46,582	$21,115	. . .
China East Indies	$1,047,385	$595,249	$261,795	$387,310	$1,352,860	$1,023,242	$305,984	$253,131	$326,183	$318,629	$135,181
Northwest of America	$827,748	$72,941	$79,515	$15,607	$23,607	$44,063	$5,383	$1,586	$13,405	$3,380	$10,362
Uncertain	. . .	. . .	. . .	. . .	. . .	. . .	$29,981	3,986	. . .	$29,275	. . .
Total	$2,315,200	$950,786	$493,381	$672,209	$1,947,147	$1,541,708	$521,776	$611,406	$619,524	$544,537	$285,527
Total Exports	$70,971,780	$78,665,822[a]	$61,526,395[a]	$57,084,924[a]	$67,374,184[a]	$47,855,546[a]	$29,655,760	$25,752,317	$20,618,014[a]	$17,571,551	$20,205,156

[a] Adjusted for internal errors in sources below.
Sources: U.S. Congress, *American State Papers: Commerce and Navigation* (1832), VII, 32, 33, 138, 248, 293, 311, 316. Timothy Pitkin, *A Statistical View of the Commerce of the United States* (1835), 260–62.

TABLE 4.193 VALUE AND ORIGIN OF UNITED STATES IMPORTS, 1795–1800

	1800	1799	1798	1797	1796	1795
England	$29,723,783	$25,896,695	$15,123,621	$24,320,599	$28,694,317	$21,124,880
Scotland	$2,624,041	$2,077,940	$1,748,600	$1,501,481	$1,241,385	$678,213
Ireland	$529,235	$1,158,584	$458,549	$1,280,987	$1,992,983	$1,510,028
British West Indies	$5,774,411	$6,083,372	$2,925,739	$3,045,045	$6,301,534	$6,426,091
Canada and Fisheries	$377,211	$225,627	$257,310	$341,012	$287,166	$303,831
British East Indies	$3,391,027	$1,521,213	$2,977,324	$1,764,290	$2,427,717	$742,523
Gibraltar	$157,882	$225,084	$225,397	$120,371	$127,972	$150,501
British Africa	. . .	$23,404	$36,701	$46,858[a]	$54,271	$36,148
Total British Empire	$42,577,590	$37,211,919	$23,753,241	$32,420,643	$41,127,345	$30,972,215
France	$74,228	$901,018	$1,371,727	$3,045,796	$1,835,066	$3,671,331
French West Indies	$9,335,111	$2,022,929	$15,380,091	$14,030,337	$15,743,774	$15,751,758
Bourbon and Mauritius	$234,984	$262,221	$1,116,284	$996,794	$1,464,174	$804,928
Total French Empire	$9,644,323	$3,186,168	$17,868,102	$18,072,927	$19,043,014	$20,228,017
Spain	$3,360,582	$2,576,988	$984,057	$1,333,056	$1,521,081	$1,232,844
Spanish Wine Islands	$217,048	$199,225	$72,962	$205,817	$380,713	$307,369
Spanish West Indies	$10,587,566	$10,974,295	$8,139,169	$4,123,362	$1,718,026	$1,739,138
Florida and Louisiana	$904,322	$507,132	$211,904	$139,535	$219,522	$593,351
Other Spanish America	$859,431	$197,960	$39,398	$27,567	$24,024	$8,593
Philippines	$142,969[a]	$24,329	. . .	$232,674	. . .	$61,150
Total Spanish Empire	$16,071,918	$14,479,929	$9,447,490	$6,062,011	$3,863,366	$3,942,445
Portugal	$787,037	$962,909	$918,443	$1,338,877	$1,298,832	$1,032,339
Portuguese Wine Islands	$508,699	$352,075	$502,903	$808,428	$829,494	$1,191,438
Total Portuguese Empire	$1,295,736	$1,314,984	$1,421,346	$2,147,305	$2,128,326	$2,223,777
Dutch West Indies	$2,800,766	$3,929,101	$2,475,494	$2,178,426	$3,703,081	$2,342,957
Swedish West Indies	$450,567	$409,054	$274,747	$545,895	$691,471	$622,514
Danish West Indies	$999,770	$2,139,870	$1,117,321	$2,416,088	$2,818,746	$2,329,273
West Indies, generally	$26,937	$101,397	$16,873	$52,898	$13,050	$85,186
Total	$4,278,040	$6,579,422	$3,884,435	$5,193,307	$7,226,348	$5,379,930

	1800	1799	1798	1797	1796	1795
Russia	$1,524,995	$2,274,913	$1,067,152	$1,418,418	$1,382,978	$1,168,715
German Ports	$5,354,732	$6,967,524	$3,738,763	$2,764,409	$2,176,486	$1,663,433
Sweden, Denmark, Norway	$400,828	$955,514	$270,381	$478,411	$524,893	$334,158
Netherlands	$775,541	$662,590	$1,757,371	$2,404,828	$943,227	$1,329,952
Italy	$1,104,833	$753,484	$726,209	$852,408	$268,237	$319,653
Europe, generally	$20,160	$16,825	$2,562	$23,171	$30,918	$1,023,068
Total Europe	$9,181,089	$11,630,850	$7,562,438	$7,941,645	$5,326,739	$5,838,979
Africa, generally	$10,988	$219	. . .	$609	$49,990	$87
Dutch East Indies	$3,556,320	$1,446,335	$2,305,344	$1,029,995	$211,626	$26,706
China, East Indies	$4,613,463	$3,219,262	$2,309,304	$2,319,964	$2,459,410	$1,144,103
Northwest of America	$23,441	. . .	. . .	. . .	. . .	. . .
Total	$8,204,212	$4,665,816	$4,614,648	$3,350,568	$2,721,026	$1,170,896
Total Imports	$91,252,908[a]	$79,069,088[a]	$68,551,700	$75,188,406[a]	$81,436,164	$69,756,259

[a] Adjusted for internal errors in source below
Source: Timothy Pitkin, *A Statistical View of the Commerce of the United States of America* (1835), 257–59.

TABLE 4.194 UNITED STATES BALANCE OF PAYMENTS, IN MILLIONS OF DOLLARS ($ M.), 1790–1800

Fiscal Year	Imports (−)	Exports[a] (+)	Net Freight Earnings[b] (+)	Specie Flows (+/−)	Interest, U.S. Debt (−)	Net Balance (+/−)
1800	$93.3 m.	$71.8 m.	$22.5 m.	+ $2 m.	$4.8 m.	− $1.8 m.
1799	$81.1 m.	$79.4 m.	$21.0 m.	+ $1 m.	$5.7 m.	+ $14.6 m.
1798	$70.6 m.	$61.9 m.	$13.8 m.	− $1 m.	$5.6 m.	− $1.5 m.
1797	$77.4 m.	$57.4 m.	$14.0 m.	0	$5.0 m.	− $11.0 m.
1796	$82.9 m.	$67.4 m.	$18.3 m.	− $1 m.	$4.7 m.	− $2.9 m.
1795	$71.3 m.	$48.3 m.	$16.1 m.	− $1.5 m.	$4.0 m.	− $12.4 m.
1794	$36.0 m.	$33.3 m.	$14.1 m.	+ $2.5 m.	$4.5 m.	+ $9.4 m.
1793	$32.6 m.	$26.3 m.	$10.6 m.	+ $2 m.	$4.6 m.	+ $1.7 m.
1792	$32.5 m.	$21.0 m.	$6.1 m.	+ $2 m.	$4.1 m.	− $7.5 m.
1791	$30.5 m.	$19.2 m.	$5.0 m.	+ $2 m.	$3.7 m.	− $8.0 m.
1790	$23.8 m.	$20.4 m.	$4.9 m.	+ $1 m.	$3.6 m.	− $1.1 m.

[a] Includes sales of ships at $200,000 from 1790 to 1793, $300,000 from 1794 to 1796, $500,000 in 1797, $400,000 in 1798, $700,000 in 1799, and $800,000 in 1800.
[b] Earnings after overseas insurance payments of $1,000,000 in 1790, $1,200,000 in 1791, $1,300,000 in 1792 and 1793, $1,400,000 in 1794, $2,900,000 in 1795, $3,300,000 in 1796, $3,100,000 in 1797, $2,800,000 in 1798, $3,200,000 in 1799, and $3,700,000 in 1800.
Source: Douglass C. North, "The United States Balance of Payments, 1790–1860," in National Bureau of Economic Research, *Trends in the American Economy in the Nineteenth Century* (1960), 600.

TABLE 4.195 VALUE OF EACH STATE'S EXPORTS IN FISCAL YEARS, 1791–1800

	1800	1799	1798	1797	1796	1795	1794	1793	1792	1791
N.H.	$431,836	$361,789	$361,453	$275,840	$378,161	$229,427	$153,860	$198,204	$181,413	$142,859
Vt.	. . .	. . .	. . .	. . .	. . .	. . .	. . .	. . .	. . .	. . .
Mass.	$11,326,876	$11,421,591	$8,639,252	$7,502,047	$9,949,345	$7,117,907	$5,292,441	$3,756,347	$2,888,104	$2,519,651
R.I.	$1,322,945	$1,055,273	$947,827	$975,530	$1,589,872	$1,222,917	$954,599	$616,432	$698,109	$470,131
Conn.	$1,114,743	$1,143,818	$763,128	$814,506	$1,452,793	$819,465	$812,765	$770,255	$879,753	$710,353
N.Y.	$14,045,079	$18,719,527	$14,300,892	$13,308,064	$12,208,027	$10,304,581	$5,442,183	$2,932,370	$2,535,790	$2,505,465
N.J.	$2,289	$9,722	$61,877	$18,161	$59,227	$130,814	$58,154	$54,179	$23,406	$26,988
Pa.	$11,949,679	$12,431,967	$8,915,463	$11,446,291	$17,513,866	$11,518,260	$6,643,092	$6,958,836	$3,820,662	$3,436,093
Del.	$418,695	$297,065	$183,727	$98,929	$201,142	$158,041	$207,985	$93,559	$133,972	$119,879
Md.	$12,264,331	$16,299,609	$12,746,190	$9,811,799	$9,201,315	$5,811,380	$5,686,191	$3,665,056	$2,623,808	$2,239,691
D.C.				. . .	. . .				. . .	
Va.	$4,430,689	$6,292,986	$6,113,451	$4,008,713	$5,268,655	$3,490,041	$3,321,636	$2,987,098	$3,552,825	$3,131,865
N.C.	$769,799	$485,921	$537,810	$540,901	$671,487	$492,161	$321,587	$365,414	$527,900	$524,548
S.C.	$10,663,510	$8,729,015	$6,994,179	$6,505,118	$7,620,049	$5,998,492	$3,867,908	$3,191,867	$2,428,250	$2,693,268
Ga.	$2,174,268	$1,396,759	$961,848	$644,307	$950,158	$695,986	$263,832	$520,955	$459,106	$491,250
	$70,971,780	$78,665,522	$61,527,097	$56,850,206	$67,064,097	$47,989,472	$33,026,233	$26,109,572	$20,753,098	$19,012,041

Note: Fiscal years began Oct. 1 and ended Sep. 30.
Source: Adam Seybert, *Statistical Annals: Embracing Views of . . . the United States of America, 1789–1818* (1818), 632.

TABLE 4.196 PERCENT OF U.S. EXPORTS SHIPPED FROM EACH STATE, 1791–1800

	1800	1798	1796	1794	1792	1791
N.H.	.6%	.6%	.6%	.5%	.9%	.8%
Mass.	16.0%	14.0%	14.8%	16.0%	13.9%	13.2%
R.I.	1.9%	1.5%	2.4%	2.9%	3.4%	2.5%
Conn.	1.6%	1.2%	2.2%	2.5%	4.2%	3.7%
N.Y.	19.8%	23.2%	18.2%	16.5%	12.2%	13.2%
N.J.	.1%	.1%	.1%	.2%	.1%	.1%
Pa.	16.8%	14.5%	26.1%	20.1%	18.4%	18.1%
Del.	.6%	.3%	.3%	.6%	.6%	.6%
Md.	17.3%	20.7%	13.7%	17.2%	12.6%	11.8%
Va.	6.2%	10.0%	7.8%	10.0%	17.1%	16.5%
N.C.	1.1%	.9%	1.0%	1.0%	2.5%	2.7%
S.C.	15.0%	11.4%	11.4%	11.7%	11.7%	14.2%
Ga.	3.0%	1.6%	1.4%	.8%	2.2%	2.6%

Note: Fiscal years began Oct. 1 and ended Sep. 30.
Source: Adam Seybert, *Statistical Annals: Embracing Views of . . . the United States of America, 1789–1818* (1818), 632.

Currency, Banking, and Finance

Currency and Money Supply

When the Revolutionary era commenced, the thirteen colonies' primary stock of currency consisted of gold or silver coins, which were earned from trade with Spanish and Portuguese possessions and then given artificial exchange values in pounds, shillings, or pence. (Since payments for American exports to England were made by crediting the financial accounts of colonial merchants rather than by shipping sterling overseas, the thirteen provinces never accumulated any substantial amount of sterling coinage, which in any event was forbidden by law to be sent outside Great Britain.) Colonial governments alleviated periodic shortages of hard money, or specie, by printing paper currency that circulated temporarily until redeemed by tax payments. Law or local custom also permitted certain commodities, most notably tobacco in the Chesapeake region, to function as de facto money for settling debts, paying church tithes, and making purchases. Notes of credit written by merchants provided some further monetary liquidity by passing at face value.

Studies of probate records indicate that the amount of ready cash per person, exclusive of commodities or private loans, was at least £1.3s. about 1775. Alexander Hamilton calculated the pre-independence money stock at about 30,000,000 Spanish dollars, or £6,750,000 sterling, which would equal £2.14s. per capita. Although America's money supply was significantly less than England's, which probably stood at £3.10s. per head in 1775, and shopkeepers often voiced frustration that a specie shortage kept them from selling customers more goods, the volume of cash in circulation was generally adequate for business conditions. A serious deficiency of cash would have generated deflationary pressures driving prices and interest rates progressively lower. Because prices rose and interest rates remained stable, it appears that the colonies successfully coped with the shortage of coins and reduced their liquidity problem to a minor inconvenience.

The thirteen colonies augmented their money supply during the Seven Years' War with large emissions of paper bills totaling £2,566,000 sterling, of which perhaps £800,000 remained outstanding in 1764. Parliament then complicated monetary affairs by passing the Currency Act of 1764, which prohibited American legislatures from issuing paper money that creditors and tax collectors could be legally obliged to accept. Although many colonies won approval to print paper bills in the 1770s, the Currency Act substantially reduced the use of fiat money and became a significant source of dissatisfaction against British imperial authority.

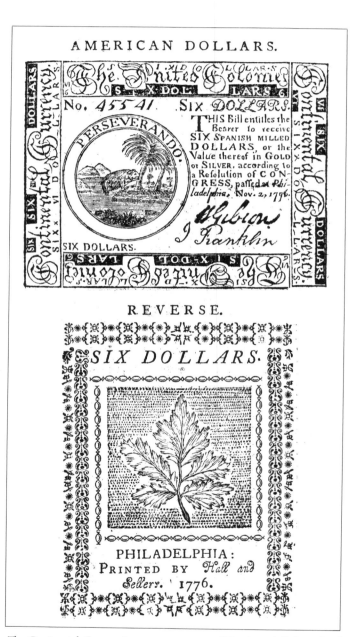

The Continental Congress's paper currency, or "Continentals," depreciated until they were worth only one cent on the dollar by 1781. This experience with hyperinflation turned American public opinion against paper money, and the U.S. Treasury issued only gold, silver, and copper coins until financial necessity forced it to resort to paper bills during the Civil War. (Courtesy Library of Congress)

The War of Independence reintroduced large amounts of paper currency into the money supply. On June 22, 1775, shortly after the Battle of Bunker Hill, the Continental Congress authorized its first printing of $2,000,000 in bills resting upon the financial credit of the state treasuries. These "Continentals" were declared equal to the Spanish dollar's silver content, which had an exchange rate of 4s.,6d. in sterling. The dollar thereafter became the basic unit of U.S. currency, but the supply of specie remained almost exclusively in Spanish or Portuguese coins.

Congress printed $241,500,000, of which it voided $41,500,000 in 1778 to counteract alleged counterfeiting. These bills of credit depreciated steadily and by December 1780 they had lost 99% of their worth. The actual specie value of this first national currency at its various times of issuance seems to have been about $52,000,000. After inflation had reduced the Continentals' buying power to nothing, Congress declared it would rely on requisitions of hard money or supplies from state treasuries for its future financial needs after 1779. By spring of 1781, each Continental dollar had sunk to about a half-cent in hard cash, and the currency passed out of existence. When the United States offered to pay off Continentals for a penny on the dollar in 1790, only $6,000,000 remained in private hands to be redeemed.

The states also issued bills of credit or various notes that became part of the money supply. State treasurers put out paper notes totaling $209,500,000, including many early emissions denominated in pounds. The state currencies also suffered from inflation, and continued to be printed through the 1780s. The resulting problems of satisfying debts with depreciated script became a major political controversy that produced demands for a stronger national government with final authority to mint coins and regulate the value of money. The Constitution of 1789 accordingly gave both these powers to the federal government.

Under Treasury Secretary Alexander Hamilton, the United States recoined its currency. Once again the American and Spanish dollars were valued closely to one another, so that each equaled about 4s., 6d. in sterling. The national mint began operating in 1794 at Philadelphia and by 1800 it had converted foreign specie into more than $2,500,000, of which all but $79,000 was in gold and silver.

TABLE 4.197   PAPER MONEY ISSUED BY CONTINENTAL CONGRESS, 1775–1779

	Face Value	Value in Specie[a]	Depreciation
1775			
Jun. 22–Nov. 29	$6,000,000	$6,000,000	none
1776			
Feb. 17–Aug. 13	$14,000,000	$14,000,000	none
Nov. 2–Dec. 28	$5,000,000	$3,300,000	1.5 to 1
1777			
Feb. 26	$5,000,000	$2,500,000	2 to 1
May 20	$5,000,000	$1,877,273	2.7 to 1
Aug. 15	$1,000,000	$333,333	3 to 1
Nov. 7–Dec. 3	$2,000,000	$500,000	4 to 1
1778			
Jan. 8–Jan. 22	$3,000,000	$750,000	4 to 1
Feb. 16–Mar. 5	$4,000,000	$800,000	5 to 1
Apr. 4–Apr. 18	$6,500,000	$1,087,666	6 to 1
May 22	$5,000,000	$1,000,000	5 to 1
Jun. 20	$1,250,000	$5,000,000	4 to 1
Jul. 30	$5,000,000	$1,111,111	4.5 to 1
Sep. 5–Sep. 26	$15,000,000	$3,000,000	5 to 1
Nov. 4–Dec. 14	$20,000,100	$3,333,367	6 to 1
1779			
Jan. 4–May 7	$50,000,100[b]	$3,055,952	16 to 1
Feb. 3–Feb. 19	$10,000,320	$1,000,000	10 to 1
Apr. 1	$5,000,160	$294,127	17 to 1
May 5	$10,000,100	$416,670	24 to 1
Jun. 4–Jul. 17	$25,000,380	$1,250,000	20 to 1
Sep. 17	$15,000,360	$625,010	24 to 1
Oct. 14	$5,000,180	$166,672	30 to 1
Nov. 17	$10,050,540	$261,053	38.5 to 1
Nov. 29	$10,000,140	$259,743	38.5 to 1
Total	$241,552,380[b]	$51,921,977	4.7 to 1

[a]Value in Spanish silver dollars worth 4s., 6d. sterling.
[b]Of this amount, approximately $25,000,000 was exchanged for old bills withdrawn allegedly for counterfeiting.
Sources: Henry Phillips, *Continental Paper Money: Historical Sketches of American Paper Currency* (1866), 198–99. E. James Ferguson, *The Power of the Purse: A History of American Public Finance, 1776–1790* (1961), 30, 43.

TABLE 4.198   PAPER MONEY ISSUED BY STATE REVOLUTIONARY GOVERNMENTS, 1776–1781

	1781[a]	1780	1779	1778	1777	1776
Mass.	£51,000	£394,000	. . .	. . .	. . .	£295,042
Conn.	. . .	£190,000	. . .	. . .	£5,250	£110,000
R.I.	. . .	£59,000	. . .	£40,000	£15,000	£176,670
N.H.	$145,000	. . .	. . .	. . .	£30,000	£43,568
Vt.	£25,155	. . .	. . .	. . .	. . .	. . .
N.Y.	$487,500	. . .	. . .	. . .	. . .	£637,500
N.J.	£30,000	£225,000	. . .	. . .	. . .	£130,000
Pa.	. . .	£100,000	. . .	. . .	£200,000	£85,000
Del.	. . .	. . .	. . .	. . .	£25,000	£30,000
Md.	£200,000	$479,433	. . .	. . .	. . .	$535,111
Va.	£9,000,000	£4,900,000	£1,000,000	£860,000	£810,000	£400,000
N.C.	£1,240,000	£500,000	£850,000	. . .	. . .	£500,000
S.C.	. . .	. . .	£1,000,000	£100,000	£696,000	£750,000
Ga.[b]	. . .	. . .	. . .	£150,000	. . .	£12,572

[a]Later issues included: 1783, £300,000 in Pa., £100,000 in N.C.; 1784, £31,259 in N.J.; 1785, £150,000 in Pa., £100,000 in N.C.; 1786, £100,000 in R.I., £200,000 in N.Y., £100,000 in N.J., £183,184 in S.C.; 1787, £64,000 in S.C.; 1788, £200,000 in N.Y., £125,000 in S.C.
[b]Exact amount of issues in 1776 and 1777 have not been determined.
Note: Currency printed to replace earlier issues not included.
Source: Eric P. Newman, *The Early Paper Money of America* (1967).

TABLE 4.199 DEPRECIATION TABLES FOR REVOLUTIONARY WAR CURRENCY, 1777–1781

Number of Bills Needed to Equal One Bill's Face Value in Gold

Date	Mass.[a]	Conn. and N.Y.	Pa. and Del.	N.J.	Md.	Va.	N.C.	S.C.
1781								
Dec.	. . .	. . .	. . .	. . .	. . .	1000	725	. . .
Nov.	. . .	. . .	. . .	. . .	. . .	800	675	. . .
Oct.	. . .	. . .	. . .	. . .	. . .	700	600	. . .
Sep.	. . .	. . .	. . .	. . .	. . .	600	550	. . .
Aug.	. . .	. . .	. . .	. . .	. . .	500	500	. . .
Jul.	. . .	. . .	. . .	. . .	. . .	400	400	. . .
Jun.	100.0	. . .	. . .	. . .	280	250	350	. . .
May	90.0	. . .	225	150	280	150	300	. . .
Apr.	82.0	. . .	160	120	160	100	260	. . .
Mar.	75.0	. . .	125	100	140	90	250	. . .
Feb.	75.0	. . .	75	90	120	80	225	. . .
Jan.	75.0	. . .	75	75	110	75	210	. . .
1780								
Dec.	74.0	. . .	75	75	100	75	200	. . .
Nov.	73.0	. . .	74	75	90	74	175	. . .
Oct.	72.0	. . .	72	75	85	73	150	. . .
Sep.	71.0	. . .	72	60	75	72	125	. . .
Aug.	70.0	. . .	70	60	65	70	100	. . .
Jul.	69.0	. . .	64.5	60	60	65	90	. . .
Jun.	62.0	. . .	61.5	60	60	65	75	. . .
May	44.0	. . .	59	60	60	60	60	52.5
Apr.	40.0	40.0	61.5	60	60	60	50	51.0
Mar.	37.4	37.3	61.5	60	60	50	40	46.6
Feb.	33.2	33.3	47.5	50	47	45	35	42.2
Jan.	29.3	29.3	40.5	42	40	42	32	37.8
1779								
Dec.	25.9	26.0	41.5	40	41.5	40	30	32.3
Nov.	23.1	23.4	38.5	36	38.5	36	27	26.0
Oct.	20.3	20.3	30	30	30	28	25	20.4
Sep.	18.0	18.0	24	24	24	24	21	16.2
Aug.	16.3	16.3	20	24	20	22	18	16.4
Jul.	14.8	14.9	19	20	20	21	15	14.6
Jun.	13.4	13.4	20	20	20	20	12.3	11.8
May	12.2	12.2	24	20	24	20	10	8.3
Apr.	11.0	11.0	17	16	17	16	10	9.7
Mar.	10.0	10.0	10.5	12	10	10	7.5	8.9
Feb.	8.7	8.7	10	10	10	10	6.5	8.3
Jan.	7.4	7.4	8	8	8	8	6	7.6
1778								
Dec.	6.3	6.3	6	7	6	6	5.5	6.3
Nov.	5.5	5.5	6	6	6	6	5	5.2
Oct.	5.0	4.6	5	5	5	5	4.8	4.1
Sep.	4.7	4.0	5	5	5	5	4.5	3.8
Aug.	4.5	3.5	5	5	5	5	4.2	3.6
Jul.	4.2	3.0	4	5	4	5	4	3.5
Jun.	4	2.6	4	5	4	5	4	3.5
May	4	2.3	5	5	5	5	4	3.3
Apr.	4	2.0	6	5	6	5	4	3.2
Mar.	3.7	1.7	5	4	5	5	3.7	2.7
Feb.	3.5	1.6	5	4	5	5	3.5	2.1
Jan.	3.2	1.5	4	4	4	4	3.5	2.2
1777								
Dec.	3.1	1.3	4	3	4	4	3.0	2.3
Nov.	3.0	1.2	3	3	3	3	2.5	2.1
Oct.	2.7	1.1	3	3	3	3	2.5	1.9
Sep.	1.7	1	3	2.7	3	3	2.2	1.7
Aug.	1.5	1	3	2.5	3	3	2.1	1.5
Jul.	1.2	1	3	2.2	3	3	2.0	1.4

Date	Mass.[a]	Conn. and N.Y.	Pa. and Del.	N.J.	Md.	Va.	N.C.	S.C.
Jun.	1.2	1	2.5	2.0	2.5	2.5	1.7	1.2
May	1.1	1	2.5	4.1	2.5	2.5	1.5	1.2
Apr.	1.1	1	2.5	3.1	2.5	2.5	1.5	1.1
Mar.	1.1	1	2.0	2.1	2.0	2.0	1.2	1
Feb.	1.1	1	1.5	1.1	1.5	1.5	1	1
Jan.	1.1	1	1.5	1.2	1.5	1.5	1	1

[a] New Hampshire and Rhode Island money depreciated at same general rate as Massachusetts currency.
Source: Eric P. Newman, *The Early Paper Money of America* (1967), 359, 360.

TABLE 4.200 EQUIVALENT VALUES OF STATE CURRENCIES WITH BRITISH STERLING, U.S. DOLLARS OF SAME PERIOD, AND WITH U.S. DOLLARS IN 1991

1766–1772	Mass.	N.Y.	Pa.	Md.	Va.	S.C.
Amount of Local Money	£1.00	£1.00	£1.00	£1.00	£1.00	£1.00
Sterling Exchange Rate	£1.31	£1.75	£1.62	£1.61	£1.24	£6.97
Value in 1791 U.S. Dollars[a]	$3.38	$2.54	$2.74	$2.76	$3.59	$.64
Value in 1991 U.S. Dollars	$56.66	$42.52	$45.99	$46.32	$60.19	$10.70
1782–1796						
Amount of Local Money Value in 1791	£1.00	£1.00	£1.00	£1.00	£1.00	£1.00
U.S. Dollars[a]	$3.33	$2.50	$2.67	$2.67	$3.33	$4.29
Value in 1991 U.S. Dollars	$43.97	$32.98	$35.18	$35.18	$43.97	$56.53

[a] A U.S. dollar was equal in gold to a Spanish dollar in 1791.
Source: John J. McCusker, " 'How Much Is That In Real Money?':" A Historical Price Index for Use as a Deflator of Money Values in the Economy of the United States," *Proceedings of the American Antiquarian Society* CI (1991–2), 333.

TABLE 4.201 COINS MINTED BY THE UNITED STATES TREASURY, 1795–1800

Gold Eagles	1800 (No.)	1799 (No.)	1798 (No.)	1797[a] (No.)	1796[b] (No.)	1795[c] (No.)
$10.	25,965	17,483	7,974	9,177	6,080	2,795
$5.	11,622	7,451	24,867	6,406	3,399	8,707
$2.50	. . .	480	614	1,756	66	. . .
Value	$317,760	$213,285	$205,610	$128,190	$77,960	$71,485
Silver						
$1.00	220,920	. . .	327,536	12,546	68,150	204,791
$.50	. . .	. . .	. . .	3,918	. . .	323,144
$.25	. . .	. . .	. . .	252	5,894	. . .
$.10	21,760	. . .	27,550	25,261	22,135	. . .
$.05	24,000	. . .	. . .	44,527	10,230	86,416
Value	$224,296	$423,515	$330,291	$86,504	$72,348	$370,683
Copper						
Cents	2,822,175	904,585	979,700	. . .	974,700	1,066,033
Half cents	211,530	12,167	. . .	. . .	115,480	142,534
Value	$29,279.40	$9,106.68	$9,797	. . .	$10,324.40	$11,373
Yearly Totals						
	$571,335	$645,907	$545,698	$147,510	$160,633	$453,542

[a] Nov. 25, 1796–Dec. 18, 1797.
[b] Jan. 1–Nov. 24, 1796.
[c] Jul. 1794–Dec. 31, 1795.
Source: U.S. Congress, *American State Papers: Finance* (1832), I, 357, 473, 505, 603, 616, 688.

TABLE 4.202 GOLD AND SILVER VALUE OF UNITED STATES DOLLAR, 1786–1800

	Gold/Silver Price Ratio	Fine-Metal Value of Dollar (Number of Grains)		Parity (Number of Dollars Equal to £1 Sterling)
		Silver	Gold	
1800	15.68	371.25	23.68	4.7727
1799	15.74	371.25	23.59	4.7910
1798	15.59	371.25	23.81	4.7453
1797	15.41	371.25	24.09	4.6905
1796	15.65	371.25	23.72	4.7636
1795				
Oct. 28–Dec. 31	15.55	371.25	23.87	4.7331
Jan. 1–Oct. 27	15.55	374.4	24.08	4.6928
1794[a]				
Oct. 15–Dec. 31	15.37	374.4	24.36	4.6388
Mar. 3–Oct. 14	15.37	371.25	24.15	4.6783
Jan. 1–Mar. 2	15.37	371	24.14	4.6815
1793	15.00	371	24.73	4.5688
1792[b]	15.17	371	24.46	4.6206
1791[c]	15.05	371	24.65	4.5840
1786[d]	15.253	. . .	. . .	. . .

[a] Metallic content set by U.S. Mint, Oct. 15, 1794 to Oct. 27, 1795. Fineness set at 11/12 for gold dollars (24.75 fine weight in grains) and 9/10 for silver dollar (374.4 fine weight in grains).
[b] Metallic content set by Act of Congress, Apr. 2, 1792. Fineness to be 11/12 for gold dollar (24.75 fine weight in grains) and 1485/1664 for silver (371.25 fine weight in grains).
[c] Metallic content set by Alexander Hamilton on Jan. 28, 1791 as market valuation based on Spanish dollar. Fineness to be .88462 to .89904 for silver (368–374 fine weight in grains) dollars. Fine weight of gold dollar to be 24.75 grains.
[d] Metallic content set by Act of Congress, Aug. 8, 1786. Fineness to be 11/12 for both gold (24.6268 fine weight in grains) and silver (375.64 fine weight in grains) dollars.
Source: Lawrence H. Officer, "Dollar-Sterling Mint Parity and Exchange Rates, 1791–1834," *Journal of Economic History* XLIII (1983), 581, 592.

Banking

Commercial and investment banking did not develop in the United States until the 1780s. Several colonial legislatures sponsored land offices that lent money against real estate guaranteed as collateral by the borrower, but these establishments never evolved into permanent financial institutions. Merchants and wealthy landowners provided virtually all the money loaned out before independence, and they continued to serve as the major source of credit well after 1800.

The Bank of North America received the earliest charter to engage in commercial finance on January 7, 1782 from the Continental Congress. The Bank of New York and Bank of Massachusetts (Boston) began operating in 1784, and commercial banks opened in Baltimore and Providence by 1791. When Congress authorized the Bank of the United States for twenty years in 1791, it created a semi-public institution with broad influence over state-chartered banks.

Banks proliferated rapidly in the federal era. Thirteen American banks were functioning in 1794, compared to just five chartered lending establishments in Great Britain. Twenty-nine banks had opened by 1800, not counting five regional branches of the Bank of the United States, and by 1816 there were 246.

New England was the greatest center of banking by 1800, when every town over 5,000 persons had a bank except Bridgewater, Massachusetts; Marblehead, Massachusetts; and Norwalk, Connecticut. New England had sixteen lending institutions—more than all of the banks in the other nine states combined. As late as 1800, the states of New Jersey, North Carolina, and Georgia remained without banks.

Given that the United States had no direct experience with commercial lending and investment, the nation's earliest banks set an admirable example of conservative management and steady profits. Five of the first eight state banks yet remain in business, and twelve of the twenty-eight founded by 1800 survived more than 190 years. Several of the largest banking establishments in the modern United States originated from lending institutions chartered before 1800, including First Pennsylvania Corporation (1782), Bank of New York (1791, seven years after it began operations), Chase Manhattan Bank (1799), and Bank of Boston (1784).

American commercial banking only emerged as a business activity after the American Revolution. The Bank of Pennsylvania, engraved here, became the country's fifteenth bank when its charter was granted in 1793. The Philadelphia bank was initially capitalized at $2,000,000 and continued in business until its failure during the panic of 1857. (I. N. Phelps Stokes Collection, Miriam & Ira Wallach Div. of Arts, Prints and Photographs. Courtesy The New York Public Library. Astor, Lenox and Tilden Foundations.)

TABLE 4.203   EXPANSION OF STATE BANKS IN THE UNITED STATES, 1782–1800

Year	Number of Banks in Operation	Authorized Capital Stock
1800	28	$17,420,000
1799	25	$16,870,000
1796–1798	22	$14,170,000
1795	20	$13,470,000
1793–1794	15	$10,470,000
1792	12	$6,310,000
1791	5	$4,600,000
1790	4	$4,100,000
1787–1789	3	$3,900,000
1786	2	$1,700,000
1784–1785	3	$2,100,000
1782–1783	1	$400,000

Note: Figures exclude Bank of the United States, but source has been amended to include Bank of New York for years 1784–1790.
Source: J. Van Fenstermaker, "The Statistics of American Commercial Banking, 1782–1818," Journal of Economic History XXV (1965), 404.

TABLE 4.204   FINANCIAL STATISTICS OF COMMERCIAL BANKS IN NEW ENGLAND, 1785–1800

	Paid-in Capital	Notes in Circulation	Deposits	Loans and Discounts	Specie
1800	$4,511,671	$1,715,804	$1,283,690	$5,318,376	$1,214,879
1799	$4,126,314	$1,584,926	$1,141,493	$4,837,027	$1,111,154
1798	$3,834,656	$1,397,456	$1,065,543	$4,360,935	$1,051,559
1797	$3,805,722	$1,401,526	$1,065,512	$4,310,099	$1,067,927
1796	$3,694,682	$1,330,791	$1,039,556	$4,269,656	$1,011,384
1795	$3,124,894	$1,042,122	$799,634	$3,614,497	$737,575
1794	$2,795,652	$892,883	$738,467	$3,286,197	$658,832
1793	$2,781,312	$894,266	$739,208	$3,260,962	$667,406
1792	$661,269	$256,878	$218,374	$823,411	$172,300
1791	$100,000	$478,603	$183,826	$168,523	$163,672
1790	$100,000	$195,417	$36,189	$42,078	$150,147
1789	$100,000	$216,075	$30,123	$57,535	$127,690
1788	$100,000	$145,375	$12,512	$40,857	$100,585
1787	$100,000	$150,618	$28,139	$38,424	$98,229
1786	$100,000	$95,643	$22,906	$31,361	$108,563
1785	$100,000	$52,484	$31,889	$15,864	$160,587

Source: J. Van Fenstermaker, John E. Filer, and Robert S. Herren, "Money Statistics of New England, 1785–1837," Journal of Economic History XLIV (1984), 441–61.

Insurance

British underwriters evidently supplied the bulk of insurance sold during the colonial era, when the greatest demand was for coverage of ship cargoes. Several merchant firms sold insurance at Boston and Philadelphia before independence, but only as a sideline when their excess capital could not be profitably used trading merchandise. Such offices usually operated with a single clerk who also worked on the merchants' other accounts.

After the Revolution, companies began appearing whose sole purpose was to write insurance. John Hurd was operating one of the earliest such firms with twenty partners at Boston in 1783. James Jeffry advertised another company at Salem, Massachusetts, in March 1784. Because most insurance concerns could eliminate the threat of personal bankruptcy by spreading financial risks among their many partners, few companies sought legal incorporation before 1794.

Most insurance companies offered coverage for marine and fire losses. Fire insurance became increasingly popular, and the first company specializing in this field opened in 1787 as the Baltimore Insurance Fire-Company. Boston's Insurance Company of North America first advertised life insurance in 1792; it approved the earliest policy (for $24,000 over 105 days to John Holker) and wrote about six similar policies by 1800. The Manhattan Insurance Company became the second company to offer life coverage in 1800.

By 1800, 32 state-chartered companies sold insurance in the United States. Most major cities had at least three such firms, while Baltimore and Philadelphia had four each. None of the incorporated firms failed before 1800, and many lasted a century.

In 1787, the Mutual Assurance Company issued this policy certificate to holders in New York. The Mutual Assurance Company was founded in 1784 in Philadelphia, when that city's only company offering fire protection declined to insure any homes near trees. Tree-loving homeowners formed a competing firm, which identified the houses it covered with a plaque termed a "firemark" designed as a tree. (I. N. Phelps Stokes Collection, Miriam & Ira Wallach Div. of Arts, Prints and Photographs. Courtesy The New York Public Library. Astor, Lenox and Tilden Foundations.)

Stock Exchange

America's earliest stock exchange originated in the habit, dating to the 1750s, of New York's merchants to meet to discuss business on lower Broad Street, often at the Royal Exchange, an open-air market where commodities were auctioned. After the Revolution, a large market developed for government bonds or other debt instruments (then referred to as "stock"), and New York merchants commonly met every week to bid upon securities issued by the United States. As yet, no formal organization existed to trade government obligations, and there was no public forum for buying the small number of shares issued by business corporations.

On March 21, 1792, New York's dealers in government bonds met at Corre's Hotel. They resolved to trade only among themselves after April 21, and they appointed a committee to propose regulations for conducting future transactions. The antecedent of the mod-

TABLE 4.205   INSURANCE COMPANIES INCORPORATED IN THE UNITED STATES, 1786–1800

	1800	1799	1798	1797	1796	1795	1794	1793	1792	1791	1787	1786
Me.	1	...	...	...	...	...	...	...	...	...	...	...
N.H.	...	1	...	...	...	...	...	...	...	...	...	...
Mass.	1	2	1	...	...	1	1	...	...	...	...	...
R.I.	4	2	...	...	...	...	...	...	...	...	...	...
Conn.	...	...	...	...	1	...	1	...	...	...	...	...
N.Y.	...	...	3	...	...	...	...	...	...	...	...	...
Pa.	...	...	...	...	...	...	2	...	...	...	...	1
Md.	...	...	1	...	...	2	1	...	...	1	1	...
Va.	...	...	...	1	...	1	1	...	...	...	...	...
S.C.	...	...	...	2	...	...	...	...	...	...	...	...
Total	6	5	6	3	0	5	5	0	0	1	1	1

Source: Joseph S. Davis, *Essays in the Early History of American Corporations* (1917), II, 235, 241.

New York's Wall Street district has been a center of investment activity since the 1790s. This etching portrays Trinity Church at the head of Wall Street in 1799. Trinity Church, at which many of the early leading figures in national finance worshiped, still remains as a reminder of Wall Street's earliest history. (I.N. Phelps Stokes Collection, Miriam & Ira Wallach Div. of Arts, Prints and Photographs. Courtesy The New York Public Library. Astor, Lenox and Tilden Foundations.)

ern New York Stock Exchange formally appeared on May 17, when twenty-four firms agreed to prefer one another in selling securities and to set minimum commissions. This organization remained essentially informal and initially chose to meet under a buttonwood tree near 68 Wall Street, where every day at noon each member or firm could auction its government bonds in rotation.

When the Tontine Coffee House was completed at the northwest corner of Wall and William streets in 1793, the brokers deserted the buttonwood tree to assemble there. Sharing the Tontine with other merchants and insurance agents, the brokers struck bargains in a leisurely atmosphere in which their various business interests were mixed. Not until 1817 did they modernize their structure by adopting the Constitution of the New York Stock Exchange Board.

TABLE 4.206   RATIFYING CONTRACT AND MEMBERS OF THE NEW YORK STOCK EXCHANGE

We the Subscribers, Brokers for the Purchase and Sale of Public Stock, do hereby solemnly promise and pledge ourselves to each other that we will not buy or sell from this day, for any person whatsoever, any kind of Public Stock, at a less rate than one quarter per cent. Commission on the specie value, and that we will give a preference to each other in our Negotiations.

In Testimony whereof we have set our hands this 17th day of May, at New York, 1792.

Leonard Bleecker	Broker	16 Wall Street
Hugh Smith	Merchant	Tontine Coffee House
Armstrong & Barnewall	Insurance Brokers	58 Broad Street
Samuel March	Broker	243 Queen Street
Bernard Hart	Broker	55 Broad Street
Alexander Zuntz	Auctioneer & Broker	97 Broad Street
Andrew D. Barclay	Merchant	136 Pearl Street
Sutton & Hardy	Stock Brokers & Auctioneers	20 Wall Street
Benjamin Seixas	Merchant	8 Hanover Square
John Henry	Broker	13 Duke Street
John A. Hardenbrook	Broker	24 Nassau Street
Samuel Beebe	Broker	21 Nassau Street
Benjamin Winthrop	Merchant	2 Great Dock Street
John Ferrers	Merchant	205 Water Street
Ephraim Hart	Broker	74 Broadway
Isaac M. Gomez	Broker	32 Maiden Lane
Guilian McEvers	Merchant	140 Greenwich Street
Augustine H. Lawrence	Warden of the Port	132 Water Street
G. N. Bleecker	Merchant	21 Broad Street
John Bush	Broker	195 Water Street
Peter Anspach	Merchant	3 Great Dock Street
Charles McEvers, Jr.	Merchant	194 Water Street
David Reedy	Insurance & Stock Broker	58 Wall Street
Robinson & Hartshorne	Merchants	198 Queen Street

Source: Joseph S. Davis, *Essays in the Early History of American Corporations* (1917), I, 36.

National Income, Wealth, Property Holding, and Poverty

National Income

Statistics on national income (gross national product) are rare for the period before 1800, and the few that exist are highly conjectural. Surviving evidence concerning periods of expansion and recession nevertheless show a strong correlation between the performance of the American and English economies, even after Britain recognized U.S. independence. It is especially difficult to estimate changes in aggregate output after 1775 because the Revolution generated enormous dislocations in domestic production and overseas commerce. Economic historians have been very reluctant to calculate the Revolution's impact on gross national incomes, but it seems certain that independence required huge financial sacrifices. Per capita exports were approximately 25% lower in 1791–1792 than they had been thirty years earlier. It does not seem improbable that from 1775 to 1790 per capita national output fell by half, a downturn comparable to the Great Depression between 1929 and 1933.

The most commonly cited research on total domestic output in the Revolutionary era concludes that by 1774 gross national product totaled a minimum of £25 million sterling, an amount equivalent in 1985 dollars to $2.25 billion. The economy experienced negative growth during most of the next fifteen years, and aggregate output may have shrunk to £14 million due to wartime destruction, exclusion from lucrative export markets, and erosion of investment capital due to high inflation and heavy taxes. Although important for long-term growth, large-scale western migration after 1785 temporarily slowed the recovery in national income because the labor of building improved farms from wilderness not only brought in little or no money for long periods, but also sharply reduced immediate cash earnings below levels in settled areas. National output rose steadily for six years after 1789 but slumped for almost three years after 1796. Gross national product most likely did not reattain the level reached in 1774 on a per capita basis until after 1820.

TABLE 4.207   COMPONENTS OF GROSS ECONOMIC OUTPUT (IN POUNDS STERLING) FOR THIRTEEN COLONIES, 1774

	New England	Mid-Atlantic Colonies	Southern Colonies	Total or Average
Export Earnings, per capita	£1.56	£1.57	£1.85	£1.70
Domestic Earnings, per capita	£8.84 to £10.54	£9.93 to £11.83	£8.55 to £10.25	£9.00 to £10.80
Total Population	607,795	640,695	1,105,477	2,353,967
High Estimate of Aggregate Output	£7,350,000	£8,590,000	£13,380,000	£29,320,000
Low Estimate of Aggregate Output	£6,320,000	£7,370,000	£11,500,000	£25,190,000
Regional % of Total Output	25.1%	29.2%	45.7%	100%

Source: Alice Hanson Jones, *Wealth of a Nation to Be: The American Colonies on the Eve of the Revolution* (1980), 37, 63, 65.

TABLE 4.208   PERIODS OF GROWTH AND DECLINE IN THE ECONOMIES OF ENGLAND AND ITS FORMER THIRTEEN COLONIES, 1761–1800

Thirteen Colonies, United States				England	
Expansion	(Peak of American Expansion)	Decline	(Bottom of American Decline)	Expansion	Decline
		1796–1799	(1798)		1796–1800
				1794–1796	1792–1794
1789–1796	(1796)			1789–1792	1787–1789
		1782–1789	(1789)	1784–1787	1783–1784
1781–1782	(1782)			1781–1783	
1779–1780	(1780)	1780–1781	(1781)		
		1778–1779	(1779)		1777–1781
1775–1778	(1778)	1773–1775	(1775)	1775–1777	1772–1775
1770–1773	(1772)	1767–1770	(1768)	1769–1772	1764–1769
1765–1767	(1766)				
		1763–1765	(1764)	1763–1764	
1761–1763	(1762)				1761–1763

Source: John J. McCusker and Russell R. Menard, *The Economy of British America, 1607–1789* (1985), 62–63. John J. McCusker, " 'How Much Is That In Real Money?': A Historical Price Index for Use as a Deflator of Money Values in the Economy of the United States," *Proceedings of the American Antiquarian Society* CI (1991–2), 360.

Wealth, Per Capita and Aggregate

Neither the British colonies nor the United States compiled data corresponding to the modern concepts of aggregate national wealth or per capita property ownership before 1800. The only thorough research into these topics concerns the year 1774, but while providing a detailed picture of late colonial living standards it offers no indication of how the Revolution affected material well-being. It nevertheless seems clear that the Anglo-American economy afforded most white families a comfortable existence, though not without much hard work and thrift.

An average farmer in 1774 held 120 acres and chattels worth £252 sterling, equivalent to $22,680 in 1985 dollars. Living standards were highest in the South, where the average property owner's possessions equalled £395 ($35,500 in 1985 dollars), a third of which consisted of slaves or indentured servants. Southern whites were so prosperous that, although they made up just 36% of all free Americans, they possessed 55% of the thirteen colonies' aggregate wealth of £109,000,000 ($9.8 billion in 1985 values). New England's notoriously bad agricultural conditions sharply limited chances to accumulate wealth, and the typical Yankee family held property amounting to just £161 ($14,500), only 40% as much as the usual southern household. Mid-Atlantic property owners on average were worth £187 ($16,800), an unexpectedly low figure that resulted from most real estate having been cleared so recently that its value had not been increased by improvements typical of farms in older colonies. Considering that their fields, garden, orchard, and livestock provided families with nearly all their diet and fuel, and even some fabric for clothing, such household wealth is nevertheless impressive by twentieth-century U.S. standards.

TABLE 4.209 TYPE AND VALUE OF PROPERTY OWNED (IN POUNDS STERLING) BY AN AVERAGE PROPERTY-OWNING MALE IN THE THIRTEEN COLONIES, 1774

Type of Property	New England	Mid-Atlantic Colonies	Southern Colonies	Average
Slaves, servants	£0.7	£7.2	£132.6	£49.4
% of net worth in slaves, servants	.4	3.9	33.6	19.6
Land	£115.1	£115.5	£181.1	£138.5
% of net worth in land	71.4	61.8	45.9	55.0
Livestock	£12.3	£21.3	£34.9	£23.3
% of net worth in livestock	7.6	11.4	8.8	9.2
Farm and home tools	£5.5	£6.1	£10.2	£7.4
% of net worth in farm-home tools	3.4	3.3	2.6	2.9
Artisan tools	£1.5	£1.3	£0.4	£1.0
% of net worth in artisan tools	.9	.7	.1	.4
Crops	£1.0	£9.3	£10.9	£7.2
% of net worth in crops	.6	5.0	2.8	2.9
Perishable (nonfarm) home-produced goods	£5.8	£8.0	£2.1	£5.2
% of net worth in home-produced goods	3.6	4.3	.5	2.1
Clothing	£3.8	£4.9	£2.9	£3.8
% of net worth in clothing	2.4	2.6	.7	1.5
Furniture, durable home goods	£14.6	£11.6	£17.2	£14.6
% of net worth in durable goods	9.1	6.2	4.4	5.8
Perishable consumer goods	£0.9	£1.3	£2.3	£1.5
% of net worth in perishable goods	.6	.7	.6	.6
Total Estate	£161.2	£186.8	£394.7	£252.0

Note: Decimal places in monetary values express percent of pound.
Source: Alice Hanson Jones, *Wealth of a Nation to Be: The American Colonies on the Eve of the Revolution* (1980), 98.

TABLE 4.210 POSSESSIONS OF A MIDDLE-CLASS, COLONIAL FARM FAMILY, 1774

Appraisal of estate left by Ann Margaret Frederick, widow, of Smithfield Township, Northampton Co., Pennsylvania. Jan. 14, 1774.

	Pa. Values £.s.d.	Sterling £.s.d.
Real Estate 120 acres	£250	£150
Cash 6 Notes due for £18.1 and £50.16.5 cash	£68.17	£41.4
Livestock 1 cow, £8, 2 steers, £5, 1 heifer, £2.10, 1 calf, £1	£16.10	£9.18
1 roan mare and 1 brown horse @ £11 and 8 sheep @ 9s.,2d.	£25.12	£15.7
Farm Tools 2 shovels, 2 axes, 2 forks, 1 hoe	16s.	9s.
1 wagon, 1 harrow, 1 flaxbrake, 1 iron hoop	£4.15	£2.17
4 sickles and 2 saddles, 1½ bu. flaxseed	£1.15	£1.1
Farm Produce 16 bu. buckwheat, 24s. and 1 stack wheat, £5, and 1 rye, £3.15	£9.19	£6
1.75 a. of wheat in ground, 4.5 a. rye ditto	£4	£2.8
1 table, 1 small box, 2 jugs, 6 beehives	£2.6	£1.11
Spinning Equipment 8 reeds, 7 pans of weaver's gears, 2 bells, and 6 bu. corn	£2.2	£1.6
1 pair cards, 1s., 1 hatchel, 3s., 1 iron, 4s.	7s.	4s.
12 lb. yarn @ 1s., 8 lb. @ 9d., and bags @ 15d.	£1.7.9	£1.1
1.5 yd. flax, 52d., 24 lb. cotton yarn @ 52d.	£5.12.6	£3.8
165.5 yd. linen, £23.7.11, 4 yds wool @ 7d.	£24.15.11	£14.17
Household Possessions Sundry clothing	£7.4	£4.7
1 bed, 1 bolster, 2 pillows, 2 sheets	£3.8	£2.1
1 bed, 1 bolster, 2 pillows, 1 rug	£5.	£3.
1 bed and blanket, £2, 2 chests @ 16s. each	£3.12	£2.3
2 iron stoves, 3 chairs, old iron and nails	£3.5	£1.19
24 knives and forks, 1 wheel, teapot, 8 milkpots	13s.	8s.
1 watering pot, 6s., 3 iron pots, 70s., and 3 tramils, 3s.	£2.9	£1.9
4 pails and 1 keg, 6s., 2 pewter basins, 12 plates, 7 spoons	£1.6	16s.
1 coffee mill, 54d., 1 tub, 1 barrel, 1 churn, small lumber	£1.6	16s.
2 lamps, candle stick, 2 wedges, mall rings	6s.	4s.
shoe leather, 24s., 12.75 lb. wool @ 18d., and 2 bu. salt	£2.9	£1.13
1 big Bible and sundry small books	£3.	£1.16
	£458.4	£275

Source: Alice Hanson Jones, *American Colonial Wealth: Documents and Methods,* 3 vols. (1978 ed.), 75.

TABLE 4.211   COMPONENTS OF AGGREGATE NATIONAL WEALTH (IN POUNDS STERLING), 1774

Type of Property	New England	Mid-Atlantic Colonies	Southern Colonies	Thirteen Colonies
Slaves, servants	£101,000	£1,032,000	£20,330,000	£21,400,000
% of all slaves and servants	.5%	4.7%	94.8%	100%
Land	£15,874,000	£16,584,000	£27,763,000	£60,221,000
% of all land	26.4%	27.5%	46.1%	100%
Livestock	£1,703,000	£3,059,000	£5,352,000	£10,114,000
% of all livestock	16.8%	30.3%	52.9%	100%
Crops and other home-produced goods	£1,911,000	£3,550,000	£3,634,000	£9,095,000
% of crops and home-produced goods	21.0%	39.0%	40.0%	100%
Furniture and consumer goods	£2,648,000	£2,590,000	£3,439,000	£8,677,000
% of furniture and consumer goods	30.5%	29.9%	39.6%	100%
Total Wealth	£22,238,000	£26,814,000	£60,518,000	£109,570,000
% of all wealth	20.3%	24.4%	55.3%	100%
Free population	582,285	585,149	652,585	1,820,019
% of population	32.0%	32.1%	35.9%	100%

Source: Alice Hanson Jones, Wealth of a Nation to Be: The American Colonies on the Eve of the Revolution (1980), 40–42, 51, 299, 308.

Property Holding

Affluence was closely connected with occupation and age during the late eighteenth century. Adults over 45 years owned 50% more property than those who were younger. The distribution of wealth was heavily skewed in favor of those 45 and up, who held perhaps two-thirds of the country's assets, but this situation was only tempo-

This dining room, as restored by the Smithsonian Institution, shows the style of furnishings owned by an upper-class family in late eighteenth-century Connecticut. The room's walls have paneling instead of bare boards. Family members sit on individual chairs rather than a bench. Linen and pewter grace the table, and a large painting decorates one wall. Furniture is custom-made, rather than roughly carved by an amateur farmer-carpenter. (Negative 86-215, courtesy Smithsonian Institution)

TABLE 4.212   AVERAGE WEALTH (STERLING) OWNED BY PROPERTY-OWNING ADULTS, 1774

Property-owning Class	New England	Mid-Atlantic Colonies	Southern Colonies	Thirteen Colonies
Men	£169	£194	£410	£260
Women	£42	£103	£215	£132
Adults 45 and older	£252	£274	£595	£361
Adults 44 and younger	£129	£185	£399	£237
Urban	£191	£287	£641	£233
Rural	£151	£173	£392	£255
Esquires, gentlemen	£313	£1,223	£1,281	£572
Merchants	£563	£858	£314	£497
Professions, sea captains	£271	£241	£512	£341
Farmers only, planters	£155	£180	£396	£262
Farmer-artisans, ship owners, fishermen	£144	£257	£801	£410
Shop and tavern keepers	£219	£222	£195	£204
Artisans, chandlers	£114	£144	£138	£122
Mariners, laborers	£52	£67	£383	£62

Source: Alice Hanson Jones, Wealth of a Nation to Be: The American Colonies on the Eve of the Revolution (1980), 224.

rary, since all the elderly's property would eventually be redistributed as inheritances after the next generation began reaching middle age.

Commerce afforded the greatest opportunities for profit, and merchants and ship captains ranked highest in property owning, although a large number in each group went either bankrupt or to a watery grave. The profession of law provided almost equal scope for making money, with much less risk, and attorneys were the wealthiest professional class, followed by doctors. A wide range of wealth existed among agriculturalists, of whom those working land with only family labor were termed farmers, yeomen, or even planters, while those with large estates requiring a dozen indentured servants or slaves were usually styled gentlemen.

Property was unevenly divided, largely due to factors related to age, but not to an extreme degree. The wealthiest 10% owned 50% to 55% of all wealth about 1775. By 1860, the richest 10% had increased their share of national wealth to 73%, and wealth remained concentrated at that level into the twentieth century. The share of property controlled by the top 10% thereafter shrank to 62% by 1962, but it still remains higher than in the 1770s.

TABLE 4.213   OWNERSHIP OF LAND AND SLAVES AMONG PROPERTY-HOLDING ADULTS, 1774

Property-owning Categories	Land Ownership % Owning Land	Land Ownership Average Value of Land	Slave Ownership % Owning Slaves	Slave Ownership Average Value of Slaves
Adult men over 44	80.3%	£222	33.7%	£60
Adult men under 45	78.4%	£123	34.4%	£48
Gentlemen	94.7%	£346	42.5%	£123
Merchants	58.2%	£260	53.5%	£39
Artisans	56.1%	£83	14.6%	£9

Source: Alice Hanson Jones, Wealth of a Nation to Be: The American Colonies on the Eve of the Revolution (1980), 225–29.

TABLE 4.214 DISTRIBUTION AND PERCENT OF WEALTH OWNED BY SOCIAL CLASSES, 1774

% of Physical Wealth Owned By:	New England Colonies		Mid-Atlantic Colonies		Southern Colonies		Thirteen Colonies	
	Value of Wealth	% Owned	Value of Wealth	% Owned	Value of Wealth	% Owned	Value of Wealth	% Owned
Richest 1%	£1,175–£992	12%	£1,087–£690	12%	£2,649–£2,113	10%	£2,027–£1,644	13%
Richest 10% (91%–100%)	£1,175–£402	47%	£1,087–£380	35%	£2,649–£1,140	47%	£2,027–£609	51%
Next 10% (81%–90%)	£401–£251	19%	£379–£284	18%	£1,139–£674	23%	£608–£334	17%
Next 30% (51%–80%)	£250–£75	27%	£283–£155	36%	£673–£148	25%	£333–£111	25%
Next 20% (31%–50%)	£74–£26	5%	£154–£31	9%	£147–£54	3%	£110–£31	5%
Lowest 30% (1%–30%)	£25–£1	2%	£30–£1	2%	£53–£1	2%	£30–£1	2%

Note: Value of servants and slaves not included in wealth, which is valued in sterling.
Source: Alice Hanson Jones, Wealth of A Nation to Be: The American Colonies on the Eve of the Revolution (1980), 165, 261, 314.

TABLE 4.215 DISTRIBUTION OF WEALTH IN UNITED STATES AND EUROPE, 1798

Country	Percent of Wealth Owned by Top Proportion of Adult Males		Percent of Adult Males Owning Land
	Top 1%	Top 10%	
United States	13%	45%	49%
Scotland	24%	64%	22%
Denmark	43%	80%	24%
Sweden	31%	65%	29%
Norway	33%	65%	38%
Finland	19%	46%	23%

Source: Lee Soltow, Distribution of Wealth and Income in the United States in 1798 (1989), 238.

TABLE 4.216 AVERAGE WEALTH OWNED BY ADULT MALES IN UNITED STATES, 1798

Region of United States	Average Wealth of Landowners	Average Wealth of Males Over 21	Percent of Males Over 21 Who Owned Land
Rural North			
Within 80 mi. of ocean	$1,868	$832	44.6%
Beyond 80 mi. of ocean	$1,002	$595	59.4%
Rural South			
Within 80 mi. of ocean	$2,314	$728	31.0%
Beyond 80 mi. of ocean	$883	$514	58.1%
Urban North			
Within 80 mi. of ocean	$3,147	$1,103	35.0%
Beyond 80 mi. of ocean	$1,753	$798	44.4%
Urban South			
Within 80 mi. of ocean	$3,001	$1,247	41.5%
National Average	$1,434	$708	49.4%

Source: Lee Soltow, Distribution of Wealth and Income in the United States in 1798 (1989), 42.

Poverty

Thomas Jefferson declared in 1787 that he had "never yet [seen] a native American begging in the streets or highways." Poverty in rural America largely stemmed from physical or mental disabilities, rather than from economic roots, and relatively few able-bodied adults found themselves in such straits. Visitors from Europe, where a large portion of the people lived on marginal incomes, often commented on how few white Americans suffered from material deprivation, even after the dislocations of the Revolutionary War.

Poverty increased from 1760 to 1800, but this growing problem was largely an urban phenomenon and untypical of American society in the late eighteenth century. Increasing indigence stemmed partly from the widows and orphans created by colonial casualties in British wars fought between 1739 and 1763, and later by the War of Independence. The poor rolls also swelled as growing numbers of immigrants landed at seaports after long voyages that had exhausted their savings, undermined their health, or created many orphans and widows. There are consequently tragic reasons to believe Jefferson was correct in writing that most of the country's paupers were foreign born.

TABLE 4.217 POOR RELIEF AND THE POVERTY RATE IN PHILADELPHIA, 1771–1776

	Population	Admittees to Almshouse	Admittees to Poor Hospital	% of Population on Relief[a]
1775–76	32,073	427	268	2.2%
1774–75	30,216	368	393	2.5%
1773–74	29,547	309	361	2.3%
1772–75	28,878	398	374	2.7%
1771–72	27,833	395	315	2.6%

[a]Does not include an unknown portion of those exempted from taxes as indigents, who averaged about 370 yearly from 1760 to 1775, and so might raise the overall percentage as much as 1.8%.
Sources: Gary B. Nash, "Poverty and Poor Relief in Pre-Revolutionary Philadelphia," William and Mary Quarterly XXXIII (1976), 3–23. Billy G. Smith, The "Lower Sort:" Philadelphia's Laboring People, 1750–1800 (1990).

By the 1760s, perhaps a sixth of property owners in Boston and a tenth of Philadelphians may have owned too few possessions to be placed on tax rolls, although most evidently managed to support themselves without public assistance. An increasing number of the infirm, crippled, aged, widowed, and orphaned burdened the budgets of the largest seaports, but the dimensions of urban poverty re-mained modest by modern standards. In the 1770s, the portion of inhabitants receiving poor relief or tax abatements for poverty equaled perhaps 5% in Philadelphia, 5% in New York, and 7% in Boston, all of which are far below the comparable number of persons receiving welfare in those cities at present.

Poverty first became a significant problem in American cities during the latter eighteenth century. Citizens consequently found it necessary to construct larger almshouses, like the one pictured above, built on Philadelphia's Spruce Street in 1799. (I. N. Phelps Stokes Collection, Miriam & Ira Wallach Div. of Arts, Prints and Photographs. Courtesy The New York Public Library. Astor, Lenox and Tilden Foundations.)

TABLE 4.218   POOR RELIEF AND POVERTY RATES IN NEW YORK AND BOSTON, 1770–1771

	Boston, 1770–1775	New York, 1771
Population	15,500	22,600
Poor relief (in sterling)	£2,478	£2,778
Highest number in almshouse	275	425
Outrelief recipients	550	700[a]
Insufficient property to pay taxes	400[b]	. . .
Total Impoverished	1,099	1,125
Percent Impoverished	7.1%	5.0%

[a] Based on inferential evidence, and may include some persons who also entered almshouse.
[b] Based on inferential evidence and includes an unknown portion of the 450 persons declared ineligible for poor relief by being "warned out" repeatedly every year.
Source: Gary B. Nash, "Urban Wealth and Poverty in Pre-Revolutionary America," *Journal of Interdisciplinary History* VI (1976), 556–65.

TABLE 4.219   CHARACTERISTICS OF PAUPERS ADMITTED TO PHILADELPHIA'S ALMSHOUSE, JUN. 20, 1800–JUN. 20, 1801

Reason Committed	380 Men	352 Woman	163 Children	Total
Old age	5.9%	8.3%	. . .	5.7%
Sick	66.2%	38.0%	. . .	43.1%
Venereal disease	9.0%	16.1%	. . .	10.2%
Alcoholic	3.6%	3.9%	. . .	3.1%
Deranged	9.0%	2.4%	. . .	4.8%
Impoverished	3.2%	8.8%	. . .	4.8%
Pregnant	. . .	13.7%	. . .	5.4%
Physically abused	. . .	1.0%	2.1%	.8%
Deserted by husband	. . .	4.9%	. . .	1.9%
Deserted by parents	. . .	. . .	12.6%	2.3%
Orphan	. . .	. . .	10.5%	1.9%
To be apprenticed	. . .	. . .	2.1%	.4%
Parents cannot support	. . .	. . .	14.7%	2.7%
Committed with parents	. . .	. . .	32.6%	5.9%
Parents in jail	. . .	. . .	16.8%	3.1%
Miscellaneous	3.2%	2.9%	8.4%	4.0%

Source: Billy G. Smith, *The "Lower Sort:" Philadelphia's Laboring People, 1750–1800* (1990), 169.

TABLE 4.220 INDEX OF COMMODITY PRICES AT PHILADELPHIA, 1770–1790

	Weighted Average of 15 Commodities[a]	Change from Previous Year	Cumulative Change from 1770[b]
1790	121.3	+22.0%	+30.8%
1789	99.4	+8.3%	+7.2%
1788	91.8	+10.5%	−1.0%
1787	102.6	−7.5%	+10.7%
1786	110.9	−2.5%	+19.6%
1785	113.7	−10.1%	+22.6%
1784	126.5	−5.5%	+36.5%
1783	133.8	−14.9%	+44.3%
1782	157.2	−97.3%	+69.6%
1781	5,762.9	−51.8%	+6,116.7%
1780	11,949.1	+255.2%	+12,790.1%
1779	3,364.3	+396.7%	+3,529.2%
1778	677.3	+81.5%	+630.6%
1777	373.3	+205.5%	+302.7%
1776	122.2	+38.4%	+31.8%
1775	88.3	−7.6%	−4.7%
1774	95.6	−3.2%	+3.1%
1773	98.8	−5.7%	+6.6%
1772	104.8	+8.8%	+13.1%
1771	96.3	+3.9%	+3.9%
1770	92.7	. . .	. . .

[a] Beef, chocolate, coffee, corn, flour (common and superfine), bar iron, molasses, pepper, pork, West Indian rum, muscavado sugar, tar, Bohea tea, wheat. Weighted by relative importance.
[b] Index designed so average of 1771–1773 equals 100.
Source: Anne Bezanson, et al., *Prices and Inflation During the American Revolution: Pennsylvania, 1770–1790* (1951), 344.

Price Indexes

Violent price fluctuations caused enormous difficulties for all Americans during the Revolutionary decades. Manufacturers had to pay more for raw materials, shopkeepers found it more difficult to pass on the cost of more expensive imported goods, consumers became increasingly unable to maintain their former standard of living, and even slaves, who purchased few goods, suffered as their own meager rations were reduced by masters struggling to keep household expenses under control. Price volatility primarily arose from imbalances in supply and demand occasioned by trade boycotts adopted to protest British laws, by wartime shortages of essential commodities, and by postwar swings between lingering depression and rapid recovery. The overissue of paper money by Congress and the states worsened these circumstances by devaluing the currency and unleashing a short, vicious snap of virulent inflation.

Based upon data from Philadelphia, which has provided the most comprehensive information concerning prices, consumption expenses began rising dramatically with a 200% increase from April 1776 to April 1777. Prices finally crested in 1781, when they stood about 12,000% higher than a decade earlier. As wartime shortages eased, the expense of basic commodities fell by more than half in 1781 and then another 97% in 1782. Prices continued declining until 1789, when they had returned to their approximate range in 1770. The American economy consequently managed to reverse hyperinflation and restore consumption costs to prewar levels. A strong business recovery thereafter pressured prices upward at a moderate rate until about 1798, after which the cost of many basic commodities again fell.

TABLE 4.221 YEARLY CHANGES IN COMMODITY PRICES AT PHILADELPHIA, 1775–1781

Commodity	1781	1780	1779	1778	1777	1776	1775
Beef	+100%	+718%	+438%	+8%	+153%	+25%	+9%
Chocolate	+93%	+180%	+100%	+400%	+153%	−4%	+23%
Coffee	+84%	+490%	+6%	+262%	+271%	+33%	−6%
Corn	+57%	+119%	+1,255%	+26%	+116%	−15%	+18%
Flour							
Common	+62%	+482%	+847%	+33%	+71%	−7%	−21%
Superfine	+99%	+425%	+466%	+116%	+94%	−27%	−4%
Bar Iron	+69%	+200%	+344%	+240%	+87%	+4%	−1%
Molasses	−48%	+1,001%	+203%	+94%	+505%	+40%	+6%
Pepper	+225%	+700%	+117%	+8%	+220%	+107%	+8%
Pork	+81%	+813%	+550%	−15%	+192%	+31%	−12%
West Indian Rum	+9%	+780%	+88%	+123%	+396%	+95%	+3%
Muscovado Sugar	+43%	+180%	+226%	+223%	+246%	+28%	−8%
Tar	+29%	+678%	+23%	+578%	+7%	+48%	−4%
Bohea Tea	+25%	+650%	+81%	+47%	+275%	+109%	−23%
Wheat	+164%	+321%	+692%	+57%	+64%	−22%	−21%
Median Change	+59%	+489%	+131%	+156%	+153%	+24%	−5%

Note: Changes measured April to April.
Source: Anne Bezanson, et al., *Prices and Inflation During the American Revolution: Pennsylvania, 1770–1790* (1951), 322.

TABLE 4.222 YEARLY INCREASES IN COMMODITY PRICES AT PHILADELPHIA, 1785–1800

	Milled Grain	Garden Produce	Meats	Dairy Goods	Fuel	Building Lumber	Textile Fabrics	Hides, Leather
1800	+17.2%	+28.8%	+7.5%	−1.6%	+5.7%	+7.9%	−2.6%	+2.1%
1799	+7.2%	−31.9%	−15.5%	+0.1%	−9.3%	+0.2%	−2.0%	+2.9%
1798	−22.7%	+0.3%	−6.5%	+17.0%	+2.2%	−7.3%	−4.0%	+19.7%
1797	−17.6%	+4.1%	−4.1%	−13.4%	−9.0%	+4.0%	+2.8%	−6.1%
1796	+17.6%	+37.2%	+11.2%	−3.9%	+6.7%	+14.9%	+7.9%	−24.0%
1795	+50.1%	+1.3%	+13.9%	+0.1%	+21.2%	+18.3%	+8.7%	+10.9%
1794	+17.5%	+2.9%	+16.9%	+19.2%	+19.7%	+5.5%	+13.1%	+3.1%
1793	+9.3%	+9.0%	+19.9%	+16.9%	+8.0%	+10.4%	+12.4%	+0.3%
1792	−1.1%	−2.4%	+2.0%	+7.0%	−2.6%	+7.8%	−0.1%	−3.3%
1791	−20.8%	+8.6%	+13.6%	+2.1%	+5.6%	+16.8%	−2.0%	−3.6%
1790	+33.9%	+11.2%	+9.8%	+36.0%	+5.6%	+1.1%	0.0	+11.9%
1789	+6.7%	−15.7%	−17.3%	−8.8%	−9.0%	+6.7%	+0.3%	+2.1%
1788	−10.1%	−24.2%	−15.8%	−12.3%	−11.5%	−3.6%	−5.8%	−2.9%
1787	−14.0%	−1.9%	−2.1%	−9.9%	+5.4%	−11.1%	+2.7%	−9.3%
1786	−2.2%	+2.5%	−2.7%	−3.9%	+3.2%	−21.7%	+7.1%	+9.4%
1785	−9.7%	+13.6%	−2.1%	−21.8%	−15.4%	−9.3%	−5.3%	−6.7%

Source: Anne Bezanson, et al., *Wholesale Prices in Philadelphia, 1784–1861* (1936), I, 424, 425.

TABLE 4.223 PRICE INDEX FOR MARYLAND FOODSTUFFS, 1763–1800

	Grains[a] (1753 = 1.00)	Meats[b] (1753 = 1.00)	Spirits[c] (1753 = 1.00)	Male Wages (1753 = 1.00)
1800	3.082	1.445	. . .	. . .
1799	2.956	1.445	4.292	. . .
1798	2.068	1.590	. . .	. . .
1797	2.531	1.632	. . .	. . .
1796	2.864	1.339	. . .	1.880
1795	1.921	1.311	3.777	. . .
1794	1.359	1.632	2.146	1.880
1793	1.753	1.381	2.384	1.252
1792	1.471	1.297	1.429	1.252
1791	1.011	1.199	. . .	1.504
1790	1.658	1.283	. . .	. . .
1789	1.288	1.255	. . .	. . .
1788	. . .	1.409	. . .	. . .
1787	1.105	1.618	. . .	.750
1786	1.749	. . .	. . .	.750
1785	1.749	1.994	2.146	.750
1784	2.585	1.702	. . .	1.000
1783	1.140	1.144	. . .	.874
1782	1.011	1.004	. . .	.750
1781	1.140	1.576	. . .	.750

	Grains[a] (1753 = 1.00)	Meats[b] (1753 = 1.00)	Spirits[c] (1753 = 1.00)	Male Wages (1753 = 1.00)
1780	1.266	1.478	.785	1.000
1779	1.391	1.063	. . .	1.000
1778	.994	5.566	. . .	1.000
1777	1.630	2.622	. . .	1.000
1776	1.073	1.148	. . .	1.000
1775	1.212	.803	. . .	1.000
1774	1.313	.767	. . .	1.000
1773	1.311	1.381	. . .	1.000
1772	1.530	1.199	. . .	1.000
1771	1.320	1.199	. . .	1.000
1770	1.352	1.213	. . .	1.000
1769	1.232	1.548	. . .	1.000
1768	1.233	1.437	. . .	1.041
1767	1.351	1.339	. . .	1.000
1766	1.245	1.144	.858	. . .
1765	1.073	1.116	1.144	1.000
1764	.993	1.297	1.144	1.252
1763	1.504	.879	1.144	1.252

[a] Corn and wheat.
[b] Beef and pork.
[b] Whiskey and rum.
Source: Donald R. Adams, Jr., "One Hundred Years of Prices and Wages: Maryland, 1750–1850," *Working Papers of the Regional Economic History Research Center* V (1982), 97–98.

Transportation and Communications

The first great period of conscious improvement in overland transportation occurred after the Revolutionary War. The colonial legislatures had financed virtually no projects to shorten or widen roads, which generally followed well-worn Indian paths, or to expand navigation along interior waterways. As long as most Americans had lived within sixty miles of the seacoast, and could send their products inexpensively to overseas markets, there had been minimal need for reducing the cost and time required for land travel. By the 1780s, however, the population had shifted so far westward that great economic incentive existed to lessen the cost of hauling farm produce to port cities and taking merchants' wares to the interior settlements.

State governments were reluctant to levy taxes or incur heavy debts for public works, so they encouraged private enterprise to assume this responsibility. Between 1783 and 1800, the legislatures chartered 219 corporations willing to improve roads or waterways. A third of these projects concerned toll bridges, another third involved turnpikes, and the rest related to inland navigation.

Toll-bridge companies were only formed to shorten routes between public highways already supported by local taxes. The first venture of this type was the Proprietors of the Charles-River Bridge, which was formed in 1785 and spent $51,000 linking Charlestown with Boston. New England made the most use of toll-bridge construction to reduce distances between markets, and New Hampshire chartered more than one quarter of all such companies. Toll bridges were relatively inexpensive, and before 1800 none cost more than the $80,000 spent to span the Raritan River at New Brunswick, New Jersey.

The earliest turnpike company formed in 1789 to renovate the road from Norwich to New London, Connecticut with lottery proceeds, and the company gained legislative permission to collect tolls three years later. Pennsylvania created the first incorporated turnpike company in 1792 when it authorized a private highway from the Schuykill's middle ferry to Lancaster. Completed in two years at a cost of $465,000, the sixty-two-mile Lancaster Pike (later enlarged by thirty miles) was the most expensive and the longest toll road built in the early national period. The average turnpike extended twenty or thirty miles and required less than $100,000 to build.

TABLE 4.224   EXPANSION OF THE UNITED STATES POST OFFICE, 1785–1800

Year	Number of Post Offices	Extent of Postal Roads	Amount of Postage Collected
1785	. . .	. . .	$29,958.00
1786	66	. . .	$27,096.00
1787	. . .	. . .	$29,243.00
1788	. . .	. . .	. . .
1789	75	. . .	. . .
1790	75	1,875	$37,934.92
1791	89	1,905	$46,294.43
1792	195	5,642	$67,443.86
1793	209	5,642	$104,746.67
1794	450	11,984	$128,947.19
1795	453	13,207	$160,629.97
1796	468	13,207	$195,066.88
1797	554	16,180	$213,998.50
1798	639	16,180	$232,977.45
1799	677	16,180	$264,846.17
1800	903	20,817	$280,804.31

Sources: Timothy Pitkin, *A Statistical Abstract of the Commerce of the United States of America* (1835), 338. Wesley E. Rich, *The History of the United States Post Office to the Year 1829* (1924), 64, 69. Jennings B. Sanders, *The Evolution of Executive Departments in the Continental Congress, 1774–1789* (1935), 165.

The most difficult undertakings concerned inland navigation. Efforts to make shallow rivers carry more traffic or to open up landlocked territories to commerce sparked an early boom in canal construction during the 1790s. Among the most ambitious projects were attempts to link the Susquehanna River with both the Delaware River and Chesapeake Bay; to build the Potomac River Canal; to clear obstructions from Virginia's James River; and to link Norfolk to North Carolina via a canal in Dismal Swamp. Most such projects underestimated numerous engineering problems and experienced long delays for lack of expertise or funds, and many were long behind schedule when finally completed in the nineteenth century. Although some inland waterways projects brought great benefits, such as in the Chesapeake where more than 600 miles were opened up to boat traffic along the Potomac and James rivers, many canals failed to produce benefits justifying their expenditures.

National communications also improved greatly during the 1790s through a rapid expansion of the post office. In place of the haphazard system of letter delivery characteristic of the colonial decades and Confederation era, the federal government undertook to create a truly extensive and efficient system of mail delivery. The number of post offices multiplied more than tenfold from 1789 to 1800 and the volume of mail, as measured by postage receipts, grew sevenfold. The post office's rapid development was especially laudable because it was accomplished despite a rudimentary road network, even in the settled districts, and in the face of hostile Indians on the frontier, where Kentucky's first mail carrier was scalped in 1793.

Although the traditional responsibility for improving and maintaining roads lay with townships and counties, states became increasingly involved in this activity after 1780. States rarely used tax money to build transportation projects, but rather chartered companies to construct roads that collected fares at tollgates like the one pictured above. (*Harper's Magazine*, November 1879)

TABLE 4.225   CORPORATIONS CHARTERED TO BUILD TRANSPORTATION PROJECTS, 1789–1800
A = Toll bridges.   B = Canals.   C = Turnpikes.

	1800	1799	1798	1797	1796	1795	1794	1793	1792	1791	1790	1789
Maine												
A	...	...	1	4	2	1	2	2	...	...	...	...
B	...	...	...	2	1	2	...	...	1	1	...	...
N.H.												
A	2	...	...	3	...	8	2	1	3	...	...	...
B	...	...	1	...	2	...	...	...	2	...	...	...
C	1	2	...	...	1	...	...	...	...	...	...	...
Vt.												
A	...	1	...	2	...	2	...	...	...	...	...	...
B	...	...	...	1	...	1	1	...	1	1	...	...
C	4	3	...	1	1	...	...	...	...	...	...	...
Mass.												
A	...	...	1	1	2	...	1	2	4	...	...	...
B	...	...	...	...	...	...	1	1	3	...	...	...
C	3	3	...	2	1	...	...	...	...	...	...	...
R.I.												
A	...	...	...	...	...	...	1	...	2	...	...	...
B	...	...	...	...	1	...	...	...	...	...	...	...
C	1	...	...	...	...	...	2	...	...	...	...	...
Conn.												
A	...	...	1	1	1	...	...	...	...	...	...	...
B	1	...	...	...	...	1	...	...	...	...	...	...
C	5	2	6	6	...	4	...	...	...	...	...	...
N.Y.												
A	...	...	...	1	...	...	...	...	...	...	...	...
B	...	...	1	...	...	...	...	...	2	...	...	...
C	5	5	2	1	...	...	...	...	...	...	...	...
N.J.												
A	...	1	1	1	...	1	...	...	1	...	...	...
B	1	...	...	1	1	1	...	...	...	...	...	...
C	...	...	...	...	...	...	...	...	...	...	...	...
Pa.												
A	...	...	2	1	...	1	...	1	...	...	...	...
B	...	...	1	...	...	...	...	2	1	1	...	...
C	...	...	1	...	2	...	1	...	1	...	...	...
Del.												
B	...	...	...	...	...	...	...	1	...	...	...	...
Md.												
A	...	...	1	...	1	1	...	...	...	1	...	...
B	...	1	...	...	1	...	...	...	...	...	...	...
C	...	...	2	...	1	...	...	...	...	...	...	...
Va.												
B	1	...	1	...	1	3	...	1	...	...	...	1
C	1	...	...	...	...	2	...	...	...	...	...	...
N.C.												
B	...	...	1	...	5	1	...	...	1	...	2	...
S.C.												
A	...	...	...	...	...	...	1	...	...	...	...	...
B	...	1	...	1	...	...	...	...	...	...	...	...
Ga.												
B	...	1	...	...	...	...	...	...	...	...	...	...
Ky.												
A	...	1	...	...	...	...	...	...	...	...	...	...
Totals												
A	2	3	7	14	6	14	7	6	10	1	...	...
B	3	3	5	5	12	9	2	5	11	3	2	1
C	20	15	11	10	6	6	3	...	1	...	...	...

Source: Joseph S. Davis, *Essays in the Early History of American Corporations* (1917), II, 118, 216, 218.

Unfree Labor

When the War of Independence began, approximately 20% of American workers were slaves and perhaps another 2% or 3% were indentured servants or convict laborers working without pay for several years. In 1774, the gross value (sterling) represented by all unfree laborers totaled about £21,400,000, nearly 20% of the collective wealth owned within the thirteen colonies. Ninety-five percent of all bonded laborers lived in the South, where the majority toiled to produce North America's most valuable exports, tobacco and rice. Indentured servants, and even many slaves, also performed a wide variety of skilled tasks that added significantly to the country's aggregate economic output.

Indentured and Convict Labor

Following the end of the Seven Years' War, which had greatly disrupted the flow of unpaid, contract laborers from Europe, Anglo-Americans resumed buying large numbers of indentured servants and convicts sentenced to overseas labor. Approximately half of the 125,000 British immigrants who arrived from 1763 to 1775 came as bonded laborers. Numerous Germans also financed their passage by selling themselves as servants popularly called "redemptioners."

Indentures were most commonly used as a means for financing immigration by people with few marketable skills and less savings. More than 10% of servants leaving England in the 1770s nevertheless possessed significant experience as artisans, and over half had learned the basics of some handicraft. Mature individuals with some useful trade frequently obtained their ship's passage in return for four years' work, during which they were housed, fed, and sometimes permitted to work for hire in their spare hours. In light of these privileges, and the financial benefits of free ocean travel and free sustenance for several years, a Scotsman named John Campbell in 1772 characterized indentured servitude as "a kind of apprenticeship into the customs of the country and the system of production that proves to be invaluable."

TABLE 4.227 IMMIGRATION OF BONDED LABORERS TO THE THIRTEEN COLONIES, 1763–1775

	Number	Percent	Value
All British immigrants	125,000	100%	. . .
Indentured servants	60,000	48%	£210,000[a]
Transported convicts	12,500	10%	£125,000[b]
German immigrants	12,000	100%	. . .
Redemptioners	4,000	35%	£14,000[a]
All European immigrants	137,000	100%	. . .
Unfree laborers	76,500	56%	£349,000

[a] Valued @ £3.10.0 sterling each.
[b] Valued @ £10 sterling each.
Sources: Bernard Bailyn, Voyagers to the West: A Passage in the Peopling of America on the Eve of the Revolution (1986), 26, 166, 295. Kenneth Morgan, "The Organization of the Convict Trade to Maryland: Stevenson, Randolph & Cheston, 1768–1775," William and Mary Quarterly XLII (1985), 221. Marianne Wokeck, "The Flow and Composition of German Immigration to Philadelphia, 1727–1775," Pennsylvania Magazine of History and Biography CV (1981), 249–78.

Each year from 1763 to 1775, the colonies also absorbed about one thousand felons (of which a fifth were women) sentenced to be transported from Britain and auctioned as servants overseas. Terms of service ranged from seven years, for those found guilty of minor offenses, to fourteen years for anyone facing a death verdict. British courts shipped the great majority of convicts to Maryland and Virginia. The main incentive for southern planters to buy criminals was that they sold for a third less than for a slave of equal age, but this discount was necessary to offset the financial risk that convicts would run away, as at least 10% of this group eventually did.

The Revolutionary War interrupted the flow of servants into the United States. When peace resumed in 1783, the importation of indentured servants never revived and this group ceased to be a significant part of America's labor force. A short-lived attempt by a few British merchants and Chesapeake planters to resume the convict trade proved abortive in the 1780s, and this commerce also failed to reestablish itself. The role of white indentured workers in the labor market thereafter dwindled to insignificance, and slaves remained the only significant group of unfree workers.

TABLE 4.226 BACKGROUNDS OF BRITISH SERVANTS SENT TO NORTH AMERICA 1773–1776

Nationality:	English	79.4%
	Scottish	15.9%
	Irish, others	4.7%
Sex:	Males	85.0%
	Females	15.0%
Age:	Average	23.7 years
	Agriculturalists	25.5 years
	Skilled craftsmen	25.7 years
	Textile workers	24.3 years
	Laborers	20.7 years
	English males	24.4 years
	English Females	22.7 years
	Scottish Males	21.8 years
	Scottish females	20.0 years
Destination:	Md.	50.6%
	Va.	15.5%
	Pa.	21.7%
	Carolinas, Ga.	5.6%
	N.Y.	6.5%

Source: Bernard Bailyn, Voyagers to the West: A Passage to the Peopling of America on the Eve of the Revolution (1986), 179, 181, 182, 213.

TABLE 4.228 PRICES (STERLING) OF INDENTURED SERVANTS AND CONVICTS, 1767–1775

Servants Sold at Philadelphia Jun.–Sep. 1774		Convicts Sold in Maryland 1767–1775			
			Percent Sold by Sex		
Category	Average Price	Price	Males	Females	Sex Unknown
Males[a]	£18.0.0	0–£4	1.9%	0.9%	34.1%
Females[b]	£15.0.0	£5–9	24.4%	71.8%	65.9%
Aged 14 to 20	£17.10.0	£10–14	57.0%	26.4%	. . .
Aged 20 to 24	£20.0.0	£15–19	12.6%	0.9%	. . .
Aged over 24	£16.10.0	£20–24	3.1%	. . .	. . .
Schoolmaster	£15.0.0	£25–34	1.0	. . .	. . .

[a] Of 14 males, 4 were farmers, 4 laborers, 5 artisans, 1 a teacher.
[b] Five of 11 females sold for £11 each.
Sources: Kenneth Morgan, "The Organization of the Convict Trade to Maryland: Stevenson, Randolph & Cheston, 1768–1775," William and Mary Quarterly XLII (1985), 221. Bernard Bailyn, Voyagers to the West: A Passage in the Peopling of America on the Eve of the Revolution (1986), 334, 345.

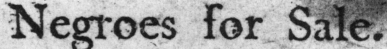

Negroes for Sale.

A Cargo of very fine ſtout Men and Women, in good order and fit for immediate ſervice, juſt imported from the Windward Coaſt of Africa, in the Ship Two Brothers.—— Conditions are one half Caſh or Produce, the other half payable the firſt of January next, giving Bond and Security if required.

The Sale to be opened at 10 o'Clock each Day, in Mr. Bourdeaux's Yard, at No. 48, on the Bay.
May 19, 1784. JOHN MITCHELL.

Thirty Seaſoned Negroes

To be Sold for Credit, at Private Sale.

AMONGST which is a Carpenter, none of whom are known to be diſhoneſt.

Alſo, to be ſold for Caſh, a regular bred young Negroe Man-Cook, born in this Country, who ſerved ſeveral Years under an exceeding good French Cook abroad, and his Wife a middle aged Waſher-Woman, (both very honeſt) and their two Children. Likewiſe, a young Man a Carpenter. For Terms apply to the Printer.

The importation of African slaves was expanding rapidly until the Revolution cut off this trade. All states had ended the overseas slave trade by the Revolution's end, but South Carolina and Georgia reopened this commerce to replace laborers who had run off to join British troops and left the country. Congress finally abolished the slave trade in 1808. [Reproduction of advertisement from newspaper, about May 19, 1784, probably from South Carolina or Georgia] (Courtesy Library of Congress)

TABLE 4.229 NUMBER AND VALUE OF SLAVES IN THE UNITED STATES, 1790–1800

	Census of 1790			Census of 1800	
	Number	Percent of Population	Estimated Value	Number	Percent Increase
U.S.	697,624	17.8%	$104,643,600	893,602	+28.1%
N.H.	157	0.1%	$23,550	8	−94.9%
Mass.	. . .	. . .	. . .	. . .	. . .
R.I.	958	1.4%	$143,700	380	−60.3%
Conn.	2,648	1.1%	$397,200	951	−64.1%
N.Y.	21,193	6.2%	$3,178,950	20,903	−1.4%
N.J.	11,423	6.2%	$1,713,450	12,422	+8.7%
Pa.	3,707	0.9%	$556,050	1,706	−53.0%
Del.	8,887	15.0%	$1,333,050	6,153	−30.8%
Md.	103,036	32.2%	$15,455,400	107,707	+4.5%
Va.	292,627	39.1%	$43,894,050	346,968	+18.6%
N.C.	100,783	25.5%	$15,117,450	133,296	+32.3%
S.C.	107,094	43.0%	$16,064,100	146,151	+36.5%
Ga.	29,264	35.5%	$4,389,600	59,232	+103.0%
Ky.	12,430	16.9%	$1,864,500	40,343	+224.6%
Tenn.	3,417	9.6%	$512,550	13,584	+297.5%
Ind.	. . .	. . .	. . .	135	. . .

Source: Bureau of the Census, *A Century of Population Growth, 1790–1900* (1909), 82, 133, 134.

TABLE 4.230 SLAVE OWNERSHIP AMONG WHITE FAMILIES, 1790

	Slave-owning Families		Average Slaves per Family	% of Slave-owning Families Possessing			
	Number	Percent		1 Slave	2–4 Slaves	5–9 Slaves	10+ Slaves
U.S.	96,168	17.2%	7.3	24.5%	30.4%	22.0%	23.1%
N.H.	123	0.5%	1.3	78.9%	19.5%	1.6%	. . .
R.I.	461	4.1%	2.1	55.3%	34.7%	9.8%	0.2%
Conn.	1,563	3.8%	1.7	62.7%	32.3%	4.2%	0.8%
N.Y.	7,796	14.2%	2.7	42.2%	39.3%	16.0%	2.5%
N.J.	4,760	16.0%	2.4	. . .	. . .	. . .	. . .
Pa.	1,858	2.5%	2.0	55.5%	35.9%	7.8%	0.8%
Del.	1,851	22.5%	4.8	. . .	. . .	. . .	. . .
Md.	13,777	38.0%	7.5	23.2%	29.6%	23.0%	24.2%
Va.	34,026	44.9%	8.5	17.0%	27.9%	25.2%	29.9%
N.C.	16,310	31.0%	6.7	27.0%	33.1%	22.5%	17.4%
S.C.	8,859	34.2%	12.1	21.8%	29.4%	20.9%	27.9%
Ga.	2,419	24.5%	12.1	. . .	. . .	. . .	. . .
Ky.	1,855	17.0%	6.7	. . .	. . .	. . .	. . .
Tenn.	510	8.8%	6.7	. . .	. . .	. . .	. . .

Source: Bureau of the Census, *A Century of Population Growth: 1790–1900* (1909), 135, 136.

Slavery

Slaves constituted the largest occupational group in late-eighteenth-century America except for white farmers. Between 1763 and 1775, the thirteen colonies imported 84,500 African laborers, or 38% of all persons arriving as new residents. Slavery was most extensive in the South, but it was legal throughout all the northern provinces; and in fact slaves composed nearly 8% of New Jersey's and 12% of New York's population. About half of all slaves belonged to a wealthy class of planters possessing at least ten (but rarely over twenty) individuals, but the institution of bondage was widely distributed within southern society. By the eve of the Revolution, every third southern white family owned at least one or two unfree blacks, who usually performed the same daily routine as their masters. An increasing number of slaves performed skilled labor as craftsmen, especially in urban areas like Charles Town, South Carolina.

The Revolution seriously undermined slavery's place in the American economy. Perhaps one of every sixteen slaves escaped their masters and joined the British, and their number could not be replaced because the war ended importations from Africa. An increasing number of whites came to view perpetual servitude as incompatible with a democratic society, and they pressed for an end to the slave trade and eventual extinction of human bondage. Few slaves were imported after 1783, and by 1804 seven northern states had either abolished slavery outright or passed laws for gradual emancipation. The number of free persons within the African-American community consequently rose from about 2% in 1775 to 11% in 1800.

CHAPTER 5 Population Statistics

The Population of the United States

The Revolutionary War strongly influenced population growth in British North America. The hostilities sharply cut population increase during the 1770s, in large part because perhaps 100,000 white Loyalists and 20,000 runaway slaves left the United States. The war also temporarily curtailed European emigration and reduced the importation of Africans to a trickle. After peace returned in 1783, the population rose quickly, and it grew at a rate of 41% during 1781–1790, two-fifths higher than during 1771–1780.

Despite the dislocations caused by the War of Independence, the American population continued to expand at rates far higher than in other eighteenth-century societies. The population almost doubled in the thirty years from 1770 to 1800, although this rate represented a decline from the previous half-century when it took just twenty-five years to double. The Revolution slowed population growth in the United States, but the country's fertility rate was so high that its effects were little more than temporary.

A major reason why the population rose so rapidly was that it was exceptionally young. Approximately half of all inhabitants were under the age of sixteen. (In 1990, by contrast, the nation's median age was thirty-two.) By 1790, only half the inhabitants had been alive when the "shot heard round the world" had exploded at Lexington, and by 1800 a majority had been born since the end of the Revolution. Under such circumstances, the population could rebound quickly once war's distractions had disappeared.

The late eighteenth century nevertheless witnessed the start of a gradual decline in the proportion of inhabitants who were nonwhite. Because Americans bought a large volume of slaves from overseas, black population growth exceeded that of whites for most of the 1700s. After 1775, when the percentage of Americans who were nonwhite reached its historical high point, at 21%, the rate of increase for African Americans slowed significantly due to the slave trade's end and the evacuation of perhaps 20,000 African Americans (4% of all) by British military authorities. The number of blacks thereafter expanded much less than the number of whites, until by 1800 the nonwhite segment of the population had fallen to 19%, and it continued declining to almost half this level in the next century.

With the enumeration of the first census in 1790, the earliest and most systematic data on population began to become available. (The only nation to institute a national census prior to the United States was Sweden, which first did so in 1749.) Although far superior to the haphazard counts of residents undertaken in the colonial period, the federal government's censuses experienced great difficulty in generating accurate figures, which always seem to have undercounted the inhabitants by at least a tenth until 1880. The earliest census data is far from perfect, although most scholars tend to accept it uncritically, and hopefully historical demographers will develop techniques to revise these statistics.

TABLE 5.1 COMPOSITION OF THE THIRTEEN COLONIES' POPULATION, 1774

	Total Number	Percent of Total	Percent of Subgroup
Total Population	2,353,967	100.0%	. . .
White Inhabitants	1,855,274	78.8%	100.0%
Status Independent	1,802,258	76.6%	97.1%
Status Indentured[a]	53,016	2.3%	2.9%
Black Inhabitants	498,693	21.2%	100.0%
Legally Free	17,761	.8%	3.6%
Slaves	480,932	20.4%	96.4%
All Males Aged 21+	511,487	21.7%	100.0%
Taxpaying Property Owners	396,162	16.8%	77.5%
All Females Aged 21+	499,299	21.2%	100.0%
Taxpaying Property Owners	38,673	1.6%	7.7%
All Youths Under 21	1,343,181	57.1%	. . .
Free Population[b]	1,820,019	77.3%	. . .
All Free Adult Males	396,158	16.8%	100.0%
Aged 21–25	87,087	3.7%	22.0%
Aged 26–44	189,673	8.1%	47.9%
Aged 45+	119,398	5.1%	30.1%
All Free Adult Females	389,405	16.5%	100.0%
Aged 21–25	89,933	3.8%	23.1%
Aged 26–44	180,941	7.7%	46.5%
Aged 45+	118,531	5.0%	30.4%
All Free Youths Under 21	1,034,456	43.9%	. . .

[a] Indentured servants and convict laborers.
[b] Includes free Negroes.
Source: Alice Hanson Jones, *American Colonial Wealth: Documents and Methods* (1978), 1787.

The most striking difference between the populations of the United States and Europe was the extraordinarily high birth rate of Anglo-Americans, who reproduced at nearly the biological maximum. This sketch by Lewis Miller recalls the baptism of a newborn child in York, Pennsylvania as follows: "Rev. Jacob Goering Administers Baptism, in the old Lutheran Church, to A Child. May 26th, 1799, was Baptist A Son of George Freinsrock And his Wife Elisabet, the Sponsors were Jacob Miller, and wife Sabina, the little Son was Born April 22d." The artist has pictured himself in the lower right-hand corner. (Courtesy The Historical Society of York County, Pennsylvania)

TABLE 5.2 FIRST CENSUS OF THE UNITED STATES, 1790

Districts	Free White Males of 16 Years and Upwards, Including Heads of Families	Free White Males Under 16 Years	Free White Females, Including Heads of Families	All Other Free Persons Except Indians Not Taxed	Slaves	Total in Each District
Vermont	22,335	22,328	40,505	225	16	85,539
New Hampshire	36,086	34,851	70,160	630	158	141,885
Maine	24,384	24,748	46,870	538	. . .	96,540
Massachusetts	95,453	87,289	190,582	5,463	. . .	378,787
Rhode Island	16,019	15,799	32,652	3,407	948	68,825
Connecticut	60,593	54,403	117,448	2,808	2,764	237,946
New York	84,700	78,122	152,320	4,654	21,324	340,120
New Jersey	45,251	41,416	73,287	2,762	11,423	184,139
Pennsylvania	110,788	106,948	206,363	6,537	3,737	434,373
Delaware	11,783	12,143	22,384	3,899	8,887	59,094
Maryland	55,916	51,339	101,395	8,043	103,036	319,728
Virginia	110,936	116,135	215,056	12,866	292,627	747,610
Kentucky	15,154	17,057	28,922	114	12,430	73,677
North Carolina	69,988	77,506	140,710	4,975	100,572	393,751
South Carolina	35,576	37,722	56,880	1,801	107,094	240,073
Georgia	13,103	14,044	25,739	398	29,264	82,548
Western Territories[a]	6,271	10,227	15,365	361	3,417	36,691
	814,396	802,077	1,476,638	59,481	697,697	3,921,326

[a] 35,691 in Tenn. See Table 5.53.
Source: Adam Seybert, *Statistical Annals: Embracing Views of . . . the United States of America, 1789–1818* (1818), 20.

TABLE 5.3 SECOND CENSUS OF THE UNITED STATES, 1800

Names of States	Free White Males					Free White Females					All Other Free Persons Except Indians Not Taxed	Slaves	Total
	Under 10 Years of Age	Of 10 and Under 16	Of 16 and Under 26	Of 26 and Under 45	Of 45 and Upwards	Under 10 Years of Age	Of 10 and Under 16	Of 16 and Under 26	Of 26 and Under 45	Of 45 and Upwards			
Vt.	29,420	12,046	13,242	16,544	8,076	28,272	11,366	12,606	15,287	7,049	557	...	154,465
N.H.	30,694	14,881	16,379	17,589	11,715	29,871	14,193	17,153	18,381	12,142	855	8	183,858
Mass.	63,646	32,507	37,905	39,729	31,348	60,920	30,674	40,491	43,833	35,340	6,552	...	422,845
Maine	27,970	12,305	12,900	15,318	8,339	26,899	11,338	13,295	14,496	8,041	818	...	151,719
R.I.	9,945	5,352	5,889	5,785	4,887	9,524	5,026	6,463	6,939	5,648	3,304	380	69,122
Conn.	37,946	19,408	21,683	23,180	18,976	35,736	18,218	23,561	25,186	20,827	5,300	951	251,002
N.Y.	100,097	44,273	49,275	61,594	31,855	95,473	39,471	48,116	56,411	28,651	10,374	20,613	586,050
N.J.	33,900	15,859	16,301	19,956	12,629	32,622	14,827	17,018	19,534	11,600	4,402	12,422	211,149
Pa.	103,226	46,061	54,262	59,333	38,585	99,624	43,789	53,947	53,846	33,395	14,564	1,706	602,545
Del.	8,250	4,437	5,121	5,012	2,213	7,628	4,277	5,543	4,981	2,390	8,268	6,153	64,273
Md.	36,751	17,743	21,929	23,553	13,712	34,703	16,787	22,915	21,725	12,180	19,987	107,707	349,692
Va.	93,327	40,820	49,191	50,819	30,442	87,993	39,148	51,209	41,746	34,179	20,507	346,968	886,149
Ky.	37,274	14,045	15,705	17,699	9,238	34,949	13,433	15,524	14,934	7,075	741	40,343	220,959
N.C.	63,118	27,073	31,560	31,209	18,688	59,074	25,874	32,989	30,665	17,514	7,043	133,296	478,105
S.C.	37,411	16,156	17,761	19,344	10,244	34,664	15,857	18,145	17,236	9,437	3,185	146,151	345,591
Ga.	19,841	8,469	9,787	10,914	4,957	18,407	7,914	9,243	8,835	3,894	1,919	59,699	162,686
Tenn.	19,227	7,194	8,282	8,352	4,125	18,450	7,042	8,554	6,992	3,491	309	13,584	105,602
N.W. Terr.	9,362	3,637	4,636	4,833	1,955	8,644	3,353	3,861	3,342	1,395	337	...	45,365
Indiana Terr.	854	347	466	645	262	791	280	424	393	115	163	135	5,641
Miss. Terr.	999	356	482	780	290	933	376	352	426	165	182	3,489	8,850
Total	713,258	342,979	392,756	477,188	262,536	725,197	323,243	402,426	405,179	254,528	109,289	893,605	5,289,573
D. Columbia	1,788	671	1,178	1,332	539	1,577	663	1,027	1,028	463	783	3,244	14,093

Source: Samuel Blodgett, Economica: A Statistical Manual for the United States of America (1806), 72.

TABLE 5.4 RATES OF POPULATION GROWTH IN UNITED STATES, 1760–1800

	From 1790 to 1800	From 1780 to 1790	From 1770 to 1780	From 1760 to 1770
Total Population[a]	5,309,858	3,929,326	2,780,369	2,148,076
Decennial increase	1,380,532	1,148,957	632,293	554,451
Rate of increase	35%	41%	29%	35%
White Population[a]	4,304,501	3,172,464	2,204,949	1,688,254
Rate of increase	36%	44%	31%	33%
Black Population[a]	1,002,037	757,181	575,420	459,822
Rate of increase	32%	25%	41%	38%
New England	1,233,000	1,009,000	713,000	581,000
Rate of increase	22%	41%	23%	29%
Mid-Atlantic	1,466,000	1,017,000	723,000	556,000
Rate of increase	44%	41%	30%	30%
South	2,549,000[b]	1,905,000[b]	1,344,000[b]	995,000
Rate of increase	34%	42%	35%	39%

[a]Population as of latest date.
[b]Includes Kentucky and Tennessee.
Source: Research of Stella H. Sutherland, in Bureau of the Census, *Historical Statistics of the United States: Colonial Times to 1957* (1960), 756.

TABLE 5.5 DISTRIBUTION OF WHITE POPULATION BY SEX, AGE, AND RACE, 1790

	Percent Male	Percent Female	Percent Aged 1–15	Percent Aged 16+	Percent Nonwhite
U.S.	50.9%	49.1%	49.0%	51.0%	19.3%
New England	49.8%	50.2%	47.0%	53.0%	1.7%
Maine	51.1%	48.9%	50.7%	49.3%	.6%
N.H.	50.3%	49.7%	48.6%	51.4%	.6%
Vt.	52.6%	47.4%	51.3%	48.7%	.3%
Mass.	49.0%	51.0%	45.5%	54.5%	1.4%
R.I.	49.2%	50.8%	46.4%	53.6%	6.4%
Conn.	49.5%	50.5%	45.4%	54.6%	2.3%
Mid-Atlantic	51.4%	48.6%	49.4%	50.6%	6.2%
N.Y.	51.6%	48.4%	49.3%	50.7%	7.6%
N.J.	51.0%	49.0%	48.7%	51.3%	7.7%
Pa.	51.4%	48.6%	49.8%	50.2%	2.4%
Del.	51.7%	48.3%	49.4%	50.6%	21.6%
South	51.5%	48.5%	50.2%	49.8%	35.6%
Md.	51.4%	48.6%	45.0%	55.0%	34.7%
Va.	51.4%	48.6%	49.7%	50.3%	40.9%
N.C.	51.1%	48.9%	51.9%	48.1%	26.8%
S.C.	52.3%	47.7%	52.2%	47.8%	43.7%
Ga.	51.3%	48.7%	53.1%	46.9%	35.9%
Ky.	52.7%	47.3%	54.5%	45.5%	17.0%
Tenn.	51.9%	48.1%	55.0%	45.0%	10.6%

Source: Bureau of the Census, *A Century of Population Growth, 1790–1800* (1909), 54–58, 82, 91–94.

TABLE 5.6 DISTRIBUTION OF WHITE POPULATION BY AGE AND SEX, 1800

	New England	New York	Mid-Atlantic States	The South
Male	48.2%	52.0%	51.7%	51.3%
Female	51.8%	48.0%	48.3%	48.7%
Adults Aged 21+	43.9%	43.6%	40.9%	39.8%
Youths Aged 16–20	9.2%	9.3%	9.2%	9.7%
Children Aged 10–15	15.5%	16.3%	15.6%	15.8%
Children to Age 9	31.4%	30.8%	34.3%	34.7%

Source: Alice Hanson Jones, *American Colonial Wealth: Documents and Methods* (1978), 1800, 1801.

Population of New England

New England experienced the slowest growth rate of any part of the United States during the Revolutionary era. The region imported virtually no slaves and attracted few immigrants. A substantial number of Yankees left the region for better land in the mid-Atlantic states during every decade but the 1780s, when New England's own internal frontier of Vermont and Maine opened up to large-scale settlement. New England's growth rates lagged consistently behind those elsewhere in the United States, in particular during the 1790s, when the usual exodus of Yankees took on the dimensions of a mass-migration into the lands abandoned by the Iroquois in upstate New York. As a result of this steady outflow of largely youthful human talent, New England entered the nineteenth century inhabited by a population relatively older and more female than was typical of the nation.

TABLE 5.7 COMPOSITION OF THE NEW ENGLAND COLONIES' POPULATION, 1774

	Total Number	Percent of Total	Percent of Subgroup
Total Population	607,795	100.0%	. . .
White Inhabitants	592,791	97.5%	100.0%
Status Independent	580,935	95.6%	98.0%
Status Indentured[a]	11,856	2.0%	2.0%
Black Inhabitants	15,004	2.5%	100.0%
Legally Free	1,350	.2%	9.0%
Slaves	13,654	2.2%	91.0%
All Males Aged 21+	129,989	21.4%	100.0%
Taxpaying Property Owners	124,536	20.5%	95.8%
All Females Aged 21+	139,872	23.0%	100.0%
Taxpaying Property Owners	13,398	2.2%	9.6%
All Youths Under 21	337,934	55.6%	. . .
Free Population[b]	582,285	95.8%	. . .
All Free Adult Males	124,534	20.5%	100.0%
Aged 21–25	26,311	4.3%	21.1%
Aged 26–44	56,424	9.3%	45.3%
Aged 45+	41,799	6.9%	33.6%
All Free Adult Females	134,001	22.0%	100.0%
Aged 21–25	28,034	4.6%	20.9%
Aged 26–44	60,430	9.9%	45.1%
Aged 45+	45,537	7.5%	34.0%
All Free Youths Under 21	323,750	53.3%	. . .

[a]Indentured servants and convict laborers.
[b]Includes free Negroes.
Source: Alice Hanson Jones, *American Colonial Wealth: Documents and Methods* (1978), 1789.

TABLE 5.8 PROVINCIAL CENSUS OF NEW HAMSPHIRE, 1773

Counties and Towns	Unmarried Men from 16 to 60	Married Men from 16 to 60	Boys 16 Years and Under	Men 60 Years and Upwards	Females Unmarried	Females Married	Widows	Male Slaves	Female Slaves	Total
Total	6,263	10,604	18,334	1,538	22,228	11,887	1,569	379	295	73,097
Rockingham county	3,132	4,835	8,363	943	11,239	5,695	1,034	260	206	35,707[1]
Allenstown	8	17	39	4	49	21	4	. . .	1	143
Atkinson	39	73	132	16	170	87	13	2	3	535
Bow	5	58	84	2	101	58	. . .	. . .	. . .	308
Brentwood	78	146	261	28	365	175	33	2	1	1,089
Candia	52	111	182	2	200	112	4	. . .	. . .	663
Canterbury	66	96	150	10	164	104	5	5	0	600
Chichester	29	44	77	2	75	46	. . .	. . .	. . .	273
Chester	151	229	355	53	453	261	43	5	2	1,552
Concord	96	151	260	30	283	154	12	8	9	1,003
Deerfield	68	143	238	8	290	151	10	2	1	911[1]
Epping	121	225	406	31	571	246	31	10	7	1,648
Epsom	18	53	86	1	109	53	4	1	1	326[1]
Exeter	129	252	366	50	539	270	59	24	25	1,714
East Kingston	29	54	93	20	118	72	13	3	. . .	402
Greenland	70	85	178	16	242	103	20	6	11	731
Hampstead	58	106	181	24	219	125	14	1	0	728
Hampton	80	120	203	36	291	151	33	2	1	917
Hampton Falls	44	146	99	21	218	96	22	1	1	648
Hawke[2]	25	71	110	8	172	81	10	1	0	478
Kensington	65	107	182	34	265	141	28	. . .	. . .	822
Kingston	110	142	201	41	295	172	23	3	2	989
Londonderry	228	299	587	84	833	357	58	12	13	2,471
Loudon	12	36	58	2	54	38	3	. . .	1	204
New Castle	58	89	128	24	167	100	22	7	6	601
Newington	46	62	114	20	172	77	21	21	15	548
Newmarket	113	178	341	22	435	188	43	8	16	1,344
Newtown	52	74	118	24	189	95	18	0	2	572
North Hampton	47	96	172	25	228	116	16	0	2	702
Northwood	9	49	58	2	77	51	4	0	0	250
Nottingham	49	139	251	14	283	139	19	5	5	904
Pelham	49	95	198	21	193	114	12	1	1	684
Pembrook	45	110	176	12	186	119	12	5	1	666
Plaistow	49	78	125	23	194	101	17	3	1	591
Poplin[3]	35	83	156	10	178	91	10	. . .	1	564
Portsmouth	617	371	868	93	1,346	682	235	100	60	4,372
Raymond	44	98	189	11	222	107	12	. . .	. . .	683
Rye	69	113	190	24	259	132	36	12	7	842
Sandown	54	81	148	15	182	95	14	1	0	590
South Hampton	39	67	96	18	153	81	17	1	1	473
Seabrook	48	94	153	17	156	103	25	. . .	. . .	596
Stratham	77	138	234	27	382	161	45	3	1	1,068
Windham	51	56	120	18	161	69	14	5	8	502
Strafford county	932	1,599	2,742	223	3,221	1,775	232	64	38	10,826
Barnstead	12	26	41	3	41	29	. . .	. . .	. . .	152
Barrington	110	223	350	7	397	223	26	4	1	1,341
Dover	172	220	393	43	514	255	42	15	11	1,665
Durham	108	138	266	52	336	183	42	15	9	1,149
East Town[4]	20	49	65	1	64	48	. . .	. . .	1	248
Gilmanton	49	105	180	2	188	105	5	1	. . .	635
Leavitts Town[5]	6	20	30	0	34	21	. . .	. . .	. . .	111
Lee	58	142	257	18	309	157	13	5	1	960
Madbury	34	84	154	29	199	107	15	. . .	3	625
Meredith	23	37	57	0	64	37	0	0	0	218
Moultonborough	28	46	68	2	68	49	2	0	0	263
New Durham	30	42	72	1	88	42	4	1	0	280
Rochester	123	210	346	26	437	241	34	. . .	1	1,420

(continued)

TABLE 5.8   (continued)

Counties and Towns	Unmarried Men from 16 to 60	Married Men from 16 to 60	Boys 16 Years and Under	Men 60 Years and Upwards	Females Unmarried	Females Married	Widows	Male Slaves	Female Slaves	Total
Strafford county										
Sandwich	9	35	64	0	61	35	0	0	0	204
Somersworth	106	140	246	34	278	161	42	20	11	1,038
Sandbornton	28	57	104	3	100	57	2	1	0	352
Wolfborough	16	25	49	2	43	25	5	. . .	. . .	165
Hillsborough county	976	2,112	3,683	207	4,016	2,243	200	39	38	13,514
Amherst	109	237	330	13	412	245	19	3	2	1,370
Bedford	54	62	121	15	49	72	7	4	4	388
Boscawen	34	76	140	11	147	90	6	0	0	504
Camden[6]	11	21	40	. . .	37	21	2	. . .	. . .	132
Derryfield[7]	28	30	77	7	92	40	3	1	1	279
Dunbarton	26	73	148	6	128	78	4	1	. . .	464
Dunstable	51	71	156	18	213	89	5	1	6	610
Goffstown	67	101	195	11	237	107	9	3	2	732
Henniker	19	60	93	2	96	62	5	0	1	338
Hillsborough	16	27	34	3	44	29	. . .	. . .	. . .	153
Hollis	104	180	287	18	355	190	25	2	1	1,162
Hopkinton	43	151	297	10	267	156	17	2	0	943
Litchfield	26	35	68	13	95	43	12	2	5	299
Mason	32	77	136	4	125	81	7	1	. . .	463
Merrimac	50	82	129	8	170	89	11	8	5	552
New Almsbury[8]	10	36	62	4	59	38	4	. . .	. . .	213
New Boston	23	61	137	6	110	64	5	2	2	410
New Britain[9]	9	26	36	2	36	26	. . .	. . .	. . .	135
New Ipswich	48	165	232	5	277	139	12	2	2	882
Nottingham W'st[10]	41	88	150	14	179	100	16	2	2	592
Peterborough	44	66	131	12	172	72	11	3	3	514
Peterborough-Slip	7	14	22	1	23	14	0	0	0	81
Salisbury	20	70	111	5	130	76	3	1	0	416
Temple	28	74	121	2	115	76	2	0	0	418
Weare	39	138	262	10	280	147	7	. . .	1	884
Wilton	37	91	168	7	168	99	8	1	1	580
Cheshire county	793	1,473	2,626	126	2 812	1,568	86	7	2	9,493[1]
Alstead	24	37	66	4	59	42	1	. . .	. . .	233[1]
Charlestown	69	83	151	3	191	85	8	. . .	. . .	590
Chesterfield	55	109	224	12	220	120	7	0	0	747
Claremont	41	66	121	2	125	66	2	0	0	423
Cornish	28	36	52	1	60	35	1	. . .	. . .	213
Croydon	13	16	21	1	23	16	1	. . .	. . .	91
Dublin	16	45	74	1	71	46	1	1	0	255
Fitzwilliam	18	44	55	. . .	53	44	. . .	. . .	. . .	214
Gilsom	17	21	32	4	37	22	2	0	0	135[1]
Hinsdale	28	28	48	5	70	31	8	1	1	220
Jaffrey	13	50	89	2	92	52	5	0	0	303
Keene	65	96	140	11	217	105	10	1	. . .	645
Lempster	11	13	16	. . .	17	9	. . .	. . .	. . .	66
Limerick[11]	16	43	62	2	49	43	. . .	. . .	. . .	215
Marlow	11	29	43	. . .	40	32	1	. . .	. . .	156
Monadnock, No. 5[12]	17	39	88	1	89	40	1	. . .	. . .	275
Monadnock, No. 6[13]	12	23	32	0	27	23	0	0	0	117
Newport	14	23	40	2	54	23	. . .	. . .	. . .	156
Plainfield	32	40	65	6	85	43	4	. . .	. . .	275
Richmond	32	112	257	5	218	115	6	. . .	. . .	745
Rindge	42	99	170	11	166	109	5	2	0	604
Saville[14]	8	16	15	0	16	16	1	0	0	72
Surry	22	30	52	2	70	32	0	0	0	208
Swanzey	42	74	148	13	164	85	9	1	0	536

Counties and Towns	Unmarried Men from 16 to 60	Married Men from 16 to 60	Boys 16 Years and Under	Men 60 Years and Upwards	Females Unmarried	Females Married	Widows	Male Slaves	Female Slaves	Total
Cheshire county										
Unity	7	18	32	. . .	32	17	. . .	. . .	. . .	106
Walpole	48	81	157	11	160	87	5	. . .	. . .	549
Westmoreland	50	109	206	13	198	117	5	0	0	698
Winchester	42	93	170	14	209	113	3	1	1	646
Grafton county	430	585	920	39	940	606	17	9	11	3,557[1]
Apthrop[15]	1	3	4	0	2	3	1	0	0	14
Bath	18	25	46	0	36	25	0	0	0	150
Campton	14	22	39	1	40	22	1	. . .	. . .	139
Canaan	12	11	16	. . .	11	12	. . .	. . .	. . .	62
Conway	40	42	39	4	37	40	1	. . .	. . .	203
Cockermouth[16]	11	22	24	. . .	28	22	. . .	. . .	. . .	107
Dorchester	23	13	33	. . .	38	14	. . .	. . .	. . .	121
New Grantham[17]	7	10	12	2	17	11	0	1	0	60
Hanover	58	49	86	7	80	54	. . .	4	4	342
Haverhill	30	66	107	1	112	66	3	1	1	387
N'w Holderness[18]	9	21	45	6	41	25	0	0	0	147
Lancaster	3	6	8	2	10	7	1	0	0	37
Lebanon	44	50	62	4	79	54	2	0	0	295
Lime	29	37	53	5	71	39	3	2	2	241
New Chester[19]	5	31	63	2	46	32	0	0	0	179
Northumberland	10	9	8	. . .	11	8	0	0	0	46
Orford	17	39	60	3	63	43	1	. . .	2	228
Plymouth	29	57	90	. . .	107	57	2	1	2	345
Stewartstown[20]	24	14	17	. . .	19	14	. . .	. . .	. . .	88
Rumney	21	31	61	1	47	29	2	0	0	192
Thornton	16	13	18	1	12	14	. . .	. . .	. . .	74
Trecothick[21]	8	8	16	. . .	18	8	. . .	. . .	. . .	58[1]
Wentworth	1	6	13	. . .	15	7	. . .	. . .	. . .	42

[1] Corrected figures.
[2] Now Danville.
[3] Now Fremont.
[4] Now Wakefield.
[5] Now Effingham.
[6] Now Washington.
[7] Now Manchester.
[8] Now Warner.
[9] Now Andover.
[10] Now Hudson.
[11] Now Stoddard.
[12] Now Marlborough.
[13] Now Nelson.
[14] Now Sunapee.
[15] Now Dalton.
[16] Now Groton.
[17] Now Grantham.
[18] Now Holderness.
[19] Now Hill.
[20] Including Cockburn and Colbrook.
[21] Now Ellsworth.
Source: Nathaniel Bouton, et al., Documents and Records Relating to the Province of New Hampshire (1867–1943), X, 625–36.

TABLE 5.9 FEDERAL CENSUS OF NEW HAMSPHIRE, 1790

County and Town	Total	White Population in 1790 — Males — 16 Years and Over	Males — Under 16 Years	Females	All Other Free Persons	Slaves
Cheshire county	28,753	7,008	7,567	14,090	70	18
Acworth	705	160	197	348	. . .	. . .
Alstead	1,112	268	285	558	1	. . .
Charlestown	1,094	307	254	531	1	1
Chesterfield	1,903	441	532	928	2	. . .
Claremont	1,423	348	389	682	2	2
Cornish	982	238	258	484	1	1
Croydon	536	121	150	262	3	. . .
Dublin	899	227	223	444	5	. . .
Fitzwilliam	1,038	255	278	505	. . .	. . .
Gilsom	298	70	64	164	. . .	. . .
Hinsdale	524	127	142	251	. . .	4
Jaffrey	1,238	285	336	606	11	. . .
Keene	1,307	319	318	663	5	2
Landgon	244	58	76	108	2	. . .
Lempster	415	110	95	207	3	. . .
Marlborough	786	175	219	392	. . .	. . .
Marlow	319	73	90	156	. . .	. . .
New Grantham	333	90	88	153	1	1
Newport	779	187	198	389	4	1
Packersfield	724	170	208	343	3	. . .
Plainfield	1,024	259	277	486	2	. . .
Protectworth	210	56	49	104	. . .	1
Richmond	1,380	332	368	680	. . .	. . .
Rindge	1,143	276	306	554	7	. . .
Stoddard	701	162	194	344	. . .	1
Sullivan	220	48	68	103	1	. . .
Surry	448	117	111	220	. . .	. . .
Swanzey	1,155	291	286	572	6	. . .
Unity	538	133	139	265	1	. . .
Walpole	1,254	327	335	589	1	2
Washington	545	137	135	273	. . .	. . .
Wendell	267	70	64	133	. . .	. . .
Westmoreland	2,000	473	524	998	4	1
Winchester	1,209	298	311	595	4	1
Grafton county	13,468	3,768	3,311	6,340	28	21
Alexandria	297	79	87	131	. . .	. . .
Bartlett	248	55	57	135	. . .	1
Bath	493	117	136	239	. . .	1
Bridgewater	281	84	62	134	. . .	1
Burton	141	34	45	62	. . .	. . .
Cambridge (not inhabited)	. . .	. . .	. . .	. . .	. . .	. . .
Campton	395	113	79	202	. . .	1
Canaan	483	137	123	223	. . .	. . .
Chatham	58	17	13	28	. . .	. . .
Cockburn	26	9	5	12	. . .	. . .
Cockermouth	373	94	104	175	. . .	. . .
Colburne	29	10	6	13	. . .	. . .
Concord (alias Gunthwaite)	313	91	75	147		
Coventry	88	21	20	47	. . .	. . .
Dalton	14	3	4	7	. . .	. . .
Dame's Location	21	4	8	9	. . .	. . .
Dartmouth	111	34	25	52	. . .	. . .
Dorchester	175	48	45	82	. . .	. . .
Grafton county (cont.)						
Dummer (not inhabited)	. . .	. . .	. . .	. . .	. . .	. . .
Enfield (alias Relhan)	724	188	173	361	2	. . .
Errol (not inhabited)	. . .	. . .	. . .	. . .	. . .	. . .
Franconia	72	22	18	32	. . .	. . .
Grafton	403	99	110	194	. . .	. . .
Hale's Location	9	3	2	4	. . .	. . .
Hanover (including 152 students at Dartmouth College)	1,379	476	297	596	8	2
Hart's Location	12	3	4	5	. . .	. . .
Haverhill	552	163	118	266	1	4
Kilkenny (not inhabited)	. . .	. . .	. . .	. . .	. . .	. . .
Lancaster	161	45	45	71	. . .	. . .
Landaff	292	75	80	137	. . .	. . .
Lebanon	1,180	375	282	515	8	. . .
Lincoln	22	8	5	9	. . .	. . .
Littleton	96	28	26	42	. . .	. . .
Lyman	202	57	39	106	. . .	. . .
Lyme	816	231	189	392	4	. . .
Millfield (not inhabited)	. . .	. . .	. . .	. . .	. . .	. . .
New Chester	312	70	103	139	. . .	. . .
New Holderness	329	96	73	160	. . .	. . .
Northumberland	117	34	27	56	. . .	. . .
Orange	131	32	37	61	. . .	1
Orford	540	140	125	272	. . .	3
Peeling (not inhabited)	. . .	. . .	. . .	. . .	. . .	. . .
Percy	48	14	11	23	. . .	. . .
Piermont	426	103	113	206	1	3
Plymouth	625	182	142	297	. . .	4
Rumney	411	97	113	201	. . .	. . .
Senter's Location	8	5	. . .	3	. . .	. . .
Shelburne	35	12	5	18	. . .	. . .
Stark's Location	29	8	5	16	. . .	. . .
Sterling's Location	9	3	2	4	. . .	. . .
Stratford	144	44	35	65	. . .	. . .
Success (not inhabited)	. . .	. . .	. . .	. . .	. . .	. . .
Thornton	385	96	98	191	. . .	. . .
Trecothick (not inhabited)	. . .	. . .	. . .	. . .	. . .	. . .
Wales's Location	6	1	3	2	. . .	. . .
Warren	206	52	64	86	4	. . .
Wentworth	241	56	73	112	. . .	. . .
Hillsborough county	32,883	8,145	8,392	16,170	176	. . .
Amherst	2,369	571	575	1,205	18	. . .
Andover	645	166	167	312	. . .	. . .
Antrim	526	138	144	244	. . .	. . .
Bedford	897	210	240	440	7	. . .
Boscawen	1,108	282	274	551	1	. . .
Bradford	217	56	60	101	. . .	. . .
Campbell's Gore	120	28	35	57	. . .	. . .
Dearing	938	213	264	459	2	. . .
Derryfield	362	92	95	175	. . .	. . .
Derryfield Gore	30	10	4	16	. . .	. . .

County and Town	Total	White Population in 1790 Males 16 Years and Over	Males Under 16 Years	Females	All Other Free Persons	Slaves
Hillsborough county						
Dunbarton	921	209	244	448	20	...
Dunstable	634	179	146	308	1	...
Duxbury Mile-slip	169	39	45	85	...	...
Fishersfield	325	68	105	152	...	...
Francestown	983	232	234	517	...	...
Goffstown	1,275	324	303	614	34	...
Hancock	634	156	160	315	3	...
Heniker	1,124	266	325	525	8	...
Hillsborough	798	193	211	393	1	...
Hollis	1,441	340	378	723	...	...
Hopkinton	1,715	445	417	852	1	...
Kersarge Gore	103	27	27	49	...	...
Litchfield	369	99	87	166	17	...
Lyndborough	1,280	313	349	618	...	...
Lyndborough Gore	38	11	8	19	...	...
Mason	922	215	242	462	3	...
Merrimac	819	209	207	393	10	...
New Boston	1,204	313	303	578	10	...
New Ipswich	1,241	338	285	614	4	...
New London	311	69	90	152	...	...
Nottingham West	1,064	267	246	544	7	...
Peterborough	861	221	213	423	4	...
Raby	338	86	89	160	3	...
Salisbury	1,362	335	385	640	2	...
Sharon	260	68	63	129	...	...
Society Land	329	84	89	156	...	...
Sutton	520	132	122	266	...	...
Temple	747	177	196	368	6	...
Warner	863	220	195	448	...	...
Weare	1,924	491	500	931	2	...
Wilton	1,097	253	270	562	12	...
Rockingham county	43,184	11,141	9,667	21,987	292	97
Allenstown	255	68	63	123	1	...
Atkinson	480	129	102	247	2	...
Bow	566	147	151	268	...	...
Brintwood	976	255	224	490	6	1
Candia	1,040	246	273	521	...	...
Canterbury	1,048	295	223	526	1	3
Chester	1,899	490	448	960	1	...
Chichester	492	137	118	237	...	...
Concord	1,738	494	405	828	7	4
Deerfield	1,613	444	358	808	1	2
East Kingston	358	90	87	179	2	...
Epping	1,255	338	256	654	2	5
Epsom	830	200	203	427	...	...
Exeter	1,722	437	343	859	81	2
Gosport (on Star Island)	93	32	22	39	...	...
Greenland	634	170	141	309	12	2
Hampstead	725	195	157	370	2	1
Hampton	852	238	174	436	3	1
Hampton Falls	540	150	96	291	3	...
Hawke	422	101	95	225	...	1
Kensington	804	222	147	435	...	...
Kingston	905	244	188	470	3	...
Londonderry	2,604	676	573	1,325	25	5
Loudon	1,074	272	274	521	5	2

County and Town	Total	White Population in 1790 Males 16 Years and Over	Males Under 16 Years	Females	All Other Free Persons	Slaves
Rockingham county						
Newcastle	534	125	117	292	...	...
Newington	542	132	109	285	2	14
Newmarket	1,137	284	235	610	7	1
Newtown	530	126	132	271	...	1
Northampton	657	184	138	333	2	...
Northfield	606	154	155	295	2	...
Northwood	746	188	181	376	...	1
Nottingham	1,069	275	249	530	4	11
Pelham	794	216	193	385	...	...
Pembrook	962	239	247	474	...	2
Pittsfield	872	204	220	444	4	...
Plaistow	516	134	123	259	...	...
Poplin	493	136	104	251	1	1
Portsmouth	4,720	1,158	973	2,487	76	26
Raymond	727	177	181	361	8	...
Rye	865	226	189	439	8	3
Salem	1,218	287	294	626	9	2
Sandown	562	138	115	309	...	...
Seabrook	715	178	178	357	2	...
South Hampton	449	125	82	241	1	...
Stratham	882	229	158	486	8	1
Windham	663	156	173	328	1	5
Strafford county	23,611	6,012	5,918	11,596	64	21
Barnstead	807	192	214	400	...	1
Barrington	2,481	608	650	1,221	2	...
Conway	574	149	146	279	...	...
Dover	1,996	547	418	1,005	18	8
Durham	1,246	336	271	634	2	3
Eaton	254	60	72	122	...	...
Effingham	153	42	43	67	...	1
Gilmantown	2,610	615	682	1,290	22	1
Lee	1,036	277	224	533	2	...
Madbury	592	167	126	295	4	...
Merideth	832	248	211	419	4	...
Middleton	617	151	162	304	...	...
Moultonborough	565	133	148	283	...	1
New Durham	554	139	140	275	...	...
New Durham Gore	445	108	118	212	7	...
New Hampton	652	171	173	306	2	...
Ossipee	339	86	82	171	...	...
Rochester	2,852	728	740	1,383	...	1
Sanborntown	1,587	415	424	748	...	...
Sandwich	905	216	243	446	...	...
Somersworth	945	248	211	481	1	4
Stark's Location	3	2	...	1	...	...
Sterling's Location	48	10	13	25	...	...
Tamworth	266	67	72	126	...	1
Tuftonborough	109	29	20	60	...	...
Wakefield	646	158	195	293	...	...
Wolfborough	447	110	120	217	...	...

Source: Bureau of the Census, *A Century of Population Growth, 1790–1900* (1909), 189, 190.

TABLE 5.10 FEDERAL CENSUS OF NEW HAMPSHIRE, 1800

	White Males	White Females	Free Blacks	Slaves	Total
Rockingham	22,076	22,991	360	. . .	45,427
Strafford	16,266	16,235	113	. . .	32,614
Hillsborough	21,662	22,032	205	. . .	43,899
Cheshire	19,483	19,230	112	. . .	38,825
Grafton	11,771	11,252	62	8	23,093
Total	91,258	91,740	852	8	183,858

Source: Census Office, Return of the Whole Number of Persons Within the Several Districts of the United States: 1800 (1802), 13.

TABLE 5.11 FEDERAL CENSUS OF VERMONT, 1790

County and Town	Total	White Population in 1790 — Males 16 Years and Over	White Population in 1790 — Males Under 16 Years	White Population in 1790 — Females	All Other Free Persons	Slaves
Addison county	6,420	1,768	1,656	2,959	37	. . .
Addison	402	108	106	186	2	. . .
Bridport	450	123	122	205	. . .	. . .
Bristol	211	53	57	101	. . .	. . .
Cornwall	825	214	218	393	. . .	. . .
Ferrisburg	481	137	119	213	12	. . .
Hancock	56	18	11	27	. . .	. . .
Kingston	101	26	31	44	. . .	. . .
Leicester	344	94	81	169	. . .	. . .
Middlebury	395	125	92	176	2	. . .
Monkton	449	122	134	193	. . .	. . .
New Haven	717	180	218	319	. . .	. . .
Panton	220	57	66	97	. . .	. . .
Salisbury	444	122	107	215	. . .	. . .
Shoreham	701	198	161	337	5	. . .
Vergennes	201	73	35	79	14	. . .
Weybridge	174	48	41	84	1	. . .
Whiting	249	70	57	121	1	. . .
Bennington county	12,206	3,103	3,205	5,865	33	. . .
Arlington	992	252	252	488	. . .	. . .
Bennington	2,350	628	601	1,101	20	. . .
Bromley	71	21	19	31	. . .	. . .
Dorsett	957	240	230	487	. . .	. . .
Glastonbury	34	6	11	17	. . .	. . .
Landgrove	31	7	4	20	. . .	. . .
Manchester	1,278	338	339	596	5	. . .
Pownal	1,732	418	498	815	1	. . .
Reedsborough	63	16	15	32	. . .	. . .
Rupert	1,034	251	289	494	. . .	. . .
Sandgate	773	198	189	386	. . .	. . .
Shaftsbury	1,990	491	528	967	4	. . .
Stamford	272	69	65	137	1	. . .
Sunderland	414	113	101	199	1	. . .
Winhall	155	39	46	69	1	. . .
Woodford	60	16	18	26	. . .	. . .
Chittenden county	7,287	2,251	1,761	3,252	23	. . .
Alburgh	446	147	106	189	4	. . .
Bakersfield	13	4	4	5	. . .	. . .
Bolton	88	21	26	41	. . .	. . .
Burlington	330	108	68	151	3	. . .
Cambridge	359	108	84	167	. . .	. . .
Cambridge Gore	15	3	6	6	. . .	. . .
Charlotte	635	189	142	301	3	. . .
Colchester	137	42	40	55	. . .	. . .
Duxbury	39	9	18	12	. . .	. . .
Elmore	12	7	1	4	. . .	. . .
Essex	354	118	76	160	. . .	. . .
Fairfax	254	85	61	108	. . .	. . .
Fairfield	126	43	28	55	. . .	. . .
Fletcher	47	13	14	20	. . .	. . .
Georgia	340	105	80	155	. . .	. . .
Highgate	103	26	31	45	1	. . .
Hinesburgh	454	127	115	212	. . .	. . .
Hungerford	40	16	8	11	5	. . .
Huntsburgh	46	25	10	11	. . .	. . .
Hydespark	43	10	12	18	3	. . .
Isle Mott	47	18	13	16	. . .	. . .
Jerico	381	115	90	176	. . .	. . .
Johnson	93	31	16	46	. . .	. . .
Middlesex	60	16	19	25	. . .	. . .
Milton	283	90	65	128	. . .	. . .
Minden	18	6	6	6	. . .	. . .
Moretown	24	10	6	8	. . .	. . .
Morristown	10	6	. . .	4	. . .	. . .
New Huntington	136	34	40	62	. . .	. . .
New Huntington Gore	31	10	7	14	. . .	. . .
North Hero	125	40	25	57	3	. . .
St. Albans	256	89	61	105	1	. . .
St. George	57	14	17	26	. . .	. . .
Shelburne	387	108	103	176	. . .	. . .
Smithfield	70	28	14	28	. . .	. . .
South Hero	537	164	128	245	. . .	. . .
Starksborough	40	15	6	19	. . .	. . .
Swanton	74	22	25	27	. . .	. . .
Underhill	59	16	12	31	. . .	. . .
Waitsfield	61	21	16	24	. . .	. . .
Waterbury	93	22	27	44	. . .	. . .
Westford	63	23	8	32	. . .	. . .
Williston	469	136	120	213	. . .	. . .
Wolcott	32	11	7	14	. . .	. . .
Orange county	10,526	2,873	2,765	4,847	41	. . .
Barnet	447	137	132	207	1	. . .
Barton (not inhabited)	. . .	. . .	. . .	. . .	. . .	. . .
Berlin	134	38	33	63	. . .	. . .
Billymead (not inhabited)	. . .	. . .	. . .	. . .	. . .	. . .
Bradford	654	158	176	313	7	. . .

County and Town	Total	16 Years and Over	Under 16 Years	Females	All Other Free Persons	Slaves
Orange county						
Braintree	221	61	66	89	5	. . .
Brookfield	419	113	116	189	1	. . .
Brownington (not inhabited)	. . .	. . .	. . .	. . .	. . .	. . .
Brunswick	66	15	15	36	. . .	. . .
Burke (not inhabited)	. . .	. . .	. . .	. . .	. . .	. . .
Cabot	122	33	37	52	. . .	. . .
Calais	45	14	11	20	. . .	. . .
Caldersburgh (not inhabited)	. . .	. . .	. . .	. . .	. . .	. . .
Canaan	19	4	5	10	. . .	. . .
Chelsea	239	77	62	100	. . .	. . .
Concord	49	18	12	19	. . .	. . .
Corinth	578	147	156	275	. . .	. . .
Danville	574	165	139	270	. . .	. . .
Dewey's Gore	48	12	18	18	. . .	. . .
Fairley	463	132	120	210	1	. . .
Ferdinand (not inhabited)	. . .	. . .	. . .	. . .	. . .	. . .
Glover (not inhabited)	. . .	. . .	. . .	. . .	. . .	. . .
Granby (not inhabited)	. . .	. . .	. . .	. . .	. . .	. . .
Greensborough	19	9	4	6	. . .	. . .
Groton	45	15	9	21	. . .	. . .
Guildhall	158	55	41	62	. . .	. . .
Hardwick	3	3	. . .	. . .	. . .	. . .
Harris Gore (not inhabited)	. . .	. . .	. . .	. . .	. . .	. . .
Hopkins Grant (not inhabited)	. . .	. . .	. . .	. . .	. . .	. . .
Lemington	31	12	7	12	. . .	. . .
Lewis (not inhabited)	. . .	. . .	. . .	. . .	. . .	. . .
Littleton	63	16	14	33	. . .	. . .
Lunenburgh	119	30	29	60	. . .	. . .
Lyndon	59	29	10	20	. . .	. . .
Maidstone	125	34	36	55	. . .	. . .
Marshfield (not inhabited)	. . .	. . .	. . .	. . .	. . .	. . .
Minehead (not inhabited)	. . .	. . .	. . .	. . .	. . .	. . .
Montpelier	118	55	19	44	. . .	. . .
Navy (not inhabited)	. . .	. . .	. . .	. . .	. . .	. . .
Newark (not inhabited)	. . .	. . .	. . .	. . .	. . .	. . .
Newbury	872	225	222	413	12	. . .
Northfield	40	10	10	20	. . .	. . .
Orange (not inhabited)	. . .	. . .	. . .	. . .	. . .	. . .
Peachum	365	102	90	173	. . .	. . .
Randolph	893	227	237	429	. . .	. . .
Orange county						
Random (not inhabited)	. . .	. . .	. . .	. . .	. . .	. . .
Roxbury	14	6	2	6	. . .	. . .
Ryegate	187	46	54	87	. . .	. . .
St. Andrews (not inhabited)	. . .	. . .	. . .	. . .	. . .	. . .
St. Johnsbury	143	54	34	55	. . .	. . .
Sheffield (not inhabited)	. . .	. . .	. . .	. . .	. . .	. . .
Strafford	844	213	228	403	. . .	. . .
Thetford	862	211	218	419	14	. . .
Topsham	162	36	56	70	. . .	. . .
Tunbridge	487	121	147	219	. . .	. . .
Vershire	439	117	118	204	. . .	. . .
Victory (not inhabited)	. . .	. . .	. . .	. . .	. . .	. . .
Walden	11	3	3	5	. . .	. . .
Walden's Gore	32	9	9	14	. . .	. . .
Washington	72	26	13	33	. . .	. . .
Westmore (not inhabited)	. . .	. . .	. . .	. . .	. . .	. . .
Wheelock	33	14	7	12	. . .	. . .
Wildersburgh	76	30	16	30	. . .	. . .
Williamstown	146	41	34	71	. . .	. . .
Winlock (not inhabited)	. . .	. . .	. . .	. . .	. . .	. . .
Woodbury (not inhabited)	. . .	. . .	. . .	. . .	. . .	. . .
Rutland county	15,590	3,990	4,098	7,470	32	. . .
Benson	658	185	182	290	1	. . .
Brandon	637	154	168	314	1	. . .
Castleton	809	210	222	376	1	. . .
Chittenden	159	38	49	72	. . .	. . .
Clarendon	1,480	343	397	740	. . .	. . .
Danby	1,206	276	333	589	8	. . .
Fair Haven	545	174	121	250	. . .	. . .
Harwich	165	38	49	78	. . .	. . .
Hubbardton	410	120	94	196	. . .	. . .
Ira	312	77	82	153	. . .	. . .
Killington	32	11	10	11	. . .	. . .
Middletown	699	169	172	358	. . .	. . .
Midway	34	7	9	18	. . .	. . .
Orwell	778	215	218	341	4	. . .
Pawlet	1,458	348	399	709	2	. . .
Philadelphia	39	12	9	18	. . .	. . .
Pittsfield	49	13	12	24	. . .	. . .
Pittsford	850	219	208	422	1	. . .
Poultney	1,120	282	292	539	7	. . .
Rutland	1,417	396	351	668	2	. . .

(continued)

TABLE 5.11 (continued)

County and Town	Total	White Population in 1790 — Males 16 Years and Over	White Population in 1790 — Males Under 16 Years	White Population in 1790 — Females	All Other Free Persons	Slaves
Rutland county						
Shrewsbury	382	98	101	183	. . .	. . .
Sudbury	258	67	69	122	. . .	. . .
Tinmouth	935	247	244	442	2	. . .
Wallingford	538	142	131	262	3	. . .
Wells	620	149	176	295	. . .	. . .
Windham county	17,572	4,416	4,672	8,426	58	. . .
Athens	450	103	138	209	. . .	. . .
Brattleborough	1,589	381	436	758	14	. . .
Dummerston	1,490	362	394	724	10	. . .
Guilford	2,422	586	646	1,177	13	. . .
Hallifax	1,209	302	342	561	4	. . .
Hinsdale	482	118	142	221	1	. . .
Jamaica	263	71	66	126	. . .	. . .
Johnson's Gore	49	15	13	21	. . .	. . .
Londonderry	362	90	99	172	1	. . .
Marlborough	629	149	176	304	. . .	. . .
New Fane	660	163	177	320	. . .	. . .
Putney	1,848	438	492	906	12	. . .
Rockingham	1,235	327	319	587	2	. . .
Somerset	111	26	35	50	. . .	. . .
Stratton	95	27	22	46	. . .	. . .
Thomlinson	561	143	165	253	. . .	. . .
Townsend	678	192	171	315	. . .	. . .
Wardsborough, North District	483	128	126	229	. . .	. . .
Wardsborough, South District	270	72	69	129	. . .	. . .
Westminster	1,599	429	387	782	1	. . .
Whitingham	442	114	119	209	. . .	. . .
Wilmington	645	180	138	327	. . .	. . .
Windsor county	15,740	4,004	4,148	7,543	45	. . .
Andover	275	75	74	126	. . .	. . .
Barnard	673	177	167	329	. . .	. . .
Bethel	473	125	118	229	. . .	. . .
Bridgwater	293	68	78	147	. . .	. . .
Cavendish	491	126	125	240	. . .	. . .
Chester	981	265	255	457	4	. . .
Hartford	988	248	250	489	1	. . .
Hartland	1,652	415	442	789	6	. . .
Ludlow	179	43	57	79	. . .	. . .
Norwich	1,158	280	322	556	. . .	. . .
Pomfret	710	177	209	319	5	. . .
Reading	747	171	211	359	6	. . .
Rochester	215	62	47	106	. . .	. . .
Royalton	748	195	190	363	. . .	. . .
Saltash	106	29	35	42	. . .	. . .
Sharon	569	147	147	275	. . .	. . .
Springfield	1,097	289	289	516	3	. . .
Stockbridge	100	32	25	43	. . .	. . .
Weathersfield	1,146	294	285	560	7	. . .
Windsor	1,542	395	406	732	9	. . .
Woodstock	1,597	390	416	787	4	. . .

Source: Bureau of the Census, *A Century of Population Growth, 1790–1900* (1909), 190, 191.

TABLE 5.12 FEDERAL CENSUS OF VERMONT, 1800

Names of Counties	Free White Males — To 10	To 16	To 26	To 45	45 &c.	Free White Females — To 10	To 16	To 26	To 45	45 &c.	All Others, &c.	Slaves
Windham	4,265	1,990	2,006	2,259	1,485	4,118	1,766	2,000	2,293	1,359	40	. . .
Windsor	5,131	2,200	2,151	2,833	1,413	4,907	2,020	2,118	2,764	1,312	95	. . .
Orange	3,661	1,348	1,439	2,045	860	3,493	1,237	1,350	1,928	791	86	. . .
Caledonia	1,865	601	836	1,111	444	1,791	605	784	980	344	16	. . .
Orleans	271	93	166	194	43	279	76	117	146	37	17	. . .
Essex	283	120	120	180	86	248	105	121	143	70	3	. . .
Bennington	2,606	1,159	1,424	1,369	925	2,539	1,124	1,290	1,314	789	78	. . .
Rutland	4,573	1,864	2,015	2,440	1,262	4,348	1,858	2,017	2,272	1,074	90	. . .
Addison	2,584	1,010	1,122	1,573	630	2,488	980	1,079	1,365	520	66	. . .
Chittenden	2,444	988	1,162	1,467	565	2,431	938	1,023	1,233	481	46	. . .
Franklin	1,737	673	801	1,073	363	1,630	657	707	849	272	20	. . .
Total 154,465	29,420	12,046	13,242	16,544	8,076	28,272	11,366	12,606	15,287	7,049	557	. . .

Source: Census Office, *Return of the Whole Number of Persons Within the Several Districts of the United States: 1800* (1802), 37.

TABLE 5.13   STATE CENSUSES OF MASSACHUSETTS 1776 AND 1777

Suffolk County

Town	Whites	Males Over 16	Town	Whites	Males Over 16
Boston	2,719	2,664	Foxboro	. . .	. . .
Roxbury	1,433	356	Brookline	502	115
Dorchester	1,513	373	Needham	912	287
Milton	1,213	259	Stoughtonham	1,261	300
Braintree	2,871	610	Stoughton	2,097	532
Weymouth	1,471	342	Medway	912	206
Hingham	2,087	504	Bellingham	627	136
Dedham	1,937	495	Hull	. . .	32
Medfield	775	188	Walpole	967	260
Wrentham	2,879	710	Chelsea	489	76
Franklin	. . .	. . .	Cohasset	754	66
			Total	27,419[a]	8,511

Essex County

Town	Whites	Males Over 16	Town	Whites	Males Over 16
Salem	5,337	1,193	Haverhill	2,810	552
Danvers	2,284	519	Gloucester	4,512	939
Ipswich	4,508	1,016	Topsfield	773	205
Newbury	3,239	704	Boxford	989	248
Newburyport	3,681	858	Amesbury	1,795	422
Marblehead	4,386	1,047	Bradford	1,240	304
Lynn-Lynnfield	2,755	431	Wenham	638	143
Andover	2,953	670	Middleton	650	159
Beverly	2,754	596	Manchester	949	220
Rowley	1,678	421	Methuen	1,326	306
Salisbury	1,666	375	Total	50,923[b]	11,328

Barnstable County

Town	Whites	Males Over 16	Town	Whites	Males Over 16
Barnstable	. . .	554	Chatham	929	210
Sandwich	1,912	362	Truro	1,227	292
Yarmouth	2,227	514	Falmouth	1,355	223
Eastham	1,899	458	Mashpee	82	. . .
Harwich	1,865	451	Provincetown	205	. . .
Wellfleet	1,235	307	Total	12,936[c]	3,371

Bristol County

Town	Whites	Males Over 16	Town	Whites	Males Over 16
Taunton	3,259	794	Attleboro	2,200	501
Rehoboth	4,191	970	Dighton	1,420	317
Swanzey	. . .	447	Freetown	1,901	414
Dartmouth	6,773	1,067	Raynham	940	223
Norton	1,329	330	Easton	1,172	293
Mansfield	944	247	Berkley	787	191
			Total	24,916[d]	5,794

Plymouth County

Town	Whites	Males Over 16	Town	Whites	Males Over 16
Plymouth	2,655	643	Plimpton	1,707	436
Scituate	2,672	663	Pembroke	1,768	418
Duxbury	1,254	316	Kingston	980	229
Marshfield	1,157	289	Hanover	1,105	253
Bridgewater	4,364	1,130	Abington	1,293	324
Middleboro	4,119	1,045	Halifax	672	148
Rochester	2,449	569	Wareham	711	151
			Total	26,906[e]	6,614

Duke's County / Nantucket County

Town	Whites	Males Over 16	Town	Whites	Males Over 16
Edgartown	1,020	. . .	Sherburne	4,412	. . .
Chilmark	769	. . .	Total	4,412[g]	. . .
Tisbury	1,033	. . .			
Total	2,822[f]	. . .			

Middlesex County

Town	Whites	Males Over 16	Town	Whites	Males Over 16
Cambridge	1,586	333	Westford	1,193	283
Charlestown	360	144	Waltham	870	174
Watertown	1,057	185	Stow	915	215
Woburn	1,691	417	Groton	1,639	398
Concord	1,927	391	Shirley	704	144
Newton	1,625	348	Pepperell	1,034	221
Reading	1,984	402	Townsend	794	177
Marlboro	1,554	391	Ashby	422	98
Billerica	1,500	348	Stoneham	319	73
Framingham	1,574	384	Natick	535	126
Lexington	1,088	213	Dracut	1,173	225
Chelmsford	1,341	319	Bedford	482	121
Sherburne	699	187	Holliston	909	216
Sudbury	2,160	522	Tewksbury	821	222
East Sudbury	. . .	. . .	Acton	769	195
Malden	1,030	221	Dunstable	679	166
Weston	1,027	222	Lincoln	775	187
Medford	967	190	Wilmington	737	187
Littleton	1,047	209	Carlisle	. . .	. . .
Hopkinton	1,134	286	Total	40,121[h]	9,140

Worcester County

Town	Whites	Males Over 16	Town	Whites	Males Over 16
Worcester	1,925	438	Harvard	1,315	338
Lancaster	2,746	672	Dudley	875	228
Mendon	2,322	524	Bolton	1,210	284
Milford	. . .	. . .	Sturbridge	1,374	338
Brookfield	2,649	655	Leominster	978	216
Oxford	1,112	275	Hardwick	1,393	346
Charlton	1,310	308	Holden	749	180
Sutton	2,644	651	Western	827	206
Leicester	1,005	212	Douglass	800	194
Spencer	1,042	257	Grafton	861	213
Paxton	. . .	116	Petersham	1,235	289
Rutland	1,006	254	Royalston	617	113
Oakham	598	135	Westminster	1,145	248
Barre	1,329	325	Athol	. . .	191
Hubbardston	488	130	Templeton	1,016	235
New Braintree	798	185	Princeton	701	153
Southboro	753	176	Ashburnham	551	122
Westboro	900	220	Winchendon	519	119
Northboro	562	127	Northbridge	481	90
Shrewsbury	1,475	384	Ward	. . .	. . .
Fitchburg	643	168	Lunenburg	1,265	284
Uxbridge	1,110	235	Upton	702	171
			Total	45,031[i]	11,005

(continued)

TABLE 5.13 (continued)

Berkshire County

Town	Whites	Males Over 16	Town	Whites	Males Over 16
Sheffield	1,722	338	Sandisfield	1,044	. . .
Great Barrington	961	231	Williamstown	1,083	257
Stockbridge	907	. . .	Becket	414	106
Pittsfield	1,132	244	Windsor	459	. . .
New Marlboro	1,087	253	Partridgefield	376	. . .
Egremont	671	150	Adams	932	150
Richmond	921	. . .	Hancock	977	127
Lennox	931	178	No. 7	. . .	. . .
Tyringham	809	. . .	Washington	750	146
West Stockbridge	370	. . .	New Ashford	215	. . .
Lowden	200	. . .	Mt. Washington	259	. . .
Alford	298	. . .	Ashuelot	. . .	. . .
Lanesboro	1,434	354	Total	17,952[j]	2,534

Hampshire County

Town	Whites	Males Over 16	Town	Whites	Males Over 16
Springfield	1,974	452	Leverett	293	79
Willbraham	1,057	260	Palmer	727	. . .
Northampton	1,790	451	Granville	1,126	268
Westhampton	. . .	. . .	New Salem	910	226
Southampton	740	199	Belchertown	972	225
Hadley	681	201	Colerain	566	144
South Hadley	584	161	Ware	. . .	150
Amherst	915	238	Warwick	766	166
Granby	491	116	Bernardstown	607	138
Hatfield	582	190	Murrayfield	405	98
Whately	410	106	Charlemont	. . .	94
Williamsburg	534	123	Ashfield	628	193
Westfield	1,488	373	Worthington	639	166
Deerfield	836	241	Shutesbury	598	147
Greenfield	735	148	Chesterfield	1,092	221
Shelburne	575	154	Chestf'd Gore	. . .	. . .
Conway	897	203	Southwick	. . .	123
Sunderland	409	116	W. Springfield	1,744	. . .
Montague	575	163	Ludlow	413	96
Northfield	580	148	No. 5	. . .	. . .
Brimfield	1,064	251	Norwich	. . .	62
South Brimfield	850	220	No. 7	244	56
Monson	813	197	Lee	. . .	. . .
Pelham	729	201	Montgomery	. . .	. . .
Greenwich	890	206	Buckland	. . .	. . .
Blandford	772	187	Total	32,701[k]	7,957

York County

Town	Whites	Males Over 16
York	2,742	607
Kittery	2,991	645
Wells	2,595	570
Berwick	3,315	671
Arundel	1,144	251
Biddeford	1,006	216
Pepperelboro	815	192
Lebanon	570	126
Sandford	810	158
Nearby Sandford	225	. . .
Buxton	698	157
Fryeburg	414	102
Brownstown	48	19
Great Falls	10	. . .
Little Ossipee	240	. . .
Massabeseek	. . .	99
Little Falls	. . .	72
Brownfield	. . .	19
Total	17,623[l]	3,904

Cumberland County

Town	Whites	Males Over 16
Falmouth	3,026	709
Cape Elizabeth	1,469	357
North Yarmouth	1,716	398
Scarborough	1,817	454
Brunswick	867	194
Harpswell	977	193
Gorham	1,471	302
Windham	550	92
New Gloucester	773	166
Piersontown	551	69
Gray	318	72
Royalboro	301	57
Bakerstown	58	. . .
Sylvester	35	. . .
Bridgetown	68	. . .
Raymondtown	113	. . .
Total	14,110[m]	3,063

Lincoln County

Town	Whites	Males Over 16	Town	Whites	Males Over 16
Pownalboro	1,424	294	Sterlington	474	. . .
Georgetown	. . .	424	Jones Plantation	49	. . .
Woolwich	695	167	Narrow Gaugus	263	. . .
Newcastle	656	159	Machias	626	. . .
Topsham	657	155	Number 4	117	. . .
Townshend	763	167	Frenchman Bay	345	. . .
Bristol	1,214	299	Union River	233	. . .
Bowdoinham	298	92	Passamaquoddy	206	. . .
Meduncook	247	. . .	Mt. Desert, etc.	235	. . .
Hallowell	554	134	Gouldsboro	293	. . .
Waldoboro	. . .	. . .	Camden	245	. . .
Vassalboro	. . .	99	Frankfort	493	. . .
Warren	272	73	Deer Island	348	. . .
Thomastown	346	. . .	Bald Hill	165	. . .
Winthrop-Readfield	307	93	Numbers 1 & 2	193	. . .
Pittstown	. . .	98	Fox Island	241	. . .
Edgecomb	677	153	Naakeag	404	. . .
Pleasant River	238	. . .	Number 6	202	. . .
Belfast	229	. . .	Penobscot	439	. . .
Lower St. George's	. . .	. . .	Blue Hill	132	. . .
Winslow	294	61	Settlements by Newcastle	582	. . .
Settlement above Winslow	390	. . .	Total	15,546[n]	2,468

Recapitulation:	White population, 1776 . . . 33,418
	Black population, 1776 . . . 5,249
	Total population, 1776 . . . 338,667
	Males over age 16, 1777 . . . 75,689[o]

[a] Also 682 blacks. [b] Also 1,049 blacks. [c] Also 171 blacks. [d] Also 585 blacks. [e] Also 487 blacks. [f] Also 59 blacks. [g] Also 133 blacks. [h] Also 702 blacks. [i] Also 432 blacks. [j] Also 216 blacks. [k] Also 245 blacks. [l] Also 241 blacks. [m] Also 162 blacks. [n] Also 85 blacks. [o] Of 343,876 whites in 1777.

Note: Data for all whites from 1776; data for adult men from 1777.

Source: Evarts B. Greene and Virginia D. Harrington, *American Population Before the Federal Census of 1790* (1932), 30–40.

TABLE 5.14 FEDERAL CENSUS OF MASSACHUSETTS, 1790

County and Town	Total	White Population in 1790 — Males — 16 Years and Over	Under 16 Years	Females	All Other Free Persons	Slaves
Essex county	57,879	14,258	12,567	30,182	872	...
Amesbury	1,801	470	384	944	3	...
Andover	2,862	741	612	1,415	94	...
Beverly	3,295	748	739	1,750	58	...
Boxford	925	247	191	481	6	...
Bradford	1,371	378	263	725	5	...
Danvers	2,424	625	486	1,279	34	...
Gloucester	5,317	1,267	1,218	2,791	41	...
Haverhill	2,404	612	535	1,250	7	...
Ipswich	4,563	1,151	920	2,414	78	...
Lynn	2,291	625	514	1,132	20	...
Lynnfield	491	119	108	261	3	...
Manchester	959	233	202	515	9	...
Marblehead	5,661	1,265	1,327	2,982	87	...
Methuen	1,295	338	293	663	1	...
Middleton	682	164	140	362	16	...
Newbury	3,970	1,038	844	2,047	41	...
Newburyport	4,817	1,153	1,072	2,525	67	...
Rowley	1,772	453	366	944	9	...
Salem	7,917	1,846	1,707	4,104	260	...
Salisbury	1,779	457	381	931	10	...
Topsfield	781	214	156	398	13	...
Wenham	502	114	109	269	10	...
Hampshire county	59,656	15,109	15,009	29,087	451	...
Amherst	1,233	335	287	609	2	...
Ashfield	1,458	354	369	734	1	...
Belchertown	1,485	370	396	713	6	...
Bernardston	690	175	172	343	...	...
Blandford	1,416	345	359	703	9	...
Brimfield	1,213	318	309	584	2	...
Buckland	718	164	191	363	...	...
Charlemont	665	166	173	326	...	...
Chester	1,119	285	300	527	7	...
Chesterfield	1,183	283	317	581	2	...
Colrain	1,418	348	371	688	11	...
Conway	2,093	500	558	1,022	13	...
Cummington	873	237	212	419	5	...
Deerfield	1,328	352	306	646	24	...
Easthampton	457	127	108	221	1	...
Goshen	681	161	185	327	8	...
Granby	596	164	154	276	2	...
Granville	1,980	497	501	969	13	...
Greenfield	1,498	391	390	714	3	...
Greenwich	1,045	271	265	504	5	...
Hadley	882	240	187	436	19	...
Hatfield	703	199	147	343	14	...
Heath	379	86	105	188	...	...
Holland	428	115	97	204	12	...
Leverett	524	126	129	268	1	...
Leyden	989	209	297	481	2	...
Longmeadow	744	200	182	356	6	...
Ludlow	560	134	158	266	2	...
Middlefield	603	154	172	277	...	...
Monson[1]	1,331	336	324	653	18	...

County and Town	Total	White Population in 1790 — Males — 16 Years and Over	Under 16 Years	Females	All Other Free Persons	Slaves
Hampshire county						
Montague	908	236	219	451	2	...
Montgomery	449	110	116	221	2	...
New Salem	1,543	390	387	765	1	...
Northampton[1]	1,628	498	341	771	18	...
Northfield	868	224	224	415	5	...
Norwich	737	186	197	350	4	...
Orange	784	186	203	395	...	...
Palmer	809	215	186	396	12	...
Pelham	1,040	246	277	517	...	...
Plainfield	443	106	118	214	5	...
Plantation No. 7	540	135	156	249	...	...
Rowe	443	119	122	202	...	...
Shelburne	1,183	300	273	598	12	...
Shutesbury	674	160	196	315	3	...
South Brimfield	606	144	171	291	...	...
South Hadley	759	209	181	359	10	...
Southampton	829	226	178	418	7	...
Southwick	841	215	217	397	12	...
Springfield	1,574	415	359	787	13	...
Sunderland	462	123	101	237	1	...
Ware	773	189	205	378	1	...
Warwick	1,244	277	308	657	2	...
Wendell	519	130	147	242	...	...
West Springfield	2,367	630	525	1,160	52	...
Westfield	2,205	527	565	1,055	58	...
Westhampton	682	162	185	333	2	...
Whately	735	184	199	351	1	...
Wilbraham	1,553	380	393	755	25	...
Williamsburgh	1,049	258	261	520	10	...
Worthington	1,117	287	278	547	5	...
Middlesex county	42,769	11,071	9,620	21,486	592	...
Acton	853	216	204	427	6	...
Ashby	751	187	194	369	1	...
Bedford	523	150	117	254	2	...
Billerica	1,191	335	256	595	5	...
Boxborough	412	100	86	217	9	...
Cambridge	2,109	534	454	1,063	58	...
Carlisle	555	149	99	305	2	...
Charlestown	1,589	395	360	809	25	...
Chelmsford	1,144	327	233	572	12	...
Concord	1,585	414	312	830	29	...
Dracut	1,217	310	284	584	39	...
Dunstable	380	107	79	193	1	...
East Sudbury	801	206	176	410	9	...
Framingham	1,598	394	350	828	26	...
Groton	1,840	477	429	929	5	...
Holliston	874	236	199	424	15	...
Hopkinton	1,316	310	329	665	12	...
Lexington	941	251	212	470	8	...
Lincoln	740	180	184	370	6	...
Littleton	854	223	177	438	16	...

(continued)

TABLE 5.14 (continued)

County and Town	Total	16 Years and Over	Under 16 Years	Females	All Other Free Persons	Slaves
Berkshire county						
Malden	1,032	239	214	559	20	. . .
Marlborough	1,552	431	335	778	8	. . .
Medford	1,036	262	215	525	34	. . .
Natick	610	141	133	300	36	. . .
Newton	1,354	332	301	696	25	. . .
Pepperell	1,132	286	245	581	20	. . .
Reading	1,802	480	386	905	31	. . .
Sherburne	858	249	211	392	6	. . .
Shirley	677	166	155	354	2	. . .
Stoneham	381	108	83	182	8	. . .
Stow	800	205	195	397	3	. . .
Sudbury	1,288	324	287	675	2	. . .
Tewksbury	955	237	231	480	7	. . .
Townsend	993	273	244	472	4	. . .
Tyngsborough on north side of Merrimack	181	44	50	87	. . .	. . .
Tyngsborough on south side of Merrimack	202	52	46	87	17	. . .
Waltham	880	232	207	431	10	. . .
Watertown	1,091	319	250	511	11	. . .
Westford	1,229	301	306	618	4	. . .
Weston	1,009	256	226	504	23	. . .
Wilmington	710	181	172	345	12	. . .
Woburn	1,724	452	394	855	23	. . .
Nantucket county	4,555	1,201	1,017	2,303	34	. . .
Sherburne	4,555	1,201	1,017	2,303	34	. . .
Plymouth county	29,512	7,493	6,536	14,984	499	. . .
Abington	1,453	357	339	742	15	. . .
Bridgewater	4,953	1,250	1,121	2,457	125	. . .
Carver	847	214	214	407	12	. . .
Duxborough	1,457	378	322	747	10	. . .
Halifax	664	178	155	329	2	. . .
Hanover	1,084	268	235	546	35	. . .
Kingston	1,006	261	222	505	18	. . .
Marshfield	1,269	386	210	645	28	. . .
Middleborough	4,524	1,165	1,051	2,284	24	. . .
Pembroke	1,954	480	433	998	43	. . .
Plymouth	2,995	749	646	1,546	54	. . .
Plympton	956	233	220	499	4	. . .
Rochester	2,642	680	606	1,302	54	. . .
Scituate	2,854	692	554	1,543	65	. . .
Wareham	854	202	208	434	10	. . .
Suffolk county	44,865	11,366	9,333	23,104	1,062	. . .
Bellingham	735	187	184	362	2	. . .
Boston	18,038	4,325	3,376	9,576	761	. . .
Boston, islands in the harbor	282	192	25	60	5	. . .
Braintree	2,775	687	640	1,430	18	. . .

County and Town	Total	16 Years and Over	Under 16 Years	Females	All Other Free Persons	Slaves
Suffolk county						
Brookline	484	152	94	225	13	. . .
Chelsea	469	133	94	221	21	. . .
Cohasset	817	188	212	417	. . .	. . .
Dedham	1,659	438	360	844	17	. . .
Dorchester	1,722	488	345	859	30	. . .
Dover	482	119	112	247	4	. . .
Foxborough	683	166	169	348	. . .	. . .
Franklin	1,101	305	235	558	3	. . .
Hingham	2,085	505	454	1,102	24	. . .
Hull	120	24	31	63	2	. . .
Medfield	731	201	120	395	15	. . .
Medway	1,040	285	208	521	26	. . .
Milton	1,039	271	205	536	27	. . .
Needham	1,109	272	269	555	13	. . .
Roxbury	2,224	618	459	1,107	40	. . .
Sharon	1,034	256	258	515	5	. . .
Stoughton	1,994	484	477	1,012	21	. . .
Walpole	1,007	254	251	497	5	. . .
Weymouth	1,469	346	368	747	8	. . .
Wrentham	1,766	470	387	907	2	. . .
Worcester county	56,764	14,600	13,664	28,091	409	. . .
Ashburnham	956	212	260	475	9	. . .
Athol	848	219	205	419	5	. . .
Barre	1,613	426	401	748	38	. . .
Berlin	512	129	138	245	. . .	. . .
Bolton	856	237	171	447	1	. . .
Boylston	841	227	183	416	15	. . .
Brookfield	3,103	784	765	1,547	7	. . .
Charlton	1,963	501	490	970	2	. . .
Douglas	1,079	267	264	548	. . .	. . .
Dudley	1,101	265	275	549	12	. . .
Fitchburgh	1,151	265	300	585	1	. . .
Fitchburgh— in the gore adjoining	14	2	6	6	. . .	. . .
Gardner	531	121	156	253	1	. . .
Gerry	739	177	182	379	1	. . .
Grafton	872	241	210	421	. . .	. . .
Hardwick	1,722	459	393	857	13	. . .
Harvard	1,387	362	298	716	11	. . .
Holden	1,077	278	267	532	. . .	. . .
Hubbardston	933	221	257	440	15	. . .
Lancaster	1,460	387	313	737	23	. . .
Leicester	1,079	286	248	537	8	. . .
Leominster	1,189	314	254	613	8	. . .
Leominster—in the gore adjoining	27	5	10	12	. . .	. . .
Lunenburgh	1,277	302	310	663	2	. . .
Mendon	1,556	389	369	795	3	. . .
Middlesex gore (adjoining Sturbridge)	64	15	20	29	. . .	. . .
Milford	839	225	175	427	12	. . .
New Braintree	939	254	188	483	14	. . .
Northborough	619	161	152	302	4	. . .

| County and Town | Total | White Population in 1790 | | | All Other Free Persons | Slaves |
| | | Males | | Females | | |
		16 Years and Over	Under 16 Years			
Worcester county						
Northbridge	569	137	140	287	5	. . .
Oakham	772	191	197	383	1	. . .
Oxford	995	271	234	485	5	
Oxford, north gore	74	19	18	37	. . .	. . .
Oxford, south gore	163	34	43	86	. . .	. . .
Paxton	558	140	139	271	8	. . .
Petersham	1,560	397	377	781	5	. . .
Princeton	1,016	258	251	504	3	. . .
Princeton— in the gore adjoining	26	5	6	15	. . .	. . .
Royalston	1,130	275	282	571	2	. . .
Rutland	1,071	294	243	526	8	. . .
Shrewsbury	963	269	209	473	12	. . .
Southborough	837	205	189	442	1	. . .
Spencer	1,321	338	316	661	6	. . .
Sterling	1,428	377	350	687	14	. . .
Sturbridge	1,703	445	400	854	4	. . .
Sutton	2,627	666	652	1,297	12	. . .
Templeton	950	232	226	492	. . .	. . .
Upton	830	210	199	392	29	. . .
Uxbridge	1,308	344	311	636	17	. . .
Ward	473	128	118	227	. . .	. . .
Westborough	929	239	256	430	4	. . .
Western	898	246	227	414	11	. . .
Westminster	1,176	310	277	585	4	. . .
Winchendon	945	238	250	455	2	. . .
Worcester	2,095	601	494	949	51	. . .
Barnstable county	17,342	4,200	4,093	8,677	372	. . .
Barnstable	2,610	631	623	1,301	55	. . .
Chatham	1,134	266	290	575	3	. . .
Eastham	1,834	426	431	974	3	. . .
Falmouth	1,639	420	365	816	38	. . .
Harwich	2,392	545	593	1,243	11	. . .
Mashpee plantation	308	35	27	72	174	. . .
Province Town	454	142	99	211	2	. . .
Sandwich	1,991	460	469	1,015	47	. . .
Truro	1,193	324	279	586	4	. . .
Wellfleet	1,115	301	252	560	2	. . .
Yarmouth	2,672	650	665	1,324	33	. . .
Berkshire county	30,263	7,356	7,790	14,794	323	. . .
Adams	2,041	473	561	1,003	4	. . .
Adams and Windsor— in the gore adjoining	425	102	121	191	11	. . .
Alford	577	142	173	262	. . .	. . .
Becket	751	195	187	362	7	. . .
Bethlehem	261	62	73	125	1	. . .
Dalton	554	129	134	283	8	. . .
Egremont	759	187	191	376	5	. . .

| County and Town | Total | White Population in 1790 | | | All Other Free Persons | Slaves |
| | | Males | | Females | | |
		16 Years and Over	Under 16 Years			
Berkshire county						
Great Barrington	1,373	328	335	664	46	. . .
Hancock	1,204	295	322	586	1	. . .
Lanesborough	2,142	522	547	1,058	15	. . .
Lee	1,170	286	310	571	3	. . .
Lenox	1,169	279	299	574	17	. . .
Loudon	344	96	84	164	. . .	. . .
Mount Washington	261	57	78	126	. . .	. . .
Mount Washington (Boston Corner)	67	13	21	33	. . .	. . .
New Ashford	464	93	126	243	2	. . .
New Marlborough	1,550	395	400	742	13	. . .
Partridgefield	1,041	250	279	509	3	. . .
Pittsfield	1,982	491	497	949	45	. . .
Richmond	1,255	336	291	624	4	. . .
Sandisfield	1,571	379	379	804	9	. . .
Sandisfield— south 11,000 acres adjoining	161	37	43	81	. . .	. . .
Sheffield	1,893	467	462	932	32	. . .
Stockbridge	1,336	311	322	639	64	. . .
Tyringham	1,397	337	368	683	9	. . .
Washington	588	143	160	283	2	. . .
West Stockbridge	1,113	260	298	545	10	. . .
Williamstown	1,769	445	454	865	5	. . .
Williamstown— in the gore adjoining	51	8	22	21	. . .	. . .
Windsor	916	222	233	454	7	. . .
Zoar plantation [1]	78	16	20	42	. . .	. . .
Bristol county	31,696	7,956	6,939	16,071	730	. . .
Attleborough	2,167	565	451	1,133	18	. . .
Berkley	850	213	179	446	12	. . .
Dartmouth	2,500	645	541	1,231	83	. . .
Dighton	1,793	416	409	879	89	. . .
Easton	1,466	366	379	704	17	. . .
Freetown	2,206	565	465	1,121	55	. . .
Mansfield	983	271	198	509	5	. . .
New Bedford	3,298	854	720	1,686	38	. . .
Norton	1,428	376	309	730	13	. . .
Raynham	1,095	301	222	543	29	. . .
Rehoboth	4,710	1,151	1,063	2,405	91	. . .
Somerset	1,151	270	234	585	62	. . .
Swanzey	1,782	429	369	912	72	. . .
Taunton	3,804	922	864	1,928	90	. . .
Westport	2,463	612	536	1,259	56	. . .
Dukes county	3,255	823	711	1,696	25	. . .
Chilmark	771	199	157	405	10	. . .
Edgartown	1,344	336	318	682	8	. . .
Tisbury	1,140	288	236	609	7	. . .

[1] Schedules missing.
Source: Bureau of the Census, *A Century of Population Growth, 1790–1900* (1909), 191–193.

TABLE 5.15 FEDERAL CENSUS OF DISTRICT OF MAINE, 1790

County and Town	Total	White Population in 1790 — Males — 16 Years and Over	Under 16 Years	Females	All Other Free Persons	Slaves
Cumberland county	25,530	6,208	6,624	12,519	179	...
Bakerstown plantation	1,270	289	370	611	...	...
Bridgton	329	100	81	147	1	...
Brunswick	1,387	355	332	662	38	...
Bucktown plantation	453	96	146	211	...	...
Butterfield plantation	189	49	55	85	...	...
Cape Elizabeth	1,356	341	324	683	8	...
Durham	722	161	215	343	3	...
Falmouth	2,995	648	815	1,504	28	...
Flintstown plantation	190	54	48	88	...	...
Freeport	1,327	333	342	650	2	...
Gorham and Scarborough	4,476	1,108	1,134	2,187	47	...
Gray	577	148	139	290	...	...
Harpswell	1,071	253	268	539	11	...
New Gloucester	1,358	320	338	694	6	...
North Yarmouth	1,923	464	488	957	14	...
Otisfield plantation	197	56	46	95	...	...
Plantation No. 4	344	89	101	154	...	...
Portland	2,239	564	537	1,122	16	...
Raymondtown plantation	345	81	92	170	2	...
Rusfield gore	102	22	30	50	...	...
Scarborough (see Gorham and Scarborough).						
Shepardsfield plantation	528	126	140	261	1	...
Standish	705	181	182	341	1	...
Turner	349	87	104	158	...	...
Waterford plantation	160	55	32	73	...	...
Windham	938	228	265	444	1	...
Hancock county	9,542	2,435	2,529	4,540	38	...
Barrettstown	173	61	44	68	...	...
Belfast	245	64	55	126	...	...
Bluehill	274	69	79	125	1	...
Camden	331	93	85	153	...	...
Canaan	132	34	39	59	...	...
Conduskeeg plantation	567	145	170	249	3	...
Deer Isle	683	175	182	318	8	...
Ducktrap	278	78	82	118	...	...
Eastern River township No. 2	240	59	63	118	...	...
Eddy township	110	19	32	59	...	...
Frankfort	891	235	235	419	2	...
Gouldsborough	267	78	64	116	9	...
Isleborough	382	90	114	177	1	...
Mount Desert	744	191	207	345	1	...
Orphan Island	124	33	31	60	...	...
Orrington	477	114	128	234	1	...
Penobscot	1,040	248	248	538	6	...
Sedgwick	569	144	155	270	...	...
Small islands not belonging to any town	66	19	17	30	...	...
Sullivan	504	126	123	254	1	...
Hancock county						
Trenton (including township No. 1, east side of Union river)	312	75	92	144	1	...
Township No. 1 (Bucks)	316	85	81	148	2	...
Township No. 6 (west side of Union river)	239	69	49	120	1	...
Vinalhaven	578	131	154	292	1	...
Lincoln county	29,733	7,668	7,679	14,245	141	...
Balltown	904	228	251	425	...	...
Bath	943	233	259	444	7	...
Boothbay	998	247	248	499	4	...
Bowdoin	970	235	261	459	15	...
Bowdoinham	455	109	127	218	1	...
Bristol	516	115	143	257	1	...
Canaan	446	99	132	215	...	...
Carratunk	105	31	35	39	...	...
Carrs plantation, or Unity	127	32	33	62	...	...
Chester plantation	70	24	19	27	...	...
Cushing	942	256	235	451	...	...
Edgecomb	843	182	259	402	...	...
Fairfield	453	122	114	217	...	...
Georgetown	1,327	342	320	654	11	...
Great Pond plantation	164	43	52	69	...	...
Greene	372	101	99	172	...	...
Hallowell	1,189	330	281	566	12	...
Hancock	278	83	64	130	1	...
Hunts Meadow	68	15	21	32	...	...
Jones plantation	244	62	63	119	...	...
Lewistown and gore adjoining	526	127	140	259	...	...
Little River	64	17	15	32	...	...
Littleborough plantation	270	71	69	123	7	...
Livermore, east side of Androscoggin river	44	15	8	21	...	...
Meduncook	321	89	79	153	...	...
New Castle	898	226	221	448	3	...
New Sandwich	296	91	65	140	...	...
Nobleborough	1,310	316	348	642	4	...
Norridgewock	332	91	89	152	...	...
Norridgewock, settlement east of	43	11	12	20	...	...
Pittston	603	182	133	281	7	...
Pownalborough	2,043	535	535	969	4	...
Prescotts and Whitchers plantation	32	12	8	11	1	...
Rockmeeko, east side of river	59	28	7	24	...	...
Sandy river, first township	493	141	127	223	2	...

County and Town	Total	White Population in 1790			All Other Free Persons	Slaves
		Males		Fe-males		
		16 Years and Over	Under 16 Years			
Lincoln county						
Sandy river, from its mouth to Carrs plantation	324	78	93	152	1	...
Sandy river, middle township	65	17	15	33	...	...
Sandy river, upper township	60	18	17	25	...	...
Seven Mile Brook	138	41	34	62	1	...
Smithtown plantation	512	142	129	240	1	...
Starling plantation	168	60	31	77	...	...
Thomaston	799	207	209	379	4	...
Titcomb	147	34	36	77	...	...
Topsham	826	215	203	398	10	...
Twenty-five Mile Pond	119	33	27	59	...	...
Union	200	53	50	94	3	...
Vassalborough	1,246	301	311	623	11	...
Waldoborough	1,720	429	454	824	13	...
Wales plantation	440	115	120	205	...	...
Warren	646	178	148	307	13	...
Washington	612	166	138	308	...	...
Winslow, with its ad-jacents	798	203	223	371	1	...
Winthrop	1,227	304	328	593	2	...
Woolwich	791	205	195	390	1	...
Between Norridge-wock and Seven Mile Brook	147	28	46	73	...	...
Washington county	2,760	754	708	1,278	20	...
Bucks Harbor Neck	61	14	18	29	...	...
Machias	818	229	210	372	7	...
Plantations east of Machias:						
No. 1	66	18	16	32	...	...
No. 2	144	41	30	67	6	...
No. 4	54	16	13	25	...	...
No. 5	84	24	26	34	...	...
No. 8	244	75	60	109	...	...
No. 9	29	9	7	13	...	...
No. 10	42	14	5	23	...	...
No. 11	37	8	10	19	...	...
No. 12	54	13	15	26	...	...
No. 13	7	1	5	1	...	...
Plantations west of Machias:						
No. 4	233	71	59	103	...	...
No. 5	177	45	49	83	...	...
No. 6	209	56	55	98	...	...
No. 11	95	22	24	49		
No. 12	8	4	1	3	...	...
No. 13	223	51	61	105	6	...
No. 22	175	43	44	87	1	...

County and Town	Total	White Population in 1790			All Other Free Persons	Slaves
		Males		Fe-males		
		16 Years and Over	Under 16 Years			
York county	29,078	7,276	7,193	14,451	158	...
Arundel	1,461	367	375	708	11	...
Berwick	3,890	978	920	1,950	42	...
Biddeford	1,018	273	233	506	6	...
Brownfield township	146	39	37	68	2	...
Brownfield town-ship—in the gore adjoining	20	6	5	9	...	...
Buxton	1,508	357	402	746	3	...
Coxhall	761	164	235	362	...	...
Francisborough plantation	409	98	101	210	...	...
Fryeburgh	549	142	138	268	1	...
Hiram	92	22	29	41	...	...
Kittery	3,205	765	696	1,705	39	...
Lebanon	1,276	310	344	622	...	...
Limerick	409	98	110	200	1	...
Little Falls	607	159	147	301	...	...
Little Ossipee	663	144	200	318	1	...
New Penacook	77	23	13	41	...	...
Parsonsfield	654	174	169	311	...	...
Pepperellborough	1,343	339	358	646	...	...
Porterfield	71	23	14	34	...	...
Sanford	1,798	449	473	876	...	...
Shapleigh	1,319	310	370	630	9	...
Sudbury-Canada	324	82	89	153	...	...
Sudbury, settlements adjoining	51	17	13	21	...	...
Suncook	85	22	25	38	...	...
Washington plan-tation	261	72	51	138	...	...
Waterborough	968	229	276	463	...	...
Waterford	154	45	35	74	...	...
Wells	3,061	819	733	1,494	15	...
York	2,898	750	602	1,518	28	...

Source: Bureau of the Census, *A Century of Population Growth, 1790–1900* (1909), 188.

TABLE 5.16 FEDERAL CENSUS OF MASSACHUSETTS AND MAINE DISTRICT, 1800

District of Maine

Names of Counties	Free White Males					Free White Females					All Others &c	Whole Number
	To 10	To 16	To 26	To 45	To &c	To 10	To 16	To 26	To 45	To &c		
York	6,504	3,238	3,292	3,257	2,402	6,445	2,791	3,946	3,277	2,577	167	37,729
Cumberland	6,817	3,104	3,159	3,987	2,057	6,622	2,978	3,073	4,030	2,091	290	37,918
Kennebec	4,869	1,833	2,031	2,744	1,095	4,675	1,806	1,921	2,506	922	169	24,402
Lincoln	5,684	2,501	2,667	3,017	1,676	5,403	2,277	2,550	2,782	1,543	125	30,100
Hancock	3,204	1,296	1,402	1,821	864	2,921	1,159	1,415	1,513	721	42	16,316
Washington	892	333	349	492	245	833	327	390	388	187	25	4,436
Total of each description in the district of Maine	27,970	12,305	12,900	15,318	8,339	26,899	11,338	13,295	14,496	8,041	818	150,901
												818
												151,719

The District of Massachusetts

Counties	Free White Males					Free White Females					All Others &c.	Slaves	Whole Number in Each Co.
	To 10	To 16	To 26	To 45	45 &c	To 10	To 16	To 26	To 45	45 &c			
Suffolk	3,429	1,629	2,741	3,412	1,601	3,455	1,691	3,252	3,448	2,119	1,238		28,015
Norfolk	3,911	1,960	2,629	2,695	2,239	3,649	1,825	2,550	2,919	2,513	326		27,216
Essex	8,662	4,594	5,565	5,816	4,169	8,189	4,348	6,198	7,006	5,747	911		61,196
Middlesex	6,917	3,551	4,325	4,393	3,853	6,653	3,406	4,445	4,627	4,288	470		46,928
Worcester	9,428	4,915	5,587	5,511	4,906	8,883	4,483	5,875	6,133	4,981	490		61,192
Plymouth	4,386	2,308	2,292	2,715	2,514	4,314	2,153	2,743	3,245	2,946	457		30,073
Bristol	4,991	2,779	2,721	2,839	2,665	4,907	2,708	3,105	3,279	3,078	808		33,880
Barnstable	3,088	1,455	1,789	1,675	1,406	2,840	1,320	1,878	1,925	1,654	263		19,293
Dukes	398	206	259	249	274	377	219	326	308	300	202		3,118
Nantucket	748	373	561	535	400	708	344	543	703	474	228		5,617
Hampshire	12,017	5,984	6,316	6,726	5,143	11,630	5,505	6,450	6,981	5,115	565		72,432
Berkshire	5,671	2,753	3,120	3,163	2,187	5,315	2,672	3,126	3,259	2,125	494		33,885
	63,646	32,507	37,905	39,729	31,348	60,920	30,674	40,491	43,833	35,340	6,452		422,845

Source: Census Office, *Return of the Whole Number of Persons Within the Several Districts of the United States: 1800* (1802), 20, 26.

TABLE 5.17 PROVINCIAL CENSUS OF RHODE ISLAND, 1774

Towns	Families	Whites				Total Whites	Indians	Blacks	Total of Each Town
		Males		Females					
		Above 16	Under 16	Above 16	Under 16				
Total	9,450	14,032	12,731	15,349	12,348	54,460	1,479	3,668	59,607
Newport	1,590	2,100	1,558	2,624	1,635	7,917	46	1,246	9,209
Providence	655	1,219	850	1,049	832	3,950	68	303	4,321
Portsmouth	220	343	341	400	285	1,369	21	122	1,512
Warwick	353	569	512	615	465	2,161	88	89	2,338
Westerly	257	421	441	443	401	1,706	37	69	1,812
New Shoreham	75	109	119	121	120	469	51	55	575
East Greenwich	275	416	345	464	338	1,563	31	69	1,663
North Kingstown	361	538	497	595	552	2,182	79	211	2,472
South Kingstown	364	550	554	597	484	2,185	210	440	2,835
Jamestown	69	110	90	118	82	400	32	131	563
Smithfield	476	742	665	769	638	2,814	23	51	2,888
Scituate	564	909	879	933	817	3,538	8	55	3,601
Glocester	525	743	724	740	719	2,926	. . .	19	2,945
West Greenwich	304	429	395	465	456	1,745	. . .	19	1,764
Charlestown	307	312	315	350	264	1,241	528	52	1,821

Towns	Families	Whites Males Above 16	Under 16	Females Above 16	Under 16	Total Whites	Indians	Blacks	Total of Each Town
Coventry	274	474	555	493	470	1,992	11	20	2,023
Exeter	289	441	415	478	446	1,780	17	67	1,864
Middletown	123	210	179	259	156	804	13	64	881
Bristol	197	272	232	319	256	1,079	16	114	1,209
Tiverton	298	418	500	438	434	1,790	71	95	1,956
Warren	168	237	251	255	185	928	7	44	979
Little Compton	218	304	254	382	220	1,160	25	47	1,232
Richmond	189	286	316	324	287	1,213	20	24	1,257
Cumberland	264	400	408	478	450	1,736	3	17	1,756
Cranston	340	476	399	517	390	1,782	19	60	1,861
Hopkinton	299	427	420	477	415	1,739	21	48	1,808
Johnston	167	242	227	254	234	957	9	65	1,031
North Providence	138	193	172	230	197	792	7	31	830
Barrington	91	142	118	162	120	542	18	41	601

Source: J. R. Bartlett, ed., *Records of the Colony of Rhode Island and Providence Plantations in New England* (1856–1865), VII, 299.

TABLE 5.18 FEDERAL CENSUS OF RHODE ISLAND, 1790

County and Town	Total	White Population in 1790 — Males 16 Years and Over	Under 16 Years	Females	All Other Free Persons	Slaves
Bristol county	3,211	778	677	1,558	100	98
Barrington	683	165	144	330	32	12
Bristol	1,412	327	292	677	52	64
Warren	1,116	286	241	551	16	22
Kent county	8,851	2,158	2,128	4,153	349	63
Coventry	2,483	645	633	1,165	35	5
East Greenwich	1,826	428	393	920	72	13
Warwick	2,490	566	516	1,151	222	35
West Greenwich	2,052	519	586	917	20	10
Newport county	14,351	3,256	2,856	7,062	805	372
Jamestown	507	100	91	232	68	16
Little Compton	1,529	357	356	771	22	23
Middletown	840	214	161	424	26	15
New Shoreham	681	154	133	290	56	48
Newport	6,744	1,460	1,244	3,393	421	226
Portsmouth	1,600	402	350	792	37	19
Tiverton	2,450	569	521	1,160	175	25

County and Town	Total	White Population in 1790 — Males 16 Years and Over	Under 16 Years	Females	All Other Free Persons	Slaves
Providence county	24,376	6,155	5,486	11,877	777	81
Cranston	1,877	444	408	942	73	10
Cumberland	1,966	503	485	970	8	. . .
Foster	2,268	528	603	1,118	15	4
Glocester	4,016	986	995	2,012	22	1
Johnston	1,320	333	280	633	71	3
North Providence	1,071	270	237	509	50	5
Providence	6,371	1,709	1,249	2,939	427	47
Scituate	2,316	563	548	1,170	29	6
Smithfield	3,171	819	681	1,584	82	5
Washington county	18,323	3,709	4,598	8,219	1,453	344
Charlestown	2,023	345	445	815	406	12
Exeter	2,496	583	613	1,176	87	37
Hopkinton	2,464	522	685	1,178	72	7
North Kingstown	2,904	601	667	1,341	199	96
Richmond	1,769	366	510	815	76	2
South Kingstown	4,369	832	999	1,813	545	180
Westerly	2,298	460	679	1,081	68	10

Source: Bureau of the Census, *A Century of Population Growth, 1790–1900* (1909), 193.

TABLE 5.19 PROVINCIAL CENSUS OF CONNECTICUT, 1774

Counties and Towns	Males Under Ten Years	Females Under Ten Years	Males Between Ten and Twenty Years, Married or Single		Females Between Ten and Twenty Years		Males Between Twenty and Seventy		Females Between Twenty and Seventy	
			Married	Single	Married	Single	Married	Single	Married	Single
Hartford county:										
Bolton	154	162	. . .	121	2	105	154	48	159	59
Chatham	420	392	. . .	276	2	276	349	129	350	127
Colchester	530	477	. . .	389	6	344	442	139	480	165
East-Haddam	447	457	4	348	9	334	412	123	429	134
East-Windsor	481	443	. . .	353	2	332	439	178	433	217
Enfield	213	225	1	131	14	126	191	91	193	120
Farmington	965	1,007	1	736	10	616	958	295	965	292
Glastenbury	331	337	1	275	8	248	283	76	293	90
Haddam	294	286	. . .	224	9	187	241	89	251	104
Hartford	770	753	11	583	11	515	715	307	715	363
Hebron	360	375	2	316	8	308	312	122	307	123
Middletown	717	766	6	591	19	529	677	276	695	316
Simsbury	671	609	6	406	12	439	591	120	597	118
Somers	146	156	. . .	133	2	130	158	51	159	56
Stafford	223	199	. . .	199	9	162	201	59	197	48
Suffield	330	331	9	244	6	212	279	101	283	143
Tolland	200	193	. . .	150	1	157	101	86	161	171
Wethersfield	490	494	5	407	18	361	492	216	493	285
Willington	178	157	. . .	119	10	122	155	39	146	46
Windsor	299	302	7	242	7	219	319	134	310	157
Total	**8,219**	**8,121**	**53**	**6,243**	**165**	**5,722**	**7,469**	**2,679**	**[1]7,616**	**3,134**
New Haven county:										
Branford	284	309	. . .	224	. . .	215	317	81	322	148
Derby	289	289	2	252	10	205	270	106	277	83
Durham	166	148	2	141	2	124	149	69	154	56
Guilford	396	372	. . .	362	. . .	286	462	170	471	237
Milford	279	289	10	241	7	214	322	110	329	100
New-Haven	1,309	1,213	1	902	25	829	1,246	618	1,246	467
Wallingford	824	799	3	623	17	544	726	189	737	217
Waterbury	619	609	5	422	19	361	568	132	569	138
Total	**4,166**	**4,028**	**23**	**3,167**	**80**	**2,778**	**4,060**	**1,475**	**4,105**	**1,446**
New London county:										
Groton	574	570	10	441	22	390	538	142	532	200
Lyme	597	601	1	430	14	422	515	448	519	231
Killingworth	311	301	. . .	247	4	249	272	120	278	122
New-London	935	917	21	599	33	593	806	207	817	343
Norwich	1,099	1,054	. . .	916	8	741	1,056	412	1,069	505
Preston	401	405	16	291	16	244	295	99	306	128
Saybrook	432	461	1	284	10	275	411	107	410	171
Stonington	913	818	4	651	16	622	714	151	721	262
Total	**5,262**	**5,127**	**53**	**3,859**	**123**	**3,536**	**4,607**	**1,686**	**4,652**	**1,962**
Fairfield county:										
Danbury	425	387	2	302	12	282	416	103	424	81
Fairfield	774	689	2	557	12	519	741	228	739	183
Greenwich	496	420	12	333	24	287	403	114	404	112
New Fairfield	199	204	. . .	170	8	182	207	51	199	44
Newtown	357	357	1	277	8	281	324	103	324	67
Norwalk	754	700	. . .	544	. . .	486	638	173	638	217
Redding	208	189	. . .	152	2	121	196	46	206	46
Ridgfield	299	269	1	214	4	189	276	59	281	57
Stamford	. . .	. . .	13	1,008	7	909	561	244	562	199
Stratford	806	795	2	655	33	618	830	292	812	240
Total	**4,318**	**4,010**	**33**	**4,212**	**110**	**3,874**	**4,592**	**1,413**	**4,589**	**1,246**

Males Above Seventy		Females Above Seventy		Negro Males Under Twenty	Negro Females Under Twenty	Negro Males Above Twenty	Negro Females Above Twenty	Indian Males Under Twenty	Indian Females Under Twenty	Indian Males Above Twenty	Indian Females Above Twenty	Total Whites	Total Blacks
Married	Single	Married	Single										
11	5	5	9	3	. . .	4	. . .	. . .	. . .	. . .	. . .	994	7
20	10	11	7	5	4	15	2	1	1	. . .	. . .	2,369	28
29	7	18	31	41	44	61	27	8	7	2	11	3,057	201
20	5	6	15	21	18	13	6	1	1	3	2	2,743	65
37	8	16	22	9	8	9	6	2	1	1	2	2,961	38
21	5	13	9	. . .	3	4	. . .	. . .	. . .	. . .	. . .	1,353	7
35	17	19	47	16	14	26	7	8	9	14	12	5,963	106
3	17	7	23	18	19	13	13	3	9	1	3	1,992	79
10	3	6	9	4	4	5	. . .	. . .	. . .	. . .	. . .	1,713	13
42	20	42	34	28	29	51	37	3	2	. . .	. . .	4,881	150
15	8	16	13	12	10	19	11	. . .	. . .	. . .	. . .	2,285	52
23	10	16	39	45	46	61	46	. . .	. . .	. . .	. . .	4,680	198
39	8	35	20	9	6	10	4	. . .	. . .	. . .	. . .	3,671	29
14	3	8	8	. . .	1	2	. . .	. . .	. . .	. . .	. . .	1,024	3
15	5	10	6	. . .	. . .	. . .	1	. . .	. . .	. . .	. . .	1,333	1
12	6	7	17	5	6	16	6	1	. . .	2	1	1,980	37
13	3	5	6	5	2	2	1	3	. . .	1	1	1,247	15
28	13	17	28	44	26	44	28	. . .	. . .	. . .	. . .	3,347	142
13	3	11	1	. . .	. . .	1	. . .	. . .	. . .	. . .	. . .	1,000	1
22	19	22	14	9	8	14	6	2	2	. . .	2	[1]2,073	43
422	175	290	358	274	248	370	201	32	32	24	34	[1]50,666	1,215
13	5	7	13	28	27	35	21	2	. . .	1	1	1,938	113
12	6	6	12	11	15	12	12	5	5	5	5	1,819	70
6	4	3	7	7	10	16	11	1	. . .	. . .	. . .	1,031	45
35	9	29	17	13	14	20	14	8	10	2	3	2,846	84
15	10	11	28	41	35	52	30	. . .	. . .	1	3	1,965	162
48	44	24	50	66	70	70	56	7	2	. . .	2	8,022	273
33	10	24	31	27	28	48	31	2	1	. . .	1	4,777	138
20	6	9	21	6	7	15	6	2	1	. . .	1	3,498	38
182	94	113	179	199	206	[2]268	[2]181	27	19	9	16	25,896	925
19	8	13	29	51	39	42	42	55	36	39	56	3,488	360
34	5	17	26	36	26	35	27	21	18	23	42	3,860	228
14	6	12	21	4	6	6	3	6	2	4	2	1,957	33
49	13	15	18	70	79	89	78	64	48	35	59	5,366	522
55	23	38	56	62	54	69	49	16	14	11	20	7,032	295
21	11	7	15	5	11	25	12	11	9	1	9	2,255	83
26	5	20	15	15	12	20	8	3	. . .	1	. . .	2,628	59
22	13	21	28	85	49	49	36	73	80	28	56	4,956	456
240	84	143	208	328	276	335	255	249	207	142	244	31,542	2,036
14	6	7	12	15	13	15	7	. . .	. . .	2	1	2,473	53
30	11	20	39	83	75	91	66	. . .	. . .	2	2	4,544	319
19	9	10	11	35	25	34	20	. . .	3	2	3	2,654	122
9	3	6	6	5	4	6	5	. . .	. . .	. . .	. . .	1,288	20
20	6	20	23	12	20	18	9	1	1	. . .	. . .	2,168	61
43	8	25	17	37	25	43	31	. . .	2	4	3	4,243	145
10	4	6	3	9	14	17	5	. . .	. . .	. . .	. . .	1,189	45
7	4	6	7	9	9	9	8	. . .	. . .	. . .	. . .	1,673	35
. . .	. . .	. . .	. . .	12	18	17	13	. . .	. . .	. . .	. . .	3,503	60
38	14	19	47	69	72	108	70	7	12	9	7	5,201	354
190	65	119	165	286	275	358	234	8	18	19	16	28,936	1,214

(continued)

TABLE 5.19 (continued)

Counties and Towns	Males Under Ten Years	Females Under Ten Years	Males Between Ten and Twenty Years, Married or Single		Females Between Ten and Twenty Years		Males Between Twenty and Seventy		Females Between Twenty and Seventy	
			Married	Single	Married	Single	Married	Single	Married	Single
Windham county:										
Canterbury	438	374	3	330	3	242	356	114	358	123
Coventry	340	290	. . .	234	. . .	259	307	97	315	137
Pomfret	334	325	2	276	5	286	314	154	320	177
Killingly	582	521	. . .	461	2	372	530	152	542	168
Lebanon	590	552	4	515	26	460	540	208	549	285
Mansfield	354	382	2	307	14	305	353	142	353	165
Plainfield	254	241	1	168	3	177	215	73	217	83
Ashford	421	375	3	277	13	263	330	67	339	93
Voluntown	242	245	. . .	202	4	156	231	57	235	45
Union	97	67	. . .	68	. . .	61	83	14	83	16
Windham	532	533	1	482	7	387	476	173	491	267
Woodstock	320	333	. . .	230	1	234	243	119	243	195
Total	4,504	4,238	16	3,550	78	3,202	3,978	1,370	4,045	1,754
Litchfield county:										
Barkhemsted	. . .	. . :	. . .	. . .	. . .	. . .	. . .	. . .	. . .	. . .
Canaan	258	273	2	194	9	190	263	63	254	47
Colebrook	. . .	. . .	. . .	. . .	. . .	. . .	. . .	. . .	. . .	. . .
Cornwall	190	160	. . .	130	1	107	152	30	155	20
Goshen	202	193	. . .	138	4	113	171	59	172	29
Hartland	. . .	. . .	. . .	. . .	. . .	. . .	. . .	. . .	. . .	. . .
Harwinton	179	163	. . .	115	. . .	119	161	50	161	50
Kent	384	352	11	176	17	166	313	141	262	78
Litchfield	428	435	1	304	7	266	399	150	403	83
New-Hartford	176	158	. . .	119	4	116	146	49	155	45
New-Milford	490	497	15	325	27	254	482	83	460	61
Norfolk	156	151	. . .	109	3	110	155	30	155	27
Salisbury	347	358	. . .	240	7	224	278	111	271	70
Sharon	343	342	. . .	259	11	236	307	77	303	56
Torrington	132	134	. . .	99	. . .	75	139	56	146	54
Westmoreland	384	352	11	176	17	166	313	141	262	78
Winchester	55	69	. . .	34	1	19	60	18	56	11
Woodbury	921	889	4	600	33	587	821	260	795	235
Total	4,645	4,526	44	3,018	141	2,748	4,160	1,318	4,010	944
Hartford county	8,219	8,121	53	6,243	165	5,722	7,469	2,679	7,616[1]	3,134
New-Haven county	4,166	4,028	23	3,167	80	2,778	4,060	1,475	4,105	1,446
New-London county	5,262	5,127	53	3,859	123	3,536	4,607	1,686	4,652	1,962
Fairfield county	4,318	4,010	33	4,212	110	3,874	4,592	1,413	4,589	1,246
Windham county	4,504	4,238	16	3,550	78	3,202	3,978	1,370	4,045	1,754
Litchfield county	4,645	4,526	44	3,018	141	2,748	4,160	1,318	4,010	944
Total for colony	31,114	30,050	222	24,049	697	21,860	28,866	9,941	[1] 29,017	10,486

Males Above Seventy		Females Above Seventy		Negro Males Under Twenty	Negro Females Under Twenty	Negro Males Above Twenty	Negro Females Above Twenty	Indian Males Under Twenty	Indian Females Under Twenty	Indian Males Above Twenty	Indian Females Above Twenty	Total Whites	Total Blacks
Married	Single	Married	Single										
19	5	10	17	6	4	22	9	1	1	7	2	2,392	52
21	1	14	17	4	6	7	5	. . .	. . .	2	. . .	2,032	24
17	8	7	16	22	11	13	7	2	4	3	3	2,241	65
36	14	22	37	12	2	14	7	2	4	1	5	3,439	47
43	9	25	35	30	19	22	27	9	5	4	3	3,841	119
17	13	11	25	3	1	4	3	3	6	1	2	2,443	23
13	4	12	18	18	9	18	13	9	8	3	5	1,479	83
17	8	7	15	2	2	7	2	. . .	. . .	. . .	. . .	2,228	13
26	2	22	9	9	3	9	8	2	3	. . .	1	1,476	35
8	5	6	4	. . .	. . .	1	1	. . .	. . .	. . .	. . .	512	2
35	3	18	32	18	10	15	29	2	7	3	7	3,437	91
11	13	11	21	3	14	15	10	13	9	7	9	1,974	80
263	85	165	246	127	81	147	121	43	47	31	37	27,494	634
. . .	. . .	. . .	. . .	. . .	. . .	. . .	. . .	. . .	. . .	. . .	. . .	[2]250	. . .
7	1	6	6	16	16	17	13	. . .	. . .	. . .	. . .	1,573	62
. . .	. . .	. . .	. . .	. . .	. . .	. . .	. . .	. . .	. . .	. . .	. . .	[2]150	. . .
3	3	3	3	2	2	5	1	1	4	2	. . .	957	17
7	. . .	4	6	3	. . .	9	1	. . .	. . .	. . .	. . .	1,098	13
. . .	. . .	. . .	. . .	. . .	. . .	. . .	. . .	. . .	. . .	. . .	. . .	[2]500	. . .
7	. . .	4	6	1	. . .	1	1	. . .	. . .	. . .	. . .	1,015	3
9	1	7	5	3	3	4	2	18	20	11	13	1,922	74
10	5	4	14	8	15	7	7	1	1	1	5	2,509	45
8	2	2	5	. . .	. . .	3	. . .	4	3	1	5	985	16
19	6	11	6	12	8	8	6	. . .	. . .	. . .	. . .	[1]2,736	34
4	1	1	4	1	2	. . .	. . .	. . .	. . .	. . .	. . .	[1]906	3
11	1	9	9	8	7	10	10	5	2	1	1	1,936	44
19	9	12	12	5	6	8	6	. . .	. . .	1	. . .	1,986	26
3	5	5	. . .	. . .	. . .	1	1	. . .	. . .	. . .	. . .	[1]848	2
9	1	7	5	. . .	. . .	. . .	. . .	. . .	. . .	. . .	. . .	1,922	. . .
1	. . .	1	2	7	1	2	2	. . .	. . .	. . .	. . .	327	12
22	16	16	25	26	19	24	11	3	2	2	2	5,224	89
139	51	92	108	92	79	99	61	32	32	19	26	[1,3]26,844	440
422	175	290	358	274	248	370	201	32	32	24	34	[1]50,666	1,215
182	94	113	179	199	206	[1]268	[1]181	27	19	9	16	25,896	925
240	84	143	208	328	276	335	255	249	207	142	244	31,542	2,036
190	65	119	165	286	275	358	234	8	18	19	16	28,936	1,214
263	85	165	246	127	81	147	121	43	47	31	37	27,494	634
139	51	92	108	92	79	99	61	32	32	19	26	[1]26,844	440
1,436	554	922	1,264	1,306	1,165	[1]1,577	[1]1,053	391	355	244	373	[1,2]191,378	6,464

[1] Corrected data.
[2] Not distributed by sex.
[3] Includes 900 not distributed by sex.
Source: J. H. Trumbull and C. J. Hoadly, eds., *Public Records of the Colony of Connecticut (1850–1890)*, XIV, 485–91.

TABLE 5.20   FEDERAL CENSUS OF RHODE ISLAND, 1800

Newport county	Free White Males					Free White Females					All Other Free Persons Except Indians Not Taxed	Slaves		
	Under 10 Years of Age	Of 10 and Under 16	Of 16 and Under 26, Including Heads of Families	Of 26 and Under 45, Including Heads of Families	Of 45 and Upwards, Including Heads of Families	Under 10 Years of Age	Of 10 and Under 16	Of 16 and Under 26, Including Heads of Families	Of 16 and Under 45, Including Heads of Families	Of 45 and Upwards, Including Heads of Families				
Towns														
Newport,	805	443	477	573	473	815	382	696	778	682	512	103	6,739	
Portsmouth	250	140	137	154	119	252	109	168	177	141	25	12	1,684	
New Shoreham,	107	42	45	57	42	99	51	55	74	49	75	18	714	
James-town,	54	33	34	39	29	71	39	38	50	34	74	6	501	
Middletown,	123	73	107	67	75	99	66	75	98	103	33	4	913	
Tiverton,	423	179	226	193	201	429	207	200	227	239	173	20	2,717	
Little Compton,	248	144	111	122	121	230	114	149	139	167	10	22	1,577	
														14,845
Providence county														
Providence,	890	499	827	726	465	848	486	774	868	575	656		7,614	
Smithfield,	434	221	309	272	237	450	236	325	322	267	46	1	3,120	
Scituate,	397	220	218	217	187	366	191	247	252	192	36		2,523	
Glocester,	658	363	297	363	290	608	338	326	387	301	78		4,009	
Cumberland,	321	173	189	176	152	307	137	193	236	165	7		2,056	
Cranston,	247	104	138	139	148	234	97	140	185	165	46	1	1,644	
Johnston,	192	95	117	128	107	186	81	143	129	124	62		1,364	
North Providence,	169	88	98	94	90	132	88	99	108	84	15	2	1,067	
Foster,	403	166	209	208	170	444	199	236	222	174	25	1	2,457	
														25,854
Washington county														
Westerly	332	243	240	177	142	344	236	207	190	163	49	1	2,329	
North Kingstown,	465	181	189	210	204	402	180	246	285	228	165	39	2,794	
South Kingstown,	506	295	264	237	196	538	294	272	240	177	375	44	3,438	
Charlestown,	227	149	110	90	95	180	119	117	128	104	129	6	1,454	
Exeter,	380	211	219	184	189	342	182	224	246	205	68	26	2,476	
Richmond,	214	97	105	115	95	220	118	114	132	123	31	4	1,368	
Hopkinton,	329	198	206	170	153	356	201	247	166	174	72	4	2,276	
														16,135
Bristol county														
Bristol,	244	119	136	154	104	220	113	155	193	127	84	29	1,678	
Warren,	226	128	123	150	78	184	104	132	189	106	42	10	1,473	
Barrington,	105	49	52	51	54	75	47	70	55	66	19	7	650	
														3,801
Kent county														
Warwick,	291	201	209	200	212	265	170	249	240	224	254	17	2,532	
East Greenwich,	232	152	127	175	112	232	154	178	204	119	88	2	1,775	
West Greenwich,	308	156	160	128	152	259	101	150	176	152	14	1	1,757	
Coventry,	365	185	210	216	195	337	186	238	223	217	51		2,423	
														8,487
	9,945	5,352	5,889	5,785	4,887	9,524	5,026	6,463	6,919	5,648	3,304	380	69,122	

Source: Census Office, *Return of the Whole Number of Persons Within the Several Districts of the United States: 1800* (1802), 38.

TABLE 5.21 FEDERAL CENSUS OF CONNECTICUT, 1790

County and Town	Total	White Population in 1790 Males 16 Years and Over	Under 16 Years	Females	All Other Free Persons	Slaves
Middlesex county	18,828	4,730	4,140	9,622	144	192
Chatham	3,218	810	729	1,642	21	16
East Haddam	2,740	702	589	1,396	34	19
Haddam	2,197	576	476	1,140	2	3
Killingworth	2,147	586	452	1,087	11	11
Middletown	5,298	1,238	1,199	2,695	57	109
Saybrook	3,228	818	695	1,662	19	34
New Haven county	30,703	7,843	6,841	15,198	434	387
Branford	2,227	558	496	1,086	40	47
Cheshire	2,332	591	504	1,193	31	13
Derby	2,960	744	722	1,399	52	43
Durham	1,071	315	214	526	7	9
East Haven	1,026	235	225	524	7	35
Guilford	3,439	951	713	1,727	23	25
Hamden	1,421	374	321	718	4	4
Milford	2,087	537	432	984	69	65
New Haven city	4,487	1,127	931	2,233	125	71
North Haven	1,235	323	272	626	8	6
Wallingford	3,355	842	783	1,659	26	45
Waterbury	2,932	733	717	1,458	14	10
Woodbridge	2,131	513	511	1,065	28	14
New London county[1]	32,918	8,189	7,148	16,268	732	581
Tolland county	13,251	3,449	3,138	6,524	94	46
Bolton	1,360	376	323	655	4	2
Coventry	2,125	513	509	1,080	16	7
Ellington	1,059	286	220	533	16	4
Hebron	2,313	639	526	1,104	25	19
Somers	1,220	322	300	591	2	5
Stafford	1,859	475	454	928	. . .	2
Tolland	1,484	387	361	717	14	5
Union	630	150	162	317	. . .	1
Willington	1,201	301	283	599	17	1
Windham county	28,881	7,436	6,547	14,373	341	184
Ashford	2,582	661	643	1,250	21	7
Brooklyne	1,327	352	302	633	30	10
Canterbury	1,885	501	391	975	16	2
Hampton	1,333	339	303	680	10	1
Killingley	2,162	541	544	1,048	20	9
Lebanon	4,156	1,042	930	2,080	53	51
Mansfield	2,635	689	610	1,320	9	7
Plainfield	1,711	468	356	817	60	10
Pomfret	1,760	461	375	885	20	19
Thompson	2,270	563	555	1,140	5	7
Voluntown	1,865	485	433	912	14	21
Windham	2,764	670	580	1,422	64	28
Woodstock	2,431	664	525	1,211	19	12

County and Town	Total	White Population in 1790 Males 16 Years and Over	Under 16 Years	Females	All Other Free Persons	Slaves
Fairfield county	36,290	9,149	8,394	17,630	318	799
Brookfield	1,012	267	219	516	7	3
Danbury	3,032	781	704	1,504	20	23
Fairfield	4,010	1,028	896	1,869	14	203
Greenwich	3,175	798	698	1,559	38	82
Huntington	2,742	671	625	1,278	48	120
New Fairfield	1,572	401	404	754	4	9
Newtown	2,788	720	637	1,350	10	71
Norwalk } Stamford {	8,810	2,187	2,099	4,324	83	117
Reading	1,501	390	327	735	17	32
Ridgefield	1,947	488	461	989	4	5
Stratford	3,222	799	724	1,552	49	98
Weston	2,479	619	600	1,200	24	36
Hartford county	38,149	9,808	8,844	18,846	395	256
Berlin	2,496	632	562	1,288	12	2
Bristol	2,468	592	615	1,242	17	2
East Hartford	3,012	787	668	1,519	7	31
East Windsor	2,581	712	561	1,274	26	8
Enfield	1,805	476	393	923	. . .	13
Farmington	2,683	678	676	1,283	39	7
Glastenbury	2,732	639	672	1,323	71	27
Granby	2,611	680	672	1,250	9	. . .
Hartford	4,072	1,056	858	2,032	79	47
Simsbury	2,679	687	663	1,316	11	2
Southington	2,104	540	502	1,033	18	11
Suffield	2,485	645	594	1,190	28	28
Wethersfield	3,790	953	818	1,909	51	59
Windsor	2,631	731	590	1,264	27	19
Litchfield county	38,635	10,135	9,237	18,747	313	203
Bethlem	1,056	275	243	534	. . .	4
Cornwall	1,475	396	318	715	27	19
Harwinton	1,367	354	334	673	. . .	6
Kent	1,317	348	317	635	11	6
Litchfield	20,278	5,302	4,914	9,782	191	89
New Milford	3,170	855	733	1,518	39	25
Southbury	1,734	485	367	847	14	21
Warren	775	195	205	364	5	6
Washington	1,677	442	405	814	11	5
Watertown	3,143	799	783	1,547	3	11
Woodbury	2,643	684	618	1,318	12	11

[1] Not returned by towns.
Source: Bureau of the Census, *A Century of Population Growth, 1790–1900* (1909), 193, 194.

TABLE 5.22 FEDERAL CENSUS OF CONNECTICUT, 1800

Names of Counties	Free White Males					Free White Females					All Others &c.	Slaves	Total of Each County
	To 10	To 16	To 26	To 45	45 &c	To 10	To 16	To 26	To 45	45 &c			
Hartford	6,412	3,421	3,779	4,042	3,047	5,999	3,139	4,004	4,179	3,315	743	67	42,147
New Haven	4,642	2,370	2,866	3,047	2,435	4,509	2,372	3,078	3,214	2,743	650	236	32,162
New London	5,304	2,554	2,893	2,995	2,488	5,087	2,359	3,247	3,475	3,036	1,236	209	34,888
Fairfield	5,020	2,863	3,150	3,663	2,837	5,442	2,713	3,464	3,929	2,985	957	276	38,208
Windham	3,890	2,283	2,626	2,417	2,380	3,671	1,952	2,736	2,804	2,794	634	35	28,222
Litchfield	6,667	3,203	3,560	4,029	2,950	6,238	2,982	3,822	4,170	2,890	656	47	41,214
Middlesex	2,847	1,575	1,628	1,762	1,681	2,710	1,593	1,875	2,044	1,809	251	72	19,874
Tolland	2,255	1,139	1,181	1,225	1,158	2,080	1,108	1,335	1,371	1,255	203	9	14,319
Total	37,946	19,408	21,683	23,180	18,976	35,736	18,218	23,561	25,186	20,827	5,330	951	251,002

Source: Census Office, *Return of the Whole Number of Persons Within the Several Districts of the United States: 1800* (1802), 30.

Population of the Middle Atlantic

Population growth in the middle-Atlantic region was fueled by large inflows of migrants from both New England, who primarily went to New York, and from Europe, who primarily went to Pennsylvania. The resulting mix of peoples produced a society unique in early America for its ethnic diversity, with the result that the mid-Atlantic states were the least Anglo-Saxon portion of the country, although the English-Welsh stock remained the largest single group everywhere but in Pennsylvania. After the years from 1760 to 1780, when its population increased at slightly less than the national average, the number of residents in the middle states grew rapidly because of vigorous urban expansion and the opportunity to settle large tracts of rich agricultural land purchased from the Indians. With the resumption of overseas emigration and a surging influx of Yankees during the 1790s, the mid-Atlantic region became the fastest growing section of the United States, with a population rising at a rate almost a third higher than in the South and twice that of New England.

TABLE 5.23 COMPOSITION OF THE MID-ATLANTIC COLONIES' POPULATION, 1774

	Total Number	Percent of Total	Percent of Subgroup
Total Population	640,695	100.0%	. . .
White Inhabitants	602,947	94.1%	100.0%
Status Independent	581,573	90.8%	96.5%
Status Indentured[a]	21,374	3.3%	3.5%
Black Inhabitants	37,748	5.9%	100.0%
Legally Free	3,576	.6%	9.5%
Slaves	34,172	5.3%	90.5%
All Males Aged 21 +	143,870	22.5%	100.0%
Taxpaying Property Owners	131,353	20.5%	91.3%
All Females Aged 21 +	133,860	20.9%	100.0%
Taxpaying Property Owners	12,223	1.9%	9.1%
All Youths Under 21	362,965	56.7%	. . .
Free Population[b]	585,149	91.3%	. . .
All Free Adult Males	131,351	20.5%	100.0%
Aged 21–25	28,097	4.4%	21.4%
Aged 26–44	64,835	10.1%	49.4%
Aged 45 +	38,419	6.0%	29.2%
All Free Adult Females	122,244	19.1%	100.0%
Aged 21–25	28,030	4.4%	22.9%
Aged 26–44	60,030	9.4%	49.1%
Aged 45 +	34,184	5.3%	28.0%
All Free Youths Under 21	331,554	51.7%	. . .

[a] Indentured servants and convict laborers.
[b] Includes free Negroes.
Source: Alice Hanson Jones, *American Colonial Wealth: Documents and Methods* (1978), 1791.

TABLE 5.24   PROVINCIAL CENSUS OF N.Y., 1771

Names of the Several Counties	Whites						Blacks						Total of Whites and Blacks
	Males Under 16	Males Above 16 & Under 60	Males 60 and Upwards	Females Under 16	Females Above 16	Total Whites in Each County	Males Under 16	Males Above 16, and Under 60	Males 60 and Upwards	Females Under 16	Females Above 16	Total of Blacks in Each County	
City & Co., of New York	3,720	5,083	280	3,779	5,864	18,726	568	890	42	552	1,085	3,137	21,863
Albany	9,740	9,822	1,136	9,086	9,045	38,829	876	1,100	250	671	980	3,877	42,706
Ulster	2,835	3,023	262	2,601	3,275	11,996	518	516	57	422	441	1,954	13,950
Dutchess	5,721	4,687	384	5,413	4,839	21,044	299	417	34	282	328	1,360	22,404
Orange	2,651	2,297	167	2,191	2,124	9,430	162	184	22	120	174	662	10,092
Westchester	3,813	5,204	549	3,483	5,266	18,315	793	916	68	776	887	3,440	21,755
Kings	548	644	76	513	680	2,461	297	287	22	261	295	1,162	3,623
Queens	1,253	2,083	950	2,126	2,332	8,744	374	511	271	546	534	2,236	10,980
Suffolk	2,731	2,834	347	2,658	3,106	11,676	350	389	59	320	334	1,452	13,128
Richmond	616	438	96	508	595	2,253	177	152	22	106	137	594	2,847
Cumberland	1,071	1,002	59	941	862	3,935	. . .	6	1	1	2	10	3,945
Gloucester	178	185	8	193	151	715	2	4	. . .	3	. . .	9	724
Totals	34,877	37,302	4,314	33,492	38,139	148,124	4,416	5,372	848	4,060	5,197	19,893	168,017

Source: Edmund B. O'Callaghan, ed., *Documentary History of the State of New York* (1849–1851), I, 697.

TABLE 5.25   FEDERAL CENSUS OF NEW YORK, 1790

County and Town	Total	White Population in 1790			All Other Free Persons	Slaves
		Males		Females		
		16 Years and Over	Under 16 Years			
Queens county	16,013	3,555	2,863	6,468	819	2,308
Flushing	1,608	325	229	587	127	340
Jamaica	1,674	397	294	697	65	221
Newtown	2,109	421	353	748	54	533
North Hempstead	2,697	550	442	1,026	172	507
Oyster Bay	4,097	949	756	1,707	304	381
South Hempstead	3,828	913	789	1,703	97	326
Richmond county	3,827	747	753	1,445	127	755
Castleton	804	178	172	314	26	114
Northfield	1,021	223	226	402	35	135
Southfield	865	151	139	306	35	234
Westfield	1,137	195	216	423	31	272
Suffolk county	16,546	3,787	3,294	7,229	1,131	1,105
Brookhaven	3,227	727	617	1,375	275	233
Easthampton	1,497	354	272	673	99	99
Huntington	3,366	791	763	1,518	75	219
Islip	607	132	126	246	68	35
Shelter Island	201	39	38	77	23	24
Smithtown	1,024	195	179	371	113	166
Southampton	3,402	781	653	1,542	280	146
Southold	3,222	768	646	1,427	198	183

County and Town	Total	White Population in 1790			All Other Free Persons	Slaves
		Males		Females		
		16 Years and Over	Under 16 Years			
Ulster county	29,370	7,050	6,783	12,462	161	2,914
Hurley	847	166	129	306	1	245
Kingston	3,923	902	742	1,549	9	721
Manakating	1,763	436	491	780	5	51
Marbletown	2,190	492	469	840	15	374
Middletown	1,019	293	259	460	1	6
Montgomery	3,564	898	834	1,578	18	236
New Marlborough	2,246	539	607	1,027	15	58
New Paltz	2,304	512	519	959	12	302
New Windsor	1,819	463	417	805	17	117
Newburgh	2,347	610	585	1,083	12	57
Rochester	1,628	374	321	638	14	281
Shawangunk	2,123	483	452	818	21	349
Wallkill	2,571	604	690	1,166	9	102
Woodstock	1,026	278	268	453	12	15
Washington county	14,077	3,616	3,789	6,623	3	46
Argyle	2,350	625	660	1,051	. . .	14
Granville	2,242	583	566	1,093	. . .	. . .
Hampton	463	108	131	224	. . .	. . .
Hebron	1,703	406	479	818	. . .	. . .
Kingsbury	1,120	299	291	529	1	. . .
Queensbury	1,080	261	275	543	. . .	1
Salem	2,198	582	573	1,021	1	21
Westfield	2,111	543	600	959	. . .	9
Whitehall	810	209	214	385	1	1

(continued)

TABLE 5.25 (continued)

County and Town	Total	White Population in 1790			All Other Free Persons	Slaves
		Males		Females		
		16 Years and Over	Under 16 Years			
Westchester county	23,978	5,934	5,318	10,952	358	1,416
Bedford	2,470	618	622	1,182	10	38
Cortlandt	1,932	484	452	905	25	66
Eastchester	741	174	161	319	12	75
Greenburgh	1,367	324	312	601	9	121
Harrison	1,007	242	220	453	38	54
Mamaroneck	452	108	98	171	18	57
Morrisania	133	43	17	41	2	30
Mt. Pleasant	1,926	501	422	911	8	84
New Rochelle	690	170	130	277	26	87
North Castle	2,470	607	591	1,200	43	29
North Salem	1,060	268	239	509	16	28
Pelham	199	45	31	84	1	38
Poundridge	1,072	247	270	548	7	. . .
Rye	986	258	164	427	14	123
Salem	1,453	366	326	728	14	19
Scarsdale	281	73	53	116	11	28
Stephen	1,297	343	297	612	7	38
Westchester	1,203	279	212	421	49	242
White Plains	505	130	100	218	8	49
Yonkers	1,125	265	220	458	12	170
York	1,609	389	381	771	28	40
Albany county	75,980	18,684	18,960	34,443	171	3,722
Albany city	3,494	803	652	1,442	26	571
First ward	1,612	392	329	672	5	214
Second ward	878	206	171	383	18	100
Third ward	1,004	205	152	387	3	257
Ballstown	7,316	1,893	2,014	3,317	23	69
Cambridge	5,009	1,246	1,312	2,408	. . .	43
Catskill	1,980	475	357	835	8	305
Coxsackie	3,401	796	821	1,474	8	302
Duanesburgh	1,469	410	369	684	1	5
Easton	2,547	569	718	1,203	. . .	57
Freehold	1,821	529	425	861	1	5
Halfmoon	3,609	865	948	1,666	7	123
Hoosick	3,031	693	839	1,454	18	27
Pittstown	2,458	567	700	1,158	. . .	33
Rennsselaerville	2,776	712	740	1,311	. . .	13
Rensselaerwick	8,305	2,024	2,087	3,632	. . .	562
Saratoga	3,071	738	867	1,405	8	53
Schaghticoke	1,650	409	387	711	. . .	143
Schenectady	756	180	170	328	. . .	78
Schenectady, south of the Mohawk	3,475	899	678	1,483	34	381
Schoharie	2,074	542	435	936	9	152
Stephentown	7,209	1,819	1,943	3,420	1	26
Stillwater	3,078	770	796	1,441	10	61
Watervliet	7,422	1,739	1,694	3,265	17	707
Island in the river not included in any town	29	6	8	9	. . .	6
Clinton county	1,615	545	356	682	16	16
Champlain	575	187	124	247	15	2
Crown Point	203	73	38	91	1	. . .
Plattsburgh	458	153	108	184	. . .	13
Wellsburgh	379	132	86	160	. . .	1

County and Town	Total	16 Yrs+	Under 16	Females	All Other Free	Slaves
Columbia county	27,496	6,554	6,739	12,518	52	1,633
Canaan	6,670	1,707	1,702	3,220	5	36
Claverack	3,257	739	747	1,419	11	341
Clermont	862	186	207	357	. . .	112
Germantown	512	117	128	227	. . .	40
Hillsdale	4,454	1,054	1,223	2,140	4	33
Hudson	2,585	616	589	1,155	26	199
Kinderhook	4,667	1,035	1,031	1,956	6	639
Livingston	4,489	1,100	1,112	2,044	. . .	233
Dutchess county	45,276	10,972	11,069	20,940	431	1,864
Amenia	3,078	768	780	1,449	29	52
Beekman	3,600	850	951	1,682	11	106
Clinton	4,607	1,173	1,113	2,115	30	176
Fishkill	5,941	1,366	1,290	2,643	41	601
Frederickstown	5,932	1,438	1,540	2,850	41	63
Northeast	3,401	839	863	1,597	22	80
Pawling	4,336	1,031	1,074	2,098	91	42
Philipstown	2,079	517	593	942	2	25
Poughkeepsie	2,529	617	573	1,092	40	207
Rhinebeck	3,662	875	756	1,544	66	421
Southeast	921	231	241	433	3	13
Washington	5,190	1,267	1,295	2,495	55	78
Kings county	4,549	903	703	1,415	46	1,482
Brooklyn	1,656	362	260	565	14	455
Bushwick	540	123	69	172	5	171
Flatbush	941	160	153	238	12	378
Flatlands	423	72	71	143	. . .	137
Gravesend	426	88	69	129	5	135
New Utrecht	563	98	81	168	10	206
Montgomery county	28,852	7,866	7,205	13,152	41	588
Canajoharie	6,155	1,647	1,538	2,868	6	96
Caughnawaga	4,261	1,128	1,068	1,928	4	133
Chemung	2,396	649	648	1,091	1	7
Chenango	45	13	12	20	. . .	. . .
German Flatts	1,307	354	301	630	2	20
Harpersfield	1,726	524	424	772	. . .	6
Herkimer	1,525	406	388	722	1	8
Mohawk	4,440	1,088	1,141	2,092	8	111
Otsego	1,702	563	427	698	6	8
Palatine	3,404	805	815	1,582	10	192
Whites	1,891	689	443	749	3	7
New York City and county	33,111	8,482	5,900	15,237	1,119	2,373
New York city	32,305	8,310	5,790	14,943	1,078	2,184
Dock ward	1,895	455	307	854	45	234
East ward	3,766	966	593	1,611	82	514
Montgomery ward	6,825	1,764	1,248	3,159	281	373
North ward	5,557	1,407	955	2,632	252	311
Out ward	5,651	1,484	1,092	2,629	178	268
South ward	1,767	451	324	822	55	115
West ward	6,844	1,783	1,271	3,236	185	369
Harlem division	806	172	110	294	41	189
Ontario county	1,074	524	192	342	6	10
Canandaigua	464	291	60	111	1	1
Erwin	168	56	36	69	. . .	7
Genesee	343	140	74	122	5	2
Jerusalem	99	37	22	40	. . .	. . .
Orange county	18,477	4,596	4,334	8,385	201	961
Goshen	2,447	616	518	1,042	59	212
Haverstraw	4,824	1,190	1,173	2,207	16	238
Minisink	2,216	552	546	1,050	17	51
New Cornwall	4,228	1,081	1,030	1,908	42	167
Orange	1,163	288	175	476	26	198
Warwick	3,599	869	892	1,702	41	95

Source: Bureau of the Census, *A Century of Population Growth, 1790–1900* (1909), 194, 195.

TABLE 5.26   FEDERAL CENSUS OF NEW YORK, 1800

Names of Counties	Free White Males					Free White Females					All Other Free Persons Except Indians Not Taxed	Slaves	Total
	Under 10 Years of Age	Of 10 and Under 16	Of 16 and Under 26, Including Heads of Families	Of 26 and Under 45, Including Heads of Families	Of 45 and Upwards, Including Heads of Families	Under 10 Years of Age	Of 10 and Under 16	Of 16 and Under 26, Including Heads of Families	Of 26 and Under 45, Heads of Families	Of 45 and Upwards, Including Heads of Families			
City & Co., of New York	8,158	3,279	4,545	8,114	2,632	8,134	3,294	5,260	7,722	2,984	3,499	2,868	60,489
Kings	668	304	310	439	300	570	274	376	391	297	332	1,479	5,740
Queens	2,211	1,228	981	1,442	1,260	2,022	989	1,158	1,487	1,154	1,431	1,528	16,893
Suffolk	2,577	1,491	1,411	1,828	1,338	2,749	1,359	1,599	1,890	1,320	1,016	886	19,464
Richmond	708	293	262	394	281	647	270	295	385	270	83	675	4,563
West Chester	4,440	2,103	2,305	2,634	1,719	4,015	2,123	2,402	2,357	1,589	482	1,259	27,428
Rockland	975	422	481	628	428	918	406	459	597	420	68	551	6,353
Clinton and Essex	1,685	672	737	1,029	382	1,608	566	604	837	274	62	58	8,514
Columbia	5,232	2,810	3,560	3,179	1,789	5,039	3,082	3,807	3,176	1,687	490	1,471	35,322
Rensselaer	5,361	2,539	2,693	2,772	1,697	5,262	2,170	2,681	2,712	1,552	113	890	30,442
Green	2,276	979	1,062	1,261	694	2,132	901	923	1,190	587	59	520	12,584
Tioga	1,299	612	610	739	342	1,212	551	499	689	276	33	17	6,889
Steuben	342	140	152	225	64	347	135	134	159	68	0	22	1,788
Montgomery	3,975	1,932	2,181	2,421	778	3,695	1,412	1,713	2,345	774	8	466	21,700
Cayuga	3,340	1,160	1,286	1,794	698	3,189	1,004	1,350	1,413	565	19	53	15,871
Onondaga	1,446	642	750	1,005	305	1,157	437	585	845	265	18	11	7,406
Ontario	3,023	1,143	1,502	1,991	592	2,630	964	1,195	1,487	525	109	57	15,218
Saratoga	4,860	2,174	1,673	2,459	1,324	4,486	1,982	1,575	2,416	1,103	73	358	24,483
Otsego	4,349	1,652	1,777	2,416	1,261	4,116	1,435	1,671	1,956	911	44	48	21,636
Delaware	1,973	770	906	1,075	582	1,969	652	806	955	494	30	16	10,228
City and County of Albany, &c.	5,780	2,552	2,330	5,631	2,066	5,622	2,374	2,146	3,521	1,860	353	1,808	34,043
Herkimer	2,866	1,132	1,185	1,736	664	2,756	874	1,121	1,476	600	8	61	14,479
Oneida	4,284	1,675	2,068	2,744	984	4,128	1,442	1,815	2,005	779	73	50	22,047
Chenango	2,999	1,314	1,436	1,942	679	2,891	1,038	1,249	1,528	534	40	16	15,666
Washington	6,810	2,894	3,065	3,562	2,011	6,482	2,623	2,958	3,287	1,683	119	80	35,574
Schohary	1,524	1,041	777	994	625	1,378	865	765	884	590	11	354	9,808
	83,161	36,953	40,015	52,454	25,497	79,154	32,822	39,086	47,710	23,161	8,573	15,602	484,065
Supplemental Return	16,936	7,320	9,230	9,140	6,358	16,319	6,649	9,030	8,701	5,490	1,801	5,011	101,985
Total	100,097	44,273	49,275	61,594	31,855	95,473	39,471	48,116	56,411	28,651	10,374	20,613	586,050

Source: Census Office, *Return of the Whole Number of Persons Within the Several Districts of the United States, 1800* (1802), 46.

TABLE 5.27   STATE CENSUS OF NEW JERSEY, 1784

	Whites	Free Blacks	Slaves	Total
Bergen co.	a	a	317	9,356
Burlington co.	15,500	467	53	15,801[b]
Cape May co.	2,093	105	33	2,231
Cumberland co.	5,000	70	30	6,300[b]
Essex co.	a	a	185	13,430
Gloucester co.	a	a	46	10,689
Hunterdon co.	17,130	970	263	18,363
Middlesex co.	a	a	210	12,005
Monmouth co.	13,216	1,228	264	14,708
Morris co.	12,925	374	117	13,416
Salem co.	a	a	41	8,473
Somerset co.	a	a	318	10,476
Sussex co.	a	a	82	14,187
Totals	a	a	1,959	149,435

[a] Not reported.
[b] Discrepancy between sources.
Source: Jedidiah Morse, *The American Geography* (1794), 284–85. State of N.J., *Compendium of Censuses, 1726–1905* (1906), 41.

TABLE 5.28   FEDERAL CENSUS OF NEW JERSEY, 1790

County and Town	Total	White Population in 1790			All Other Free Persons	Slaves
		Males		Females		
		16 Years and Over	Under 16 Years			
Morris county	16,216	4,092	3,938	7,502	48	636
Hanover Mendham Morristown Pequanack Roxbury	16,216	4,092	3,938	7,502	48	636

(continued)

TABLE 5.28 (continued)

County and Town	Total	White Population in 1790			All Other Free Persons	Slaves
		Males		Females		
		16 Years and Over	Under 16 Years			
Salem county	10,437	2,679	2,396	4,816	374	172
Elsingborough ⎫ Lo Penn's Neck ⎪ Low Aloway Cr ⎪ Mannington ⎪ Piles Grove ⎬ Pitts grove ⎪ Salem ⎪ Up Aloway's Cr ⎪ Up Penn's Neck ⎭	10,437	2,679	2,396	4,816	374	172
Somerset county	12,296	2,819	2,390	5,130	147	1,810
Bedminster	1,197	275	260	489	4	169
Bernardstown	2,377	601	560	1,115	8	93
Bridgewater	2,578	586	462	1,119	34	377
Eastern Precinct	2,068	481	298	795	26	468
Hillsborough	2,201	463	465	868	19	386
Western Precinct	1,875	413	345	744	56	317
Sussex county	19,500	4,963	4,939	9,094	65	439
Greenwich	2,035	507	510	944	10	64
Hardwicke ⎫ Independance ⎬ Newton ⎭	6,490	1,641	1,681	3,023	16	129
Hardyston	2,393	610	637	1,110	10	26
Knowlton	1,937	488	490	935	11	13
Mansfield	1,482	377	368	700	2	35
Montague	543	150	124	241	3	25
Oxford	1,905	471	468	892	9	65
Sandyston	519	131	122	239	1	26
Wallpack	496	129	102	233	2	30
Wantage	1,700	459	437	777	1	26
Bergen county	12,601	2,865	2,299	4,944	192	2,301
Bergin ⎫ Franklin ⎪ Hackinsack ⎬ Harrington ⎪ N. Barbadoes ⎪ Saddle River ⎭	12,601	2,865	2,299	4,944	192	2,301
Burlington county	18,095	4,625	4,164	8,481	598	227
Burlington ⎫ Chester ⎪ Chesterfield ⎪ Evansham ⎪ Little Egghar ⎪ Mansfield ⎬ New Hanover ⎪ Northampton ⎪ Notingham ⎪ Springfield ⎪ Willingboro' ⎭	18,095	4,625	4,164	8,481	598	227
Cape-May county	2,571	631	609	1,176	14	141
Lower Precinct ⎫ Middle Precinct ⎬ Upper Precinct ⎭	2,571	631	609	1,176	14	141
Cumberland county	8,248	2,147	1,966	3,877	138	120
Deerfield ⎫ Downs ⎪ Fairfield ⎪ Greenwich ⎬ Hopewell ⎪ Maurice River ⎪ Stowenuk ⎭	8,248	2,147	1,966	3,877	138	120
Essex county	17,785	4,339	3,972	8,143	160	1,171
Acquacknack ⎫ Elizabethtown ⎬ Newark ⎭	17,785	4,339	3,972	8,143	160	1,171
Gloucester county	13,363	3,287	3,311	6,232	342	191
Deptford ⎫ Eggharbor ⎪ Galloway ⎪ Glou town ⎪ Glou. townsh ⎬ Greenwich ⎪ Newtown ⎪ Waterford ⎪ Woolwich ⎭	13,363	3,287	3,311	6,232	342	191
Hunterdon county	20,153	4,966	4,379	9,316	191	1,301
Alexandria	1,503	377	401	685	. . .	40
Amwell	5,201	1,249	1,173	2,480	16	283
Bethleham	1,335	331	329	643	1	31
Hopewell	2,320	579	448	1,041	19	233
Kingwood	2,446	603	574	1,161	4	104
Maidenhead	1,032	237	189	432	14	160
Lebanon ⎫ Readington ⎬ Tewksbury ⎭	4,370	1,092	919	2,033	58	268
Trenton	1,946	498	346	841	79	182
Middlesex county	15,956	3,995	3,375	7,128	140	1,318
Amboy	582	149	108	246	31	48
North Brunswick	2,312	638	456	1,010	3	205
Piscataway	2,261	537	514	982	10	218
South Amboy	2,626	642	597	1,196	8	183
South Brunswick	1,817	439	361	789	10	218
Windsor	2,838	719	565	1,318	46	190
Woodbridge	3,520	871	774	1,587	32	256
Monmouth county	16,918	3,843	3,678	7,448	353	1,596
Dover	910	237	231	422	6	14
Lower Freehold	3,785	819	778	1,549	12	627
Middletown	3,225	711	618	1,343	62	491
Shrewsbury	4,673	1,094	1,041	2,161	165	212
Stafford	883	219	221	441	. . .	2
Upper-Freehold	3,442	763	789	1,532	108	250

Source: Bureau of the Census, *A Century of Population Growth, 1790–1900* (1909), 195, 196.

TABLE 5.29   FEDERAL CENSUS OF NEW JERSEY, 1800

Counties	Free White Males					Free White Females					All Other Free Persons Except Indians Not Taxed	Slaves	Total Number
	Under 10 Years of Age	Of 10 and Under 16	Of 16 and Under 26, Including Heads of Families	Of 26 and Under 45, Including Heads of Families	Of 45 and Upwards, Including Heads of Families	Under 10 Years of Age	Of 10 and Under 16	Of 16 and Under 26, Including Heads of Families	Of 26 and Under 45, Including Heads of Families	Of 45 and Upwards, Including Heads of Families			
Hunterdon	3,363	1,558	1,698	1,872	1,366	3,031	1,509	1,929	1,965	1,230	520	1,220	21,261
Sussex	4,080	1,981	1,926	2,061	1,381	3,779	1,717	2,013	1,853	1,127	102	514	22,534
Burlington	3,569	1,637	1,742	2,229	1,289	3,459	1,418	1,933	2,166	1,121	770	188	21,521
Essex	3,343	1,663	1,928	2,084	1,285	3,344	1,718	1,857	2,088	1,240	198	1,521	22,269
Monmouth	3,144	1,353	1,375	1,864	1,190	3,106	1,309	1,412	1,736	1,282	468	1,633	19,872
Morris	2,998	1,318	1,405	1,563	1,197	2,905	1,277	1,564	1,616	1,032	100	775	17,750
Middlesex	2,819	1,307	1,419	1,564	1,088	2,619	1,278	1,397	1,577	995	263	1,564	17,890
Gloucester	2,861	1,332	1,230	1,578	936	2,661	1,169	1,285	1,511	845	646	61	16,115
Bergen	2,087	920	665	1,560	925	2,048	1,008	649	1,410	857	202	2,825	15,156
Somerset	1,798	819	879	1,027	822	1,804	767	968	1,115	778	175	1,863	12,815
Salem	1,759	946	856	1,329	500	1,876	745	895	1,276	497	607	85	11,371
Cumberland	1,672	783	844	961	453	1,541	685	844	941	459	271	75	9,529
Cape May	487	242	334	264	197	449	227	272	279	137	80	98	3,066
	33,980	15,859	16,301	19,956	12,629	32,622	14,827	17,018	19,533	11,600	4,402	12,422	211,149

Source: Census Office, *Return of the Whole Number of Persons Within the Several Districts of the United States: 1800* (1802), 48.

TABLE 5.30   NUMBER OF TAXPAYERS IN PENNSYLVANIA COUNTIES, 1760–1786

Counties	1760	1770	1779	1786
Philadelphia	8,321	10,455	10,747	9,392
Bucks	3,148	3,177	4,067	4,273
Chester	4,761	5,483	6,378	6,286
Lancaster	5,635	6,608	8,433	5,839
York	3,302	4,426	6,281	6,254
Cumberland	1,501	3,521	5,092	3,939
Berks	3,016	3,302	4,662	4,732
Northampton	1,989	2,793	3,600	3,967
Bedford	. . .	. . .	1,201	2,632
Northumberland	. . .	. . .	2,111	2,166
Westmoreland	. . .	. . .	2,111	2,653
Washington	. . .	. . .	. . .	3,908
Fayette	. . .	. . .	. . .	2,041
Franklin	. . .	. . .	. . .	2,237
Montgomery	. . .	. . .	. . .	3,725
Dauphin	. . .	. . .	. . .	2,881

Note: The state took no censuses prior to 1790. Taxpayers equaled about one-fifth or one-sixth of the total population.
Source: Evarts B. Greene and Virginia D. Harrington, *American Population Before the Federal Census of 1790* (1932), 113.

TABLE 5.31   FEDERAL CENSUS OF PENNSYLVANIA, 1790

County and Town	Total	White Population in 1790			All Other Free Persons	Slaves
		Males		Females		
		16 Years and Over	Under 16 Years			
Allegheny county	10,203	2,524	2,745	4,763	12	159
Depreciation tract	206	50	59	97	. . .	. . .
Elizabeth	1,498	368	398	711	. . .	21
Pitt	1,468	380	365	681	2	40
Pittsburgh town	376	100	80	195	1	. . .
Plum	402	104	105	192	. . .	1
Versailles	414	94	114	203	. . .	3
That part of Allegheny county taken from Washington county	5,839	1,428	1,624	2,684	9	94
Bedford county [1]	13,132	2,887	3,840	6,325	34	46
Berks county	30,189	7,711	7,551	14,666	201	60
Albany	773	191	180	402	. . .	. . .
Alsace	836	207	226	400	3	. . .
Amity	869	229	215	413	11	1
Bern	2,268	528	651	1,069	18	2
Bethel	950	234	234	481	1	. . .
Brecknock	324	78	85	161	. . .	. . .
Brunswick and Manheim	1,504	368	399	736	. . .	1
Caernarvon	509	137	123	240	5	4
Colebrookdale	553	149	135	265	4	. . .
Cumru	1,450	371	363	706	10	. . .
Douglass	480	123	120	230	6	1
Earl	527	136	136	252	2	1
East District	634	150	166	313	5	. . .
Exeter	893	236	215	432	3	7
Greenwich	724	187	164	373	. . .	. . .

(continued)

TABLE 5.31 (continued)

County and Town	Total	White Population in 1790			All Other Free Persons	Slaves
		Males		Females		
		16 Years and Over	Under 16 Years			
Heidelberg	2,095	528	511	1,026	24	6
Hereford	969	240	236	489	3	1
Longswamp	739	185	194	359	1	...
Maiden Creek	735	205	168	353	9	...
Manheim (see Brunswick and Manheim).						
Maxatany	1,022	274	241	498	9	...
Oley	973	267	217	469	16	4
Pinegrove	900	214	251	435	...	...
Reading borough	2,225	583	512	1,118	3	9
Richmond	654	190	160	291	9	4
Robeson	1,088	289	276	514	8	1
Rockland	744	199	184	358	3	...
Ruscomb	472	119	121	228	4	...
Tulpehocken	2,315	603	553	1,123	21	15
Union	704	182	169	334	16	3
Windsor	1,260	309	346	598	7	...
Bucks county[1]	25,216	6,529	5,894	11,951	581	261
Chester county	27,829	7,486	6,590	13,065	544	144
Birmingham	221	58	53	109	1	...
Brandywine	740	214	178	343	5	...
Charlestown	1,260	319	312	582	40	7
Coventry	1,168	308	271	545	43	1
East Bradford	836	221	226	378	11	...
East Caln	702	191	158	329	21	3
East Fallowfield	517	141	136	239	1	...
East Marlborough	811	226	183	388	14	...
East Nantmill	1,154	281	298	546	21	8
East Nottingham	820	221	195	390	12	2
East Town	423	113	111	197	...	2
East Whiteland	491	136	114	219	20	2
Fallowfield	792	229	159	384	11	9
Goshen	1,272	359	272	604	33	4
Honeybrook	794	193	205	380	3	13
Kennet	658	180	164	298	14	2
London Britain	247	70	50	107	12	8
Londonderry	588	163	132	282	4	7
Londongrove	786	203	203	370	5	5
New Garden	742	191	186	349	15	1
New London	746	211	164	333	18	20
Newlin	534	120	147	260	7	...
Oxford	1,004	277	226	465	16	20
Pennsbury	595	145	150	286	14	...
Pikeland	817	185	221	392	19	...
Sadsbury	607	168	143	281	8	7
Thornbury	123	40	27	51	5	...
Trediffrin	988	277	217	466	25	3
Uwchland	976	258	221	465	28	4
Vincent	1,230	339	274	609	7	1
West Bradford	723	182	195	337	9	...
West Caln	840	229	214	394	3	...
West Marlborough	678	208	144	309	16	1
West Nantmill	903	294	177	414	11	7
West Nottingham	432	102	110	197	20	3
West Town	366	95	74	179	18	...
West Whiteland	457	118	106	213	16	4
Willistown	788	221	174	375	18	...

County and Town	Total	White Population in 1790			All Other Free Persons	Slaves
		Males		Females		
		16 Years and Over	Under 16 Years			
Cumberland county	18,208	4,816	4,514	8,449	206	223
Hopewell, Newton, Tyborn, Westpensboro	7,599	1,991	1,867	3,550	93	98
Eastern portion of county	10,609	2,825	2,647	4,899	113	125
Dauphin county	18,155	4,651	4,434	8,801	59	210
Harrisburgh town	880	259	184	411	1	25
Lebanon town	960	245	240	471	2	2
Remainder of county	16,315	4,147	4,010	7,919	56	183
Delaware county	9,469	2,530	2,109	4,494	287	49
Ashton	444	114	107	210	13	...
Bethel	224	50	67	99	7	...
Birmingham	428	98	109	202	15	4
Chester	673	200	128	323	22	...
Concord	674	168	160	305	35	6
Darby	641	168	137	313	15	8
Edgmont	437	104	106	213	9	5
Haverford	465	130	102	218	6	9
Lower Chichester	501	135	94	257	15	...
Lower Providence	216	68	50	97	1	...
Marple	471	120	105	235	11	...
Middletown	582	167	127	265	20	3
Newtown	451	126	101	218	5	1
Radnor	681	191	164	320	4	2
Ridley	502	137	106	229	29	1
Springfield	335	89	72	142	28	4
Thornbury	401	99	92	198	12	...
Tinicum	158	46	27	58	24	3
Upper Chichester	265	66	63	132	3	1
Upper Darby	571	164	113	282	12	...
Upper Providence	349	90	79	178	1	1
Fayette county	13,318	3,415	3,420	6,155	46	282
Bullskin	754	192	186	356	1	19
Franklin	1,854	443	488	881	11	31
Georges	1,371	350	359	658	...	4
German	1,299	319	355	622	...	3
Luzerne	1,113	285	281	515	5	27
Menallen	1,668	439	442	737	7	43
Springhill	1,321	325	330	626	2	38
Tyrone	730	210	183	316	...	21
Union	1,538	424	360	717	9	28
Washington	1,241	319	311	532	11	68
Wharton	429	109	125	195	...	...
Franklin county	15,662	4,021	3,874	7,162	279	326
Fannet, Hamilton, Letterkenney, Montgomery, Peters	7,212	1,862	1,838	3,230	134	148
Remainder of county	8,450	2,159	2,036	3,932	145	178
Huntingdon county[1]	7,558	1,871	2,089	3,531	24	43

Compared to contemporary western Europe, population density in the United States was exceptionally low. John J. Holland's view of Philadelphia (1796) shows that it required just a relatively short walk for residents of the country's largest city to find pleasing rural scenery. (I. N. Phelps Stokes Collection, Miriam & Ira Wallach Div. of Arts, Prints and Photographs. Courtesy The New York Public Library. Astor, Lenox and Tilden Foundations.)

| County and Town | Total | White Population in 1790 | | | All Other Free Persons | Slaves |
| | | Males | | Females | | |
		16 Years and Over	Under 16 Years			
Lancaster county	36,081	9,714	8,067	17,411	542	347
Bart	873	214	218	421	15	5
Brecknock	636	142	161	326	7	. . .
Caernarvon	766	168	185	348	36	29
Cocalico	3,023	767	714	1,539	3	. . .
Colerain	665	196	145	321	3	. . .
Conestogo	1,091	286	284	514	7	. . .
Donegal	533	155	111	247	10	10
Drumore	1,025	316	189	466	20	34
Earl	3,050	670	717	1,506	137	20
Elizabeth	546	147	120	273	5	1
Elizabeth town	196	52	42	102	. . .	. . .
Heidelberg	69	21	19	29	. . .	. . .
Hempfield	1,605	440	378	776	7	4
Lampeter	1,541	447	356	730	7	1
Lancaster	297	93	63	139	1	1
Lancaster borough	3,762	1,049	790	1,830	36	57
Leacock	1,405	395	296	683	13	18
Little Britain	1,291	357	271	589	32	42
Manheim	780	215	192	372	. . .	1
Manheim town	367	108	75	184	. . .	. . .

| County and Town | Total | White Population in 1790 | | | All Other Free Persons | Slaves |
| | | Males | | Females | | |
		16 Years and Over	Under 16 Years			
Lancaster county						
Manor	1,635	414	380	798	43	. . .
Martick	1,290	374	280	614	13	9
May town	1,134	314	256	521	20	23
Mountjoy	849	230	172	436	4	7
Rapho	1,606	469	316	784	26	11
Sadsbury	720	203	151	340	15	11
Salisbury	1,368	367	291	612	52	46
Strasburg	1,689	510	376	781	16	6
Warwick	2,269	595	519	1,130	14	11
Luzerne county[1]	4,892	1,237	1,328	2,303	13	11
Mifflin county	7,562	1,954	1,955	3,552	42	59
That portion south of the river Juniata	2,187	586	557	1,030	5	9
Remainder of county	5,375	1,368	1,398	2,522	37	50
Montgomery county	22,918	6,001	5,382	10,982	440	113
Abington	881	265	177	424	10	5
Cheltenham	620	103	138	272	45	2

(continued)

TABLE 5.31   (continued)

County and Town	Total	White Population in 1790			All Other Free Persons	Slaves
		Males		Females		
		16 Years and Over	Under 16 Years			
Montgomery county						
Manor of Moreland	1,283	345	273	588	60	17
Springfield	446	121	95	222	8	. . .
Remainder of county	19,688	5,107	4,699	9,476	317	89
Northampton county	24,238	6,007	6,404	11,675	132	20
Allen	1,456	382	352	717	5	. . .
Bethlehem	960	258	160	537	4	1
Chestnut Hill	709	150	222	337	. . .	. . .
Cosikton District	327	99	88	139	1	. . .
Delaware	421	110	104	201	6	. . .
Easton town	708	173	170	349	11	5
Forks	741	175	217	343	4	2
Hamilton	595	143	179	272	1	. . .
Heidelberg	962	244	254	464	. . .	. . .
Lehigh	626	146	181	299	. . .	. . .
Lower Mount Bethel	896	230	211	453	1	1
Lower Saucon	997	268	222	489	18	. . .
Lower Smithfield	1,436	359	364	647	59	7
Lowhill	419	97	115	206	1	. . .
Lynn	1,016	225	308	483	. . .	. . .
Macunge	1,263	335	330	596	1	1
More	752	200	170	382	. . .	. . .
Nazareth	889	252	231	403	3	. . .
Penn	607	151	167	287	2	. . .
Plainfield	886	193	245	448	. . .	. . .
Salisbury	1,010	257	248	505	. . .	. . .
Towamensink	395	102	97	195	. . .	1
Upper Milford	1,149	273	279	597	. . .	. . .
Upper Mount Bethel	1,040	254	301	478	6	1
Upper Saucon	851	200	255	396	. . .	. . .
Upper Smithfield	352	101	94	155	1	1
Wallen Papack	170	44	43	82	1	. . .
Welsenbergh	626	133	195	297	1	. . .
Whitehall	1,253	266	394	593	. . .	. . .
Williams	726	187	208	325	6	. . .
Northumberland county [1]	17,147	4,191	4,729	8,051	89	87
Philadelphia county	54,388	14,497	10,896	26,523	2,099	373
Blockley	883	244	179	434	22	4
Bristol	723	191	179	331	19	3
Byberry	586	148	141	278	13	6
Germantown town	2,769	752	597	1,394	21	5
Kingsessing	542	149	107	225	54	7
Lower Dublin	1,267	318	263	610	57	19
Manor of Moreland	376	93	79	181	15	8
Moyamensing and Passyunk	1,393	377	299	682	27	8
Northern Liberties town	9,907	2,537	2,206	4,884	219	61
Oxford	979	258	215	463	26	17
Passyunk. (See Moyamensing and Passyunk.)						
Roxborough	778	205	220	350	2	1
Southwark	5,663	1,486	1,141	2,808	204	24
Philadelphia city	28,522	7,739	5,270	13,883	1,420	210
Northern district (between Vine and Race streets from the Delaware to the Schuylkill)	3,938	1,048	733	2,045	85	27

County and Town	Total	White Population in 1790			All Other Free Persons	Slaves
		Males		Females		
		16 Years and Over	Under 16 Years			
Philadelphia county						
Middle district (from the north side of Chestnut street to the south side of Race street from the Delaware to the Schuylkill)	13,674	3,655	2,623	6,713	612	71
Southern district (from the south side of Chestnut street to the north side of South street from the Delaware to the Schuylkill)	10,910	3,036	1,914	5,125	723	112
Washington county [1]	23,892	5,333	7,279	11,005	12	263
Westmoreland county	16,019	4,013	4,359	7,480	39	128
Armstrong	1,452	389	403	647	8	5
Derry	1,623	399	434	778	6	6
Donegal	727	191	183	352	1	. . .
Fairfield	639	147	170	311	3	8
Franklin	778	207	210	360	1	. . .
French Creek	93	56	13	24	. . .	. . .
Hempfield	2,200	534	621	1,032	7	6
Mount Pleasant	1,059	272	304	474	. . .	9
North Huntingdon	1,581	372	428	763	1	17
Rostraver	1,087	253	290	495	. . .	49
Salem	795	203	197	387	4	4
South Huntingdon	1,647	390	467	772	4	14
Unity	1,246	305	352	579	1	9
Washington	706	197	184	323	1	1
Wheatfield	386	98	103	183	2	. . .
York county	37,535	9,171	9,469	17,542	850	503
Chanceford	1,690	457	399	772	35	27
Codorus	1,485	359	390	707	17	12
Dover	1,478	330	377	756	15	. . .
Fawn	1,307	342	299	610	13	43
Hellam	769	183	176	365	38	7
Hopewell	1,184	292	323	540	18	11
Manchester	1,686	381	428	835	29	13
Monaghan	1,463	343	374	673	61	12
Newberry	2,216	521	631	1,051	13	. . .
Paradise	1,179	263	307	575	30	4
Reading	978	219	247	435	52	25
Shrewsbury	1,258	300	337	579	27	15
Warrington	1,469	342	374	702	43	8
Windsor	1,447	336	395	705	8	3
York	1,381	288	385	664	34	10
York borough	2,076	462	451	1,008	125	30
Huntington, Manallen, Manheim, and Tyrone	4,669	1,202	1,200	2,206	23	38
Berwick, Cumberland, Franklin, Germany, Hamiltonban, Heidelberg, Mount Pleasant, Mountjoy, and Straban	9,800	2,551	2,376	4,359	269	245

[1] Not returned by townships.

Source: Bureau of the Census, *A Century of Population Growth, 1790–1900* (1909), 196–98.

TABLE 5.32 FEDERAL CENSUS OF PENNSYLVANIA, 1800

The Eastern District of Pennsylvania

Names of Counties	Free White Males					Free White Females					All Others &c	Slaves	Total
	To 10	To 16	To 26	To 45	45 &c	To 10	To 16	To 26	To 45	45 &c			
City Philad.	4,485	2,256	4,518	5,247	2,118	4,736	2,424	4,626	4,233	2,312	4,210	55	41,220
Co. of ditto	5,915	2,480	3,204	4,198	2,635	5,877	2,439	3,713	4,114	2,599	2,585	30	39,789
Montgom'y	3,887	1,869	2,269	2,349	1,744	3,699	1,797	2,196	2,144	1,636	527	33	24,150
Bucks	4,753	2,243	2,296	2,755	1,853	4,220	2,205	2,326	2,567	1,609	610	59	27,496
Delaware	1,958	1,217	1,221	1,108	796	1,808	1,140	1,055	1,022	832	645	7	12,809
Chester	5,117	2,407	2,852	3,224	2,323	4,865	2,201	2,868	2,963	2,082	1,145	46	32,093
Lancaster	7,080	3,235	4,110	4,277	2,970	6,853	3,154	4,263	3,928	2,569	786	178	43,403
Berks	5,934	2,659	2,598	3,271	2,002	5,783	2,425	2,776	3,056	1,719	165	19	32,407
Northampt.	5,333	2,288	2,686	2,821	1,919	5,447	2,098	2,588	2,741	1,892	241	8	30,062
Luzerne	2,450	1,029	1,125	1,256	787	2,439	940	1,016	1,104	597	78	18	12,839
Dauphin	4,082	1,955	1,730	2,465	1,057	3,804	1,891	1,783	2,233	1,011	166	93	22,270
Northum. (part)	1,293	570	542	624	447	1,243	538	465	567	359	41	10	6,699
Wayne	480	230	242	269	174	402	175	204	220	112	54	1	2,562
	52,767	24,438	29,393	33,864	20,824	51,176	23,427	29,879	30,892	19,329	11,253	557	327,799

The Western District of Pennsylvania

Names of Counties	Free White Males						Free White Females						All Others &c.	Slaves	Total
	To 10	To 16	To 26	To 45	45 &c	Total Males	To 10	To 16	To 26	To 45	45 &c	Total Females			
Adams	2,302	1,002	1,163	1,183	985	6,635	2,152	975	1,227	1,040	840	6,234	189	114	13,172
Allegheny	2,814	1,163	1,345	1,326	1,053	7,701	2,754	1,009	1,257	1,311	720	7,051	256	79	15,087
Armstrong	513	197	208	241	114	1,273	471	177	186	197	94	1,125	. . .	1	2,399
Beaver	1,118	422	499	554	364	2,957	1,136	395	505	473	271	2,780	35	4	5,776
Bedford	2,475	982	1,062	924	811	6,254	2,297	888	1,070	902	599	5,756	24	5	12,039
Butler	780	310	343	386	249	2,068	727	247	330	339	202	1,845	2	1	3,916
Crawford	427	154	312	326	116	1,335	394	126	218	178	85	1,001	5	5	2,346
Cumberland	4,251	2,347	2,268	2,267	1,694	12,827	4,188	2,280	2,144	2,135	1,255	12,002	329	228	25,386
Fayette	3,799	1,517	1,935	1,870	1,214	10,335	3,623	1,397	1,751	1,558	1,076	9,405	327	92	20,159
Franklin	3,411	1,395	1,701	1,833	1,289	9,629	3,357	1,354	1,787	1,665	1,001	9,164	664	181	19,638
Green	1,671	655	717	844	482	4,369	1,701	624	706	764	361	4,156	58	22	8,605
Huntingdon	2,366	974	1,181	1,198	934	6,653	2,349	985	1,194	1,061	634	6,223	100	32	13,008
Lycoming	1,010	448	395	463	293	2,609	977	420	401	446	259	2,503	263	39	5,414
Mercer	596	248	370	390	181	1,785	545	186	294	268	137	1,430	8	5	3,228
Mifflin & Center	2,572	1,039	1,220	1,308	889	7,028	2,419	989	1,181	1,193	650	6,432	126	23	13,609
Northumberland	4,143	1,593	1,855	2,025	1,286	10,902	3,782	1,515	1,911	1,849	1,026	10,083	94	19	21,098
Sommerset	2,138	788	889	898	631	5,344	1,929	711	870	828	481	4,819	26	. . .	10,188
Venango	221	81	175	133	41	651	184	70	103	81	35	473	6	. . .	1,130
Warren	47	17	37	31	11	143	36	16	19	15	4	90	. . .	. . .	230
Washington	5,024	2,139	2,659	2,501	1,952	14,275	5,098	1,992	2,562	2,346	1,601	13,599	340	84	28,298
Westmoreland	4,231	1,959	2,190	2,052	1,390	11,822	3,828	1,887	2,018	1,890	1,054	10,677	91	136	22,726
York	4,280	2,126	2,146	2,480	1,726	12,758	4,243	2,061	2,202	2,305	1,645	12,456	352	77	25,643
Erie	270	67	199	236	56	828	258	58	159	110	36	621	17	2	1,468
Total	50,459	21,623	24,869	25,469	17,761	140,181	48,448	20,362	24,095	22,954	14,066	129,925	3,311	1,149	274,566

Source: Census Office, *Return of the Whole Number of Persons Within the Several Districts of the United States: 1800* (1802), 56, 64.

TABLE 5.33 DELAWARE POPULATION STATISTICS, 1774–1784

County	1774 Estimated Population Whites	1774 Estimated Population Blacks	1774 Taxables Both Races	1782 Census Both Races	1784 Taxables Both Races
Kent	8,210	786	1,642	9,782	1,827
Sussex	13,180	748	. . .	12,660	2,926
New Castle	13,829	466	. . .	. . .	. . .
Total	35,219	2,000	. . .	. . .	. . .

Source: Stella H. Sutherland, *Population Distribution in Colonial America* (1936), 135.

TABLE 5.34 FEDERAL CENSUS OF DELAWARE, 1790

County	Free White Males Above 16	Free White Males Under 16	Free White Females	Other Free Persons	Slaves	Totals
Kent	3,705	3,467	6,878	2,570	2,300	18,920
Sussex	4,105	3,929	7,739	690	4,025	20,488
Newcastle	3,973	4,747	7,767	639	2,562	19,686
Total	11,783	12,143	22,384	3,899	8,887	59,094

Source: Bureau of the Census, *A Century of Population Growth, 1790–1900* (1909), 198.

TABLE 5.35 FEDERAL CENSUS OF DELAWARE, 1800

Names of Counties, & Townships	Free White Males — Under 10 Years of Age	Free White Males — Of 10 and Under 16	Free White Males — Of 16 and Under 26, Including Heads of Families	Free White Males — Of 26 and Under 45, Including Heads of Families	Free White Males — Of 45 and Upwards, Including Heads of Families	Free White Females — Under 10 Years of Age	Free White Females — Of 10 and Under 16	Free White Females — Of 16 and Under 26, Including Heads of Families	Free White Females — Of 26 and Under 45, Including Heads of Families	Free White Females — Of 45 and Upwards, Including Heads of Families	All Other Free Persons Except Indians Not Taxed	Slaves	Total
New Castle Co.													
Brandywine	343	155	183	230	139	322	163	195	218	120	62	53	
Christiana	816	466	556	544	268	784	574	642	562	303	624	186	
Mill Creek	326	202	168	167	141	272	250	199	183	119	85	82	
New Castle	292	183	164	216	91	280	189	168	201	96	323	235	
White Clay Creek	229	120	115	137	78	207	154	122	148	85	107	105	
Pencader	290	200	137	161	87	260	135	177	167	106	201	211	
Redlion	105	54	80	73	13	88	66	66	74	23	88	142	
St. Georges	397	243	243	253	77	335	274	238	241	99	484	481	
Appoquinimink	591	340	267	363	109	485	266	236	344	121	780	343	25,361
Kent Co.													
Duck Creek	418	224	277	297	90	382	189	284	281	106	892	345	
Little Creek	225	113	105	157	47	187	88	142	121	44	546	133	
St. Jones's	131	66	92	95	39	87	73	94	84	29	583	138	
Murderkill	834	425	573	523	209	840	372	627	549	233	1,546	383	
Mispillion	712	401	566	239	109	662	405	568	264	145	679	486	19,554
Sussex Co.													
Ceader Creek	299	159	209	188	101	294	159	247	189	119	169	382	
Broad Kilne	383	170	240	222	102	335	144	256	227	103	140	255	
Nanticoke	251	136	153	143	70	256	101	185	143	38	117	239	
N. W. Forke	330	167	195	182	87	307	152	246	185	93	138	459	
Little Creek	310	131	195	188	70	303	127	239	178	74	94	255	
Broad Creek	249	123	164	155	73	250	106	155	160	76	73	235	
Baltimore	165	104	103	132	52	191	71	103	133	53	32	256	
Lewis & Rehoboth	183	89	99	104	52	172	75	116	101	54	230	239	
Dagsborough	177	72	129	121	55	156	65	111	117	55	90	270	
Indian River	194	94	108	122	54	173	79	127	115	56	185	240	19,358

A Recapitulation of the aggregate amount of each description of Persons in the whole District.

	Free White Males — Under 10 Years of Age	Of 10 and Under 16	Of 16 and Under 26	Of 26 and Under 45	Of 45 and Upwards	Free White Females — Under 10 Years of Age	Of 10 and Under 16	Of 16 and Under 26	Of 26 and Under 45	Of 45 and Upwards	All Other Free Persons	Slaves	Total
New Castle	3,389	1,963	1,913	2,144	1,003	3,033	2,071	2,043	2,138	1,072	2,754	1,838	25,361
Kent	2,320	1,229	1,613	1,311	494	2,158	1,127	1,715	1,299	557	4,246	1,485	19,554
Sussex	2,541	1,245	1,595	1,557	716	2,437	1,079	1,785	1,544	761	1,268	2,830	19,358
Aggregate amount of each description	8,250	4,437	5,121	5,012	2,213	7,628	4,277	5,543	4,981	2,390	8,268	6,153	64,273

Total amount in the whole District. Sixty-Four Thousand, Two Hundred and Seventy-Three Inhabitants.

Source: Census Office, *Return of the Whole Number of Persons Within the Several Districts of the United States: 1800* (1802), 63.

Population of the South

Population growth in the South outstripped the remainder of the country during the late eighteenth century. Southerners imported more than 80,000 Africans during the dozen years before independence and drew thousands of pioneers from the middle colonies who settled in the frontier districts from Hagerstown, Maryland, to Ninety Six, South Carolina. The South grew more slowly after 1780 because the slave trade ended with the Revolution and perhaps 4% of the region's slaves departed with British forces when the war ended, but many northern whites and an unknown number of foreign immigrants continued moving to the southern backcountry until the 1790s. Only after 1790, when almost half of all Americans lived below the Mason-Dixon Line, did the mid-Atlantic states replace the South as the nation's fastest developing region. After 1790, the number of northerners and foreigners who moved to the South was negligible, and during the nineteenth century southern growth rates would fall increasingly behind those in the North.

TABLE 5.37   STATE CENSUS OF MARYLAND, 1782

County	Whites	County	Whites
Anne Arundel	9,370	Kent	6,165
Baltimore	17,878	Montgomery	10,011
Calvert	4,012	Prince Georges	9,864
Caroline	6,230	Queen Ann's	7,767
Cecil	7,749	St. Mary's	8,459
Charles	9,804	Somerset	7,787
Dorchester	8,927	Talbot	6,744
Frederick	20,495	Washington	11,488
Harford	9,377	Worcester	8,561
Total White Population, 170,688			

Source: Jedidiah Morse, *The American Geography; or a View of the Present Situation of the United States of America* (1792), 350.

TABLE 5.36   COMPOSITION OF THE SOUTHERN COLONIES' POPULATION, 1774

	Total Number	Percent of Total	Percent of Subgroup
Total Population	1,105,477	100.0%	. . .
White Inhabitants	659,536	59.7%	100.0%
Status Independent	639,750	57.9%	97.0%
Status Indentured[a]	19,786	1.8%	3.0%
Black Inhabitants	445,941	40.3%	100.0%
Legally Free	12,835	1.2%	2.9%
Slaves	433,106	39.1%	97.1%
All Males Aged 21 +	237,628	21.5%	100.0%
Taxpaying Property Owners	140,723	12.7%	59.2%
All Females Aged 21 +	225,567	20.4%	100.0%
Taxpaying Property Owners	13,052	1.2%	5.8%
All Youths Under 21	642,282	58.1%	. . .
Free Population[b]	652,585	59.0%	. . .
All Free Adult Males	140,273	12.7%	100.0%
Aged 21–25	32,679	3.0%	23.3%
Aged 26–44	68,414	6.2%	48.8%
Aged 45 +	39,180	3.5%	27.9%
All Free Adult Females	133,160	12.0%	100.0%
Aged 21–25	33,869	3.1%	25.4%
Aged 26–44	60,481	5.5%	45.5%
Aged 45 +	38,810	3.5%	29.1%
All Free Youths Under 21	379,152	34.3%	. . .

[a] Indentured servants and convict laborers.
[b] Includes free Negroes.
Source: Alice Hanson Jones, *American Colonial Wealth: Documents and Methods* (1978), 1793.

TABLE 5.38   FEDERAL CENSUS OF MARYLAND, 1790

County and Town	Total	White Population in 1790 Males 16 Years and Over	White Population in 1790 Males Under 16 Years	White Population in 1790 Females	All Other Free Persons	Slaves
Western shore	212,089	38,573	35,748	69,187	4,136	64,445
Allegany county	4,809	1,068	1,283	2,188	12	258
Anne Arundel county	22,598	3,142	2,850	5,672	804	10,130
Baltimore county	25,434	5,184	4,668	9,101	604	5,877
Baltimore town and precincts	13,503	3,866	2,556	5,503	323	1,255
Calvert county	8,652	1,091	1,109	2,011	136	4,305
Charles county	20,613	2,565	2,399	5,160	404	10,085
Frederick county	30,791	7,010	7,016	12,911	213	3,641
Harford county	14,976	2,872	2,812	5,100	775	3,417
Montgomery county	18,003	3,284	2,746	5,649	294	6,030
Prince Georges county	21,344	2,653	2,503	4,848	164	11,176
St. Marys county	15,544	2,100	1,943	4,173	343	6,985
Washington county	15,822	3,738	3,863	6,871	64	1,286
Eastern shore	107,639	17,342	15,591	32,208	3,907	38,591
Caroline county	9,506	1,812	1,727	3,389	421	2,057
Cecil county	13,625	2,847	2,377	4,831	163	3,407
Dorchester county	15,875	2,541	2,430	5,039	528	5,337
Kent county	12,836	1,876	1,547	3,325	655	5,433
Queen Anns county	15,463	2,158	1,974	4,039	618	6,674
Somersett county	15,610	2,185	1,908	4,179	268	7,070
Talbot county	13,084	1,938	1,712	3,581	1,076	4,777
Worcester county	11,640	1,985	1,916	3,725	178	3,836

Source: Bureau of the Census, *A Century of Population Growth, 1790–1900* (1909), 198.

TABLE 5.39 FEDERAL CENSUS OF MARYLAND, 1800

Counties, & c.	Free White Males					Free White Females					All Other Free Persons Except Indians Not Taxed	Slaves
	Under 10 Years of Age	Of 10 and Under 16	Of 16 and Under 26, Including Heads of Families	Of 26 and Under 45, Including Heads of Families	Of 45 and Upwards, Including Heads of Families	Under 10 Years of Age	Of 10 and Under 16	Of 16 and Under 26, Including Heads of Families	Of 26 and Under 45, Including Heads of Families	Of 45 and Upwards, Including Heads of Families		
Baltimore City	3,035	1,849	3,180	2,519	711	2,675	1,621	2,418	2,126	766	2,771	2,843
Baltimore co.	3,820	1,790	2,295	2,600	1,894	3,845	1,752	2,375	2,414	1,365	1,536	6,830
Allegany	1,121	498	454	551	337	1,094	402	482	494	270	101	499
Washington	2,975	1,272	1,509	1,681	1,036	2,848	1,206	1,351	1,463	767	342	2,200
Frederick	4,679	1,995	2,452	2,542	1,846	4,537	1,901	2,554	2,409	1,563	473	4,572
Montgomery	1,451	619	760	824	584	1,409	826	835	702	498	262	6,288
Prince George's	1,294	593	718	911	623	1,307	486	996	846	572	648	12,191
Charles	1,369	669	783	916	597	1,365	795	1,047	954	548	571	9,558
St. Mary's	1,023	569	563	689	451	873	514	746	797	453	622	6,399
Calvert	648	311	322	415	192	633	332	425	413	198	307	4,101
Ann Arundle	1,962	879	944	1,178	756	1,730	862	1,004	1,039	676	1,833	9,760
Harford	2,074	992	1,047	1,095	921	1,918	917	1,147	1,102	805	1,344	4,264
Cœcil	1,117	490	614	689	528	1,026	421	602	602	453	373	2,103
Caroline	1,082	575	752	689	327	1,072	529	768	633	332	602	1,865
Kent	824	474	575	633	310	770	290	711	600	324	1,786	4,474
Queen Ann's	1,158	577	778	810	356	1,117	560	880	765	314	1,025	6,517
Talbot	1,099	554	754	766	393	1,047	496	842	719	400	1,591	4,775
Dorchester	1,611	816	910	947	456	1,485	718	1,025	1,040	407	2,365	4,566
Somerset	1,511	747	915	994	480	1,330	846	1,072	920	525	586	7,432
Worcester	1,999	1,123	909	1,329	596	1,715	963	1,087	1,132	670	449	4,398
District of Columbia	899	351	695	775	318	907	350	548	555	274	400	2,072
Total	36,751	17,743	21,929	23,553	13,712	34,703	16,787	22,915	21,725	12,180	19,987	107,707

Source: Census Office, *Return of the Whole Number of Persons Within the Several Districts of the United States: 1800* (1802), 66.

TABLE 5.40 ENUMERATION OF VIRGINIANS SUBJECT TO POLL TAX, 1782–1789

Counties	Whites	Blacks	Total	Date	
Accomac	812	2,749	3,561	1787	Tithables
Albemarle	908	4,409	5,317	1782	Tithables
Amelia	5,549	8,749	14,298	1782	
Amherst	5,964	3,852	9,816	1783	
Augusta	1,311	1,182	2,493	1782	Tithables
Bedford	5,497	1,653	7,150	1783	
Berkeley	1,315	1,921	3,236	1782	Tithables
Botetourt	922	823	1,745	1785	Tithables
Brunswick	. . .	. . .	6,449	1782	Tithables
Buckingham	759	3,160	3,919	1782	Tithables
Campbell	1,307	1,059	2,366	1785	Tithables
Caroline	965	3,712	4,677	1783	Tithables
Charles City	472	2,729	3,201	1787	Tithables
Charlotte	3,790	3,442	7,232	1783	
Chesterfield	4,885	5,961	10,846	1783	
Culpepper	1,863	6,352	8,215	1782	Tithables
Cumberland	2,670	3,882	6,552	1782	
Dinwiddie	840	5,746	6,586	1782	Tithables
Elizabeth City	904	648	1,552	1782	Tithables
Essex	2,489	2,817	5,306	1785	
Fairfax	5,154	3,609	8,763	1782	
Fauquier	1,747	5,168	6,915	1782	Tithables
Fluvanna	1,985	1,330	3,315	1782	
Frederick	4,786	767	5,553	1782	
Gloucester	3,151	2,764	5,915	1783	

Counties	Whites	Blacks	Total	Date	
Goochland	614	3,852	4,466	1782	Tithables
Greenbriar	515	167	682	1783	Tithables
Greensville	1,845	2,691	4,536	1783	
Halifax	5,335	3,290	8,625	1782	
Hampshire	7,469	513	7,982	1782	
Hanover	3,707	5,184	8,891	1782	
Henrico	1,339	6,961	8,300	1787	Tithables
Henry	1,168	1,723	2,891	1782	Tithables
Isle of Wight	3,760	2,948	6,708	1782	
James City	493	1,832	2,325	1782	Tithables
King and Queen	549	2,827	3,376	1782	Tithables
King George	450	2,040	2,490	1782	Tithables
King William	877	3,443	4,320	1782	Tithables
Lancaster	1,541	2,567	4,108	1783	
Loudon	947	8,704	9,651	1783	Tithables
Louisa	No figures available				
Lunenburg	750	3,406	4,156	1782	Tithables
Mecklenburg	6,397	4,927	11,324	1782	
Middlesex	1,167	2,282	3,449	1783	
Monongalia	2,302	81	2,383	1782	
Montgomery	1,560	319	1,879	1787	Tithables
Nansemond	2,842	2,567	5,409	1783	
New Kent	1,617	2,957	4,574	1782	
Norfolk	5,365	3,096	8,461	1782	
Northumberland	3,809	3,925	7,734	1782	

Counties	Whites	Blacks	Total	Date	
Orange	3,410	2,848	6,258	1782	
Pittsylvania	5,304	1,835	7,139	1782	
Powhatan	1,468	2,669	4,137	1783	
Prince Edward	1,552	1,468	3,020	1783	
Prince George	476	3,303	3,779	1782	Tithables
Prince William	877	3,443	4,320	1782	Tithables
Princess Anne	3,999	2,656	6,655	1783	
Richmond	2,947	3,885	6,832	1783	
Rockbridge	755	471	1,226	1782	Tithables
Rockingham	2,947	3,885	6,832	1783	Tithables
Shenandoah	7,908	347	8,255	1783	
Southampton	5,286	4,953	10,239	1784	
Spotsylvania	696	4,714	5,410	1782	Tithables
Stafford	2,483	428	2,911	1785	
Surry	2,389	2,729	5,118	1782	
Sussex	2,923	3,696	6,619	1782	
Warwick	569	776	1,345	1782	
Westmoreland	410	4,536	4,946	1782	
Washington	1,062	383	1,445	1782	Tithables
Williamsburg, city of	722	702	1,424	1782	
York	2,063	699	2,762	1782	Tithables

Source: Evarts B. Greene and Virginia D. Harrington, *American Population Before the Federal Census of 1790* (1932), 152, 153.

TABLE 5.41 FEDERAL CENSUS OF VIRGINIA, 1790

County and Town	Total	White Population in 1790			All Other Free Persons	Slaves
		Males		Females		
		16 Years and Over	Under 16 Years			
Accomack	13,959	2,297	2,177	4,502	721	4,262
Albemarle	12,585	1,703	1,790	3,342	171	5,579
Amelia, including Nottoway, a new county	18,097	1,709	1,697	3,278	106	11,307
Amherst	13,703	2,056	2,235	3,995	121	5,296
Augusta, the part east of the North Mountain	10,886	2,048	1,665	3,438	40	1,222
Part west of do		551	572	986	19	345
Bedford	10,531	1,785	2,266	3,674	52	2,754
Berkley	19,713	4,253	4,547	7,850	131	2,932
Botetourt, as it stood previous to the formation of Wythe from it & Montg'ry	10,524	2,247	2,562	4,432	24	1,259
Brunswick	12,827	1,472	1,529	2,918	132	6,776
Buckingham	9,779	1,274	1,537	2,685	115	4,168
Campbell	7,685	1,236	1,347	2,363	251	2,488
Caroline	17,489	1,799	1,731	3,464	203	10,292
Charles-City	5,588	532	509	1,043	363	3,141
Charlotte	10,078	1,285	1,379	2,535	63	4,816
Chesterfield	14,214	1,652	1,557	3,149	369	7,487
Culpeper	22,105	3,372	3,755	6,682	70	8,226
Cumberland	8,153	885	914	1,778	142	4,434
Dinwiddie	13,934	1,790	1,396	2,853	561	7,334

County and Town	Total	White Population in 1790			All Other Free Persons	Slaves
		Males		Females		
		16 Years and Over	Under 16 Years			
Elizabeth-City	3,450	390	388	778	18	1,876
Essex	9,122	908	869	1,766	139	5,440
Fairfax	12,320	2,138	1,872	3,601	135	4,574
Fauquier	17,892	2,674	2,983	5,500	93	6,642
Fluvanna	3,921	589	654	1,187	25	1,466
Franklin	6,842	1,266	1,629	2,840	34	1,073
Frederick division }	19,681	1,757	1,653	3,041	49	1,319
Ditto		2,078	2,517	4,269	67	2,931
Gloucester	13,498	1,597	1,523	3,105	210	7,063
Goochland	9,053	1,028	1,059	2,053	257	4,656
Greenbrier, including Kanawa, a new county	6,015	1,463	1,574	2,639	20	319
Greensville	6,362	669	627	1,234	212	3,620
Halifax	14,722	2,214	2,320	4,397	226	5,565
Hampshire	7,346	1,662	1,956	3,261	13	454
Hanover	14,754	1,637	1,412	3,242	240	8,223
Hardy	7,336	1,108	2,256	3,192	411	369
Harrison	2,080	487	579	947	. . .	67
Henrico	12,000	1,823	1,170	2,607	581	5,819
Henry	8,479	1,523	1,963	3,277	165	1,551
Isle of Wight	9,028	1,208	1,163	2,415	375	3,867
James City	4,070	395	359	765	146	2,405
King George	7,366	757	781	1,585	86	4,157
King & Queen	9,377	995	1,026	2,138	75	5,143
King William	8,128	723	732	1,438	84	5,151
Lancaster	5,638	535	542	1,182	143	3,236
Loudon	18,962	3,677	3,992	7,080	183	4,030
Louisa	8,467	957	1,024	1,899	14	4,573
Lunenburg	8,959	1,110	1,185	2,252	80	4,332
Mecklenburg	14,733	1,857	2,015	3,683	416	6,762
Middlesex	4,140	407	370	754	51	2,558
Monongalia	4,768	1,089	1,345	2,168	12	154
Montgomery, as it stood previous to the formation of Wythe from it and Botetourt	13,228	2,846	3,744	5,804	6	828
Nansemond	9,010	1,215	1,167	2,331	480	3,817
New-Kent	6,239	605	587	1,199	148	3,700
Norfolk	14,524	2,650	1,987	4,291	251	5,345
Northampton	6,889	857	743	1,581	464	3,244
Northumberland	9,163	1,046	1,137	2,323	197	4,460
Ohio	5,212	1,222	1,377	2,308	24	281
Orange	9,921	1,317	1,426	2,693	64	4,421
Pendleton	2,452	568	686	1,124	1	73
Pittsylvania	11,579	2,008	2,447	4,083	62	2,979
Powhatan	6,822	623	548	1,115	211	4,325
Prince Edward	8,100	1,044	1,077	1,961	32	3,986
Prince George	8,173	965	822	1,600	267	4,519
Princess Anne	7,793	1,169	1,151	2,207	64	3,202
Prince William	11,615	1,644	1,797	3,303	167	4,704
Randolph	951	221	270	441	. . .	19

(continued)

TABLE 5.41 (continued)

County and Town	Total	White Population in 1790 — Males — 16 Years and Over	Under 16 Years	Females	All Other Free Persons	Slaves
Richmond	6,985	704	697	1,517	83	3,984
Rockbridge	6,548	1,517	1,552	2,756	41	682
Rockingham	7,449	1,816	1,652	3,209	. . .	772
Russell	3,338	734	969	1,440	5	190
Shannandoah	10,510	2,409	2,779	4,791	19	512
Southampton	12,864	1,632	1,546	3,134	559	5,993
Spotsylvania	11,252	1,361	1,278	2,532	148	5,933
Stafford	9,588	1,341	1,355	2,769	87	4,036
Surry	6,227	732	651	1,379	368	3,097
Sussex	10,549	1,215	1,174	2,382	391	5,387
Warwick	1,690	176	158	333	33	990
Washington	5,625	1,287	1,440	2,440	8	450
Westmoreland	7,722	815	754	1,614	114	4,425
York	5,233	530	461	1,124	358	2,760

Source: Bureau of the Census, *A Century of Population Growth, 1790–1900* (1909), 198.

TABLE 5.42   FEDERAL CENSUS OF VIRGINIA, 1800

Eastern District

Names of Cities, Counties, and Towns	Free White Males — Under 10 Years of Age	Of 10 and Under 16	Of 16 and Under 26, Including Heads of Families	Of 26 and Under 45, Including Heads of Families	Of 45 and Upwards, Including Heads of Families	Free White Females — Under 10 Years of Age	Of 10 and Under 16	Of 16 and Under 26, Including Heads of Families	Of 26 and Under 45, Including Heads of Families	Of 45 and Upwards, Including Heads of Families	All Other Free Persons Except Indians Not Taxed	Slaves
Amelia	480	184	306	308	170	415	190	300	272	164	58	6,585
Albemarle	1,669	721	863	821	547	1,590	657	859	644	425	207	7,436
Amherst	1,723	689	846	989	525	1,603	614	897	852	467	134	7,462
Accomack	1,462	797	947	966	468	1,483	756	1,117	1,132	595	1,541	4,429
Bedford	1,889	819	858	873	611	1,796	758	864	819	539	202	4,097
Buckingham	1,255	544	664	622	410	1,155	505	702	577	390	229	6,336
Brunswick	1,157	518	737	670	361	939	548	698	658	361	270	9,422
Caroline	1,148	457	545	648	356	1,068	497	737	629	407	365	10,581
Chesterfield	1,028	471	612	684	363	976	510	627	685	361	319	7,852
Campbell	1,019	472	582	604	343	1,002	405	618	538	310	302	3,671
Culpeper	1,878	806	938	1,011	708	1,768	726	1,041	956	647	273	7,348
Cumberland	700	273	434	397	218	668	302	369	355	229	183	5,711
Charlotte	1,005	382	562	569	324	918	413	556	480	297	123	6,283
Charles City	333	142	167	206	116	291	160	182	245	112	398	3,013
Dinwiddie	816	360	516	458	302	712	339	513	439	286	246	6,866
Elizabeth City	190	94	112	160	58	184	107	142	145	46	18	1,522
Essex	570	241	326	360	214	474	250	397	381	252	276	5,767
Fairfax	1,230	694	589	668	475	1,172	580	666	635	326	204	6,078
Fauquier	2,190	957	1,127	1,087	815	2,083	915	1,335	1,135	800	131	8,754
Franklin	1,540	668	700	715	405	1,436	557	713	599	368	27	1,574
Fluvanna	464	211	227	258	181	442	221	278	217	160	44	1,920
Goochland	794	327	368	430	277	771	333	467	443	270	413	4,803
Greensville	408	171	260	280	100	365	177	283	205	149	213	4,116
Gloster	551	270	269	377	150	546	280	338	322	134	35	4,909
Hanover	993	418	421	649	371	950	470	621	627	432	259	8,192

Eastern District											
	Free White Males					Free White Females					
Names of Cities, Counties, and Towns	Under 10 Years of Age	Of 10 and Under 16	Of 16 and Under 26, Including Heads of Families	Of 26 and Under 45, Including Heads of Families	Of 45 and Upwards, Including Heads of Families	Under 10 Years of Age	Of 10 and Under 16	Of 16 and Under 26, Including Heads of Families	Of 26 and Under 45, Including Heads of Families	Of 45 and Upwards, Including Heads of Families	All Other Free Persons Except Indians Not Taxed	Slaves
Henry	692	319	398	283	235	670	286	347	313	172	129	1,415
Henrico	686	252	335	409	242	636	334	447	382	276	542	4,608
Halifax	2,082	760	1,060	1,060	644	1,902	884	1,199	980	597	298	7,911
Isle of Wight	712	341	602	531	233	703	389	471	513	240	578	4,029
James City	216	82	185	140	76	179	104	160	166	66	168	2,389
King William	517	251	254	352	165	495	269	316	344	176	172	5,744
King George	437	207	215	280	142	379	198	271	298	171	164	3,987
King and Queen	694	361	356	455	246	665	341	449	486	282	164	5,380
Louisa	1,072	459	483	559	377	922	416	595	524	361	132	5,992
Louden	2,706	1,205	1,343	1,489	936	2,687	1,277	1,431	1,285	841	333	4,990
Lunenberg	740	335	447	428	258	727	365	425	419	228	133	5,876
Lancaster	329	140	197	240	94	296	166	276	218	134	159	3,126
Matthews	510	245	216	327	166	489	250	292	318	172	17	2,804
Madison	848	362	394	474	305	856	350	532	413	302	50	3,436
Middlesex	262	104	138	183	76	270	130	153	189	98	84	2,516
Mecklinberg	1,368	579	801	746	451	1,297	519	822	750	446	553	8,676
Norfolk	1,159	599	748	990	216	1,095	651	763	994	336	207	4,735
Northampton	461	232	288	334	145	412	207	367	335	150	654	3,178
Nansemond	847	606	681	584	263	761	629	621	526	291	910	4,408
Northumberland	587	273	348	385	170	570	272	474	412	188	221	3,903
New Kent	443	193	209	289	118	388	174	276	300	133	218	3,622
Nottoway	547	243	357	334	175	557	256	351	309	182	107	5,983
Orange	1,077	423	560	598	381	1,073	426	607	641	374	47	5,242
Prince Edward	887	374	522	492	274	841	335	528	448	277	63	5,921
Prince George	482	203	236	344	161	402	171	289	317	190	250	4,380
Powhatan	443	179	212	263	131	411	163	226	221	144	345	5,031
Pittsylvania	1,599	707	818	769	479	1,499	696	777	752	407	61	4,133
Princess Ann	916	458	465	565	205	845	376	531	581	258	85	3,574
Patrick	674	295	310	275	218	659	318	341	278	184	130	649
Prince William	1,160	507	710	706	423	1,167	500	720	663	419	342	5,416
Richmond and Westmoreland	907	432	457	554	275	854	387	601	582	285	584	7,826
Surry	442	232	266	312	138	412	190	322	292	171	500	3,258
Stafford	904	419	477	511	336	940	423	535	544	346	193	4,343
Spotsylvania	968	490	603	550	403	881	397	694	529	360	297	6,830
Sussex	706	350	459	481	245	722	338	447	498	286	542	5,988
Southampton	1,049	440	651	727	341	977	479	644	765	388	839	6,625
Warwick	121	47	50	75	26	84	44	70	75	22	21	1,024
York	209	90	84	146	59	163	71	153	129	62	45	2,020
City of Richmond	351	174	512	440	150	337	154	337	279	103	607	2,293
Norfolk Borough	354	261	735	793	169	378	198	454	398	110	352	2,724
Petersburg	181	83	286	305	72	189	66	173	185	66	428	1,487
	57,837	25,998	32,444	34,588	19,087	54,597	25,469	34,807	32,641	18,821	18,194	322,199
Alexandria	578	250	420	489	189	546	269	410	416	160	369	875
Part of the co. of Fairfax in the District of Columbia	111	70	63	68	32	124	44	69	57	29	14	297

(continued)

TABLE 5.42 (continued)

	Western District											
	Free White Males					Free White Females					All Other Free Persons Except Indians Not Taxed	Slaves
Names of Cities, Counties, and Towns	Under 10 Years of Age	Of 10 and Under 16	Of 16 and Under 26, Including Heads of Families	Of 26 and Under 45, Including Heads of Families	Of 45 and Upwards, Including Heads of Families	Under 10 Years of Age	Of 10 and Under 16	Of 16 and Under 26, Including Heads of Families	Of 26 and Under 45, Including Heads of Families	Of 45 and Upwards, Including Heads of Families		
Bottetourt	1,568	646	727	794	533	1,491	590	808	777	432	116	1,343
Fincastle	60	32	60	51	16	74	29	37	39	9	19	176
Washington	1,731	653	624	619	439	1,556	645	722	674	387	307	817
Abington	56	16	6	30	4	41	8	11	28	3	79	83
Kenawa	594	230	289	350	149	576	167	255	281	110	7	231
Hamshire	1,433	579	661	610	456	1,370	609	512	580	392	108	587
Romney	44	6	12	21	7	30	6	14	24	6	9	26
Springfield	21	1	4	9	6	13	3	4	12	2	1	10
Frankfort	30	14	10	17	4	39	8	6	20	3	2	7
Greenbrier	765	312	334	334	262	704	294	354	312	221	2	271
Lewisburgh	16	11	28	26	5	27	12	14	13	2	. . .	26
Monroe	788	315	387	329	266	735	307	349	315	196	12	189
Rockingham	1,868	723	805	884	479	1,781	721	643	930	432	56	1,052
Pendleton	714	311	330	282	265	723	246	315	277	178	13	124
Franklin	26	9	30	21	10	27	5	25	15	7	1	8
Bath	1,001	492	445	365	233	925	414	440	312	203	17	661
Frederick	2,837	1,397	1,373	1,324	1,241	2,744	1,279	1,515	1,366	761	420	5,118
Winchester	293	141	209	180	111	255	131	176	167	95	22	348
Stephensburgh	83	38	40	40	33	73	36	30	47	26	3	64
Fort Royal	33	23	24	23	6	38	11	17	23	6	3	47
Middletown,	29	9	12	19	8	33	6	18	14	6	. . .	12
Berry Ville	6	10	18	6	3	11	3	8	2	4	1	59
Keins town	14	7	11	8	3	17	6	4	9	4	3	14
Pugh town	12	3	10	8	7	12	4	4	10	5	1	1
Ohio	840	353	348	487	265	895	325	370	399	186	15	257
Wythe	1,128	437	600	428	332	1,006	392	568	402	245	11	831
Russel	970	398	428	360	236	830	296	373	367	185	13	352
Tazewell	410	127	169	176	88	396	134	189	126	80	13	219
Montgomery	1,629	648	733	680	484	1,489	582	760	646	386	39	968
Randolph	343	163	155	159	79	372	106	150	143	69	2	85
Monongalia	1,677	644	722	755	517	1,662	564	744	687	387	18	163
Barclay	2,804	1,139	1,410	1,293	1,021	2,579	1,069	1,386	1,213	824	156	3,679
Smithfield	32	9	16	21	6	24	11	14	17	4	. . .	2
Middletown	25	15	22	19	3	28	7	16	11	5	3	14
Muhlenburgh	152	60	95	100	63	178	68	99	85	48	17	112
Bath	37	13	20	15	22	37	10	21	18	18	2	11
Darksville	19	15	12	10	8	21	5	19	8	6	2	7
Shepherdstown	193	90	87	97	73	160	70	91	100	57	15	75
Charlestown	89	37	50	66	18	90	34	51	43	11	8	71
Grayson	740	299	350	285	259	710	266	368	275	189	1	170
Lee	740	241	308	303	132	650	261	304	256	97	3	243
Augusta	1,708	696	938	934	736	1,624	685	913	867	570	95	1,946
Hardy	1,083	573	635	529	261	966	525	579	567	175	111	623
Brooke	904	342	379	389	280	827	339	383	358	201	16	288
Harrison	992	378	372	437	254	901	304	378	368	214	5	245
Wood	240	82	109	115	67	238	79	78	97	50	1	61
Shanandoah	2,261	1,032	990	982	762	2,166	934	949	1,015	634	84	738
Strasburgh	54	20	24	36	32	68	18	27	46	12	. . .	15
Woodstock	128	52	54	78	29	101	35	41	64	32	1	19
New Market	56	11	29	35	9	59	15	21	32	4	. . .	19
Rockbridge	1,325	650	760	535	552	1,349	692	750	712	453	97	1,070
	34,601	14,502	16,264	15,674	11,134	32,726	13,366	15,923	15,169	8,632	1,930	23,597

Source: Census Office, Return of the Whole Number of Persons Within the Several Districts of the United States: 1800 (1802), 69–71.

TABLE 5.43 STATE CENSUS OF NORTH CAROLINA, 1786 [INCOMPLETE]

Counties	Whites — Males 21–60	Whites — Other Males	Whites — Females	Blacks — From 12 to 60	Blacks — Other Blacks	Total
Franklin	740	1,069	1,814	931	913	5,475
Tyrrell	552	966	1,488	374	379	3,859
Pasquotank	615	1,023	1,551	789	815	4,793
Northampton	763	1,329	1,966	1,721	1,564	7,043
New Hanover	579	722	1,397	1,332	1,012	5,042
Duplin	734	1,356	1,997	605	548	5,248
Warren	735	1,399	2,499	1,792	1,870	8,295
Addition to above						701
Richmond	380	757	1,126	168	154	2,585
Caswell	1,273	2,748	3,611	1,110	1,097	9,839
Chowan	463	641	970	992	716	3,782
Nash	650	1,269	1,850	799	709	5,277
Edgecomb	1,045	1,977	2,985	1,271	1,202	8,480
Halifax	1,088	814	3,145	2,638	2,552	10,327
Gates	543	901	1,361	927	1,183	4,917
Granville	733	1,486	2,149	925	954	6,247
Addition to above						4,055
Sampson	565	1,197	1,786	384	338	4,268
Hyde	496	584	1,282	430	376	3,421
Surry	340	837	436	105	94	1,559
	12,294	21,075	33,413	17,293	16,476	105,213
Total whites	66,782					
Total blacks				33,769		
Total whites and blacks			105,213			

Note: Census does not include 25 other counties inhabited by 18,572 persons.
Source: Walter Clark, ed., State Records of North Carolina, 1777–1790 (1895–1905), XVIII, 433–34.

TABLE 5.44 FEDERAL CENSUS OF NORTH CAROLINA, 1790

District, County, and Town	Total	White Population in 1790 — Males — 16 Years and Over	White Population in 1790 — Males — Under 16 Years	White Population in 1790 — Females	All Other Free Persons	Slaves
Edenton district	53,769	8,405	8,653	16,510	1,048	19,153
Bertie county	12,462	1,719	1,802	3,442	378	5,121
Camden county	4,022	725	754	1,475	30	1,038
Chowan county, excluding Edenton town	3,413	457	438	865	7	1,646
Edenton town	1,575	181	113	306	34	941
Currituck county	5,220	1,018	1,024	1,960	115	1,103
Gates county	5,386	790	772	1,514	93	2,217
Hertford county	5,949	813	824	1,632	232	2,448
Pasquotank county	5,477	951	1,035	1,804	87	1,600
Perquimans county	5,439	884	921	1,714	37	1,883
Tyrrell county	4,826	867	970	1,798	35	1,156
Fayette district	34,393	7,111	7,324	13,677	608	5,673
Anson county	5,235	1,035	1,183	2,147	41	829
Cumberland county, excluding Fayetteville town	7,195	1,458	1,366	2,656	49	1,666
Fayetteville town	1,535	394	195	398	34	514
Moore county	3,870	850	965	1,672	12	371
Richmond county	5,053	1,096	1,205	2,114	55	583
Robeson county	5,343	1,132	1,138	2,263	277	533
Sampson county	6,162	1,146	1,272	2,427	140	1,177
Halifax district	64,848	9,215	10,130	18,610	1,364	25,529
Edgecombe county	10,265	1,663	1,878	3,487	70	3,167
Franklin county	7,502	1,076	1,381	2,307	37	2,701
Halifax county, including Halifax town	14,310	1,873	1,826	3,471	443	6,697
Martin county	6,010	1,067	1,010	2,008	96	1,829
Nash county	7,390	1,134	1,434	2,621	193	2,008
Northampton county	9,992	1,335	1,283	2,502	458	4,414
Warren county	9,379	1,067	1,318	2,214	67	4,713
Hillsborough district	59,971	10,937	12,903	21,980	702	13,449
Caswell county [1]	10,096	1,801	2,110	3,377	72	2,736
Caswell district	. . .	. . .	. . .	. . .	. . .	. . .
Gloucester district	. . .	. . .	. . .	. . .	. . .	. . .
Nash district	. . .	. . .	. . .	. . .	. . .	. . .
Richmond district	. . .	. . .	. . .	. . .	. . .	. . .
St. David's district	. . .	. . .	. . .	. . .	. . .	. . .
St. James district	. . .	. . .	. . .	. . .	. . .	. . .
St. Lawrence district	. . .	. . .	. . .	. . .	. . .	. . .
St. Lukes district	. . .	. . .	. . .	. . .	. . .	. . .
Chatham county	9,161	1,761	2,168	3,664	10	1,558
Granville county [1]	10,982	1,581	1,873	3,050	315	4,163
Abraham's Plains district	. . .					
Beaver Dam district	. . .					
Dutch district	. . .	. . .	. . .	. . .	. . .	. . .
Epping Forest district	. . .					74
Fishing Creek district	. . .	. . .	. . .	. . .	. . .	. . .
Fort Creek district	. . .	. . .	. . .	. . .	. . .	. . .
Goshen district	. . .	. . .	. . .	. . .	. . .	. . .
Henderson district	. . .	. . .	. . .	. . .	. . .	. . .
Island Creek district	. . .					
Knap of Leeds district	. . .	. . .	. . .	. . .	. . .	. . .
Oxford district	. . .	. . .	. . .	. . .	. . .	182
Ragland district	. . .	. . .	. . .	. . .	. . .	. . .
Tabb's Creek district	. . .					
Tar River district	. . .	. . .	. . .	. . .	. . .	. . .

(continued)

TABLE 5.44 (continued)

District, County, and Town	Total	White Population in 1790 Males 16 Years and Over	Males Under 16 Years	Fe-males	All Other Free Persons	Slaves
Orange county[1]	12,216	2,433	2,709	4,913	101	2,060
Caswell district	. . .	. . .	. . .	. . .	. . .	. . .
Chatham district	. . .	. . .	. . .	. . .	. . .	. . .
Hillsboro district	. . .	. . .	. . .	. . .	. . .	. . .
Hillsboro town	. . .	. . .	. . .	. . .	. . .	. . .
Orange district	. . .	. . .	. . .	. . .	. . .	. . .
St. Asaph's district	. . .	. . .	. . .	. . .	. . .	. . .
St. Mark's district	. . .	. . .	. . .	. . .	. . .	. . .
St. Mary's district	. . .	. . .	. . .	. . .	. . .	. . .
St. Thomas' district	. . .	. . .	. . .	. . .	. . .	. . .
Randolph county	7,318	1,590	1,952	3,292	24	460
Wake county	10,198	1,771	2,091	3,684	180	2,472
Morgan district	33,317	6,953	8,773	14,961	13	2,617
Burke county	8,106	1,705	2,108	3,684	9	600
First company	833	169	216	356	. . .	92
Second company	525	90	148	263	. . .	24
Third company	607	120	156	248	7	76
Fourth company	441	99	129	203	. . .	10
Fifth company	596	124	146	275	. . .	51
Sixth company	677	141	169	306	2	59
Seventh company	631	124	152	268	. . .	87
Eighth company	685	150	183	324	. . .	28
Ninth company	677	147	187	317	. . .	26
Tenth company	459	99	126	213	. . .	21
Eleventh company	559	133	119	266	. . .	41
Twelfth company	481	94	155	217	. . .	15
Thirteenth company	935	215	222	428	. . .	70
Lincoln county	9,246	2,057	2,293	4,041	. . .	855
First company	492	110	124	215	. . .	43
Second company	509	114	127	229	. . .	39
Third company	503	118	146	221	. . .	18
Fourth company	733	166	180	349	. . .	38
Fifth company	602	130	167	289	. . .	16
Sixth company	1,099	250	261	494	. . .	94
Seventh company	735	170	174	281	. . .	110
Eighth company	653	148	184	303	. . .	18
Ninth company	1,427	318	308	610	. . .	191
Tenth company	718	145	189	333	. . .	51
Eleventh company	1,010	202	227	351	. . .	230
Twelfth company	765	186	206	366	. . .	7
Rutherford county	7,808	1,576	2,119	3,502	2	609
First company	573	105	110	218	. . .	140
Second company	581	110	147	244	. . .	80
Third company	390	70	110	150	. . .	60
Fourth company	361	70	99	168	. . .	24
Fifth company	603	121	163	291	. . .	28
Sixth company	686	127	192	323	. . .	44
Seventh company	514	111	138	230	. . .	35
Eighth company	527	103	154	248	2	20
Ninth company	584	119	167	287	. . .	11
Tenth company	598	114	165	259	. . .	60
Eleventh company	955	186	287	431	. . .	51
Twelfth company	692	139	209	305	. . .	39
Thirteenth company	358	93	93	163	. . .	9
Fourteenth company	386	108	85	185	. . .	8

District, County, and Town	Total	White Population in 1790 Males 16 Years and Over	Males Under 16 Years	Fe-males	All Other Free Persons	Slaves
Wilkes county	8,157	1,615	2,253	3,734	2	553
First company	535	111	132	237	. . .	55
Second company	609	101	164	268	. . .	76
Third company	505	100	134	233	2	36
Fourth company	541	106	157	265	. . .	13
Fifth company	466	88	145	222	. . .	11
Sixth company	601	121	169	291	. . .	20
Seventh company	392	76	100	162	. . .	54
Eighth company	319	76	105	128	. . .	10
Ninth company	631	118	150	297	. . .	66
Tenth company	488	109	132	224	. . .	23
Eleventh company	600	109	149	246	. . .	96
Twelfth company	443	88	122	199	. . .	34
Thirteenth company	723	152	205	332	. . .	34
Fourteenth company	377	75	96	188	. . .	18
Fifteenth company	369	78	114	173	. . .	4
Sixteenth company	558	107	179	269	. . .	3
Newbern district	55,683	9,595	9,876	19,329	841	16,042
Beaufort county	5,405	910	924	1,821	128	1,622
Carteret county	3,734	718	709	1,505	93	709
Craven county, including Newbern town	10,474	1,710	1,538	3,226	337	3,663
Dobbs county	6,994	1,164	1,293	2,479	46	2,012
Hyde county	4,204	792	714	1,518	37	1,143
Johnston county	5,691	1,040	1,177	2,081	65	1,328
Jones county	4,796	736	794	1,541	70	1,655
Pitt county	8,270	1,461	1,508	2,912	25	2,364
Wayne county	6,115	1,064	1,219	2,246	40	1,546
Salisbury district	66,927	14,003	15,932	28,490	249	8,253
Guilford county	7,300	1,615	1,807	3,235	27	616
Iredell county	5,430	1,118	1,218	2,223	3	868
Mecklenburg county	11,360	2,364	2,563	4,758	67	1,608
Montgomery county	5,039	942	1,220	2,029	11	837
Rockingham county	6,211	1,188	1,411	2,489	10	1,113
Rowan county, including Salisbury town	15,972	3,399	3,828	6,902	102	1,741
Stokes county	8,423	1,846	2,122	3,665	12	778
Surry county	7,192	1,531	1,763	3,189	17	692
Wilmington district	26,097	3,953	4,062	7,799	216	10,067
Bladen county	5,100	837	834	1,685	58	1,686
Brunswick county	3,070	380	398	778	3	1,511
Duplin county	5,663	1,035	1,187	2,052	3	1,386
New Hanover county, including Wilmington town	6,837	834	702	1,496	68	3,737
Onslow county	5,427	867	941	1,788	84	1,747

[1] Names taken from county tax lists.
Source: Bureau of the Census, *A Century of Population Growth, 1790–1900* (1909), 199.

TABLE 5.45   FEDERAL CENSUS OF NORTH CAROLINA, 1800

Names of Counties & Townships	Free White Males					Free White Females					All Other Free Persons Except Indians Not Taxed	Slaves	Total Amount
	Under 10 Years of Age	Of 10 and Under 16	Of 16 and Under 26, Including Heads of Families	Of 26 and Under 45, Including Heads of Families	Of 45 and Upwards, Including Heads of Families	Under 10 Years of Age	Of 10 and Under 16	Of 16 and Under 26, Including Heads of Families	Of 26 and Under 45, Including Heads of Families	Of 45 and Upwards, Including Heads of Families			
Morgan District													
Burke county	1,817	652	725	777	586	1,703	676	774	839	422	52	776	9,799
Morganton	19	4	19	8	5	9	3	6	5	2	. . .	50	130
Buncombie county	1,092	415	475	485	289	1,133	368	504	420	225	34	334	5,774
Ashville	7	1	4	4	. . .	4	. . .	3	2	. . .	. . .	13	38
Lincoln	2,212	949	865	1,061	631	2,131	792	918	974	538	18	1,479	12,568
Lincolnton	7	2	5	5	2	7	5	7	3	5	. . .	44	92
Rutherford county	1,995	764	895	785	528	1,832	694	909	782	453	12	1,047	10,696
Rutherfordton	3	. . .	4	11	1	3	. . .	3	3	3	1	25	57
Wilkes county	1,272	501	592	518	354	1,221	453	613	534	335	64	790	7,247
Ashe county	575	197	226	208	144	560	200	234	189	110	55	85	2,783
Total	8,999	3,485	3,810	3,862	2,540	8,603	3,191	3,971	3,751	2,093	236	4,643	49,184
Salisbury District													
Rowan county	3,194	1,487	1,516	1,599	1,008	2,755	1,379	1,594	1,446	875	30	2,532	19,415
Salisbury	48	22	51	38	20	51	23	39	29	12	5	307	645
Guilford county	1,560	668	931	777	512	1,487	582	909	612	459	40	905	9,442
Rockingham ditto	1,244	485	624	581	338	1,200	516	644	551	345	116	1,633	8,277
Surry ditto	1,677	736	725	743	508	1,471	706	716	709	431	21	962	9,405
Huntsville	7	3	2	3	1	8	2	. . .	5	2	. . .	20	53
Rockford	5	2	2	3	2	3	4	1	. . .	2	. . .	23	47
Stokes county	1,767	791	820	841	519	1,571	723	838	782	454	51	1,359	10,516
Germantown	10	4	3	11	2	12	3	6	8	1	1	33	94
Bethany	17	4	15	15	9	15	7	10	14	5	. . .	42	153
Bethabara	7	3	3	6	1	2	2	1	7	3	. . .	2	37
Salem	17	7	29	22	24	21	19	23	18	32	11	3	226
Iredell county	1,297	560	680	685	497	1,218	558	739	625	405	16	1,481	8,761
Statesville	16	1	4	9	2	15	1	5	8	6	1	27	95
Cabarras county	808	384	355	405	275	776	365	394	390	212	2	695	5,061
Concord	7	2	6	6	2	1	. . .	2	2	1	. . .	4	33
Montgomery co	1,205	538	569	557	335	1,256	461	559	500	304	20	1,373	7,677
Mecklenberg co.	1,574	677	648	861	469	1,532	694	688	779	449	15	1,931	10,317
Charlotte	10	6	11	3	5	5	6	4	8	7	. . .	57	122
Total	14,470	6,380	6,994	7,165	4,529	13,399	6,051	7,172	6,493	4,005	329	13,389	90,376
Hillsborough District													
Orange county	2,755	976	1,247	829	677	1,985	852	1,304	1,042	555	108	3,327	15,657
Hillsborough	58	21	31	35	14	50	21	16	36	9	8	175	474
University	18	22	67	13	5	15	5	9	10	4	. . .	63	231
Randolph county	1,663	691	788	754	441	1,525	580	743	771	469	202	607	9,234
Wake ditto	1,596	654	802	770	474	1,530	706	849	747	428	306	3,906	12,768
Raleigh, City of	41	28	39	50	15	39	22	39	28	15	18	335	669
Caswell county	1,211	396	599	568	297	1,039	415	568	524	270	26	2,788	8,701
Parson ditto	813	327	396	362	239	797	276	430	348	209	123	2,082	6,402
Granville ditto	1,414	570	771	705	382	1,413	539	733	693	360	329	6,106	14,015
Chatham ditto	1,659	878	985	524	453	1,552	865	897	615	407	102	2,708	11,645
Pittsborough	11	9	9	2	1	6	13	4	1	2	. . .	77	135
Haywood	14	11	9	8	. . .	7	3	3	2	. . .	. . .	24	81
Total	11,253	4,583	5,743	4,620	2,998	9,958	4,297	5,595	4,817	2,728	1,222	22,198	80,012

(continued)

TABLE 5.45 (continued)

Names of Counties & Townships	Free White Males					Free White Females					All Other Free Persons Except Indians Not Taxed	Slaves	Total Amount
	Under 10 Years of Age	Of 10 and Under 16	Of 16 and Under 26, Including Heads of Families	Of 26 and Under 45, Including Heads of Families	Of 45 and Upwards, Including Heads of Families	Under 10 Years of Age	Of 10 and Under 16	Of 16 and Under 26, Including Heads of Families	Of 26 and Under 45, Including Heads of Families	Of 45 and Upwards, Including Heads of Families			
Halifax District													
Hallifax county	1,032	480	560	591	293	929	458	641	592	344	623	7,020	13,563
Hallifax town	17	5	35	28	2	21	12	14	13	4	12	219	382
Nash county	753	309	401	403	230	748	342	402	417	231	143	2,596	6,975
Warren ditto	833	436	499	449	394	787	347	513	462	290	131	5,905	11,046
Warrenton	16	40	21	14	2	13	3	9	6	2	5	107	238
Franklin county	886	417	438	433	272	878	377	455	413	237	. . .	3,667	8,473
Louisburg	3	. . .	8	4	1	3	. . .	2	2	2	. . .	31	56
Northampton co	988	427	552	540	289	903	430	582	559	317	538	6,206	12,331
Princeton	1	3	1	4	1	4	1	2	1	. . .	1	3	22
Edgecombe county	1,091	479	615	590	329	1,101	455	687	531	335	105	3,580	9,898
Tarborough	18	17	36	32	9	18	16	28	16	7	1	325	523
Martin county	630	325	303	180	194	658	257	367	369	211	172	1,646	5,312
Williamston	22	4	11	17	4	19	4	13	11	6	10	127	248
Jameston	11	. . .	3	13	1	10	1	6	8	2	1	13	69
Total	6,301	2,942	3,483	3,298	2,021	6,092	2,703	3,721	3,400	1,988	1,742	31,445	69,136
Edenton District													
Chowan county	365	154	166	229	115	326	156	187	240	104	28	1,760	3,830
Edenton	73	40	53	77	26	74	46	53	75	33	39	713	1,302
Perquimons county	630	283	356	363	166	597	280	354	360	180	60	1,980	5,609
Hertford	9	7	8	4	4	5	6	6	3	6	1	40	99
Pasquotank	551	268	316	334	108	560	242	338	271	229	227	1,593	5,037
Nixonton	17	4	22	13	2	7	8	17	8	5	3	104	210
Elizabeth city	9	7	12	13	1	9	3	4	11	1	4	58	132
Camden county	534	259	287	223	144	507	244	287	284	126	56	1,170	4,191
Currituck ditto	944	391	526	540	257	902	407	510	516	291	114	1,530	6,928
Gates ditto	507	252	325	290	196	471	218	317	326	209	82	2,688	5,881
Hertford	540	235	344	347	166	517	242	351	345	199	429	2,733	6,448
Murfreesborough	17	9	15	21	3	18	3	11	17	2	6	131	253
Bertie county	852	406	535	504	278	882	409	617	623	310	195	5,387	10,998
Windsor	9	10	12	12	5	16	12	16	14	4	8	119	237
Colerain	1	. . .	1	2	. . .	1	1	2	. . .	. . .	. . .	6	14
Washington co	239	114	130	145	79	266	102	166	159	71	49	645	2,165
Plymouth	23	9	15	19	4	13	7	17	18	2	14	116	257
Tyrrell county	449	209	207	284	106	454	185	247	239	122	12	849	3,363
Elizabeth	5	1	2	4	. . .	2	. . .	3	4	. . .	1	10	32
Total	5,474	2,658	3,332	3,524	1,660	5,627	2,571	3,503	3,513	1,894	1,298	21,632	56,986
Newbern District													
Craven county	813	354	417	471	246	806	361	457	543	263	184	2,863	7,778
Newbern	131	79	102	147	41	137	81	102	146	59	144	1,298	2,467
Jones county	381	196	237	206	113	326	211	253	236	119	64	1,899	4,241
Trenton	9	4	8	4	3	5	2	7	4	2	. . .	50	98
Carterel county	546	238	250	285	181	492	269	327	313	158	107	796	3,962
Beaufort	46	25	25	43	13	56	22	29	39	16	1	122	437
Hyde county	601	244	259	380	152	613	268	341	354	140	45	1,386	4,783
Jarmington	7	1	. . .	5	. . .	6	2	3	3	. . .	1	18	46
Beaufort county	624	305	313	374	280	604	272	369	382	212	182	1,674	5,541
Washington	29	17	47	45	11	34	22	38	36	9	8	305	601
Bath	6	1	1	4	4	7	4	1	6	1	. . .	65	100
Pitt county	1,064	454	519	516	290	1,116	458	704	658	307	32	2,792	8,910
Greensville	11	3	13	14	. . .	13	6	9	9	3	. . .	93	174
Green county	436	183	222	243	114	462	311	351	258	115	27	1,496	4,218
Lenoir ditto	416	198	250	199	120	386	193	250	237	137	55	1,457	3,898
Kingston	3	3	4	9	2	6	2	4	3	2	. . .	69	107
Wayne county	851	399	454	434	231	834	383	464	394	256	84	1,988	6,772
Johnston ditto	853	356	435	422	236	775	353	460	373	241	34	1,763	6,301
Total	6,827	3,060	3,556	3,801	1,987	6,678	3,220	4,169	3,994	2,040	968	20,134	60,434

Names of Counties & Townships	Free White Males					Free White Females					All Other Free Persons Except Indians Not Taxed	Slaves	Total Amount
	Under 10 Years of Age	Of 10 and Under 16	Of 16 and Under 26, Including Heads of Families	Of 26 and Under 45, Including Heads of Families	Of 45 and Upwards, Including Heads of Families	Under 10 Years of Age	Of 10 and Under 16	Of 16 and Under 26, Including Heads of Families	Of 26 and Under 45, Including Heads of Families	Of 45 and Upwards, Including Heads of Families			
Wilmington District													
New Hanover co	402	169	182	260	139	437	192	215	242	125	75	2,933	5,371
Wilmington	64	39	59	105	32	70	29	58	63	26	19	1,125	1,689
Brunswick county	446	148	219	264	129	416	178	184	234	115	163	1,614	4,110
Bladen, ditto	812	351	370	447	263	797	353	467	437	244	144	2,278	6,963
Elizabeth	5	2	2	5	1	6	4	3	6	2	8	21	65
Duplin county	880	389	473	425	289	836	383	488	435	279	55	1,864	6,796
Onslow ditto	760	300	374	365	205	396	333	421	367	196	. . .	1,757	5,474
Swansborough	11	8	7	10	8	11	5	21	7	4	. . .	57	149
Total	3,380	1,406	1,686	1,881	1,066	2,969	1,477	1,857	1,791	991	464	11,649	30,617
Fayetteville District													
Cumberland co	874	416	541	547	379	886	377	562	539	338	52	2,097	7,608
Fayetteville	128	71	111	127	42	134	84	109	120	37	67	626	1,656
Moore county	830	341	392	381	218	747	264	372	353	230	31	608	4,767
Richmond ditto	890	425	425	439	277	834	395	393	396	249	25	875	5,623
Anson ditto	1,379	531	611	612	333	1,294	507	590	546	322	131	1,290	8,146
Robeson ditto	1,032	374	461	486	362	935	352	541	475	348	340	960	6,666
Lumberton	28	10	12	17	6	23	8	10	16	4	1	38	173
Sampson county	953	391	403	449	270	895	377	424	461	247	137	1,712	6,719
Total	6,114	2,559	2,956	3,058	1,887	5,748	2,364	3,001	2,906	1,775	784	8,206	41,358

Source: Census Office, *Return of the Whole Number of Persons Within the Several Districts of the United States: 1800* (1802), 71–73.

TABLE 5.46   ESTIMATES OF SOUTH CAROLINA'S POPULATION, 1766–1787

Date	Whites	Blacks	Militia	Total	Source
1785	108,000	80,000	. . .	188,000	Noah Webster
1775	60,000	90,000	. . .	150,000	Henry Laurens
1770	. . .	75,178	10,000	. . .	Lt. Gov. Bull
1769	45,000	80,000	. . .	125,000	Lt. Gov. Bull
1766	. . .	. . .	10,000	. . .	Gov. Montagu

Source: Evarts B. Greene and Virginia D. Harrington, *American Population Before the Federal Census of 1790* (1932), 175, 176.

TABLE 5.47   FEDERAL CENSUS OF SOUTH CAROLINA, 1790

District, County, and Parish	White Population in 1790				All Other Free Persons	Slaves
	Total	Males		Females		
		16 Years and Over	Under 16 Years			
Beaufort district [1]	18,753	1,266	1,055	2,043	153	14,236
Camden district	38,265	6,941	8,694	13,607	158	8,865
Chester county	6,866	1,446	1,604	2,831	47	938
Claremont county	4,548	517	841	1,080	. . .	2,110
Clarendon county	2,392	444	516	830	. . .	602
Fairfield county	7,623	1,335	1,874	2,929	. . .	1,485
Lancaster county	6,302	1,253	1,537	2,074	68	1,370
Richland county	3,930	596	710	1,173	14	1,437
York county	6,604	1,350	1,612	2,690	29	923

(continued)

TABLE 5.47   (continued)

District, County, and Parish	Total	White Population in 1790 Males 16 Years and Over	Males Under 16 Years	Females	All Other Free Persons	Slaves
Charleston district	66,985	5,060	3,177	7,165	950	50,633
Berkley county, St. Johns parish	5,922	209	152	331	60	5,170
Colleton county, St. Johns parish	5,312	209	104	272	22	4,705
Dorchester county, St. Georges parish	4,299	337	311	604	25	3,022
Christ Church parish	2,954	156	138	272	11	2,377
St. Andrews parish	2,947	125	71	174	31	2,546
St. Bartholomes parish	12,606	625	491	1,017	135	10,338
St. James Goose Creek parish	2,787	158	79	202	15	2,333
St. James Santee parish	3,797	140	110	187	15	3,345
St. Pauls parish	3,433	65	48	103	15	3,202
St. Phillips and St. Michaels parish	16,359	2,810	1,561	3,718	586	7,684
St. Stephens parish	2,733	81	45	100	1	2,506
St. Thomas parish	3,836	145	67	185	34	3,405
Cheraw district[1]	10,706	1,779	1,993	3,646	59	3,229
Georgetown district	22,122	2,356	2,467	4,055	113	13,131
All Saints parish	2,225	104	102	223	1	1,795
Prince Fredericks parish	8,135	907	915	1,596	32	4,685
Prince Georges parish	11,762	1,345	1,450	2,236	80	6,651
Ninety-six district	73,729	14,973	17,165	30,324	198	11,069
Abbeville county	9,197	1,904	1,948	3,653	27	1,665
Edgefield county	13,289	2,333	2,571	4,701	65	3,619
Greenville county	6,503	1,400	1,627	2,861	9	606
Laurens county	9,337	1,969	2,270	3,971	7	1,120
Newberry county	9,342	1,992	2,232	3,962	12	1,144
Pendleton county	9,568	2,007	2,535	4,189	3	834
Spartanburgh county	8,800	1,868	2,173	3,866	27	866
Union county	7,693	1,500	1,809	3,121	48	1,215
Orangeburgh district	18,513	3,201	3,171	6,040	170	5,931
North part	11,281	1,780	1,693	3,258	21	4,529
South part	7,232	1,421	1,478	2,782	149	1,402

[1] Not returned by counties.
Source: Bureau of the Census, *A Century of Population Growth, 1790–1900* (1909), 200.

TABLE 5.48   FEDERAL CENSUS OF SOUTH CAROLINA, 1800

	Free White Males	Free White Females	Free Blacks	Slaves	Total
Charleston District					
St. Michael	1,434	1,404	299	3,504	6,641
St. Philip in city	3,155	2,826	652	5,549	12,182
outside city	441	369	73	786	1,669
St. Stephen	161	143	26	2,156	2,486
St. James, Santee	216	179	2	3,843	4,240
St. John, Berkeley	350	311	53	6,479	7,193
St. Thomas	119	88	19	2,328	2,554
Christ Church	233	199	17	3,585	4,034
St. James, Goose Creek	771	742	9	3,161	4,683
St. Andrew	287	295	3	4,543	5,128
St. John, Colleton	340	310	8	6,031	6,689
	7,508	6,866	1,161	41,945	57,480
Colleton District					
St. Bartholemew	1,439	1,289	20	9,110	11,858
St. Paul	405	344	12	6,383	7,144
St. George	497	420	6	4,978	5,901
	2,341	2,053	38	20,471	24,903
Beaufort District					
St. Helena	175	137	1	2,657	2,970
Beaufort Town	152	262	11	421	846
St. Luke	413	310	1	5,887	6,611
St. Peter	739	801	134	2,669	4,343
Pr. William	676	646	51	4,397	5,770
	2,195	2,004	198	16,031	20,428
Georgetown District					
Wicyau	835	726	68	9,012	10,641
Wacamau	317	282	20	3,394	4,013
Kingston	969	926	3	708	2,606
Williamsburg	1,177	1,043	4	3,454	5,678
	3,298	2,977	95	16,568	22,938
Orangeburgh District					
Orange	2,392	1,860	9	2,409	6,670
Lewisbourg	888	787	79	1,701	3,455
Lexington	1,911	2,027	7	1,246	5,191
	5,191	4,674	95	5,356	15,316
Sumpter District					
Clarendon	1,018	900	123	2,333	4,374
Salem	1,136	1,047	3	1,385	3,571
Claremont	1,118	1,020	175	2,845	5,158
	3,272	2,967	301	6,563	13,103

	Free White Males	Free White Females	Free Blacks	Slaves	Total
Ninety-Six District					
Marion	2,412	2,209	138	2,155	6,914
Barnwell	2,751	2,734	111	1,690	7,286
York	4,299	4,118	27	1,804	10,248
Chester	3,524	3,495	2	1,164	8,185
Fairfield	4,127	3,969	23	1,968	10,087
Laurens	5,542	5,328	20	1,919	12,809
Pendleton	9,081	8,679	68	2,224	20,052
Greenville	5,119	4,910	36	1,439	11,504
Spartanburg	5,422	5,187	46	1,467	12,122
Union	4,305	4,167	68	1,697	10,237
Edgefield	6,757	6,306	61	5,006	18,130
Abbeville	5,440	5,108	41	2,964	13,553
Richland	1,504	1,425	135	3,033	6,097
Lancaster	2,515	2,383	38	1,076	6,012
Kershaw	2,438	2,268	104	2,530	7,340
Newberry	5,016	4,691	95	2,204	12,006
	70,252	66,977	1,013	34,340	172,582
Cheraw District					
Marlborough	1,997	1,883	179	1,393	5,452
Chesterfield	2,066	1,929	73	1,148	5,216
Darlington	2,706	2,557	32	2,336	7,631
	6,769	6,369	284	4,877	18,299
Total					
	100,916	95,339	3,185	146,151	345,591

Source: Census Office, *Return of the Whole Number of Persons Within the Several Districts of the United States: 1800* (1802), 77, 78.

TABLE 5.50   FEDERAL CENSUS OF GEORGIA, 1800

County	Free White Males	Free White Females	Free Blacks	Slaves	Total
Wilkes	4,184	3,848	63	5,008	13,103
Lincoln	1,745	1,581	7	1,433	4,766
Greene	3,716	3,381	7	3,657	10,761
Oglethorpe	3,479	3,207	5	3,089	9,780
Richmond	1,503	1,225	54	2,691	5,473
Jackson	3,259	3,069	8	1,400	7,736
Effingham	718	592	. . .	762	2,072
Jefferson	2,066	1,942	34	1,642	5,684
Washington	3,739	3,442	451	2,668	10,300
Warren	3,263	2,989	19	2,058	8,329
Franklin	3,079	2,813	8	959	6,859
Bryan	286	242	2	2,306	2,836
Liberty	762	584	27	3,940	5,313
McIntosh	460	371	10	1,819	2,660
Camden	496	440	10	735	1,681
Hancock	5,205	4,400	16	4,835	14,456
Montgomery	1,445	1,297	3	435	3,180
Burke	3,358	3,167	14	2,967	9,506
Chatham	2,077	1,596	224	9,049	12,946
Elbert	3,709	3,546	23	2,816	10,094
Glynn	445	334	3	1,092	1,874
Bullock	871	758	15	269	1,913
Scriven	1,253	1,000	. . .	766	3,019
Columbia	2,848	2,473	16	3,008	8,345
Total	53,968	48,293	1,919	59,699	162,686

Source: Census Office, *Return of the Whole Number of Persons Within the Several Districts of the United States: 1800* (1802), 79–82.

TABLE 5.49   FEDERAL CENSUS OF GEORGIA, 1790

District, County, and Parish	Total	White Population in 1790			All Other Free Persons	Slaves
		Males		Females		
		16 Years and Over	Under 16 Years			
Lower district	19,266	2,050	1,160	2,637	158	13,261
Camden	305	81	44	96	14	70
Chatham	10,769	846	480	1,130	112	8,201
Effingham	2,424	627	336	711	. . .	750
Glyn	413	70	36	87	5	215
Liberty	5,355	426	264	613	27	4,025
Middle district	25,336	4,649	4,790	8,643	52	7,202
Burke	9,467	1,808	1,841	3,415	11	2,392
Richmond	11,317	1,894	1,925	3,343	39	4,116
Washington	4,552	947	1,024	1,885	2	694
Upper district	37,946	6,404	8,094	14,459	188	8,801
Franklin	1,041	225	243	417	. . .	156
Greene	5,405	1,027	1,111	1,882	8	1,377
Wilks	31,500	5,152	6,740	12,160	180	7,268

Source: Bureau of the Census, *A Century of Population Growth, 1790–1900* (1909), 200.

The West

Anglo-Americans did not establish themselves across the Appalachians until 1775, when they began erecting forts in Kentucky's bluegrass plain. Settlement of Tennessee's transmontane region commenced in 1779 at Nashboro, and in 1788 white pioneers founded the first U.S. community in modern Ohio at Marietta. Anglo-Americans began drifting into Indiana and Mississippi during the 1790s.

No accurate counts exist for Kentucky and Tennessee before the first census. Their population grew rapidly after the Revolution's end and had surpassed 100,000 by 1790. After 1795, when the Treaty of Greenville ended Indian warfare in the Ohio Valley and Indian hostilities began subsiding in the Tennessee territory, migration from the east accelerated sharply. By 1800, more than 400,000 Americans, 7.5% of all inhabitants, lived beyond the Appalachian crest.

Geographic mobility was a defining characteristic of the late-eighteenth-century population. Frontier expansion and military service habituated large numbers of people to traveling long distances. Stagecoaches became a more common sight on the country's rutted roads and tavernkeepers built larger inns to accommodate more customers. (*Harper's Magazine*, November 1879)

TABLE 5.51   FEDERAL CENSUS OF KENTUCKY, 1790

District, County, and Parish	Total	White Population in 1790		Females	All Other Free Persons	Slaves
		Males				
		16 Years and Over	Under 16 Years			
Beards Town, in Nelson county	216	52	49	85	1	29
Bourbon	7,837	1,645	2,035	3,249	...	908
Danville, in Mercer county	150	49	28	51	...	22
Fayette county	17,576	3,241	3,878	6,738	30	3,689
Jefferson	4,565	1,008	997	1,680	4	876
Lexington, in Fayette county	834	276	203	290	2	63
Lincoln	6,548	1,375	1,441	2,630	8	1,094
Louisville, in Jefferson county	200	49	44	79	1	27
Madison	5,772	1,231	1,421	2,383	...	737
Mason	2,267	431	676	952	...	208
Mercer	6,941	1,411	1,515	2,691	7	1,317
Nelson	11,099	2,456	2,746	4,644	34	1,219
Washington, in Mason county	462	163	95	183	...	21
Woodford	9,210	1,767	1,929	3,267	27	2,220

Source: Bureau of the Census, *A Century of Population Growth, 1790–1900* (1909), 200.

As population spread westward, more people found themselves inhabiting stockades such as Boonesborough, Kentucky, which is pictured here. Stockades were designed not only to be defensive—largely secured by fire from the blockhouses constructed at each corner—but also to serve as corrals where the maximum number of livestock could be penned in case of attack. (Lewis Collins, *History of Kentucky* [1843].)

TABLE 5.52   FEDERAL CENSUS OF KENTUCKY, 1800

	Free White Males	Free White Females	Free Blacks	Slaves	Total
Barren co.	2,223	2,056	. . .	505	4,784
Boone co.	641	553	15	325	1,534
Bourbon co.	5,342	4,962	58	1,994	12,356
Millersburg	40	44	. . .	8	92
Paris	136	103	4	134	377
Bracken co.	1,161	1,026	4	191	2,382
Augusta	48	47	10	38	143
Germantown	35	32	. . .	14	81
Breckinridge co.	383	336	1	33	753
Hardinsburg	26	20	. . .	3	49
Bullitt co.	1,378	1,115	9	944	3,446
Shepherdsville	43	28	. . .	25	96
Campbell co.	791	778	10	258	1,837
Newport	44	39	2	21	106
Clark co.	3,052	2,922	14	1,535	7,523
Winchester	51	50	3	26	130
Christian co.	1,101	920	. . .	297	2,318
Cumberland co.	1,618	1,394	36	236	3,284
Fayette co.	4,254	4,128	65	3,786	12,233
Lexington	805	528	23	439	1,795
Fleming co.	2,492	2,152	9	240	4,893
Flemingsburg	58	50	1	14	123
Floyd co.	240	203	. . .	29	472
Prestonburg	3	1	. . .	2	7
Franklin co.	1,734	1,590	17	1,109	4,450
Frankfort	209	154	5	260	628
Gallatin co.	428	372	2	276	1,078
Port William	87	73	. . .	53	213
Garrard co.	2,503	2,341	5	1,234	6,083
Lancaster	43	34	1	25	103
Green co.	2,719	2,487	3	816	6,025
Greensburg	27	24	. . .	20	71
Hardin co.	1,733	1,545	9	310	3,597
Elizabethtown	24	15	2	15	56

	Free White Males	Free White Females	Free Blacks	Slaves	Total
Harrison co.	2,026	1,825	19	393	4,263
Cynthianna	41	33	. . .	13	87
Henderson co.	472	451	. . .	340	1,263
Henderson	84	69	2	50	205
Henry co.	1,489	1,359	4	406	3,258
Jefferson co.	3,224	2,819	22	2,330	8,395
Louisville	158	124	1	76	359
Jessamine co.	1,995	1,869	21	1,553	5,438
Nicholasville	6	9	. . .	8	23
Knox co.	540	504	3	62	1,109
Lincoln co.	3,500	3,282	23	1,750	8,555
Stanford	28	12	. . .	26	66
Livingston co.	1,291	1,048	4	444	2,787
Eddyville	34	23	. . .	12	69
Logan co.	2,573	2,295	92	730	5,690
Russellville	51	20	1	45	117
Madison co.	4,397	4,292	3	1,688	10,380
Richmond	44	28	. . .	38	110
Mason co.	5,078	4,678	46	1,603	11,405
Maysville	66	52	3	16	137
Washington	213	193	39	125	570
Williamsburg	31	36	. . .	3	70
Mercer co.	3,637	3,406	30	2,169	9,242
Danville	115	54	. . .	101	270
Harrodsburg	47	38	3	46	134
Montgomery co.	3,310	2,924	11	749	6,994
Mt. Sterling	34	31	. . .	18	83
Muhlenberg co.	768	530	3	116	1,417
Greenville	10	5	2	9	26
Nelson co.	3,875	3,664	13	1,735	9,287
Bardstown	230	179	3	167	579
Nicholas co.	1,351	1,184	6	322	2,863
Newtown	27	35	. . .	. . .	62

(continued)

TABLE 5.52 (continued)

	Free White Males	Free White Females	Free Blacks	Slaves	Total
Ohio co.	520	478	3	122	1,123
Hartford	29	17	. . .	28	74
Vienna	12	13	. . .	1	26
Pendleton co.	711	621	2	239	1,573
Falmouth	18	21	. . .	1	40
Pulaski co.	1,525	1,403	1	232	3,161
Scott co.	3,010	2,851	11	1,787	7,659
Georgetown	131	93	1	123	348
Shelby co.	3,356	3,143	21	1,409	7,929
Shelbyville	107	75	2	78	262
Warren co.	2,117	2,107	4	417	4,645
Bowling Green	16	11	. . .	14	41
Washington co.	3,812	3,679	14	1,382	8,887
Springfield	66	54	3	40	163
Woodford co.	2,243	2,137	14	2,058	6,452
Versailles	66	56	1	49	172
Total	93,956	85,915	741	40,343	220,955

Source; Census Office, *Return of the Whole Number of Persons Within the Several Districts of the United States: 1880 (1802),* 83, 84.

TABLE 5.54 FEDERAL CENSUS OF TENNESSEE TERRITORY, 1790

	Free Whites			Other Free Persons	Slaves	Total
	Males		Females			
Counties	Over 16	Under 16	Females			
Washington	1,009	1,792	2,524	12	535	5,872
Sullivan	806	1,242	1,995	107	297	4,447
Greene	1,293	2,374	3,580	40	454	7,741
Hawkins	1,204	1,970	2,921	68	807	6,970
South of Fr. Broad River	681	1,082	1,627	66	163	3,619
Davidson	639	855	1,288	18	659	3,459
Sumner	404	582	854	8	348	2,196
Tennessee	235	380	576	42	154	1,387
Total	6,271	10,277	15,365	361	3,417	35,691

Source: Stella H. Sutherland, *Population Distribution in Colonial America* (1936), 209.

TABLE 5.53 FEDERAL CENSUS OF MISSISSIPPI TERRITORY, 1800

Names of Counties & Townships	Free White Males					Free White Females					All Other Free Persons Except Indians Not Taxed	Slaves	Total
	Under 10 Years of Age	Of 10 and Under 16	Of 16 and Under 26, Including Heads of Families	Of 26 and Under 45, Including Heads of Families	Of 45 and Upwards, Including Heads of Families	Under 10 Years of Age	Of 10 and Under 16	Of 16 and Under 26, Including Heads of Families	Of 26 and Under 45, Including Heads of Families	Of 45 and Upwards, Including Heads of Families			
Washington Co.													1,250
Jefferson	54	19	22	52	15	73	29	23	25	11	2	112	
Shamburgh	36	12	16	19	16	29	11	20	10	9	21	194	
Steele	49	18	15	29	17	39	21	17	21	6	. . .	188	
Pickering Co.													2,959
Fair Child's Creek	60	16	29	43	10	48	18	23	23	9	1	72	
Ellicottsville	8	4	12	9	. . .	5	. . .	4	2	. . .	. . .	12	
Union Town	4	. . .	5	6	3	4	2	3	3	. . .	. . .	11	
Cole's Creek	235	77	107	148	49	219	67	74	87	32	1	397	
Baie Pairre	110	40	49	84	29	112	49	37	52	17	2	198	
Big Black	17	15	16	18	3	23	13	13	11	. . .	. . .	29	
Walnut Hills	6	6	3	10	1	7	. . .	2	6	20	. . .	19	
Adams Co.													4,641
Sandy Creek	110	33	25	55	24	99	40	23	55	7	29	140	
Homo Chito	52	17	21	42	25	62	21	15	30	4	12	462	
Pine Ridge	19	5	5	8	4	13	8	1	3	26	7	26	
Natchez & St. Catharine's	136	57	97	151	54	123	54	45	51	12	83	833	
Second Creek	40	16	30	50	21	48	21	14	28	11	20	481	
Buffaloe & Baie Sarah	63	21	30	56	19	48	22	38	19	. . .	4	315	
Aggregate amount of each description	999	356	482	780	290	953	376	352	426	165	182	3,489	8,850

Source: Census Office, *Return of the Whole Number of Persons Within the Several Districts of the United States: 1800 (1802),* 85.

TABLE 5.55 FEDERAL CENSUS OF TENNESSEE, 1800

Names of Districts, Towns, & Counties	Free White Males					Free White Females					All Other Free Persons Except Indians Not Taxed	Slaves
	Under 10 Years of Age	Of 10 and Under 16	Of 16 and Under 26, Including Heads of Families	Of 26 and Under 45, Including Heads of Families	Of 45 and Upwards, Including Heads of Families	Under 10 Years of Age	Of 10 and Under 16	Of 16 and Under 26, Including Heads of Families	Of 26 and Under 45, Including Heads of Families	Of 45 and Upwards, Including Heads of Families		
Mero District												
Nashville	21	10	42	50	8	20	5	22	9	4	3	151
Davidson county	1,348	460	728	753	265	1,288	485	622	509	212	14	2,936
Summer county	658	254	373	306	175	625	269	274	271	127	. . .	1,284
Smith County	762	255	389	388	141	747	250	318	342	101	4	597
Wilson county	571	171	239	268	78	527	180	200	203	86	9	729
Williamson county	483	127	196	256	72	434	149	196	180	81	1	693
Robertson county	715	246	315	358	145	653	246	316	293	127	3	863
Montgomery county	462	160	227	222	87	371	160	137	172	80	. . .	821
	5,020	1,683	2,509	2,601	971	4,665	1,744	2,085	1,979	818	34	8,074
Hamilton District												
Knox county	2,351	826	1,062	955	481	2,172	734	980	848	431	19	1,122
Knoxville town	35	16	51	32	10	37	13	22	17	8	. . .	146
Kingston	9	5	5	8	. . .	10	1	1	8	. . .	. . .	30
Iredell	. . .	. . .	. . .	1	. . .	. . .	. . .	. . .	. . .	. . .	. . .	. . .
Blount county	1,000	405	517	485	238	962	443	523	414	188	2	339
Maryville town	13	8	14	12	4	2	3	5	3	1	. . .	6
Sevier county	623	280	291	372	167	643	239	267	236	137	2	162
Grainger county	1,493	585	562	477	325	1,542	593	544	457	293	. . .	496
Jefferson & Cooke counties	1,719	671	731	706	456	1,584	642	762	662	362	27	695
	7,243	2,796	3,233	3,048	1,681	6,952	2,668	3,104	2,645	1,420	50	2,996
Washington District												
Hawkins county	1,195	398	334	702	269	1,159	404	405	604	197	85	811
Carter county	1,103	408	324	326	111	1,035	419	400	278	105	96	208
Sullivan county	2,077	853	708	634	341	2,185	814	1,277	500	321	17	491
Washington county	1,140	477	555	459	340	1,110	463	542	442	293	25	533
Green county	1,449	579	619	582	412	1,344	530	741	544	337	2	471
	6,964	2,715	2,540	2,703	1,473	6,833	2,630	3,365	2,368	1,253	225	2,514
District of Mero	5,020	1,683	2,509	2,601	971	4,665	1,744	2,085	1,979	818	34	8,074
Ditto of Hamilton	7,243	2,796	3,233	3,048	1,681	6,952	2,668	3,104	2,645	1,420	50	2,996
Ditto of Washington	6,964	2,715	2,540	2,703	1,473	6,833	2,630	3,365	2,368	1,253	225	2,514
	19,227	7,194	8,282	8,352	4,125	18,450	7,042	8,554	6,992	3,491	309	13,584

Sources: Census Office, *Return of the Whole Number of Persons Within the Several Districts of the United States: 1800* (1802), 88.

TABLE 5.56 ESTIMATED POPULATION OF NORTHWEST TERRITORY, 1792

Settlements	Whites and Slaves
Ohio co. Purchase [Ohio]	2,500
Col. Symmes's settlements [Ohio]	2,000
Gallipolis [Ohio]	1,000
Vincennes and nearby [Indiana]	1,500
Kaskaskias and Cahokia [Illinois]	680
Grand Ruisseau, St. Philip, and Prairie-du-Rochers [Illinois]	240
Total	7,920

Source: Jedidiah Morse, *The American Gazeteer* (1797).

TABLE 5.57 FEDERAL CENSUS OF NORTHWEST TERRITORY, 1800

The whole number of inhabitants in the Territory, 45,365

Names of Counties & Townships	Free White Males					Free White Females					All Other Free Persons Except Indians Not Taxed	Slaves	Total
	Under 10 Years of Age	Of 10 and Under 16	Of 16 and Under 26, Including Heads of Families	Of 26 and Under 45, Including Heads of Families	Of 45 and Upwards, Including Heads of Families	Under 10 Years of Age	Of 10 and Under 16	Of 16 and Under 26, Including Heads of Families	Of 26 and Under 45, Including Heads of Families	Of 45 and Upwards, Including Heads of Families			
Jefferson	1,937	758	749	731	417	1,768	719	718	606	328	35	. . .	8,766
Washington	1,035	379	568	642	292	991	328	474	507	193	18	. . .	5,427
Adams	727	273	319	341	177	664	261	267	273	115	15	. . .	3,432
Hamilton	3,273	1,335	1,503	1,251	480	3,090	1,165	1,297	954	344	. . .	. . .	14,691
Wayne	540	201	332	584	198	467	193	252	198	102	139	. . .	3,206
Ross	1,648	630	928	1,061	336	1,458	604	760	698	292	125	. . .	8,540
Trumbull	202	71	238	223	55	206	83	93	106	21	5	. . .	1,303
Aggregate amount of each description	9,362	3,647	4,636	4,833	1,955	8,644	3,353	3,861	3,342	1,395	337	. . .	45,365

Source: Census Office, *Return of the Whole Number of Persons Within the Several Districts of the United States: 1800* (1802), 85.

TABLE 5.58 FEDERAL CENSUS OF INDIANA TERRITORY, 1800

Names of Counties, Towns, or Other Civil Divisions	Free White Males					Free White Females					All Other Free Persons Except Indians Not Taxed	Slaves
	Under 10 Years of Age	Of 10 and Under 16	Of 16 and Under 26, Including Heads of Families	Of 26 and Under 45, Including Heads of Families	Of 45 and Upwards, Including Heads of Families	Under 10 Years of Age	Of 10 and Under 16	Of 16 and Under 26, Including Heads of Families	Of 26 and Under 45, Including Heads of Families	Of 45 and Upwards, Including Heads of Families		
Knox Co.												
Town of St. Vincennes,	104	55	79	90	45	112	58	72	50	25	16	8
Neighbourhood of St. Vincennes	144	65	78	80	40	134	50	78	58	22	55	15
Traders on the Wabash river	4	. . .	17	22	5	1	. . .	1	. . .	. . .	. . .	5
Illinois Grant	184	75	61	108	33	191	55	83	106	17	16	. . .
Randolph Co.												
Kaskaskias Town & Township	99	18	40	63	23	66	14	30	35	10	22	47
Praire de Roche Township	33	5	20	26	4	30	1	7	16	6	4	60
Mitchel Township	53	38	33	43	22	49	26	28	28	8	6	. . .
Massac	20	3	14	13	11	9	4	7	5	2	2	. . .

Names of Counties, Towns, or Other Civil Divisions	Free White Males					Free White Females					All Other Free Persons Except Indians Not Taxed	Slaves
	Under 10 Years of Age	Of 10 and Under 16	Of 16 and Under 26, Including Heads of Families	Of 26 and Under 45, Including Heads of Families	Of 45 and Upwards, Including Heads of Families	Under 10 Years of Age	Of 10 and Under 16	Of 16 and Under 26, Including Heads of Families	Of 26 and Under 45, Including Heads of Families	Of 45 and Upwards, Including Heads of Families		
St. Clair Co. Eahokia Town and Township	135	47	64	119	49	106	32	60	55	10	42	. . .
Belle Fountaine	44	24	35	44	14	46	18	28	26	7	. . .	. . .
L'Aigle Township	34	17	25	37	16	47	22	30	14	8	. . .	. . .
Total	854	347	466	645	262	791	280	424	393	115	163	135

Source: Census Office, *Return of the Whole Number of Persons Within the Several Districts of the United States: 1800* (1802), 87.

Birthrates, Family Size, and Population Growth

The demographic history of the Revolutionary era has been researched much less intensively than the colonial period's, for which there exist a small—but excellent—number of local studies. Because little attention has been given to this topic in the post-colonial decades, it is difficult to determine whether fertility remained approximately as high after 1760 as before, because the average number of births per woman varied from six in some parts of New England to eight in Pennsylvania. The first census reported a wide variation in family sizes across the nation, with smaller households characteristic of New England and larger families typical of whites in the mid-Atlantic and western regions. Scholars nevertheless agree that the U.S. population grew rapidly during the late eighteenth century because its families raised larger numbers of children than did those in Europe.

Data from the 1800 federal census indicate that, at any given moment, the normal white household would contain nearly 6 members, which exceeded the 4.5 persons usually found in contemporaneous English families by almost a third. Early marriage, a relatively benign disease environment, and a high standard of living enabled the United States to attain the highest rate of natural reproduction known for any society in the Atlantic world in the late eighteenth century.

American families produced substantially more children than European households because women married four to five years earlier in the New World than in the Old World, and this additional span of fertility enabled them to conceive an extra two babies. Although perhaps every fifth American childbirth resulted in its mother's premature death before 1800, this rate was evidently lower than in Europe, where far fewer women lived long enough to bear the maximum number of children biologically possible. Survival rates for infants and adolescents were also significantly more favorable in the United States than in Europe, reaching perhaps 85%. (Only in the five largest American cities did adolescent death rates rival those in densely peopled regions of Europe, in some of which half of all children died before age 20, but this circumstance had little impact on population growth because barely 4% of U.S. citizens lived in urban areas.) White families evidently produced an average of seven children about 1800, and raised six of these to adulthood, when they would themselves resume the cycle.

TABLE 5.59 AVERAGE MARRIAGE AGE AND TOTAL BIRTHS PER WHITE WIFE IN U.S., 1760–1800

Community	Period	Age at First Marriage		Children per Completed Family[a]	Children Surviving to Age 20[b]
		Women	Men		
Hingham, Mass.	1761–1780	23.5	24.6	6.4	5.1
Hingham, Mass.	1781–1800	23.7	26.4	6.2	5.0
Sturbridge, Mass.	1760–1779	22.8	. . .	7.3	5.8
Sturbridge, Mass.	1780–1799	22.5	. . .	7.3	5.8
Quakers[c]	1775–1800	. . .	. . .	6.2	5.0
Lancaster co., Pa.	1771–1800	21.9[d]	25.8[d]	8.0[d]	6.4[d]
Tidewater, Md.	1750–1800	22.2	. . .	6.9	4.6
U.S. Average	ca. 1800	22.5	26.1	6.9	5.5

[a] Total births to women who reached age 40.
[b] Assumes 80% survival rate except for Maryland, which was 67%.
[c] Sample of 276 families from N.Y., N.J., and Pa.
[d] Median figures.
Sources: Daniel Scott Smith, "The Demographic History of Colonial New England," *Journal of Economic History* XXXII (1972), 177. Nancy Osterud and John Fulton, "Family Limitation and Age at Marriage: Fertility Decline in Sturbridge, Mass., 1730–1850," *Population Studies* XXX, 483, 484. Robert V. Wells, "Family Size and Fertility Control in Eighteenth-Century America: A Study of Quaker Families," *Population Studies* XXV (1971), 75. Rodger C. Henderson, "Demographic Patterns and Family Structure in Eighteenth-Century Lancaster Co., Pa.," *Pennsylvania Magazine of History and Biography* CXIV (1990), 357, 373. Allan Kulikoff, *Tobacco and Slaves: The Development of Southern Cultures in the Chesapeake, 1680–1800* (1986), 60.

The Revolutionary War resulted in at least 25,000 fatalities among young men, besides an unknown number of deaths among women, and it forced many couples to delay marriage from 1776 to 1782, yet it had little long-term impact on family formation and fertility rates. The return of peace in 1783 triggered a resumption in the rates for both marriages and childbirth that almost entirely offset the previous period of slow growth. The family of Daniel Boone provides an isolated, but revealing, example of how the United States recovered from its wartime losses and resumed growing through natural increase at a rapid rate. Boone lost two sons killed by Indians between 1773 and 1782, but his other eight children were so prolific (producing him 68 grandchildren) that when he died at age 87, there were about 400 people among his descendants' various households.

TABLE 5.60 NUMBER AND AVERAGE SIZE OF FREE HOUSEHOLDS IN UNITED STATES, 1790

	Free Households	Average Size	Average Size in Largest City
New England	174,017	5.7	. . .
Maine	17,009	5.6	. . .
N.H.	24,065	5.9	5.2 (Portsmouth)
Vt.	14,992	5.7	. . .
Mass.	65,779	5.7	4.9 (Boston)
R.I.	11,296	5.9	4.5 (Providence)
Conn.	40,876	5.7	4.8 (New Haven)
Middle Atlantic	166,762	5.8	. . .
N.Y.	54,878	5.7	5.6 (New York)
N.J.	29,779	5.8	. . .
Pa.	73,874	5.8	4.4 (Philadelphia)
Del.	8,231	6.1	. . .
The South	217,110	5.7	. . .
Md.	36,228	5.6	4.1 (Baltimore)
Va.	75,830	6.0	4.6 (Norfolk)
N.C.	52,613	5.6	3.6 (Edentown)
S.C.	25,872	5.5	4.1 (Charleston)
Ga.	9,867	5.4	. . .
Tenn.	5,763	5.6	. . .
Ky.	10,937	5.6	. . .
United States	557,889	5.7	4.6 (average)

Note: Free households include both whites and free blacks. Data estimated for N.J., Del., Va., Ga., Ky., and Tenn. Size is number in 1790 only, not completed family size. See Table 5.61.
Sources: Bureau of the Census, *A Century of Population Growth, 1790–1900* (1909), 96, 100. Jim Potter, "Demographic Development and Family Structure," in Jack P. Greene and J. R. Pole, eds., *Colonial British America: Essays in the New History of the Early Modern Era* (1984), 147.

TABLE 5.61 PERCENT DISTRIBUTION OF FREE HOUSEHOLDS, IN UNITED STATES, 1790

Household Size	New England	Middle Atlantic[a]	The South[b]	United States
1	3.0%	2.8%	6.1%	3.7%
2	7.8%	7.5%	8.1%	7.8%
3	11.7%	11.8%	11.6%	11.7%
4	13.7%	13.9%	13.8%	13.8%
5	13.9%	14.3%	13.5%	13.9%
6	13.4%	13.4%	12.6%	13.2%
7	11.5%	11.4%	10.7%	11.2%
8	9.2%	9.1%	8.6%	9.0%
9	6.7%	6.5%	6.2%	6.5%
10	4.3%	4.2%	4.1%	4.2%
11 +	4.9%	5.0%	4.8%	4.9%

[a] Data not available for N.J. and Del.
[b] Data not available for Va., Ga., Ky., and Tenn.
Note: Figures exclude any slaves in households. See Table 5.60.
Source: Bureau of the Census, *A Century of Population Growth, 1790–1900* (1909), 98.

European Immigration and Ethnicity

Immigration to British America fell off sharply during the Seven Years' War (1754–1763) but immediately afterward reached its peak during the dozen years prior to the Revolution. From 1763 to 1775, the thirteen colonies absorbed more than 130,000 migrants from Europe, besides importing a minimum of 50,000 (perhaps 75,000) Africans. This surge of newcomers equaled about one quarter of the white population's increase during those years, and it accounted for at least one third of the rise in the number of slaves.

Besides temporarily disrupting European immigration and the slave trade, the Revolution precipitated the only significant out-migration from the United States. By 1783, perhaps 100,000 white Tories and 20,000 African Americans resettled in either Canada or the West Indies. The only significant addition to the country's population during the Revolution resulted from the decision of about 5,000 Hessian mercenaries, plus an unknown number of former British soldiers, to remain permanently in the United States.

Postwar economic depression discouraged European emigration after 1783, and most states refused to allow the slave trade to resume before it was prohibited in 1808. Emigration from Great Britain and Germany fell sharply, and even though a rising tide of Catholic Irish and French colonials from Haiti somewhat offset this decline, the contribution of overseas migration to American population growth dwindled dramatically. Just 155,000 Europeans and about 6,000 Africans landed in the United States from 1783 to 1799, and they contributed less than a tenth to population growth in the nation during those two decades.

TABLE 5.62 EUROPEAN IMMIGRATION TO THIRTEEN COLONIES/UNITED STATES, 1763–1799

Immigrant Groups	1790–1799	1783–1789	1775–1782	1763–1775[a]
English, Welsh	15,200[b]	6,500[b]	. . .	30,000
Scots	. . .	. . .	. . .	40,000
Irish	61,500[c]	45,300	. . .	55,000[d]
Germans, Swiss, Dutch	5,100	3,600	5,000[e]	12,000
French	1,700	200	. . .	. . .
French from Haiti	12,800	1,300	. . .	. . .
Others	1,000	600	. . .	. . .
Total	97,300	57,500	5,000	137,000

[a] Data includes immigration to Nova Scotia.
[b] Includes Scots.
[c] Primarily Catholics.
[d] Primarily Ulster Protestants.
[e] Hessian mercenaries remaining in U.S.
Sources: Hans-Jurgen Grabbe, "European Immigration to the United States, 1783–1820," *Proceedings of the American Philosophical Society* CXXXIII (1989), 194. Bernard Bailyn, *Voyagers to the West: A Passage in the Peopling of America on the Eve of the Revolution* (1986), 26.

TABLE 5.63 PROFILE OF BRITISH IMMIGRANTS LANDING IN NORTH AMERICA, 1773–76

	English–Welsh Immigrants	Scottish Immigrants
Sex		
Male	83.8%	59.9%
Female	16.2%	40.1%
Age		
1–14 years	5.6%	24.7%
15–19 years	18.1%	16.4%
20–24 years	34.8%	19.4%
25–29 years	18.7%	15.1%
30–34 years	10.1%	8.9%
35–39 years	6.1%	6.0%
40–44 years	3.9%	4.3%
45–49 years	1.7%	2.7%
50 + years	1.0%	2.5%

(continued)

The Revolution constituted the only period in early American history when more people left the United States than came as immigrants. The Revolution created a large number of political refugees, like this family leaving their home amid the jeers of their neighbors. Perhaps 100,000 whites, in large part recent British immigrants, went into exile, plus at least 20,000 African Americans. (Howard Pyle Collection, courtesy Delaware Art Museum, Wilmington, Delaware)

TABLE 5.63 (continued)

	English–Welsh Immigrants	Scottish Immigrants
Familial Status		
Traveled alone	80.1%	52.1%
Traveled in a family	19.9%	47.9%
Occupations or Status		
Gentleman, gentlewoman	2.1%	1.0%
Learned profession (law, etc.)	.4%	.2%
Merchandising	5.2%	5.2%
Agriculture	17.8%	24.0%
Craftsmen, artisans	54.2%	37.7%
Laborers, servants	20.3%	31.9%
Indentured Servants		
Indentured	68.4%	18.4%
Financed own passage	31.6%	81.6%
Destination		
New England	.9%	.8%
N.Y.	5.3%	43.0%
Pa.	15.8%	13.4%
Md.	41.3%	1.0%
Va.	13.6%	1.0%
N.C.	.2%	27.8%
S.C.	1.4%	.6%
Ga.	2.5%	5.1%
Canada and West Indies	19.0%	7.3%

Source: Bernard Bailyn, *Voyagers to the West: A Passage in the Peopling of America on the Eve of the Revolution* (1986), 128, 131, 140, 150, 168, 206.

TABLE 5.64 ANCESTRAL ORIGINS OF WHITE POPULATION IN UNITED STATES, 1790

State	English	Welsh	Scotch-Irish	Scottish	Irish	German	Dutch	French	Swedish
Maine	77.6%	2.2%	8.4%	4.2%	4.8%	1.2%		1.6%	
N.H.	81.4%	2.3%	8.0%	4.0%	3.7%	.1%		.5%	
Vt.	81.4%	3.5%	7.3%	3.6%	3.6%	.2%	.2%	.2%	
Mass.	84.4%	3.5%	5.3%	2.7%	2.5%	.3%	.1%	1.2%	
R.I.	79.9%	2.3%	7.0%	3.5%	2.6%	.1%		4.6%	
Conn.	87.1%	3.1%	4.5%	2.2%	2.1%	.4%	.1%	.5%	
N.Y.	50.3%	3.4%	8.7%	4.3%	4.1%	9.1%	15.9%	4.2%	
N.J.	50.6%	3.6%	6.8%	3.4%	4.1%	6.5%	20.1%	3.8%	1.1%
Pa.	25.8%	3.6%	15.1%	7.6%	7.1%	38.0%	1.3%	.9%	.6%
Del.	63.3%	5.5%	9.2%	4.6%	8.0%	2.6%	1.3%	1.7%	3.8%
Md.	52.5%	4.6%	10.4%	5.2%	10.9%	12.7%	.4%	3.0%	.3%
Va.	61.3%	6.5%	11.7%	5.9%	6.8%	4.5%	.7%	2.4%	.2%
N.C.	53.2%	6.2%	15.8%	7.9%	8.6%	5.1%	.4%	2.5%	.3%
S.C.	47.6%	6.2%	18.9%	9.4%	8.2%	5.5%	.2%	3.7%	.3%
Ga.	58.6%	7.9%	12.2%	6.1%	8.6%	3.5%	.1%	2.6%	.4%
Ky.	54.8%	3.6%	16.5%	8.3%	9.0%	4.9%	1.2%	1.5%	.2%
Tenn.	50.6%	4.8%	17.8%	8.9%	8.7%	6.6%	1.3%	.9%	.4%
U.S.	59.7%	4.3%	10.5%	5.3%	5.8%	8.9%	3.1%	2.1%	.3%

Source: Thomas L. Purvis, "The European Ancestry of the United States Population, 1790," *William and Mary Quarterly* XLI (1984), 98.

Slave Importations and Population Growth

The purchase of slaves from overseas reached its peak from 1763 to 1775. Following a sharp decline during the Seven Years' War, the slave trade rapidly revived after 1760. Surviving records document the arrival of 50,000 blacks from 1763 to 1775, and the actual total probably approached 75,000. Slave imports accounted for over 40% of the African-American population's rise from 1760 to 1775. Because slave imports were unusually high during that period, the rate of growth for blacks outpaced that of whites 38% to 33% in the 1760s, and by 41% to 31% in the 1770s.

All states abolished the slave trade during the Revolution, although South Carolina and Georgia briefly reopened this traffic after the war's end. Once slaves could no longer be brought in from overseas in substantial numbers, the African-American growth rate dropped significantly. The rate of increase for blacks thereafter consistently trailed that of whites. Although the number of whites rose by 95% from 1780 to 1800, the number of blacks was only 74% higher in the same period. African Americans declined from 21% of all inhabitants in 1770 to just 19% in 1800.

No accurate statistics exist to detail slave imports after 1780, but the best estimates indicate that 50,000 overseas blacks were purchased from then until 1800. Within the short span of four decades, the North American slave trade reached its zenith, having brought perhaps 100,000 Africans to the United States (and cost the lives of another 7,500 to 10,000 who died crossing the Atlantic), and then rapidly passed into oblivion.

TABLE 5.65   ORIGINS OF SLAVES IMPORTED TO THIRTEEN COLONIES, 1763–1775

Colony	Slaves Imported Number	From Africa Number	From Africa Percent	From West Indies Number	From West Indies Percent
N.Y.	359	282	78.6%	77	21.4%
Md.	2,349	2,173	92.5%	176	7.5%
Va.	6,661	5,509	82.7%	1,152	17.3%
N.C.	608	43	7.1%	565	92.9%
S.C.	35,555	29,102	81.9%	6,453	18.1%
Ga.	4,131	2,831	68.5%	1,300	31.5%
Total	49,663	39,940	80.4%	9,723	19.6%

Note: Based on incomplete records. Africans distributed as following: Gambia, 12%; Senegal, 26%; Angola, 14%; Windward and Gold Coasts, 15%; and Africa in general, 33%.
Sources: Elizabeth Donnan, *Documents Illustrative of the Slave Trade to America* (1935), IV, 612–33. Bureau of the Census, *Historical Statistics of the United States* (1975), 1173, 1174. Darold D. Wax, "Black Immigrants: The Slave Trade in Colonial Maryland," *Maryland Historical Magazine* LXXIII (1978), 36, 37. James G. Lydon, "New York and the Slave Trade, 1700–1774," *William and Mary Quarterly* XXXV (1978), 382. Susan Westbury, "Slaves of Colonial Virginia: Where Did They Come From," *William and Mary Quarterly* XLII (1985), 235, 236.

TABLE 5.66   AFRICAN ORIGINS OF MARYLAND AND SOUTH CAROLINA SLAVES, 1760–1775

	2,173 Africans Imported to Md. 1763–1775	276 Runaway Slaves in S.C. 1760–1769	419 Runaway Slaves in S.C. 1770–1775
Senegal-Gambia	38.0%[a]	29.0%	11.0%
Windward Coast-Sierra Leone	5.5%[b]	3.6%	18.9%
Gold Coast	8.6%[c]	5.4%	5.3%
Dahomey-Togo	. . .	2.5%	3.1%
Niger Delta	. . .	6.9%	6.9%
Angola-Congo	14.5%	29.7%	24.6%
Guinea	. . .	21.0%	28.9%
Unknown	33.4%	1.8%	1.4%

[a] 12.0% from Gambia and 26.0% from Senegal.
[b] Windward Coast only.
[c] Including some from Windward Coast.
Sources: Daniel C. Littlefield, *Rice and Slaves: Ethnicity and the Slave Trade in Colonial South Carolina* (1981), 125. Darold D. Wax, "Black Immigrants: The Slave Trade in Colonial Maryland," *Maryland Historical Magazine* LXXIII (1978), 36.

TABLE 5.67   AFRICAN AND CARIBBEAN SLAVES IMPORTED TO UNITED STATES, 1763–1800

	Ga.	S.C.	N.C.	Va.	Md.	N.Y.	Other Imports[a]
1800	. . .	. . .	. . .	. . .	. . .	. . .	3,600
1799	. . .	. . .	. . .	. . .	. . .	. . .	3,600
1798	252	. . .	. . .	. . .	. . .	. . .	3,348
1797	515	. . .	. . .	. . .	. . .	. . .	3,085
1796	717	. . .	. . .	. . .	. . .	. . .	2,883
1795	. . .	. . .	. . .	. . .	. . .	. . .	3,600
1794	52	. . .	. . .	. . .	. . .	. . .	3,548
1793	. . .	. . .	. . .	. . .	. . .	. . .	3,600
1792	560	. . .	. . .	. . .	. . .	. . .	3,040
1791	. . .	. . .	. . .	. . .	. . .	. . .	3,600
1790	. . .	. . .	. . .	. . .	. . .	. . .	3,600
1789	. . .	. . .	. . .	. . .	. . .	. . .	1,780
1788	. . .	. . .	. . .	. . .	. . .	. . .	1,780
1787	. . .	26	. . .	. . .	. . .	. . .	1,754
1786	. . .	87	. . .	. . .	. . .	. . .	1,693
1785	. . .	1,252	. . .	. . .	. . .	. . .	. . .
1784	. . .	2,140	. . .	. . .	. . .	. . .	. . .
1783	. . .	194	. . .	. . .	. . .	. . .	. . .
1775	204	. . .	. . .	550	. . .	. . .	. . .
1774	140	4,474	. . .	550	. . .	. . .	. . .
1773	. . .	7,799	. . .	550	5	. . .	. . .
1772	. . .	4,683	145	550	163	23	6
1771	120	1,991	75	550	214	8	7
1770	710	1,580	103	549	660	69	. . .
1769	537	4,642	115	351	16	. . .	20
1768	510	4	170	221	166	19	85
1767	404	. . .	. . .	62	125	. . .	. . .
1766	899	. . .	. . .	444	31	. . .	. . .
1765	291	6,447	. . .	137	18	. . .	10
1764	201	2,597	. . .	967	277	35	93
1763	115	1,338	. . .	1,180	674	205	170
Total	6,227	39,254	608	6,661	2,349	359	44,902

[a] Includes Anstey's average imports after 1785 (see Source, below)
Source: Elizabeth Donnan, *Documents Illustrative of the Slave Trade to America* (1935), IV, 474–77, 490–92, 612–33. Bureau of the Census, *Historical Statistics of the United States* (1975), 1174. Darold D. Wax, "Black Immigrants: The Slave Trade in Colonial Maryland," *Maryland Historical Magazine* LXXIII (1978), 36, 37. James G. Lydon, "New York and the Slave Trade, 1700–1774," *William and Mary Quarterly* XXXV (1978), 382. Susan Westbury, "Slaves of Colonial Virginia: Where They Came From," *William and Mary Quarterly* XLII (1985), 235, 236. Darold D. Wax, "Negro Imports Into Pennsylvania, 1720–1766," *Pennsylvania History* XXXII (1965), 286–87. Roger Anstey, "The Volume of the North American Slave-Carrying Trade from Africa, 1761–1810," *Revue Française d'Histoire d'Outre-Mer* LXII (1975), 64–65.

CHAPTER 6 Diet and Health

Diet

Anglo-Americans lived comfortably by eighteenth-century standards and consequently could afford a sound diet. Relatively little information has survived about what an average farm family consumed, however, and generalizations about eating habits largely derive from records concerning groups untypical of Revolutionary society, such as soldiers, servants, and widows. Historians assume that average caloric intake was more than adequate before 1800, but they remain unsure whether most individuals chose a nutritionally balanced mix of foods.

Few dietary records have survived in sufficient completeness to calculate caloric intake on a daily basis before 1800. Nearly all of these sources are military, workhouse, or prison menus that sacrificed variety and nutritional balance to reduce expenditures and simplify purchasing. Despite their unrepresentative nature, these records indicate that the amount of food believed appropriate for adult male workers was quite high in Revolutionary America. The majority of diets exceeded the recommended daily food allowance of 2,900 calories set by the National Research Council in 1968, and most did so by several hundred calories. Even slaves sometimes received rations in excess of 3,700 calories. Food provided in such large amounts was certainly sufficient to replenish calories expended by vigorous work and lengthy exposure to weather outdoors.

The typical American family ate an ample diet in the late 1700s but may not have balanced its intake properly among meat, grains, and vegetables. New England farmers commonly guaranteed their widows a minimum daily allowance of 2,900 calories, of which half came from Indian corn and a fifth from salted meat. By the 1760s, however, it had become customary for New England farmers to reserve allowances of vegetables and fruit for their widows.

Whether most Americans chose diets that were rich or deficient in vitamins remains unknown. Without air-tight seals or artificial refrigeration, it was impossible to preserve fruit or vegetables for long periods. All families experienced shortages of fresh food between winter and spring. The scientific study of nutrition was still in its infancy, and so average people relied on folk tales for their ideas on how to eat properly. Many urban families unable to raise their own food would have had to expend more than half their income to stay well fed, according to the latest research; they certainly ate more carbohydrates, which were filling and cheap, than meat and vegetables. By the late 1700s, however, Dr. Benjamin Rush of Philadelphia noted a decline in meat consumption in favor of vegetables, which had become less expensive and more common due to improvements in transportation. If Rush was correct, then diets may have been evolving in the direction of greater variety and more vitamin intake.

In the absence of any direct statistics on diet, figures on average adult heights can provide some quantitative measure of the food supply's adequacy and nutritional value. Because a strong correlation exists between adolescent growth rates and a sound diet, a population's average height can serve as a rough index of its overall nutritional status. Muster rolls from the Continental Army's archives provide the necessary data to compare the typical stature of young adult males with foreign soldiers and Americans in the twentieth century. Americans born between 1745 and 1755 evidently enjoyed a healthy diet, for they were about two to four inches taller than British soldiers, who themselves matured in a society considered prosperous by European standards. This disparity almost certainly arose from the high level of meat consumption among early Americans. Protein accelerates human growth, and daily consumption of meat may have averaged eight ounces per adult in the thirteen colonies by 1763.

By the Revolution, adult American males had attained an average size of five feet, eight inches. The average height of English males would not reach this level until after 1900. Americans of the Revolutionary generation had already reached modern stature, and were as tall as members of the U.S. military serving in World War II. These statistics indicate an exceptionally high level of nutrition in late-eighteenth-century America, marked in particular by a protein-rich diet of red meat. Although animal fats are now linked with circulatory disease and intestinal cancer, early Americans may have faced reduced levels of risk from these dangers because they raised cattle and hogs far leaner than modern livestock, which are fattened to an

TABLE 6.1   BASIC WEEKLY DIETS OF AMERICANS, 1770–1800

	Calories per Day	Weekly Allowances		
		Grains	Meat	Dairy/ Liquor
Slaves at Mt. Vernon				
(1790)	3,752	14.4 lb. cornmeal	3.6 lb. fish 0.55 lb. meat	. . .
Continental Army Rations				
(1780)	2,478– 3,741	7 lb. bread 7 lb. flour 1.75 pt. cornmeal	7 lb. beef or 6.125 lb. pork	. . .
(1775)	3,032– 4,058	7 lb. bread 1 pt. cornmeal 3 pt. peas	7 lb. beef or 7 lb. fish or 5.25 lb. pork	.875 gal. milk, 1.75 gal. beer or .36 gal. molasses
Continental Navy Rations				
(1776)	4,137ᵃ	7 lb. bread 0.5 pt. rice 1.5 pt. peas 3 lb. potatoes, turnips, or pudding	3 lb. beef 3 lb. pork	12 oz. cheese 2 oz. butter 3.5 pt. rumᵇ
Tory Prisoners in Maryland				
(1776)	3,226– 3,917	7 lb. bread 1 qt. cornmeal 3 pts. peas	7 lb. beef or 5.25 lb. pork	7 gills molasses 7 gills vinegar
Convicts Sent to Maryland for Sale as Servants				
(1770)	2,061	4.67 lb. bread 1.67 lb. oatmeal 1 lb. peas	0.67 lb. beef 0.5 lb. pork	0.67 lb. cheese 0.33 gill gin 1.25 lb. molasses

ᵃ2,961 calories excluding rum.
ᵇAlso 1.5 pt. of vinegar weekly for sick men.
Source: Research of Austin White, printed in Bureau of the Census, *Historical Statistics of the United States: Colonial Times to 1957* (1960), 774. Nathan Miller, *Sea of Glory: The Continental Navy Fights for Independence, 1775–1781* (1974), 526–27.

Folk artist Lewis Miller preserved his memories of early American cuisine by sketching a Pennsylvania Dutch cook and her "old style cooking," preparing bread, sausage, and "ballone." "The York Hotels, Kept In 1800. No Better, And good Cooks can be found no where to prepare Victuals for the table, as these Taverns. See the names—Mrs. Abraham Miller, Mrs. Polly Wattermyer, Mrs. Gostler, Mrs. Lamb, Mrs. Upp, Mrs. Rummel, Mrs. Balters Spangler, Mrs. George Hay, Mrs. Beard, and Mrs. Eichelberger. Not far from Town, the two last names. The[y] had plenty of raw materials to cook them, Beef, Veal, ham, Mutton, Pork, and fish, oysters, Poultry, Eggs, Butter, Cheese, milk, and honey, and all kind of vegetables—and fruit. See Mrs. Hersh in 1804. She could take every bone out of a chicken, for the table it was good to carve for the customers at her tavern." (Courtesy The Historical Society of York County, Pennsylvania)

Lewis Miller's childhood memories included sweet potatoes cooked in sausage grease. "Mrs Lottman Frying Sweet potatoes and give to Lewis Miller. Some of them the first I ever tasted. The[y] were good Eating. It was in her Tavern, South George Street, 1799." (Courtesy The Historical Society of York County, Pennsylvania)

excessive degree. The majority of evidence indicates that the typical white American enjoyed a very nutritious and reasonably balanced diet, which—in conjunction with the vigorous work of farming— contributed greatly to higher levels of fertility among women, lower rates of mortality, and longer life expectancy than Europeans enjoyed at the same time.

TABLE 6.2 ESTIMATED DIET AND COST OF FOOD FOR A PHILADELPHIA LABORER, 1762

Foodstuff	Annual Quantity Consumed in Pounds	Daily Caloric Intake	1762 Cost[d] per Week in Pence
Wheat flour[a]	365.0	1,600	12.73
Cornmeal	45.0	199	.71
Rice	15.7	68	.68
Bran	52.6	110	.69
Meat			
Beef	100.2	528	11.65
Mutton	18.2	. . .	. . .
Pork	9.1	. . .	. . .
Veal	47.0	. . .	. . .
Potatoes	6.6	7	.19
Turnips	27.6	12	.50
Butter	12.8	117	5.09
Milk	38.1	281	7.81
Salt	21.9[b]	c	.37
Pepper	.1	c	.06
Sugar	16.8	83	2.16
Molasses	4.9[b]	174	3.16
Beverages			
Coffee	.7	c	.92
Tea	.2	c	. . .
Chocolate	.2	c	. . .
Total		3,179	46.72

[a] Includes both "middling" and "common" flour.
[b] In gallons.
[c] Not included in caloric calculations.
[d] In Pa. currency with pence given as percent of shillings.
Source: Billy G. Smith, The "Lower Sort:" Philadelphia's Laboring People, 1750–1800 (1990), 98.

TABLE 6.3 AVERAGE HEIGHTS OF SOLDIERS, AGED 24–35, BORN IN AMERICA AND EUROPE WHO SERVED IN AMERICAN REVOLUTION

American Born		European Born	
Where Born	Inches Tall	Where Born	Inches Tall
N.Y.	69.111	Scotland[b]	67.747
N.J.	69.111	Germany[b]	67.391
Carolinas	69.030	Ireland[b]	67.236
Va.	68.847	England[b]	66.649
Md.	68.525	Other Europe[b]	66.300
Pa.[a]	68.312	Urban-born[b]	67.297
Rural New England	68.249	British Royal Marines[c]	64.700
Urban-born	67.872		
Non-whites	67.643		
Southern non-whites	67.198		
Average	68.100		66.760

[a] Includes Del.
[b] In Continental Army.
[c] Serving 1776–1782.
Source: Kenneth L. Sokoloff and Georgia C. Villaflor, "The Early Achievement of Modern Stature in America," Social Science History VI (1982), 457, 458, 462.

TABLE 6.4 AVERAGE FOOD ALLOWANCES PROVIDED FOR NEW ENGLAND WIDOWS IN THEIR HUSBANDS' WILLS, 1766–1799

	1766–1778		
	Annual Amount		Daily Caloric Intake[b]
	bu.	lb.[a]	
Grains			
Indian corn	10.6	335.2	1,485
Rye	5.3	167.6	574
Wheat	1.3	41.1	179
Average total[c]	16.1	543.9	2,238
Meat			
Salt pork	. . .	128.0	. . .
Salt beef	. . .	82.0	. . .
Average total[c]	. . .	183.5	553
Total daily caloric intake[d]	. . .	. . .	2,791
1781–1799			
Grains			
Indian corn	10.9	344.7	1,527
Rye	6.3	199.2	682
Wheat	1.5	47.4	208
Average total[c]	17.1	591.3	2,417
Meat			
Salt beef	. . .	118.5	. . .
Salt pork	. . .	75.3	. . .
Average total[c]	. . .	195.9	591
Total daily caloric intake[d]	. . .	. . .	3,008

[a] Expressed as flour remaining after miller received toll of 15% for grinding. One bu. of grain yielded about 37.2 lb. of flour, based on yield of 17 to 21 barrels (of 196 lb. each) milled from 100 bu. wheat (i.e., 6,000 lb. wheat yielded about 3,724 lb. flour before tolls). Greville Bathe and Dorothy Bathe, Oliver Evans: A Chronicle of Early American Engineering (1935), 28.
[b] 1 lb. wheat flour = 1,600 cal. 1 lb. cornmeal = 1,618 cal.
1 lb. ryemeal = 1,250 cal. 1 lb. meat = 1,100 cal.
See source for Table 6.2.
[c] Averages include other meats not identified in source.
[d] Source does not provide information on other allowances specified in the wills, but notes on pp. 57–59 that in the period 1781–1799, the percentage of widows receiving additional allotments was as follows: dairy products, 95.9%; vegetables, 91.8%; fruit, 55.1%.
Source: Sarah F. McMahon, "A Comfortable Subsistence: The Changing Composition of Diet in Rural New England, 1620–1840," William and Mary Quarterly XLII (1985), 54, 56.

Medical Practice and Disease Environment

In the late eighteenth century, medicine still remained a science based far more upon unverified theories than empirical research. Many important discoveries had been made since 1600, such as identifying germs ("animalculae") under the microscope and adding greatly to anatomical knowledge, but the medical profession failed to realize how these advances might prevent or cure illness. Like their European counterparts, American doctors not only had little understanding of how disease spread but even employed treatments that impaired the body's immune system.

Eighteenth-century physicians did not realize that most illness resulted from external infections that attacked the body, although they did recognize the contagious character of many diseases such as smallpox. Medical theory instead taught that sickness resulted from internal imbalances of the body's four primary "humors": blood, phlegm, choler, or black bile. Therapy consisted of returning these fluids to their natural equilibrium or ridding them of impurities. For diseases believed to result from an excess or contamination of humors, treatment involved purging, sweating, or bleeding these fluids away. For disorders presumed to originate from a deficiency of humors, doctors prescribed diet or drugs thought to restore the depleted substances to their proper levels.

Doctors typically divided diseases according to their primary symptoms—such as fevers, fluxes, breathing problems, or heart ailments—and prescribed similar treatment for all varieties of each category. Because they believed most diseases arose from an excess of body fluids, physicians usually tried to restore health by laxatives, forced vomiting, or bleeding. Such "cures" retarded recovery by leaving the patient malnourished or weak.

Bleeding seems to have been the most often prescribed cure, and it did enormous damage by carrying off a great volume of the white blood cells needed to combat infection. Many Americans studied medicine at the University of Edinburgh, where they learned from Dr. William Cullen that up to four-fifths of the body's blood might be drained to restore balance to the patient's humors. Dr. Benjamin Rush, a pupil of Cullen's, advocated so profuse an amount of bleeding as a cure during Philadelphia's yellow fever epidemic of 1793 that he became the object of public ridicule. Journalist William Cobbett scorned Rush's insistence upon bleeding victims of an exceptionally debilitating disease as "one of the great discoveries which are made from time to time for the depopulation of the earth." Such open skepticism about bleeding was nevertheless rare, and this procedure remained one of the most common treatments for illness well into the nineteenth century.

Surgeons were general practitioners who repaired broken bones or flesh, amputated diseased limbs, removed superficial cancers, restored sight by removing cataracts, and pulled teeth. Internal surgery rarely occurred until diseases or growth reached an advanced state, since the danger of infection counterbalanced the benefits, even though the medical profession had developed the instruments, techniques, and anatomical knowledge to perform such operations. Without any anesthetic except alcohol, surgery produced fearful agony, but skillful practitioners usually managed to complete the painful portion of amputations and other operations in about two minutes. Although ranked below doctors in status, surgeons undoubtedly accomplished more practical good for the public than their more distinguished colleagues. The first American to write a surgical textbook was John Jones, who published his *Remarks on the Treatment of Wounds and Fractures* in 1775.

Access to medical treatment expanded in the late 1700s as more hospitals became established. Prior to 1763, Anglo-Americans had built just one public institution for health care, the Pennsylvania Hospital at Philadelphia, which formally opened in 1756. The New York Hospital, designed to accommodate eighty beds, opened to patients in 1776, and by the century's end its staff numbered six physicians and four surgeons. Although not chartered as such, the Philadelphia Almshouse's medical department operated as a de facto hospital since 1772; it had a staff of five doctors by 1788, and in 1835 it was officially designated the Philadelphia Hospital. In 1791, twelve New York physicians organized a dispensary to provide char-

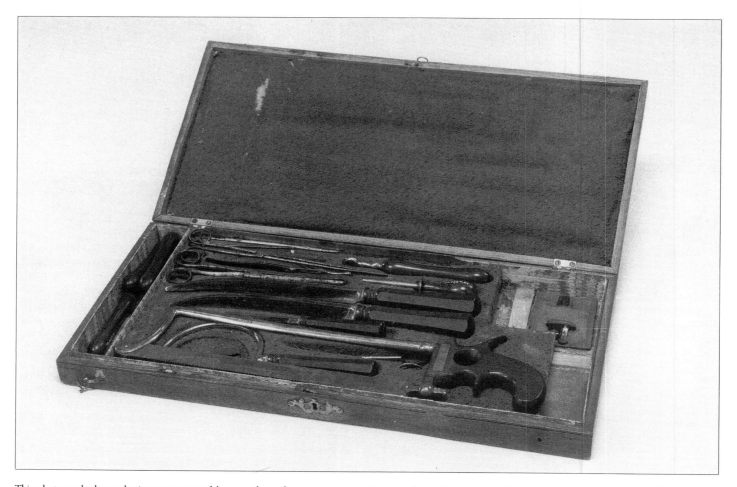

This photograph shows the instruments used by an eighteenth-century surgeon. Surgeons learned to operate with a relatively small number of tools for slicing into flesh and sawing through bones. Speed took priority over bedside manner, and good surgeons were supposed to finish an operation's painful procedures in less than two minutes. (Negative 83-30057-26, courtesy Smithsonian Institution)

Anglo-America's earliest hospital was the Pennsylvania Hospital, which opened at Philadelphia in 1756. By the time its Pine Street building was sketched in 1799, it was clearly the preeminent medical institution in North America. (I. N. Phelps Stokes Collection, Miriam & Ira Wallach Div. of Arts, Prints and Photographs. Courtesy The New York Public Library. Astor, Lenox and Tilden Foundations.)

ity treatment on an out-patient basis; the dispensary operated with branches in all the city's districts, and its caseload grew to 536 by 1795. Philadelphia and New York were nevertheless far ahead of other cities in providing institutionalized health care; even Boston would not open its first hospital until 1821.

Care for the insane still remained in its infancy. Those with severe mental or emotional disorders became the wards of public hospitals, sat in jails, or stayed in almshouses. Hospitals primarily acted as their custodians and saw their main duties as preventing acts of violence or escape with as much lenity as each case permitted. A major break with this tradition occurred on October 12, 1773, when the nation's earliest "insane asylum" opened as the Public Hospital under Dr. John de Sequeyra at Williamsburg, Virginia. The Public Hospital admitted only those deemed curable (except for a few deemed too dangerous to remain in society) and tried to restore the patients' emotional balance; it was the country's first step toward devising treatment more therapeutic and humane for the mentally disturbed.

The most systematic source of quantitative information about disease and the success rates of doctors in Revolutionary America was compiled at the Pennsylvania Hospital in Philadelphia. Aside from mental disorders, which afflicted almost one fifth of all patients in 1762–1763, half of the hospital's diagnoses concerned these seven disorders: scurvy (15%), fevers (9%), venereal disease (9%), dropsy (6%), flux (5%), eye disease (4%), and respiratory ailments (4%). Despite the limitations of eighteenth-century medical science, 59% of all admittees left the hospital cured and another 11% had their symptoms relieved, although 13% died under care. A significant need for medical attention evidently existed in early America's urban centers, for during the decade 1768–1777 approximately every sixth Philadelphian (4,175 people) sought treatment at the Pennsylvania Hospital, and 65% of these patients were handled as charity cases.

Epidemic diseases became an increasingly serious problem in the late eighteenth century. Rural New England, which had the country's highest population density, experienced many outbreaks of diphtheria, scarlet fever, measles, and whooping cough. These disorders increased adolescent mortality and on rare occasions struck hard at farming communities such as Oxford, Massachusetts, which lost about 10% of its inhabitants to diphtheria from 1766 to 1769. The middle-Atlantic countryside experienced relatively few epidemics, however, and the rural South was largely spared from them.

Urban centers fell prey to contagion most frequently because disease spread most rapidly among their concentrated populations. Smallpox infested most major cities about every decade, and unless

TABLE 6.5   DISEASES DIAGNOSED AT THE PENNSYLVANIA HOSPITAL, PHILADELPHIA, APR. 4, 1762–MAY 1, 1763

Diseases	Admitted	Cured	Symptoms Relieved	Died	Left Hospital Uncured[a]	Remain Under Care
Agues	6	5				1
Asthma	1		1			
Burn	1	1				
Consumption	4			4		
Contusion	2	1				1
Cough	4	3	1			
Deafness	1	1				
Dislocation	1					1
Dropsy	17	10	1	3		3
Drunken madness	1	1				
Epilepsy	1					1
Eyes diseased	13	7	2			4
Fevers	21	11	3	3	1	3
Fistula	3			1		2
Flux	15	9		4		2
Fractures	4	2	1		1	
Guinea worm	1	1				
Jaundice	2					2
Imposthume	3	1		1		1
Inflammations	2	2				
Lues Venerea	25	20		1	1	3
Lunacy	52	6	7	7	7	23
Melancholy	3				1	2
Mortification	4	2			1	1
Palsy	10	3	3	1		3
Pleurisy	3	1		1		1
Rheumatism	10	8				2
Ruptures	2					2
Scirrous swellings	1	1				
Scrophulous ulcers	1					1
Scorbutic disorders	44	20	7	1	3	13
Smallpox	2	1		1		
Sprain	6	3	1		1	1
Stone	2				1	1
Vertigo	1	1				
Viscera obstructed	11	6	1	2	1	1
Ulcers, carious bones	3	1		1		1
Uterine disorders	3	3				
Wounds	6	4		1	1	
Totals	292	135	28	32	19	76

[a]Includes those taken out by friends and those who escaped or were discharged for irregularity.
Source: Samuel Hazard, et al., eds., *Pennsylvania Archives* (1852–1949), 8th Ser., VI, 5454–55.

TABLE 6.6   PATIENTS TREATED AT PENNSYLVANIA HOSPITAL, 1753–1802

Period	Whole Number Treated			Number Discharged			City Population
	Free	Pay	Total	Free	Pay	Total	
1798–1802	398	571	969	371	501	872	41,220
1793–1797	426	628	1,054	404	580	984	42,000
1788–1792	212	394	606	186	357	543	43,282
1783–1787	175	604	779	154	568	722	40,000
1778–1782	514	164	678	499	153	652	36,946
1773–1777	1,807	329	2,136	1,759	309	2,068	33,290
1768–1772	1,802	237	2,939	1,706	228	1,934	28,042
1763–1767	1,358	246	1,604	1,269	232	1,501	26,460
1758–1762	552	160	712	511	149	660	18,756
1753–1757	268	71	339	249	66	315	16,182

Sources: Thomas G. Morton and Frank Woodbury, *The History of the Pennsylvania Hospital, 1751–1895* (1895), 241. P. M. G. Harris, "The Demographic Development of Philadelphia in Some Comparative Perspective," *Proceedings of the American Philosophical Society* CXXXIII (1989), 274.

TABLE 6.7 NUMBER OF CURES AND DISCHARGES FOR PATIENTS ADMITTED TO PENNSYLVANIA HOSPITAL, 1753–1802

Period	Treated	Cured	Symptoms Relieved	Incurable	Died	Left Hospital Uncured[a]	Kept Under Care
1798–1802	969	552	120	2	143	55	97
1793–1797	1,054	577	172	4	151	80	70
1788–1792	906	253	120	13	74	83	63
1783–1787	779	326	135	10	90	161	57
1778–1782	678	328	113	5	108	98	26
1773–1777	2,136	1,361	186	24	314	186	68
1768–1772	2,039	1,350	138	8	241	197	105
1763–1767	1,604	1,099	107	13	181	101	103
1758–1762	712	426	62	9	75	88	52
1753–1757	339	204	32	18	41	20	24

[a]Includes those removed at request of themselves or others outside, those discharged for misconduct, or lunatics who escaped.
Source: Thomas G. Morton and Frank Woodbury, *The History of the Pennsylvania Hospital, 1751–1895* (1895), 242.

it was identified quickly, it was certain to take several hundred lives. Yellow fever, which had rarely appeared in the colonial era, suddenly became a major killer during the 1790s. In 1793, yellow fever, for which no medicinal cure has yet been found, carried off 10% to 15% of Philadelphia's population, or about 4,500 to 6,500 people. The disease struck Philadelphia three more times by 1799 and killed at least 3,500; it also afflicted New York, New Haven, New London, Baltimore, Norfolk, and Charleston.

Hoping to prevent recurrences of yellow fever, most port cites founded health boards between 1793 and 1810. These organizations also moved to protect water purity, improve sewage disposal, and drain pools of stagnant water that bred disease-carrying insects. Because health officials were unaware of how germs transmitted sickness, many of their improvements only reduced, rather than eliminated, the danger of infection by water or other sources.

TABLE 6.8 OUTBREAKS OF EPIDEMIC DISEASE IN REVOLUTIONARY AMERICA, 1763–1800

Year	Disease	Location
1763	Typhus	Nantucket, Mass. (222 Indians died)
1763	Smallpox	South Carolina
1763	Diphtheria	Philadelphia, Pa.
1764	Smallpox	Charleston, Mass.; Newport, R.I.
1764	Scarlet Fever	Philadelphia, Pa.
1764	Typhus	Talbot Co., Md.
1764–65	Smallpox	Ga., among the Creek, Chickasaw, and Choctaw
1765	Diphtheria	Boston, Mass.
1765–66	Whooping Cough	New England
1765	Smallpox	Annapolis, Md., and seven counties
1765–66	Smallpox	Philadelphia, Pa.
1766–69	Diphtheria	Mass.
1768	Smallpox	Reading, Pa. (60 children died)
1768	Smallpox	Southeast Va.
1769	Dysentery	Boston, Mass. (179 deaths)
1769	Scarlet Fever	Philadelphia
1769	Smallpox	Philadelphia, Pa.
1769	Diphtheria	New York, N.Y.
1770–71	Influenza	Philadelphia, Pa.
1771	Whooping Cough	New England; Philadelphia
1771	Scarlet Fever	Duxboro, Mass.
1772	Measles	Charles Town, S.C., to Philadelphia (hundreds dead)
1773	Typhus	Va.
1773	Smallpox	Philadelphia, Pa. (300 deaths)
1773	Scarlet Fever	New Haven and East Haven, Conn.; Salem, Mass.

Year	Disease	Location
1775	Smallpox	New England
1775	Diphtheria	New England, especially Middletown, Conn.
1778	Measles	New York, N.Y.; Philadelphia, Pa.
1781	Influenza	U.S.
1783	Measles	New England
1783	Scarlet Fever	Philadelphia, Pa.
1783–84	Scarlet Fever	New England; Charleston, S.C.
1785	Canine Rabies	Northern states
1787	Diphtheria	Northampton, Mass.
1789	Influenza	New England, N.Y., Philadelphia
1789	Scarlet Fever	West N.J.; Philadelphia, Pa.
1789	Canine Rabies	U.S.
1793	Yellow Fever	New York, N.Y. (525 deaths)
1793	Yellow Fever	Philadelphia, Pa. (4,500–6,500 deaths)
1793–94	Scarlet Fever	Northern states
1794	Yellow Fever	New Haven, Conn.
1795	Yellow Fever	Norfolk, Va. (220 deaths)
1795–96	Dysentery	Mass., N.Y.
1797	Yellow Fever	Philadelphia, Pa. (1,000 deaths); Baltimore (545 deaths); Providence, R.I.; Charles Town, S.C.
1798	Yellow Fever	Philadelphia, Pa. (3,521 deaths); New London, Conn. (81 deaths)
1799	Yellow Fever	Philadelphia, Pa.

Sources: John Duffy, *Epidemics in Colonial America* (1972), passim. Francis R. Packard, *History of Medicine in the United States* (1931), I, 95–158.

Americans benefited from a few significant improvements in health care during the Revolutionary era. Benjamin Franklin's invention of bifocal lenses greatly eased vision problems for older people. Through the efforts of Dr. Hall Jackson of Portsmouth, New Hampshire, in the 1780s, the usefulness of digitalis to treat dropsy (congestive heart failure) became known in America simultaneously with that drug's introduction in England, where it had been first recognized as strengthening the heart's muscles.

Mortality from smallpox inoculation also dropped significantly during the Revolution. American doctors adopted advanced English procedures that used a very small dose of virus taken from recently erupted pustules, which were far less virulent than older pus and less likely to develop into the full disease. Whereas during the early 1700s, it was usual for 2% or 3% of all persons inoculated to die, the death rate evidently declined to less than 1% after 1760. Dr. Hall Jackson inoculated more than 300 people at Marblehead, Massachusetts, in 1773 without losing a single patient. It was only with the development of vaccination by cowpox, a procedure developed by Edward Jenner of England in 1798, that smallpox could be prevented without undue risk. When Dr. Benjamin Waterhouse of Boston introduced vaccination to the United States in July 1800, he took the first step in the eventual eradication of this disease.

White Americans probably enjoyed a level of health care equal to that available to the average European. The general level of eighteenth-century medicine was nevertheless rather low, aside from a reasonably competent cadre of surgeons, and so most patients owed their recovery from disease to the immune system's restorative powers rather than to being cured by physicians. Rural Americans enjoyed good health, but largely because they were well nourished and dispersed in a manner that limited the risk of contagion.

Medical Aspects of the Revolutionary War

Dr. Benjamin Rush, a member of the Continental Army's Medical Department, expressed perfectly the major danger facing soldiers during the American Revolution. "Fatal experience has taught the people of America," Rush wrote, "that a greater proportion of men have perished with sickness in our armies than have fallen by the sword." Although no reliable count was ever made of total deaths during the War of Independence, the best estimate indicates that of the 25,700 American soldiers who died, 18,500 succumbed to disease (including 8,500 who fell sick while in prison camps). Germs killed twice as many troops as did British bullets.

In both the Continental and British armies, soldiers fell prey to the same basic disorders. Half of all American troops treated at army hospitals in 1781 and 1782 suffered from miscellaneous fevers (23%),

TABLE 6.10 **DIAGNOSES OF AMERICAN AND BRITISH SOLDIERS RECEIVING MEDICAL TREATMENT IN REVOLUTIONARY WAR**

	449 Diagnoses at U.S. General Hospital, Albany (1777)	3,248 Diagnoses in British 1st Regiment of Foot (1776–1783)
Dysentery	18.04%	18.93%
Intermittent Fever	17.59%	19.92%
Inflammatory Fever	. . .	10.13%
Diarrhea	13.59%	.89%
Cough	5.57%	.65%
Rheumatism	4.90%	3.48%
Convalescent	3.79%	. . .
Debility	3.79%	. . .
Lues Venerea	3.12%	3.57%
Fever	2.90%	. . .
Whooping Cough	2.23%	. . .
Head Itch	2.00%	. . .
Measles	1.78%	. . .
Putrid Fever	1.34%	. . .
Bilious Fever	.89%	. . .
Dropsy	.89%	.03%
Scorbutic (Scurvy)	.89%	3.20%
Pleurisy	.67%	.03%
Nephritis	.67%	.22%
Scrofula	.67%	.06%
Jaundice	.45%	.15%
Hernia	.45%	.45%
Hemoptysis	.45%	. . .
Palsy	.45%	.06%
Hemorrhoids	.22%	.49%
Asthma	.22%	.06%
Cholera	.22%	.58%
Hypochondria	.22%	. . .
Ophthalmia (sore eyes)	.22%	2.89%
Surgical Patients	11.80%	20.84%
Consumption	. . .	2.87%
Cutaneous Eruption	. . .	2.09%
Stomach Complaints	. . .	1.82%
Vertigo	. . .	1.17%
Sore Throat	. . .	1.14%
Erysipelas	. . .	.80%
Other	. . .	3.48%

Source: J. Worth Estes, *Hall Jackson and the Purple Foxglove: Medical Practice and Research in Revolutionary America, 1760–1820* (1979), 70–72.

TABLE 6.9 EFFECTIVENESS OF SMALLPOX INOCULATION IN BOSTON, 1764–1792

	1764	1776	1778	1792
City Population	15,500	. . .	. . .	19,300
Natural smallpox				
Cases	699	304	122	232
Deaths	124	29	40	69
Deaths per 1,000 cases	177	95	328	298
Inoculated smallpox				
Cases	4,977[a]	4,988[b]	2,121	9,152[c]
Deaths	46[d]	28[d]	19	179[d]
Deaths per 1,000 cases	9	6	9	20
Total smallpox				
(Boston residents only)				
Cases	5,276	4,063	2,243	8,346
Deaths	170	57	59	248
Deaths per 1,000 cases	32	14	26	30
Cases per 1,000 population	340	. . .	. . .	432
Deaths per 1,000 population	11	. . .	. . .	13
Percent of cases inoculated	87%	90%	95%	97%
Persons who left town	1,537	. . .	. . .	262
Escaped disease in town	519	. . .	. . .	221
Had smallpox before	8,200	. . .	. . .	10,300

[a]Including about 400 nonresidents inoculated in Boston.
[b]Including 1,329 nonresidents inoculated in Boston.
[c]Including 1,038 nonresidents inoculated in Boston.
[d]Additional deaths may have occurred among nonresidents.
Source: John B. Blake, *Public Health in the Town of Boston, 1630–1822* (1959), 244.

smallpox (18%), or diarrhea and dysentery (10%). These same disorders also afflicted half the patients treated in Britain's First Regiment of Infantry, but in different proportions (30% fevers, 0.4% smallpox, and 20% diarrhea or dysentery). Fewer than 4% of American soldiers were treated for wounds or accidents in 1781–1782, while 21% of the British First Regiment's casualties required surgery for that cause during the entire war.

The main threat to soldiers' health came from the transmission of germs through contaminated water, poor sewage disposal, insects, or overcrowded living conditions. Although the role of germs in spreading sickness was not then understood, all competent military physicians advocated practical measures that would have reduced the spread of disease. Army doctors urged that soldiers wash daily, clean their linen frequently, wear their hair short to inhibit lice infestation, change their straw bedding often, eat more vegetables, not be crowded into sleeping quarters, and be encamped away from marshy areas that bred mosquitos. Together with proper concern for water purity and waste disposal, these policies had great potential to restrain the spread of typhus, malaria, dysentery, cholera, typhoid, tuberculosis, pneumonia, and influenza.

It was nevertheless difficult to enforce elementary rules of hygiene and sanitation, even in army hospitals. During the winter of 1777–1778, doctors at Bethlehem, Pennsylvania, had no choice but to house 700 sick soldiers in quarters designed for 400. Lack of money and supplies resulted in such poor sanitation, that four or five men sometimes died on the same straw bedding before it was changed. At least half the troops treated at Bethlehem died that winter, and almost all the hospital's staff became dangerously ill.

Composed mostly of New Englanders with a high degree of immunity from the local disease environment, Washington's army experienced low rates of illness, generally below 13%, at the siege of Boston. After mid-1776, however, sickness among American troops usually ranged from 20% to 33% until September of 1778, and mortality was undoubtedly high. Increased attention to problems of hygiene and sanitation thereafter managed to cut in half the proportion of soldiers too sick for duty. From March 1779 through the war's end, the number of Continental soldiers too ill for duty rarely exceeded 11%, except in winter when the troops' diet was most deficient in vitamins. Had Washington and his medical staff not managed to instill high standards of sanitation and personal hygiene as part of military discipline, the Continental Army might have withered away from disease before independence could be secured.

Battle casualties often strained the Continental Army's medical facilities. In 1777, soldiers wounded at the Battle of Brandywine had to be evacuated to Ephrata, Pennsylvania. While there, they were nursed at the "Sisters' House" (pictured here) by women of the Dunker faith. (*Harper's Magazine,* October 1889)

TABLE 6.11   PERCENT OF CONTINENTAL ARMY RECORDED AS SICK, 1775–1783

1775		1779 (cont.)	
Jul.	11.0%	Jul.	9.4%
Aug.	17.1%	Aug.	8.7%
Sep.	14.8%	Sep.	9.8%
Oct.	12.8%	Oct.	10.0%
Nov.	12.2%	Nov.	9.4%
Dec.	10.6%	Dec	10.8%
1776		**1780**	
Jan.	12.3%	Jan.	11.1%
Feb.	14.8%	Feb.	11.0%
Mar.	16.1%	Mar.	9.7%
Apr.	12.2%	Apr.	10.2%
May	9.9%	May	9.7%
Jun.	9.7%	Jun.	9.8%
Jul.	16.6%	Jul.	8.3%
Aug.	25.3%	Aug.	9.6%
Sep.	31.9%	Sep.	8.9%
Oct.	30.3%	Oct.	8.2%
Nov.	27.0%	Nov.	9.7%
Dec.	31.9%	Dec.	9.5%
1777		**1781**	
Jan.	. . .	Jan.	10.4%
Feb.	. . .	Feb.	10.4%
Mar.	. . .	Mar.	10.6%
Apr.	21.7%	Apr.	14.9%
May	24.8%	May	8.3%
Jun.	21.6%	Jun.	5.4%
Jul.	21.6%	Jul.	6.6%
Aug.	21.0%	Aug.	. . .
Sep.	. . .	Sep.	16.2%
Oct.	17.7%	Oct.	14.3%
Nov.	26.3%	Nov.	. . .
Dec.	32.2%	Dec.	. . .
1778		**1782**	
Jan.	28.0%	Jan.	24.3%
Feb.	35.5%	Feb.	24.8%
Mar.	33.5%	Mar.	16.0%
Apr.	28.0%	Apr.	11.9%
May	27.1%	May	12.1%
Jun.	27.3%	Jun.	11.8%
Jul.	21.6%	Jul.	11.9%
Aug.	20.4%	Aug.	12.2%
Sep.	20.6%	Sep.	11.9%
Oct.	17.5%	Oct.	11.2%
Nov.	16.0%	Nov.	10.6%
Dec.	16.8%	Dec.	10.6%
1779		**1783**	
Jan.	15.2%	Jan.	10.2%
Feb.	13.0%	Feb.	11.0%
Mar.	10.9%	Mar.	10.7%
Apr.	9.6%	Apr.	10.7%
May	9.2%	May	10.5%
Jun.	9.6%	Jun.	12.1%
		Jul.	11.0%

*Note: There are no figures for the rest of 1783 because the war had ended and the army disbanded.
Source: Charles H. Lessing, ed., *The Sinews of Independence: Monthly Strength Reports of the Continental Army* (1976), xxxi.

Life Expectancy and Mortality

Conclusions about life expectancy and mortality depend on a few studies for the Revolutionary era. In addition to having relatively little data about these subjects, very much of the information available is unreliable or unrepresentative of the population. Historians have long depended on mortality data from Massachusetts, which attempted to register deaths well before other states did, but the state's record-keeping efforts did not become reasonably complete until 1849. Early demographers attempted to adjust these sources for underregistration, but they probably overcompensated and estimated life expectancy at too low a level. A major reason why existing research may have significantly underestimated life expectancy is an overreliance on statistics from urban areas, whose inhabitants evidently died of contagious diseases at a higher rate than the rural population, which was more typical of society in general.

The primary difference between life expectancy in the eighteenth and twentieth centuries is that a far higher percentage of children died 200 years ago than today. It would seem that at least one of every eight babies died within a year, and that one of every five or six died before reaching maturity. The death rate was much higher in cities, where perhaps half of all children died before age twenty. Life expectancy at birth was consequently less than half its present level.

Individuals who attained adulthood nevertheless approached the lifespan of Americans in the 1980s. Males who reached their twenty-first year in eighteenth-century Lancaster County, Pennsylvania, could expect to survive to age sixty-one, while a white American in 1986 would probably live to age seventy-three. If that Pennsylvanian remained alive at sixty-one, he would most likely not die until age seventy-five, while a modern American who reaches sixty-one would outlive him by just a few years, to age seventy-eight.

Life expectancy among women has increased much more than among men in the previous two centuries. A twenty-one-year-old woman in Lancaster County, Pennsylvania, would probably live to fifty-seven in the eighteenth century, but a white woman aged twenty-one would likely survive to eighty now. A steep reduction in maternal mortality resulting from childbirth must account for such a dramatic change, but this explanation has yet to be documented. In one of the few studies on maternal death rates, only 0.5% of 998 pregnancies in Augusta, Maine, ended in the mother's death from 1777 to 1812. If this rate was typical for a society in which the average wife bore eight children, then about one of every twenty-five adult woman died giving birth. Mortality among women has declined to such a degree, that men have ceased to outlive them and now die six years younger than the typical woman.

Although it is certain that crude death rates have declined during the past two centuries, there is little evidence regarding how steeply they have fallen. The best studies of mortality in Revolutionary America concern urban populations, which enjoyed less health than the rural areas that were home to most people. In the late 1700s, annual death rates in Boston and Philadelphia ranged from 30 to 40 per 1,000, higher than the level that then prevailed in England and most of Europe. Mortality in Revolutionary America's farming communities may have been less than half or a third of that found in cities or contemporary Europe. If figures collected by New Jersey's government in 1772 were accurate, then deaths among that colony's whites equaled just 10 per 1,000, a figure equal to the death rate for the United States in 1956. Such comparisons suggest that mortality rates in the countryside during the 1700s may have approximated levels of the twentieth century.

TABLE 6.12 LIFE EXPECTANCY IN REVOLUTIONARY AMERICA

Year of Age	Lancaster Co., Pa. 1741–1770		Hampton, N.H. 1735–1792	Salem, Mass. 1781–1782	United States 1986	
	Male	Female	Both Sexes	Both Sexes	Male	Female
	Age at Death	Age at Death	Age at Death	Age at Death	Age at Death	Age at Death
0–1	37.2	35.2	20	19	72.0	78.8
6	55.1	51.5	30	39	72.9	79.6
11	55.0	54.1	54	43	72.9	79.6
21	61.1	57.2	60	47	73.5	79.9
31	64.7	61.6	68	53	74.2	80.2
41	67.5	66.6	72	63	74.0	80.6
51	71.3	70.9	75	70	76.2	81.3
61	75.6	75.4	78	76	79.2	83.6
71	80.7	79.8	82	80	82.7	86.1
81	87.0	86.7	89	86	87.9	89.8

Sources: Rodger C. Henderson, "Demographic Patterns and Family Structure in Eighteenth-Century Lancaster County, Pennsylvania," Pennsylvania Magazine of History and Biography CXIV (1990), 379–80. J. Worth Estes, Hall Jackson and the Purple Foxglove: Medical Practice and Research in Revolutionary America, 1760–1820 (1979), 126–27. Department of Commerce, Statistical Abstract of the United States, 1989 (1989), 73.

TABLE 6.13 CRUDE DEATH RATES AND INFANT MORTALITY IN REVOLUTIONARY AMERICA

	Annual Deaths per 1,000	Infant Mortality per 1,000[a]	Stillbirths per 1,000 Births[b]
Andover, Mass.			
1760–1764	13.5	. . .	. . .
1765–1769	5.6	. . .	. . .
1770–1774	3.8	. . .	. . .
Boston, Mass.			
1760–1764	32.2	. . .	. . .
1765–1769	32.8	. . .	. . .
1770–1774	34.2	. . .	. . .
Philadelphia, Pa.			
1760–1764	45.3	173	. . .
1765–1769	38.5	118	. . .
1770–1774	36.3	109	. . .
1780–1800	. . .	187	. . .
N.J., 1772			
All Whites	10.1	. . .	. . .
All Blacks	15.7	. . .	. . .
Salem Co.	16.8	. . .	. . .
Sussex Co.	6.9	. . .	. . .
Portsmouth, N.H., 1775–1794	. . .	. . .	24
Bradford, Vt., 1768–1819	. . .	. . .	29
Augusta, Me., 1785–1812	. . .	. . .	18
England-Wales 1760–1800	27.3	129	. . .
United States, 1986			
Whites	8.5	8.9	0.1
Blacks	9.0	18.0	0.3

[a] Deaths to age one.
[b] Includes fetal deaths of 20 weeks gestation.
Sources: Billy G. Smith, "Death and Life in a Colonial Immigrant City: A Demographic Analysis of Philadelphia," Journal of Economic History XXXVII (1977), 879, 888. Susan E. Klepp, "Fragmented Knowledge: Questions in Regional Demographic History," Proceedings of the American Philosophical Society CXXXII (1989), 230. Peter O. Wacker, Land and People, A Cultural Geography of Preindustrial New Jersey (1975), 161. Laurel Thatcher Ulrich, " 'The Living Mother of a Living Child': Midwifery and Mortality in Post-Revolutionary New England," William and Mary Quarterly XLVI (1989), 33. E. A. Wrigley and R. S. Schofield, The Population History of England, 1541–1871 (1981), 249, 534. Department of Commerce, Statistical Abstract of the United States, 1989 (1989), 74, 76.

Medical Education

During the colonial period, aspiring physicians attained professional competence either through apprenticeship to a doctor or by enrolling at European universities. Of an estimated 3,500 practitioners about 1775, no more than 400 had attended medical school, and many—if not most—of that minority had not earned the M.D. degree. Because most Americans who studied abroad went to the University of Edinburgh, a college lectureship program emerged as the model for medical education in the thirteen colonies, rather than the English system of training doctors at schools attached to the wards of major hospitals. The primary incentive for founding medical schools in America was to cultivate an elite minority of learned doctors capable of raising the profession's standards by their example. Medical schools were consequently intended to augment rather than replace training by apprenticeship, and classroom training did not become the expected background for physicians until the late nineteenth century.

TABLE 6.14 MEDICAL DEGREES EARNED BY RESIDENTS OF THIRTEEN COLONIES OR UNITED STATES AT EDINBURGH UNIVERSITY OR IN UNITED STATES, 1740–1800

	Edinburgh University	Colleges in United States	
	Doctor of Medicine	Bachelor of Medicine[a]	Doctor of Medicine[a]
1791–1800	42	36	113
1781–1790	23	69	6
1771–1780	22	23	7
1761–1770	25	21	1
1740–1760	6	. . .	. . .
Totals	118	149	127

[a] Honorary and Ad Eundum degrees not included.
Source: J. Worth Estes, Hall Jackson and the Purple Foxglove: Medical Practice and Research in Revolutionary America, 1760–1820 (1979), 4. Frederick C. Waite, "Medical Degrees Conferred in the American Colonies and in the United States in the Eighteenth Century," Annals of Medical History, IX (1937), 317–318.

Dr. John Morgan, an Edinburgh graduate, and Dr. William Shippen organized the thirteen colonies' first medical school on May 3, 1765 at the College of Philadelphia (later the University of Pennsylvania). Three years later, King's College (later Columbia) established its own medical faculty in New York. On June 21, 1768, the College of Philadelphia awarded the first medical degrees given in America, ten Bachelors of Medicine, and in 1770, King's College conferred the country's first Doctor of Medicine degree on Robert Tucker.

TABLE 6.15   MEDICAL DEGREES AWARDED WITHIN UNITED STATES, 1768–1800

Institution	M.B.	Hon. M.B.[a]	Ad E. M.B.[b]	M.D.	Hon. M.D.[a]	Ad E. M.D.[b]	Total
University of Pennsylvania	96	. . .	. . .	102	. . .	1	199
Columbia	12	. . .	. . .	18	. . .	4	34
Rutgers	3	. . .	. . .	6	3	3	15
Harvard	29	1	. . .	1	16	4	51
Dartmouth	9	. . .	1	. . .	3	. . .	13
Yale	. . .	. . .	. . .	. . .	5	2	7
William and Mary	. . .	. . .	. . .	. . .	1	. . .	1
Washington College	. . .	. . .	. . .	. . .	1	. . .	1
Connecticut State Medical Society	. . .	. . .	. . .	. . .	10	4	14
Totals	149	1	1	127	39	18	335
Duplications[c]							23
Total Individuals							312

[a] Honorary degree.
[b] Ad Euendum degree, awarded to persons who had already earned the same degree from another medical faculty.
[c] Individuals receiving multiple degrees.
Source: Frederick C. Waite, "Medical Degrees Conferred in the American Colonies and in the United States in the Eighteenth Century," *Annals of Medical History* IX (1937), 317–18.

TABLE 6.16   REQUIREMENTS FOR MEDICAL DEGREES AT COLLEGE OF PHILADELPHIA, 1766

College of Philadelphia, Jul. 27, 1767.

For a Bachelor's Degree in Physic:
1. It is required that such students as have not taken a Degree in any College shall, before admission to a degree in Physic, satisfy the Trustees and Professors of the College concerning their knowledge in the Latin tongue, and in such branches of Mathematics, Natural and Experimental Philosophy as shall be judged requisite to a medical education.
2. Each student shall attend at least one course of lectures in Anatomy, Materia medica, Chemistry, the Theory and Practice of Physic, and one course of Clynical Lectures, and shall attend the Practice of the Pennsylvania Hospital for one year, and may then be admitted to a Public Examination for a Bachelor's Degree in Physic.
3. It is further required that each student previous to the Bachelor's Degree, shall have served a sufficient apprenticeship to some reputable Practitioner in Physic, and be able to make it appear that he has a general knowledge in Pharmacy.

For a Doctor's Degree in Physic:
It is required for this Degree that at least three years have intervened from the time of taking the Bachelor's Degree, and the Candidate be full twenty-four years of age, and that he shall write and defend a Thesis in the College.

Source: Francis R. Packard, *History of Medicine in the United States* (1931), 355–56.

Morgan and the earliest pioneers of medical education envisioned an intensive program of undergraduate training, culminating in a Bachelor of Medicine, after which the Doctor of Medicine would be earned by a written thesis. By the 1790s, however, both Columbia and the University of Pennsylvania had ceased awarding M.B.s and concentrated on training physicians through post-graduate lectures. Training for the M.D. comprised lectures in seven general areas:

1. anatomy and surgery;
2. theory and practice of medicine;
3. clinical medicine;
4. botany;
5. chemistry;
6. medical matters and pharmacy; and
7. natural and experimental philosophy.

At a major school like the University of Philadelphia, teaching these subjects required a faculty of six to eight members.

The Revolution seriously disrupted medical education in the United States, but the return of peace not only saw colleges reopen at Philadelphia and New York but also spurred interest in founding medical schools elsewhere. By 1800, additional medical departments had been established at Harvard (1783), Dartmouth (1796), and even in frontier Kentucky at Transylvania College (1799). Prior to that decade, the number of Americans earning M.D.s at Edinburgh had exceeded the number of doctors produced domestically by a wide margin, but after 1790s, far more American physicians earned doctorates in the United States than overseas. On August 8, 1797, Samuel L. Mitchell began editing the first regularly published American medical journal, the *Medical Repository.* By 1800, the United States had become self-sufficient in medical education.

CHAPTER 7 Religion

A major realignment of religious loyalties occurred during the late eighteenth century. Ever since the extended revival known as the Great Awakening of the 1740s, evangelical churches such as the Presbyterians, Baptists, and Methodists had gained members at the expense of larger groups such as the Anglicans and Congregationalists. This trend accelerated after 1763 as evangelical ministers mounted a sustained effort to win converts among the frontier's largely unchurched settlers. Presbyterians, Methodists, and Baptists held a near monopoly in organizing congregations in the very areas where the country's population was growing most rapidly, especially in the southern backcountry and the Ohio Valley. By 1800, Anglicans and Congregationalists no longer ranked as the nation's largest religious bodies, while Methodists, Baptists, and Presbyterians had emerged as America's "mainstream" Protestant denominations, a distinction they would retain for the next two centuries.

By winning political independence, the Revolution unleashed latent dissatisfaction against the subordination of many American churches to European hierarchies. After 1783, the Lutherans, Dutch Reformed, Methodists, and Anglicans began severing their foreign links and created their own structures for self-governance. Those denominations that failed to Americanize themselves (such as the Mennonites, Moravians, and various German-speaking sects), lapsed gradually into obscurity over the next century.

The Revolution greatly reduced the role of government in religious affairs. The Anglican establishment everywhere lost its former legal privileges, but Congregational churches continued to be state-supported in New England well into the nineteenth century. The Bill of Rights furthermore forbade the national government from promoting or interfering with the affairs of any denomination. Although many links remained between religion and state at both the local and national levels, when the Bill of Rights was ratified in 1791, the Revolution instituted changes that endowed the vast majority of Protestants with equal rights, and significantly enhanced the legal standing of Catholics and Jews.

By 1800, no religion enjoyed any special relationship with the national government and no church could claim the allegiance of more than a quarter of the population. Out of this situation, Americans fashioned a practical attitude to religious diversity now termed "denominationalism." Denominationalism rejected the concept that any single church deserved special status for monopolizing theological truth; it accorded equal respect to all faiths that worshiped sincerely and admonished belief in the scriptures. In conjunction with disestablishment, denominationalism created an environment in which the clergy did not appear either as a threat to individual rights or a privileged class, and consequently the American Revolution did not spawn a wave of anticlerical hysteria as resulted from the French Revolution. Denominationalism helped ameliorate tension between faiths and created a compelling argument that the United States could cohere only as a pluralistic society.

Denominational Affiliation

Statistical information on church membership remains extremely poor for the late eighteenth century. Aside from educated guesses, the only quantitative measure of relative size among denominations is a count of congregations organized by 1775. Using the broadest definition of a church—any religious organization that regularly met for worship—the country then contained approximately 3,228 congregations, although they included many small groups without a church that gathered in private homes or chapels serving distant parts of extensive parishes. Since more than one third of all churches were Congregational or Anglican, it seems probable that these two faiths composed about 45% of the population, but estimates of actual membership are highly conjectural.

No similar survey of churches yet exists for the United States in 1800. All indications nevertheless indicate that Methodists and Baptists both experienced extraordinarily high rates of growth, and that Presbyterians also made large numbers of converts. These three groups had certainly emerged as the leading denominations by 1800, and may have comprised a majority of all whites. The Evangelicals' success came at the expense of the Congregationalists, who lost great numbers to the Baptists in New England, and of the Anglicans,

TABLE 7.1 ESTIMATED CHURCH MEMBERSHIP IN UNITED STATES, 1775

Religious Preference	Number[a]	Percent of Population[a]	Number of Churches	Persons per Church
Congregationalists	575,000	24.0%	668	861
Anglicans	500,000	20.8%	495	1,266
Presbyterians	410,000	17.1%	588	697
Dutch Reformed	75,000	3.1%	120	625
Lutherans	75,000	3.1%	150	500
German Reformed	50,000	2.1%	159	314
Miscellaneous German Churches	75,000	3.1%	71	1,056
Friends	40,000	1.7%	310	129
Baptists	25,000	1.0%	494	51
Catholics	25,000	1.0%	56	446
Methodists	5,000	.2%	65	77
Jews	2,000	.1%	5	400
Unchurched slaves	543,000	22.6%	. . .	. . .

[a] Includes persons unattached to a specific congregation.
Sources: Richard B. Morris, ed., *Encyclopedia of American History* (rev. ed., 1961), 582. Research of Marcus W. Jernegan in Charles O. Paullin, *Atlas of the Historical Geography of the United States* (1932), 50.

whose pro-British clergy largely abandoned their parishioners during the Revolution. Most minor denominations experienced moderate growth, but Roman Catholics may have doubled by 1800 due to a greater supply of priests and an upsurge in Irish immigration.

Religious affiliation varied significantly by region. New England included 98% of all Congregational churches but only 10% of Presbyterian churches and just 2% of Methodist organizations. The South contained more than half of congregations that were Anglican, Methodist, or Baptist. The mid-Atlantic states held more than half of all churches that were Presbyterian, the vast majority of those that were Lutheran or German Reformed, and virtually every one that was Dutch Reformed. These patterns continued to characterize the geographical distribution of religions in the nineteenth century.

TABLE 7.2 DISTRIBUTION OF CHURCHES IN NEW ENGLAND, 1776

Denomination	Me.	N.H.	Vt.	Mass.	Conn.	R.I.
Congregational	26	78	13	310	222	9
Separatist-Congregational	...	1	1	7	14	1
Presbyterian	11	27	2	7	4	1
Episcopal	6	2	2	17	46	5
Baptist	3	13	2	51	25	26
Methodist	...	...	...	1	...	...
Friends	4	4	...	31	4	11
Sandemanian	...	...	...	1	4	1
Rogerene	...	...	...	...	2	...
Lutheran	1	...	...	...	...	...
Jewish	...	...	...	...	...	1
Total	51	125	20	425	321	55

Sources: Lester J. Cappon, *Atlas of Early American History: The Revolutionary Era, 1760–1790* (1976), 36–37. Bruce E. Steiner, "Anglican Officeholding in Pre-Revolutionary Connecticut: The Parameters of New England Community," *William and Mary Quarterly* XXXI (1974), 396, n. 52.

TABLE 7.3 DISTRIBUTION OF CHURCHES IN MID-ATLANTIC STATES, 1776

Denomination	N.Y.	Pa.	N.J.	Del.
Congregational	6	2	2	...
Presbyterian	46	112	78	26
Episcopal	29	24	29	15
Baptist	16	24	28	3
Methodist	9	7	9	3
Friends	28	64	41	17
German Reformed	8	126	8	...
Lutheran	17	142	18	1
Moravian	5	13	2	...
German Baptist Brethren	...	22	1	...
Mennonite	...	64	...	...
Dutch Reformed	84	3	26	1
French Reformed	3	...	...	...
Rogerene	...	...	1	...
Sandemanian	...	...	...	...
Catholic	1	11	3	5
Jewish	1	2	...	...
Total	253	616	246	71

Source: Lester J. Cappon, *Atlas of Early American History: The Revolutionary Era, 1760–1790* (1976), 37–39.

Disestablishment of State Religions

The Revolution dealt a mortal wound to legally established churches in the ten states where they existed. When the war began, the great majority of Anglican clerics strongly supported Britain, and most eventually left the United States. This Tory heritage so alienated public opinion that Anglicanism lost its entitlement to tithes from taxpayers and its exclusive standing as the officially recognized church in every southern state and New York. Unlike the Anglicans, Congregational ministers had lent such strong support to the Revolutionary movement that they earned the nickname of America's black regiment. Its reputation for patriotism enabled the Congregational establishment to survive in New England, and not until after 1815 were its legal privileges repealed.

TABLE 7.4 DISTRIBUTION OF CHURCHES IN THE SOUTH, 1776

Denomination	Md.	Va.	N.C.	S.C.	Ga.
Congregational	...	...	...	3	1
Presbyterian	29	95	46	45	3
Episcopal	51	94	23	37	3
Baptist	5	101	71	40	7
Methodist	21	10	2	...	...
Friends	26	42	30	7	3
German Reformed	16	14	12	4	...
Lutheran	16	17	3	9	5
Moravian	2	...	5	...	...
German Baptist Brethren	5	2	...	...	...
Mennonite	1	2	...	...	...
Dutch Reformed	2	...	...	...	...
French Reformed	...	...	...	2	...
Catholic	30	...	...	...	...
Jewish	...	...	...	1	1
Total	204	377	192	148	23

Source: Lester J. Cappon, *Atlas of Early American History: The Revolutionary Era, 1760–1790* (1976), 37–39.

The Constitution furthered the cause of disestablishment once the Bill of Rights was adopted in 1791. The First Amendment specifically enjoined Congress from either establishing a national religion or interfering with freedom of worship. Because states regulated elections under the Constitution, their legislatures could require congressional or senatorial candidates to worship in certain denominations. The Sixth Amendment ended this possibility by forbidding any religious tests for federal officials.

Although majority opinion soon came to favor disestablishment, no consensus emerged in favor of separating church and state, or of eliminating all distinctions among religions. When Virginia's government cut its ties with Anglicanism, its legislature almost adopted Patrick Henry's "Bill Establishing a Provision for Teachers of the Christian Religion," which would have required all taxpayers to pay tithes that would be divided among all their counties' Christian ministers. South Carolina's constitution of 1778 placed Anglicanism on

TABLE 7.5 DISESTABLISHMENT OF STATE RELIGIONS IN UNITED STATES, 1776–1833

Anglican Disestablishment		Congregational Disestablishment	
Date	State	Date	State
1776	Va.[a]	1818	Conn.
1776	Md.	1819	N.H.
1777	N.Y.	1820	Maine
1777	N.C.	1833	Mass.
1777	Ga.[b]		
1778	S.C.[c]		

[a] Supplemented by Jefferson's Act for Establishing Religious Freedom (1785) and legislation selling glebe lands (1801).
[b] Supplemented by legislation in 1789.
[c] Supplemented by legislation in 1790.
Note: There were no established churches in R.I., N.J., Pa., and Del.
Source: Richard B. Morris, ed., *Encyclopedia of American History* (rev. ed., 1961), 582, 584.

The disestablishment of state-sponsored churches was Revolutionary America's seminal religious event. This impulse to minimize any connections between church and state expressed itself in the American "meeting house," in which exterior design provided few hints of the building's religious function. St. Anne's Protestant Episcopal Church, at Middletown, Delaware, exemplifies that tradition by emphasizing Georgian symmetry and abandoning traditional religious motifs such as bell towers and sharply angled lines directed toward the sky. The cemetery provides the sole hint of St. Anne's religious function. (Compare with photos on pages 110 and 200.) (Courtesy National Images of North American Living, Research and Archival Center, Washington)

an equal level with all other faiths, but it also declared Protestantism to be the state's official religion. Although the states moved to grant full political rights to all Protestants, Catholics were excluded from public office in Georgia, South Carolina, New Jersey, Massachusetts, and New Hampshire during the 1770s and 1780s. Every state but Rhode Island required officeholders to swear religious oaths, and in 1790 Pennsylvania specifically excluded atheists from office.

In general, however, a greater degree of religious freedom existed within the United States than in any other country when the eighteenth century ended. Nowhere else did such a wide array of Protestant denominations coexist in a spirit of mutual toleration. Catholics might be excluded from public office in a few states, but they enjoyed greater political privileges under the Constitution than were accorded them in any other Protestant country. Although proponents of unpopular groups such as Deists or Unitarians might have difficulty winning acceptance for their views, they could publicize their ideas free of censorship. Most important, opinion was rapidly shifting toward the position enunciated by Thomas Jefferson in his Act for Establishing Religious Freedom (1786): "that all men shall

be free to profess, and by argument to maintain, their opinion in matters of religion, and that the same shall in no wise diminish, enlarge, or affect their civil capacities."

New Religions

Several new denominations took root in the United States during the latter eighteenth century. Immigration carried Sandemanians, Shakers, and Universalists to American soil. Dissension within the Methodists, produced two new churches, the Republican Methodists, who objected to the manner of appointing ministers, and the embryo of the African Methodist Episcopal church, whose members refused to stay in segregated seating arrangements during prayer. Arising from spiritual impulses nurtured on American soil were the River Brethren, the Evangelical church, and the United Brethren in Christ. Through their diverse origins, these new faiths illustrated how American religious life has long been enriched by charismatic leaders from overseas, by an independent, questioning spirit among American laymen, and by a readiness to promote spiritual renewal by founding new churches.

African Methodist Episcopal Church

During the Revolutionary era, it became increasingly common for black Christians to worship in white congregations. Many blacks felt attracted to Methodist theology and services. After the Methodist church condemned slavery in 1784 and admonished its members to set their slaves free within a year, African Americans had even more reason to see this denomination as a sympathetic body where they would be welcome.

Not all Methodist congregations accepted blacks on equal terms, however. One such institution was St. George's Church in Philadelphia, which included a substantial black membership. The most notable black parishioner was Richard Allen, a former slave from Delaware who had bought his own freedom. Allen held separate prayer meetings and preached to other African Americans at St. George's after he moved to Philadelphia in 1786. In response to the increasing black membership at St. George's, white congregants decided to hold segregated services. When Allen and two other black worshippers defied the hierarchy by attempting to pray with whites, ushers dragged them from their knees back to their assigned area.

Richard Allen and his followers left St. George's and organized the Free African Society. In 1793 he founded Bethel Church and received ordination as Methodism's first black deacon. He also encouraged free blacks in Baltimore, Wilmington, and Salem to form independent congregations within the Methodist fellowship. The Bethel Church became the nucleus of the African Methodist Episcopal church, which held its first general conference in 1816 and elected Richard Allen as bishop.

Evangelical United Brethren

The United Evangelical Brethren originated in two separate groups, the United Brethren in Christ and the Evangelical church, which began evolving in the 1790s. The United Brethren appeared first under the leadership of Philip W. Otterbein and Martin Boehm. Although Otterbein was a German Reformed minister and Boehm was a Mennonite preacher, they conducted joint revivals among the German-speaking population of Pennsylvania, Maryland, and Vir-

New York City's Methodist church on John Street, as depicted by Joseph Smith in 1817, was that denomination's first church in America. Completed in 1768, the John Street Church was constructed just twenty-nine years after John Wesley opened Bristol's New Room, England's earliest Methodist house of worship, which still stands. The John Street Church was demolished in 1817. (I. N. Phelps Stokes Collection, Miriam & Ira Wallach Div. of Arts, Prints and Photographs. Courtesy The New York Public Library. Astor, Lenox and Tilden Foundations.)

ginia. By 1800, Otterbein and Boehm had created an organizational structure under themselves, but not until after 1810 did their successors adopt a formal creed and statement of discipline.

Jacob Albright founded the Evangelical church in 1800 in Lancaster County, Pennsylvania. Although raised a Lutheran, Albright gravitated toward Methodism and modeled his organization closely upon that faith. Within three years of being established, the denomination consisted of sixteen congregations.

The United Brethren and Evangelical church arose from similar roots and developed along parallel lines. They proselytized among the diaspora of German-speaking settlers extending from Pennsylvania to the Ohio Valley. They appealed to individuals drawn to a more introspective, even mystical, religious experience than the more traditional churches encouraged. Both sought to expand by winning converts among the unchurched settlers of the West; they grew so quickly from their modest origins, that within seven decades of their founding they had spawned over 2,200 congregations. The two denominations merged in 1946 under their present name.

Methodist Episcopal Church

Methodism originated as a revival movement within the Church of England during the mid-eighteenth century. Its leading spirit, John Wesley, briefly ministered (as an Anglican cleric) in the thirteen colonies during the 1730s, but no Methodist societies existed in America before the Revolutionary period. Until 1784, American Methodists considered themselves part of the Anglican fold and received the sacraments from its clerics. Their most meaningful religious activities nevertheless occurred at revivals and prayer meetings led by themselves rather than priests.

Because few Anglican priests sympathized with Methodism, laymen had to spread its message. It was a layman who founded the John Street Church, the sect's first in America, at New York City, in 1766 (the building was not consecrated until October 30, 1768), and that same year another layman introduced Methodism into Maryland. By July 14, 1773, when the first yearly conference of American Methodists was held at Philadelphia, membership was estimated at 1,160. John Wesley began dispatching lay preachers from England in 1769 to augment the American evangelists, and by 1776 twenty-four Methodist preachers energetically rode itinerant circuits. The South proved especially receptive to their preaching, and by 1784 that region included about 80% of all members, mostly in Virginia and Maryland.

The Revolution left Methodists forsaken by both the Anglican clergy and their own English lay preachers, both of whom abandoned the United States for Britain. This situation forced Methodists to decide whether to remain within the Anglican fellowship or found an autonomous church with a clergy to administer the sacraments. By 1784, American leaders and John Wesley recognized that the United States required an independent episcopal establishment to ordain ministers for those whom Wesley termed "the desolate sheep in America." In that year, Wesley's emissaries ordained Francis Asbury as first bishop of the Methodist Episcopal church. The denomination affirmed its close ties with British Methodism by adopting Wesley's twenty-four articles of faith as its creed and his "Sunday Service" for worship.

No other church expanded as rapidly as did the Methodists. Numbering just 2,073 in 1774, they increased to 8,504 by 1780, despite having lost many English lay preachers as refugees, and by 1792 they totaled 65,980. On December 6, 1787, Methodists founded their first center of higher learning, Cokesbury College, in Abingdon, Maryland. Methodists were always among the first itinerants to preach among unchurched western pioneers, and they were consequently poised to add members quickly as large numbers of easterners moved to the frontier. This exceptionally rapid growth rate continued during the early nineteenth century, when Methodist membership doubled every decade.

Republican Methodist Church

Methodism experienced its first major schism when James O'Kelly challenged the authority of Francis Asbury, the denomination's first bishop. O'Kelly had been a circuit rider in southern Virginia since emigrating from Ireland in 1778. By 1789 he had concluded that the presiding bishop was accumulating unwarranted power at the expense of the General Conference of clergy. The first issue on which he opposed episcopal authority concerned the appointment of ministers to circuits. O'Kelly introduced a resolution at the 1792 General Conference in Baltimore that would have allowed any rider an appeal to the General Conference if he objected to his assigned circuit, and then would have required the bishop to give him another posting if that appeal was upheld.

After a week's debate, O'Kelly's proposition lost by a wide margin. O'Kelly and many followers then withdrew from the Methodist Episcopal church and formed the Republican Methodists. Bishop Asbury's efforts to reverse the schism failed, and the Methodists lost about 9,000 members to the dissenting body over the next six years. The Republican Methodists were most numerous near O'Kelly's circuit, in southern Virginia and North Carolina. Within a few years of the schism, however, the number of converts to the church dropped sharply, and by the time O'Kelly died in 1826, his following had shrunk into relative obscurity. The Republican Methodists nevertheless continued as an independent denomination until 1934, when they reunited with the Methodist Episcopal church.

River Brethren

The River Brethren originated during a period of pietistic revivals in Lancaster County Pennsylvania, held in the 1770s among that area's Mennonite population. A minority of Mennonites increasingly felt that their church had grown too formalistic and gave insufficient spiritual guidance on personal salvation. Such individuals began attending revivals held by visiting preachers and found their emphasis on spiritual rebirth more meaningful than the guidance offered by settled Mennonite ministers; they also came to believe that their church erred in not performing baptism by immersion. The dissenters nevertheless did not feel entirely comfortable about joining any of the pietistic German sects because they did not wish to break completely with their Mennonite upbringing.

In 1778, Jacob Engel and other leaders proposed to solve this dilemma by establishing an independent consociation called "The Brethren" that combined pietistic and Mennonite practices. To distinguish Engel's followers from groups with similar titles, such as the United Brethren in Christ, local residents started calling them the Brethren by the River, or River Brethren, because of their concentration along the Susquehanna River. This name continued in use until the Civil War, when the group redesignated itself as the Brethren in Christ. The Brethren remained a minor denomination that was highly concentrated in Pennsylvania, although a large group migrated to Canada in 1788 and became numerous in Ontario province.

Sandemanians

Robert Sandeman was a Scottish cleric influenced by his father-in-law, John Glas. Glas formed several independent congregations in the 1730s after advocating complete independence of church from state. Glas wished to restore Christian practices as they had existed in the early church, and he advocated weekly communion, baptism by immersion, and full autonomy for every congregation. Sandeman authored several pamphlets that circulated in the thirteen colonies, and he emigrated to New England in 1764 after receiving encouragement that Americans were receptive to his ideas.

Sandemanian theology nevertheless proved far more controversial than popular. Sandeman belittled revivalists for trying to effect salvation through emotional experiences by arguing that only the intellectual act of accepting Christianity's truths merited saving grace; he also argued that such belief was only possible for those whom God had predestined for heaven. His ideas on absolute congregational independence, rule by church elders, infant baptism, and a weekly communion modeled exactly upon the Last Supper also drew rebuke from orthodox ministers.

Sandeman died at Danbury, Connecticut, only seven years after arriving in the colonies. By 1776, his followers had founded six congregations in Connecticut, New Hampshire, and Massachusetts. Sandemanians became highly unpopular during the Revolution because their beliefs prevented them from supporting war. Tainted with Toryism and frequently harassed for their pacifism, the group lost many members during the Revolution and completely vanished during the nineteenth century.

Shakers

The United Society of Believers in Christ's Second Coming, or Shakers, developed from an eighteenth-century English sect termed the "Shaking Quakers," because their worship included vigorous and emotional dancing. They believed that Christ's second coming would be as a woman and that the millennium would arrive after humanity had been gathered in Shaker communities. They insisted that the root of all sin had been sexual relations and that their followers practice absolute celibacy.

The charismatic Mother Ann Lee landed at New York City on August 6, 1774 with seven followers. They settled near Albany in 1776 but made very few converts over the next three years. In 1779, they started to acquire believers by evangelizing people who had been "born again" at revivals, and they were especially successful in winning over Freewill Baptists. By the time Ann Lee died in 1784, the church was adding members rapidly, and by 1794 it had organized twelve self-supporting communities in New York and New England.

After American-born Joseph Meacham became the sect's leader in 1787, Shakers perfected a highly efficient communal organization, complete with separate lines of authority for men and women. All work and responsibilities were minutely scheduled to avoid wasted effort. Regularity prevailed and life was simple, but members never lacked abundant food or comfortable clothing. All property was owned in common. Aside from separate male and female dormitories, both sexes worked, ate, and prayed together. By 1800, the church had grown from eight souls in 1774 to several hundred and it was poised to begin building communities in the West.

Universalism

Although a few pietistic sects and some liberal Congregational ministers espoused Universalist beliefs during the colonial period, no formal church structure existed until John Murray immigrated to America and began preaching this theology in 1770. Murray was an Englishman who had been excommunicated from Methodism for asserting that Christ's death atoned for the sins of all humanity, not merely an elect chosen personally by God. Murray combined John Wesley's promise of "grace to all" with the argument that eternal punishment for sin was inconsistent with a benevolent God's nature. His belief in salvation for all nevertheless denied Calvinist assumptions on predestination and guilt incurred for sin.

Murray conducted an itinerant ministry from 1770 to 1779, when he founded the first Universalist congregation at Gloucester, Massachusetts. As Universalists increased in numbers, they engaged in an extended controversy over the soul's status after death. "Restorationists" argued that all individual sins required atonement by punishment after death, while "Ultra-Universalists" insisted that Christ's death and God's benevolence had already prepared the soul for divine reconciliation when life ended. The church finally affirmed the Restorationist position as its dogma at a convention in 1803.

Universalists often attracted many followers in frontier areas. They also converted numerous New Englanders dissatisfied with the Congregational establishment. By opposing predestination with universal salvation, the church appealed to the Revolutionary era's concern with equality, while its deemphasis on spiritual depravity resonated well with Enlightenment attitudes regarding human perfectablity. Universalism never developed into a major church, although it actively proselytized for converts, and it remained largely limited to New England and the upper midwestern states.

Survey of Major Denominations

As would be expected in a pluralistic society, the experiences of religious denominations varied considerably in the late 1700s. In general, however, the religious bodies can be distinguished from one another by their ability to attract new members or stem losses from their own ranks. Least successful in this regard were the Anglicans, whose members defected in tens of thousands, and the Congregationalists, who barely held their own against the inroads of evangelicals. Quakers, Lutherans, and the continental European Reformed churches lacked appeal to outsiders, but they grew modestly as their families raised children. Most successful in winning converts were Baptists and Presbyterians, who increased more rapidly than any denomination except the Methodists (see previous section). A portent of the future also could be seen in the above-average growth for Catholicism, whose numbers doubled from 1785 to 1800, and Judaism, which added two new congregations and built two new synagogues from 1780 to 1800.

Baptists

The Baptist church had grown slowly through most of the colonial period. After the Great Awakening of the 1740s, the denomination's use of revivalistic techniques and lay preachers attracted many who viewed Anglican and Congregational worship as too formalistic and spiritually dry. Although the number of Baptists may have tripled in the three decades after 1740, on the eve of independence all

This photograph of Virginia's Mill Creek Meeting House shows the stark interior where its Baptist congregation held services. The spare furnishings reflect not poverty, but a conviction that Calvinist simplicity best fostered soul-searching spirituality. The atmosphere within this meeting house, with its splintered wood rafters and raw beams, contrasts sharply with the ornate columns and airy lightness found in the interior of Philadelphia's Christ Church and the decor of York, Pennsylvania's Lutheran Church (see photos on page 207 and 206). (Howard Wickliffe Rose Papers, courtesy Manuscripts and Archives, Yale University Library)

people in Baptist families may have totaled just 25,000, about the size of the colonies' tiny Roman Catholic population.

While yet in its infancy, the Baptist church established the seventh oldest college in the thirteen colonies. The Philadelphia Association envisioned this project in 1763, but positioned it in Rhode Island, whose government showed the least inclination to meddle in religious matters. Chartered in 1764, the College of Rhode Island graduated its first class five years later. In 1804 it took the name Brown University to honor patron Nicholas Brown.

It was during the period 1775–1790, when their members more than doubled, that Baptists began emerging as one of the country's largest religions. In the 1770s alone, sixty-seven new Baptist churches appeared in Virginia. By 1790, 266 Baptist churches existed in New England, compared to just twenty-five a half-century earlier. The church not only grew rapidly in the South and on the frontier,

but also made numerous converts in the settled areas of the East. In 1791, the denomination included 564 clergy, 748 churches, and 60,970 laymen. By 1800, the number of Baptists exceeded 100,000, and over the next thirty years they increased at the rate of 66% per decade.

Catholicism

During the years preceding 1776, anti-Catholic sentiment increased because of fears that a conspiracy existed to restore Catholicism in all of Anglo-America, as had been done in Canada by the Quebec Act of 1774. Although several Catholics served in high office during the Revolution, including one signer of the Declaration of Independence, Protestant suspicion of Catholicism survived the war, although in muted form. Catholics could vote everywhere, and faced no disabilities under the Constitution, but they remained ineligible for public office in several states.

The end of British rule opened the way for a bishopric in the United States, but the Vatican initially hesitated and instead appointed Rev. John Carroll, a Jesuit priest from Maryland, as Superior of Missions for the country in 1784. Apprehensive that a French diocese would be given jurisdiction over the United States, American priests pressed the pope to appoint a bishop chosen by themselves. Rome soon acquiesced, and in 1790 the clergy voted for the ordination of Reverend Carroll, whose see was located at Baltimore but included all territory east of the Mississippi.

Writing to Rome in 1785, Reverend Carroll had estimated that the United States contained about 25,000 practicing Catholics, including 15,800 in Maryland, 7,000 in Pennsylvania, 1,500 in New York, and 200 in Virginia. Carroll had only about thirty priests, mostly Jesuits like himself, to care for the laity, or one per 800 parishioners. To alleviate the shortage of clergy, Carroll founded St. Mary's seminary at Baltimore in 1791 by offering asylum to the Society of Saint Sulpice from the anticlericalism of the French Revolution on the condition that they provide the faculty. That same year, Carroll established the first American Catholic college, a Jesuit venture, at Georgetown, Maryland. Under Carroll's direction, the church made steady progress in expanding its clergy and laity, and by 1800 its membership seems to have exceeded 50,000, twice the number of parishioners in 1785.

Congregationalism

Of all major denominations, Congregationalism was changed the least by the struggle with Britain. Its ministers, both liberal and conservative, defended American rights so unanimously, that they stood out as the most prominent of all the patriot clergy whom Britain's defenders termed the "black regiment." Its laymen likewise endorsed Toryism to a far less degree than did any other religious body. Congregationalism consequently emerged from the War of Independence with enhanced public esteem.

This newfound prestige was critical in enabling Congregationalism to keep its status as an established church throughout New England (except in Rhode Island, where it had never been state-supported). New England's failure to end Congregationalism's privileged status nevertheless sparked discontent. This unrest led Connecticut to pass a Toleration Act in 1784 that lessened the establishment's ability to harass sectarians. The high court of Massachusetts also issued several decisions between 1785 and 1800 that enlarged the ability of dissenters to escape paying Congregational tithes. Such actions weakened the strictures of establishment, but, by making it less burdensome and offensive, these compromises quieted many critics and helped Congregationalism endure as a state-church until the nineteenth century.

Congregational membership increased far less than that of the Baptists, Methodists, and Presbyterians. In part, its slow growth resulted from the aggressiveness of Baptists and Methodists in evangelizing people dissatisfied with New England's established religion. Congregationalism furthermore was backward in meeting the spiritual needs of the West's unchurched pioneers. The church expanded little farther than upstate New York before 1800, and even there its clergy frequently arrived well after evangelical circuit riders had already converted much of the population as Baptists, Methodists, or Presbyterians. This reluctance to follow their flock as they moved west eventually resulted in Congregationalism's slow decline relative to competing faiths, and it would leave the denomination a narrowly regional church concentrated in New England and the upper midwest during the nineteenth century.

Dutch Reformed

By the mid-eighteenth century, tensions frayed the harmony between the colonial Dutch Reformed church and the Amsterdam Classis (central governing body) of its mother church in the Netherlands. Most of its churches in New York and New Jersey wanted the Classis to empower American clerics to settle intra-congregational disputes without having to appeal for decisions on such matters to Amsterdam. The colonists also wish to examine and ordain their own clergy, rather than having to accept ministers appointed for them by the Classis. Although a large majority of colonial churchmen favored this program for more local autonomy, the Amsterdam Classis had resisted surrendering any of its power since this controversy had emerged in the 1720s.

After mid-century, an increasing shortage of Dutch Reformed clergy for colonial churches led to demands that a seminary be established in America to assure an adequate supply of ministers. The Amsterdam Classis finally relented its opposition and permitted the colonists to proceed, providing they bore all expenses. In 1766, the Dutch Reformed church obtained a charter from New Jersey to found Queen's College (later Rutgers) at New Brunswick, which awarded its first theological degrees in 1774.

In 1771, the Amsterdam Classis allowed its colonial clerics to organize a governing board authorized to license ministers from Queen's College and to take jurisdiction over local disputes without having to appeal overseas. The American congregations still professed a spiritual communion with the Reformed Church of the Netherlands, and acknowledged the Amsterdam Classis to have a higher authority and prestige. During the years 1792–1794, a fully autonomous Reformed Dutch Church in America came into being with the adoption of a presbyterian church government like that of the mother church.

Its struggle for equality with the Classis strengthened the Dutch Reformed church. The denomination gained greater allegiance from its parishioners by showing firm determination to fight for their spiritual welfare. The founding of a seminary at Queen's College eventually relieved the shortage of clergy and reduced the danger that unchurched members would join other faiths. Once freed from overseas interference, the clergy could adapt religious practices more suited to the needs of their American fold, especially by conducting services in English and deemphasizing liturgy in favor of vigorous preaching capable of sparking a desire for redemption. Had it not accomplished these changes, the Reformed Dutch church would surely have become increasingly irrelevant to its members and suffered decline after 1800.

German Reformed

German Reformed churches had functioned under the jurisdiction of the Amsterdam Classis of the Reformed Church of the Netherlands since the early eighteenth century. In 1793, they were reorganized as an independent denomination named the German Reformed Church. In that year, their membership stood at approximately 15,000, who were gathered into 178 congregations ranging from Virginia to New York—but mostly centered in Pennsylvania.

The German Reformed church suffered from a lack of clergy because it failed to establish a seminary until 1825. Its members often joined with Lutherans to form union congregations, which shared the expense of building a common church and then accepted the first minister available from either faith. Both denominations also cooperated in founding Franklin College, at Lancaster, Pennsylvania, in 1787. The church's reluctance to abandon services in German not only limited its evangelical appeal to one nationality, but also encouraged defections by succeeding generations in German Reformed families whose first language was English. The church consequently tended to lag behind the growth of most religious groups.

Judaism

The Revolutionary ideal of equal rights, combined with the Enlightenment's rejection of intolerance, weakened the hold of anti-Jewish prejudices among Anglo-Americans, especially among the better educated. The most striking example of changing attitudes was the first election of a practicing Jew to public office by a western Christian community: the choice of Francis Salvador to represent Charles Town at South Carolina's Provincial Assembly in 1776. Although Jews had not been prohibited from voting in any colony except Rhode Island, after independence they enjoyed this right universally. No religious tests existed for federal offices, but Maryland, North Carolina, and Georgia prescribed oaths that were worded to bar Catholics, Deists, or atheists from office, and these laws had the practical result of excluding Jews as well.

Few in the Christian majority expressed any reservations about extending more civil rights to Jews. A major reason would seem to be that few overt differences separated themselves from the Hebrew minority. "There are many Jews now resident in America," wrote the Hessian officer Johan Conrad Dohla in 1777, "who are not easily distinguishable from Christians." Dohla then elaborated:

> The Jews, however, are not like the ones we have in Europe and Germany, who are recognizable by their beards and their clothes, for these are dressed like other citizens, get shaved regularly, and also eat pork, although that is forbidden by their Law. Also Jews and Christians intermarry without scruple. The women also go about with curled hair and in French finery such as is worn by the ladies of the other religions.

The Revolutionary era produced both disruption and growth for American Judaism. Truro Synagogue at Newport, Rhode Island, ceased services after the British captured the town, and it again closed during the 1790s when economic depression led many merchants to shut their businesses. Many refugees fleeing British occupation in Newport and New York joined Philadelphia's Congregation Mikveh Israel, and they provided much of the funds to erect that city's earliest building for Jewish worship in 1782. Other Jewish refugees founded Baltimore's first synagogue that same year, and Congregation Beth Shalom at Richmond soon after. The Jewry of Savannah dispersed after British troops captured their city, and their congregation was not reestablished until 1790. The membership of Charleston's synagogue, the nation's largest in 1800, grew so fast that a new structure had to built in 1794. At the first census of 1790, there were probably 1,500 to 2,000 Americans who practiced Judaism, mostly of Sephardic origin, but increased immigration by Ashkenazic families from Europe was starting to make substantial additions to this community's size.

Lutheranism

The American Revolution had little direct affect on the Lutheran church, aside from the benefit its congregations gained from Anglicanism's disestablishment in the South and New York. Lutheranism faced several difficulties in retaining its status as a major denomination. Although independent of any European episcopate, the Lutheran church stubbornly clung to German and could only expand within one ethnic group. Its traditions emphasized formal liturgy, but Americans—including those of German background—responded most enthusiastically to revivalism and spontaneous worship.

The most serious problem undermining Lutheranism was its failure to develop a distinctive identity. Its ministers tended to compromise their faith rather than provoke controversy among their parishioners or with neighboring denominations. Lutherans also diluted their image by close cooperation with other churches, including Protestant Episcopalians, with whom New York Lutherans tentatively considered uniting. Lutherans forged especially strong links with Reformed Germans, a body that shared most of their basic beliefs. The two denominations established many union congregations that shared the same church and accepted ministers indiscriminately from either faith. In 1787, both denominations cooperated to found Franklin College, although the first president was Lutheran.

Unsure of their own identity, Lutherans found it difficult to articulate a compelling reason for converts to accept their faith. They consequently grew at a steady rate, but no more than would be expected from normal population increase and immigration. The church nevertheless positioned itself for wider acceptance through belated reforms, such as permitting laymen to vote on church affairs in 1792 and slowly discarding the use of German after then.

Presbyterianism

The Presbyterian church underwent no significant change as a direct result of the Revolution, aside from making additional converts at the expense of the disestablished Anglican religion. Presbyterians earned an exaggerated reputation for rebelliousness; although most of their laymen supported independence, in particular those of Scotch-Irish and New England stock, their ranks included a substantial minority of Tories, especially among recently arrived Scottish immigrants. The core of truth underlying the legend of Presbyterian patriotism concerned its clergy. This denomination's ministers united more solidly behind the Continental cause than any other's, except possibly the Congregationalists, and they provided the only cleric to vote for independence, John Witherspoon, president of the College of New Jersey.

After the Revolution, the most significant problem facing the denomination was its outdated form of government. The number of congregations had, not only grown too large for the annual synod to represent the full range of Presbyterian opinion, but they had also become so widely dispersed into the backcountry that attendance at synod was perennially poor due to the great distances most members had to travel. After three years of deliberation, the synod of 1788 ratified a Plan of Government and Discipline. This document established an annual General Assembly, four synods (New York-New Jersey, Philadelphia, Virginia, and the Carolinas), and sixteen presbyteries, which held the authority to ordain. The same synod also approved a new Directory of Public Worship and a revised confession of faith. With church government reorganized more democratically, Presbyterians turned again to expanding their denomination, which then included 420 congregations (of which 214 had ministers) and 188 clergy (including 11 awaiting licenses).

Protestant Episcopal

Although two-thirds of the signers of the Declaration of Independence were nominal Anglicans, Anglican priests were almost unanimously pro-British. Most Anglican rectors were natives of Britain, and they left the United States in droves after 1776. Virginia lost two-thirds of its priests, and Pennsylvania briefly had but one resident Anglican rector. Infuriated by this clerical Toryism, Americans disestablished the Church of England in every state where it had been legally supported.

Meeting at Woodbury, Connecticut, in 1783, ten New England priests requested that the Church of England create a separate episcopate in the United States by making Rev. Samuel Seabury a bishop. British law required all bishops to swear allegiance to the British Crown, which Seabury could not do as an American, so in 1784 Seabury obtained the office from three Scottish bishops who had received ordination outside the Church of England, but never-

Folk artist Lewis Miller titled this sketch "In Side of the old Lutheran Church in 1800, York, Pa." As Rev. Jacob Goering preaches from the pulpit, latecomers sneak in and the sexton Henry Bannix chases out a stray dog. The atmosphere is decidedly liturgical Protestant, rather than Calvinist, with ornamentation depicting Hebrew prophets, the four evangelists, and Luther himself. The traditional seating arrangement not only separates men from women but also provides a separate section for the smallest children, who can then misbehave among themselves as long as they do so discreetly. (Courtesy The Historical Society of York County, Pennsylvania)

As the spiritual heirs of England's established church, Protestant Episcopalians struggled to preserve religious traditions that the ancestors of most Anglo-Americans had emigrated to escape. Typical of this heritage was the splendidly designed interior of Philadelphia's Christ Church, restored to its original whiteness after 1953. Although it was visually stunning, most eighteenth-century American Protestants would have associated the decor with the ornate style and decoration of Roman Catholic churches. (Compare with photo on page 203.) (Courtesy National Images of North American Living, Research and Archival Center, Washington)

theless stood in the proper line of apostolic succession and had sacramental powers of ordination. Seabury returned a bishop, only to discover that other Anglicans were organizing a rival church structure.

In 1785, Anglicans from the southern and mid-Atlantic states convened at Philadelphia to elect candidates for bishoprics, in hopes that Parliamentary legislation then pending would allow ordination of Americans by the Church of England. Once Parliament passed the necessary exception, Dr. William White and Rev. Samuel Provoost were ordained in 1787 with orthodox rites in England. Anglicans then had to choose between two competing claims to episcopal legitimacy, and it appeared the laity would be split between the two factions.

When Massachusetts Anglicans requested that Seabury, White, and Provoost consecrate their choice as bishop, the two parties began seriously investigating how to compromise their differences on church government and doctrine. In 1789, the two sides found a

middle ground and voted to unite. The Protestant Episcopal church then assumed its mature form as an American institution.

The new church's most serious problem was its precipitous decline in membership. In the wake of being abandoned by most of their former Anglican clergy during the war, perhaps half of all Anglicans had joined the Baptists, Methodists, or Presbyterians. The Revolution had generated enormous prejudice against the Church of England, and few Americans could give serious thought to joining its Protestant Episcopal successor. The Protestant Episcopal church was poorly positioned to win back its former members because it suffered from a severe lack of clergy and could reopen only a portion of its parishes. In 1796 an English visitor to Virginia, Isaac Weld, summed up the denomination's situation by writing that he "scarcely observed one [church] that was not in a ruinous condition, with the windows broken, and doors dropping off the hinges, and lying open to the pigs."

Quakerism

The American Revolution had long-lasting consequences for the Society of Friends. They had previously composed the largest religious body in the Pennsylvania and New Jersey assemblies, aside from the period of the Seven Years' War, during which Quakers recused themselves from the Pennsylvania house (but not New Jersey's) as part of their peace testimony. They regained their former political influence after 1763 but again felt compelled to withdraw from legislative politics in both states during the Revolution in order to escape complicity in making war. Both sides interpreted their pacifism as support for their enemies, and many Quakers suffered harassment, fines, or confiscations of property simply for trying to stay neutral. When peace returned in 1783, few Quakers sought elective office, and their denomination's political influence shriveled to a mere shadow of its former self.

During the Revolutionary era, the Society of Friends showed greater concern for humanitarian issues than did other denominations, which emphasized personal piety. New Jersey Quakers founded the Association for Helping the Indians in 1757. Pennsylvania Quakers became such prominent apologists for the Indians during Pontiac's War that they provoked an armed confrontation with hundreds of exasperated frontiersmen who marched on Philadelphia and threatened to burn the city in December 1763. The Society of Friends later financed several missions among the Iroquois in the 1790s.

The Quakers made their foremost contribution to social reform as the first church to repudiate slaveholding. At the prodding of John Woolman of New Jersey, Philadelphia's Yearly Meeting condemned human bondage as immoral in 1754, but it did not compel manumission. The decision to forbid slave ownership, on pain of expulsion, was taken by the yearly meetings of New England (1770), New York (1774), and Philadelphia (1776). By 1779, 80% of slaves formerly held by Friends had gained their freedom, and by 1796 none of the Society's members owned any bondsmen. Although other denominations declared slavery to be immoral in the late eighteenth century, only the Society of Friends succeeded in forcing its members to abandon the institution or be disowned.

CHAPTER 8 Government

Constitutional Developments

During the quarter century after 1775, Americans not only overthrew British authority, but also created six provisional congresses or legislatures, wrote twenty state constitutions, instituted two national governments, and ratified eleven amendments to the federal constitution. This burst of political creativity occurred when Americans enjoyed a unique chance to break with the past, yet few states departed drastically from their old form of government. Aside from Georgia and Pennsylvania, which adopted unicameral assemblies and—in the latter's case—eliminated the governorship, the states retained bicameral legislatures and entrusted civil administration to a single chief executive.

Although hardly radical, the revised state governments did make important changes. Governors everywhere lost most of their former authority and prerogatives, even including the veto. The upper houses, which had previously been filled with executive appointees everywhere except New England, now became elective. Reversing a late-colonial trend toward making judges subject to summary dismissal, most states vested judgeships with lifetime tenure. The state constitutions also pioneered the concept of protecting basic liberties through an explicit bill of rights. Most of the earliest constitutions required major revisions before 1800 to equalize relations between the executive, legislative, and judicial branches. From this process of trial and error came a recognition of the need for a balance of powers in government.

National government began as a temporary expedient termed the Continental Congress. Beginning in late 1774, Congress began enforcing its policies through various committees that were elected by citizens in their counties and coordinated through provincial congresses in the colonies. None of these bodies, including the Continental Congress, had any lawful standing to usurp British authority. Even after Congress voted for independence on July 2, 1776, it remained an extra-legal body with no constitutional power to compel compliance from either state governments or individual citizens. The United States fought virtually all of the Revolution without a legally constituted national authority, before its first frame of government—the Articles of Confederation—went into effect six months before the decisive battle of Yorktown in 1781.

The Articles of Confederation was a weak alliance of states, all of which retained their essential sovereignty. Dependent upon the states for finances, Congress found it increasingly difficult to obtain their cooperation as Britain's military threat subsided. By 1787, calls for stronger central government resulted in a convention at Philadelphia that wrote a new constitution, which was ratified on June 21, 1788. This federal constitution established an equilibrium between the president, Congress, and judiciary based on a sophisticated system of checks and balances; it also devised an innovative system of dual representation to apportion the lower house into districts of equal population and give each state two senators. The Constitution finally created a federal system of dual sovereignty between the states and national government, yet defined the Constitution as the supreme law of the land.

TABLE 8.1 CONSTITUTIONAL REORGANIZATION OF AMERICAN GOVERNMENTS, 1774–1800

Government	Royal Authority Effectively Ended	First Constitution Officially Adopted	When Replaced
U.S.	Jul. 2, 1776	Mar. 1, 1781	Jun. 21, 1788
N.H.	Jan. 5, 1776	Jun. 2, 1784	. . .[a]
Vt.	. . .	Jul. 8, 1777	Jul. 4, 1786
Mass.	Sep. 9, 1774	Jun. 16, 1780	. . .[a]
R.I.	May 4, 1776	kept charter[b]	Nov. 23, 1842
Conn.	Apr. 26, 1775	kept charter[c]	Oct. 5, 1818
N.Y.	Jul. 8, 1776	Apr. 20, 1777	Feb. 1822
N.J.	Jan. 8, 1776	Jul. 2, 1776	Aug. 13, 1844
Pa.	Jun. 19, 1776	Sep. 28, 1776	Sep. 2, 1790
Del.	Jun. 15, 1776	Sep. 20, 1776	Jun. 12, 1792
Md.	Jun. 24, 1776	Nov. 9, 1776	Jun. 4, 1851
Va.	Jun. 8, 1775	Jun. 29, 1776	Apr. 1830
N.C.	May 24, 1775	Dec. 18, 1776	Apr. 23, 1868
S.C.	Sep. 15, 1775	Mar. 19, 1778	Jun. 3, 1790
Ga.	Jan. 18, 1776	Feb. 5, 1777	May 16, 1789
Ky.	. . .	Apr. 19, 1792	Aug. 17, 1799
Tenn.	. . .	Feb. 6, 1796	Mar. 6, 1835

[a] Remains in effect, with amendments.
[b] On May 4, 1776, Rhode Island altered the 1663 charter's authority, but retained its form of government.
[c] In October 1776, Connecticut altered the 1662 charter's authority, but retained its form of government.
Source: Francis N. Thorpe, ed., *The Federal and State Constitutions, Colonial Charters, and Other Organic Laws of the States, Territories, and Colonies Now or Heretofore Forming the United States of America,* 7 vols. (1909).

TABLE 8.2 APPOINTMENTS AND DURATION OF POST-REVOLUTIONARY STATE OFFICIALS

State	Date of Constitution	Governor Chosen by	Term	Supreme Court Chosen by	Tenure
Vt.	1786	voters	1 year	legislature	lifetime
N.H.	1784	voters	1 year	governor & executive council	lifetime
Mass.	1780	voters	1 year	governor & upper house	lifetime
R.I.	1663	voters	1 year	governor & upper house	1 year
Conn.	1662	voters	1 year	legislature	1 year
N.Y.	1777	voters	3 years	council of appointment	lifetime
N.J.	1776	legislature	1 year	legislature	7 years
Pa.	1776	legislature[b]	1 year	council of appointment	lifetime
Del.	1776	voters	3 years	governor	lifetime
Md.	1776	legislature	1 year	governor & senate	lifetime
Va.	1776	legislature	1 year	legislature	lifetime
N.C.	1776	legislature	1 year	none[c]	. . .
S.C.	1778	legislature	2 years	legislature	3 years
Ga.	1777	legislature	1 year	none[d]	. . .
Tenn.	1796	voters	2 years	none[e]	. . .
Ky.	1792	College of Electors	4 years	governor & senate	lifetime

(continued)

TABLE 8.2 (continued)

State	Date of Constitution	Senators — Chosen by	Senators — Term	Representatives — Chosen by	Representatives — Term
Vt.	1786	(unicameral)		voters	1 year
N.H.	1784	voters	1 year	voters	1 year
Mass.	1780	voters	1 year	voters	1 year
R.I.	1663	voters	1 year	voters	1 year
Conn.	1662	voters	1 year	voters	6 months
N.Y.	1777	voters	4 years	voters	1 year
N.J.	1776	voters	1 year	voters	1 year
Pa.	1776	(unicameral)		voters	1 year
Del.	1776	voters	3 years	voters	1 year
Md.	1776	College of Electors	5 years	voters	1 year
Va.	1776	voters	1 year	voters	1 year
N.C.	1776	voters owning 50 acres	1 year	all voters	1 year
S.C.	1778	voters	4 years	voters	2 years
Ga.	1777	(unicameral)		voters	1 year
Tenn.	1796	voters	2 years	voters	2 years
Ky.	1792	College of Electors	4 years	voters	1 year

[a] Lifetime tenure was contingent upon good behavior.
[b] Pennsylvania's chief executive was Chair of Executive Council.
[c] Until 1818, the state had separate superior courts for its three judicial districts, but no supreme court as such.
[d] Judgments appealed from the superior courts of the state's three judicial districts were decided by a ''special jury'' impaneled for that purpose, and so no supreme court was established.
[e] A separate court of appeal existed for each of the state's three judicial districts, rather than a single supreme court.
Source: Samuel Blodget, Economica: A Statistical Manual of the United States of America (1806), 56, amended to delete errors.

TABLE 8.3 SIZE OF ASSEMBLIES AND RATIO OF REPRESENTATIVES TO ADULT WHITE MALES, 1770 AND 1790

	1770 — Number of Members	1770 — Members per Adult White Males[a]	1790 — Number of Members	1790 — Members per Adult White Males[a]
N.H.	34	1:363	92[b]	1:293
Vt.	. . .	. . .	112[b]	1:152
Mass.	125	1:368	290[b]	1:304
R.I.	65	1:167	65	1:186
Conn.	138	1:258	138	1:316
N.Y.	27	1:1,065	70	1:880
N.J.	24	1:910	39	1:844
Pa.	36	1:1,301	69	1:1,198
Del.	18	1:374	21	1:433
Md.	58	1:478	80	1:509
Va.	118	1:439	163[c]	1:530
N.C.	81	1:315	108	1:520
S.C.	51	1:192	124	1:225
Ga.	25	1:102	34	1:303
Tenn. (1796)	. . .	. . .	22	1:286
Ky. (1792)	. . .	. . .	40	1:306

[a] Figures show members of lower house only.
[b] Figure is only approximate, because Constitution did not set exact number of representatives, allowed representation to vary due to population changes, and did not require eligible towns to hold legislative elections. Based partly on delegations seated in 1790.
[c] Excluding representatives from Kentucky.
Source: Jack P. Greene, ''Legislative Turnover in British America, 1696–1775,'' William and Mary Quarterly XXXVIII (1981), 461, which does not include 1790 figures.

TABLE 8.4 RATIFICATION OF THE FEDERAL CONSTITUTION, 1787–1791

State and Rank	Voted on Ratification	Votes at Convention — Ayes	Votes at Convention — Nays	% of Adult White Males Who Votes in Ratification Elections
1. Del.	Dec. 7, 1787	30	0	. . .
2. Pa.	Dec. 12, 1787	46	23	16.7%
3. N.J.	Dec. 18, 1787	38	0	. . .
4. Ga.	Jan. 2, 1788	25	0	. . .
5. Conn.	Jan. 9, 1788	128	40	. . .
6. Mass.	Feb. 6, 1788	187	168	27.0%
7. Md.	Apr. 28, 1788	63	11	15.0%
8. S.C.	May 23, 1788	149	73	. . .
9. N.H.	Jun. 21, 1788	57	47	. . .
10. Va.	Jun. 25, 1788	89	79	26.5%
11. N.Y.	Jul. 26, 1788	30	27	43.4%
12. N.C.	Aug. 1, 1788	84	184	. . .
	Nov. 21, 1789	194	77	. . .
13. R.I.	Apr. 1788	237	2,708[a]	24.4%
	May 29, 1790[b]	34	32	. . .

[a] Referendum conducted at town meetings rather than a convention.
[b] The legislature defeated seven resolutions to call a ratifying convention from Feb. 1788 to Dec. 1789.
Sources: Forrest McDonald, We the People: The Economic Origins of the Constitution (1958), 113–322. Robert J. Dinkin, Voting in Revolutionary America: A Study of Elections in the Original Thirteen States, 1776–1789 (1982), 122, 125, 129.

Location of Capitals

As America's largest city and central seaport, Philadelphia was the natural choice to be first capital of the United States. Congress eventually convened in seven other cities while fleeing British occupation or threats of mutiny by unpaid Continental soldiers. Had the capital not been relocated so many times, it might still be in Philadelphia, but its impermanence encouraged southerners to press for the creation of a "federal district" below the Mason-Dixon Line. In 1790, the idea of a "southern capital" seemed so alluring that several Virginia congressmen agreed to vote for Alexander Hamilton's plan to convert state debts into U.S. bonds (a proposal bitterly opposed by their constituents) in return for his ability to gain the necessary northern support to move the capital to land donated by Maryland on the Potomac River, which became the District of Columbia.

The location of state capitals also became a political issue after 1775. Because transportation to, and lodging at, capitals was expen-

TABLE 8.5 CAPITALS OF THE UNITED STATES OF AMERICA, 1776–1800

City	Congress in Session
Philadelphia, Pa.	Sep. 5, 1774–Dec. 12, 1776
Baltimore, Md.	Dec. 20, 1776–Mar. 4, 1777
Philadelphia, Pa.	Mar. 5, 1777–Sep. 19, 1777
Lancaster, Pa.	Sep. 27, 1777
York, Pa.	Sep. 30, 1777–Jun. 27, 1778
Philadelphia, Pa.	Jul. 2, 1778–Jun. 21, 1783
Princeton, N.J.	Jun. 30, 1783–Nov. 4, 1783
Annapolis, Md.	Nov. 26, 1783–Jun. 3, 1784
Trenton, N.J.	Nov. 1, 1784–Dec. 24, 1784
New York, N.Y.	Jan. 11, 1785–Aug. 12, 1790
Philadelphia, Pa.	Dec. 6, 1790–May 14, 1800
Washington, D.C.	Nov. 17, 1800 to present

Source: Mark M. Boatner III, Encyclopedia of the United States Revolution (1974), 274.

TABLE 8.6 RELOCATION AND ROTATION OF STATE CAPITALS, 1776–1812

State	Date Removal Act Passed	Old and New Capitals
Del.	May 12, 1777	Newcastle to Dover
Va.	Jun. 12, 1779	Williamsburg to Richmond
Ga.	Jan. 26, 1786	Savannah to Louisville (Augusta interim capital to 1795)
	Dec. 12, 1804	Louisville to Milledgeville
S.C.	Mar. 22, 1786	Charleston to Columbia
N.C.	Aug. 4, 1788	New Bern to Raleigh
N.J.	(since 1703)	Alternate sessions at Burlington and Perth Amboy
	Nov. 25, 1790	to Trenton
N.Y.	Mar. 10, 1797	New York to Albany
Pa.	Mar. 30, 1788	Philadelphia to Lancaster
	Feb. 21, 1810	Lancaster to Harrisburg
N.H.	1808 (de facto)	Portsmouth to Concord
R.I.	(since 1600s)	Rotated among Newport, Providence, Bristol, East Greenwich, South Kingston until 1854, then between Newport and Providence
Conn.	(since 1701)	Rotated between Hartford and New Haven until October 1873, when Hartford was named sole capital
Tenn.	1812	From Knoxville to Nashville (except 1817–19, when both were co-capitals), then in 1819 to Murphreesboro

Source: Rosemarie Zagarri, *The Politics of Size: Representation in the U.S., 1776–1850* (1987), 151.

sive, demands surfaced that the legislature and superior courts be held nearer to the center of each state's population (which in every state was shifting rapidly westward), so that government would be more accessible than it was at seaports. As a result of these demands, nine of the original thirteen states relocated their capitals to more central locations that would lessen the time and money needed to attend sessions of the assembly or testify at the supreme court. Ever since, it has been axiomatic among Americans that a democratic society requires a capital that is convenient for the citizens.

Elections and Voter Turnout

Prior to independence, Americans rarely voted except to elect members of their legislature's lower house. Royal governors called elections at their discretion in all but four colonies, and half the voters often did not attend the poll. Perhaps 40% of adult free males could not meet the property qualifications for voters, and well over 60% lacked the wealth required to be candidates.

The Revolution introduced significant modifications in electoral practices, but not radical change. All states but Rhode Island and Connecticut liberalized property requirements for officeholding and voting, but only Vermont and Kentucky enfranchised all free men. Elections were everywhere set at regular, frequent intervals. Only two colonies had elected governors and members of the upper house before 1776, yet by 1800 all but six elected their governors and all but one allowed citizens to choose state senators. Few states allowed voters to pick sheriffs or other county officials, however.

Voter participation remained low after independence, and it fell short of 25% in most of 1789's congressional races. Voter turnout tended to increase during the 1790s because of conscious efforts to mobilize supporters by leaders of the newly organized Federalist and Democratic-Republican parties. Turnout tended not to rise in areas where voters had to travel long distances or where one party was so dominant that its victory was assured. In the cities, where voting was convenient, and in the middle-Atlantic states, where opinion was more evenly split between the opposing parties, the number of citizens drawn into politics steadily increased. By the late 1790s, voter turnout exceeded 50% in many districts of New York, Pennsylvania, and Maryland, which became the swing states that determined presidential elections and control of Congress.

TABLE 8.7 ELECTORAL TURNOVER IN COLONIAL ASSEMBLY ELECTIONS, 1763–1776

Percentage of New Members							
Year	N.H.	Mass.	Conn.a	R.I.	N.Y.	Pa.	Del.
1776	...	...	46%	71%	22%	90%	...
1775	...	...	48%–50%	54%	...	.22%	50%
1774	38%	25%	42%–41%	36%	...	20%	8%
1773	...	32%	34%–40%	44%	...	15%	17%
1772	...	30%	31%–42%	67%	...	29%	17%
1771	29%	32%	44%–41%	52%	...	8%	28%
1770	...	22%	43%–40%	0%–48%a	...	22%	22%
1769	...	35%	50%–37%	69%	35%	6%	17%
1768	16%	32%	42%–41%	72%	48%	14%	17%
1767	...	23%	35%–40%	65%	...	25%	11%
1766	...	40%	50%–46%	49%	...	14%	17%
1765	30%	27%	43%–50%	45%	...	25%	28%
1764	...	39%	50%–48%	29%	...	28%	33%
1763	...	32%	45%–33%	55%	...	17%	22%

Year	N.J.	Md.	Va.	N.C.	S.C.	Ga.
1775	...	...	21%	21%	...	...
1774	...	...	...	...	...	...
1773	...	47%	...	48%–31%a	24%–25%a	...
1772	46%	...	32%	...	41%–22%a	52%–53%a
1771	...	50%	...	34%	...	31%
1770	...	...	...	56%	...	...
1769	54%	...	40%–19%a	...	45%	60%
1768	...	45%	...	...	51%	40%
1767	...	...	...	...	...	...
1766	...	...	35%	49%	...	...
1765	...	31%	...	...	46%	...
1764	...	...	...	47%	...	64%
1763	...	...	...	...	...	...

[a]Two elections in one year.
Note: Turnover is calculated by the formula:

$$\% \text{ replacements} = \frac{(\text{number new members}) - (\text{number new seats})}{(\text{number seats}) - (\text{number new seats})}$$

Source: Data compiled by Jack P. Greene for "Legislative Turnover in British America, 1696–1775," *William and Mary Quarterly* XXXVIII (1981), 442–61, but not printed in that source.

TABLE 8.8 QUALIFICATIONS FOR VOTING UNDER THE FIRST STATE CONSTITUTIONS

State	Pre-1776 Property Requirement	Post-1776 Property Requirement	Free Blacks Eligible	Women Taxpayers Eligible
N.H.	Estate of £50	All taxpayers	Yes	No
Vt.	...	All adult males	Yes	No
Mass.	Land rentable for £2 yearly, or any property worth £40	Land rentable for £3 yearly, or any property worth £60	Yes	No

(continued)

TABLE 8.8 (continued)

State	Pre-1776 Property Requirement	Post-1776 Property Requirement	Free Blacks Eligible	Women Taxpayers Eligible
R.I.	Land rentable for £2 yearly, or worth £40	For representative, land worth £40 or payment of £2 rent; for senator, land worth £100	Yes (to 1822)	No
Conn.	Land worth £40 or £2 yearly rent	Land worth £40 or £2 yearly rent	Yes (to 1814)	No
N.Y.	Landed estate worth £50	Landed estate worth £20 or payment of £2 rent for lower house, but landed estate worth £100 for senate	Yes	No
N.J.	Landed estate worth £50	Any property worth £50	Yes (to 1807)	Yes (to 1807)
Pa.	50 acres or any property worth £40	All taxpayers	Yes (to 1838)	No
Del.	50 acres or any property worth £40	50 acres or any property worth £40[a]	Yes (to 1792)	No
Md.	50 acres or any property worth £40	50 acres or any property worth £30	Yes (to 1802)	No

State	Pre-1776 Property Requirement	Post-1776 Property Requirement	Free Blacks Eligible	Women Taxpayers Eligible
Va.	25 acres and house, or 100 acres of unimproved land	25 acres and house, or 100 acres of unimproved land[b]	No	No
N.C.	50 acres	All taxpayers for lower house, 50 acres for senate	Yes (to 1835)	No
S.C.	50 acres or land worth £2 rent	50 acres, or paying tax equal to levy on 50 acres	No	No
Ga.	50 acres	Any property worth £10	No[c]	No
Ky.	. . .	All adult males	Yes (to 1799)	No
Tenn.	. . .	All adult males	Yes (to 1834)	No

[a] Liberalized to all taxpayers and any sons under age 23 in 1792.
[b] In 1785, the voting qualification for improved land was reduced from 100 acres to 50.
[c] Expressly banned in constitution of 1777, but not in constitutions of 1792 and 1798, when custom barred nonwhite suffrage.
Note: Qualifications are those specified in first constitution adopted officially (not provisionally) after independence.
Sources: Francis N. Thorpe, ed., *The Federal and State Constitutions, Colonial Charters, and Other Organic Laws of the States, Territories, and Colonies Now or Heretofore Forming the United States of America*, 7 vols. (1909). Winthrop D. Jordan, *White Over Black: American Attitudes Toward the Negro, 1550–1812* (1968), 412–14.

Howard Pyle's drawing of women voting in New Jersey depicts the sole instance in Revolutionary America when property qualifications for suffrage were defined without regard to sex, from 1790 to 1807. Any New Jersey woman could vote, as long as she owned the minimum amount of property required by law. Female suffrage was uncontroversial until 1800, when the Federalists used female voters—including a black woman escorted to the poll by Sen. Jonathan Dayton—to carry the state against Thomas Jefferson. In 1807, the Democrats solidified political control over New Jersey by taking the vote away from both women and African Americans. (Howard Pyle Collection, courtesy Delaware Art Museum, Wilmington, Delaware)

TABLE 8.9 PERCENT OF ADULT WHITE MALES ELIGIBLE TO VOTE IN U.S., 1792

New England	Eligible to Vote
N.H.	90%+
Vt.	100%
Mass.	
seaports	60%–70%
rural towns	80%–90%
R.I.[a]	74%
Conn.	75%

Mid-Atlantic	Eligible to Vote
N.Y.	
for assembly	58%
for senate	29%
N.J.	85%–90%
Pa.	90%+
Del.	80%+

South	Eligible to Vote
Md.	70%+
Va.	70%–75%
N.C.[a]	90%+
S.C.	80%+
Ga.	90%+
Ky.	100%

[a] State had dual qualifications to vote in legislative elections.
Source: Robert J. Dinkin, *Voting in Revolutionary America: A Study of Elections in the Original Thirteen States, 1776–1789* (1982), 36–39.

TABLE 8.10 PROPERTY QUALIFICATIONS FOR STATE OFFICEHOLDERS

State	(Date)	Governor	Representative	Senator
N.H.	(1783)	Landed estate worth £500	Landed estate worth £100	Landed estate worth £200
Vt.	(1777)	None	None	(unicameral)
Mass.	(1780)	Landed estate worth £1,000	Landed estate worth £100, or any property worth £200	Landed estate worth £300, or any property worth £600
R.I.	(1663)	Land worth £2 yearly rent	Land worth £2 yearly rent	Land worth £2 yearly rent
Conn.	(1662)	Landed estate worth £40 or £2 yearly rent	Landed estate worth £40 or £2 yearly rent	Landed estate worth £40 or £2 yearly rent
N.Y.	(1777)	Any landowner	Landed estate worth £20 or tenant paying £2 yearly rent	Landed estate worth £100
N.J.	(1776)	None	Landed estate worth £500	Landed estate worth £1,000 (unicameral)
Pa.	(1776)	None	Any taxpayer	
Del.	(1776)	None	Any landowner	Any landowner
Md.	(1776)	None	Any property worth £500	Landed estate worth £1,000
Va.	(1776)	None	25 acres and house 100 acres	25 acres and house 300 acres
N.C.	(1776)	Landed estate worth £1,000		
S.C.	(1778)	Landed estate worth £10,000	500 acres and 10 slaves, or landed estate worth £1,000	Landed estate worth £2,000
Ga.	(1777)	250 acres or any goods worth £250	250 acres or any goods worth £250	(unicameral)

State	(Date)	Governor	Representative	Senator
Tenn.	(1796)	500a.	200a.	200a.
Ky.	(1792)	None	None	None

Note: All monetary values given in local currency.
Source: Francis N. Thorpe, ed., *The Federal and State Constitutions, Colonial Charters, and Other Organic Laws of the States, Territories, and Colonies [of] the United States,* 7 vols. (1909).

TABLE 8.11 AVERAGE PERCENT OF ADULT WHITE MALES WHO VOTED IN ELECTIONS FOR GOVERNOR, 1764–1800

	N.H.	Mass.	R.I.	Conn.	N.Y.	Pa.	Del.	Ky.
1800	44.0%	31.0%	. . .	. . .	. . .	. . .	. . .	59.1%
1799	32.0%	28.0%	. . .	. . .	. . .	56.0%	. . .	. . .
1798	33.0%	18.0%	. . .	. . .	35.0%	. . .	46.0%	. . .
1797	30.0%	22.0%	10.0%	. . .	. . .	. . .	. . .	. . .
1796	30.0%	24.0%	. . .	15.0%	. . .	26.0%	. . .	. . .
1795	27.0%	16.0%	. . .	. . .	33.3%	. . .	47.0%	. . .
1794	31.0%	22.0%	. . .	. . .	. . .	. . .	. . .	. . .
1793	29.0%	18.0%	. . .	. . .	. . .	27.0%	. . .	. . .
1792	27.0%	17.0%	. . .	. . .	27.0%	. . .	50.0%	. . .
1791	28.0%	17.0%	. . .	. . .	. . .	. . .	. . .	. . .
1790	24.0%	17.0%	. . .	. . .	. . .	31.0%	. . .	. . .
1789	32.3%	23.3%	25.5%	. . .	20.0%	. . .	. . .	. . .
1788	36.9%	25.2%	16.2%	. . .	. . .	. . .	. . .	. . .
1787	43.1%	29.3%	33.3%	. . .	. . .	. . .	. . .	. . .
1786	44.9%	10.3%	30.0%	13.1%	. . .	. . .	. . .	. . .
1785	37.1%	11.9%	12.4%	. . .	. . .	. . .	. . .	. . .
1784	30.0%	10.6%	10.6%	16.1%	. . .	. . .	. . .	. . .
1783	. . .	12.7%	24.4%	17.0%	. . .	. . .	. . .	. . .
1782	. . .	10.8%	22.5%	14.9%	. . .	. . .	. . .	. . .
1781	. . .	12.1%	13.5%	16.8%	. . .	. . .	. . .	. . .
1780	. . .	. . .	15.0%	17.9%	. . .	. . .	. . .	. . .
1779	. . .	. . .	. . .	. . .	. . .	. . .	. . .	. . .
1778	. . .	. . .	15.0%	. . .	. . .	. . .	. . .	. . .
1777	. . .	. . .	. . .	. . .	15.0%	. . .	. . .	. . .
1776	. . .	. . .	. . .	. . .	10.5%	. . .	. . .	. . .
1775	. . .	. . .	. . .	13.0%	. . .	. . .	. . .	. . .
1774	. . .	. . .	. . .	14.5%	. . .	. . .	. . .	. . .
1773	. . .	. . .	. . .	. . .	. . .	. . .	. . .	. . .
1772	. . .	. . .	. . .	17.4%	. . .	. . .	. . .	. . .
1771	. . .	. . .	. . .	. . .	. . .	. . .	. . .	. . .
1770	. . .	. . .	34.8%	27.4%	. . .	. . .	. . .	. . .
1769	. . .	. . .	. . .	22.0%	. . .	. . .	. . .	. . .
1768	. . .	. . .	32.2%	23.0%	. . .	. . .	. . .	. . .
1767	. . .	. . .	45.9%	24.8%	. . .	. . .	. . .	. . .
1766	. . .	. . .	41.7%	. . .	. . .	. . .	. . .	. . .
1765	. . .	. . .	47.2%	. . .	. . .	. . .	. . .	. . .
1764	. . .	. . .	43.9%	. . .	. . .	. . .	. . .	. . .

Sources: Robert J. Dinkin, *Voting in Revolutionary America: A Study of Elections in the Original Thirteen States, 1776–1789* (1982), 109–28, and *Voting in Provincial America: A Study of Elections in the Thirteen Colonies, 1689–1776* (1977), 149–80. J. R. Pole, *Political Representation in England and the Origins of the American Republic* (1966), 544–53. Congressional Quarterly, *Guide to U.S. Elections* (2d ed., 1985), 493–530.

TABLE 8.12 AVERAGE PERCENT OF ADULT WHITE MALES WHO VOTED IN LEGISLATIVE ELECTIONS, 1762–1800

Year	% Voting	Year	% Voting
	New Hampshire		
1775	25% in Portsmouth	1768	16% in Portsmouth
1774	28% in Portsmouth	1765	25% in Portsmouth

(continued)

TABLE 8.12 (continued)

Year	% Voting	Year	% Voting
New Hampshire			
1772	80% in Goffstown 63% in Raymond		
Massachusetts			
1787	23.0% statewide	1769	23.0% in Boston
1785	9.0% statewide	1768	19.9% in Boston
1774	24.2% in Boston	1767	28.0% in Boston
1773	19.0% in Boston	1766	33.8% in Boston
1772	32.8% in Boston	1765	29.1% in Boston
1771	18.6% in Boston	1764	20.1% in Boston
New York			
1800	85.0% in New York City	1768	53.6% in New York City
1769	40.6% in New York City		40.0% in Queens Co.
	37.0% in Dutchess Co.		18.3% in Westchester Co.
Pennsylvania			
1788	25.0% statewide	1774	35.6% in Philadelphia
1787	24.9% statewide	1771	12.4% in Philadelphia Co.
1786	27.3% statewide	1766	45.8% in Philadelphia
1785	22.1% statewide		31.4% in Philadelphia Co.
1784	22.7% statewide	1765	61.8% in Philadelphia
1783	24.8% statewide		47.7% in Lancaster Co.
1780–82	18–20%ᵃ statewide		46.1% in Philadelphia Co.
1778–79	10–15%ᵃ statewide		45.8% in Bucks Co.
1775	29.9% in Philadelphia Co.		22.4% in Chester Co.
	26.6% in Philadelphia	1764	42.2% in Philadelphia Co.
			42.2% in Philadelphia
New Jersey			
1788	35.3% in Essex Co.	1784	29.2% in Hunterdon Co.
1787	7.5% in Burlington Co.	1783	11.0% in Burlington Co.
1785	66.6% in Essex Co.	1782	33.7% in Hunterdon Co.
	43.1% in Hunterdon Co.	1762	51.6% in Perth Amboy
	25.9% in Sussex Co.		
	18.1% in Monmouth Co.		
Virginia			
1789	43.4% in Essex Co.	1786	35.1% in Essex Co.
	36.3% in Orange Co.		26.4% in Orange Co.
	24.7% in Princess Anne Co.		17.1% in Stafford Co.
1788	48.3% in Essex Co.		8.7% in Fairfax Co.
	33.1% in Buckingham Co.	1771	48.7% in Spotsylvania Co.
1787	53.3% in Essex Co.		45.5% in Lancaster Co.
	36.1% in Accomac Co.		44.4% in Surry Co.
	30.2% in Princess Anne Co.		38.5% in Northumberland Co.
			36.9% in Richmond Co.
			33.5% in Essex Co.
North Carolina			
1769	54.3% in Orange Co.		
South Carolina			
1788	26.8% in Charles Town	1768	63.4% in Charles Town
1786	22.4% in Charles Town		
Georgia			
1788	49.8% in Chatham Co.	1784	36.3% in Chatham Co.
1787	59.2% in Chatham Co.	1783	39.9% in Chatham Co.

ᵃEstimate based on probable turnout.

Sources: Robert J. Dinkin, *Voting in Revolutionary America: A Study of Elections in the Original Thirteen States, 1776–1789* (1982), 115–27, and *Voting in Provincial America: A Study of Elections in the Thirteen Colonies, 1689–1776* (1977), 149–80. Thomas L. Purvis, *Proprietors, Patronage, and Paper Money: Legislative Politics in New Jersey, 1703–1776* (1986), 101. Van Beck Hall, *Parties Without Politics: Massachusetts, 1780–1791* (1972), 90, 238.

TABLE 8.13 PERCENT OF ADULT WHITE MALES WHO VOTED IN CONGRESSIONAL ELECTIONS, 1789–1800

Year	% Voting
Vermont	
1795	23.5% in 1st Dist.
New Hampshire	
1789	21.4% statewide
Massachusetts	
1789	13.1% statewide
Connecticut	
1800	14.0% statewide
1798	10.0% statewide
1794	7% statewide
1790	2% statewide

New York

	1800	1798	1796	1794	1792	1790	1789
Dist. 1	...	...	43.5%	40.5%	33.9%	6.9%	29.1%
Dist. 2	...	...	27.6%	31.1%	42.1%	16.8%	12.6%
Dist. 3	...	...	36.0%	36.0%	34.1%	11.9%	11.6%
Dist. 4	...	...	34.5%	21.3%	31.0%	18.4%	uncontested
Dist. 5	...	...	24.1%	27.3%	20.3%	19.5%	21.2%
Dist. 6	...	...	30.0%	28.5%	50.5%	16.5%	17.8%
Dist. 7	...	...	39.7%	20.7%	30.4%	...	...
Dist. 8	...	...	6.0%	10.3%	20.5%	...	...
Dist. 9	...	...	23.5%	32.7%	37.5%	...	...
Dist. 10	...	...	43.0%	41.0%	33.0%	...	...
Average	...	...	31.5%	29.2%	32.5%	16.5%	17.5%

Pennsylvania

Year	% Voting
1795	47.5% in 10th Dist.
1794	48.6% in 4th Dist.
1789	18.0% statewide

New Jersey

Year	% Voting	
1789	95.1% in Gloucester Co.	41.3% in Salem Co.
	86.0% in Essex Co.	34.0% in Hunterdon Co.
	76.4% in Burlington Co.	28.6% in Middlesex Co.
	44.0% in Somerset Co.	19.7% in Monmouth Co.
	42.5% in Morris Co.	16.0% in Bergen Co.

Delaware

Year	% Voting
1794	47.5% statewide

Maryland

County	1800	1798	1796	1794	1792	1790	1789
Allegheny	56%	76%	...	69%	14%	46%	...
Anne Arundel	49%	64%	...	48%	54%	7%	...
Baltimore	8%	50%	...	1%	31%	57%	...
Calvert	50%	...	...	69%	57%	27%	...
Caroline	18%	58%	...	38%	36%	50%	...
Cecil	25%	95%	...	66%	57%	40%	...
Charles	43%	48%	...	61%	55%	46%	...
Dorchester	18%	6%	...	59%	28%	26%	...
Frederick	45%	47%	...	16%	7%	12%	...
Harford	35%	70%	...	51%	49%	54%	...
Kent	23%	86%	...	51%	55%	44%	...
Montgomery	47%	43%	...	48%	46%	54%	...
Prince Georges	51%	80%	...	31%	57%	46%	...
Queene Annes	25%	98%	...	61%	67%	29%	...
St. Mary's	24%	49%	...	31%	29%	20%	...

Year		% Voting					
			Maryland				
County	1800	1798	1796	1794	1792	1790	1789
Somerset	14%	. . .	. . .	25%	14%	10%	. . .
Talbot	14%	87%	. . .	42%	71%	19%	. . .
Washington	59%	67%	. . .	37%	10%	37%	. . .
Worcester	11%	12%	. . .	36%	44%	17%	. . .
Average	36%	59%	. . .	37%	37%	39%	18%

	Virginia	
1795	15.0% in 13th Dist.	
1789	44.6% in Louisa Co.	22.3% in Fluvanna Co.
	32.2% in Goochland Co.	21.3% in Orange Co.
	29.1% in Princess Anne Co.	20.5% in Albemarle Co.
	27.9% in Spotsylvania Co.	14.9% in Essex Co.
	25.6% in Cumberland Co.	13.3% in Culpeper Co.
	23.8% in Amherst Co.	11.2% in Greensville Co.

South Carolina	
1789	12.2% statewide

Sources: Robert J. Dinkin, *Voting in Revolutionary America: A Study of Elections in the Original Thirteen States, 1776–1789* (1982), 106–30. J. R. Pole, *Political Representation in England and the Origins of the American Republic* (1966) 544–56. David A. Bohmer, "Stability and Change in Early National Politics: The Maryland Voter and the Election of 1800," *William and Mary Quarterly* XXXVI (1979), 32. Alfred F. Young, *The Democratic Republicans of New York: The Origins, 1763–1797* (1967), 590–92. U.S. Congress, *American State Papers: Miscellaneous* (1834), I, 76, 135, 136, 139, 142.

TABLE 8.14 PERCENT OF ADULT WHITE MALES WHO VOTED IN ELECTIONS TO CHOOSE PRESIDENTIAL ELECTORS, 1789–1800

	1800	1796	1792	1789
N.H.	a	unknown	unknown	17%
Mass.	a	14%	unknown	10%
R.I.	unknown	unknown	unknown	a
Pa.	a	19%	a	8%
Md.	49%	36%	2%	17%
Va.	25%	a	a	a
N.C.	unknown	unknown	a	a
Ga.	a	a	unknown	a
Ky.	unknown	unknown	unknown	a

[a] No popular election.

Sources: Robert J. Dinkin, *Voting in Revolutionary America: A Study of Elections in the Original Thirteen States, 1776–1789* (1982), 108–30. J. R. Pole, *Political Representation in England and the Origins of the American Republic* (1966), 544–62. Donald A. Bohmer, "Stability and Change in Early National Politics: The Maryland Voter and the Election of 1800," *William and Mary Quarterly* XXXVI (1979), 32. John T. Wills, *Presidential Elections in Maryland* (1984), 13–18.

TABLE 8.15 STATE PROCEDURES FOR CHOOSING PRESIDENTIAL ELECTORS, 1788–1800

	1788–89	1792	1796	1800
Conn.	Legislature	Legislature	Legislature	Legislature
Del.	Voters elect separately in 3 districts	Legislature	Legislature	Legislature
Ga.	Legislature	Legislature	Voters choose all electors by state ticket	Legislature
Ky.	As part of Virginia	Voters elect separately in 4 districts	Voters elect separately in 4 districts	Voters elect separately in 4 districts
Md.	Voters choose all electors by state ticket	Voters choose all electors by state ticket	Voters elect separately in 10 districts	Voters elect separately in 10 districts
Mass.	8 by voters, 2 by legislature	5 by voters, 11 by legislature	7 by voters, 9 by legislature	Legislature
N.H.	Voters choose all electors by state ticket	Voters choose all electors by state ticket	Voters choose all electors by state ticket	Legislature
N.J.	Legislature	Legislature	Legislature	Legislature
N.Y.	Not appointed	Legislature	Legislature	Legislature
N.C.	Not in union	Legislature	Voters elect separately in 12 districts	Voters elect separately in 12 districts
Pa.	Voters choose all electors by state ticket	Voters choose all electors by state ticket	Voters choose all electors by state ticket	Voters choose all electors by state ticket
R.I.	Not in union	Legislature	Legislature	Legislature
S.C.	Legislature	Legislature	Legislature	Legislature
Tenn.	As part of N.C.	As part of N.C.	In caucus of electors named by legislature	In caucus of electors named by legislature
Vt.	Not eligible	Legislature	Legislature	Legislature
Va.	Voters elect separately in 12 districts	Voters choose separately in 21 districts	Voters choose all electors by state ticket	Voters choose all electors by state ticket

Source: Congressional Quarterly, *Guide to United States Elections* (2d ed., 1985), 1222.

TABLE 8.16 ELECTORAL TURNOVER IN CONGRESS, 1789–1800

	1st Congress, 1789–1791					
	House of Representatives			Senate		
	Newly Elected in 1789[a]	Seated in By-Election	New Members as Percent of All	Newly Elected in 1789[a]	Seated in By-Election	New Members as Percent of All
Conn.	4	. . .	60%	2	. . .	100%
Del.	1	. . .	100%	2	. . .	100%
Ga.	2	. . .	67%	1	. . .	50%
Md.	4	. . .	67%	2	. . .	100%
Mass.	6[b]	. . .	75%	2	. . .	100%
N.H.	2	. . .	67%	1	. . .	50%
N.J.	4	. . .	100%	1	1	67%
N.Y.	5	. . .	83%	2	. . .	100%
N.C.	4	. . .	80%	2	. . .	100%
Pa.	8	. . .	100%	2	. . .	100%

(continued)

TABLE 8.16   (continued)

	1st Congress, 1789–1791					
	House of Representatives			Senate		
	Newly Elected in 1789[a]	Seated in By-Election	New Members as Percent of All	Newly Elected in 1789[a]	Seated in By-Election	New Members as Percent of All
R.I.	1	...	100%	2	...	100%
S.C.	3	...	60%	2	...	100%
Va.	7	1	73%	2	2	100%
Total	51	1	80%	23	3	90%

[a] A new member is one who had not sat in session of the Continental Congress immediately preceding this one in 1788. About half of all representatives and two-thirds of senators had served in the Continental Congress at some time from 1775 to 1789.
[b] One member resigned in August 1790, but no by-election was held.

	2nd Congress, 1791–1793					
	House of Representatives			Senate		
	Newly Elected in 1791	Seated in By-Election	New Members as Percent of All	Newly Elected in 1791	Seated in By-Election	New Members as Percent of All
Conn.	2	...	40%	...	1	33%
Del.	...	...	...	...	...	...
Ga.	2	1	75%	...	...	...
Ky.	...	2	100%	...	2[a]	100%
Md.	5	2	88%	...	1	33%
Mass.	2	...	29%	1	...	50%
N.H.	1	...	33%	...	...	...
N.J.	3	...	75%	1	...	50%
N.Y.	3	...	50%	1	...	50%
N.C.	2	...	40%	...	...	...
Pa.[b]	4	...	50%	...	...	...
R.I.	...	...	...	...	...	...
S.C.	1	...	20%	...	...	...
Vt.	...	2[c]	100%	...	2[c]	100%
Va.	1	...	10%[d]	...	1	33%
Total	26	7	46%[d]	3	7	30%[e]

[a] Delegation first seated 1792.
[b] One Senate seat was vacant.
[c] Delegation seated 1791.
[d] Excluding four members from newly admitted states, turnover would have equaled 43% of all members seated.
[e] Excluding four members from newly admitted states, turnover would have equaled 21% of all members seated.

	3rd Congress, 1793–1795					
	House of Representatives[a]			Senate		
	Newly Elected in 1793	Seated in By-Election	New Members as Percent of All	Newly Elected in 1793	Seated in By-Election	New Members as Percent of All
Conn.	3	...	43%	...	1	33%
Del.	1	1	100%	...	1	33%
Ga.	1	...	50%	1	...	50%

	3rd Congress, 1793–1795					
	House of Representatives[a]			Senate		
	Newly Elected in 1793	Seated in By-Election	New Members as Percent of All	Newly Elected in 1793	Seated in By-Election	New Members as Percent of All
Ky.	...	...	...	...	...	...
Md.	4	2	60%	...	...	...
Mass.	8	...	57%	...	...	...
N.H.	2	...	50%	1	...	50%
N.J.	2	1	50%	1	...	50%
N.Y.	8	...	80%	...	...	...
N.C.	7	...	70%	1	...	50%
Pa.	6	...	46%	1	1	67%
R.I.	1	...	50%	1	...	50%
S.C.	5	1	86%	...	...	...
Vt.	...	...	...	...	...	...
Va.	11	...	58%	...	2	50%
Total	59	5	58%	6	5	34%

[a] Reapportionment increased the House's size from 65 to 105.

	4th Congress, 1795–1797					
	House of Representatives			Senate		
	Newly Elected in 1795	Seated in By-Election	New Members as Percent of All	Newly Elected in 1795	Seated in By-Election	New Members as Percent of All
Conn.	3	2	55%	1	2	75%
Del.	...	...	...	...	...	...
Ga.	1	...	50%	...	2	50%
Ky.	...	...	...	1	...	50%
Md.	1	2	30%	...	1	33%
Mass.	7	2	56%	...	2	50%
N.H.	1	...	25%	...	...	...
N.J.	3	...	60%	...	1	33%
N.Y.	5	...	50%	...	1	33%
N.C.	5	1	55%	1	...	50%
Pa.	7	1	50%	1	...	50%
R.I.	...	1	33%	...	...	...
S.C.	2	...	33%	1	1	67%
Tenn.	...	1[a]	100%	...	2[a]	100%
Vt.	1	...	50%	1	1	67%
Va.	4	...	22%	...	...	...
Total	40	10	47%[b]	6	13	43%[c]

[a] Delegation first seated in 1796.
[b] Excluding new delegation from Tennessee, turnover would have equaled 47% of all members seated.
[c] Excluding new delegation from Tennessee, turnover would have equaled 40% of all members seated.

	5th Congress, 1797–1799					
	House of Representatives			Senate		
	Newly Elected in 1797	Seated in By-Election	New Members as Percent of All	Newly Elected in 1797	Seated in By-Election	New Members as Percent of All
Conn.	2	1	37%	...	...	...
Del.	1	...	100%	...	2	50%
Ga.	...	...	...	...	...	...
Ky.	2	...	100%	...	...	...
Md.	3	...	38%	...	1	33%
Mass.	5	1	43%	...	...	...
N.H.	2	1	60%	...	...	...
N.J.	3	...	60%	...	1	33%

	5TH Congress, 1797–1799					
	House of Representatives			Senate		
	Newly Elected in 1797	Seated in By-Election	New Members as Percent of All	Newly Elected in 1797	Seated in By-Election	New Members as Percent of All
N.Y.	4	. . .	40%	1	3	80%
N.C.	3	1	36%	. . .	. . .	. . .
Pa.	3	3	37%	. . .	. . .	. . .
R.I.	1	1	67%	. . .	1	33%
S.C.	3	1	57%	. . .	1	33%
Tenn.	1	. . .	100%	. . .	3	60%
Vt.	2	. . .	100%	. . .	1	33%
Va.	9	1	50%	. . .	. . .	. . .
Total	44	10	46%	1	13	31%

	6TH Congress, 1799–1801					
	House of Representatives			Senate		
	Newly Elected in 1799	Seated in By-Election	New Members as Percent of All	Newly Elected in 1799	Seated in By-Election	New Members as Percent of All
Conn.	4	1	62%	. . .	. . .	. . .
Del.	. . .	. . .	. . .	. . .	1	33%
Ga.	2	. . .	100%	1	. . .	50%
Ky.	. . .	. . .	. . .	. . .	. . .	. . .
Md.	3	. . .	37%	. . .	1	33%
Mass.	5	3	47%	1	2	75%
N.H.	1	1	40%	. . .	. . .	. . .
N.J.	4	. . .	80%	2	1	75%
N.Y.	5	1	55%	. . .	2	50%
N.C.	5	. . .	50%	1	. . .	50%
Pa.	4	1	36%	. . .	. . .	. . .
R.I.	1	. . .	50%	. . .	. . .	. . .
S.C.	2	. . .	33%	. . .	. . .	. . .
Tenn.	. . .	. . .	. . .	. . .	. . .	. . .
Vt.	. . .	. . .	. . .	. . .	. . .	. . .
Va.	8	1	45%	1	. . .	50%
Total	44	8	46%	6	7	33%

Below: The 1792 official engraved plan of Washington, D.C., indicates how the location of government branches reflected Republican ideology. Congress's placement on "Capitol Hill" symbolized the legislative branch's supremacy and kept lawmaking in open view. The president's offices were isolated at a distance from Congress to thwart power-hungry executives from seducing legislators from the people's wishes. Broad avenues converged on the executive offices and legislative chambers to facilitate the flow of public opinion from citizens, but the Supreme Court was eventually tucked away in an isolated corner to prevent temporary passions or popular prejudices from bending the justices' interpretation of the Constitution. (I. N. Phelps Stokes Collection, Miriam & Ira Wallach Div. of Arts, Prints and Photographs. Courtesy The New York Public Library. Astor, Lenox and Tilden Foundations.)

Source: John F. Hoadley, *Origins of American Political Parties, 1789–1800* (1986), 199–218.

TABLE 8.17　PRESIDENTIAL ELECTION OF 1789

	Conn.	Del.	Ga.	Md.[a]	Mass.	N.H.	N.J.	N.Y.[b]	N.C.[c]	Pa.	R.I.[c]	S.C.	Va.[d]	Totals
Electoral Votes	(14)	(6)	(10)	(16)	(20)	(10)	(12)	(16)	(14)	(20)	(6)	(14)	(24)	
Washington	7	3	5	6	10	5	6	...	...	10	...	7	10	69
Adams	5	...	...	...	10	5	1	...	...	8	...	...	5	34
Jay	...	3	...	...	...	...	5	...	...	...	...	...	1	9
Harrison	...	...	...	6	...	...	...	...	...	...	...	...	...	6
Rutledge	...	...	...	...	...	...	...	...	...	...	...	6	...	6
Hancock	...	...	...	...	...	...	...	...	...	2	...	1	1	4
Clinton	...	...	...	...	...	...	...	...	...	...	...	...	3	3
Huntington	2	...	...	...	...	...	...	...	...	...	...	...	...	2
Milton	...	...	2	...	...	...	...	...	...	...	...	...	...	2
Armstrong	...	...	1	...	...	...	...	...	...	...	...	...	...	1
Lincoln	...	...	1	...	...	...	...	...	...	...	...	...	...	1
Telfair	...	...	1	...	...	...	...	...	...	...	...	...	...	1

[a]Two Maryland electors abstained.
[b]Abstained from voting.
[c]Had not ratified Constitution and was ineligible to vote.
[d]Two Virginia electors abstained.
Source: Congressional Quarterly, *Guide to United States Elections* (2d ed., 1985), 269.

TABLE 8.18　PRESIDENTIAL ELECTION OF 1792

	Conn.	Del.	Ga.	Ky.	Md.[a]	Mass.	N.H.	N.J.	N.Y.	N.C.	Pa.	R.I.	S.C.	Vt.[b]	Va.	Totals
Electoral Votes	(18)	(6)	(8)	(8)	(20)	(32)	(12)	(14)	(24)	(24)	(30)	(8)	(16)	(8)	(42)	(270)
Washington	9	3	4	4	8	16	6	7	12	12	15	4	8	3	21	132
Adams	9	3	...	...	8	16	6	7	...	...	14	4	7	3	...	77
Clinton	...	...	4	...	...	...	...	...	12	12	1	...	...	...	21	50
Jefferson	...	...	...	4	...	...	...	...	...	...	...	...	...	...	...	4
Burr	...	...	...	...	...	...	...	...	...	...	...	...	1	...	...	1

[a]Two Maryland electors abstained.
[b]One Vermont elector abstained.
Source: Congressional Quarterly, *Guide to United States Elections* (2d ed., 1985), 270.

TABLE 8.19　PRESIDENTIAL ELECTION OF 1796

	Conn.	Del.	Ga.	Ky.	Md.	Mass.	N.H.	N.J.	N.Y.	N.C.	Pa.	R.I.	S.C.	Tenn.	Vt.	Va.	Totals
Electoral Votes	(18)	(6)	(8)	(8)	(20)	(32)	(12)	(14)	(24)	(24)	(30)	(8)	(16)	(6)	(8)	(42)	(276)
J. Adams	9	3	...	...	7	16	6	7	12	1	1	4	...	...	4	1	71
Jefferson	...	...	4	4	4	...	...	...	...	11	14	...	8	3	...	20	68
T. Pinckney	4	3	...	...	4	13	...	7	12	1	2	...	8	...	4	1	59
Burr	...	...	...	4	3	...	...	...	...	6	13	...	...	3	...	1	30
S. Adams	...	...	...	...	...	...	...	...	...	...	...	...	...	...	15		15
Ellsworth	...	...	...	...	...	1	6	...	...	...	...	4	...	...	...	...	11
Clinton	...	...	4	...	...	...	...	...	...	...	...	...	...	...	...	3	7
Jay	5	...	...	...	...	...	...	...	...	...	...	...	...	...	...	...	5
Iredell	...	...	...	...	...	...	...	...	...	3	...	...	...	...	...	...	3
Henry	...	...	...	...	2	...	...	...	...	...	...	...	...	...	...	...	2
Johnston	...	...	...	...	...	2	...	...	...	...	...	...	...	...	...	...	2
Washington	...	...	...	...	...	...	...	...	...	1	...	...	...	...	...	1	2
C. Pinckney	...	...	...	...	...	...	...	...	...	1	...	...	...	...	...	...	1

Source: Congressional Quarterly, *Guide to United States Elections* (2d ed., 1985), 271.

TABLE 8.20　PRESIDENTIAL ELECTION OF 1800

	Conn.	Del.	Ga.	Ky.	Md.	Mass.	N.H.	N.J.	N.Y.	N.C.	Pa.	R.I.	S.C.	Tenn.	Vt.	Va.	Totals
Electoral Votes	(18)	(6)	(8)	(8)	(20)	(32)	(12)	(14)	(24)	(24)	(30)	(8)	(16)	(6)	(8)	(42)	(276)
Jefferson[a]	...	...	4	4	5	...	...	...	12	8	8	...	8	3	...	21	73
Burr[a]	...	...	4	4	5	...	...	...	12	8	8	...	8	3	...	21	73
Adams	9	3	...	...	5	16	6	7	...	4	7	4	...	...	4	...	65
Pinckney	9	3	...	...	5	16	6	7	...	4	7	3	...	...	4	...	64
Jay	...	...	...	...	...	...	...	...	...	...	...	1	...	...	...	...	1

[a]Tie vote decided by House of Representatives.
Source: Congressional Quarterly, *Guide to United States Elections* (2d ed., 1985), 272.

The Executive Department

No governmental position inspired more distrust among Americans than that of chief executive, which evoked memories of innumerable quarrels with royal governors. The earliest state constitutions eviscerated the office and reduced its occupants to figureheads whose authority depended on their ability to elicit voluntary cooperation from the legislature. Americans consequently refused to entrust the national government to a chief executive until 1789.

Under the Articles of Confederation, Congress elected one of its own delegates as a president, but this individual remained part of the legislature and did not function as a true president. To carry on its financial, military, and diplomatic affairs, the Continental Congress organized standing committees (sometimes called boards), to operate in executive fashion. This system worked poorly because the delegates inevitably sacrificed their committee responsibilities to fulfill other legislative obligations. By 1781, Congress replaced the committee system with boards staffed and headed by nonmembers of Congress. These boards performed executive business for Congress and were the forerunners of the departments of state, treasury, war, and post office established in 1789.

Americans increasingly viewed the absence of a chief executive as a political liability. The federal constitution created a strong presidency possessing extensive powers in 1788. Had it not been for the widespread anticipation that George Washington would serve as first president, it is questionable whether Americans would have overcome their lingering doubts about the office and ratified a constitution that made the chief executive co-equal in authority with Congress.

TABLE 8.21   PERSONAL CHARACTERISTICS OF UNITED STATES PRESIDENTS, 1789–1800

President (Term)	Span of Life	Religion, Occupation	Family
George Washington (1789–1797)	b. Feb. 22, 1732 at Pope's Creek, Va.	Episcopal	married Martha Dandridge Custis
	d. Dec. 14, 1799 at Mt. Vernon, Va.	Planter	(no children)
John Adams (1797–1801)	b. Oct. 30, 1735 at Braintree, Mass.	Unitarian	married Abigail Smith (3 sons, 2 daughters)
	d. Jul. 4, 1826 at Quincy, Mass.	Lawyer	

Source: John and Alice Durant, *The Presidents of the United States,* 2 vols. (1974), II, 356.

TABLE 8.22   BACKGROUNDS OF MAJOR CABINET AND DIPLOMATIC APPOINTEES, 1789–1800[a]

Education	Had Some College	Had No College	Graduated Harvard, Yale or Princeton	Graduated Other U.S. College	Graduated College Abroad
	13.1%	13.1%	43.5%	8.6%	21.7%

Residence	Mass.	Other New England	N.Y.	Pa.	Va.	Other South
	15.4%	7.2%	11.5%	15.4%	26.9%	23.1%

Occupation	Agriculture	Lawyer with Rural Estate	Urban Lawyer	Businessman, Professional
	8.7%	34.8%	30.4%	26.1%

Prior Government Service	None	Relatively Little	Considerable
	4.3%	4.3%	91.4%

[a] Based on backgrounds of 23 appointees.
Source: Gary King and Lyn Ragsdale, *The Elusive Executive: Discovering Statistical Patterns in the Presidency* (1988), 240–46.

PRESIDENTIAL CABINET MEMBERS

President	Vice President	Secretary of State	Secretary of the Treasury	Secretary of War	Attorney General	Postmaster General
George Washington, April 30, 1789–March 3, 1797	**John Adams,** Massachusetts, April 21, 1789	**John Jay,** New York, (acting in former capacity as the Confederation's Secretary for Foreign Affairs until Jefferson took office) **Thomas Jefferson,** Virginia, March 22, 1790 **Edmund Randolph,** Virginia, January 2, 1794 **Timothy Pickering,** Pennsylvania, December 10, 1795	**Alexander Hamilton,** New York, September 11, 1789 **Oliver Wolcott,** Connecticut, February 2, 1795	**Henry Knox,** Massachusetts, September 12, 1789 **Timothy Pickering,** Pennsylvania, January 2, 1795 **James McHenry,** Maryland, February 6, 1796	**Edmund Randolph,** Virginia, February 2, 1790 **William Bradford,** Pennsylvania, January 29, 1794 **Charles Lee,** Virginia, December 10, 1795	**Samuel Osgood,** Massachusetts, September 26, 1789 **Timothy Pickering,** Pennsylvania, August 19, 1791 **Joseph Habersham,** Georgia, February 25, 1795
John Adams, March 4, 1797–March 3, 1801	**Thomas Jefferson,** Virginia, March 4, 1797	**Timothy Pickering,** Pennsylvania, continued from previous administration **John Marshall,** Virginia, June 6, 1800	**Oliver Wolcott,** Connecticut, continued from previous administration **Samuel Dexter,** Massachusetts, January 1, 1801	**James McHenry,** Maryland, continued from previous administration **Samuel Dexter,** Massachusetts, June 12, 1800 **Secretary of the Navy** **Benjamin Stoddert,** Maryland, June 18, 1798	**Charles Lee,** Virginia, continued from previous administration	**Joseph Habersham,** Georgia, continued from previous administration

Congress

The Continental Congress enjoyed little real power under the Articles of Confederation. It relied on the voluntary cooperation of state legislatures to supply troops for the Continental Army and collect taxes for the treasury. As long as independence was in jeopardy, the legislatures upheld their obligations, but once peace returned they became preoccupied with their own internal problems and tended to ignore the common welfare.

By 1787, Congress operated under severe financial constraints because it could not levy taxes without approval from every state, and unanimous consent was impossible to obtain. Congress found it increasingly difficult to find the necessary quorum to conduct business because attendance by the state delegations was haphazard. Aside from passing two landmark ordinances to organize settlement of the West, the national legislature in fact did little after 1783 and inspired even less confidence. Popular dissatisfaction with Congress's weakness finally expressed itself in the adoption of a new constitution, which created a bicameral legislature empowered to impose taxes and to override state laws with federal statutes. The new Congress first met in 1789 and immediately proved itself equal to the task of enacting laws to restore the government's public credit, defend the frontier, and revive overseas commerce.

Until 1789, the U.S. government possessed neither an executive nor a judicial branch. Government by Congress meant that legislative committees performed most executive functions and that legal disputes between states could only be resolved by arbitrators appointed by Congress. In the sketch below, the Second Continental Congress adjourns to hear the first public reading of its Declaration of Independence. (*Harper's Weekly,* July 10, 1880)

Few representatives or senators relocated their families to the capital for sessions, during which they received no salary but only a living allowance. Congress consequently tended to keep its agenda limited so that the members could spend half the year, if not more, at home and resume their normal occupations. Congress rarely enacted more than forty laws a year, and it performed little of what has become known as "constituent services," except for helping a small number of disabled war veterans to obtain pensions. For similar reasons, congressmen tended not to continue in office for more than a few sessions, and so turnover generally amounted to 20% of senators and 40% of representatives per session. This ethos of limited government, undertaken by non-professional politicians, was the essential principle of Jeffersonian democracy.

TABLE 8.23   OCCUPATIONAL BACKGROUNDS OF CONTINENTAL CONGRESSMEN, 1777–1779

Lawyers	35.4%	Slave-owning Planters	16.7%
Professionals[a]	18.7%	Non-slave-owning Farmers	4.2%
Merchants	16.7%	Government Officeholders	8.3%

Source: H. James Henderson, *Party Politics in the Continental Congress* (1974), 173.

TABLE 8.24 OFFICERS OF CONGRESS, 1764–1800

Stamp Act Congress. Oct. 7–25, 1765.

President:	Timothy Ruggles, Mass.

Continental Congress, 1774–1789.

President	Date Elected
Peyton Randolph, Va.	Sep. 5, 1774
Henry Middleton, S.C.	Oct. 22, 1774
Peyton Randolph, Va.	May 10, 1775
John Hancock, Mass.	May 24, 1775
Henry Laurens, S.C.	Nov. 1, 1777
John Jay, N.Y.	Dec. 10, 1778
Samuel Huntington, Conn.	Sep. 28, 1779
Thomas McKean, Del.	Jul. 10, 1781
John Hanson, Md.	Nov. 5, 1781
Elias Boudinot, N.J.	Nov. 4, 1782
Thomas Mifflin, Pa.	Nov. 3, 1783
Richard H. Lee, Va.	Nov. 30, 1784
John Hancock, Mass.	Nov. 23, 1785 (declined to serve)
Nathaniel Gorham, Mass.	Jun. 6, 1786
Arthur St. Clair, Pa.	Feb. 2, 1787
Cyrus Griffin, Va.	Jan. 22, 1788

First Congress. Mar. 4, 1789–Mar. 3, 1791.

Speaker of the House:	Frederick A. C. Muhlenberg, Pa., Pro-Admin.
President Pro Tempore:	John Langdon, N.H., Anti-Admin.

Second Congress. Mar. 4, 1791–Mar. 3, 1793.

Speaker of the House:	Jonathan Trumbull, Conn., Fed.
President Pro Tempore:	John Landgon, N.H., Dem.

Third Congress. Mar. 4, 1793–Mar. 3, 1795.

Speaker of the House: President Pro Tempore:	Frederick A. C. Muhlenberg, Pa., Fed. Ralph Izard, S.C. Fed. Henry Tazewell, Va., Dem.

Fourth Congress. Mar. 4, 1795–Mar. 3, 1797.

Speaker of the House: President Pro Tempore:	Jonathan Dayton, N.J., Fed. Henry Tazewell, Va. Dem. Samuel Livermore, N.H., Fed. William Bingham, Pa., Fed.

Fifth Congress. Mar. 4, 1797–Mar. 3, 1799.

Speaker of the House: President Pro Tempore:	Jonathan Dayton, N.J., Fed. William Bradford, R.I., Fed. Jacob Read, S.C., Fed. Theodore Sedgwick, Mass., Fed. John Laurance, N.Y., Fed. James Ross, Pa., Fed.

Sixth Congress. Mar. 4, 1799–Mar. 3, 1801.

Speaker of the House: President Pro Tempore:	Theodore Sedgwick, Mass., Fed. Samuel Livermore, N.H., Fed. Uriah Tracy, Conn., Fed. John E. Howard, Md., Fed. James Hillhouse, Conn., Fed.

Source: Linda S. Hubbard, *Notable Americans: What They Did, From 1620 to the Present* (1988), 1, 3, 41–45.

TABLE 8.25 CONGRESSIONAL SESSIONS AND LEGISLATION, 1789–1800

Congress	Session	Date Begun	Date Adjourned	Days	Statutes Passed		
					Public Laws	Private Laws	Vetoes
1st	1	Mar. 4, 1789	Sep. 29, 1789	210	26	1	. . .
1st	2	Jan. 4, 1790	Aug. 12, 1790	221	40	7	. . .
1st	3	Dec. 6, 1790	Mar. 3, 1791	88	28	. . .	. . .
2nd	1	Oct. 24, 1791	May 8, 1792[a]	197	36	8	1[b]
2nd	2	Nov. 5, 1792	Mar. 2, 1793	119	69	7	. . .
3rd	1	Dec. 2, 1793	Jun. 9, 1794	190	48	17	. . .
3rd	2	Nov. 3, 1794	Mar. 3, 1795	121	40	13	. . .
4th	1	Dec. 7, 1795	Jun. 1, 1796	177	47	7	. . .
4th	2	Dec. 5, 1796	Mar. 3, 1797	89	24	4	. . .
5th	1	May 15, 1797	Jul. 10, 1797	57	17	. . .	1[c]
5th	2	Nov. 13, 1797	Jul. 16, 1798	246	74	15	. . .
5th	3	Dec. 3, 1798	Mar. 3, 1799	91	43	5	. . .
6th	1	Dec. 2, 1799	May 14, 1800	164	62	9	. . .
6th	2	Nov. 17, 1800	Mar. 3, 1801	107	29	6	. . .

[a] Both houses recessed Dec. 23–30, 1800.
[b] Congressional Apportionment Act of Apr. 5, 1792 (sustained).
[c] Military establishment act of Feb. 28, 1797 (sustained).
Sources: Congressional Quarterly, *Guide to Congress* (4th ed., 1991), 113-A. Richard E. Parks, ed., *The Public Statutes at Large of the United States . . . 1789 to Mar. 3, 1845*, 6 vols. (1856), I–VI.

TABLE 8.26 APPORTIONMENT OF STATE DELEGATIONS IN 1ST THROUGH 6TH CONGRESSES

	1789 Representatives Prescribed by Sec. 2, Art. I of Constitution [a]	1791 According to 1790 Census [b]		
		Free Population	3/5 of Slave Population	Size of Delegation
Conn.	5	235,182	1,658	7
Del.	1	50,209	5,332	1
Ga.	3	53,284	17,558	2
Ky.	...	61,247	7,458	2
Md.	6	216,692	61,822	8
Mass.	8	475,327	none	14
N.H.	3	141,727	95	4
N.J.	4	172,716	6,854	5
N.Y.	6	318,796	12,794	10
N.C.	5	293,179	60,343	10
Pa.	8	430,636	2,242	13
R.I.	1	67,877	569	2
S.C.	5	141,979	64,256	6
Tenn.	...	32,274	2,050	1
Vt.	...	85,539	none	2
Va.	10	454,983	175,576	19
Total	65	3,052,587	409,099	106

[a] Used to apportion 1st and 2nd Congresses, 1789–1793.
[b] Used to apportion 3rd through 6th Congresses, 1793–1801.
Sources: Merrill Jensen and Robert A. Becker, *The Documentary History of the First Federal Elections, 1788–1790,* 3 vols. (1976), I, xxiv.

TABLE 8.27 PARTY AFFILIATION OF HOUSE OF REPRESENTATIVES, 1789–1801

1st Congress, 1789–1791			
	Pro-Administration	Anti-Administration	Interim Elections
Conn.	5	...	...
Del.	1	...	...
Ga.	...	3	...
Ky.	...	...	...
Md.	6	...	...
Mass.	6	2	...
N.H.	2	1	...
N.J.	4	...	...
N.Y.	4	2	...
N.C.	2	3	...
Pa.	5	3	...
R.I.	1	...	...
S.C.	1	4	...
Vt.	...	...	...
Va.	2	8	1 (no change)
Total	39	26	1 (no change)

2nd Congress, 1791–1793			
	Pro-Admin. or Federalist	Anti-Admin. or Republican	Interim Elections
Conn.	5	...	...
Del.	1	...	...
Ga.	...	3	1 (no change)
Ky.	...	2	...
Md.	4	2	2 (+1 Dem.)
Mass.	7	1	...
N.H.	2	1	...
N.J.	3	1	...
N.Y.	4	2	...
N.C.	3	2	...
Pa.	4	4	...
R.I.	1	...	...
S.C.	3	2	...
Vt.	...	2	...
Va.	3	7	...
Total	40	29	3 (+1 Dem.)

3rd Congress, 1793–1795			
	Federalist	Republican	Interim Elections
Conn.	7	...	...
Del.	1	...	+1 Dem.
Ga.	...	2	...
Ky.	...	2	...
Md.	3	5	2 (no change)
Mass.	11	3	...
N.H.	3	1	...
N.J.	4	1	+1 Fed.
N.Y.	6	4	...
N.C.	1	9	...
Pa.	5	8	...
R.I.	2	...	...
S.C.	1	5	+1 Fed.
Tenn.	...	...	...
Vt.	...	2	...
Va.	4	15	...
Total	48	57	5 (+1 Fed.)

4th Congress, 1795–1797			
	Federalist	Republican	Interim Elections
Conn.	7	...	2 (no change)
Del.	...	1	...
Ga.	...	2	...
Ky.	...	2	...
Md.	3	5	2 (+1 Fed.)
Mass.	10	4	2 (+1 Dem.)
N.H.	3	1	...
N.J.	5	...	...
N.Y.	5	5	...
N.C.	1	9	+ 1 Fed.
Pa.	4	9	+1 Fed.
R.I.	2	...	1 (no change)
S.C.	2	4	...
Tenn.	...	1	...
Vt.	1	1	...
Va.	2	17	...
Total	45	61	9 (+2 Fed.)

5th Congress, 1797–1799

	Federalist	Republican	Interim Elections
Conn.	7	. . .	2 (no change)
Del.	1	. . .	. . .
Ga.	. . .	2	. . .
Ky.	. . .	2	. . .
Md.	6	2	. . .
Mass.	11	3	1 (no change)
N.H.	4	. . .	1 (no change)
N.J.	5	. . .	. . .
N.Y.	6	4	. . .
N.C.	1	9	1 (no change)
Penn.	6	7	3 (+1 Dem.)
R.I.	2	. . .	+1 Dem.
S.C.	3	3	1 (no change)
Tenn.	. . .	1	. . .
Vt.	1	1	. . .
Va.	4	15	1 (no change)
Total	57	49	10 (+2 Dem.)

6th Congress, 1799–1801

	Federalist	Republican	Interim Elections
Conn.	7	. . .	1 (no change)
Del.	1	. . .	. . .
Ga.	1	1	. . .
Ky.	. . .	2	. . .
Md.	5	3	. . .
Mass.	12	2	3 (+1 Dem.)
N.H.	4	. . .	1 (no change)
N.J.	2	3	. . .
N.Y.	4	6	1 (no change)
N.C.	5	5	. . .
Pa.	5	8	+1 Dem.
R.I.	2	. . .	. . .
S.C.	5	1	. . .
Tenn.	. . .	1	. . .
Vt.	1	1	. . .
Va.	8	11	+1 Dem.
Total	62	44	8 (+3 Dem.)

Source: John F. Hoadley, *Origins of American Political Parties, 1789–1803* (1986), 199–214.

TABLE 8.28 PARTY AFFILIATION OF SENATE, 1789–1801

1st Congress, 1789–1791

	Pro-Administration	Anti-Administration	Interim Elections
Conn.	2	. . .	. . .
Del.	2	. . .	. . .
Ga.	. . .	2	. . .
Ky.	. . .	. . .	. . .
Md.	1	1	. . .
Mass.	2	. . .	. . .
N.H.	1	1	. . .
N.J.	2	. . .	1 (no change)
N.Y.	2	. . .	. . .
N.C.	2	. . .	. . .

1st Congress, 1789–1791

	Pro-Administration	Anti-Administration	Interim Elections
Pa.	1	1	. . .
R.I.	1	1	. . .
S.C.	1	1	. . .
Vt.	. . .	. . .	. . .
Va.	. . .	2	2 (no change)
Total	17	9	3 (no change)

2nd Congress, 1791–1793

	Pro-Admin. or Federalist	Anti-Admin. or Republican	Interim Elections
Conn.	2	. . .	1 (no change)
Del.	2	. . .	. . .
Ga.	. . .	2	. . .
Ky.	. . .	2	. . .
Md.	1	1	1 (no change)
Mass.	2	. . .	. . .
N.H.	1	1	. . .
N.J.	2	. . .	. . .
N.Y.	1	1	. . .
N.C.	2	. . .	. . .
Pa.	1 [a]	. . .	. . .
R.I.	1	1	. . .
S.C.	1	1	. . .
Vt.	. . .	2	. . .
Va.	. . .	2	1 (no change)
Total	16	13	3 (no change)

3rd Congress, 1793–1795

	Federalist	Republican	Interim Elections
Conn.	2	. . .	1 (no change)
Del.	2	. . .	1 (no change)
Ga.	. . .	2	. . .
Ky.	. . .	2	. . .
Md.	1	1	. . .
Mass.	2	. . .	. . .
N.H.	1	1	. . .
N.J.	2	. . .	. . .
N.Y.	1	1	. . .
N.C.	1	1	. . .
Pa.	1	1	+1 Fed.
R.I.	2	. . .	. . .
S.C.	1	1	. . .
Tenn.	. . .	. . .	. . .
Vt.	. . .	2	. . .
Va.	. . .	2	2 (no change)
Total	16	14	5 (+1 Fed.)

4th Congress, 1795–1797

	Federalist	Republican	Interim Elections
Conn.	2	. . .	2 (no change)
Del.	2	. . .	. . .
Ga.	. . .	2	2 (no change)
Ky.	1	1	. . .
Md.	1	1	1 (no change)

(continued)

TABLE 8.28 (continued)

	4th Congress, 1795–1797		
	Federalist	Republican	Interim Elections
Mass.	2	...	2 (no change)
N.H.	1	1	...
N.J.	2	...	1 (no change)
N.Y.	1	1	1 (no change)
N.C.	...	2	...
Pa.	2	...	...
R.I.	2	...	...
S.C.	1	1	+1 Fed.
Tenn.	...	2	...
Vt.	1	1	+1 Fed.
Va.	...	2	...
Total	18	14	11 (+2 Fed.)

	5th Congress, 1797–1799		
	Federalist	Republican	Interim Elections
Conn.	2	...	...
Del.	2	...	2 (no change)
Ga.	...	2	...
Ky.	1	1	...
Md.	1	1	1 (no change)
Mass.	2	...	...
N.H.	1	1	...
N.J.	2	...	1 (no change)
N.Y.	2	...	2 (no change)
N.C.	...	2	...
Pa.	2	...	...
R.I.	2	...	2 (no change)
S.C.	2	...	+1 Dem.
Tenn.	...	2	3 (no change)
Vt.	2	...	1 (no change)
Va.	...	2	...
Total	21	11	13 (+1 Dem.)

	6th Congress, 1799–1801		
	Federalist	Republican	Interim Elections
Conn.	2	...	...
Del.	2	...	1 (no change)
Ga.	1	1	...
Ky.	1	1	...
Md.	1	1	+1 Fed.
Mass.	2	...	2 (no change)
N.H.	1	1	...
N.J.	2	...	1 (no change)
N.Y.	1	1	2 (no change)
N.C.	...	2	...
Pa.	2	...	...
R.I.	2	...	...
S.C.	1	1	...
Tenn.	...	2	...
Vt.	2	...	...
Va.	...	2	...
Total	20	12	7 (+1 Fed.)

[a]One seat vacant from Pa., 1791–1793.
Source: John F. Hoadley, *Origins of American Political Parties, 1789–1803* (1986), 215–18.

John Jay became the Supreme Court's first Chief Justice in 1791. He had served as president of the Continental Congress in 1778, had played a leading role in drafting New York's initial constitution, and then had become that state's first Chief Justice. This engraving, based on a portrait by Gilbert Stuart, presents the austere, grave, and incisive manner for which Jay was known. (Courtesy Library of Congress)

The Federal Judiciary

The first national constitution, the Articles of Confederation, established no judicial department. In case of disputes arising among the states, the document merely authorized Congress to oversee arbitration of the controversy, provided each party agreed. Appeals from decisions in lower tribunals went no farther than each state's superior court, since every state enjoyed complete legal autonomy.

Once the Constitution was established as the supreme law of the land, a federal judiciary became essential. In 1789 Congress created a hierarchy of district and circuit courts, capped by a Supreme Court of six justices. The primary forum of appeal was the Circuit Court, where two Supreme Court justices joined a District Court judge in hearing cases. The Supreme Court's members largely spent their time "riding circuit," a chore so burdensome that in 1791 Justice John Rutledge resigned from the nation's highest bench to become a state judge, and two men refused to succeed him rather than spend their lives trudging endlessly between circuit sessions. Chief Justice Jay characterized his duties as "intolerable" in 1794 and ran for New York's governorship.

No cases reached the Supreme Court, in its role as highest tribunal, until its fourth term, and so few appeals came from lower jurisdictions that it rarely issued more than three rulings per term in the 1790s. The early Supreme Court's most notable achievement was its refusal to issue advisory rulings when requested by Congress or the president. The justices wisely reasoned that such opinions would entangle the court in making political policy, compromise its ability to render impartial verdicts, and blur the constitutional separation of powers.

The United States Supreme Court enjoyed much less prestige in the early national period than it does today. Three of the first sixteen men nominated to the court declined to serve, including two named

TABLE 8.29 ORGANIZATION OF FEDERAL JUDICIARY, BY ACT OF SEPT. 24, 1789 AND LATER AMENDMENTS

Court and Personnel	Schedule of Yearly Sessions
I. Supreme Court. 1 chief justice and 5 associate justices	Two sessions at national capital, held first Monday in February held first Monday in August
II. Circuit Courts. any 2 justices of Supreme Court and 1 District-Court judge	1. Eastern Circuit Sessions held at: N.H. (Portsmouth and Exeter), Mass. (Boston), R.I. (Providence and Newport), Conn. (New Haven and Hartford), N.Y. (New York City), Vt. (Bennington). 2. Middle Circuit Sessions held at: N.J. (Trenton), Pa. (Philadelphia and York), Del. (New Castle and Dover), Md. (Annapolis and Easton), Va. (Charlottesville and Williamsburg). 3. Southern Circuit Sessions held at: N.C. (New Bern), S.C. (Columbia and Charleston[a]), Ga. (Savannah and Augusta).
III. District Courts.[b] 1 judge each	Fifteen districts established (one per state), with courts held four times yearly by a single district judge.

[a] Held October 1 at Charleston.
[b] Courts for Me., Ky., and Tenn. given jurisdiction over all cases hearable in circuit courts except appeals from itself and writs of error.
Source: Richard Peters, ed., *The Public Statutes at Large of the United States of America . . . 1789 to March 3, 1845,* 6 vols. (1856), I, 119, 222, 241, 366, 430, 483, 552, 604.

TABLE 8.30 NOMINATIONS TO THE SUPREME COURT

	Nominated to Office	Date of Senate Vote	End of Service
John Jay (N.Y.)[a]	9/24/1789	9/26/1789	resigned 6/29/1795
John Rutledge (S.C.)	9/24/1789	9/26/1789	resigned 3/5/1791
William Cushing (Mass.)	9/24/1789	9/26/1789	died 9/13/1810
James Wilson (Pa.)	9/24/1789	9/26/1789	died 8/21/1798
John Blair (Va.)	9/24/1789	9/26/1789	resigned 1/27/1796
Robert H. Harrison (Md.)	9/24/1789	9/26/1789	declined to serve
James Iredell (N.C.) (for Harrison)	2/8/1790	2/10/1790	died 10/20/1799
Thomas Johnson (Md.) (for Rutledge)	11/1/1791	11/7/1791	resigned 3/4/1793
William Paterson (N.J.) (for Johnson)	2/27/1793	3/4/1793[b]	died 9/9/1806
John Rutledge (S.C.)[a] (for Jay)	7/1/1795	12/15/1795	rejected by Senate
William Cushing (Mass.)[a] (for Jay)	1/26/1796	1/27/1796	declined to serve
Samuel Chase (Md.) (for Blair)	1/26/1796	1/27/1796	died 6/19/1811
Oliver Ellsworth (Conn.)[a] (for Jay)	3/3/1796	3/4/1796	resigned 12/15/1800
Bushrod Washington (Va.) (for Wilson)	12/19/1798	12/20/1798	died 11/26/1829
Alfred Moore (N.C.) (for Iredell)	12/6/1799	12/10/1799	died 1/26/1804
John Jay (N.Y.) (for Ellsworth)	12/18/1800	12/19/1800	declined to serve

[a] Chief Justice.
[b] Withdrew and was confirmed after renomination.
Source: Congressional Quarterly, *Chief to the U.S. Supreme Court* (2d ed., 1990), 995.

for the chief justiceship. Three others resigned after less than five years on the bench. The Court finally won recognition as a major force in government under Chief Justice John Marshall (1801–1835).

TABLE 8.31 SUPREME COURT TERMS AND CASES HEARD, 1789–1800

Term	Cases Heard
Feb. 1790	none
Aug. 1790	none
Feb. 1791	none
Aug. 1791	2
Feb. 1792	1
Aug. 1792	3
Feb. 1793	3
Aug. 1793	none
Feb. 1794	2
Aug. 1794	none
Feb. 1795	4
Aug. 1795	2
Feb. 1796	5
Aug. 1796	11
Feb. 1797	4
Aug. 1797	4
Feb. 1798	3
Aug. 1798	2
Feb. 1799	4
Aug. 1799	3
Feb. 1800	7
Aug. 1800	3

Source: Alexander J. Dallas, *Reports of Cases Ruled and Adjudged in the Several Courts of the United States, and of Pennsylvania,* 4 vols. (1795–1807).

Finances

British Imperial Finances

Only at the end of the colonial era did the British government collect significant amounts of tax revenue in North America. Parliament levied no direct taxes on the provinces before 1763 and indirect taxes collected while certifying trade reportedly totaled about £1,800 per year, which was less than the budget of the colonial customs service. Beginning in 1764, Parliament imposed several new taxes designed to offset the cost of maintaining troops overseas. Americans ultimately forced Parliament to repeal the Stamp Act and

TABLE 8.32 EXPENDITURES BY BRITISH GOVERNMENT IN THIRTEEN COLONIES, 1764–1775

Government Department	Expenditures 1764–1775	Yearly Average
Army	£3,369,000	£280,750
Ordnance Board	£552,000	£46,000
Navy Board	£421,266	£35,106
Naval Victualling Board	£250,569	£20,881
Colonial Administration	£391,000	£32,583
Privy Purse	£18,000	£1,500
Total	£5,001,835	£416,820

Source: Julian Gwyn, "British Government Spending and the North American Colonies, 1740–1775," *Journal of Imperial and Commonwealth History,* VIII (1980), 77–78.

TABLE 8.33 TOTAL TAXES COLLECTED IN THE THIRTEEN COLONIES UNDER PARLIAMENTARY REVENUE LAWS, 1765–1774

Year	Stamp Act of 1764	Sugar Act of 1764	Revenue Act of 1767	Other Customs Duties	Total
1765	£3,292	£14,091	. . .	£2,954	£17,383
1766	. . .	£26,696	. . .	£7,373	£26,696
1767	. . .	£33,844	£197	£3,905	£34,041
1768	. . .	£24,659	£13,202	£1,160	£37,861
1769	. . .	£39,938	£5,561	£1,294	£45,499
1770	. . .	£30,910	£2,727	£1,828	£33,637
1771	. . .	£27,086	£4,675	£1,446	£31,761
1772	. . .	£42,570	£3,300	£1,490	£45,870
1773	. . .	£39,531	£2,572	£2,517	£42,103
1774	. . .	£27,074	£921	£672	£27,995
Total	£3,292	£306,399	£33,155	£24,639	£342,846

Source: Oliver M. Dickerson, *The Navigation Acts and the American Revolution* (1951), 201.

most of the Townshend duties (except those on tea), but they could not block collections under the Sugar Act since it could be enforced at sea by the Royal Navy. The Sugar Act furnished the royal treasury with £306,000, or almost 90% of all American revenues paid to the Crown from 1764 to 1774.

Although Britain's efforts to establish an American revenue sparked a rebellion to end taxation without representation, the monies collected were so small that they never offset the expenses of royal government. During the decade after the Seven Years' War, Parliament disbursed £5,000,000 in North America, or almost fifteen times as much as it collected in taxes. These payments helped alleviate the chronic shortage of hard money in the provinces, counterbalanced the colonists' tendency to import more consumer items than the value of their exports, and so enabled the people to afford a slightly higher standard of living. The net effect of the British government's fiscal policies consequently seems to have been positive for the American economy.

United States Government Finances

The Continental Congress and the states shared responsibility for financing the Revolutionary War. Neither level of government possessed a sophisticated staff of experienced financiers, and eventually this system degenerated into economic chaos. Accounts remained unorganized, taxes went uncollected, and Continental money inflated so wildly that the expression "not worth a Continental" endured as a folk-saying for generations. Official record keeping was so erratic that no exact figure can be given for the cost of winning independence, although it seems that Congress and the states together spent from $158,000,000 to $168,000,000 in specie (the designated exchange rate in Spanish dollars), which had a value in sterling equal to approximately £35,000,000.

Congress initially tried to avoid raising heavy taxes and resorted to printing paper money denominated in the specie value of Spanish dollars. This expedient worked remarkably well for the war's first three years. Continentals passed at official worth through 1776 and circulated at a mere 6% discount in early 1777; thereafter they steadily declined, and when the printing presses halted in 1781 after eleven emissions, their purchasing power was almost nonexistent. Congress thereafter assessed the states for requisitions, which were to be paid in Spanish gold or silver.

European loans and subsidies contributed to the American war effort, but their overall significance was minor. By 1781, the United States had received only $2,212,972 in foreign aid, just 4% of the treasury's income. These loans were primarily important because they allowed the United States to buy military supplies in Europe, where continental currency was not accepted. After the war ended, European speculators bought a large amount of the national debt at depressed prices in anticipation that the United States would honor its obligations and redeem the debt at face value. Their gamble paid off in 1790, and they reaped windfall profits.

Congress and the states both issued large amounts of interest-bearing loan certificates. There were an infinite variety of these domestic IOUs, which were supported by taxes and congressional assessments upon the states. By the war's end, most states found it difficult to raise the hard money needed to pay interest and retire these loans, and so they fell behind in their requisitions to Congress. Congress consequently had to default on its loans, could not pay interest on schedule, and fell behind in retiring its own debt. The states assumed some of the national debt held by their own citizens and paid interest to the creditors with local taxes. The national and state debts consequently became mixed, and after 1781 many states accumulated large sums of congressional loan certificates and expended more than half of their budgets in paying interest.

The United States was still defaulting on the national debt when Alexander Hamilton became treasurer in 1789, and yet enormous progress had been made in managing the Revolution's expenses. Of approximately $160,000,000 spent during the war, about $91,000,000, or 57%, had been liquidated, although unpaid interest had risen to $15,000,000. In his Report on the Public Credit of January 9, 1790, Hamilton itemized the unpaid national debt as $54,000,000, which included overdue interest of $15,000,000; he proposed reissuing that amount in U.S. bonds, together with $21,500,000 in state loan certificates to be assumed as part of the national debt. Congress complied and the subsequent refunding of $75,600,000 in revolutionary debt was handled so responsibly, that U.S. bonds became eagerly sought as the safest way to protect capital during the chaotic period spawned by the French Revolution. The U.S. government established itself as a model of fiscal responsibility in the 1790s. It enjoyed sterling credit on overseas stock exchanges, and by 1800 it not only was meeting heavy interest payments on the national debt, but also was balancing the federal budget and had run a small surplus in most years after 1793.

TABLE 8.34 EXPENDITURES BY CONTINENTAL CONGRESS, 1775–1781

	Disbursements at Face Value		Value in Specie
1775–76	$20,064,666	(Continentals)	$20,064,666
1777	$26,426,333	(Continentals)	$24,986,646
1778	$66,965,269	(Continentals)	$24,289,438
1779	$149,703,856	(Continentals)	$10,794,620
1780	$82,908,320	(Continentals)	$2,500,000
	$891,236	(new currency)	$500,000
1781	$11,408,095	(Continentals)	$285,202
	$1,179,249	(new currency)	$589,624
	$320,049	(specie)	$320,049
	$747,590	(treasury accounts)	$747,590
Totals	$360,614,663		$85,077,835

Note: Specie value denominates a U.S. dollar in gold equal to a Spanish dollar, which was worth 22.5% of £1 sterling, or 4s., 6d.
Source: E. James Ferguson, *The Power of the Purse: A History of American Public Finance, 1776–1790* (1961), 28–29.

TABLE 8.35 INCOME OF CONTINENTAL CONGRESS (SPECIE VALUE) TO 1780

Domestic Income	
Issues of Continental Currency	
1775	$6,000,000
1776	$17,300,000
1777	$4,530,000
1778	$11,695,000
1779	$5,964,000
Subtotal	$45,489,000
Loan Certificates	
To March 1, 1778	$2,437,301
March 1, 1778 to March 1, 1779	$2,506,143
March 1, 1779 to March 18, 1780	$988,607
Subtotal	$5,932,051
State Credits	
Requisitions	$378,456
Payments of Federal Drafts	$397,522
Payments of Specie	$61,696
Various Credits	$881,641
Subtotal	$1,719,315

Foreign Aids	
France	
Subsidies	2,000,000 livres
Loans	4,000,000 livres
Supplies	5,107,594 livres
Tobacco Contract	1,000,000 livres
(Repaid by 1780	−705,340 livres)
Subtotal (in Dollars)	11,402,254 livres ($2,111,528)
Spain	
1777 Subsidy	187,500 livres
1778 Loan	187,500 livres
Subtotal (in Dollars)	375,000 livres ($69,444)
Netherlands	
Private loans through 1779	80,000 florin
Subtotal (in Dollars)	($32,000)
Total Foreign Aids	$2,212,972
Total Domestic Income	$53,140,366
Total Income	$55,353,338

Note: Specie value denominates a U.S. dollar in gold equal to a Spanish dollar, which was worth 22.5% of £1 sterling, or 4s., 6d.
Source: E. James Ferguson, *The Power of the Purse: A History of American Public Finance, 1776–1790* (1961), 40–43.

TABLE 8.36 EXPENDITURES AND INCOME OF UNITED STATES GOVERNMENT, 1784–1789

Receipts and Expenditures, November 1, 1784 to 1789, (excluding indents)

Receipts				Expenditures			
Nov. 1, 1784 (end of Morris's administration) to Dec. 31, 1784							
Balance in Treasury, Nov. 1		$21,986		Administrative expenses		$16,245	
				Army		$6,275	
Payments from or credits to states		$54,740		Others		$6,145	
Other domestic incomes		$2,758		Anticipations		$32,379	
				Balance in Treasury		$18,440	
Total			$79,484				$79,484
1785							
Balance in Treasury, Jan. 1		$18,440		Domestic:			
Domestic incomes:				Administration	$85,715		
Payments from or credits to states	$378,866			Army	$132,372		
Others	$26,278			Others	$65,084		
				Debts and anticipations	$97,439		
		$405,144		Balance in Treasury	$41,902		
						$422,512	
Foreign incomes:				Foreign:			
Dutch loan, etc.		$208,802		Interest on Dutch loan		$209,874	
Total			$632,386				$632,386
1786							
Balance in Treasury, Jan. 1		$41,902		Domestic:			
				Administration	$117,430		
Domestic incomes:				Army	$145,530		
Payments from or credits to states	$328,872			Others	$24,223		
				Credit to South Carolina for supplies	$27,730		
Others	$9,249			Past debts	$49,681		
		$338,121				$364,594	
Foreign incomes:		None		Foreign:			
Payments over receipts:		$59,571		Interest on Dutch loan		$75,000	
Total			$439,594				$439,594

(continued)

TABLE 8.36 (continued)

TABLE 8.36 (continued)

Receipts				Expenditures			
1787							
Domestic incomes:				Accumulated deficit:		$59,571	
Payments from or				*Domestic:*			
credits to state	$276,639			Administration	$128,332		
Others	$41,931			Army	$160,406		
		$318,570		Others	$39,675		
				Payment of old accounts	$9,318		
Foreign incomes:		$4,909					$337,731
Payments over receipts				*Foreign:*			
and accumulated deficit:		$105,815		Interest on Dutch loan		$31,992	
Total			$429,294				$429,294
1788							
Domestic incomes:				Accumulated deficit:		105,815	
Payments from or				*Domestic:*			
credits to states	$261,679			Administration	$94,610		
Others	$77,909			Army	$196,404		
		$339,588		Others	$96,104		
				Payment of old accounts	$10,248		
Foreign incomes:		$1,645					$397,366
Payments over receipts				*Foreign:*		None	
and accumulated deficit:		$174,189		*Discrepancy in*			
				indent account:		$12,241	
Total		$515,422					$515,422
1789 (incomplete)							
Domestic incomes:				Accumulated deficit:		$174,189	
Payments from or				*Domestic:*			
credits to states	$127,837			Administration	$55,741		
Others	$14,432			Army	$78,311		
		$142,269		Others	$23,339		
				Payment of old accounts	$595		
Foreign incomes:		none					$157,986
Payments over receipts							
and accumulated deficit:		$189,906					
Total		$332,175					$332,175

Source: E. James Ferguson, *The Power of the Purse: A History of American Public Finance, 1776–1790* (1961), 236–37.

TABLE 8.37 UNITED STATES TREASURY ACCOUNTS WITH STATE GOVERNMENTS, 1786–1793

	Value of U.S. Loan Certificates Assumed[a]	State War Expenses Refunded by U.S.	State War Expenses Not Funded by U.S.	Balance due State from U.S. in 1793[b]	Balance due U.S. from State in 1793[b]
N.H.	$33,148	$440,974	$466,544	$75,055	. . .
Mass.	. . .	$1,245,737	$3,167,020	$1,248,801	. . .
R.I.	. . .	1,028,511	$310,395	$299,611	. . .
Conn.	$8,647	$1,016,273	$1,607,295	$619,121	. . .
N.Y.	$2,300,000	$822,803	$1,545,889	. . .	$2,074,846
N.J.	interest only[c]	$366,729	$512,916	$49,030	. . .
Pa.	$6,044,000	$2,087,276	$2,629,410	. . .	76,709
Del.	. . .	$63,817	$208,878	. . .	$612,428
Md.	$661,000	$609,617	$945,537	. . .	$151,640
Va.	$22,000	$482,881	$1,963,811	. . .	$100,879
N.C.	. . .	$788,031	$219,835	. . .	$501,082
S.C.	. . .	$1,014,808	$499,325	$1,205,978	. . .
Ga.	. . .	$679,412	$122,744	$19,998	. . .
Total	$9,038,795	$10,646,869	$14,199,599	3,517,584	$3,517,584

[a]Assumption of interest-bearing U.S. securities held by creditors, who then received interest from their respective state governments.
[b]As of final settling of state accounts on June 29, 1793. Balances were calculated after deducting state credits for interest payments and congressional requisitions.
[c]Paid interest on $424,000 of U.S. debt from 1786 to 1790.
Sources: E. James Ferguson, *The Power of the Purse: A History of American Public Finance, 1776–1790* (1961), 230–34. U.S. Congress, *American State Papers: Finance* (1834), I, 55, and *Miscellaneous* (1834), I, 69.

TABLE 8.38 FUNDING AND ASSUMPTION OF REVOLUTIONARY DEBT BY U.S. TREASURY, 1790

National Debt to be Funded	Principal	Unpaid Interest to Dec. 31, 1789	Total to be Reissued as U.S. Bonds
Foreign Held	$10,070,307.00[b]	$1,640,071.62	$11,710,378.62
Held in U.S.	$27,383,917.74	$13,030,168.20	$40,414,085.94
Unliquidated[a]	$2,000,000.00	...	$2,000,000.00
Subtotals	$39,454,224.74	$14,670,239.82	$54,124,464.56

State Debts to be Assumed	Authorized to be Assumed[c]	Amount Exchanged for U.S. Debt by 1791[d]	Estimate of State Debts Not Assumed
N.H.	$300,000	$242,501.25	$100,000.000
Mass.	$4,000,000	$4,000,000.00	$1,838,540.66
R.I.	$200,000	$200,000.00	$349,259.69
Conn.	$1,600,000	$1,455,331.81	$458,436.52
N.Y.	$1,200,000	$1,028,238.75	$195,639.79

National Debt to be Funded	Principal	Unpaid Interest to Dec. 31, 1789	Total to be Reissued as U.S. Bonds
N.J.	$800,000	$599,703.56	$207,647.78
Pa.	$2,200,000	$675,101.33	$500,000.00
Del.	$200,000	$53,305.84	none
Md.	$800,000	$299,225.40	$430,000.00
Va.	$3,500,000	$2,552,570.88	$1,172,555.25
N.C.	$2,400,000	$1,166,355.57	$713,192.30
S.C.	$4,000,000	$4,000,000.00	$1,965,756.33
Ga.	$300,000	$300,000.00	$400,000.00
Subtotal	$21,500,000	$17,072,334.39[e]	$8,331,028.32

Total Debt to be funded and assumed..$75,624,464.56

[a]Chiefly Continental bills of credit, but exact value unknown.
[b]$6,296,296 borrowed on French credit (40% in Dutch hands), $174,011 on Spanish credit, and $3,600,000 lent in Netherlands.
[c]Not all state debts were assumed, and state accounts would still have to be settled with U.S. Treasury (see Table 8.37).
[d]Undersubscribed because some states paid creditors higher interest than they would receive after exchanging their debt for U.S. bonds.
[e]Subscriptions after Sept. 30, 1791 raised total to $18,200,000.
Source: "Report on the Public Credit," Jan. 9, 1790, in U.S. Congress, *American State Papers: Finance* (1834), I, 19–29, 149–50.

TABLE 8.39 EXPENDITURES OF U.S. GOVERNMENT, 1791–1800

From 4th Mar. 1789 to 31st Dec.	Civil List	Foreign Intercourse	Miscellaneous	Military Establishment — Military Services, including Fortifications, Arsenals, Armories, Ordnance, Internal Improvements, etc.	Other Pensioners	Indian Department	Naval Establishment	Public Debt	Total	Balances in the Treasury at the end of the year
1791	$757,134	$14,733	$311,533	$632,804	$175,813	$27,000	$570	$5,287,949	$7,207,539	$973,905
1792	$380,917	$78,766	$194,372	$1,100,702	$109,243	$13,648	$53	$7,263,665	$9,141,569	$783,444
1793	$358,241	$89,500	$24,709	$1,130,249	$80,087	$27,282	. .	$5,819,505	$7,529,575	$753,661
1794	$440,946	$146,403	$118,248	$2,639,097	$81,399	$13,042	$61,408	$5,801,578	$9,302,124	$1,151,924
1795	$361,633	$912,685	$92,718	$2,480,910	$68,673	$23,475	$410,562	$6,084,411	$10,435,059	$516,442
1796	$447,139	$184,859	$150,476	$1,260,263	$100,843	$113,563	$274,784	$5,835,846	$8,367,776	$888,895
1797	$483,233	$669,788	$103,880	$1,039,402	$92,256	$62,496	$382,631	$5,792,421	$8,626,012	$1,021,899
1798	$504,605	$457,428	$149,004	$2,009,522	$104,845	$16,470	$1,381,347	$3,990,294	$8,613,517	$617,451
1799	$592,905	$271,374	$175,111	$2,466,946	$95,444	$20,302	$2,858,081	$4,596,876	$11,077,943	$2,161,867
1800	$748,688	$395,288	$193,636	$2,560,878	$64,130	$31	$3,448,716	$4,578,369	$11,989,739	$2,623,311

Source: Timothy Pitkin, *A Statistical Abstract of the Commerce of the United States of America* (1835), 342.

TABLE 8.40 INCOME OF THE UNITED STATES GOVERNMENT, 1791–1800

From 4th Mar. 1789 to 31st Dec.	Customs	Internal Revenue	Direct Taxes	Postage	Public Lands	Loans, and Treasury Notes, etc	Dividend and Sales of Bank Stock and Bonus	Miscellaneous	Total
1791	$4,399,473	. . .	. . .	. . .	. . .	$5,791,112	. . .	$19,440	$10,210,025
1792	$3,443,070	$208,942	. . .	. . .	. . .	$5,070,806	$8,028	$9,918	$8,740,766
1793	$4,255,306	$337,705	. . .	$11,020	. . .	$1,067,701	$38,500	$10,390	$5,720,624
1794	$4,801,065	$274,089	. . .	$29,478	. . .	$4,609,196	$303,472	$23,799	$10,041,101
1795	$5,588,461	$337,755	. . .	$22,400	. . .	$3,305,268	$160,000	$5,917	$9,419,802
1796	$6,567,987	$475,289	. . .	$72,909	$4,836	$362,800	$1,240,000	$16,506	$8,740,329
1797	$7,549,649	$575,491	. . .	$64,500	$83,540	$70,135	$385,220	$30,379	$8,758,916
1798	$7,106,061	$644,357	. . .	$39,500	$11,963	$308,574	$79,920	$18,692	$8,209,070
1799	$6,610,449	$779,136	. . .	$41,000	. . .	$5,074,646	$71,040	$45,187	$12,621,459
1800	$9,080,932	$809,396	$734,223	$78,000	$443	$1,602,435	$71,040	$74,712	$12,451,184

Source: Timothy Pitkin, *A Statistical Abstract of the Commerce of the United States of America* (1835), 340.

State and Local Taxation

Prior to the Revolution, no society in Europe or Europe's American possessions enjoyed a lower level of per capita taxation than the thirteen colonies. Since their bureaucracies were minimal and their defense was borne by Britain, the provincial governments needed little revenue. The amount of money Parliament collected per Englishman was twenty-five to fifty times greater than the revenues imposed by North American legislatures, while taxpayers in Holland and many parts of France paid at even higher rates. Counties and towns levied significantly higher taxes than the provincial assemblies, since most government services were provided at that level, but local taxes nevertheless remained relatively light.

The American Revolution had the ironic result of necessitating taxes far higher than any Parliament would have dared enact. The ensuing rise in tax burdens inspired the country's first wave of revenue reform. As long as citizens did not have to sacrifice much of their income, they voiced few complaints that the usual practice of assessing taxes on a uniform basis, rather than by ability to pay, allowed the upper class to escape paying their fair share of the government expenses. The enormous cost of winning independence ended this complacency and sparked demands that the war be financed more equitably among the population. By 1780, most states assessed property according to its value, had abandoned the regressive poll tax, and levied duties on luxury items. After the Revolution, Americans would insist that taxes be assessed not only as low as possible, but also as equitably as possible.

TABLE 8.41 SUMMARY OF BALANCE IN THE FEDERAL BUDGET, 1791–1800

	Income	Expenditures	Net Balance	Amount Borrowed
1800	$12,413,978.34	$11,952,534.12	+$461,444.22	$1,565,229.24
1799	$12,546,813.31	$11,002,396.97	+$1,544,416.34	$5,000,000.00
1798	$8,179,170.80	$8,583,618.41	−$404,447.61	$200,000.00
1797	$8,758,780.99	$8,625,877.37	+$132,903.62	$70,000.00
1796	$8,740,329.26	$8,367,776.84	+$372,552.42	$320,000.00
1795	$9,515,758.59	$10,151,240.15	−$635,481.56	$3,300,000.00
1794	$9,439,855.65	$9,041,593.17	+$398,262.48	$4,600,000.00
1793	$6,450,195.15	$6,479,977.97	−$29,782.82	$1,000,000.00
1792	$8,772,458.76	$8,962,920.00	−$190,461.24	$4,936,595.56
1791	$4,771,342.43	$3,797,436.78	+$973,905.65	$5,552,475.31

Source: Adam Seybert, *Statistical Annals: Embracing Views of . . . the United States of America* (1818), 536, 715.

TABLE 8.43 CIVILIAN EMPLOYEES (NON-ELECTED) OF U.S. GOVERNMENT, 1790–1800

	1800	1799	1798	1797	1796	1795
State Dept.						
Domestic	8	8	8	8	8	8
Foreign	6	6	6	6	6	6
Treasury Dept.						
Staff and Mint	166	166	166	166	166	166
Revenue Officers	459	396	400	408	334	323
War and Navy						
Depts.	32	32	32	32	32	32
Attorney General	33	33	33	33	33	33
Post Office						
Postmasters	903	677	639	554	468	453
Mail Carriers[a]	210	160	160	160	130	130
Congress	14	14	14	14	14	14
Judiciary	38	38	38	38	38	37
Other[b]	28	28	28	28	28	28
Totals	1,897	1,558	1,524	1,447	1,257	1,230

	1794	1793	1792	1791	1790	
State Dept.						
Domestic	8	8	8	7	6	
Foreign	6	6	6	4	3	
Treasury Dept.						
Staff and Mint	155	155	155	95	39	
Revenue Officers	504	504	504	100	. . .	
War and Navy						
Depts.	32	32	32	25	23	
Attorney General	33	33	33	1	1	
Post Office						
Postmasters	450	209	195	89	75	
Mail Cariers[a]	120	56	56	19	19	
Congress	14	14	14	12	13	
Judiciary	37	37	37	21	19	
Other[b]	28	28	28	9	5	
Totals	1,387	1,082	1,068	382	203	

[a] One carrier per 100 miles of post road.
[b] Territorial government, lighthouse keepers, etc.
Note: Data on civil list is incomplete. If employment was unknown, figures from the next earliest year were used.
Source: U.S. Congress, *American State Papers: Finance* (1834), I, 33–35, 57–68, 400, 574, 577–578, 617, 682.

TABLE 8.42 NATIONAL DEBT OF THE UNITED STATES, 1791–1800

Years	Gross or Nominal Debt United States	Debt after Deducting Sinking Fund and Reimbursements	Net Debt After the Further Offsets of Bonds and Cash in the Treasury	Comparative Debt for Each Person After Reference to Depreciation and Increase of Population
1791	$76,781,953	$76,081,969	$73,670,259	$18.25
1792	$77,124,300	$75,924,300	$72,797,970	$18.05
1793	$78,402,946	$76,383,762	$70,379,950	$16.50
1794	$79,424,668	$77,159,646	$69,185,090	$15.00
1795	$84,980,438	$81,726,203	$71,785,132	$14.60
1796	$83,404,139	$80,803,795	$70,862,624	$14.00
1797	$81,324,139	$76,774,512	$63,432,545	$12.40
1798	$81,244,139	$76,010,965	$63,616,936	$11.10
1799	$88,456,038	$80,291,805	$65,385,826	$10.50
1800	$89,443,437	$80,161,207	$59,767,483	$ 8.00

Source: Samuel Blodget, *Economica: A Statistical Manual of the United States of America* (1806), 187.

This picture, showing the last boatload of British troops evacuated from their occupation of New York City, is indicative of the widespread disruption experienced by American governments in the Revolution. British forces occupied every major seaport but Baltimore, marched into ten state capitals, and even forced the Continental Congress to flee from its chambers in 1777. (*Harper's Magazine,* November 1883)

TABLE 8.44 ANNUAL PER CAPITA TAXES LEVIED IN BRITISH NORTH AMERICA AND EUROPE (IN ENGLISH SHILLINGS)

British Colonies	About 1765	About 1785	Europe	About 1785
Mass.	1s.	18s.	United Provinces	35s.
Conn.	7d.	. . .	France	21s.
N.Y.	8d.	. . .	Paris	56s.
N.J.	6d.	. . .	Rouen	31s.
Pa.	1s.	. . .	Lyon	25s.
Md.	1s.	. . .	Strasbourg	12s.
Va.	5d.	10s.	Rennes	10s.
N.C.	4s.,7d.	. . .	Austrian Empire	12s.
			Austria	21s.
Great Britain			Bohemia-Moravia	14s.
			Hungary	12s.
			Translvania	7s.
England	26s.	34s.	Spain	10s.
Ireland	6s.,8d.	10s.	Sweden	9s.
			Russia	8s.
			Prussia	6s.
			Poland	1s.

Note: Figures for America do not include town or county taxes, except North Carolina, of which about 60% (2s.,9d.) were local rather than provincial levies. New Jersey's per capita figure is based on estimated payments of 3s. per taxpayer.
Sources: Robert R. Palmer, *The Age of the Democratic Revolution: I, The Challenge* (1959), 155. Marvin L. Michael Kay, "The Payment of Provincial and Local Taxes in North Carolina, 1748–1771," *William and Mary Quarterly* XXVI (1969), 240. Thomas L. Purvis, *Proprietors, Patronage, and Paper Money: Legislative Politics in New Jersey, 1703–1776* (1986), 198.

TABLE 8.45 PROVINCIAL TAXES COLLECTED IN THE THIRTEEN COLONIES, 1760–1775

	N.H.[a]	Mass.[a]	R.I.[a]	Conn.[a]	N.Y.[c]	N.J.[a]
1775	. . .	. . .	. . .	[£2,500][b]	. . .	. . .
1774	£1,000	£10,312	£4,000	[£10,000]	£5,200	. . .
1773	£2,000	£20,625	£4,000	[£7,500]	£5,078	. . .
1772	£2,000	£27,500	£12,000	[£12,500]	£3,875	. . .
1771	£2,500	£27,300	£12,000	(no tax)	£3,615	£12,465
1770	£2,000	£25,000	£12,000	[£10,000]	£4,814	. . .
1769	£3,000	£30,000	£6,000	(no tax)	£4,678	. . .
1768	£2,200	(no tax)	(no tax)	(no tax)	£4,895	£12,449
1767	£2,200	£40,000	(no tax)	(no tax)	. . .	. . .
1766	. . .	£40,000	£6,000	(no tax)	£7,271	. . .
1765	. . .	£50,000	£12,468	[£5,000]	£4,920	. . .
1764	. . .	£50,000	£12,000	[£40,000]	£7,597	. . .
1763	. . .	£50,000	£12,000	[£30,000]	£8,574	. . .
1762	. . .	£78,447	. . .	. . .	£7,109	. . .
1761	. . .	. . .	. . .	. . .	£10,319	. . .
1760	. . .	. . .	. . .	. . .	£10,346	. . .

(continued)

TABLE 8.45 (continued)

	Pa. Taxes		N.C.[d]	S.C. Taxes		Ga.[e]
	Property	Excises		Property	Excises	
1775	£22,750	£8,239	. . .	. . .	. . .	. . .
1774	£24,000	£9,156	. . .	. . .	. . .	. . .
1773	£22,869	£9,360	none	. . .	. . .	£5,172
1772	£24,014	£6,607	none	. . .	£98,000	. . .
1771	£24,491	£4,791	none	. . .	. . .	. . .
1770	£24,800	£4,705	none	. . .	£68,525	£3,355
1769	£22,365	£5,187	£2,573	£73,326	£95,604	£3,047
1768	£26,317	£5,162	£2,336	£105,733	£41,543	£3,375
1767	£28,097	£4,465	£9,334	£85,950	£187,984	£1,843
1766	£22,225	£3,241	£8,762	£35,529	£50,979	£1,925
1765	£23,032	£3,698	£8,215	£102,927	£111,425	£1,599
1764	£18,419	£3,916	£8,117	£220,307	£77,681	£2,117
1763	£21,235	£4,022	£3,733	. . .	. . .	£1,934
1762	. . .	. . .	. . .	£162,000	. . .	. . .
1761	. . .	. . .	. . .	£284,758	. . .	. . .

[a] General property or poll taxes.
[b] Estimates based on source.
[c] Impost duties only.
[d] Poll taxes received by treasury.
[e] Total from all taxes.
Note: Taxes given in local currency or proclamation money, which usually traded at 40% discount to sterling.
Source: Robert A. Becker, Revolution, Reform, and the Politics of American Taxation, 1763–1783 (1980), 234–46.

TABLE 8.46   SYSTEMS OF PERSONAL TAXATION USED BY STATES, 1785

	Poll Taxes		Property Taxes		
	Paid by All Taxpayers	% Raised by Poll Tax	Manner of Taxing Land[b]	Unsettled Tracts Taxed[f]	Luxury Goods Taxed[g]
N.H.	Yes	. . .	ad valorem	Yes	. . .
Mass.	Yes	33%–40%	ad valorem	No	. . .
R.I.	Yes	20%	ad valorem[c]	Yes	Yes
Conn.	Yes	33%	ad valorem	Yes	Yes
N.Y.	No	0	ad valorem[c]	Yes	Yes
N.J.	No	0	ad valorem[c]	Yes	Yes
Pa.	No	0	ad valorem	Yes	Yes
Del.	No	0	ad valorem	No	. . .
Md.	No	0	ad valorem	No	Yes
Va.	Yes	. . .	ad valorem	No[d]	Yes
N.C.	Yes	50%?	equally by acre[e]	Yes	Yes
S.C.	No[a]	. . .	ad valorem	No	Yes
Ga.	No[a]	. . .	equally by acre	No	. . .

[a] Only levied on free blacks.
[b] Ad valorem rates set taxes by ability to pay and assessed property by its value, but rates set equally by acre taxed all land the same regardless of worth.
[c] Rates were not uniform across state because county or towns had to collect predetermined amounts to meet quotas set by legislature.
[d] Speculative tracts had been taxed from 1781 to 1785.
[e] Modified ad valorem rates were reinstituted in 1787.
[f] Large holdings held for land speculation.
[g] Such as carriages, billiard tables, watches, or silver plate.
Source: Robert A. Becker, Revolution, Reform, and the Politics of American Taxation, 1763–1783 (1980), passim.

TABLE 8.47   AVERAGE ANNUAL TAXES IMPOSED BY COUNTIES IN TIDEWATER VIRGINIA AND TOWNS IN EASTERN MASSACHUSETTS, 1765–1773 AND 1790–1799

State	Per Poll	Per Capita	Per Free Capita
Mass.			
1765–1773	27.73s.[a]	5.41s.[b]	5.57s.[c]
1790–1799	$8.77	$1.71	$1.71
Va.			
1765–1773	9.76s.[d]	3.07s.[e]	5.64s.[f]
1790–1799	$1.04	$.33	$.61

[a] Equal to $5.55.
[b] Equal to $1.08.
[c] Equal to $1.11.
[d] Equal to $1.95.
[e] Equal to $.61.
[f] Equal to $1.13.
Note: Colonial taxes expressed in shillings of local currency, both of which were exchanged at nearly equal rates with sterling.
Source: H. James Henderson, "Taxation and Political Culture: Massachusetts and Virginia, 1760–1800," William and Mary Quarterly XLVII (1990), 95, 103.

TABLE 8.48   AVERAGE ANNUAL TAXES PAID IN MASSACHUSETTS AND VIRGINIA, 1794–1796

State	Per Free Capita U.S. Taxes	Per Free Capita State Taxes	Per Free Capita Local Taxes	Total Per Free Capita	Total Per Capita
Mass.	$1.57	$.35	$1.71	$3.63	$3.63
Va.	$2.26	$.35	$.61	$3.22	$1.74

Note: Per capita burden of U.S. customs calculated equally for all free consumers, with slaves calculated at 60% of free population.
Source: H. James Henderson, "Taxation and Political Culture: Massachusetts and Virginia, 1760–1800," William and Mary Quarterly XLVII (1990), 112.

TABLE 8.49   EXPENDITURE OF TAXES (IN LOCAL SHILLINGS) LEVIED BY MASSACHUSETTS TOWNS AND VIRGINIA COUNTIES, 1765–1773

Purpose	Va. % of Total	Va. Per Poll	Va. Per Free Capita	Mass. % of Total	Mass. Per Poll	Mass. Per Free Capita
County[a]	19.9%	1.93s.	1.12s.	5.8%	1.61s.	.32s.
Roads	21.5%	2.10s.[b]	1.20s.[b]	22.6%	6.27s.	1.26s.
Welfare	12.9%	1.26s.	.74s.	16.4%	4.55s.	.91s.
Religion	41.1%	4.02s.	2.32s.	28.2%	7.82s.	1.57s.
Schools	. . .	. . .	. . .	15.6%	4.32s.	.87s.
Other[c]	4.6%	.45s.	.26s.	11.4%	3.16s.	.64s.
Total	100.0%	9.76s.	5.64s.	100.0%	27.73s.	5.57s.

[a] Virginia county expenditures exclude labor for repairing highways.
[b] Estimated at two days work (5s.) per eligible white and four days work (2.68s.) per eligible slave.
[c] Collection fees, processing costs, repairs, salaries, legal costs.
Source: H. James Henderson, "Taxation and Political Culture: Massachusetts and Virginia, 1760–1800," William and Mary Quarterly XLVII (1990), 97.

TABLE 8.50

TABLE 8.50 PERCENT OF COUNTY OR TOWN TAXES PAID BY ECONOMIC CLASSES IN TIDEWATER VIRGINIA AND EASTERN MASSACHUSETTS, 1770–1799[a]

Economic Status	Va. % of Taxes Paid	Mass. % of Taxes Paid
Wealthiest 10%	41.2%	29.1%
Top Middle (11%–50%)	38.8%	46.7%
Bottom Half (1%–50%)	20.0%	24.1%

[a]Massachusetts estimates from tax lists of 1770–1772. Virginia estimates from tax lists of 1782–1799.
Source: H. James Ferguson, "Taxation and Political Culture: Massachusetts and Virginia, 1760–1800," William and Mary Quarterly XLVII (1990), 101.

Foreign Affairs

The country's diplomatic history began on November 29, 1775, when the Continental Congress named a Committee on Secret Correspondence to determine the prospects for negotiating treaties with France if independence became necessary. Ambassador Benjamin Franklin and the French monarchy signed two treaties, one of alli-

TABLE 8.51 U.S. DIPLOMATIC AGREEMENTS WITH FOREIGN NATIONS, 1778–1800

Treaty or Convention	When Signed	When Ratified by Congress
Treaty of alliance with France[a]	Feb. 6, 1778	May 4, 1778
Treaty of amity and trade with France[a]	Feb. 6, 1778	May 4, 1778
Treaty of amity and commerce with the States General of the Netherlands	Oct. 8, 1782	Jan. 22, 1783
Convention with the States General of the Netherlands on recaptured ships	Oct. 8, 1782	. . .
Provisional peace articles with Britain	Nov. 30, 1782	. . .
Armistice declared with Great Britain	Jan. 20, 1783	. . .
Treaty of amity and commerce with Sweden	Apr. 3, 1783	Jul. 29, 1783
Treaty of Peace with Great Britain	Sep. 3, 1783	Jan. 14, 1784
Treaty of amity and trade with Prussia	Sep. 1785	May 17, 1786
Treaty of peace and amity with Morocco	Jan. 1787	Jul. 18, 1787
Convention with France on consuls	Nov. 14, 1788	. . .
Jay's Treaty of amity, naviagation,[b] and trade with Britain	Nov. 19, 1794	Jun. 24, 1795
Treaty of peace and amity with Algiers	Sep. 5, 1795	May 6, 1796
Pinckney's Treaty of boundaries, navigation, and trade with Spain [Treaty of San Lorenzo]	Oct. 27, 1795	Mar. 15, 1796
Treaty of peace and amity with Tripoli	Nov. 4, 1796	. . .
Treaty of peace and amity with Tunis	Mar. 26, 1799	. . .
Treaty of amity and trade with Prussia	Jul. 11, 1799	Jun. 22, 1800
Convention to end hostilities with France[c]	Sep. 30, 1800	Feb. 3, 1801

[a]Annulled by Congress Jul. 7, 1798.
[b]Additional articles were added May 4, 1796 and Mar. 15, 1798.
[c]Second Article expunged, and U.S. ratified this change Dec. 19, 1801.
Source: Richard Peters, ed., The Public Statutes at Large of the United States of America, from . . . 1789 to Mar. 3, 1845, 83 vols. (1857), VIII, ix, x.

ance and the other for friendship and trade, on February 6, 1779. Although Spain declared war on Britain, it did so as an ally of France and refused to enter into formal diplomatic arrangements with the United States. The Netherlands, another belligerent against Britain, also withheld formal recognition but finally signed a treaty in 1782.

The Constitution vested responsibility for conducting diplomacy in the president, but required him to consult with the Senate and obtain the concurrence of two-thirds of its members to ratify treaties. The Senate has claimed the right of changing the terms of treaties before ratification but has rarely done so. Treaties have the force of law when signed by duly authorized commissioners, and ratification becomes retroactive in the event of delays.

The Washington administration's greatest accomplishment was to compel Britain and Spain, by diplomacy rather than war, to remove

TABLE 8.52 U.S. AMBASSADORS, 1775–1800

Peace Commissioners for the Treaty of Paris
1782–1783	Benjamin Franklin, John Adams, John Jay, Henry Laurens
1782	Thomas Jefferson (appointment withdrawn)

Ambassadors to France
1776–1778	Joint commission of Benjamin Franklin, Silas Deane, and Arthur Lee, with John Adams added in 1778.
1778–1785	Benjamin Franklin, minister.
1785–1789	Thomas Jefferson, minister.
1790–1792	William Short (acting minister, chargé d'affaires)
1792–1794	Gouverneur Morris
1794–1796	James Monroe
1796	Charles Cotesworth Pinckney (credentials as ambassador not accepted by French government and he served as an envoy extraordinary)
1797	John Marshall (envoy extraordinary)
1797–1798	Elbridge Gerry (envoy extraordinary)
1799–1800	William Vans Murray (envoy extraordinary)
1799–1800	Oliver Ellsworth and William Davie (envoys extraordinary)

Ambassadors to Great Britain
1785–1788	John Adams
1792–1796	Thomas Pinckney
1794	John Jay (envoy extraordinary)
1796–1803	Rufus King

Ambassadors to Prussia
1777–1779	William Lee (unrecognized)
1785	John Adams (envoy to negotiate commercial treaty)
1797–1801	John Quincy Adams

Ambassadors to Netherlands
1779–1780	Henry Laurens (captured at sea and imprisoned at London)
1781–1788	John Adams (not recognized until April 22, 1782 and resident in London, 1785–1788)
1792–1794	William Short
1794–1797	John Quincy Adams
1797–1801	William Vans Murray

Ambassadors to Portugal
1791–1797	David Humphreys
1797	William L. Smith

Ambassadors to Russia
1780–1783	Francis Dana (not officially recognized)

Ambassadors to Spain
1779–1782	John Jay (unrecognized)
1790–1794	William Carmichael
1794–1795	William Short
1794–1795	Thomas Pinckney (envoy extraordinary)
1796–1801	David Humphreys

Ambassadors to Sweden
1782	Benjamin Franklin (minister plenipotentiary)
1798	John Quincy Adams (minister plenipotentiary)

their garrisons from U.S. soil, respect the nation's boundaries, and cease inciting Indian attacks, through Jay's Treaty (1795) and Pinckney's Treaty (1796). Improved relations with those nations generated friction with France, however, and in 1798 Congress annulled its alliance with France. None of the earliest American treaties survived the Napoleonic Wars except Pinckney's Treaty, a remarkably durable pact that lasted for more than a century.

Military Affairs

Americans have long underappreciated the Revolutionary War's social impact because they failed to consider the scale of that conflict in proportion to the number of persons affected. Since the country had a free population of just 2,000,000, there were barely 450,000 men of military age (from 16 to 45), and many of these were not fit for campaign duty. The total number who served was not calculated by the government, but the government received more than 80,000 pension applications after 1818, a date so long after the war that most veterans would have already been dead. It appears that perhaps 220,000 individuals joined the regular army, served in the field for at least three months with the militia, or sailed on warships.

The war effort consequently mobilized about half of all adult white males below age forty-five. Most of this burden fell upon young, single men, who were the prime source of manpower not only because they were most physically fit, but also because their deaths would not burden society with widows and orphans. Perhaps 66% to 75% of men between the ages of 18 and 29 fought with the Revolutionary forces. With manpower needs so high, virtually every state had to institute a draft.

Although the final numbers may seem light by modern standards, the war resulted in a heavy casualty rate for a small population. The Continental forces sustained almost 26,000 fatalities by 1783, or approximately one death for every ten soldiers. One of every twenty males between sixteen and forty-five perished in the conflict. Casualties on such a scale would suggest that at least half the free population experienced the loss of either a brother, nephew, or first cousin in the course of the struggle. Relative to the population of that time, the Revolutionary War's casualty rate was about four times higher than the per capita rate for American deaths in World War II.

Once peace was declared, the United States demobilized rapidly. The last naval vessel was sold in 1785 and by 1789 the army had been reduced to fewer than 900 men. The country's military strength was altogether inadequate to its needs, however, since Britain occupied five military posts within U.S. borders, Spain effectively controlled large amounts of American territory adjacent to its colony of Florida, and both nations encouraged Indians to raid the frontier. The Washington administration steadily expanded the army until it could inflict a decisive defeat upon the Indians, as it eventually did at the Battle of Fallen Timbers in 1794, and pose a credible threat to compel the peaceful evacuation of foreign garrisons from U.S. soil, as happened in 1796.

Once the danger of armed conflict with Britain and Spain receded, relations with France deteriorated rapidly and resulted in attacks on American merchant shipping. The Adams administration responded by augmenting the navy, which had been revived on March 27, 1794, and elevated its status to cabinet level in 1798. The Marine Corps was formally reestablished on July 11, 1798, and the army's authorized strength was increased to 12,660. By 1800, France had been bested in an undeclared naval war in which it lost 93 privateers and took just one U.S. ship, and the threat of war subsided. The United States then drastically cut both the army and navy and managed to enjoy a dozen years of peace before war broke out with Britain in 1812.

TABLE 8.53   REQUISITIONS AND TROOPS PROVIDED FOR CONTINENTAL ARMY, 1775–1783

Statement of the troops furnished by the following states, taken from actual returns of the army, for the year 1775. (The Continentals were to serve to December's last day.)

States	Quotas Required		Furnished		Total of Militia and Continental Troops
	Number of Battalions of 522 Men Each	Number of Men	Number of Continental Troops	Number of Militia	
N.H.	. . .	. . .	2,824	. . .	. . .
Mass.	. . .	. . .	16,444	. . .	. . .
R.I.	. . .	. . .	1,193	. . .	. . .
Conn.	. . .	. . .	4,507	. . .	. . .
N.Y.	. . .	. . .	2,075	. . .	. . .
Pa.	. . .	. . .	400	. . .	. . .
Total	. . .	. . .	27,443	. . .	. . .
Conjectural estimate of militia employed in addition to above					
Va., for six months				2,000	. . .
Va., state corps for eight months				1,180	. . .
N.C., for three months				2,000	. . .
S.C., for six months				2,500	. . .
S.C., state troops				1,500	. . .
Ga., for nine months				1,000	. . .
Total Conjectural				10,180	. . .

Statement of the troops furnished by the following states, taken from actual returns of the army, for the year 1776

States	Quotas Required		Furnished		Total of Militia and Continental Troops
	Number of Battalions of 522 Men Each	Number of Men	Number of Continental Troops	Number of Militia	
N.H.	. . .	. . .	3,019		
Mass.	. . .	. . .	13,372	4,000	17,372
R.I.	. . .	. . .	798	1,102	1,900
Conn.	. . .	. . .	6,390	5,737	12,127
Del.	. . .	. . .	609	145	754
Md.	. . .	. . .	637	2,592	3,329
Va.	. . .	. . .	6,181	. . .	
N.C.	. . .	. . .	1,134	. . .	
S.C.	. . .	. . .	2,069	. . .	
Ga.	. . .	. . .	351	. . .	
N.Y.	. . .	. . .	3,629	1,715	5,344
Pa.	. . .	. . .	5,519	4,876	10,395
N.J.	. . .	. . .	3,193	5,893	9,086
Total			46,891	26,060	72,951
Conjectural estimate of militia employed in addition to above					
N.H., averaged at four months				1,000	
Mass., averaged at four months				3,000	
Conn., averaged at four months				1,000	
N.Y., averaged at four months				2,750	
Va. averaged at four months				. . .	
N.C. averaged at eight months				3,000	
S.C. averaged at six months				4,000	
Ga. State troops				1,950	
Total Conjectural					16,700
Grand Total					89,651

Quotas fixed by Congress, September 1776, for three years or during the war. Statement of the troops furnished by the following states, taken from the actual returns of the Army, for the year 1777

States	Quotas Required		Troops Furnished		Total of Militia and Continentals
	Number of Battalions, 680 Men Each	Number of Men	Number of Continentals	Number of Militia	
N.H.	3	2,040	1,172	1,111—3 months,	2,283
Mass.	15	10,200	7,816	2,775—3 do.	10,591
R.I.	2	1,360	548	. . .	548
Conn.	8	5,440	4,563	. . .	4,563
N.Y.	4	2,720	1,903	929—6 do.	2,832
N.J.	4	2,720	1,408	. . .	1,408
Pa.	12	8,160	4,983	2,481—5 do.	7,464
Del.	1	680	299	. . .	299
Md.	8	5,440	2,030	1,535—3 do.	3,565
Va.	15	10,200	5,744	1,269—5 do.	7,013
N.C.	9	6,120	1,281	. . .	1,281
S.C.	6	4,080	1,650	. . .	1,650
[a]Ga.	1	680	1,423	and State troops	1,423
Besides the above Congress authorized the commander-in-chief, on the 27th Dec., 1776, to raise sixteen additional regiments of infantry	16	10,880			

(continued)

TABLE 8.53 (continued)

States	Quotas Required		Troops Furnished		Total of Militia and Continentals
	Number of Battalions, 680 Men Each	Number of Men	Number of Continentals	Number of Militia	
Returns of May, 1778, of artillery	3	2,040			
Cavalry	. . .	3,000			
Total	107	75,760	34,820	10,100	44,920

[a]By the resolve of the 15th July, 1776, Ga. was authorized to raise in Va., North and South Carolina, two regiments of infantry, and also two companies of artillery, of fifty men each. These troops were chiefly enlisted for one year, and the time expired in 1777.

Conjectural estimate of militia employed in addition to the above

N.H. and Vt., for 2 months				2,200	
Mass., for 2 months				2,000	
Conn., for 2 months				2,000	
N.Y., for 6 months				2,500	
N.J., for 2 months				1,500	
Pa., for 3 months				2,000	
Del., for 2 months				1,000	
Md., for 2 months				4,000	
Va., for 2 months				4,000	
S.C., for 8 months				350	
Ga., for 8 months				750	
R.I., for 6 months				1,500	
Total Conjectural					23,800
Grand Total					68,720

February 26, 1778, Congress resolved to have the following number of men furnished by each State. Statement of the troops furnished by the following states, taken from actual returns of the Army for the year 1778

States	Quotas Required		Furnished		Total of Militia and Continental Troops
	Number of Battalions of 522 Men Each	Number of Men	Number of Continental Troops	Number of Militia	
N.H.	3	1,566	1,283	. . .	1,283
Mass.	15	7,830	7,010	*1,927	8,937
R.I.	1	522	630	†2,426	3,056
Conn.	8	4,176	4,010	. . .	4,010
N.Y.	5	2,610	2,194	. . .	2,190
N.J.	4	2,088	1,586	. . .	1,580
Pa.	10	5,220	3,684	. . .	3,684
Del.	1	522	349	. . .	349
Md., including the German battalion	8	4,176	3,307	. . .	3,307
Va.	15	7,830	5,230	. . .	5,236
N.C.	9	4,698	1,287	. . .	1,287
S.C.	6	3,132	1,650	. . .	1,650
Ga.	1	522	673	. . .	673
Total	86	44,892	32,899	4,353	37,252
Total from returns					37,252

Conjectural estimate of the Militia employed in addition to the preceding information

N.H., for 2 months				500	
Mass., for 2 months				4,500	
N.J.				1,000	
Va., for 2 months				2,000	
Va., guarding convention troops				600	
S.C., for 3 months				2,000	
Ga., 2,000 militia 6 months and 1,200 State troops				3,200	
Total Conjectural					13,800
Grand Total					51,052

*Guarding Convention troops.
†Short levies and militia for six months.

March 9, 1779, Congress resolved that the infantry of these States, for the next campaign, be composed of eighty battalions, viz.

Statement of the troops furnished by the following states, taken from actual returns of the Army, for the year 1779

States	Quotas Required		Furnished		Total Number of Continentals and Militia
	Number of Battalions, 522 Men Each	Number of Men	Number of Men	Militia	
N.H.	3	1,566	1,004	222	
Mass.	15	7,830	6,287	1,451	
R.I.	2	1,040	507	756	
Conn.	8	4,176	3,544	. . .	
N.Y.	5	2,610	2,256	. . .	
N.J.	3	1,566	1,276	. . .	
Pa.	11	5,742	3,476	. . .	
Del.	1	522	317	. . .	
Md.	8	4,176	2,849	. . .	
Va.	11	5,742	3,973	. . .	
N.C. (8 months)	6	3,132	1,214	2,706	
S.C.[a]	6	3,132	909	. . .	
Ga.	1	522	87	. . .	
Total	80	41,756[a]	27,699	5,135	
Total from returns					32,834

[a]Corrected from original.

Conjectural estimate of militia, employed in addition to the above

N.Y., for 3 months				1,500	
Va., for 2 months				3,000	
Va., for 6 months				1,000	
Va., guarding convention troops				600	
N.C., for 8 months				1,000	
S.C., for 9 months				4,500	
Ga.				750	
Total Conjectural					12,350
Grand Total					41,584

(continued)

TABLE 8.53 (continued)

Resolved, That the States furnished by draught, or otherwise, the deficiencies of their respective quotas of eighty battalions, apportioned by a resolve of Congress of 9th March, 1779.

Statement of the troops furnished by the following states, taken from actual returns of the Army, for the year 1780

States	Quotas Required		Furnished		Total Number of Continentals and Militia
	Number of Battalions of 522 Men Each	Number of Men	Number of Men	Militia	
N.H.	3	1,566	1,017	760	
Mass.	15	7,830	4,453	3,436	
R.I.	2	1,044	915	. . .	
Conn.	8	4,176	3,133	544	
N.Y.	5	2,610	2,179	668	
N.J.	3	1,566	1,105	162	
Pa.	11	5,742	3,337	. . .	
Del.	1	522	325	231	
Md.	8	4,176	2,065	. . .	
Va.	11	5,742	2,486	. . .	
N.C.	6	3,132		. . .	
S.C.	6	3,132		. . .	
Ga.	1	522		. . .	
Total	80	41,756[a]	21,015	5,811	
Totals from returns					26,826

[a]Corrected from original.

Conjectural estimate of militia employed in addition to the above

N.Y., 2 months				2,000	
Va. 12 months				1,500	
Va., 3 months				3,000	
N.C., average 12 months				3,000	
S.C., 4 months				5,000	
S.C., 8 months				1,000	
Ga.				750	
Total Conjectural					16,000
Grand Total					42,826

Statement of the troops furnished by the following states, taken from actual returns of the Army, for the year 1781

States	Quotas Required		Furnished		Total Number of Continentals and Militia
	Number of Battalions, 576 Men Each	Number of Men	Number of Men	Militia	
N.H.	2	1,152	700	. . .	
Mass. (4 months' men)	11	6,366	3,732	1,566	
R.I.	1	576	464	. . .	
Conn. (4 months' men)	6	3,456	2,420	1,501	
N.Y.	3	1,728	1,178	. . .	
N.J.	2	1,152	823	. . .	
Pa.	9	5,184	1,346	. . .	
Del.	1	576	89	. . .	
Md.	5	2,880	770	1,337[a]	
Va.	11	6,336	1,225	2,894[b]	
N.C.	4	2,304	545	. . .	
S.C.	2	1,152	. . .	. . .	
Ga.	1	576	. . .	. . .	
Total	58	33,408	13,292	7,298	
Total from returns					20,590

Conjectural estimate of Militia employed in addition to the preceding information

Va. N.C. S.C. Ga.				2,000 ⎫c 3,000 ⎬ 3,000 750	
Total Conjectural					8,750
Grand Total					29,340

[a]With General Green.
[b]Before York Town.
[c]The average number employed during ten months of the year may be estimated at six thousand.

Statement of the troops furnished by the following states, taken from actual returns of the Army, for the year 1782

States	Quota Required		Furnished		Total Number of Continentals and Militia
	Number of Battalions, 576 Men Each	Number of Men	Number of Men	Militia	
N.H.	2	1,152	744	. . .	
Mass.	11	6,336	4,423	. . .	
R.I.	1	576	481	. . .	
Conn.	6	3,456	1,732	. . .	
N.Y.	3	1,728	1,198	. . .	
N.J.	2	1,152	660	. . .	
Pa.	9	5,184	1,265	. . .	
Del.	1	576	164	. . .	
Md.	5	2,880	1,280	. . .	
Va.	11	6,336	1,204	. . .	
N.C.	4	2,304	1,105	. . .	
S.C.	2	1,152	. . .	. . .	
Ga.	1	576	. . .	. . .	
Total	58	33,408	14,256	. . .	
Total, from returns					14,256

Conjectural estimate of militia, employed in addition to the above

Va. S.C. for 4 months Ga.				1,000 2,000 750	
Total Conjectural					3,750
Grand Total					18,006

(continued)

TABLE 8.53 (continued)

Statement of the troops furnished by the following states, taken from the actual returns of the Army, for the year 1783

| States | Quota Required | | Furnished | | Total Number of Continentals and Militia |
	Number of Battalions, of 576 Men Each	Number of Men	Number of Men	Militia	
N.H.	2	1,152	733	. . .	
Mass.	11	6,336	4,370	. . .	
R.I.	1	576	372	. . .	
Conn.	6	3,456	1,740	. . .	
N.Y.	3	1,728	1,169	. . .	
N.J.	2	1,152	676	. . .	
Pa.	7	5,184	1,598	. . .	
Del.	1	576	235	. . .	
Md.	5	2,880	974	. . .	
Va.	11	6,336	629	. . .	
N.C.	4	2,304	697	. . .	
S.C.	2	1,152	139	. . .	
Ga.	1	576	145	. . .	
Total	58	33,408	13,476	. . .	13,476

Note: The Army in the Northern Department discharged November 5, 1783, and that in the Southern States, on November 15, 1783.
Source: U.S. Congress, *American State Papers: Military Affairs* (1832), I, 14–19.

The U.S. attempt to annex Canada forcibly as a fourteenth state ended when Gen. Richard Montgomery's forces failed to capture Quebec on New Year's Eve of 1775. John Trumbull's art has here interpreted Montgomery's death in the heroic style of eighteenth-century history painting. Montgomery, who had resigned from the British army to take a Continental commission, emerged as one of the Revolution's earliest heroes and had communities named for him in every state. (Courtesy Library of Congress)

TABLE 8.54 MEN UNDER ARMS SERVING WITH CONTINENTAL ARMY, 1775–1783

	Continentals			State Militia on Campaign	Total
	Infantry[a]	Artillery	Cavalry		
Dec. 1775	20,041	551	. . .	943	21,535
Jul. 1776	21,728[b]	471	. . .	10,329	32,528[a]
Dec. 1776	9,402	. . .	. . .	2,021	11,423[c]
Oct. 1777	26,546	550	401	11,946	39,443
Dec. 1777	25,470	. . .	515	. . .	25,985
Jul. 1778	24,166	1,213	214	3,045	28,638
Dec. 1778	28,136	929	. . .	4,346	33,411
Jul. 1779	25,813	1,278	318	1,536	28,945
Jan. 1780	19,431	1,177	653	. . .	21,261
Aug. 1780	16,589	1,137	300	6,802	24,828[d]
Nov. 1780	17,482	1,038	228	1,283	20,031
Oct. 1781	13,232	456	280	2,801[e]	16,769[f]
Mar. 1782	13,317	997	705	66	15,085
Dec. 1782	12,705	895	373	. . .	13,973
May 1783	10,588	916	293	. . .	11,797[g]

[a] Infantry includes small number of invalids, sappers, and miners.
[b] Includes 6,922 Continentals retreating from Canada on June return.
[c] Includes only troops under Washington near Bristol, Pa.
[d] Not including Southern Department under Horatio Gates.
[e] Not including 2,894 Virginia militia at Yorktown under Nelson.
[f] Not including Southern Department under Nathanael Greene.
[g] Not including Southern Department.
Source: Charles H. Lesser, ed., *The Sinews of Independence: Monthly Strength Reports of the Continental Army* (1976), 12–13, 25–27, 43, 50, 54–55, 76–77, 96–98, 124–26, 148–49, 176–77, 188–98, 210–11, 216, 240, 252.

TABLE 8.55 COMMISSIONED VESSELS OF THE CONTINENTAL NAVY

Name, Guns	Type Vessel	Years in Service	End of Service
Alfred, 24	Ship	Purchased 1775	Captured 1778
Columbus, 20	Ship	Purchased 1775	Destroyed 1778
Andrew Doria, 14	Brig	Purchased 1775	Destroyed 1777
Cabot, 14	Brig	Purchased 1775	Captured 1777
Providence, 12	Sloop	Purchased 1775	Destroyed 1779
Hornet, 10	Sloop	Purchased 1775	Destroyed 1777
Wasp, 8	Schooner	Purchased 1775	Destroyed 1777
Fly, 8	Schooner	Purchased 1775	Destroyed 1777
Lexington, 16	Brig	Purchased 1776	Captured 1777
Reprisal, 16	Brig	Purchased 1776	Lost at Sea 1777
Hampden, 14	Brig	Purchased 1776	Sold 1777
Independence, 10	Sloop	Purchased 1776	Wrecked 1778
Sachem, 10	Sloop	Purchased 1776	Destroyed 1777
Mosquito, 4	Sloop	Purchased 1776	Destroyed 1777
Raleigh, 32	Frigate	Launched 1776	Captured 1778
Hancock, 32	Frigate	Launched 1776	Captured 1777
Warren, 32	Frigate	Launched 1776	Destroyed 1779
Washington, 32	Frigate	Launched 1776	Destroyed 1777
Randolph, 32	Frigate	Launched 1776	Lost in action 1778
Providence, 28	Frigate	Launched 1776	Captured 1780
Trumbull, 28	Frigate	Launched 1776	Captured 1781
Congress, 28	Frigate	Launched 1776	Destroyed 1777
Virginia, 28	Frigate	Launched 1776	Captured 1778
Effingham, 28	Frigate	Launched 1776	Destroyed 1777
Boston, 24	Frigate	Launched 1776	Captured 1780
Montgomery, 24	Frigate	Launched 1776	Destroyed 1777
Delaware, 24	Frigate	Launched 1776	Destroyed 1777
Ranger, 18	Ship	Launched 1777	Captured 1780
Resistance, 10	Brigantine	Launched 1777	Captured 1778
Surprise	Sloop	Purchased 1777	[a]
Racehorse, 12	Sloop	Captured 1776	Destroyed
Repulse, 8	Xebec	Pennsylvania State gunboat lent to Continental Navy—1777	Destroyed 1777
Champion, 8	Xebec	Pennsylvania State gunboat lent to Continental Navy—1777	Destroyed 1777
L'Indien, 40	Frigate	Built in Holland 1777	Sold to France: later acquired by South Carolina Navy as *South Carolina*— Captured 1782
Deane (Later Hague), 32	Frigate	Purchased 1777	Sold 1783
Queene of France, 28	Frigate	Purchased 1777	Sunk 1780
Dolphin, 10	Cutter	Purchased 1777	[a]
Surprise, 10	Lugger	Purchased 1777	Seized by France
Revenge, 14	Cutter	Purchased 1777	Sold 1779
Alliance, 32	Frigate	Launched 1778	Sold 1785
General Gates, 18	Ship	Purchased 1778	Sold 1779
Retaliation	Brigantine	Purchased 1778	[a]
Pigot, 8	Schooner	Captured 1778	[a]
Confederacy, 32	Frigate	Launched 1779	Captured 1781
Argo, 12	Sloop	Purchased 1779	Sold 1779
Diligent, 12	Brig	Captured 1779	Destroyed 1779
Bonhomme Richard, 42	Ship	Purchased 1779	Lost in action 1779
Pallas, 32	Frigate	Lent by France 1779	Returned
Cerf, 18	Cutter	Lent by France 1779	Returned
Vengeance, 12	Brig	Lent by France 1779	Returned
Serapis, 44	Frigate	Captured 1779	Sold 1779
Ariel, 20	Ship	Lent by France 1780	Returned 1781
Saratoga, 18	Ship	Launched 1780	Lost at sea 1781
America, 74	Ship of the line	Launched 1782	Given to France
General Washington, 20	Ship	Captured 1782	Sold 1784
Duc de Lauzun, 20	Ship	Purchased 1782	Sold 1783
Bourbon, 36	Frigate	Launched 1783	Sold 1783

Packets:

Active	Georgia Packet
Baltimore	Horn Snake
Despatch	Mercury
Enterprise	Phoenix
Fame	

Washington's Fleet, 1775–1776

Name	Type Vessel
Hannah	schooner
Lynch	schooner
Franklin	schooner
Lee	schooner
Harrison	schooner
Warren	schooner
Washington	brigantine
Hancock	schooner
General Schuyler	sloop
General Mifflin	sloop
Lady Washington	galley

Lake Champlain, 1776

Name, Guns	Type Vessel
Enterprise, 12	sloop
Royal Savage, 12	schooner
Revenge, 8	schooner
Liberty, 8	schooner
New Haven, 3	gondola
Providence, 3	gondola
Boston, 3	gondola
Spitfire, 3	gondola
Philadelphia, 3	gondola
Connecticut, 3	gondola
Jersey, 3	gondola
New York, 3	gondola
Lee, 6	galley
Trumbull, 8	galley
Congress, 8	galley
Washington, 8	galley
Gates, 8	galley

(continued)

TABLE 8.55 (continued)

Mississippi River, 1778–1779	
Name	Type Vessel
Morris	ship
West Florida	sloop
Morris	schooner

[a] Disposition unknown.

Source: Nathan Miller, *Sea of Glory: The Continental Navy Fights for Independence, 1775–1781* (1974), 528–29. Gardiner W. Allen, *A Naval History of the American Revolution* (1913), 700–03.

TABLE 8.56 PRIVATEERS COMMISSIONED BY CONGRESS, 1776–1783

Privateers Commissioned by Year, Type, and State

Year	No.	Type Vessel	No.	State	No.
1776	34	Ships	301	N.H.	43
1777	69	Brigs and		Mass.	626
1778	129	brigantines	541	R.I.	15
1779	209	Schooners and		Conn.	218
1780	301	sloops	751	N.Y.	1
1781	550	Boats and		N.J.	4
1782	383	galleys	104	Pa.	500
1783	22			Md.	225
		Total	1,697	Va.	64
Total	1,697			S.C.	1
Number of crewmen	58,400				
Number of guns	14,872			Total	1,697

Note: 216 U.S. privateers were captured by British forces. U.S. privateers captured 2,208 British ships with 16,000 crewmen, not counting 879 other prizes regained at sea by the Royal Navy.

Source: Gardiner W. Allen, *A Naval History of the American Revolution* (1913), 716–17.

TABLE 8.57 COMMANDERS-IN-CHIEF OF U.S. ARMY, NAVY, AND MARINES, 1775–1800

Commanders-in-Chief of the Army			
Commander	State	Years	Rank
Artemas Ward	Mass.	1774–1775	General
George Washington	Va.	1775–1783	General
Henry Knox	Mass.	1783–1784	Major-General
Josiah Harmar	Pa.	1784–1791	Lieutenant-Colonel
Arthur St. Clair	Pa.	1791–1792	Major-General
Anthony Wayne	Ga.	1792–1796	Major-General
James Wilkinson	Ky.	1796–1798	Brigadier-General
George Washington	Va.	1798–1799	Lieutenant-General
Alexander Hamilton	N.Y.	1799–1800	Major-General
James Wilkinson	Ky.	1800–1812	Brigadier-General
Commander-in-Chief of the Navy			
Esek Hopkins [a]	R.I.	1775–1778	
Commandants of the Marines			
Samuel Nicholas	Pa.	1776–1783	Major
William Ward Burrows	Pa.	1798–1804	Lieutenant Colonel

[a] No officer succeeded Hopkins to this rank when he was discharged from the service on January 2, 1778.

TABLE 8.58 CASUALTIES SUSTAINED BY CONTINENTAL FORCES IN REVOLUTIONARY WAR

Year	Engagements		Killed	Wounded	Captured	Missing
1775	Land	143	323	436	519	5
	Naval	14	4	5	74	
1776	Land	251	600	562	5,365	1
	Naval	66	29	71	224	
1777	Land	266	1,493	2,053	2,084	38
	Naval	42	24	45	671	
1778	Land	138	753	443	1,212	139
	Naval	27	462	38	620	
1779	Land	127	657	824	859	18
	Naval	29	252	178	218	
1780	Land	152	984	1,886	4,661	9
	Naval	13	18	36	58	
1781	Land	196	1,003	1,454	761	1,216
	Naval	14	263	31	675	
1782	Land	53	277	124	80	
	Naval	9	31	44	490	
1783	Land	5		1	1	
	Naval	4	1	10		
Total for 1,331 land engagements			6,090	7,783	15,542	1,426
Total for 218 naval engagements			1,084	458	3,030	
Total for all engagements			7,174	8,241	18,572	1,426
Estimated deaths from disease			10,000			
Estimated prisoners who died			8,500			
Total estimate of deaths			25,674			

Source: Howard H. Peckham, ed., *The Toll of Independence: Engagements and Battle Casualties of the American Revolution* (1974), 130.

CHAPTER 9 The States and Territories

Connecticut

Having been first permanently settled in 1633, Connecticut had been inhabited by five generations of Yankees when the Revolution began. Total area equaled 4,872 square miles after the state's final cession of land claims in the Ohio Valley to the United States in 1795. It entered the Union as the fifth ratifying vote for the Constitution on January 9, 1788. This "land of steady habits" continued the colonial custom of convening its legislature alternately at Hartford and New Haven until 1873, when Hartford was named sole capital. Between 1770 and 1800, the population increased from 183,181 (40 persons per square mile) to 251,002 (51 persons per square mile). It was the eighth most populous state by 1800. African-Americans equaled about 3% of all residents. In 1800 there were 107 towns; the largest were Hartford (5,347), New London (5,150), New Haven (4,049), and Norwich (3,475).

Connecticut supplied less than 4% of American goods sold abroad in 1791, but it ranked first in the export of salted pork (19% of all) and second in salted beef (30% of all). Most residents were small farmers who produced for markets in New England and New York. A significant publishing industry developed at Hartford, New Haven, and New London, which together turned out approximately 10% of all American imprints from 1765 to 1783. Connecticut's eventual rise as a major firearms producer had its inception in 1798, when Eli Whitney founded a gunworks to mass-produce muskets at New Haven.

During the Revolution, little major fighting occurred in Connecticut except for British raids on Danbury (1777), New Haven (1779), and New London (1781). Sentiment was almost unanimous for independence. During most of the war, Connecticut provided eight of the Continental Army's eighty regiments; it also outfitted 218 privateers to prey on the British merchant marine. When peace resumed, a major outmigration ensued to New York, Pennsylvania, and Ohio. Its citizens voted overwhelmingly Federalist in politics and did not elect any Democratic-Republicans to Congress from 1789 to 1801. Revolutionary Connecticut's notable figures included Samuel Huntington (president of the Continental Congress), Uriah Tracy (president pro-tempore of the Senate), Oliver Ellsworth (chief justice of the Supreme Court), Jonathan Trumbull (speaker of the House of Representatives), and Eli Whitney (inventor).

Governors
1754—Thomas Fitch
1766—William Pitkin
1769—Jonathan Trumbull
1784—Matthew Griswold
1786—Samuel Huntington
1796—Oliver Wolcott
1797—Jonathan Trumbull, II

Chief Justices of Supreme Court
1754—William Pitkin
1766—Jonathan Trumbull
1769—Matthew Griswold
1784—Samuel Huntington
1785—Richard Law
1789—Eliphalet Dyer
1793—Andrew Adams
1798—Jesse Root

Delaware

Despite a long history extending to its first permanent settlement in 1638, Delaware remained a political appendage of Pennsylvania until 1776. Still officially termed "The Three Lower Counties on the Delaware," the province lay under the executive authority of Pennsylvania's governor and the jurisdiction of Pennsylvania's superior court until 1776, when Delawareans wrote their own constitution. It was the first state to ratify the federal constitution, on December 7, 1787. New Castle, the former colonial capital, remained its seat of government until 1777, when Dover took its place. Between 1770 and 1800, the population increased from 35,496 (19 persons per square mile) to 64,273 (33 persons per square mile). It was the smallest state in population by 1800, and the second smallest in land area (1,932 square miles). New Castle was its major urban center (2,438) in 1800.

African Americans equaled 5% of all residents in 1770 and by 1800 had increased to 22%. Slavery remained legal, although the number in bondage dropped by 31%, from 8,887 to 6,153, during the 1790s. Slaves made up just one-tenth of the population by 1800. The state would not outlaw slavery until the Civil War.

Less than 1% of American exports went overseas from Delaware ports. Most residents were small farmers who produced for nearby markets such as Philadelphia. Delaware began to industrialize in the 1790s, when the Brandywine Creek area became a regional center for flour milling and the nation's largest producer of gunpowder.

Delaware escaped major fighting during the Revolution. It furnished just one of the Continental Army's eighty regiments, but these men (commanded by Col. William Smallwood) received universal acclaim as one of the army's most intrepid fighting units. A large postwar migration drained the state's young people, and Delaware suffered the nation's slowest population growth in the 1790s. Federalists usually represented the state at Washington. Notable Delawareans included John Dickinson (father of the Articles of Confederation), Oliver Evans (designer of the first fully automated factory) and Eleuthere du Pont (pioneering munitions industrialist).

Governors
1777—John McKinley
1777—George Read
1777—Thomas McKean
1778—Caesar Rodney
1781—John Dickinson
1783—Nicholas Van Dyke
1786—Thomas Collins
1789—Joshua Clayton
1796—Gunning Bedford
1797—Daniel Rogers
1799—Richard Bassett

Chief Justices (Officially Termed Chancellors)
1776—William Killen
1800—Richard Bassett

Georgia

English colonization had started so late in Georgia (not until 1733), that Indians still outnumbered whites in 1776. The state's total area originally included the northern two-thirds of present-day Alabama and Mississippi, but when Georgia ceded that area to the United States in 1802, it attained its present size of 58,056 square miles. It entered the Union as the fourth state to ratify the Constitution on January 2, 1788. Its colonial capital, Savannah, remained the seat of government until 1786, when Augusta became temporary capital pending a final move to Louisville, which took place in 1795. Between 1770 and 1800, the population increased from 23,375 (1 person per square mile) to 162,686 (9 persons per square mile). Its population was the nation's fourth smallest by 1800. African Americans made up 45% of residents (excluding Indians) in 1770, and 38% in 1800. The only significant cities in 1800 were Savannah (5,166) and Augusta (2,215).

Georgia supplied about 3% of American goods sent overseas in 1791; it ranked second in the export of rice (9% of all), third in tobacco and pine boards, and fourth in shingles. Agricultural output shifted rapidly to cotton after a practical gin came into use after 1793. From 1791 to 1801, Georgia's cotton harvest rose from 500,000 to 10,000,000 pounds. By 1800, Georgia stood second among the states in cotton production and produced 20% of that crop.

The presence of large numbers of recent British immigrants gave Georgia a large body of Tory sentiment during the Revolution. British troops captured Savannah in 1778 and repulsed an American siege in 1779. The British occupied Georgia until 1782, when they left with 3,100 Tories (about 15% of all whites). Georgia's congressional delegation was consistently Democratic-Republican. Among its prominent citizens were Revolutionary generals Elisha Clarke and Lachlan MacIntosh.

Governors

1760—Sir James Wright
1773—James Habersham (President of Council)
1773—Sir James Wright
1776—Archibald Bullock
1777—Button Gwinnett
1777—John A. Treutlen
1778—John Houstoun
1778—John Wereat
1779—George Walton
1780—Richard Howley
1781—Stephen Heard
1781—Nathan Brownson
1782—John Martin
1783—Lyman Hall
1784—John Houstoun
1785—Samuel Elbert
1786—Edward Telfair
1787—George Mathews
1788—George Walton
1789—Edward Telfair
1793—George Mathews
1796—Jared Irwin
1798—James Jackson

Chief Justice

1769—Anthony Stokes (to 1776)

(*Note:* Following independence, Georgia established a superior court for each of its three judicial districts, but no supreme court for the state. Appeals were heard by a "special jury" specifically impaneled for that purpose, not by a court of appeals.)

Kentucky

The name *Kentucky* derived from *Kentaten,* which may have been Iroquoian for "tomorrow's land." After its boundaries were definitively surveyed in the early 1800s, it included 39,669 square miles. Originally a county of Virginia, it became the fifteenth state—and first west of the Appalachians—on June 1, 1792. In 1792, the capital moved from Danville to Frank's Ford, now known as Frankfort. The population increased from perhaps 15,000 in 1780 to 220,955 (6 persons per square mile) in 1800, by which time it ranked as the ninth most populous state. Slaves equaled 17% of residents in 1790 and 19% in 1800. By 1800, only 2% of inhabitants lived in towns of 500 or more, of which the largest were Lexington (1,795), Frankfort (628), Bardstown (579), and Washington (570). The state rapidly developed a plantation economy like Virginia's and sent its tobacco and foodstuffs to market via New Orleans.

Kentucky became the first area beyond the Appalachians to be settled by Anglo-Americans because no Indians lived there in the 1770s. The Iroquois, Cherokee, and Shawnee signed treaties renouncing their claims by 1774. Harrodsburg became the first permanently occupied settlement in 1775. As allies of the British, Indians launched unrelenting waves of attacks on Kentucky during the Revolution. It was Kentucky's militia that broke Britain's hold on the territory north of the Ohio River by seizing Kaskaskia, Illinois, and Vincennes, Indiana. The Indians continued their harassment until their decisive defeat by U.S. regulars and Kentucky militia at Fallen Timbers, Ohio, in 1794. In the five years after Indian hostilities ended, more than 100,000 settlers moved to the state. Every congressman elected from Kentucky in the 1790s was a Democratic-Republican. The legislature's Kentucky Resolutions of 1798 and 1799 stand among the boldest denunciations of Federalist misgovernment. Prominent citizens included Daniel Boone (explorer), George Rogers Clark (frontiersman and Revolutionary hero), and John Fitch (inventor).

Governors

1792—Isaac Shelby
1796—James Garrard (to 1803)

Chief Justices

1792—Harry Innes
1792—George Muter

Maine

Maine continued its status as a district of Massachusetts, even though it had been settled since 1624. Its boundaries with Canada would not be resolved until 1842, but Maine's inhabited area probably covered 8,000 square miles in 1800. Between 1770 and 1800, the population quintupled from 31,257 (6 persons per square mile) to 151,719 (19 persons per square mile). African Americans composed less than 1% of residents. Of the 220 towns or settlements in 1800, just twelve had populations exceeding 2,000. The largest towns were Berwick (3,891), Portland (3,704), Wells (3,692), Falmouth (3,422), and Kittery (3,114).

Bad weather and poor soil made it difficult for farmers to turn a good profit, so most adults supplemented agriculture with work in the lumber industry or part-time fishing. The Revolution's first naval engagement occurred at Machias in June 1775, when two armed vessels from the town captured the royal schooner *Margaretta*. The only significant military campaign occurred in 1779 when the British occupied Penobscot Bay and repulsed an expedition under Paul Revere to expel them. An influx of settlers from Massachusetts founded 35 new towns from 1775 to 1790, and another 55 came into existence during the next decade. New settlers often could not obtain clear title to land because rival speculators or real estate companies had filed so many overlapping claims for the best land. Numerous assaults and mobbings resulted when enraged farmers who had unknowingly poured their life savings into faulty titles used violence to avoid being evicted from their property. Among Maine's notable citizens were Peleg Wadsworth (Revolutionary general) and James Sullivan (historian and political leader).

Maryland

The second oldest southern colony, founded by English Catholics in 1634, Maryland's territory included 9,837 square miles after its true boundary with Pennsylvania was verified in 1768 by the Mason-Dixon Line. It was the seventh state to ratify the Constitution on April 28, 1788. Its colonial capital, Annapolis, remained the seat of government. Between 1770 and 1800, the population increased from 202,599 (25 persons per square mile) to 341,548 (36 persons per square mile). It was the sixth largest state in population by 1800. African Americans composed 31% of all residents in 1770 and 36% in 1800. Baltimore was its largest city (26,514) by 1800.

Maryland ranked second in tobacco output and produced a quarter of the domestic crop, but it was diversifying rapidly away from its traditional dependence on that commodity. By 1791, it had emerged as the country's second leading exporter of flour (23% of all) and third largest exporter of both wheat (16% of all) and corn (12% of all). Baltimore had emerged as the country's fourth largest harbor by 1800 and had become a major center of shipbuilding.

During the Revolution, Maryland escaped any major fighting; it had few Tories. For most of the war, Maryland provided eight of the eighty Continental regiments, and its troops earned the nickname of "the bayonets of the Continental Army" by their fighting spirit. Maryland also outfitted 225 privateers to prey upon Britain's shipping. After 1783, the state's population growth lagged the national average because of a large out-migration to Kentucky and the Carolinas. Political sentiment divided rather evenly between Federalists and Democratic-Republicans, but Federalists dominated Maryland's congressional elections in every year but 1793 and 1795. Revolutionary Maryland's notable public figures included Daniel Carroll "of Carrollton" (signer of the Declaration), John Hanson (president of the Continental Congress), James McHenry (secretary of war), and John Eager Howard (president pro-tempore of the Senate).

Governors
1753—Horatio Sharpe
1769—Robert Eden
1774–1777—Committee chairmen
1777—Thomas Johnson
1779—Thomas Sim Lee
1782—William Paca
1785—William Smallwood
1789—John Eager Howard
1791—George Plater
1792—Thomas Sim Lee
1794—John H. Stone
1797—John Henry
1798—Benjamin Ogle

Chief Justices
1771—William Hayward
1778—Benjamin Rumsey (to 1805)

Massachusetts

Massachusetts had been inhabited by Anglo-Saxons longer than any other northern state, and its small land area (7,824 square miles, excluding Maine) had become thickly populated by 1800. From 1770 to 1800, the population of present-day Massachusetts grew from 235,308 (37 persons per square mile) to 422,845 (54 persons per square mile). African Americans made up 1% of all residents. Out of 279 towns in 1800, only six had more than 5,000 residents: Boston (24,937), Salem (9,457), Newburyport (5,946), Gloucester (5,313), Marblehead (5,211), and Bridgewater (5,200). Its colonial capital, Boston, remained the government's seat. It entered the Union as the sixth state on February 6, 1788.

Most families lived on farms, but stony soil and a short growing season kept agricultural yields so low that the state had to import foodstuffs. In 1791, Massachusetts ranked first in the export of fish (90% of all), whale oil (71% of all), pine boards (55% of all), oak boards (43% of all), and shingles (20% of all). Its 156 stills made 57% of all whiskey taxed in 1792. Massachusetts possessed the nation's largest merchant marine, and overseas trade was the most dynamic element of its economy. The volume of exports from the state grew 350% from 1791 to 1800, and its share of all U.S. exports rose from 13% to 16% during those years.

Although the Revolution began in Massachusetts at the Battle of Lexington, the state remained the scene of major fighting only until the British evacuated Boston in March 1776. Fifteen of the Continental Army's eighty regiments were from Massachusetts, and—despite ranking third in the number of free males of military age—it mustered more troops each year than did any other state. It also outfitted 626 privateers to prey upon British shipping. After the war, the state's economy spiraled into depression as the nation's trade plummeted, and hard economic times climaxed in Shays's Rebellion, an armed uprising by hard-pressed farmers trying to keep the courts from ordering any further foreclosures on farms to settle unpaid debts or taxes. The insurrection collapsed in early 1787, but the legislature allayed further discontent by reducing taxes. Massachusetts experienced a high rate of outmigration to upstate New York and Ohio, and so its population growth lagged the national average.

Every state suffered from an extended commercial depression during the 1780s, but economic troubles were greatest in Massachusetts. Severely vexed by a wave of court suits for unpaid debts and back taxes, Massachusetts farmers rallied around Daniel Shays to enforce a moratorium on court actions to seize property from hard-pressed citizens until prosperity returned. In the above etching, a crowd of Shaysites takes possession of a courthouse to halt its proceedings at Springfield, Massachusetts, in autumn 1786. (*Harper's Magazine,* January 1884)

The voters chose a majority of Federalist congressmen in every election of the 1790s. The state's notable public figures included President John Adams, John Hancock (president of the Continental Congress), Henry Knox (secretary of war), and Samuel Osgood (postmaster general).

Governors

1760—Sir Francis Bernard
1769—Thomas Hutchinson (acting)
1770—Thomas Hutchinson
1774—Gen. Thomas Gage
1775—The next chief executive held office under the constitution of 1780.
1780—John Hancock
1785—James Bowdoin
1787—John Hancock
1794—Samuel Adams
1797—Increase Sumner
1800—Caleb Strong

Chief Justices

1761—Thomas Hutchinson
1769—Benjamin Lynde
1772—Peter Oliver
1775—John Adams
1777—William Cushing
1789—Nathaniel P. Sargeant
1791—Francis P. Dana

New Hampshire

New Hampshire grew slowly for a century and a half after its first English settlement in 1623, in large part because most of its 8,993 square miles was rugged terrain ill-suited for farming. A period of rapid growth nevertheless occurred from 1770 to 1800, when the population tripled from 62,396 (7 persons per square mile) to 183,858 (20 persons per square mile). Even after this burst of in-migration, New Hampshire ranked as the sixth smallest state in 1800. It entered the Union as the ninth state on June 21, 1788. Less than 1% of inhabitants were African Americans. Just 13 of 206 towns had more than 2,000 people; the largest were the capital of Portsmouth (5,339), Gilmantown (3,752), Barrington (2,773) and Londonderry (2,650).

New Hampshire furnished less than 1% of American exports. The state produced 40% of all domestic oak boards sent overseas, 14% of pine boards, 4% of staves, and 5% of dried fish. Most residents were small farmers who found agriculture just marginally profitable and supplemented their income with work in the lumber industry.

During the Revolution, New Hampshire escaped any major fighting; its people supported independence almost unanimously. It furnished three of the Continental Army's eighty regiments and outfitted 43 privateers to prey upon Britain's shipping. The state's voters always sent a majority of Federalist representatives to Congress. Revolutionary New Hampshire's notable public figures included John Sullivan (Revolutionary general), John Landgon (first president pro-tempore of the Senate), and Samuel Livermore (president pro-tempore of the Senate).

Governors

1741—Benning Wentworth
1767—John Wentworth
1776—Meshech Ware

1785—John Langdon
1786—John Sullivan
1788—John Langdon
1789—John Sullivan
1790—Josiah Bartlett
1794—John T. Gilman

Chief Justices

(*Note:* Prior to Independence, the governor and council acted as the colony's final court of appeal.)

1789—Josiah Bartlett
1790—John Pickering
1795—Simeon Olcott

New Jersey

New Jersey entered the Union as the third state to ratify the Constitution on December 18, 1787. After its disputed boundary with New York was accurately surveyed in the 1770s, the colony's total area equaled 7,468 square miles. Between 1770 and 1800, the population increased from 117,431 (16 persons per square mile) to 211,149 (28 persons per square mile), but its population ranked seventh smallest among the sixteen states in 1800. Eight percent of residents were African Americans. It continued the colonial custom of having the legislature meet alternately at Perth Amboy and Burlington until 1790, when Trenton became sole capital.

New Jersey produced great amounts of grain and livestock for export. Its iron industry was second only to that of Pennsylvania, and it was America's largest producer of glass for much of the late eighteenth century. New Jersey had been the colonies' main source of copper, but output from its mines dropped sharply after 1775.

New Jersey was the scene of major fighting early in the Revolution when Washington retreated across the state and then won important victories at Trenton (1776) and Princeton (1777). The state's people were badly divided in their loyalties; they provided four of the eighty Continental regiments, plus the British army's largest Tory organization, a brigade of four battalions known as the New Jersey Volunteers. After 1783, the state's population growth lagged the national average because of a large out-migration to upstate New York and the Ohio Valley. The state's voters elected a majority of Federalists to Congress in every election before 1800 except 1799. Revolutionary New Jersey's notable residents included Jonathan Dayton (speaker of the House of Representatives), William Livingston (longest serving governor in Revolutionary America), and Patience Wright (first American sculptor to win European acclaim).

Governors

1761—Josiah Hardy
1763—William Franklin
1776—William Livingston
1790—William Paterson
1793—Richard Howell

Chief Justices

1761—Robert Hunter Morris
1764—Charles Read (acting)
1764—Frederick Smyth
1777—Robert Morris
1779—David Brearley
1789—James Kinsey

New York

For most of the time since it had been first occupied by the Dutch in 1614, New York had experienced only modest growth, but it began to expand dramatically after the Revolution. Its population increased from 162,920 (4 persons per square mile) to 598,051 (12 persons per square mile) during the thirty years after 1770. By 1800, New York was the third most populous state and the third largest in land area (47,377 square miles after it gave up its land claim in the Ohio Valley in 1780). African Americans numbered 12% of all residents in 1770, but just 5% in 1800. The population was about 88% rural in 1800, and the largest cities were New York (60,515), Albany (5,289), and Schenectady (also 5,289). New York became the eleventh state to ratify the Constitution on July 26, 1788. Albany replaced New York as the capital in 1797.

New York agriculturalists sold large amounts of farm products abroad. In 1791, New York ranked first in the export of flaxseed (47% of all), second in wheat (22% of all), and fourth in both flour (13% of all) and corn (12% of all); it also shipped off 19% of all domestic staves and 7% of all pine boards. The volume of New York's exports increased 460% from 1791 to 1800, and its share of all U.S. exports rose from 13% to 20% as well.

New York entered the Revolution badly divided. It usually mustered five of the eighty Continental regiments, but it also provided five major units of Tories, including the three battalions of De-Lancey's Brigade. In 1776, British forces captured New York City, which they occupied for six years. The war's turning point came at Saratoga in 1777, where an entire British army surrendered. In retaliation for devastating frontier raids by Iroquois warriors, Continental forces drove most of the Iroquois to Canada in 1779. With the Iroquois removed, upstate New York attracted a flood of migrants from New England and New Jersey. The Federalists and Democratic-Republicans closely contested the state in the 1790s. Notable citizens included Chief Justice John Jay, Vice President Aaron Burr, and Treasury Secretary Alexander Hamilton.

Governors

1762—Robert Monckton
1763—Lt. Gov. Cadwallader Colden
1765—Sir Henry Moore
1769—Lt. Gov. Cadwallader Colden
1770—John Murray, Earl of Dunmore
1771—William Tryon
1774—Lt. Gov. Cadwallader Colden
1775—William Tryon
1776—George Clinton
1795—John Jay

Chief Justices

1763—Daniel Horsmanden
1777—John Jay
1789—Richard Morris
1790—Robert Yates
1798—John Lansing, Jr.

North Carolina

North Carolina entered the Union as the twelfth state on November 21, 1789. The seat of government moved from New Bern, the colonial capital, to Raleigh in 1788. Between 1770 and 1800, its population increased from 197,200 (5 persons per square mile) to 478,103 (10 persons per square mile). By 1800, it had the fifth largest population of all sixteen states and was the second largest in land area (with 48,843 square miles after it ceded jurisdiction over Tennessee). African Americans equaled 35% of all residents in 1770, but only 29% in 1800. Only 2% of the population lived in communities exceeding 500 people, of which the largest in 1800 were New Bern (2,467), Wilmington (1,689), and Fayetteville (1,656).

About 3% of American goods were shipped abroad in 1791 from North Carolina. The state ranked first in the export of pitch (49% of all) and tar (31% of all), second in turpentine (20% of all), and fifth in tobacco (3% of all). By 1800, direct exports from the state amounted to just 1% of America's total. After 1793, many farmers began shifting to cotton, which had rarely been grown before then, and by 1801, North Carolinians were raising 10,000,000 pounds, about 10% of the domestic crop.

North Carolina was the scene of much serious fighting in the Revolution. In 1776, the patriot militia defeated an uprising of Scottish Tories at Moore's Creek Bridge and then repulsed an invasion of the frontier by the Cherokee. In 1780–1781, the armies of both sides crisscrossed the state and small bands of guerrillas waged war in a chaotic fashion. North Carolina usually furnished nine of the eighty Continental regiments. During the political struggles of the 1790s, North Carolinians strongly supported the Democratic-Republicans over the Federalists. Prominent citizens included James Iredell (Supreme Court justice) and Francis Nash and Jethro Sumner (Revolutionary generals).

Governors

1754—Arthur Dobbs
1765—William Tryon
1771—James Hasell (President of Council)
1771—Josiah Martin
1775—Pres. Cornelius Harnett
1776—Pres. Samuel Ashe
1776—Pres. Willie Jones
1776—Richard Caswell
1780—Abner Nash
1781—Thomas Burke
1782—Alexander Martin
1784—Richard Caswell
1787—Samuel Johnston
1789—Alexander Martin
1792—Richard Dobbs Spaight
1795—Samuel Ashe
1798—William R. Davie
1799—Benjamin Williams

(*Note:* Cornelius Harnett, Samuel Ashe, and Willie Jones served as presidents of the Revolutionary Council in 1775 and 1776.)

Chief Justice

1761—Martin Howard (to 1776)

(*Note:* From 1776 to 1818, the state had separate superior courts in each of its three judicial districts but no supreme court as such.)

Pennsylvania

Pennsylvania continued the rapid expansion that had characterized its history since English Quakers first landed in 1681. The population increased from 240,057 (6 persons per square mile) in 1770 to 602,365 (13 persons per square mile) in 1800. It was the second most populous state in 1800. After its boundary dispute with Maryland was resolved in 1768 and New York surrendered a small tract

When the Revolution ended, all states faced the question of what to do for large numbers of discharged soldiers, such as these Continentals trudging home in their "regimentals," or uniforms. Those states with vacant western lands, including New York and most of the South, rewarded returning Continentals with land grants, but veterans from elsewhere had to be content with the esteem of their fellow citizens. [from *Harper's Magazine,* September 1896] (Howard Pyle Collection, courtesy Delaware Art Museum, Wilmington, Delaware)

including Erie harbor, Pennsylvania contained 44,888 square miles. It was the second state to ratify the Constitution on December 12, 1787. Lancaster replaced Philadelphia, the old colonial capital, as the seat of government in 1788. About 2% of inhabitants were African Americans. The five largest towns in 1800 were Philadelphia (61,559), Lancaster (4,292), York (2,503), Pittsburgh (1,565), and Harrisburg (1,472).

The state sent large amounts of farm produce overseas. In 1791, Pennsylvania ranked first in the export of flour (42% of all), second in corn (21% of all) and flaxseed (19% of all), and fourth in wheat (15% of all). It also possessed the greatest concentration of ironworks (69 as the Revolution began) in Anglo-America and manufactured more guns than any other state. The volume of Pennsylvania's exports increased 250% from 1791 to 1800, but its share of the nation's exports held constant at about 17%.

Pennsylvania usually provided ten of the eighty Continental regiments, the third greatest contribution of troops during the Revolution; it also furnished 500 privateers to attack British commerce. Pennsylvania became a major war theater only in 1777, when the British won victories at Brandywine Creek and Germantown before occupying Philadelphia for about eight months. Indians inflicted heavy losses on the state's frontier until 1794. Frontier violence also erupted when federal revenue collectors were mobbed while trying to enforce excise laws on whiskey distillers near Pittsburgh. Washington quelled the Whiskey Rebellion by calling up 15,000 militia from four states to arrest the ringleaders. In politics, Pennsylvania was closely contested by the Federalists and Democratic-Republicans but tilted toward the latter. Notable citizens included Benjamin Franklin (statesman), Robert Morris (Revolutionary financier), Frederick Muhlenberg (first speaker of the House of Representatives), Anthony Wayne (commander-in-chief of the Army), and Samuel Nicholas (first commandant of the Marines).

Governors

1763—John Penn
1771—Pres. James Hamilton
1771—Richard Penn
1773—Pres. James Hamilton
1773—John Penn
1777—Thomas Wharton, Jr.
1778—George Bryan (acting president)
1778—Joseph Reed
1781—William Moore
1782—John Dickinson
1785—Benjamin Franklin
1789—Thomas Mifflin

1799—Thomas McKean

(*Note:* Prior to 1773, all resident chief executives were deputies of the governor or the Council's president acting in a vacancy. From 1777 to 1790, all chief executives were the Supreme Executive Council's presidents.)

Chief Justices
1750—William Allen
1778—Thomas McKean
1799—Edward Shippen

Rhode Island

Having first been settled in 1636, and owning an area of just 1,497 square miles (72% land and 28% water or tidal water beach), Rhode Island led the nation in population density in 1800, with 65 persons per square mile. Its population increased slowly between 1770 and 1800, from 58,196 to 69,122, and by the latter date it ranked second last among states in number of residents. About 21% of the people lived in the urban communities of Providence (7,614) and Newport (6,739). Rhode Island was the last state to ratify the Constitution on May 29, 1790. It retained the colonial custom of having the legislature meet alternately at Bristol, Newport, Providence, East Greenwich, and South Kingston.

Rhode Island furnished about 2% of American goods sent abroad; in 1791, it exported 30% of all rum, 9% of whale oil, and 5% of dried fish. From its stills came 19% of all whiskey taxed in 1792. Farmers were known for raising cattle and breeding cattle. In 1793, an English immigrant named Samuel Slater built America's earliest textile factory to harness water power and made Rhode Island the birthplace of the country's industrial revolution.

Rhode Islanders had been so enthusiastic for independence that their legislature renounced the colony's allegiance to George III on May 4, 1776, two months before the Continental Congress did so. The state provided two of the eighty Continental regiments during most of the war and outfitted fifteen privateers to attack British shipping. The most significant military event occurred in December 1776 when a British force seized the undefended town of Newport, which remained under occupation until 1779. Rhode Island ceased sending taxes or representatives to the Continental Congress during the late 1780s and lapsed into semi-autonomy. It refused to enter the Union for six months after the Constitution had received its twelfth ratification, during which time Rhode Island was technically an independent government. Population grew slowly because of a large out-migration to New York's frontier. Rhode Islanders sent only Federalists to Congress from 1790 to 1801. Among the state's prominent citizens were Nathanael Greene (Revolutionary general), Esek Hopkins (first commander-in-chief of the Navy), and Samuel Slater (industrial pioneer).

Governors
1762—Samuel Ward
1763—Stephen Hopkins
1765—Samuel Ward
1767—Stephen Hopkins
1768—Josias Lyndon
1769—Joseph Wanton
1775—Nicholas Cooke, Jr.
1778—William Greene, Jr.
1786—John Collins
1790—Arthur Fenner

Chief Justices
1761—Samuel Ward
1762—Jeremiah Niles
1763—Joshua Babcock
1764—John Cole
1765—Joseph Russell
1767—James Helm
1768—Joseph Russell
1769—James Helm
1770—Stephen Hopkins
1776—Metcalf Bowler
1777—William Greene
1778—Shearjashub Bourne
1781—Jabez Bowen
1781—Paul Mumford
1785—William Ellery
1786—Paul Mumford
1788—Othniel Gorton
1790—Daniel Owen
1795—Peleg Arnold

South Carolina

Settled barely a century when the Revolution commenced, South Carolina included its present area of 30,203 square miles and a small strip of land extending to the Mississippi River south of Tennessee, which the state gave to the United States in 1787. It entered the Union as the eighth state on May 23, 1788. Its colonial capital, Charles Town (modern Charleston), remained the seat of government until 1786, when Columbia took its place. Between 1770 and 1800, the population nearly tripled from 124,244 (4 persons per square mile) to 345,591 (11 persons per square mile) and made South Carolina the seventh most populous state. African Americans equaled 61% of all residents in 1770 and 43% in 1800. Charles Town was the largest city (20,565).

South Carolina supplied about 14% of American goods sent overseas in 1791; it ranked first in the export of rice (75% of all) and fourth in tobacco (5% of all). Agriculture shifted rapidly to cotton after a practical gin became available in 1793. South Carolina's cotton crop skyrocketed from 2,000,000 to 20,000,000 pounds, a level that equaled 40% of domestic production and stood first among all the states.

A British naval assault on Charles Town was repulsed in 1776, but the British returned in 1780 and captured the city. The British would occupy South Carolina until 1782, when they left with about 4,000 Tories (about 5% of the prewar white population). South Carolina usually mustered six of the Continental Army's eighty regiments during the Revolution. Such extensive damage resulted from military operations that the state's economy remained anemic into the 1790s. South Carolina politics were initially dominated by Federalists, but the Democratic-Republicans were emerging as the majority party by the late 1790s. Among the state's prominent citizens were Henry Laurens (president of the Continental Congress), Ralph Izard and Jacob Read (presidents pro-tempore of the Senate), Francis Marion (the "Swamp Fox"), and Thomas Pinckney (diplomat).

Governors
1761—Thomas Boone
1764—William Bull, Jr. (Lieutenant Governor)
1766—Charles Greville Montagu
1768—William Bull, Jr. (Lieutenant Governor)
1769—Charles Greville Montagu
1773—Lt. Gov. William Bull

1775—Lord William Campbell
1776—Pres. John Rutledge
1778—Pres. Rawlins Lowndes
1779—John Randolph
1782—John Mathews
1783—Benjamin Guerard
1785—William Moultrie
1787—Thomas Pinckney
1792—Arnoldus Vander Horst
1794—William Moultrie
1796—Charles Pinckney
1798—Edward Rutledge
1800—John Drayton

Chief Justices

1761—Charles Shinner
1768—Rawlins Lowndes (acting)
1771—Thomas Knox Gordon
1789—William H. Drayton
1791—John Rutledge

(*Note:* from 1795 to 1859 the office of chief justice did not exist.)

Tennessee

Tennessee took its name from the Tennessee River; its original Cherokee meaning is unknown. Total area equaled 41,155 square miles after North Carolina gave up its title to the region in 1790. It entered the Union as the sixteenth state on June 1, 1796. Its capital moved from Jonesboro to Knoxville in 1796. The population rose from a few hundred to 105,602 (3 persons per square mile) in the three decades after 1770, but in 1800, Tennessee was still the third least populous state. African Americans composed 11% of residents in 1790 and 14% in 1800. The largest towns in 1800 were Knoxville (387) and Nashville (345).

When North Carolinians and Virginians began drifting into the Watauga River valley of east Tennessee in 1769, the entire area north of the Tennessee River had no permanent Indian inhabitants. With Nashboro's founding in 1779, the settlements broke clear of the mountains and occupied the great central plain. The Revolution unleashed an avalanche of Indian raids, which Tennesseeans had to endure until 1795, despite their frequent expeditions to compel the Indians to make peace by burning their villages. Discontented with North Carolina's apparent insensitivity to their problems, east Tennesseeans tried to join the Union as the state of Franklin, but Congress refused to admit them. Most residents of the mountain counties were small farmers who grew grain for local consumption and raised livestock that could be driven to eastern markets. Central Tennessee developed a plantation economy devoted to tobacco and cotton. The state's entire congressional delegation was Democratic-Republican through 1800. Notable citizens included John Sevier (first governor) and Andrew Jackson (first congressman).

Governors

1790—William Blount (territorial)
1796—John Sevier

Chief Justices

(*Note:* The state's first constitution established a separate court of final appeal for each of its three judicial districts and as such had no supreme court or chief justice.)

Vermont

Vermont's permanent settlement by English colonists dated from 1724. Its name derived from *vert mont,* French for "green mountain." Total area equaled 9,273 square miles. Vermont became the fourteenth state on March 4, 1791; its capital was Montpelier. Between 1770 and 1800, the population increased from perhaps 10,000 (1 person per square mile) to 154,465 (16 persons per square mile). It was the fourth least populous state in 1800. Less than 1% of the residents were African Americans. There were 242 settlements or towns in 1800, of which Windsor (2,211) was the largest.

Most Vermonters were small farmers who supplemented their income by cutting lumber or working at handicrafts. It was Green Mountain Boys from Vermont who captured Ft. Ticonderoga's enormous arsenal of artillery and firearms for the Continental Army in 1776. During the Revolution, Vermont was the scene of one major battle, at Bennington, when its militia defeated and captured 900 Hessians in 1777. Vermonters adopted the first constitution to abolish slavery and allow every man to vote. By the late 1790s, political sentiment was almost evenly split between Democratic-Republicans and Federalists. Notable citizens included Revolutionary generals Ethan Allen and John Stark.

Governors

1791—Thomas Chittenden
1797—Isaac Tichenor
1797—Paul Brigham

Chief Justices

1778—Moses Robinson
1782—Paul Spooner
1784—Moses Robinson
1785—Nathaniel Chapman
1791—Samuel Knight
1794—Isaac Tichenor
1796—Nathaniel Chapman
1797—Israel Smith
1798—Enoch Woodbridge

Virginia

Virginia entered the Union as the tenth state to ratify the Constitution on June 25, 1788. After ceding its land claims north of the Ohio River and ending its jurisdiction over Kentucky, Virginia retained 63,823 square miles. It was the largest state in both area and population. Between 1770 and 1800, the population doubled from 447,016 (7 persons per square mile) to 886,149 (14 persons per square mile). African Americans equaled 42% of residents. Williamsburg, its colonial capital, remained the seat of government until 1779, when Richmond took its place. The largest cities in 1800 were Norfolk (6,926), Richmond (5,737), Alexandria (4,971), and Petersburg (3,521).

Virginia ranked first in tobacco output and grew more than half the domestic crop, but its economy increasingly diversified. It had emerged by 1791 as the country's leading exporter of wheat (46% of all), corn (35% of all), and staves (25% of all); it stood second in shingle exports (17% of all) and third in flour (13% of all). The state was also the leading producer of coal and lead.

Virginians supported independence almost unanimously; they furnished fifteen of the Continental Army's eighty regiments and more generals than any other state. It was at Yorktown, Virginia, that Washington ensured American victory by capturing Cornwallis's army in 1781. After the war, settlement rapidly expanded in the southwestern counties and in present-day West Virginia, both of which experienced much Indian warfare. Democratic-Republicans dominated state politics. Notable citizens included President George Washington, Vice President Thomas Jefferson, Governor Patrick Henry, and three presidents of the Continental Congress: Peyton Randolph, Richard Henry Lee, and Cyrus Griffith.

Governors

1758—Lt. Gov. Francis Fauquier
1768—John Blair (President of Council)
1768—Gov. Norborne Berkeley, Baron of Botetourt
1770—William Nelson (President of Council)
1771—Gov. John Murray, Earl of Dunmore
1775—Edmund Pendleton (Chairman of Committee of Safety)
1776—Patrick Henry
1779—Thomas Jefferson
1781—Pres. William Fleming
1781—Thomas Nelson
1781—Benjamin Harrison
1784—Patrick Henry

1786—Edmund Randolph
1789—Beverly Randolph
1791—Henry Lee
1794—Robert Brooke
1796—James Wood
1799—James Monroe

(*Note:* Prior to 1768, all resident chief executives were either deputy governors or presidents of the Council. Captain General John Campbell, Earl of Loudoun, who was governor-in-chief from 1756 to 1763, and Captain General Sir Jeffery Amherst who was governor-in-chief from 1763 to 1768, were absent as army commanders-in-chief.

Chief Justice

1779—Edmund Pendleton (to 1803)

(*Note:* As a colony, the governor and council held final jurisdiction over appeals when sitting as the General Court. After 1779 the President of the Court of Appeals was the highest judicial officer.)

CHAPTER 10 The Cities

At the end of the colonial era, 132,105 Americans, 5.5% of all, lived in cities. By the century's finish, their numbers had risen to 283,897, but that figure still made up less than 6.0% of the population (5.4%). The cities' role in national life loomed much larger than can be indicated by their relatively small number of inhabitants. The cities provided the critical mercantile services that distributed the hinterland's agricultural surpluses among overseas and domestic markets; they also served as cultural centers for the diffusion of European styles and manners that enhanced the sophistication of colonial society.

By imperial standards, provincial cities were respectable in size, but not large. As of 1775, no urban center in America exceeded the population of the six largest British cities: London (700,000), Dublin (130,000), Edinburgh (70,430), Norwich (36,000), Bristol (35,440), and Liverpool (34,407). Philadelphia (with an estimated 33,500 denizens) ranked as the empire's seventh largest city, New York (with 22,000) as the tenth, Boston (with 16,000) as the fifteenth, Charles

Town (with 14,000) as the eighteenth, and Newport (with 9,209) as the nineteenth. Although the scale of Britain's urban life dwarfed that in the provinces, it nevertheless is noteworthy that two of the empire's ten largest cities then lay in America. Philadelphia and New York were furthermore growing at such a rapid rate, that they would soon have eclipsed all British cities except the three biggest had the Revolution not intervened.

In the late eighteenth century, it was war, rather than peace, that formed the background for urban life. Because the destruction of enemy commerce was an integral part of that era's warfare, the American cities (which were above all centers for overseas trade) repeatedly experienced the dislocation of their economies when armed conflict erupted. During the Revolution, British troops occupied every major harbor in the nation but Baltimore. Boston and Charles Town furthermore suffered great physical damage during lengthy sieges.

Economic prospects improved slowly for the cities after the Revolution ended. Urban prosperity depended upon overseas trade, but most foreign governments erected a multitude of restrictions against American merchants and ship captains after 1783. Trade with the British Isles became highly circumscribed, and Americans found themselves legally excluded from exporting to the Anglo-Caribbean islands, which had been a highly profitable market before 1776. The United States found it difficult to develop alternative outlets for trade because many countries, including France and Spain, refused to dismantle their customs barriers to improve economic relations. New opportunities appeared slowly, and the seaports languished in depression for most of the 1780s.

The outbreak of the Napoleonic Wars in 1793 presented great opportunities to the United States to expand its commerce because Spanish and French colonial harbors were opened to neutral ships. The United States nevertheless found it difficult to win universal acceptance of its rights as a neutral carrier, and foreign powers seized more than 600 merchant vessels during the 1790s. This situation improved after the ratification in 1795 of Jay's Treaty, which extended many trading privileges within the British Empire. Although Jay's Treaty offended the French, and worsened commercial relations with them, it stimulated a dramatic expansion of overseas trade. Despite the difficulties of maintaining its neutrality while caught between belligerent powers, the United States more than doubled its exports during the six years after 1794, and the late 1790s ended as a decade of economic prosperity and population growth for major cities.

During the Revolutionary era, the United States contained six urban centers with populations that would have ranked among Great Britain's twenty large cities: Philadelphia, New York, Boston, Charles Town, Newport, and Baltimore. Newport underwent such a precipitous decline during the 1780s that it never again emerged as a major seaport. Taking Newport's place was Baltimore, which rose from a regional center for exporting tobacco and grain into the South's largest city by 1800. The following profiles summarize the history of each city from 1763 to 1800.

TABLE 10.1 POPULATION OF AMERICAN URBAN CENTERS, 1760–1800

	1760	1775	1780	1790	1800
Albany, N.Y.	a	3,700	3,050	3,494	5,289
Baltimore, Md.	a	6,734	8,000	13,503	26,514
Boston, Mass.	15,631	16,000	10,000	18,038	24,937
Charleston (Charles Town), S.C.	8,000	14,000	10,000	16,359	20,565
Gloucester, Mass.	a	a	a	3,000 b	5,313
Hartford, Conn.	a	3,000 b	3,000 b	3,000 b	5,347
Lancaster, Pa.	a	a	3,190	3,762	4,292
Marblehead, Mass.	4,954	4,812	4,142	5,661	5,211
New Haven, Conn.	a	a	3,350	4,487	4,049
New London, Conn.	a	a	a	3,000 b	5,150
New York City, N.Y.	14,000	22,000	18,000	32,305	60,515
Newburyport, Mass.	a	3,000	3,080	4,817	5,946
Newport, R.I.	6,500	9,209	5,530	6,744	6,739
Norfolk, Va.	d	6,000	a	3,000	6,926
Norwich, Conn.	a	3,000 b	3,000 b	3,000 b	3,475
Philadelphia, Pa.c	18,756	33,482 e	27,565	42,520	61,559
Portsmouth, N.H.c	d	4,590	4,222	4,720	5,339
Providence, R.I.	d	d	4,321	4,310	7,614
Richmond, Va.	a	a	a	3,761	5,737
Salem, Mass.c	4,469	5,000	4,008	7,917	9,457
Savannah, Ga.	a	3,000 b	a	a	5,166

a Not a city.
b Estimate.
c Includes suburbs.
d No information.
e Corrected from original, see Source, p. 98.
Source: Lester J. Cappon, ed., *Atlas of Early American History: The Revolutionary Era, 1760–1790* (1976), 97.

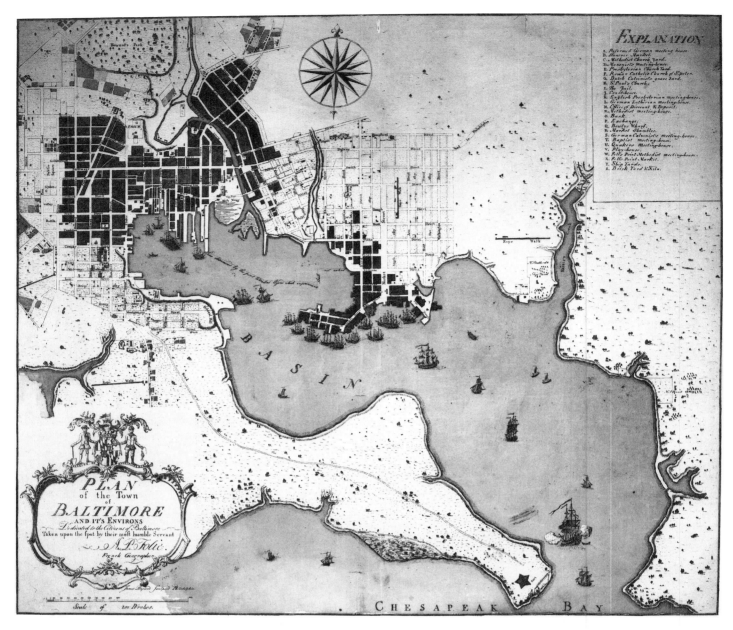

Baltimore was the country's most rapidly growing city during the 1790s. This print shows the extent of urban development around its harbor at the mouth of the Patapsco River as of 1792. (I. N. Phelps Stokes Collection, Miriam & Ira Wallach Div. of Arts, Prints and Photographs. Courtesy The New York Public Library. Astor, Lenox and Tilden Foundations.)

Baltimore, Maryland

Founded: 1729 (incorporated 1797)
Population in 1800: 26,514
U.S. Rank in 1800: third
Elevation: sea level to 490 ft.
Average Temperatures: not known for 1800
Average Annual Precipitation: not known for 1800
Type of Government: board of city commissioners until charter of 1797, then a mayor chaired commission meetings

No colonial city grew more rapidly during the eighteenth century than Baltimore. A mere village of 200 people in 1752, it numbered almost 7,000 in 1775. Baltimore primarily owed its prosperity to a few prescient merchants who saw in the late 1750s that its location was ideally suited for tapping the produce of a prosperous rural

hinterland and sending agricultural commodities to market with the least amount of transportation overhead. Once that point began to be appreciated, Baltimore became a magnet for merchants eager for new markets to conquer. By 1765, its trading network not only included central and western Maryland, but also extended far up the Susquehanna River, and it had consequently begun to win a large part of the grain trade that had once been sent overseas from Philadelphia. So alarmed were Philadelphia's businessmen at Baltimore's inroads, that they started laying plans to dig canals connecting the Delaware River with the Susquehanna River and Chesapeake Bay, so that backcountry traffic from these areas could be intercepted before it came within the Maryland city's grasp. Before these projects could be undertaken, however, the Revolution intervened, and Baltimore's rise continued apace.

When the Revolution commenced, Baltimore was the sixth largest urban center in the United States. Because it was the only major seaport to escape occupation by the British army, Baltimore alone managed to survive the war without having its population suffer a sharp decline. The Continental Congress sought its safety between December 1776 and March 1777 when Philadelphia seemed threatened by British troops pursuing Washington's retreat across New Jersey. Besides stimulating its commerce by offering the opportunity to provision Continental forces, the war hastened the development of a large shipbuilding industry at the suburb of Fell's Point.

By 1790, Baltimore had passed Newport in population and was the country's fifth largest city. It attracted a substantial influx of European immigrants and other newcomers through the next decade. By 1790, the city's white population divided into the following ethnic groups: English-Welsh, 48%; Scotch-Irish, 13%; Irish, 16%; German 13%; Scottish, 6%; French, 2%; and 1% Dutch or Swedish. Blacks composed 21% of the inhabitants, and almost half of this group was free.

From 1790 to 1800, Baltimore's population increased by 96%, the highest rate of growth among the major cities. During this period it passed Boston and Charleston in size to become the third largest urban center in 1800. It also ranked fourth in the size of its merchant marine, which equaled 11% of all permanent tonnage registered to U.S. vessels.

Mayors of Baltimore

1797—James Calhoun

Boston, Massachusetts

Founded: 1630 (incorporated 1800)
Population in 1800: 24,937
U.S. Rank in 1800: fourth
Elevation: sea level to 330 ft.
Average Temperatures (1784–88): January, 22.5°F; April, 45.1°F; July, 69.9°F; October, 50.1°F; Annual average, 50.8°F
Average Annual Precipitation: not known for 1763–1800
Type of Government: Town Meeting, chaired by an elected Moderator, with decisions made by majority vote of the citizens in attendance.

Boston experienced serious difficulties prior to the Revolution. It took several years to rebound from a disastrous fire in 1760 that incinerated 176 warehouses and destroyed a tenth of all homes. Boston lost much of its fishing industry to outlying ports, and new British taxes on imported rum cut deeply into the profitability of the town's 36 distilleries. One of every six property-holders evidently owned too few possessions to be placed on the tax rolls, and payments for poor relief rose steadily.

The city's economy rebounded during the late 1760s and early 1770s as the amount of goods clearing the harbor rose 40% over levels of the 1750s. Boston nevertheless lost ground relative to other seaports. Long the busiest harbor in North America, Boston lost this distinction by 1770, when, for the first time, the amount of tonnage

it handled fell behind Philadelphia's imports and exports. Already reduced to the second-ranked urban center by Philadelphia in the 1750s, Boston dropped to third place by 1775 when New York's population surpassed its own.

Boston set the pace for opposition to unconstitutional British taxes, but it paid a heavy price for its stubbornness in defending the rights of Englishmen. In 1768, four regiments of redcoats occupied the city to cow the residents into submission, and Boston stayed a garrison town for the next eight years. Tensions between the citizens and "bloodybacks" finally exploded in the Boston Massacre of 1770, when troops fired into a riotous crowd and killed five people. After the Battle of Lexington in April 1775, New England militia kept Boston under siege for eleven months. During that time, the population shrank by perhaps 75% to just 4,000. The British army abandoned Boston on March 17, 1776. The merchants exploited their location north of Britain's blockade to make Boston the greatest center of privateering against enemy shipping. The population trickled back from their relatives' homes in the country, but by 1780 it stood at only 10,000. The city felt much privation during the postwar depression, but it steadily reclaimed much of its old commerce (in large part by smuggling goods to the West Indies) and pioneered new markets, in particular the China trade. By 1788, the tonnage clearing Boston had risen 30% over the peak levels achieved before independence. Highly indicative of this newfound prosperity was the 1786 opening of the Charles River Bridge, a span of 1,503 feet measuring 42 feet wide, which was followed in 1792 by the even more colossal West Boston Bridge, which measured 3,483 feet long and was the most ambitious such project yet built in America. These thoroughfares above all marked the end of Boston's isolation as a peninsula virtually cut off from the mainland and inaugurated its period of geographic expansion.

Although the city had recovered significantly by 1790, its population in that year—18,038—was just slightly higher than the 16,382 inhabitants it had contained in 1743. Boston attracted newcomers from the neighboring countryside, but few immigrants from abroad. By 1790, its population was 96% white, of whom 78% were English or Welsh in descent. About 15% of whites were Irish, although two-thirds of this group were Protestants of Scotch-Irish stock, and the only other significant minority were Scots (5%).

Boston won a significant share of the international carrying trade during the Napoleonic Wars. By 1800, 12.4% of all registered tonnage in the United States docked permanently at Boston. The volume of commerce in its harbor, as measured by customs receipts, quadrupled from 1792 to 1801. Boston nevertheless ranked third in tonnage, behind Philadelphia and fifth in the volume of exports it handled. By 1800, it had slipped behind Baltimore to stand just fourth in population.

Moderators of Boston

The office of mayor did not exist until 1822. Civic decisions were made by voters at town meetings and administrative business between meetings was conducted by selectmen. The citizens annually chose a moderator to preside over town meetings.

1763—James Otis
1764—Thomas Hubbard
1765—James Otis
1770—Thomas Cushing
1770—Joshua Henshaw (pro tempore)

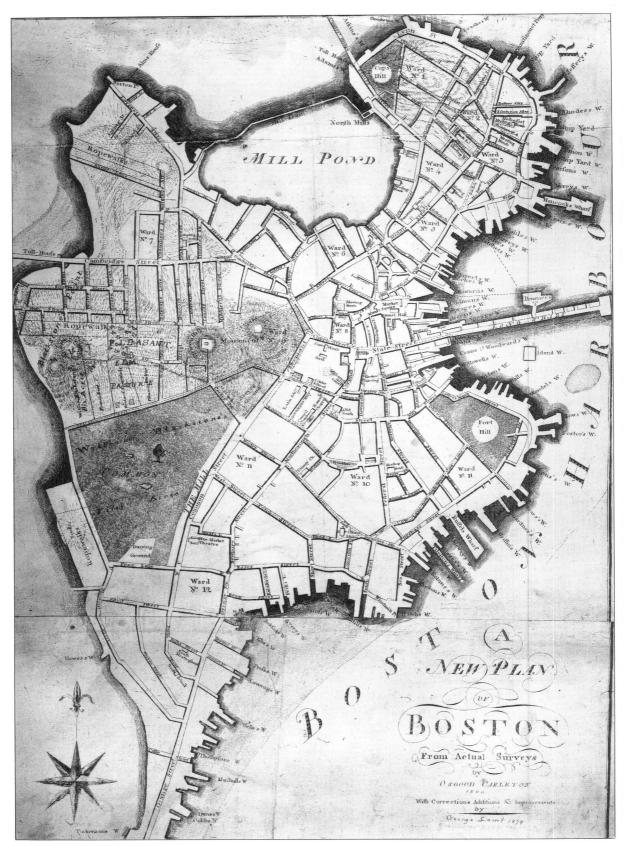

By 1799, when Osgood Carleton prepared this map, Boston's growth had become highly constricted by the peninsula on which it lay. Bostonians responded by building bridges to unite their economy more closely to the mainland. (I. N. Phelps Stokes Collection, Miriam & Ira Wallach Div. of Arts, Prints and Photographs. Courtesy The New York Public Library. Astor, Lenox and Tilden Foundations.)

1771—Thomas Cushing
1772—John Hancock
1774—Thomas Cushing
1774—Samuel Adams
1775—John Hancock
1776—Thomas Cushing
1778—John Hancock
1781—John Brown
1783—Ezekiel Price
1784—Stephen Higginson (pro tempore)
1784—John Brown
1785—Stephen Higginson
1786—Samuel Adams
1788—Thomas Dawes
1789—Samuel Adams
1790—Caleb Davis
1791—Thomas Dawes
1794—Thomas Crafts
1797—Thomas Dawes
1802—Joseph Russell

Charleston, South Carolina

Founded: 1670 (incorporated 1783)
Population in 1800: 20,565
U.S. Rank in 1800: fifth
Elevation: sea level to 330 ft.
Average Temperatures: not known for 1800
Average Annual Precipitation: not known for 1800
Type of Government: city council and intendant (mayor)

Charles Town—the city's proper title until 1783—possessed Anglo-America's wealthiest population and suffered its least healthy disease environment. Although strict quarantines of ship passengers prevented smallpox from reappearing after 1764, the residents endured whooping cough, mumps, diphtheria, scarlet fever, and measles in epidemic proportions from then until the Revolution; they also faced a wide variety of generalized fevers and dysentery that sometimes proved fatal as well. Many of the residents, however, were wealthy absentee rice planters who could afford to spend the unhealthy summer months at Newport, Rhode Island, which acquired the nickname of the "Carolina Hospital."

The rice trade ultimately determined how well Charles Town's inhabitants lived, and it allowed them to live very well in the decade before 1775. The commodity's price remained high and yields were usually excellent. By the early 1770s, as many as 350 ships might be seen waiting outside the harbor to load during the harvest season. The tonnage passing through Charles Town surpassed that of New York, and in 1772–1773 alone, 10,000 imported slaves were auctioned off in the city. The rice trade's profits also sparked a building boom that created several new suburbs filled with fashionable homes.

The Revolutionary War arrived at Charles Town's doorstep in June 1776, when a British task force carrying 3,000 soldiers anchored off the harbor. After a furious exchange of fire with the city's artillery batteries, the ships left, having received far more punishment than they had inflicted. The British returned in 1780, and this time they capped a forty-two-day siege with a full week of firing explosive shells and red-hot cannonballs into Charles Town. They marched victorious into the city on May 12 and did not leave until October 27, 1782, when they made off with everything worth looting—including the church bells of St. Michael's Parish.

In August 1783, the legislature passed the first act of incorporation for the city, which also changed its official name to Charleston. The charter vested government in a committee of thirteen wardens, so called because each of the thirteen wards elected one individual, and allowed the voters to choose one of them as an executive chairman, who was called the intendant. In effect, it was a variant of the mayor and city council system.

Charleston recovered more slowly from the postwar economic depression than did any other major harbor but Newport. By 1790, its population (which was 50% black) had increased just 17% over its level in 1775. Its recovery continued to lag behind its sister seaports during the 1790s. By 1800, it ranked fifth in the size of its merchant marine, which equaled 6% of all tonnage registered to U.S. vessels. Between 1790 and 1800, its total population increased by 26%, but this gain was much less than in other cities, and Charleston ended the century fifth in number of inhabitants.

Mayors of Charleston

When Charleston incorporated in 1782, its highest executive official was termed the intendant rather than mayor.

1782—Richard Hutson
1783—Arnoldus Vander Horst
1786—John F. Grimke
1788—Rawlins Lowndes
1789—Thomas Jones
1790—Arnoldus Vander Horst
1792—John Huger
1794—John B. Holmes
1795—John Edwards
1797—Henry W. de Saussure
1799—Thomas Roper
1801—John Ward

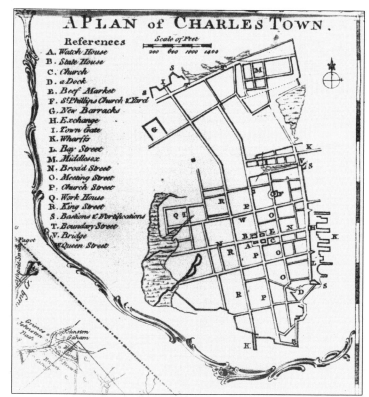

Charleston, South Carolina, was fortunate to be situated on the broad estuary of the Ashley and Cooper rivers. The confluence of the two rivers permitted as many as 350 ships to congregate offshore to await cargoes of rice and indigo after planters had harvested their year's crops. In 1773, its street plan appeared thus in James Cook's Map of South Carolina. (Courtesy South Caroliniana Library, Columbia, South Carolina)

New York City, New York

Founded: 1626 (incorporated 1731)
Population in 1800: 60,515
U.S. Rank in 1800: second
Elevation: sea level to 410 ft.
Average Temperatures (1782–84): January, 25.2°F; April, 49.3°F;
    July, 81.0°F; October, 54.3°F; Annual Average, 58.4°F
Average Annual Precipitation: not known for period
Type of Government: A chartered open corporation, in which voters
    of each ward annually elected an alderman and a councilman, but
    the city council chose the mayor.

Although it possessed a well-sheltered harbor able to service many hundreds of ships, New York remained a modest seaport in 1763. Its economic hinterland along the Hudson River had not yet begun to produce the great volume of foodstuffs necessary for New York to emerge as a first-rate exporter. This situation changed in the next dozen years as settlers swarmed to the Hudson Valley and began shipping progressively larger volumes of grain overseas through New York. By the colonial period's end, the amount of tonnage clearing New York was approaching the level of trade conducted in Boston, and it was only a matter of time before Boston would be overtaken. As the port's business increased, the city added 1,000 homes from 1760 to 1776 to accommodate a population rise of about 60%.

New York's expansion came despite the political turmoil and economic dislocation of the Revolutionary era. On November 1, 1765, major bloodshed was narrowly averted when British troops nervously fingering loaded muskets managed to refrain from firing on a howl-ing mob of 2,000 attempting to storm Ft. George and destroy the printed forms needed to implement the Stamp Act. On January 19, 1770, forty redcoats with drawn bayonets brawled with hundreds of citizens carrying clubs in a hard-fought clash called the Battle of Golden Hill. The economic burden of protesting unconstitutional taxation proved exceptionally high for the city, which sustained an 85% drop in imports during 1769 while enforcing a trade boycott against the Townshend taxes passed in 1767.

For most of the summer and fall of 1776, heavy fighting swirled around Manhattan Island. The British captured the city on September 15, and on the 21st a massive fire broke out that destroyed 300 buildings, a quarter of all homes. A second conflagration spread through the city in August 1778 and burned another 100 homes. In its first four years of military occupation, the city's population declined more than one-fifth. New York continued under military rule, its civilian government suspended, until November 25, 1783, which was long celebrated as Evacuation Day.

Upon returning from Europe in the 1780s, merchant Samuel Breck described New York as "a neglected place, built chiefly of wood, and in a state of prostration and decay." The task of rebuilding the gutted city and resurrecting its commerce started while a severe postwar depression gripped the nation. One factor that initially helped underpin the local economy was the selection of New York as U.S. capital from 1785 to 1790. By 1790 a strong recovery was under way and the population stood 66% higher than the low point of 18,000 reached a decade earlier. Substantial numbers of immigrants arrived from Europe, and by 1790 the city's white population divided along these ethnic lines: English-Welsh, 42%; Dutch,

This engraving by Benjamin Taylor shows the extent of New York's development by 1796. New York almost overtook Philadelphia as the country's largest city during the 1790s. By 1796, the city was still concentrated at the tip of Manhattan, however, and most of the island remained farmland. (I. N. Phelps Stokes Collection, Miriam & Ira Wallach Div. of Arts, Prints and Photographs. Courtesy The New York Public Library. Astor, Lenox and Tilden Foundations.)

17%; Scotch-Irish, 15%; Irish, 8%; Scottish, 7%; and German, 6%. A tenth of inhabitants were black, of whom two-thirds were enslaved.

New York boomed in the 1790s as its merchants took advantage of the shortages of grain that plagued Europe and the West Indies during the Napoleonic Wars. In 1792, its merchants and brokers also founded the country's first organized market for stocks—an institution that remained modest for the next twenty years but would evolve into the New York Stock Exchange. Although New York ranked slightly behind Philadelphia in registered tonnage (with 14% of the nation's merchant marine), by 1796–97 it had surpassed its rival in the volume of goods imported and exported, and from then on it continued to extend its edge as America's leading shipyard. By 1800, New York's population had nearly doubled over the previous decade and stood second only to that of Philadelphia. Had New York not been afflicted by an outbreak of yellow fever that cost 2,000 lives in 1798, it would certainly have held the largest urban population in the United States in 1800.

New York Mayors

1757—John Cruger, Jr.
1766—Whitehead Hicks
1776—David Matthews
1777–1783—New York under British military authority
1784—James Duane
1789—Richard Varick
1801—Edward Livingston

Newport, Rhode Island

Founded: 1639 (incorporated in 1800)
Population in 1800: 6,739
U.S. Rank in 1800: eighth
Elevation: sea level to 200 ft.

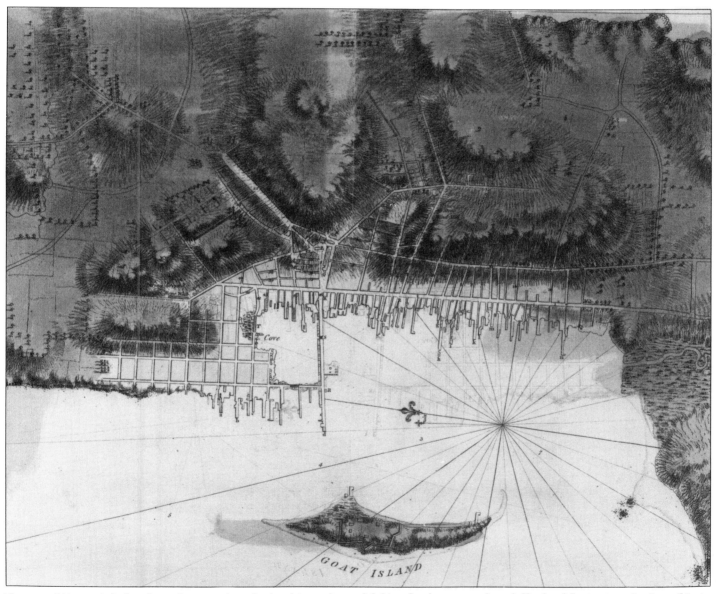

This map of Newport's harbor shows the city to have developed in an elongated fashion, for about one and one-half miles, following its main thoroughfare. British occupation crippled the city's commerce and Newport's economy contracted after the Revolution. (Courtesy Geography and Maps Div., Library of Congress.)

Average Temperatures: not known for period

Average Annual Precipitation: not known for period

Type of Government: Town meeting, chaired by an elected moderator, with decisions made by majority vote of the citizens in attendance.

In 1760, Newport was the fifth largest city in the thirteen colonies, with 6,500 people. Its principal physical assets were 888 houses, 439 warehouses, and 6 windmills. The number of vessels based in its harbor equaled no more than 140 in the 1760s. Its central street extended one and a half miles. During the next fifteen years, its population increased to 9,209, a figure that made the unpretentious town the British Empire's nineteenth largest urban center.

A British amphibious force captured Newport without encountering any resistance in December 1776. Although the city escaped physical destruction, the resulting occupation was an unmitigated disaster. The population shrank by half as families of rebel sympathizers fled to American lines. The British commandeered livestock at will for rations; they not only denuded the region of trees, but also burned all the town's fences and tore down many frame houses for fuel. Since Newport lay on an island, a small British naval force could frustrate any American attack, and the city remained in enemy hands until the British voluntarily left in October 1779.

Newport never really recovered from the occupation. By 1790, its population still remained at just three-quarters of its size in 1775. Much of its commerce was taken over by merchants and ship captains in Providence, whose population rose by almost 50% from 1775 to 1790. By 1800, Newport ranked eighth among American cities in population (Providence was sixth), and its merchant marine stood just eleventh in total registered tonnage of the vessels based permanently at its wharves.

Philadelphia, Pennsylvania

Founded: 1682 (incorporated 1789)

Population in 1800: 61,559

U.S. Rank in 1800: first

Elevation: sea level to 440 ft.

Average Temperatures (1798–1804): January, 33.3° F; April, 52.9° F; July 76.4° F; October, 57.1° F; Annual average, 58.7° F

Average Annual Precipitation (1800): 41.61 inches

Type of Government: Mayor and bicameral city council elected by voters.

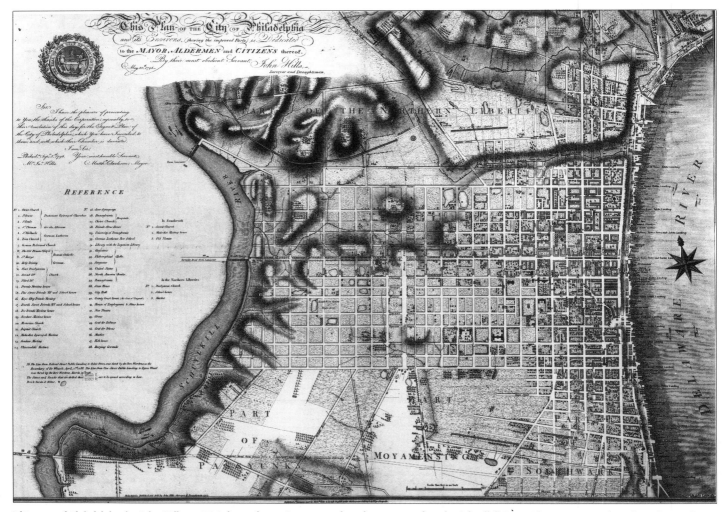

This map of Philadelphia by John Hills in 1796 shows the city's streets to have been surveyed to the Schuylkill River (then its western boundary), but it shows also that the population remained concentrated near the docks, well east of 10th Street. Philadelphia was evolving into a metropolitan area, with a significant urban population living outside the city's boundaries in the Northern Liberties and Southwark. (I. N. Phelps Stokes Collection, Miriam & Ira Wallach Div. of Arts, Prints and Photographs. Courtesy The New York Public Library. Astor, Lenox and Tilden Foundations.)

In 1765, Philadelphia was experiencing prosperity and rapid growth. Over the next decade, its carpenters built 2,000 new houses, an increase of two-thirds over the number standing in 1760, and launched 246 vessels into the Delaware. By 1775, Philadelphia had replaced Boston as the leading producer of ships in America. Severe droughts in southern Europe stimulated demand for colonial grain after 1764, and Philadelphia's location near a highly fertile and productive hinterland allowed it to expand its commerce sharply by satisfying this market. Immigrants flooded to the city, and from 1760 to 1775, the population increased by 44%.

As the country's largest city, Philadelphia was the logical choice for holding sessions of the Continental Congress. Congress first met at Philadelphia in September 1774, and by July 1776 the city had become the de facto capital for the nation. The British army marched into the city on September 26, 1777, and occupied it until the next summer.

In 1776, the city's charter was judged void because it rested on the authority of an English proprietor loyal to George III. For the next thirteen years, Philadelphia went without any formal structure of government. In 1789, the legislature granted another charter that allowed citizens to elect city officials for the first time. The municipal charter created a mayor whose only clear authority related to control over law enforcement. Responsibility for other areas of administration lay with a bicameral council, which consisted of the select council, comprising one member elected from each ward, and the common council, which had a member for every 1,200 taxpayers. Although far more democratic than the previous municipal government, in which the city council had appointed its own replacements and new mayors, the new system ultimately degenerated into an inefficient bureaucracy due to its unwieldly structure and its failure to prescribe clear lines of authority.

Congress remained in Philadelphia until June 1783, when it began a series of moves that ultimately led it to New York in 1785. The national capital returned provisionally to Philadelphia from 1790 to 1800 pending its relocation to the District of Columbia. As the site of the Bank of the United States (the country's first commercial lending institution, which was founded in 1782), and the location of the U.S. Mint, which started operations in 1794, Philadelphia emerged as the nation's true financial center.

The overseas commerce of Philadelphia was languishing by 1785 but then revived strongly. By 1788, its harbor was clearing 60% more tonnage than it had in prosperous years of the early 1770s. The city's population grew by more than 50% from 1780 to 1790, as immigrants once again began pouring into the city. By 1790, the city's white population divided into the following ethnic groups: Germans, 34%; English-Welsh, 26%; Scotch-Irish, 17%; Irish, 11%; Scottish, 9%; Swedish, 2%; and French, 1%. Almost 4% of inhabitants were black, of whom one of every eight was enslaved.

Philadelphia fell prey to several outbreaks of epidemic disease during the late eighteenth century. Scarlet fever struck in 1769 and 1783, smallpox in 1769 and 1773, influenza in 1770 and 1789, whooping cough in 1771, and measles in 1772. Yellow fever, which evidently arrived in ships from Haiti, panicked the federal government into fleeing the capital in terror during 1793 and then carried off 10% to 15% of the inhabitants, or about 4,500 to 6,500 people. The disease later killed at least of 3,000 people when it recurred in 1797, 1798, and 1799.

During the 1790s, Philadelphia became the primary outlet for selling American foodstuffs to Europe, which faced serious grain shortages due to crop failures and war. The harbor's exports increased 235% from 1790 to 1795. By 1800, Philadelphia had more registered shipping tonnage than any other harbor, 14.7% of the country's merchant marine, and it still remained the largest city in the United States. It had fallen behind in one critical respect, however, that of total tonnage passing through its harbor. New York, whose population lagged behind Philadelphia's by only a thousand people, had emerged as the country's busiest seaport, and within another decade it would overtake its rival as the largest urban center.

Mayors of Philadelphia

1763—Thomas Willing
1764—Thomas Lawrence
1765—John Lawrence
1767—Isaac Jones
1769—Samuel Shoemaker
1771—John Gibson
1773—William Fisher
1774—Samuel Rhoads
1775—Samuel Powel
1776–1789—No mayors chosen, as the city's proprietary charter was judged void.
1789—Samuel Miles
1791—John Barclay
1792—Mathew Clarkson
1796—Hillary Baker
1798—Robert Wharton
1800—John Inskeep

CHAPTER 11 Prominent and Representative Americans

The accomplishments of the Revolutionary era culminated from the efforts of three classes of Americans: "founding fathers" such as George Washington, Thomas Jefferson, and Benjamin Franklin; second-echelon leaders such as Nathanael Greene and George Rogers Clark; and rank-and-file citizens with exceptional talents such as Mercy Otis Warren and Benjamin Banneker. This chapter will outline the achievements of representative individuals from each group to indicate the diverse range of people who enriched the quality of life in late-eighteenth-century America.

John Adams

John Adams was born on October 30, 1735 at Braintree, Massachusetts. He became a lawyer upon graduating from Harvard in 1755. He became deeply involved in politics after 1768 when he moved to Boston, where his distant cousin Samuel Adams was the town's most influential citizen. Although he was unalterably opposed to the use of British troops to uphold Parliamentary taxes, John Adams defended the redcoats charged with murder in the Boston Massacre (1770) and got them acquitted. He attended the first and second Continental Congresses and served on the committee charged with drafting the Declaration of Independence. In 1776, he published *Thoughts on Government,* in which he prefigured the shape of the U.S. Constitution by arguing that the best form of republican government would assign executive, lawmaking, and judicial functions to different branches of itself, and that the legislature should be divided into two separate houses. He performed diplomatic duties as commissioner to France during 1777–1778, ambassador to the Netherlands from 1780 to 1782, commissioner to negotiate peace with Britain during 1782–1783, and envoy to Britain from 1785 to 1788. He served as vice president from 1789 to 1797 and as president from then until he was replaced by Thomas Jefferson in 1801. After a long retirement, he died in 1826 at Quincy, Massachusetts, on the fiftieth anniversary of the Fourth of July, within a few hours of Thomas Jefferson's death.

Benjamin Banneker

Born on November 9, 1731 near Baltimore, Maryland, to a family of free African Americans, Benjamin Banneker attended school with white children and soon showed great talent in mathematics, engineering, and science. While still an adolescent, he built a clock made from original wooden pieces. A local mill owner, George Ellicott, recognized him as a prodigy, allowed him the use of his own large library, and tutored him in mechanics and astronomy. Banneker issued a highly successful series of almanacs under his own name, and with a woodcut of his face on the cover, from 1791 to 1802, in which he put to use his skill in making astronomical predictions. Banneker's most important public service was to serve on the board of surveyors charged with marking the boundary line of the District of Columbia and laying out the capital's streets. He won this honor through the patronage of whites who respected him for his abilities, such as George Ellicott, who designed the layout of Washington, and James McHenry, a Maryland politician who later became secretary of war. Banneker used his position to publicize arguments denouncing slavery and warfare. He died on October 9, 1806 at Oella, Maryland.

Daniel Boone

Daniel Boone was born on November 2, 1734 near Reading, Pennsylvania. At age sixteen he moved with his family to the North Carolina backcountry. While serving as a teamster with the British army in 1755, his imagination was stirred by accounts of Kentucky. He spent two years after 1769 exploring the bluegrass region. He led thirty men and several families to settle Kentucky in 1773 but gave up the effort after Indians killed his son and three other boys. In 1775, he blazed the Wilderness Road through the Cumberland Gap and built a fort on the Kentucky River named Boonesborough, the second settlement established in the bluegrass. He commanded the fort's sixty defenders in repulsing 400 Indians and French-Canadian militia in September 1778. He served as a colonel of Kentucky militia during the Revolution and sat several terms in Virginia's House of Burgesses. In the course of two decades of frontier warfare he experienced the death of a brother and two sons, plus the theft of more than forty horses. Boone survived many hairbreadth escapes from Indians in ambushes and skirmishes, but he later said that he was only positive of having killed one warrior, whom he shot at the Battle of Blue Licks in 1782. He entered claims for 12,000 acres but lost virtually all of them because of faulty titles or improper surveys during the 1780s. In 1799, he moved to the Femme Osage valley of Missouri, where he died on September 26, 1820.

George Rogers Clark

George Rogers Clark was born in Albemarle County, Virginia, on November 19, 1752. He began learning how to survey at age nineteen but had little formal education. He explored the upper Ohio River with an eye toward land speculation during 1772–1773, and in 1774 he participated in Lord Dunmore's War against the Shawnee of Ohio. When just twenty-three, Clark secured Virginia's financial support for a campaign to extend American control over the French settlers living in Illinois and Indiana, and if possible to take the British fort at Detroit. In June 1778, Clark headed west from the falls of the Ohio with about 200 frontiersmen, and by July's end he had persuaded the French inhabitants at Kaskaskia, Cahokia, and Vincennes to swear allegiance to the United States. In February 1779, however, Clark learned that a sizeable force of British and Indians had retaken Vincennes and threatened his own headquarters at Kaskaskia. Although outnumbered by the enemy, Clark launched a counteroffensive in mid-winter across 200 miles of icy, flooded plains in southern Illinois. After marching for eighteen days on half rations, the Americans scared off several hundred Indians camped nearby, besieged the British fort, and accepted its surrender on February 25. Clark's victory ended British authority south of Detroit (which remained in British hands until 1796) and denied Britain the chance to retain the territory south of the Great Lakes after the war. Clark led several expeditions against the Indians north of the Ohio River through 1786 but then fell into obscurity. He died at Louisville, Kentucky, on February 13, 1818.

Peter Francisco

Peter Francisco began life as a foundling abandoned near Hopewell, Virginia, about 1760. Rumors later circulated that his parents were distinguished Portuguese aristocrats, but his background may also have been French. He matured into a giant of six and a half feet and weighed over 250 pounds. He enlisted in the 10th Virginia Regiment at about age sixteen. After suffering wounds in the battles of Brandywine, Pennsylvania, and Monmouth Courthouse, New Jersey, Francisco won renown as the Continental Army's "Goliath." Washington directed that a special five-foot broadsword be made for Francisco's personal use. As part of a twenty-man suicide squad assigned to pierce British defenses at Stony Point, New York, in 1779, he was one of just four survivors who got within enemy lines, despite having received a bayonet slash across his abdomen. During the American rout at Camden, South Carolina, he rescued his colonel who was surrounded by a crowd of British and lugged off a cannon barrel weighing 1,000 pounds to prevent its capture. He reportedly killed nine enemy troops at the Battle of Guilford Courthouse, North Carolina; at Ward's Corner, Virginia, in 1781, he singlehandedly extricated himself from a surprise attack by nine mounted Tories and left two of them dead. Francisco received four wounds during the war. When peace returned, he became a blacksmith, tavern keeper, and country squire, and he served as sergeant at arms for Virginia's House of Delegates. He died at Richmond in 1836.

Benjamin Franklin

Benjamin Franklin was born in Boston, Massachusetts, on January 17, 1706. In 1723, he settled in Philadelphia, where he became a highly successful printer and set an example as a public-spirited citizen. By the 1760s, he had retired from business to devote himself to politics and science. Between 1768 and 1774, he lived in London while representing the interests of Pennsylvania, New Jersey, Georgia, and Massachusetts to the British government, and he was influential in having his son William appointed governor of New Jersey in 1763. He returned to America in May 1775 and sat in the Continental Congress. He helped draft the Declaration of Independence, and he never forgave his son William for remaining loyal to the crown. Benjamin Franklin served as the first U.S. postmaster general during 1775–1776. He received appointment as first ambassador to France in 1776 and as commissioner to negotiate the peace settlement in 1782. At age eighty-one, he was the oldest delegate to the Constitutional Convention at Philadelphia in 1787. He lived to see the Constitution go into effect but died on April 17, 1790.

Simon Girty

Born in the Pennsylvania backwoods about 1741, Simon Girty (originally Garrity) was captured in 1756 by Indians, who also took his three brothers and murdered his parents. He lived with the Seneca for about a decade. He drifted between the Indian world, in which he married another white captive and raised children, and Anglo-American society, for which he served as an interpreter. When the Revolution began, he enlisted as a ranger for frontier militia, but he deserted to the British side in 1778. He led many raids against settlers in the Ohio Valley, including the destruction of Col. David Rogers's seventy-man party carrying $600,000 worth of supplies to Ft. Pitt in October 1779. His harassment of numerous outposts in Kentucky and western Virginia earned him unremitting hatred among frontiersmen as the "white savage," but he was also responsible for saving some white prisoners from being burned to death, and he seems to have been misidentified as the perpetrator of several grisly tortures and atrocities committed by his brother James, who also took the British side as an Indian warrior. After the Revolution, he helped rout Gen. Arthur St. Clair's U.S. army in Novem-

ber 1791 and fought with the Indians defeated at the Battle of Fallen Timers in August 1794. Having acquired one of the most universally reviled reputations in the western territories, Girty emigrated to Canada. He degenerated into alcoholism during old age and survived on a British pension for his war services until his death on February 18, 1818.

Mary Katherine Goddard

Born June 16, 1738 at New London, Connecticut, Mary Goddard learned the printer's trade from her mother, Sarah Updike Goddard, who financed the family's entry into printing and eventually edited the *Providence* [R.I.] *Gazette*. In late 1768, Mary Goddard moved to Philadelphia, where she helped her brother William operate his newly founded *Pennsylvania Chronicle*. Mary Goddard ran the print shop during much of the early 1770s when William moved south to establish Baltimore's first paper, the *Maryland Journal*. In February 1774, Goddard closed the Philadelphia shop and took over the Baltimore printing business while her brother became involved in other financial enterprises, and on May 10, 1775, she altered the newspaper's letterhead to read, "Published by M. K. Goddard." In January 1777, she produced the first typeset edition of the Declaration of Independence that included the signers' names. By 1784, Mary and her brother had become so antagonistic over managing the family business that they produced rival almanacs under the titles of *William Goddard's* and *Mary K. Goddard's*. In the meantime, in 1775, she had been named Baltimore's postmaster (the first woman to hold that position in the U.S. Post Office); she retained the appointment until 1789. She then operated a bookstore in Baltimore until her death on August 12, 1816.

Nathanael Greene

Born on August 7, 1742 to a Quaker family of Potowmut, Rhode Island, Nathanael Greene was disowned by the Society of Friends in 1773 for attending a military drill. He led a brigade of Rhode Island troops to reinforce Washington at New York in June 1775 and became the Continental Army's youngest brigadier general on June 22 at age thirty-three. He commanded Washington's left wing at the battle of Trenton, became quartermaster general on February 1778, and led the right flank at Monmouth Courthouse. He took command of Continental forces in the South after the American defeat at Camden, South Carolina, in October 1780. After losing three closely contested engagements at Guilford Courthouse, North Carolina, Hobkirk's Hill, South Carolina, and Eutaw Springs, South Carolina, Greene summarized his campaign by writing, "we fight, get beat, rise, and fight again." The "fighting Quaker" nevertheless slowly turned the tide of war by inflicting more casualties on the British than they could afford to lose without relaxing their grip on the southern countryside. By January 1782, the British held little of the south except Savannah, Georgia, and Charles Town, South Carolina. After the war, Greene built a plantation near Savannah on land given him by the state of Georgia. Sunstroke killed him at age forty-four on June 19, 1786.

Alexander Hamilton

Alexander Hamilton was born on the island of Nevis on January 11, 1755. He enrolled at King's College (now Columbia University) shortly before the Revolution and discontinued his studies to become an artillery officer in 1776. He demonstrated great coolness under

John Trumbull here depicts the Second Continental Congress receiving the preamble to the Declaration of Independence. President John Hancock accepts the draft from its author, Thomas Jefferson. Surrounding Jefferson are John Adams, Robert Livingston, Roger Sherman, and Benjamin Franklin, who were appointed to the committee for drafting the Declaration's preamble but left the Virginian to do the writing. (United States Capitol Art Collection, courtesy Architect of the Capitol, Washington.)

fire during Washington's retreat across New Jersey and commanded the battery that broke the Hessian ranks at the Battle of Trenton. He served for most of the Revolution as a colonel on Washington's staff. He returned to New York and practiced law after 1783. Hamilton attended the Constitutional Convention at Philadelphia in 1787, and he helped shift public opinion in its favor by authoring many of the *Federalist* papers under the pen name Publius. Appointed as the first secretary of the treasury, he prepared the legislation that reorganized the national debt, restored the country's credit with international lenders, recoined the currency, and established the Bank of the United States. He resumed private life in 1795, became a leading figure in the Federalist Party, and received appointment as second in command of the U.S. Army (as major general) in 1798. He died on July 12, 1804, at age forty-seven, of wounds received in a duel fought at New Jersey with his bitter political enemy, Vice President Aaron Burr.

John Hancock

The son of a country minister who died when he was seven, John Hancock was born at North Braintree, Massachusetts, on January 12, 1737. A childless uncle, who made a fortune in trade, raised John, put him through Harvard (class of 1754), and trained him to take over his business. At age twenty-seven, John Hancock inherited £80,000 and became New England's richest man. He fully shared the antagonism toward Parliamentary taxation felt by Boston's political leadership and took an early lead in opposing measures such as the Stamp Tax and Townshend Duties. Such activities led to his being victimized by customs officers, who confiscated several of his cargoes for technical infractions of the highly complex regulations governing overseas trade. When customs officials seized his ship *Liberty* on June 10, 1768, Boston's wharf exploded in rioting that forced the revenue officers to flee the city for their own safety. (It was in response to this violence that the British government ordered 1,700 redcoats to be garrisoned in Boston.) Following the Boston Massacre in March 1770, Hancock headed the citizens' committee that induced the governor to remove most of the troops from Boston. Several participants in the Boston Tea Party named him as one of those involved, but he never claimed the honor. Massachusetts sent Hancock to the Continental Congress in 1774, and the next year he became its presiding officer. The Congress's presidency left Hancock unsatisfied, however, and he hoped to be appointed commander-in-chief of the forces besieging the British at Boston; he responded to George Washington's selection for this post with "mortification and resentment" according to one observer. He evidently attempted to salve his injured feelings by trying to ensure that the fledgling American navy named its largest ship (a thirty-two-gun frigate) the USS *Hancock*. He was the first to sign the Declaration of Independence and did it with such an oversized flourish that the term *John Hancock* entered the language as slang for signature. He served as the first governor of the state of Massachusetts from 1780 to 1785 and resumed that position from 1787 until his death at Quincy on October 8, 1793.

Thomas Jefferson

Thomas Jefferson was born in Albemarle County, Virginia, on April 13, 1743. Orphaned by his father's death at age fourteen, he became heir to more than thirty slaves and more than 3,000 acres. He began studying Latin, Greek, and French at age nine, entered the College of William and Mary at seventeen, started clerking for a Williamsburg lawyer at nineteen, commenced the practice of law at twenty-four, and won election to the House of Burgesses at twenty-six. Virginia sent him to the Continental Congress in 1775, and he wrote the Declaration of Independence in 1776. He served as Virginia's governor during 1779–1781, and as ambassador to France from 1785 to 1789. In 1787, he authorized a London printer to publish his *Notes on the State of Virginia*, which was the first book by an American to become a best-seller in Europe. He maintained a passion for music throughout his life and practiced three hours a day on his violin through much of the 1780s. Washington appointed him the first secretary of state in 1789. Jefferson resigned in 1793 and became a leading figure among the Democratic-Republicans who opposed Federalist policies. He ran for president in 1796 and received enough electoral votes to become vice president to John Adams. In 1798, he authored the Virginia and Kentucky Resolutions. He defeated Adams for president in 1800 and served until 1809. During his career, he expressed a view of how government should operate that has since become the core of Jeffersonian Democracy: that government should treat all citizens equally by refusing to bestow special privileges or rights on individuals or groups; that government finances should be kept to their absolute minimum to avoid unnecessary burdens on the taxpayers; that government functions should be kept narrow to leave citizens the broadest latitude in their personal and business affairs. He died on the fiftieth anniversary of the Declaration of Independence, within a few hours of John Adams, on July 4, 1826, at his estate, Monticello.

Little Turtle

Little Turtle, or Michikinikwa, was born near modern Fort Wayne, Indiana, in the Miami Nation about 1752. Little Turtle was pro-British during the Revolution, and in November 1780 he organized his village's defense against a raiding party of pro-American French militia from Illinois and helped repulse the invaders. Little Turtle became the leading figure behind Indian resistance to Anglo-American expansion into the Ohio Valley by 1790. After drawing Gen. Josiah Harmar beyond the limits of American supply lines, Little Turtle compelled Harmar to retreat after luring several large reconnaissance parties into ambushes in late 1790. A year later, his warriors inflicted the worst defeat ever sustained by the U.S. Army at Indian hands, killing 632 of Gen. Arthur St. Clair's troops and wounding 283 others, at a loss of just 60 Indians. Little Turtle met his match against Gen. Anthony Wayne, whose security was so tight that the Indians termed him the soldier who never slept. After being repulsed from an assault on Ft. Recovery, Ohio, in July 1794, Little Turtle advised negotiating a peace but failed to persuade his allies. A month later, Wayne defeated the Indians at Fallen Timbers, a battle in which Little Turtle fought but did not command. Upon signing the Treaty of Greenville in 1795, Little Turtle declared, "I am the last to sign it, and will be the last to break it." He never

warred again. He traveled through eastern cities on several occasions and met George Washington in 1797. The United States paid him an annuity because he advocated peace. He died at Fort Wayne, Indiana, in 1812.

Francis Marion

Francis Marion was born in St. John's Parish, South Carolina, about 1732. After being shipwrecked at age sixteen, he abandoned his plans to be a sailor. He earned praise for bravery in a campaign against the Cherokee in 1761, when he dispersed an enemy ambush despite having lost two-thirds of his men. During the Revolution, he commanded a militia regiment until Charles Town fell in 1780. He then organized a small band of guerrillas to harass the king's soldiers. On August 20, 1780, he routed 250 Tories with just 52 followers at Blue Savannah, South Carolina. During the next year, he fought a dozen more skirmishes or ambushes with redcoats and Tories, in which he sustained only three losses. His successes won him the nickname "Swamp Fox" (an allusion to his base at marshy Snow's Island) and command of a full brigade of South Carolina militia. Marion led his brigade at the Battle of Eutaw Springs, where his men fought like professionals against British regulars. Marion lost nearly all his personal property when Tories plundered his plantation. After the war, he married a wealthy cousin, sat in the state legislature, and died on February 27, 1795.

Mary Ludwig Hays McCauley

Mary Ludwig was born October 13, 1754 near Trenton, New Jersey. In 1769 she moved to Carlisle, Pennsylvania, where she worked as a domestic servant and married George Hays. Hays enlisted in Pennsylvania's Continental Artillery in 1775, and Mary joined him in 1777 as a camp follower, in which capacity she earned extra money by cleaning clothes for soldiers and doing odd jobs. On June 28, 1778, at the Battle of Monmouth, New Jersey, which was fought under exceptionally trying conditions caused by blistering temperatures, she carried pitchers of water to the parched American ranks, for which she received the nickname "Molly Pitcher" according to a tradition that cannot be entirely verified. At some point, however, her own husband fell victim to heat prostration and she evidently took his place as a gunner's mate on an artillery piece for the rest of the engagement. When the war ended, Mary and George Hays returned to Carlisle, Pennsylvania. Three years after George died in 1789, she married John McCauley. Her second marriage proved unhappy, and by 1820 she had again been widowed. The Pennsylvania Legislature voted her a special annuity of $40 per year in 1821 in recognition of her military services at the Battle of Monmouth. After her death at Carlisle on January 22, 1832, she was remembered as an earthy, good-hearted charwoman who chewed tobacco and swore like a trooper.

Timothy Murphy

Timothy Murphy grew up on the Pennsylvania frontier, where he was born in 1751 near the Delaware Water Gap. In 1775, he enlisted to fight the British at Boston. He later joined Daniel Morgan's elite corps of riflemen as a sharpshooter. Murphy has been credited with a major role in the American victory at Bemis Heights, New York (Second Battle of Saratoga) for having fired the rounds that killed British commanders Gen. Simon Fraser and Sir Francis Clerke at a range of 300 yards. Murphy's exploit was particularly significant, since the engagement compelled Gen. John Burgoyne to surrender his army soon after at Saratoga; the surrender is considered to be the Revolution's military turning point. While patrolling on the day after the Battle of Monmouth Courthouse, New Jersey, he helped capture the British commanding officer's carriage. He fought Indians in upstate New York during 1778 and 1779. While scouting in spring of 1780 in Pennsylvania, he and another man were captured by eleven Indians. The two prisoners managed to escape from their bonds while their captors slept; they collected all of their weapons and tomahawked ten of the Indians as they lay on the ground. When the war ended, Murphy became a prosperous farmer and miller in Pennsylvania, where he died in 1818.

Thomas Paine

Thomas Paine was born at Thetford, Norfolk, England, on January 29, 1737 to a struggling Quaker family and was apprenticed as a corset maker at age 13. He served on a privateer vessel stalking French merchant ships when Britain declared war on France in 1756. After having pursued the occupations of tax collector, teacher, store keeper, and printer, he ranked as little more than a self-educated failure by age thirty-seven; he emigrated to Philadelphia in 1774 and became a newspaperman. He achieved fame in January 1776 by publishing *Common Sense,* a pamphlet of forty-seven pages that made the most uncompromising argument for independence yet articulated in the colonies. It was ironic that Paine, a recent English emigrant, could write with such directness and compelling argument what no American leader had yet been able to say: that kingship was inherently unsuitable for a democratic society and that postponing independence merely raised the risk of ultimate military defeat. Perhaps 100,000 copies of *Common Sense* rolled off American presses within a hundred days (making it the eighteenth century's best-selling publication), and it decisively shifted public opinion toward accepting independence as inevitable. Paine continued publicizing the American cause in a series of pamphlets titled *The Crisis,* in which he sustained civilian morale with stirring language. "These are the times that try men's souls," he wrote in 1776, "yet we have this consolation with us, that the harder the conflict, the more glorious the triumph." Paine became actively involved in the French Revolution, and wrote *The Rights of Man* (1791) and *The Age of Reason* (1794) in its defense, but he left France when political parties began executing their enemies. He returned to America and passed his life poor but honored until he died at New York City, New York, on June 8, 1809.

Charles Willson Peale

Charles Willson Peale was born April 15, 1741 in Queen Annes County, Maryland. At age twenty-three, after thirteen years of working as a saddler, he was inspired to become a painter after viewing some especially polished portraits at a plantation, although he had never before mixed any paints or even held a brush in his hand. Peale's sudden passion to produce art was fortunately accompanied by a latent talent that revealed itself at once. He traveled in 1767 to London, where he studied under the former Pennsylvanian, Benjamin West, who was reckoned one of the most proficient painters in the metropolis. Peale's abilities blossomed so rapidly that upon returning to Maryland in 1769, just five years after he embarked upon painting, he secured enough commissions to support his family. In 1776, he relocated to Philadelphia, where he found liberal patronage. He opened a public portrait gallery, later added a museum of natural history filled with zoological curiosities, and deserved much of the credit for the Philadelphia Academy of Fine Arts' founding in 1805.

Peale's paintings showed craftsmanship of a high degree, which deserves special admiration because he came to art rather late from humble origins. He died February 22, 1827 at Philadelphia.

Haym Salomon

Haym Salomon was born about 1740 into a Jewish family at Lissa, Poland. He emigrated to New York in 1772 and established a merchant's business. During the British occupation of that city, he was arrested as a spy on September 22, 1776; he was paroled to serve as an interpreter for Hessian officers, was rearrested in August 1777, and managed to escape by bribing his jailer. He became a leading broker in government securities at Philadelphia, paymaster for the French army in America, and primary broker for the issue of U.S. Treasury notes. By 1784, Salomon had used his personal credit to furnish the government with approximately $660,000 in gold or silver in loans and in effect emerged as the Revolution's lender of last resort at the very time when the U.S. Treasury most needed money. When peace returned, Salomon suffered heavy losses, which were aggravated by having so much of his assets frozen in loans to the government. When he died prematurely on January 6, 1785, his estate was insolvent because its major asset, money owed him by the U.S. Treasury, could not be collected because the government lacked the funds to honor it debts. Despite Salomon's example of unhesitating sacrifice to keep the government solvent, his heirs never obtained any restitution from Congress for his losses.

Friedrich Wilhelm Augustus von Steuben

Friedrich W. A. von Steuben was born at Magdeburg, Prussia, on September 17, 1730 and spent much of his early youth in Russia. He served on Frederick the Great's general staff during the Seven Years' War and left the army as a captain in 1763. Without employment and badly in debt, he presented himself to Benjamin Franklin, then ambassador to France, in 1777 and exaggerated his military experience, even to the extent of claiming to have held lieutenant general's rank. With Franklin's encouragement, he entered the Continental Army as an unpaid volunteer pending a decision to award him suitable rank. Washington immediately appointed him drillmaster to the army at Valley Forge. Steuben proved to be a genius in finding common-sense solutions for complex problems. He devised a simplified drill that could be learned quickly and organized a training program that allowed large numbers of men to learn it simultaneously by imitating demonstration squads, companies, and battalions. By the summer of 1778, he had brought the Continental Army's battlefield proficiency to a level roughly equal to the British army's for the first time in the war, for which he was appointed inspector general, with rank of major general, on May 5, 1778. Steuben remained a staff officer until he was discharged in March 1784. He died at Utica, New York on November 28, 1794.

Mercy Otis Warren

Mercy Otis was born on September 25, 1728 at Barnstable, Massachusetts, and married James Warren in 1754. She educated herself in politics and became a fierce supporter of America's right to remain exempt from Parliamentary taxation. She wrote a series of plays that mercilessly satirized British politicians and soldiers, which included *The Adulateur* (1772), *The Defeat* (1773), *The Group* (1775), and *The Blockheads* (1776). All these works appeared anonymously because she doubted that the public would accept their harsh critique of apologists and defenders of Parliament, including some material that risked offending genteel sensibilities by obscene and scatological subject matter. As sister of James Otis (one of Boston's most impassioned anti-British spokesmen), wife of a man elected president of the rebellious Massachusetts Provincial Congress, and close friend of John Adams, she became thoroughly familiar with the arguments and events that led to independence. She published a significant work in verse, *Poems Dramatic and Miscellaneous* (1790), and the three-volume narrative *History of the Rise, Progress, and Termination of the American Revolution* (1805). Her dramatic, literary, and historical writings rank among the most effective works of patriotic literature and give her some claim to be considered the Revolution's de facto poet laureate. She died October 19, 1814 at Plymouth, Massachusetts.

George Washington

Only eleven years after he was born in Westmoreland County, Virginia, on February 22, 1732, George Washington was orphaned by his father's death. He was trained as a surveyor, but he hoped for a military career in the British army. In 1754, he was commissioned a lieutenant colonel of Virginia militia and was ordered to resist French encroachments near the forks of the Ohio, but he returned home after being defeated at Ft. Necessity, Pennsylvania. A year later, his courage at Braddock's Defeat made him a minor hero in the British Empire. He resigned from the militia in 1758 and became a planter. Service in Virginia's House of Burgesses turned him into a determined, if underspoken, opponent of Parliamentary taxation, and he attended the First Continental Congress during 1774–1775. Appointed commander-in-chief on June 17, 1775, he directed the successful siege of Boston. Driven by superior enemy forces from New York in 1776, he reinvigorated the American cause with victories at Trenton and Princeton, New Jersey, by January 1777. He experienced setbacks at Brandywine Creek and Germantown, Pennsylvania the next year, but he used the encampment at Valley Forge to remake his Continentals into a professional army and then fought the British to a standstill at Monmouth Courthouse,

New Jersey in August 1778. He then kept the British pinned down in New York until 1781, when he captured Lord Cornwallis's army at Yorktown, Virginia. He presided over the Constitutional Convention at Philadelphia in the summer of 1787 and served as U.S. president from 1789 to 1797. His administration restored the country's financial credit, ended the Indian wars in the West, and negotiated treaties that removed foreign troops from American soil and expanded overseas markets for American exports. He died at Mt. Vernon, Virginia on December 14, 1799.

Phillis Wheatley

Phillis Wheatley was born about 1753 in Africa, and she was taken to Boston in a slaving ship in 1761. John Wheatley, a prosperous Boston tailor, bought her as a maidservant for his wife Susannah. The Wheatleys found Phillis to be such a quick learner that after just sixteen months of personal instruction at home, she not only attained complete fluency in English but also had mastered reading and could read all parts of the Bible with little difficulty. The Wheatleys recognized her precocious abilities, raised her like a daughter, and freed her before she became an adult. Phillis read avidly among literature, history, geography, and even the classics in Latin; she also began composing poetry and developed her writing skills to a high degree while a teenager. She published her first poem at age 13. In 1773, the Wheatleys financed her passage to England, where she arranged for publication of her first book, *Poems on Various Subjects, Religious and Moral,* the earliest work of verse by an African American. In 1775, the *Pennsylvania Magazine* printed her ode "His Excellency General Washington." Washington thanked her by letter and added, "If you should ever come near headquarters, I shall be happy to see a person so favored by the Muses." The poetess accepted his invitation and visited the general while he besieged Boston. Phillis Wheatley suffered from a weak physique and died at the early age of thirty in 1784 at Boston.

In this painting, T. P. Rossiter commemorates the 1787 signing of the Constitution by the convention's members, presided over by George Washington. By traditional definition, the country's "founding fathers" include those who signed either the Declaration of Independence or the Constitution; eight men signed both. (Courtesy Library of Congress)

CHAPTER 12 Education

The financial burdens spawned by the Revolutionary War made the states reluctant to expand support for public education. Thomas Jefferson introduced a bill that would provide three years of free education for Virginia children in 1779, but the legislature never adopted it. Massachusetts amended its education statute to permit many towns the option of avoiding the expense of hiring teachers capable of preparing students to meet college-entrance requirements. Pennsylvania's legislature almost enacted a system of free county schools in 1794, but the bill never received final approval. New York began appropriating treasury funds to local school districts in 1795 but ended all state aid to localities in 1800. By 1800, the concept of universal public education was accepted nowhere outside of New England, and even there, no commitment existed to furnish free education to all children. Americans viewed secondary schooling as a parental responsibility and thought the state should assist private efforts only as a last resort.

Some states nevertheless believed that spending taxes on higher education would serve the public interest. Georgia, North Carolina, and Vermont consequently established state university systems prior to 1800. New York and Maryland likewise created state boards of regents to have responsibility for setting standards for colleges and private academies. Public support contributed relatively little to the expansion of higher education from 1760 to 1800, however, and it was largely through the efforts of churches that most new colleges opened during the forty years from 1760 to 1800.

Pre-Collegiate Education

No systematic information has yet been collected to measure the number of pre-collegiate schools, students, and teachers in late-eighteenth-century America. The parents of most upper-class children hired private tutors who taught not only basic skills in grammar, literacy, and numeracy, but also music, dancing, fencing, bookkeeping, foreign languages, and occasionally navigation or surveying. For the typical child, however, access to education varied widely according to geographical region. Almost every New England town sponsored basic instruction in reading, writing, and arithmetic— mostly at taxpayer expense, but usually contingent upon a small fee—as did many church congregations in the mid-Atlantic region. In the South, educational opportunities were meager for white children (and virtually nonexistent for blacks), and most learning took place in "dame schools," where a local woman charged fees for teaching neighborhood youngsters the alphabet in her home.

Even in New England, which had developed the most thorough system of public education, many students must have received a marginal education for lack of personal attention. Dedham, Massachusetts had established four precinct schools by 1765, and yet it still had a rate of 120 educable adolescents (ages 5 to 15) per teacher. Students in this country town were still more fortunate than those in New York City, which had only one teacher (including private tutors) for every 307 school-age children at about the same time. Although not all adolescents took instruction simultaneously, it appears that late-eighteenth-century teachers taught two or three times as many students as do teachers in the twentieth century.

The educational experience of most students consisted of four to six years' attendance at an English school (so named because it taught no classical languages). English schools gave instruction for six months out of twelve and generally had two terms of three months each in the summer and winter. Older children attended in the winter when they had little farm work to do. Because students were not organized into grades, they progressed by listening to personal instruction at the teacher's desk and then completing assignments at their seats, after which they would be summoned again to show their work or recite the lesson. A large part of each class inevitably wasted much time in silent boredom waiting for their next trip to the teacher's desk. Parents could withdraw children from classes whenever they were satisfied with their level of literacy, and school attendance rarely went beyond age twelve.

TABLE 12.1 NUMBER OF TEACHERS PER SCHOOL-AGE CHILDREN IN REVOLUTIONARY AMERICAN COMMUNITIES

	Dedham, Mass. (1765)	New York, N.Y. (1765–74)	Philadelphia, Pa. (1765–74)	Elizabeth City Co., Va. (1782)
Population	1,919	20,700	13,000[b]	1,425[c]
Households	309	3,622	2,281	248
School-Age Children	500[a]	4,856	3,050	350[a]
English Schools	4	. . .	. . .	5
Teachers	4	16	22	5
Children per Teacher	120	307	137	70

[a] Ages 5 to 15, assumed to be 25% of population given in source.
[b] Excludes suburbs.
[c] Whites only (46% of county).
Source: Lawrence A. Cremin, American Education: The Colonial Experience, 1607–1783 (1970), 526, 534, 539.

Learning proceeded under spartan conditions, in which a single teacher supervised all his or her charges in a poorly heated, single-room building. Up to seventy children might be packed into an enclosure measuring eighteen by twenty feet. Students perched for almost six hours on benches that had no backs and were too high to allow their feet to touch the ground. The youngest scholars sat nearest to the stove and tried to keep their balance while fighting off drowsiness induced by the hot temperature. By custom, teachers had to instruct from whatever textbooks the children brought to school and group instruction was almost impossible. Four years of this ordeal would convey the ability to write simple sentences and enable one to stumble through the Scriptures or an almanac, but did little more.

English schools did not provide sufficient preparation for higher education, so tax-supported grammar schools were set up to qualify students in the larger towns for college admission. The chief characteristic of a grammar school was instruction in Latin and Greek for older scholars. Boys as young as seven might enter after two years at an English school to perfect their skills at reading, penmanship, and arithmetic, but at about age nine or ten they began three or four years of reading classical literature from Rome and Greece. Typical of grammar instruction was the following curriculum adopted by Boston Public Latin School in 1789.

1st Year. Cheever's *Latin Accidence. Colloquies of Corderius* (Latin with English translation). *Nomenclator*, Aesop's *Fables* (Latin with English translation). Ward's *Latin Grammar* or Eutropius.
2nd Year. Eutropius, continued. Ward's *Latin Grammar*. Clarke's *Introduction to Latin* (with English translation). Castillo's *Dialogues*, or *Selecte e Veteri Testamento Historiae. Making of Latin*, from Garretson's *Exercises*.
3rd Year. Caesar's *Commentaries*. Ovid's *Metamorphoses*. Tully's *Epistles*, or *Offices*. Virgil. Greek Grammar. *Making of Latin*, from King's *History of the Heathen Gods*.

Most education in early America resembled the one-room "English school" pictured here by R. H. Curran. While the teacher led recitation by one group, other children tried to ignore the distraction and study their assignments. Physical discomfort was inevitable in an overheated room furnished only with backless, crude benches. (Courtesy Library of Congress)

4th Year. Virgil continued. *Making of Latin,* continued. Tully's *Orations.* Horace. *Gradus ad Parnassum.* Homer. Greek Testament.

The number of grammar schools declined sharply during the Revolutionary era. Every New England colony but Rhode Island had passed laws requiring towns of a certain size (usually fifty families) to hire teachers trained in the classics, who commanded much higher salaries than instructors of the English curricula, but many taxpayers resisted establishing grammar schools because they benefited a minority of students whose parents could, in many cases, afford private tutors. By 1775, about 85 New England communities had established permanent grammar schools, little more than half the number required by law, and about 65 were in Massachusetts. In 1789, however, Massachusetts exempted 117 towns with fewer than 200 families from maintaining a classics instructor, and New Hampshire likewise excused all but nine towns from teaching Latin and Greek. Most towns either reduced their curricula to the level of English schools or found ways of evading the law without being charged with noncompliance. By 1800 in Massachusetts, for example, classical studies were funded in only 30 of the 110 towns required to maintain grammar schools. The number of New England communities supporting pre-collegiate training evidently dropped from about 85 in 1775 to approximately 45 by the century's end.

Offsetting the loss of grammar schools was a sharp increase of small, tuition-based schools called academies, which became the most important provider of secondary education after 1780. These institutions first appeared in the early eighteenth century as denominational schools, but after 1780 most originated as secular bodies. Massachusetts and Vermont encouraged their founding by offering land grants up to thirty-six square miles as endowments. The typical academy was a private school taught by a single master, who rented a building for classes, adopted rules that fit his own philosophy of learning, and in many cases migrated from town to town in search of more pupils. The master invariably taught two curricula, a program akin to that of common English schools and courses modeled after a free grammar school.

After 1780, many academies obtained state incorporation and established boards of trustees that enabled them to become self-perpetuating. A few also created an administrative body for making personnel decisions, determining rules of conduct, overseeing finances, and conserving the estate. Such academies often expanded by hiring assistants to the master, and a few established separate departments for mathematics, classics, and English. It was the more sophisticated institutions that became distinguished centers of college-preparation, such as New Hampshire's Phillips Exeter.

Academies pioneered a different curriculum than the traditional core of classical literature found in grammar schools. In its constitution, Phillips Andover (Massachusetts) proclaimed its goal to be "instructing youth, not only in English and Latin grammar, writing, arithmetic, and those sciences, wherein they are commonly taught; but more especially to learn them the great and real business of living." Academies consequently taught a wider range of subjects than were offered by grammar schools. All taught rhetoric, mathematics, geography, and English grammar; some offered logic, natural philosophy, astronomy, and music; and a few provided vocational training in navigation, bookkeeping, and surveying. Because most parents paid tuition so their boys could gain entrance to college, instruction still remained heavily weighted toward making the scholars fluent in Latin and Greek.

TABLE 12.2   PRIVATE ACADEMIES CHARTERED IN UNITED STATES, 1775–1800

	1775–1789	1790–1800	1775–1800
N.H.	2	7	9
Vt.	1	16	17
Mass.	5	16	21
Conn.	14	8	22
R.I.	...	3	3
N.Y.	2	17	19
N.J.	1	...	1
Pa.	6	5	11
Md.	3	4	7
Va.	8	12	20
N.C.	15	...	15
Ga.	5	...	5
Tenn.	2	...	2
Ky.	1	...	1
Total	65	88	153

Sources: Robert Middlekauff, *Ancients and Axioms: Secondary Education in Eighteenth-Century New England* (1963), 151. Emit D. Grizzell, *Origin and Development of the High School in New England Before 1865* (1923), 31. Lester J. Cappon, ed., *Atlas of Early American History: The Revolutionary Era, 1760–1790* (1976), 115.

Few English schools admitted girls until the late eighteenth century, and no grammar schools allowed them to enter. Even after they began attending common schools, girls frequently attended classes separately from boys. Grammar schools universally excluded girls, since girls were ineligible for college. A few academies accepted female students, but education for girls usually stopped after a few years at an English common school. In most of the cities, however, women established schools to provide daughters of wealthy families with social graces. Many of these schoolmistresses devised curricula that included history, geography, English grammar and literature, French language, music, and the visual arts. Enos Hitchcock, writing in the *Memoirs of the Bloomsgrove Family* of 1790, summed up the prejudices of his generation (including those of many women) against women's education by stating that "learned lady" was an "epithet" that no woman "should ever acquire."

Collegiate Education

On April 5, 1770, President Ezra Stiles of Yale made a diary entry detailing four current projects to found colleges in the thirteen colonies, and he ended the note approvingly by exclaiming "college enthusiasm." In the years from 1763 to 1800, Americans founded twenty-seven colleges. Not all these institutions endured, however, and six either never began classes or closed shortly after opening. By 1800, nineteen colleges were fully operational and had conferred their first baccalaureate degrees.

Prior to the Revolutionary era, no state-supported colleges existed in Anglo-America, although Massachusetts and Virginia had given endowments and occasional financial aid to Harvard and the College of William and Mary. The majority of colleges begun before 1785 had originated as denominational enterprises, although all had charters obliging them to admit students of any church. In that year, Georgia created the first state college by chartering and endowing Franklin College, which served as the nucleus for the University of Georgia. Because of the time involved in getting Franklin organized, the University of North Carolina (founded four years later) was the first state institution to open and award degrees. Vermont established a state university in 1791, and Blount College, which began

as a private school in 1794, was rechartered as the University of Tennessee in 1879.

College faculties were small, and as late as 1800, Yale authorized just two permanent professorships (one for divinity and another for mathematics and natural science). In 1750, the total number of faculty (excluding tutors) at America's four colleges was only ten. A sharp rise in professors resulted from the gradual replacement of

TABLE 12.3   AMERICAN COLLEGES FOUNDED, 1763–1800

Original Name	Present Name	First Charter	First Degrees
College of Rhode Island	Brown University	1764	1769
Queen's College	Rutgers University	1766	1774
Dartmouth College	(same)	1769	1771
Washington College (Md.)	(same)	1782	1783
Liberty Hall Academy	Washington and Lee University	1782	1785
Hampden-Sidney College	(same)	1783	1786
Dickinson College	(same)	1783·	1787
Transylvania Seminary	Transylvania College	1783	1802
St. John's College	(same)	1784	1793
College of Charlestown	(same)	1785	1794
Franklin College (Ga.)	University of Georgia	1785	1804
College of Ninety-Six, S.C.	(never opened)	1785	...
College of Winnsboro, S.C.	(never opened)	1785	...
Franklin College (Pa.)	Franklin and Marshall College	1787	1853
University of North Carolina	(same)	1789	1798
University of Vermont	(same)	1791	1804
College of Bethesda, Md.	(never opened)	1791	...
Williams College	(same)	1793	1795
Bowdoin College	(same)	1794	1806
Blount College	University of Tennessee	1794	1806
Greenville College (Tenn.)	Tusculum College	1794	1808
Cokesbury College (Md.)	(burned 1796)	1794	...
Union College (N.Y.)	(same)	1795	1797
Washington College (Tenn.)	(defunct)	1795	1796
College of Beaufort, S.C.	(defunct)	1795	...
College of Alexandria, S.C.	(defunct)	1797	...
Middlebury College	(same)	1800	1802

Source: Walter Crosby Eells, *Baccalaureate Degrees Conferred by American Colleges in the Seventeenth and Eighteenth Centuries,* U.S. Office of Education Circular No. 528 (May 1958), 4–35.

tutorial instruction by specialized lectures on assigned subjects. By 1800, the country's nineteen colleges needed approximately 100 teachers of professorial rank, about five per institution, of which one would be president. Most colleges recruited their faculty from the clergy or medical profession, and nearly half of all professors taught for fewer than fifteen years. Most American professors merited respect for their intellectual and scholarly attainments; 40% of them earned their degrees in Europe and 11% belonged to the country's three distinguished cultural organizations: the American Philosophical Society, American Academy of Arts and Sciences, and American Academy of Fine Arts.

American colleges awarded 4,371 baccalaureate degrees from 1775 to 1800. Harvard and Yale conferred 44% of these degrees, in almost equal numbers. Although nine-tenths of all baccalaureates were issued by "Ivy League" institutions that antedated the Revolu-

TABLE 12.4 NUMBER OF PROFESSORS ON COLLEGE FACULTIES, 1750–1800

Years[a]	Active Professors	Years[a]	Active Professors
1796–1800	94	1771–1775	33
1791–1795	105	1766–1770	41
1786–1790	78	1761–1765	26
1781–1785	53	1756–1760	20
1776–1780	49	1751–1755	16
		1750	10

[a]Average for five-year period, except 1750.
Source: William D. Carrell, "American College Professors: 1750–1800," History of Education Quarterly VIII (1968), 290, 297.

TABLE 12.5 BACCALAUREATE DEGREES AWARDED BY AMERICAN COLLEGES, 1776–1800

College	A.B. Degrees Awarded	Percent of Total
Harvard University	982	22.5%
Yale University	957	21.9%
Dartmouth College	623	14.3%
Princeton University	455	10.4%
Brown University	301	6.9%
University of Pennsylvania	296	6.8%
Columbia University	217	5.0%
Dickinson College	166	3.8%
Williams College	94	2.2%
Rutgers University	55	1.2%
Washington College (Md.)	53	1.2%
Hampden-Sidney College	35	.8%
St. John's College	31	.7%
Union College	30	.7%
College of William and Mary	26	.6%
University of North Carolina	19	.4%
Washington College (Va.)	19	.4%
College of Charleston	6	.1%
Washington College (Tenn.)	6	.1%
Total	4,371	100.0%

Source: Walter Crosby Eells, *Baccalaureate Degrees Conferred by American Colleges in the Seventeenth and Eighteenth Centuries*, U.S. Office of Education Circular No. 528 (May 1958), 22.

I. Johnson's *View of Columbia College in the City of New York* (about 1790) shows a typical eighteenth-century "campus." Except for older institutions such as Harvard, Yale, and William and Mary, most colleges carried out all their functions within the walls of a single, multi-story building. At Columbia, this building included the classrooms, faculty and administrative offices, the library, student dormitory rooms, and probably a chapel. (I. N. Phelps Stokes Collection, Miriam & Ira Wallach Div. of Arts, Prints and Photographs. Courtesy The New York Public Library. Astor, Lenox and Tilden Foundations.)

tion, several colleges formed after independence quickly surpassed them in the number of degrees granted. William and Mary, the second oldest college in the country, produced fewer than 1% of all graduates, while Dartmouth, which received its charter only in 1769, accounted for 14% of all degree recipients. Dickinson College, the first class of which left in 1787, graduated three times as many students as Rutgers, which was its senior by seventeen years.

Prior to the Revolution, American colleges graduated about a thousand individuals per decade, and by the 1790s that rate had more than doubled. The number of baccalaureates rose steadily from 1760 to 1800, but it lagged behind the overall population growth, and so the ratio of all living college graduates fell from 11.8 per

10,000 persons in 1760 to 10.6 in 1800. At 10.6 per 10,000, the proportion of living college graduates in 1800 was far lower than the previous high of 14.0, attained in both 1670 and 1740.

Most college students commenced their studies at about age 17 and earned their degree when 21 in the period 1775–1800. At many colleges, including Princeton, Columbia, and the University of Pennsylvania, students earned their bachelors' degrees at age 19. Students left Dartmouth at 23, however, in large part because many came from modest circumstances and lacked the funds to finish their classes without leaving for short periods to earn tuition money.

The Revolution prompted Americans to question how relevant was the traditional college curriculum's emphasis on the classics and belles lettres. "It is not indeed the fine arts which our country requires," wrote John Adams, "the useful, the mechanic arts, are those which we have occasion for in a young country." Americans also perceived a political dimension for higher education that would serve, as Thomas Jefferson hoped, to "form the statesmen, legislators and judges, on whom public prosperity and individual happiness are so much to depend." Faculties consequently expanded instruction in the sciences, mathematics, American geography, recent history, English grammar, modern foreign languages, and even vocational skills such as surveying; they furthermore introduced many overtly political topics as the subjects for student disputations and discourses, and chose to teach the classics more through works about government or public service than through literary subjects.

Such changes modified higher education but did not change it radically. Although the students wrote and declaimed less Latin than before, instruction in the classics remained the core of their studies. Typical of the collegiate curriculum was the course of education adopted by Columbia in 1785.

TABLE 12.6   BACCALAUREATE DEGREES AWARDED YEARLY, 1763–1800

Year	A.B.s Awarded	Number of Men Alive Holding A.B. Degree
1800	223	5,605
1799	234	5,459
1798	252	5,319
1797	222	5,152
1796	174	5,014
1795	241	4,908
1794	213	4,759
1793	206	4,620
1792	245	4,489
1791	194	4,304
1790	199	4,163
1789	185	4,033
1788	169	3,909
1787	212	3,806
1786	190	3,650
1785	164	3,518
1784	158	3,416
1783	134	3,339
1782	110	3,271
1781	119	3,219
1780	86	3,160
1779	84	3,125
1778	95	3,096
1777	124	3,066
1776	138	3,023
1775	150	2,961
1774	127	2,879
1773	126	2,806
1772	117	2,740
1771	133	2,667
1770	102	2,595
1769	107	2,534
1768	106	2,470
1767	85	2,408
1766	131	2,369
1765	144	2,290
1764	90	2,192
1763	111	2,140

Note: Number of institutions granting degrees was as follows: 6 in 1763–68; 7 in 1769–70; 8 in 1771–73; 9 in 1774–82; 10 in 1783–84; 11 in 1785; 12 in 1786; 13 in 1787–92; 14 in 1793; 15 in 1794; 16 in 1795; 17 in 1796; 18 in 1797; 19 in 1798–1800.
Source: Walter Crosby Eells, Baccalaureate Degrees Conferred by American Colleges in the Seventeenth and Eighteenth Centuries, U.S. Office of Education Circular No. 528 (May 1958), 36.

ADMISSION REQUIREMENTS
No candidate shall be admitted into the College unless he shall be able to render into English Caesar's Commentaries of the Gallic War, the four orations of Cicero against Catiline, the first four books of Virgil's Aenead, and the Gospels from the Greek; to explain the government and connection of the words; to turn English into grammatical Latin; and shall understand the first four rules of arithmetic, with the rule of three.
Freshman Class
Professor of Languages—twice a day
      Xenophon's Cyropedia. Lucian. Demosthenes.
Professor of Mathematics—once a week
      Vulgar and decimal fractions. Extracting roots.
      Algebra as far as quadratic equations.
Professor of Logic and Rhetoric—once a week
      English grammar, together with the art of reading and speaking English with propriety and elegance.
Freshman Assignments
To deliver every day to the Professor of Languages a written Latin exercise, and once a week to the President a translation out of Latin into English, in which, after expressing the sense of the author, the freedom, spirit and elegance of the translation are principally to be regarded; and the writing is to be neat and correct; this is to be considered as an English rather than a Latin exercise.

Sophomore Class

Professor of Languages—once a day
>   Demosthenes, Tacitus, Homer, Sallust, Euripides, Sophocles, Virgil.

Professor of Mathematics—once a day
>   Euclid's *Elements*. Plain and Spherical Trigonometry. Conic Sections. The higher branches of Algebra.

Professor of Geography—three times a week
>   Description of the globe and present state of world. Rise, extent, and fall of ancient empires to Roman Empire. Origin of present states and kingdoms, their extent, power, commerce, religion, and customs. Modern chronology.

Sophomore Assignments

To continue to make Latin every day, and once a week to deliver to the President an English composition upon a subject to be assigned. Such students as happen not to be sufficiently well grounded in arithmetic, and in the inferior parts of Algebra, may this year attend that lecture of the Professor of Mathematics for a second time, for which purpose the different Professors will so arrange their hours of Lecture so as not to interfere with each other.

Junior Class

Professor of Logic and Rhetoric—once a week
>   Logic.

Professor of Languages—twice a week
>   Latin and Greek authors as chosen by professor.

Professor of Natural Philosophy—three times a week
>   General properties of matter, laws of motion, mechanical powers, hydrostatics, hydraulics, pneumatics, optics, astronomy, electricity, magnetism.

Junior Assignment

To deliver once a week, to the President, an English or Latin composition, upon a subject to be assigned, which compositions are expected to be longer and more correct as the students advance. Such students as wish it may this year attend the principal course of the Professor of Mathematics for a second time.

Senior Class

Professor of Moral Philosophy—three times a week
>   Ethics, with historical view of ancient philosophers.

Professor of Logic and Rhetoric—twice a week
>   Rise and progress of language—universal grammar.
>   Rise and progress of the written character—criticism.

Senior Assignments

To deliver, once a week, an English or Latin composition to the President upon a subject of their own choosing; and to read in their chambers such parts of Longinus *On the Sublime*, Cicero's *Oratory*, Quintillian, Cicero's *Offices*, etc., as the Professors of Rhetoric and Moral Philosophy shall direct. Such students as choose may this year attend the lectures in Natural Philosophy again.

Students earned their degrees through weekly written assignments and performing public exercises. To demonstrate their proficiency in foreign languages and rhetoric, seniors conducted debates or gave orations every month. The president certified their progress at quarterly examinations, during which he evaluated their fluency in addressing an audience in Latin or Greek.

As the eighteenth century ended, higher education remained largely the same as it had been prior to independence. The scope of learning had been expanded in the name of practicality and civic virtue, but the curriculum continued to focus on classical languages and rhetoric. Collegiate education primarily served the purpose of preparing men for the ministry, medicine, or the law, but it had yet to develop a curriculum that would directly benefit individuals outside these careers.

Literacy

Remarkably little research exists on the subject of literacy in Revolutionary America. Because no government statistics were compiled to measure educational attainment before 1800, historians have defined literacy as the ability to sign one's name, a skill that presumes exposure to formal schooling in excess of two years. All major studies of literacy have used the percent of testators able to sign wills as their measure of how many persons could read and write. Relying upon wills is unfortunate, since historians have long realized that only a small minority transferred their property at death through written documents, and that literate individuals were far more likely to do so than were those without writing skills, who tended to settle their affairs orally on their deathbed. At some future date, historians hope to exploit the 80,000 pension applications submitted by Revolutionary soldiers and their widows, who constituted a far more representative cross-section of the country's population than any group previously examined in any study of literacy.

Literacy was highest in New England, where every state but Rhode Island had enacted laws mandating the establishment of local schools. By the late eighteenth century, New England had arrived at the threshold of universal white male literacy. If Pennsylvania and Virginia are typical of the mid-Atlantic and southern states, then the portion of adult white males who could read and write ranged from 68% in rural areas to 85% in large cities.

If slaves are excluded, Americans possessed more education than did western Europeans. Only in Scotland and Sweden did adult male literacy approach the level of New England, while only in the Netherlands did the percentage of men able to sign their names equal that of the middle-Atlantic and southern states. About 75% of all white adult males were literate in the original thirteen states, compared to 60% in England and 55% among the French and Germans.

Illiteracy was far more prevalent among American women than among men. Fewer than half of all females who prepared wills could sign them, even in New England. Since community and church

TABLE 12.7 LITERACY IN THE UNITED STATES AND EUROPE, 1760–1790

United States	Percent Literate[a] Male	Percent Literate[a] Female	Europe	Percent Literate[a] Male
New England, 1760	89%	46%	Scotland, 1790	90%
New York City, 1760–75	87%	67%	Sweden, 1790	90%
Pennsylvania, 1775	70%	. . .	Netherlands, 1790	70%
Philadelphia, 1773–75	82%	80%	Belgium, 1790	61%
Virginia,[b] 1790	68%	. . .	England-Wales, 1790	60%
Average, 1760	75%	40%	France, 1790	55%
			German states, 1790	55%

[a] Ability to sign name.
[b] Whites only.
Sources: Kenneth A. Lockridge, *Literacy in Colonial New England: An Inquiry into the Social Context of Literacy in the Early Modern West* (1974), 17, 76, 77, 99, 140. Lawrence J. Cremin, *American Education: The Colonial Experience, 1607–1783* (1970), 540. J. E. Craig, "The Expansion of Education," *Review of Research in Education*, IX (1981), 170.

schools rarely admitted girls before 1780, the disparity between male and female literacy is less surprising than is the fact that such a large minority of women did acquire the skill of writing. Numerous women obviously learned to write for their mothers, brothers, and husbands, but the dynamics and stages of this important educational phenomena have never been investigated. Illiteracy may have been high among American women, but all researchers have concluded that it was far lower than among women in western Europe.

Although the level of literacy among Anglo-Americans was high about 1760, it had not increased greatly during the previous half-century. By 1710, about two-thirds of adult white males were able to sign their names and only slight differences existed in literacy rates among New England, the middle-Atlantic region, or the South. Virtually no progress was made in reducing illiteracy among free men anywhere except New England, where the portion of adult men capable of writing expanded from 67% to 89%. Most of this gain evidently came among farmers, whose rate of signing wills increased from 60% in about 1710 to almost 85% by 1790. Literacy among New England women improved slightly during the same period from 41% to 46%, and, in major cities such as Boston, almost 65% of women were able to write by 1790. Except for New England, which apparently reduced male illiteracy to its lowest practical level soon after 1800, the ability to read and write among Anglo-Americans stagnated for most of the century following 1710 and would not show appreciable improvement until after 1800.

It remains unclear whether most Americans had progressed beyond the bare level of functional literacy sufficient to pick painfully through an almanac or the Bible, and it seems probable that the majority had not. Most inventories of probated estates did not include books, and very few mentioned writing paper, ink, or pens. The primary reason why ordinary people mastered and retained the skills of reading and writing was probably for keeping accurate records of finances for their farm or workshop. Below the ranks of the cultured elite and the sophisticated middle class, there was nevertheless a sizeable minority of farmers and craftsmen who read regularly and thoughtfully. The average citizen struck observers, such as Professor Jacob Duche of the University of Pennsylvania, as more literate than Europeans in general. "The poorest laborer on the shore of the Delaware," wrote Duche, "thinks himself entitled to deliver his sentiments in matters of religion or politics with as much freedom as the gentleman or scholar." Duche certainly exaggerated the extent of popular learning, but his explanation for why ordinary Americans seemed better informed than Europeans held a kernel of truth: "such is the prevailing taste for books of every kind, that almost every man is a reader."

Libraries

By the Revolutionary era, circulating libraries had become well established. No tax-supported libraries existed until 1803, and before then books largely circulated through private organizations funded by individual contributions and donations. Such subscription libraries assessed an entry payment and annual borrowing fees. The initial cost of membership could be as much as £2, with yearly dues of ten shillings. Membership was an expensive luxury for most Americans but still was affordable to many in the middle class. Some libraries nevertheless allowed nonmembers to read for free during the few hours when their collection was available for use.

Subscription libraries proliferated rapidly after Benjamin Franklin helped found the Library Company of Philadelphia in 1731. During the next four decades, new lending libraries appeared at a rate of almost two per year. The chance to borrow books became almost universal in cities, increasingly common in small towns, and not un-

TABLE 12.8   ESTABLISHMENT OF LIBRARIES IN NEW ENGLAND, 1761–1800

State	Dates Established						
	1796–1800	1791–1795	1786–1790	1781–1785	1776–1780	1771–1775	1761–1770
Maine	8	4	2	. . .	. . .	. . .	1
N.H.	54	18	1	. . .	. . .	. . .	. . .
Vt.	10	4	2	. . .	. . .	1	. . .
Mass.	34	35	15	6	5	6	4
R.I.	6	3	. . .	. . .	. . .	1	. . .
Conn.	29	61	24	9	3	6	8
Total	141	125	44	15	8	14	13

Source: Jesse H. Shera, *Foundations of the Public Library: The Origins of the Public Library Movement in New England, 1629–1855* (1949), 55, 69.

usual in the countryside. All but a few libraries operated out of a member's house, which was kept open for this purpose an afternoon each week. A few accumulated respectable collections, such as the Redwood Library at Newport, Rhode Island, which was just seventeen years old in 1764 but owned 700 titles. By 1775, a minimum of sixty-four libraries existed in the thirteen colonies, including thirty-eight in New England, twenty-three in the mid-Atlantic region, and three in the South. By 1800, New Englanders had founded 325 libraries since 1781, and the total within the United States probably approached 500.

Even as late as 1800, the typical library remained extremely small. One-fifth of the collections whose size is known held fewer than a hundred books, and half possessed fewer than three hundred. Only one of every seven libraries contained more than a thousand titles.

The only surviving charge-out ledger from before 1800 was compiled at the New York Society Library during 1789–1790. Novels composed 17% of the titles that circulated, but they accounted for 35% of all borrowings. The next most frequently borrowed subjects were history at 17%, travel-geography at 13%, reference works or periodicals at 10%, biography at 8%, essays at 7%, drama-poetry at 4%, religion-philosophy at 3%, and science at 3%.

Some college libraries suffered severe setbacks in the late 1700s. Harvard experienced its worst disaster on January 26, 1764, when fire engulfed its entire collection except for about four hundred items out on loan. Princeton lost a portion of its books when British and Continental troops fought over the campus on January 3, 1777,

TABLE 12.9   SUBJECT ANALYSIS OF NEW ENGLAND LIBRARY TITLES, 1785–1794

	Farmington, Conn. (1785)	Brookfield, Vt. (1791)	New Haven, Conn.[a] (1793)	Norwich, Conn.[b] (1794)
Theology, religion	22%	28%	9%	32%
History, biography	27%	29%	25%	16%
Literature, drama	28%	9%	20%	24%
Travel, geography	10%	11%	17%	9%
Science, agriculture	. . .	. . .	1%	7%
Fiction	5%	12%	22%	10%
Miscellaneous[c]	8%	11%	6%	2%
(Number of Titles)	(197)	(248)	(204)	(194)

[a] Mechanic's Library.
[b] Franklin Library.
[c] Magazines, law, politics.
Source: Jesse H. Shera, *Foundations of the Public Library: The Origins of the Public Library Movement in New England, 1629–1855* (1949), 103.

and much of William and Mary's library was pilfered by Continental troops garrisoned on the campus in 1781.

These losses proved temporary, even at Harvard, which received such an outpouring of bequests that by 1766 it again possessed the colonies' largest educational library. By 1790, the nine pre-Revolutionary colleges held about 27,000 titles. Harvard owned half of all books in college libraries, while the next largest library, William and Mary's with 3,000 titles, contained 11% of the total. The country's entire college library stock remained in a rudimentary state, with barely thirty books for each of the nine hundred students enrolled for study at Ivy League institutions.

All libraries, including those at colleges, had been privately supported or endowed through the eighteenth century. The beginning of the public library movement came in 1800 with the establishment of the Library of Congress. Envisioned solely as a service for representatives and senators, the library grew slowly until its purchase of Thomas Jefferson's library in 1814. Congress soon authorized the library to perform services for its constituents, and it consequently evolved into a national public library with the obligation to maintain two copies of every book printed in the United States for the use of civil servants and private scholars.

TABLE 12.10   LIBRARY HOLDINGS OF IVY LEAGUE COLLEGES IN 1790

Institution	Library Started	Number of Volumes	Annual Rate of Acquisitions
Harvard	1764[a]	12,000	462
William and Mary	1693	3,000	30
Yale	1700	2,700	30
Princeton	1750	2,300	58
Columbia	1756	2,000	60
Pennsylvania	1749	1,500	40
Brown	1768	2,156	100
Rutgers	1792	[b]	?
Dartmouth	1763	1,000	58
Total	. . .	26,656	. . .

[a] Date fire destroyed all but 400 books.
[b] Under 100.
Source: Louis Shores, *Origins of the American College Library, 1638–1800* (1966), 56.

The Franklin Library, a bequest of Philadelphia's first citizen, Benjamin Franklin, is pictured on 5th Street as of 1799. The library held the largest non-academic collection of books in North America, with over 5,000 titles, and had furnished reading material for the delegates who attended the Constitutional Convention in 1787. (I. N. Phelps Stokes Collection, Miriam & Ira Wallach Div. of Arts, Prints and Photographs. Courtesy The New York Public Library. Astor, Lenox and Tilden Foundations.)

CHAPTER 13 Arts and Letters

American cultural life suffered only temporary disruption during the Revolutionary War. In 1763, journalism and publishing remained small-scale and unsophisticated, and the colonies still had not produced a major literary work or piece of art. From then until 1800, newspapers and magazines multiplied dramatically, the press's annual output of imprints quadrupled, the first novels appeared, the earliest studios for instructing painters opened, and the country's intellectual elite began founding learned societies. By 1800, the United States was taking on the trappings, however rudimentary, of a worldly metropolitan culture like London's.

Journalism

Although the thirteen colonies possessed just twenty-one papers and one magazine in 1760, journalism was poised on the brink of its first major period of expansion. Rapid population growth, increasing cultural sophistication, and recurring political crises greatly accelerated the demand for news and other reading material. The number of papers multiplied almost tenfold in the four decades after 1760, and magazines started appearing regularly rather than intermittently. Journalism also underwent important qualitative changes that made the press an important influence upon political and cultural life for the first time in American history.

The number of colonial newspapers rose from twenty-one to thirty-seven and their circulation swelled enormously during the period 1760–1775. No longer small organs lucky to be supported by 600 subscribers, the most popular papers in 1775 attracted up to 3,500 paying readers, plus several times that number who perused copies secondhand. Competition for readers became so feverish in the cities that there appeared a new occupation, the paperboy, to peddle the latest editions in the streets to passersby. As early as 1773, the *New York Gazette and Weekly Mercury* was being distributed by the very prototype of today's street vendor, America's earliest known paperboy, whom a competitor identified as "the egregious and clamorous Lawrence Sweeney." The greatest potential for expanding readership lay in the countryside, however, and more frequent mail service allowed editors to win large numbers of rural customers.

TABLE 13.1 COMPARISON OF NEWSPAPER SUBSCRIPTION RATES IN BRITISH EMPIRE, 1775

	Number of Newspapers	Estimated Subscribers	Population	Subscribers per 1,000 Persons[b]
London, England	23	57,500	788,000	72.0
Other England and Wales	44	55,000	6,456,000	8.5
Total England and Wales	67	112,500	7,244,000	15.5
Ireland	16	16,000	3,678,000	4.3
13 Colonies	37	35,000	1,855,000[a]	18.9

[a] Free population only.
[b] Total population, not just adults.
Source: Lawrence A. Cremin, *American Education: The Colonial Experience, 1607–1783* (1970), 547.

On the eve of independence, per capita newspaper subscription among white Americans was over four times higher than in Ireland and slightly higher than in England and Wales. When the *Connecticut Courant*'s circulation reached 8,000 in 1778, it rivaled the readership of many of London's larger papers. By 1780, the number of paying customers for the country's thirty-eight papers equaled every tenth adult free male, and it is unlikely that the press of any European country reached a wider audience.

TABLE 13.2 RISE IN AMERICAN NEWSPAPER CIRCULATION, 1770–1800

Year	Number of Papers	Number of Subscribers	White Adult Males Over 16	Subscribers per 1,000 White Adult Males	Annual Newspapers Printed
1770	29	23,200[a]	422,000	55.0	672,800
1775	48	35,000[b]	464,000	75.4	1,196,000
1780	38	53,700	551,250	97.4	2,004,000
1800	197[c]	160,600[d]	1,074,000	149.6	13,078,000

[a] Estimated at 800 per paper.
[b] See Table 13.1.
[c] See Table 13.6.
[d] Adjusted from source to reflect actual number of papers in print.
Sources: Sidney Kobre, *The Development of the Colonial Newspaper* (1960), 97. Clarence S. Brigham, *Journals and Journeymen: A Contribution to the History of Early American Newspapers* (1950), 3.

Americans founded more than sixty newspapers during the 1780s and by 1790 the number in operation had reached eighty-four, including the first two papers west of the Appalachians: the Pittsburgh *Gazette* (1786) and the *Kentucke Gazette* (1787). In the next decade, 450 papers started publication, and although most did not survive, the country had 197 papers by 1800. The 1790s witnessed the proliferation of "country journals" through rural districts. Greater competition reduced average subscription to about 700 customers, but total paid circulation approximated 15% of all adult white males. If there were two secondhand readers for each subscriber, then total circulation approached half the voting-age population. How many people actually consulted papers is unknown, but access to printed news was within the reach of a substantial majority of free adults.

Newspapers not only became more numerous but also appeared more frequently. All colonial papers printed one issue per week until 1768, when several Massachusetts editors experimented with semiweekly publications on an irregular basis. The earliest triweekly premiered on July 4, 1770 as the *Pennsylvania Packet,* and it continued this format for a decade. The *Pennsylvania Evening Post* launched the country's first daily newspaper on May 30, 1783, but this venture soon failed. Publication of the first successful daily began on September 21, 1784 with the *Pennsylvania Packet and Daily Advertiser,* which was quickly followed by New York's *Daily Advertiser* a few months later. By 1800, the country had sixteen dailies, including six in Philadelphia, five in New York, three in Baltimore, and two in Charleston. Although three-quarters of all papers were weeklies in 1800, they accounted for fewer than half of all individual issues produced. It was largely because of the rise of dailies and other multiweekly editions that yearly newspaper production soared twentyfold, from

TABLE 13.3 INCREASE IN FREQUENCY OF NEWSPAPER ISSUES, 1769–1785

First Semiweeklies (1768–1781)		
Early Attempts	Massachusetts Gazette & Post-Boy, News-Letter	(May 23, 1768–Oct. 2, 1769)
	Boston Chronicle	(Jan. 9, 1769–Jun. 25, 1770)
	Massachusetts Spy	(Nov. 5, 1770–Feb. 1, 1771)
	New York Constitutional Gazette	(Aug. 2, 1775–Aug. 20, 1776)
	Rind's Virginia Gazette	(Dec. 6, 1775–Feb. 3, 1776)
	Pennsylvania Ledger	(Dec. 23, 1777–May 23, 1778)
	Pennsylvania Evening Post	(Jan. 7, 1779–Oct. 1779)
	Newport Mercury	(Jan. 20, 1776–Jul. 1, 1776)
	Providence American Journal	(Jan. 1, 1781–Aug. 29, 1781)
Longer Lasting Semiweeklies	N.Y. Royal American Gazette	(May 19, 1778–Jul. 31, 1783)
	Rivington's Royal Gazette	(May 13, 1778–Nov. 1783)
	Royal South Carolina Gazette	(Mar. 3, 1781–Sep. 28, 1782)
	Pa. Independent Gazeteer	(Sep. 17–Dec. 17, 1782)
	Pennsylvania Packet	(Apr. 8, 1780–Jan. 9, 1781)
First Successful Semiweeklies	Pennsylvania Journal	(Jun. 17, 1781–1788)
	Maryland Journal	(Mar. 14, 1783–1800+)
	(N.Y.) Independent Journal	(Dec. 25, 1783–1800+)
First Triweeklies (1770–1784)		
Early Attempts	Massachusetts Spy	(Jul. 17, 1770–Oct. 30, 1770)
First Successful Triweeklies	Royal South Carolina Gazette	(1780–1782)
	Pennsylvania Evening Post	(Jan. 24, 1775–Jan. 1, 1779)
	Pennsylvania Packet	(June 12, 1781–Sep. 18, 1784)
First Dailies (1783–1784)		
Early Attempts	Pennsylvania Evening Post	(irregular 1783–1784)
First Successful Daily	Pennsylvania Packet and Daily Advertiser	(Sep. 1784)

Source: Sidney Kobre, The Development of the Colonial Newspaper (1960), 158.

TABLE 13.4 MAGAZINES PUBLISHED IN THE UNITED STATES, 1769–1800

Year	Number of Magazines[a]	Where Published
1800	14	Walpole, N.H.; Northampton, Mass.; Boston; Hartford, Conn.; New York (4); Philadelphia (2); Baltimore (2); Richmond (2).
1799	11	Portland, Me.; Walpole, N.H.; Boston; New York (3); Newark, N.J.; Philadelphia (3); Richmond.
1798	20	Portland, Me.; Walpole, N.H.; Fairhaven, Vt.; Danbury, Conn.; Bridgeport, Conn.; New York (4); Newark, N.J.; Philadelphia (7); Frederick, Md.; Baltimore; Charleston.
1797	20	Walpole, N.H.; Haverhill, N.H.; Exeter, N.H.; Concord, N.H.; New York (9); Philadelphia (4); West Chester, Pa.; Baltimore; Charleston.
1796	16	Walpole, N.H.; Rutland, Vt.; Boston (2); Hartford, Conn.; Sagg Island, N.Y.; New York (8); Philadelphia (2).
1795	8	Walpole, N.H.; Rutland, Vt.; Boston; New York (3); Philadelphia (2).
1794	7	Walpole, N.H.; Bennington, Vt.; Boston; New York (2); Newark, N.J.; Baltimore.
1793	8	Walpole, N.H.; Concord, N.H.; Boston; New York (2); Philadelphia (2); Baltimore.
1792	6	Boston (2); New York; Philadelphia (3).
1791	5	Boston; New York; Elizabeth-Town, N.J.; Philadelphia (2).
1790	7	Boston (2); New York; Elizabeth-Town, N.J.; Philadelphia (3).
1789	8	Boston (2); New Haven, Conn.; Hartford, Conn.; Elizabeth-Town, N.J.; Philadelphia (3).
1788	5	Worcester, Mass.; New Haven, Conn.; New York; Philadelphia (2).
1787	6	Worcester, Mass.; New Haven, Conn.; New York; New Brunswick, N.J.; Philadelphia (2).
1786	6	Worcester, Mass.; Boston; New Haven, Conn. (2); New Brunswick, N.J.; Philadelphia.
1785	2	Boston (2).
1784	2	Boston (2).
1783	1	Boston.
1779	1	Philadelphia.
1776	1	Philadelphia.
1775	2	Boston; Philadelphia.
1774	1	Boston.
1772	1	Boston.
1771	2	Boston; Philadelphia.
1769	1	Philadelphia.

[a]Includes magazines published during any part of calendar year.
Source: Frank L. Mott, A History of American Magazines, 1741–1850 (1957), 787–91.

672,800 in 1770 to 13,078,000 in 1800.

Journalism was one of the eighteenth century's most risky ventures, and few papers lasted more than two years. Of thirty-seven papers in print when the Revolution began in April 1775, seventeen had failed by Cornwallis's surrender in October 1781, as did eighteen of the thirty-four papers that had been founded during that same period (including eleven edited by Tories). Although about 450 new papers went to press during the 1790s, only 197 still existed by 1800. The only papers published during the eighteenth century to survive more than fifty years were the eight listed below.

Pennsylvania Gazette (1728–1815)
Maryland Gazette (1745–1820+)
Boston News-Letter (1704–1776)
New Hampshire Gazette (1756–1820+)
Newport Mercury (1758–1820+)
Providence Gazette (1762–1820+)
Connecticut [New London] Gazette (1763–1820+)
Connecticut [Hartford] Courant (1764–1820+)
Connecticut [New Haven] Journal (1767–1820+)
Pennsylvania Journal (1742–1793)

The late eighteenth century also marked the period when magazine editing became an established fixture of American culture. Since the appearance of the colonies's first magazine in 1741, these ventures had experienced little success. Just five monthly magazines were printed during the Revolutionary War, in large part as experiments, and none survived longer than nineteen months. From 1783 to 1801, however, Americans produced about seventy-five magazines, of which several enjoyed more than five years of successful sales.

Most magazines offered an eclectic mixture of subjects. The *Massachusetts Magazine* (1789–1796), for instance, promoted itself as a "Monthly Museum of Knowledge and Rational Entertainment, Poetry, Musick, Biography, Physicks, Geography, Morality, Criticism, Philosophy, Mathematicks, Agriculture, Architecture, Chemistry, Novels, Tales, Romances, Translations, News, Marriages and Deaths, Meteorological Observations, Etc." The first journal designed for female readers, *Gentlemen and Ladies' Town & Country Magazine,* appeared at Boston in May 1784. The earliest regular musical publication, Daniel Read's *American Musical Magazine,* debuted at New Haven in May 1786. *Children's Magazine,* the first U.S. periodical for adolescents, premiered in January 1789 at Hartford, Connecticut. The typical journal contained sixty-four pages and often serialized long articles into several monthly installments. Illustrations became an increasingly common feature after January 1774, when the *Royal American Magazine* became the first colonial magazine to use them extensively. By the 1790s, the United States usually had at least three magazines being simultaneously produced.

American journalism underwent a significant transformation from 1763 to 1800. During most of the colonial period, newspapers had primarily functioned as advertising vehicles. Advertisements for local customers consumed at least a quarter of the four pages that constituted the typical paper. Local events usually received much less coverage than foreign news, especially court gossip from the major European capitals, which was appropriated wholesale from the latest British newspapers available for reading. Any remaining space featured reprints of essays or poetry from overseas magazines on subjects such as English politics, literature, or science. Aside from the solicitation and preparation of paid notices, an editor compiled the bulk of each issue by cannibalizing segments from overseas publications to fill whatever space remained after the advertising was typeset.

Because of the constitutional disputes between Britain and the thirteen colonies, the American press developed an unprecedented political dimension after 1763. Advertising continued to be paramount for a paper's financial health, and European news took precedence over local events more often than not, but for the first time in colonial history, newspapers became self-conscious agents for influencing political behavior. Prior to this time, politicians had generally expressed their views through pamphlets, circulars, or broadsides rather than papers. By 1770, newspapers had emerged as a major force in molding public opinion.

Editors altered their traditional format to provide heightened coverage of the controversies between Britain and its colonies. They deemphasized news from the European continent in favor of reports concerning British and American affairs. Although editors seldom published statements of their personal views, they printed essays by authors with positions like their own. They also carried an increasing number of political cartoons (rare occurrences before 1760), highlighted important developments with bold headlines, and often increased their page-size to accommodate the greater volume of information. It was during this period that publishers began providing news at more frequent intervals by issuing the first semiweeklies and triweeklies, or by printing "extras" to cover especially significant events.

The onset of war created an enormous demand for information about battles and diplomacy, but the press was ill-equipped to satisfy its readers' curiosity. Newspapers never developed any systematic means of reporting about the Revolution. All editors depended overwhelmingly on the random arrival of stories already printed by papers nearer to the scene of events, and to a lesser extent on private correspondence. Without a corps of reporters to provide accurate facts, newspapers had no way to distinguish rumor from reality unless there were eyewitnesses to an event among their correspondents or close neighbors. The press could do little more than publish stories as they drifted in and hope that their sources were knowledgeable.

Military operations and the British blockade increased the time lag normally experienced in reporting news. Even before the Revolution, colonial papers described events from Britain seven to eight weeks after the fact. Word that independence was voted in Philadelphia on July 2 spread more rapidly than any other occurrence, and yet the first newspaper coverage did not appear until July 9 in Maryland, July 10 in New York, July 12 in Connecticut, July 13 in Rhode Island, July 16 in Massachusetts, July 19 in Virginia, and August 13 in London, England. War conditions delayed the travels of post riders, upon whom editors were dependent for most news, and greatly reduced the flow of British newspapers, which had formerly supplied perhaps half the information printed in colonial papers.

Only in a relative sense did the most important news travel swiftly. The Treaty of Paris, which ended the Revolution on September 3, 1783, for example, did not become known to journalists in Boston until October 22, and most Americans certainly did not learn of this event for another month. George Washington's death on

TABLE 13.5 COMPARATIVE SPEED (IN ELAPSED DAYS) WITH WHICH SOUTHERN NEWSPAPERS REPORTED CONTEMPORARY EVENTS, 1763–1775

News From	Maryland Gazette (days)	Virginia Gazette [a] (days)	N.C. Gazette (days)	S.C. Gazette [b] (days)	Georgia Gazette (days)
Great Britain	84	78	83	71	69
Mass.	21	22	27	26	31
R.I.	22	30	16	24	. . .
N.Y.	16	19	28	23	40
Pa.	12	15	23	23	28
Md.	. . .	14	. . .	24	. . .
Va.	19	. . .	19	33	15
N.C.	49	4	. . .	20	11
S.C.	43	44	25	. . .	15
Ga.	48	. . .	. . .	13	. . .

[a] Edited by Rind and Pinkney.
[b] *South Carolina Gazette & Country Journal.*
Source: Robert M. Weir, "The Role of the Newspaper Press in the Southern Colonies on the Eve of the Revolution: An Interpretation," in Bernard Bailyn and John B. Hench, eds., *The Press and the American Revolution* (1980), 128.

December 14, 1799 received first notice in the *Alexandria [Va.] Times* on December 16. All subsequent press coverage printed firsthand or secondhand accounts from this source, and the news traveled only as fast as post riders could. New York papers managed to report Washington's death by December 21, while Boston's papers did so on Christmas. Residents of New Hampshire did not learn of the president's demise until December 30 from the *Farmer's Weekly Museum,* although the *Kentucke Gazette* put the story out rather quickly west of the mountains on January 2, 1800.

The Revolution marked an important turning point in American journalism. Nearly all papers established earlier had been founded as advertising auxiliaries to printing shops, and their purpose was purely financial. After 1760, newspapers assumed the additional task of rallying support for political causes. Having proved its usefulness in marshaling public opinion against British policies, it was inevitable that the press would be drawn into the struggle between Federalists and Democratic-Republicans to control the federal government during the 1790s.

Journalism had a far greater impact on politics during the 1790s

TABLE 13.6   NEWSPAPERS PUBLISHED IN UNITED STATES, 1775–1800

	In 1775	In 1784	In 1790	In 1800
Conn.	4	5	7	15
Del.	. . .	. . .	1	1
D.C.	. . .	. . .	1	2
Ga.	1	1	2	5
Ky.	. . .	. . .	1	4
Maine	. . .	1	1	5
Md.	2	3	3	11
Mass.	8	8	11	19
N.H.	1	1	4	12
N.J.	. . .	2	3	7
N.Y.	3	6	13	29
N.C.	2	1	3	6
Ohio	. . .	. . .	. . .	2
Pa.	7	8	16	39
R.I.	2	3	4	5
S.C.	3	3	3	6
Tenn.	. . .	. . .	. . .	2
Vt.	. . .	2	2	6
Va.	3	4	9	21
Totals	36	48	84	197

Note: Figures refer only to newspapers published during Jan. of each year, some of which discontinued later in year.
Source: Lester J. Cappon, ed., *Atlas of Early American History: The Revolutionary Era, 1760–1790* (1976), 109–112. Clarence S. Brigham, *History and Bibliography of American Newspapers, 1690–1820*, 2 vols. (1962 ed.).

than it had during the years leading to independence. The number of papers multiplied more than five times from 1776 to 1800, and total circulation rose to reach almost half of all adult voters. Newspapers furthermore ceased advocating broad principles capable of enlisting support from a wide spectrum of political views, and became aligned with specific parties. The Revolutionary press had rarely taken stands on elections prior to 1776, but the partisan press of the 1790s emerged as an important arm of each party's campaign machinery.

As newspapers became more closely aligned with politics, journalism acquired new prestige and editors became figures of considerable stature. For most of the eighteenth century, newspaper editors were little more than mere printers who patched together large amounts of advertising with a hodgepodge of public-interest items to fill a four-page issue. After 1790, editors consciously molded their papers into an expression of their own values—and sometimes as an extension of their own personality. This background underlay the evolution of the editorial column. Although earlier editors had often written anonymous essays or bogus letters, they had avoided making explicit statements of opinion in their paper's name. The classic editorial form evidently originated with Noah Webster's *American Minerva* and Boston's *Columbian Centinel* during 1796–1797. By 1800, numerous papers were reserving a block of space for the editor's commentary as a standard part of their format.

The expanded coverage given to politics broadened the scope of American journalism during the early national era, but papers remained otherwise similar to their colonial antecedents. Profits still depended on advertising revenue, and successful papers filled anywhere from half to three-quarters of their columns with paid notices. Yankees retained a fascination with news from Britain and Europe, so editors liberally sprinkled their pages with articles gleaned from foreign journals. So well did the press report on European affairs, that the Englishman John Bernard wrote in 1797 of finding men "leading secluded lives in the woods of Virginia perfectly *au fait* as to the literary, dramatic and personal gossip of London and Paris." The fact that even a few individuals could acquire such sophistication certainly testified that the country's paper and magazines wrote at a relatively high level for people eager to improve themselves by avid and discriminating reading.

Publishing and Literature

The American publishing industry expanded rapidly during the late eighteenth century. The number of print shops rose steadily from thirty-eight in 1764 to fifty-six in 1775. A strong indicator of publishing's newfound significance in colonial society was the emergence of the earliest type-founders between 1769, when Abel Buell cast the first Roman type at Killingworth, Connecticut, and 1771, when Christopher Sauer began manufacturing type for German script at Philadelphia.

The pace of expansion accelerated after the Revolution's end. The number of presses doubled from sixty-one in 1780 to 126 in 1790, and then doubled again in just five years. Publishing thereafter grew at a more modest rate, but by 1799 the United States had 274 printing establishments. The demand for printers far exceeded the supply of domestic journeymen and the trade could not have expanded had large numbers of British printers not brought their presses to America. Just as Americans were beginning to create a distinctive national literature, the country found itself dependent on foreign talent to develop its publishing industry.

Boston, Philadelphia, and New York were the preeminent centers of American publishing. These cities produced over two-thirds of all imprints that rolled off presses in the thirteen colonies from 1761 to 1776. Boston remained the largest center of publishing through the colonial period, but after being besieged in 1775–1776 it was surpassed by Philadelphia. Smaller centers of printing also existed in Rhode Island and Connecticut before the Revolution, and their output expanded significantly from 1785 to 1800. Southern presses largely limited their production to government documents, newspapers, or almanacs, and consequently they turned out barely a tenth of all American imprints.

The amount of available reading material increased dramatically due to the expansion of printing establishments. From an average of 475 imprints per year from 1764 to 1773, the country's presses had raised output to an annual average of almost 2,000 imprints by the decade 1791–1800. Along with higher volume came a shift toward producing works of greater length. Prior to 1775, only about 5% of all imprints contained at least 150 pages, but in the 1790s this figure more than doubled to 11% of all printed matter, of which nearly half comprised substantial books of 300 or more pages. In 1788, William Perry put out the earliest American-made dictionary at Worcester, Massachusetts. Two years later, in Philadelphia, Thomas Dobson began typesetting the first encyclopedia published in America, an eighteen-volume pirated version of the *Encyclopaedia Britannica* known as Dobson's *Encyclopaedia*. In 1796, there appeared the first complete edition of Shakespeare's plays printed in the United States.

Certain types of reading material served as the economic mainstay of eighteenth-century publishers. The largest category within these staples of the press comprised government documents, which included over a third of all imprints dating from 1774 to 1785. Next in importance were almanacs, which had the potential for enormous profitability if they developed a faithful following. Sales for Benjamin Franklin's *Poor Richard's Almanac* peaked at 10,000 annually. Legal handbooks for magistrates and sheriffs generated a regular, though not large cash flow. Schoolbooks rarely failed to turn a profit, if printed in modest editions, and a few even turned into roaring successes, as did Noah Webster's *Grammatical Institute of the English Language* . . . (1790), which reputedly sold 3,000,000 copies by 1803. Such standbys of the book trade normally would account for about 40% of late-eighteenth-century imprints.

The largest category of discretionary reading material produced in the United States concerned religion, although the percentage of imprints on theological subjects fell sharply after 1776. The next largest class of imprints concerned information useful to leaders in government on topics such as political affairs, geography, history, or military science. Books that helped prepare the upper class for public service represented about a fifth of all titles after 1765.

American publishers offered relatively little fiction for their customers to purchase. Literature and belles lettres formed just 4% of all works published between 1765 and 1785, in large part because widespread prejudice existed against using one's leisure to read for enjoyment rather than self-improvement. Even Thomas Jefferson, always an avid reader, criticized the "inordinate passion for novels." "When this poison infects the mind," he wrote, "the result is a bloated imagination, sickly judgment, and disgust towards all the real businesses of life." A widespread undercurrent of fascination nevertheless existed for novels, and printers began increasing their output of pirated English fiction after 1789. Following the earliest American reprint of a foreign novel—Samuel Richardson's *Pamela*—in 1744, the press offered just 56 editions of British fiction through 1788, but it flooded the country with 350 of them from 1789 to 1800.

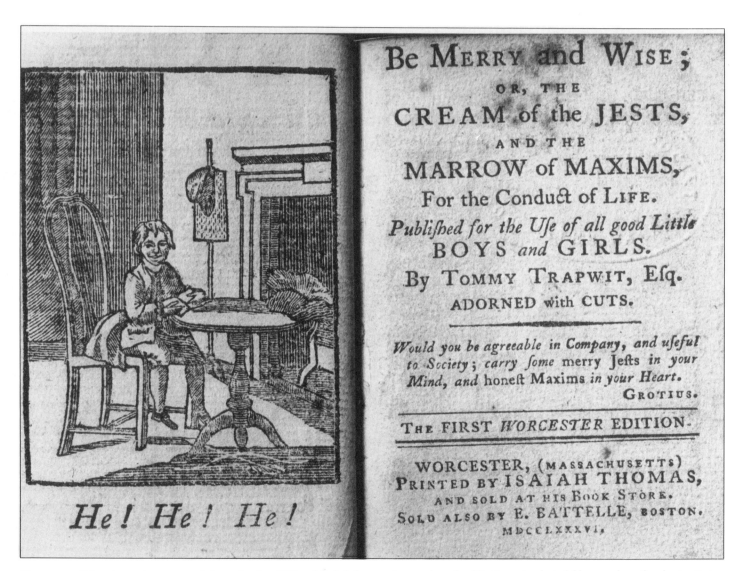

The output of American printers expanded greatly after 1780 and included a growing number of publications aimed at children, such as the classics *Mother Goose* and *Goody Twoshoes* from Isaiah Thomas's press. Tommy Trapwit's joke-book, complete with a woodcut of Master Trapwit drawing inspiration from his own work, is a reminder that some of childhood's pleasures are timeless. (Courtesy American Antiquarian Society)

TABLE 13.7 OUTPUT OF UNITED STATES PRINTERS, 1764–1800

Year	Number of Print Shops	Total Imprints[a]	% Equaling 150–299 Pages	% Exceeding 300 Pages
1800	. . .	2,604	5.3%	3.5%
1799	274	1,952	5.6%	4.9%
1798	. . .	2,300	5.3%	5.1%
1797	. . .	2,792	5.1%	4.2%
1796	. . .	1,280	12.7%	7.9%
1795	251	2,227	6.8%	5.2%
1794	. . .	2,061	6.9%	5.1%
1793	. . .	1,762	5.8%	3.5%
1792	. . .	1,398	5.6%	5.4%
1791	. . .	1,206	5.1%	5.0%
1790	126	1,136	4.0%	3.8%
1789	. . .	1,092	4.1%	3.9%
1788	. . .	941	4.6%	2.6%
1787	. . .	950	2.9%	1.9%
1786	. . .	985	3.5%	1.3%
1785	. . .	715	3.2%	1.4%
1784	73	737	3.0%	1.8%
1783	. . .	754	2.8%	1.7%
1782	. . .	593	2.5%	1.8%
1781	. . .	568	2.3%	1.2%
1780	61	574	1.4%	1.0%
1779	. . .	688	1.3%	1.3%
1778	. . .	664	.9%	1.2%
1777	. . .	705	1.8%	1.0%
1776	. . .	841	1.5%	1.0%
1775	56	1,119	1.0%	1.3%
1774	. . .	927	2.6%	2.5%
1773	. . .	625	3.4%	1.6%
1772	. . .	433	4.1%	1.8%
1771	. . .	455	3.1%	3.3%
1770	49	588	3.4%	1.2%
1769	. . .	547	2.4%	1.3%
1768	43	461	3.7%	1.5%
1767	. . .	382	3.1%	2.1%
1766	. . .	403	3.2%	1.5%
1765	. . .	421	3.3%	1.0%
1764	38	431	2.6%	1.8%

[a] An imprint is a separately typecast publication, but multivolume works and each year's run of newspapers count as one imprint.
Sources: Charles Evans, American Bibliography: A Chronological Dictionary of All Books, Pamphlets, and Periodical Publications Printed in the United States . . . 1630 . . . to . . . 1820, 12 vols. (1910), VI–XII. Roger P. Bristol, Supplement to Charles Evans' American Bibliography (1970). G. Thomas Tanselle, "Some Statistics on American Printing, 1764–1783," in Bernard Bailyn and John B. Hench, eds., The Press and the American Revolution (1980), 324.

TABLE 13.8 PERCENT OF IMPRINTS PRODUCED AT LEADING CITIES, 1768–1783

Year	Phila-delphia	Boston	New York	Provi-dence	Hart-ford	New Haven	New London
1783	30%	10%	7%	5%	4%	3%	2%
1780	22%	16%	6%	9%	8%	2%	2%
1777	28%	13%	5%	7%	4%	1%	3%
1774	22%	23%	18%	2%	3%	2%	2%
1771	32%	23%	10%	3%	3%	3%	4%
1768	15%	32%	13%	5%	3%	4%	4%

Source: G. Thomas Tanselle, "Some Statistics on American Printing, 1764–1783," in Bernard Bailyn and John B. Hench, eds., The Press and the American Revolution (1980), 337.

TABLE 13.9 SUBJECT MATTER OF IMPRINTS PUBLISHED IN UNITED STATES, 1765–1785

Category	1765–1773	1774–1778	1779–1785	Average
Government Documents	13.2%	34.6%	34.1%	27.3%
Theology	29.4%	9.9%	17.8%	19.1%
Political Science	11.3%	9.8%	11.4%	10.9%
Almanacs	9.4%	6.5%	6.8%	7.6%
History	10.1%	8.6%	4.7%	7.7%
Law	6.8%	5.2%	8.3%	6.8%
Literature	3.9%	4.6%	4.2%	4.2%
Social Science	4.9%	2.3%	4.4%	3.9%
Useful Arts[a]	2.7%	3.3%	3.8%	3.2%
In Foreign Languages	3.4%	2.8%	2.1%	2.8%
Biography	4.5%	1.5%	2.1%	2.7%

[a] Agriculture, theater, music, military and naval science.
Source: G. Thomas Tanselle, "Some Statistics on American Printing, 1764–1783," in Bernard Bailyn and John B. Hench, eds., The Press and the American Revolution (1980), 328–29.

By 1789, several factors encouraged American authors to write novels. Between 1783 and 1786, every state but Delaware vested authors with copyright protection for their works, and the federal government enacted its own statute in 1790. Authors thereafter had an important legal weapon to prevent their books from being pirated by unscrupulous printers. The influx of foreign fiction showed the prospects for commercial success to be more likely than before, while the rapid expansion of domestic publishers greatly multiplied the opportunities to get manuscripts before the public. These developments enabled authorship to emerge as a financially viable profession for the first time in American history.

America's premier novel, William Hill Brown's Power of Sympathy, imitated the conventions of British "sentimental" fiction when it appeared in 1789. The sentimental genre exploited romantic plots that usually cast a heroine trying to find true love while fending off the advances of unscrupulous seducers. In a country such as the United States, whose literary culture had long emphasized religiosity, practicality, or self-instruction, such works invited censure as frivolous at best and scandalous at worst. In 1797, for example, the magazine Monthly Mirror presented the essay "Novel Reading, a Cause of Female Depravity," which warned ominously that "those who first made novel-reading an indispensable branch in forming the minds of young women, have a great deal to answer for."

Sentimental novels did indeed target young, unmarried women as their audience. They portrayed young, spirited, attractive heroines confronting moral dilemmas during courtship. Such plots provided vicarious adventure and triumph, but they also gave their readers strong role models for character and shrewdness. Through the vehicle of intelligent female conversations on politics, law, or business, sentimental novels furthermore gave women a positive self-image as the intellectual equals of men. It is not surprising then that young women provided the primary market for the earliest American novels. "I have a family of three daughters," wrote a distraught mother in the opening volume of Lady's Magazine in 1792, "who are mad upon reading novels, and I can seldom prevail upon them to read anything else." In 1800, a Maryland mother tried to save her daughter from novels by forcing her to spend her spare time knitting, only to find herself presented with a sampler that read, "Patty Polk did this and she hated every stitch she did in it. She loves to read much more."

TABLE 13.10 FIRST EDITIONS AND BEST-SELLERS BY AMERICAN AUTHORS, 1789–1800

Year	Novels Printed	Best-Sellers (Editions Known to be Published)
1800	5[a]	. . .
1799	5[a]	. . .
1798	5	. . .
1797	8	Hannah Foster, *The Coquette* (30 eds. by 1840)
1796	. . .	. . .
1795	2	Anonymous, *The History of Constantius and Pulchrea* (9 eds. by 1831)
1794	3[a]	Susanna Rowson, *Charlotte: A Tale of Truth* (78 eds. by 1850)
1793	4[a]	Susanna Rowson, *The Fille de Chambre*[b] (6 eds. by 1831)
1792	1	Hugh Brackenridge, *Modern Chivalry*[c] (9 eds. by 1846)
1791	. . .	. . .
1790	. . .	. . .
1789	1	. . .

[a]One title printed in London.
[b]Retitled as *Rebecca; or the Fille de Chambre* in 1814.
[c]Published serially, 1792–1797.
Sources: Lillie D. Loshe, *The Early American Novel, 1789–1830* (1907), 106–10. Lyle H. Wright, "A Statistical Survey of American Fiction," *Huntington Library Quarterly* II (1938–9), 309–18.

Americans authored thirty-five novels from 1789 to 1800. The most commercially successful writers were Hannah Webster Foster, whose *Coquette* sold thirty editions from 1797 to 1840, and Susanna Haswell Rowson, whose *Charlotte: A Tale of Truth* sold 78 editions from 1794 to 1850. American authors produced far too little for the domestic market, however, and British novelists provided most of the books read in the United States long after 1800. Because British booksellers generally exported their less popular, unsold titles overseas, however, the authors most often read in America—Samuel Richardson, Henry Fielding, Laurence Sterne, and Henry Brooks—were not England's most popular writers, who were then Robert Bage, Ann Radcliffe, and Matthew "Monk" Lewis. The rising popularity of novels, both foreign and domestic, marked a decisive stage in American literary history, for it dramatically expanded the growth of the reading public and made possible the eventual appearance of the country's earliest full-time writers (such as James Fenimore Cooper) in the next generation.

Painting and Sculpture

The period 1763–1800 is notable for the international acclaim accorded to American painters. The first American to achieve fame in Europe was the Pennsylvania Quaker Benjamin West (1738–

Benjamin West's *Death of General Wolfe* (1771) became renowned as the finest specimen of historical painting of its time. The setting is the Battle for Quebec of 1759, and among the Americans portrayed by West are a ranger, an Indian, and the physician treating Wolfe, Dr. Thomas Hinde, who remained in the colonies and died in Newport, Kentucky. West's painting inspired many imitations, such as John Trumbull's *Death of General Montgomery.* (photo on page 240) (Courtesy William L. Clements Library, Ann Arbor, Michigan)

1820), who set up his studio in London in 1763. The exhibition of West's *Death of General Wolfe* (1771), a huge, panoramic masterpiece of heroic romanticism, won him lasting renown as Britain's greatest artist of the historical genre. West became court painter to George III the next year, and he succeeded Joshua Reynolds as president of the Royal Academy [of Painting] in 1792.

The reputation of John Singleton Copley (1738–1815) ranked just below that of West. A self-taught Massachusetts portrait-maker, he startled London's artistic circles in 1766 with his *Boy with Squirrel,* which gained him election to the Society of Artists of Great Britain the next year. In 1774 Copley left Boston for London, where he joined West at his studio, and three years later he gained admission to the Royal Academy. When premiered in 1780, Copley's *Death of Chatham* drew 20,000 paying visitors in six weeks, far more than attended a competing exhibition by the Royal Academy. Copley's *Death of Major Peirson* (1784), which George III reportedly studied for three straight hours, brought Copley to the height of his fame and resulted in commissions to paint the king's daughters.

European respect for American talent also increased due to the reputation of Patience Wright (1725–1786), who earned fame as the country's first major sculptor. A New Jersey Quaker, Wright had exhibited wax-works in Charles Town, Philadelphia, and New York before relocating to London in 1772. She achieved instantaneous recognition as the capital's most accurate sculptor and could afford to choose the commissions she cared to accept from the most exclusive levels of British society, including the royal family.

Studying with Benjamin West at London were several Americans who returned home to become the most distinguished painters of

This anonymous portrait of Miss [Matilda?] Denison of Stonington, Connecticut (about 1790) is characteristic of American folk painting. Offsetting a stiff pose, arms that appear too long, and hands that appear flat and limp, the face emerges as the work's focal point, gives a strong hint of personality through the eyes, and imparts a sense of charm by its modest smile. Folk artists often used birds or small animals for contrast, but this painter has overdone that motif by including both a bird and a squirrel. Compare this girl with squirrel with Copley's *Boy With Squirrel* (left). (Joseph Steward [probably], *Miss Denison of Stonington, Conn.* Gift of Edgar William and Bernice Chrysler Garbisch, c. 1993. National Gallery of Art, Washington)

John Singleton Copley's portrait of his half-brother Henry Pelham, *Boy With Squirrel* (1765), was the first truly great painting by an American and won the artist renown in London. Contrast its sophisticated style with the portrait of Matilda Denison (right). (Gift of the artist's great-granddaughter. Courtesy Museum of Fine Arts, Boston)

the early Republic. Charles Willson Peale (1741–1827), a former Maryland saddlemaker who rose to be Philadelphia's most noted portraitist and executed some of the best likenesses of the founding fathers, sired America's greatest dynasty of painters. The Rhode Islander Gilbert Stuart (1755–1828) achieved success in London between 1781 and 1793, but he returned to the United States and painted perhaps the most accurate likenesses of the republic's political leaders. John Trumbull (1756–1843), a Connecticut Yankee, became America's dean of historical painting through such masterpieces as *The Battle of Bunker's Hill* (1785), *Death of General Montgomery at Quebec* (1787), and *The Declaration of Independence* (1794).

The late eighteenth century also witnessed a sudden blooming of folk art in the countryside and small towns. A very common expression of popular culture evolved from individually designed samplers and quilts sewn to represent patriotic themes or embellish ethnic symbols. Quilt-making seems to have emerged as a highly creative outlet through which women could explore variations in design and coloration by the 1790s. Another folk craft that merged into art was shipcarving. Shipcarvers were half-tradesmen and half-artists whose figureheads often displayed imagination, ingenuity, and technical skill, especially those fashioned by the noted artisan William Rush (1756–1833).

Portraiture was the major form in which folk art expressed itself. Folk artists divided into the ranks of amateurs, who only painted for pleasure when they had leisure time, and professionals, who worked as artisans after learning elementary skills during brief periods of study with established painters. Because of their limited education, they often had to work out difficult problems unassisted, and they frequently resolved them by improvising unique solutions that imparted a distinctly personal style.

Revolutionary folk artists invariably rendered their subjects in static poses and flat or shadowless forms. Their work shows much awkwardness in rendering curved shapes, developing perspective, and depicting the human body accurately—aside from faces. Folk artists were familiar with contemporary conventions of portraiture (such as suggesting personality by symbolic embellishment, stock poses, and idealized scenery as background) and often incorporated those elements, although they were notably reluctant to employ sensuous imagery that might seem sexually suggestive. Despite these weaknesses, folk artists often executed works of surprising merit. By their curious juxtaposition of unbalanced shoulders, gangling arms, and grotesque hands, folk portraits frequently created fascinating compositions that focused attention irresistibly on the subject's face.

Unlike the American School of Benjamin West, folk artists did not paint on a grand scale. They instead portrayed life in a human dimension appropriate to the everyday life of their subjects. They showed middle-class citizens in rustic settings compatible with their everyday experiences and consequently provide a unique window to the past. Folk artists recorded a people who seem honest and straightforward, even as they assume stock poses or stare uncomfortably above disproportionate bodies. Their draftsmanship frequently appears poor in plasticity, proportion, or anatomy, but these drawbacks can be dramatically offset by a remarkable individuality of expression. As a result, the best folk paintings from the late eighteenth century convey a strong aesthetic flavor that combines simplicity, vibrancy, and power of expression.

Learned Societies

American learned societies developed in imitation of English organizations such as the Royal Society of London (for science), the Society of Antiquarians (for history), and the Society for the Encouragement of Arts, Manufactures and Commerce (for promoting practical inventions). The Royal Society's interests included the study of natural science in the western hemisphere, and it had afforded the colonists an opportunity to publish papers on natural science since the seventeenth century; it admitted nine residents of the thirteen colonies as members from 1764 to 1800. The Society of Arts also showed an interest in American affairs by offering cash prizes or honorary awards for entrepreneurial projects to develop colonial production of potash, hemp, silk, grapes, and olives. By 1775, forty-one colonists belonged to the Society of Arts.

Between 1769 and 1800, Americans founded five learned societies. Two of these, the Connecticut Society of Arts and Sciences and the New York Society for Promoting Useful Knowledge, never incorporated and disbanded before 1800 because of insufficient public support. Three others still remain in existence: the American Philosophical Society, the American Academy of Arts and Science, and the Massachusetts Historical Society. Among those founding the latter three were internationally known scientists, Benjamin Franklin, David Rittenhouse, and John Bartram—all of whom belonged to the Royal Society—and their early presidents included John Adams and

Thomas Jefferson. Membership in these three groups also overlapped.

In 1769, two rival groups of amateur scientists—the American Society Held at Philadelphia for Promoting and Propagating Useful Knowledge and the Philosophical Society—joined ranks to form the American Philosophical Society, Held at Philadelphia, for Promoting Useful Knowledge. (An earlier organization by the same name had briefly flourished in 1743–1744.) The founders included Benjamin Franklin, David Rittenhouse, John Bartram, Cadwallader Colden, John Dickinson, and Joseph Galloway. Restricting its focus to scientific pursuits, the society's first bylaws created these six committees on inquiry: 1. geography, mathematics, natural philosophy, and astronomy; 2. medicine and anatomy; 3. natural history and chemistry; 4. trade and commerce; 5. mechanics and agriculture; and 6. husbandry and American improvements. Regular publication of research reports began in 1771 with the first issue of the society's *Transactions*. The society not only organized its own library, but opened a museum in the 1790s. It normally elected fewer than thirteen new fellows yearly, but it sought out the most talented Americans regardless of residence, so that by 1790 its members lived in every state except New Hampshire and Rhode Island.

Having become familiar with the American Philosophical Society while at Philadelphia with the Continental Congress, John Adams envisioned creating a similar organization at Boston. Adams, James Bowdoin, James Sullivan, and James Winthrop formed the American Academy of Arts and Sciences at Boston in 1780. Their stated purpose was "to cultivate every art and science, which may tend to advance the interests, honour, dignity and happiness of a free, independent, and virtuous people." To accomplish this goal, the academy

TABLE 13.11   LEARNED SOCIETIES FOUNDED IN UNITED STATES, 1769–1800

	American Philosophical Society	American Academy of Arts and Sciences	Massachusetts Historical Society
Founded	Jan. 2, 1769	1780	Jan. 24, 1791
Chartered	Mar. 15, 1789	May 4, 1780	Feb. 19, 1794
Location	Philadelphia	Boston	Boston
Founders	Benjamin Franklin	John Adams	Jeremy Belknap
	David Rittenhouse	James Bowdoin	Rev. John Eliot
	John Bartram	James Sullivan	James Sullivan
	Cadwallader Colden	James Winthrop	Rev. Peter Thacher
	John Dickinson		William Tudor
			James Winthrop
Presidents	Benjamin Franklin	John Adams	James Sullivan
	1769–1790	1791–1814	1791–1808
	David Rittenhouse		
	1791–1796		
	Thomas Jefferson		
	1797–1815		

	Connecticut Society of Arts and Sciences	New York Society for Promoting Useful Knowledge
Founded	1786	1784
Chartered	no	no
Location	Hartford, New Haven[a]	New York
Founders	Ezra Stiles	Thomas Paine
		John Jay
		James Duane
Presidents	Oliver Wolcott	George Clinton
	1786	1784–1788
		John S. Hobart
		1788–?

[a] Met alternately at both

began publishing its *Memoirs* on a regular basis in 1785. By 1785, the academy had ninety members, who represented every New England state plus New Jersey, Philadelphia, and Virginia.

Two members of the academy, James Sullivan and James Winthrop, also gave strong support to Jeremy Belknap's efforts to organize an American equivalent to England's Society of Antiquarians. Under Belknap's leadership, Bostonians founded the Historical Society in 1791 (renamed the Massachusetts Historical Society when chartered by that state's legislature in 1794). It initially limited its membership at sixty, divided equally between Bostonians and correspondents living at a distance. The society articulated its purpose as "the preservation of books, pamphlets, manuscripts and records, containing historical facts, biographical anecdotes, temporary projects, and beneficial speculations." Belknap and his fellow antiquarians

began publishing the documents they rescued from family attics on a regular basis through their *Collections* series in 1792. The Massachusetts Historical Society inspired the founding of the New-York Historical Society in 1804 and the American Antiquarian Society in 1818.

Music

English folk traditions remained the dominant form of musical expression in the United States during the late eighteenth century. Among inherited English songs commonly heard in the colonies were "Chevy Chase," "Children in the Wood," "Spanish Lady," and "Lillibullero." It is a testament to the hold of English culture on Anglo-

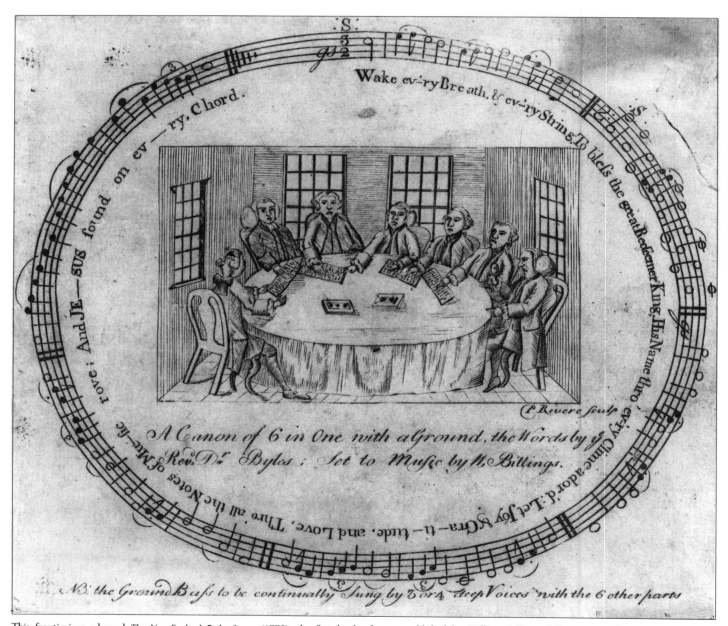

This frontispiece adorned *The New-England Psalm-Singer* (1770), the first book of songs published by William Billings. Billings was early America's premier composer of music, the leading figure in the movement to raise the standard of choral singing, and its most successful composer; he primarily wrote religious tunes. Not until the mid-eighteenth century would the American public begin to spend more money on secular than church music. (Courtesy William L. Clements Library, Ann Arbor, Michigan)

Americans that these ballads endured because their unusual length ("Chevy Chase" had almost a hundred stanzas) made them difficult to transmit across generations. Other popular tunes included many variants of the Robin Hood legend and doleful accounts of romances with tragic ends known as "love songs about murder."

The earliest authentic American voice in music emerged from New England psalm compositions. According to a 1782 index of vocal works by Americans, the most influential and prolific composer was William Billings, to whom were credited 226 of 264 religious songs of Yankee origin. Billings achieved this distinction despite serious handicaps. Born with a withered arm, he matured with legs of different lengths and went blind in one eye by 1790. Supporting himself as a leather tanner, street cleaner, and a hogreeve (town officer responsible for impounding stray hogs) in Boston, he sometimes startled his choir's sensibilities with the lingering odors of his tannery vats and brushes with truant hogs.

Billings began his publishing career in 1770 with *The New-England Psalm-Singer*. Many of his works were fugues, which Billings once described as "notes flying after each other, altho' not always after the same sound." His most famous composition, a patriotic march known as "Chester" that was popular with the Continental Army, rang out:

Let tyrants shake their iron rod,
And slavery clank her galling chains,
We fear them not, we trust in God,
New England's God forever reigns.

As choirmaster for several Boston congregations, Billings set an influential example in bringing polish and sophistication to the performance of church music. Billings fought the traditional New England belief that synchronized gospel singing smacked of Roman Catholicism and created new standards for choral performance. He fined members who came late for practice, blew a whistle so every participant could start on the same note, and invented a machine to beat out time so his singers could stay in rhythm. Although many of his followers sang no better than himself, which is to say they could do no more than bellow, Billings helped popularize hymns as a form of uplifting entertainment by infusing them with joy and energy. The hymns authored by Billings and lesser Yankee composers became a key component of the American folk tradition of shape-note choir singing that flowered immediately after 1800.

Concerts in the high tradition of European music also took root during the post-Revolutionary era. Every major city from Charleston to Boston acquired a cadre of trained instrumentalists who could entertain frequently. Americans favored composers popular in England, so scores by Handel and Haydn became standard events, especially their sacred music. In 1787, Philadelphia's Uranian Society (founded to improve church music) treated over 2,000 patrons to eighteenth-century America's greatest concert: a performance by 250 singers and a fifty-piece orchestra that capped a program of concertos, overtures, hymns, and anthems with Handel's "Hallelujah Chorus." By 1800, for the first time, the United States had developed a cultural infrastructure capable of supporting public programs of music by Baroque and early Classical composers on a regular basis.

TABLE 13.12   INNOVATIONS IN AMERICAN MUSICAL HISTORY, 1767–1796

1796	Third and fourth American-written operas performed at New York: *The Archers, or the Mountaineers of Switzerland* (libretto by William Dunlap, music by Benjamin Carr) and *Edwin and Angelina* (libretto by Elihu Smith, music by Victor Pelissier).
1794	The second American-authored opera, James Hewitt's *Tammany,* opened at New York on Mar. 3.
1791	The first opera house in New Orleans, Le Théâtre de St. Pierre, held its premier.
1790	Alexander Reinagle of Philadelphia composed the earliest known piano music written in the United States: four sonatas.
1790	The first U.S. singing contest pitted the Stoughton Musical Society against Dorchester's First Parish at Dorchester, Mass.
1789	John Friedrich Peter composed first American-authored music for strings: six quintets for two violins, two violas, and cello.
1788	Francis Hopkinson published the earliest American-composed secular songbook, his *Seven Songs for the Harpsichord or Forte Piano,* in Nov.
1786	First regularly-issued musical publication, Daniel Read's *American Musical Magazine,* appeared on Jan. 16 at New Haven.
1787	First pipe organ west of Allegheny Mountains built in Cookstown, Pa.
1774	First American pianoforte made at Philadelphia by John Behrent.
1771	David Propert gave first American piano concert at Boston.
1770	First performance in colonies of nearly-complete version of Handel's *Messiah* at Trinity Church, New York.
1769	First American harpsichord made (in Sep.) at Boston by John Harris.
1767	Andrew Barton published libretto to first American-written opera, *The Disappointment* (two acts), at New York City.

Sources: Richard B. Morris, *Encyclopedia of American History* (1961), 645–48. Kenneth Silverman, *A Cultural History of the American Revolution: Painting, Music, Literature, and the Theatre, from the Treaty of Paris to the Inauguration of George Washington, 1763–1789* (1976), 469–84, 587. Gilbert Chase, *America's Music: From the Pilgrims to the Present* (1992 ed.), 51–52.

CHAPTER 14 Science and Technology

Scientific endeavors during the Revolutionary era were closely associated with research on astronomy and natural history, the term that then comprehended botany and zoology. Science was absent from the standard college curriculum, except at medical schools, which were the only institutions that taught courses in natural history, botany, chemistry, or mineralogy. Since science was essentially a part-time avocation pursued by a few, largely self-educated, men of leisure, it is remarkable that anyone in the thirteen colonies could manage to do significant work in the natural or experimental sciences. Several Americans nevertheless managed to establish an international reputation for themselves (including Benjamin Franklin for his work on electricity, naturalists John and William Bartram, and astronomers John Winthrop IV and David Rittenhouse), and in 1775 six mainland colonists belonged to Britain's most elite scientific organization, the Royal Society. Americans primarily excelled as inventors, and during the late eighteenth century, they produced the first successful steamboat, an operational submarine, the first automated mill, and the cotton gin.

Astronomy

No area of scientific endeavor elicited wider interest among Anglo-Americans than astronomy. Sir Isaac Newton's portrayal of the solar system ranked as the most impressive achievement of that era's Scientific Revolution, and so most educated gentlemen felt obliged to acquire a rudimentary knowledge of the celestial bodies and their movements. Astronomical research also offered practical benefits, by lessening the margin of error in land surveys and marine navigation. More articles appeared in the publications of the American Philosophical Society and the American Academy of Arts and Sciences on astronomy than on any other subject.

Two men of exceptional ability conducted astronomical research during the late eighteenth century: John Winthrop (1714–1779) and David Rittenhouse (1732–1796). Both published numerous reports in scientific journals, acquired an international reputation, and became members of Britain's Royal Society. Winthrop was professor of mathematics and natural philosophy at Harvard; between 1739 and 1779, he authored many significant articles on sunspots, planetary transits across the Sun's face, lunar eclipses, and Halley's Comet. Rittenhouse was a self-taught prodigy who built clocks and optical instruments at Philadelphia; he first won fame in 1767 for making a mechanical planetarium, or orrery, that depicted planetary orbits over a 5,000-year period with less than one degree's margin of error, which was far more accurate than any such device that had yet been produced in Europe.

The first major chance for astronomers in the thirteen colonies to prove their collective competence came on June 3, 1769, during the Transit of Venus, when that planet created an eclipse while passing between the Earth and the Sun. Among the rarest of solar phenomena, transits of Venus gave observers the chance to work out the Earth's exact parallax angle with the Sun and verify estimates of the Earth's orbit. Measuring the transit of 1769 became that century's greatest example of international cooperation in science, and numerous expeditions set sail from Europe to record the event.

The transit sparked enormous interest among British colonists. Despite the difficulty of collecting suitable instruments for the project (only Harvard had owned a telescope appropriate for viewing this event before 1768), Americans organized twenty-two stations to take readings, of which the American Philosophical Society sent out

half. Winthrop and Rittenhouse collected data separately, and with extreme care, but the quality of the other observations varied greatly according to the participants' experience and the instruments' precision. Most of the observations became known to the public through the American Philosophical Society's printed *Transactions*. Rittenhouse's figures allowed him to calculate the Earth's distance from the Sun to be 93,000,000 miles, approximately the same as twentieth-century estimates.

Europeans praised the sophistication and care with which most Americans had recorded the Transit of 1769. The French scientist Jean Bernoulli praised the American Philosophical Society on the comprehensiveness of its reports, which he declared to be "well worthy of imitation by those European astronomers who are so sparing of detail and who speak only in general terms of their instruments and their observations." "No astronomers could better deserve all possible encouragement," pronounced the *Gentleman's Magazine* in September 1771, "whether we consider their care and diligence in making the observations, their fidelity in relating what was done, or the clearness and accuracy of their reasonings on this curious and difficult subject." American science had won its first significant measure of international recognition.

After the Transit of Venus, the most important celestial event reported by Americans was the solar eclipse of October 27, 1780. The newly formed American Academy of Arts and Sciences dispatched an expedition under Samuel Williams to Penobscot Bay, Maine, where the Moon's shadow would completely obscure the Sun. With permission from the British, who then occupied the region, Williams fixed his camp just outside the region of total obscuration, evidently due to the poor quality of his map. His error nevertheless had a fortunate consequence because the party could then discern the finest line of light on the Sun's edge as it broke up into tiny drops or beads of light. Williams was the first scientist to publish a report on this phenomenon, now known as Bailey's beads.

The most active astronomer in post-Revolutionary America was David Rittenhouse. Although deeply involved in public service as Pennsylvania's treasurer and surveyor, he made the first sighting of Uranus by an American in 1781, kept a daily record of noteworthy events in the Solar System from 1788 to 1796, and published many reports on planetary transits, comets, and eclipses. He also developed technical innovations to improve telescopic accuracy such as using spiderwebs for crosshairs and devising lenses that made far more accurate adjustments for line of sight. Rittenhouse corresponded with prominent European astronomers such as Joseph Laland and Franz von Zach, both of whom incorporated his data on 1791's solar eclipse and the Sun's meridian time into their own published books.

For most of the eighteenth century, it was still possible for self-taught scientists using rather unsophisticated tools to make noteworthy astronomical observations. This circumstance enabled a few American part-time scientists—mostly professors, instrument makers, surveyors, and leisured gentlemen—to win international recognition for their research into celestial phenomena. The development of more powerful telescopes, both reflecting and refracting, transformed astronomy into a science requiring the sort of sophisticated optical equipment used by William Herschel to discover Uranus in 1781. Because such telescopes lay beyond the financial means of individual scientists, American atronomers soon found themselves without the technical tools to do path-breaking work. Plans by the American Philosophical Society to establish an observatory at Philadelphia never materialized because of the prohibitive costs. Calls for the federal government to build a national observatory also fell on deaf ears. Until Yale acquired the country's first modern telescope in 1828, Americans lacked the technology to advance the science of celestial mechanics, and the country produced no one whose international stature could rival that enjoyed by Rittenhouse and Winthrop at the height of their fame between 1768 and 1796.

Botany and Zoology

In 1789, Thomas Jefferson outlined the contemporary state of knowledge regarding the country's flora and fauna in a letter to Harvard's president. "The botany of America is far from being exhausted; it's Mineralogy is untouched, and it's Natural history or Zoology totally mistaken and misrepresented," he wrote. "It is the work to which the young men, whom you are forming, should lay their hands." There were few naturalists to carry on the task of cataloguing the continent's vegetation and wildlife, however, and they found it difficult to interrupt their occupations to perform research in the field. Progress came slowly as isolated, part-time scientists conducted intensive studies near home and relayed their findings to fellow naturalists in the United States and Europe.

None of the colonial era's important naturalists survived the Revolution. John Clayton, author of *Flora Virginica,* died in 1774. Cadwallader Colden and John Bartram, both founding fathers of the American Philosophical Society, died in 1776 and 1777, respectively. Alexander Garden, member of the Royal Society and an implacable Tory, left South Carolina and returned to England. In their place arose a new generation of naturalists led by William Bartram (1739–1823), Manasseh Cutler (1742–1823), Samuel Latham Mitchill (1764–1831), and Henry Muhlenberg (1753–1815).

John and William Bartram were the only scientists who traveled extensively to collect botanical material. Having accompanied his father John from North Carolina to Florida during 1765 and 1766, William rambled alone from Cape Fear in North Carolina to the Mississippi River from March 1773 to January 1777. After his father died in 1777, William found himself bereft of the patronage needed to finance field work and beset by creditors. Since his forte was

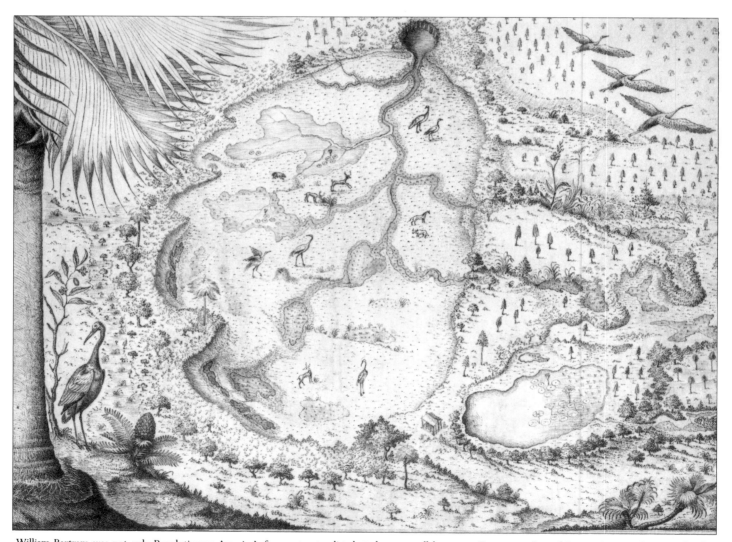

William Bartram was not only Revolutionary America's foremost naturalist, but also was well known to Europeans. One of Bartram's more elaborate sketches is this view, which he titled *The Great Alachua Savanna, in East Florida.* The savannah was 60 miles in circumference, about 100 miles west from St. Augustine, and 45 miles west of the St. Johns River. (Courtesy American Philosophical Society)

collecting specimens, rather than classifying data, William's talents could only blossom in the wilderness. The younger Bartram continued cultivating his father's botanical garden—the best in North America—distributed seeds to other naturalists, and kept in contact with European scientists, but his talents languished for the rest of his career while he remained trapped in Philadelphia's civilized society.

Bartram's listlessness deprived the scientific world of full access to his specimens, sketches, and journals until 1791, when they were published as *Travels Through North and South Carolina, Georgia, East and West Florida.* Bartram provided a wealth of new information on both vegetation and wildlife. His commentary on reptiles and amphibians had no parallel at that time, and American ornithology is considered to have begun with his catalogue of 215 species of birds. Bartram's *Travels* exercised enormous influence after 1791 and went through numerous editions at home and abroad.

Nothing of significance appeared in print on the vegetation of New England until 1785, when Manasseh Cutler authored a botanical arrangement of the region's flora: "An Account of Some of the Vegetable Productions, Naturally Growing in this Part of America, Botanically Arranged." Compared to the rest of America, little was known about plant life in New England, where Cutler observed "that Botany has never been taught in any of our Colleges." Cutler's monograph was the first systematic survey of botany published about the northeastern United States, and it brought the self-taught scientist much acclaim for its thoroughness and familiarity with the best contemporary scholarship. Cutler continued gathering specimens for a complete botany of New England and corresponded with leading European naturalists, but he found himself constantly distracted by his political and business activities. He abandoned all hope of writing a definitive description of New England plants during his retirement in 1812, when he was seventy, after a fire consumed most of the materials he had accumulated over the course of his lifetime.

Botany and zoology first entered the college curriculum during the Revolutionary period as part of the instruction given medical students. Adam Kuhn offered the earliest course in botany at the College of Philadelphia in 1768. It was through professorships of natural history on medical faculties that botany and zoology became an accepted part of academic life. Shortly after his appointment as Columbia University's professor of natural history in 1792, Samuel Latham Mitchill emerged as the country's foremost zoologist. Once described as "a chaos of knowledge," Mitchill turned out a stream of publications ranging from insects to dissecting skunks, but he was primarily known for his work on the fish of New York State, to which he devoted a quarter-century of his life after 1789.

Of all the post-Revolutionary naturalists, none ultimately accomplished more in the areas of cataloguing and description than the botanist Henry Muhlenberg, a Lutheran minister in Lancaster, Pennsylvania, and later president of Franklin College. Heeding his father's advice "not to buy a large library, but to read the book of nature," Muhlenberg began teaching himself the techniques of species classification and field observation during the Revolution. Muhlenberg eventually identified 1,380 separate plants in the vicinity of Lancaster; he accumulated a sizeable scientific library, and created the country's largest herbarium (over 5,000 specimens) before he died. He corresponded with every major botanist in the United States and Europe. Muhlenberg endeavored to catalogue the flora of North America; he finally completed this task in 1815, when he published *A Catalogue of the Hitherto Unknown and Naturalized Plants of North America,* which listed 853 genera of plants and approximately 3,670 species. Muhlenberg's magnum opus was the first botanical codex of American flora since that of Carolus Linnaeus, whose list of American plants had barley numbered 2,000 species, and it marked the high point of natural history in the early United States.

Chemistry and Physics

Although America's scientific community produced a few men who achieved foreign recognition for their work in the observational sciences of astronomy, botany, and zoology, it failed to make any equivalent contributions in the experimental fields of chemistry and physics between 1763 and 1800. The primary accomplishment of chemists and physicists was to absorb the latest scientific advances from Europe and disseminate them within the country. Chemistry first attained academic recognition in medical education. In 1769, Dr. Benjamin Rush became the country's first professor of chemistry in the College of Philadelphia's medical faculty, and Dr. James Smith assumed that title at King's College soon after. No professorships of physics existed before 1800.

While some potentially useful experimentation was conducted within the United States from 1763 to 1800, none of it compared remotely to Benjamin Franklin's work on electrical theory between 1747 and 1752, which constituted the best experimental science done in early America. Electricity remained a major focus of American physicists, who were particularly fascinated with how certain eels generated and transmitted electric charges, a phenomenon they never fully explained. The most important publication on electricity was David Rittenhouse's report on the magnetization of steel, in which he outlined a molecular theory that presumed an atomic structure within steel controlled by the attraction of positive and negative forces; similar ideas were current as Rittenhouse wrote, but no scientist had ever described them as lucidly as he did in 1786.

American scientists also conducted experiments and theorized about the nature of light. Benjamin Franklin broke with Sir Isaac Newton's conception of light as a stream of particles emitted from a source, and hypothesized that light moved in waves. David Rittenhouse constructed a primitive spectroscope that dispersed rays of light according to the principles of diffraction grating, which produced results incompatible with Newton's corpuscular theory, but he abandoned this line of inquiry before he could realize that Newton's theory was in error. Like Rittenhouse, most Americans were predisposed to accept Newton's explanation of light as a hail of particles, and scientists did not vindicate Franklin's theory of light as a pulsating ray until the 1820s.

In contrast to the gradual evolution of theoretical and experimental physics during the late eighteenth century, chemistry underwent a conceptual revolution. In 1783—after centuries of deference to Aristotle's dictum that all physical matter divided into four basic substances of earth, water, air, and fire—Antoine Lavoisier introduced the modern nomenclature of chemical elements and redefined this discipline as the quantitative analysis of how these elements combined to build molecular structures. Lavoisier's reformulation of chemistry influenced the United States almost immediately; by 1788 it had entered the curriculum of Harvard's medical program. Samuel Latham Mitchill authored the first book-length summary of the French School by an American academic in 1794 in his *Nomenclature of the New Chemistry.*

Not all Americans accepted the French School uncritically. Thomas Jefferson expressed skepticism about Lavoisier's theories as early as 1788. Joseph Priestley, who ranked as the most famous chemist in the United States after leaving England in 1794, railed against Lavoisier's ideas until his death in 1804, but his attacks on the new chemistry failed to prevent its rapid acceptance in the United States. The controversy between Priestley and Lavoisier's American disciples, though short-lived, was a noteworthy sign of intellectual progress, for it marked the first occasion when Americans actively joined in an international debate on a major scientific controversy.

Cartography and Earth Sciences

During the eighteenth century, geography comprehended several fields that would later emerge as separate disciplines in the earth sciences. Westward expansion and national independence inevitably stimulated research on mapmaking and its related topics. The years after 1763 saw not only the rapid improvement of cartography, but also the beginnings of field work on hydrography, geology, and mineralogy.

As the colonial period ended, exploring, surveying, mapmaking, and charting the coast proceeded with renewed energy. Between 1763 and 1768, Charles Mason and Jeremiah Dixon made the first exact longitudinal determinations for many points between the Delaware and Monongahela rivers while marking the border of Pennsylvania and Maryland, which thereafter became known as the Mason-Dixon Line and passed into the language as a metaphor expressing the cultural differences between North and South. A less famous expedition ran the boundary between New York and New Jersey in the 1770s. The British Admiralty Department completed the earliest survey of Florida's harbors and Atlantic coastline from 1764 to 1772, during which time its cartographers wrote some of the earliest reports about the hydrography of Florida.

The best-informed cartographer of this period was Thomas Hutchins, a New Jersey native who served as a British army officer. Hutchins became the chief authority on western territories while charting the Ohio River and much of the Illinois country in 1766, after which he aided with surveys in the Southeast. In 1778, his *Topographical Description of Virginia, Pennsylvania, Maryland, and North Carolina* appeared, with maps and elementary information about mineralogy and geology. It was followed six years later by his *Historical Narrative and Topographical Description of Louisiana and West-Florida.* Hutchins left the British service and became the Continental Army's expert on geographical intelligence until he became geographer-general for the United States in 1781. Assigned to survey the national domain's initial ranges in the Northwest Territory, he failed to complete a projected general topographical account of the United States before his death in 1789.

The last great accomplishment of eighteenth-century cartography was the delineation of the nation's southern boundary with Spanish Florida along the thirty-first parallel of latitude from the Mississippi to the Atlantic coast. Andrew Ellicott, who succeeded Hutchins as geographer-general, supervised the survey. A demanding Quaker who believed that "observations accurately made never become obsolete," Ellicott trudged through forests, swamps, and flooded rivers from 1798 to 1800. Not content to perform a mere survey, Ellicott took copious notes on the terrain, waterways, and natural resources so that his journal, when published in 1803, added to the country's stock of information on mineralogy and hydrography.

Knowledge of geology progressed slowly during the eighteenth century because both Europeans and Americans spent far more effort speculating about how the Earth's crust formed than in conducting field research on minerals, rock formations, and terrain features. No agreement existed on how the planet originated or the length of that process. Biblical accounts of the world's creation and later inundation by the great flood remained a plausible model for the planet's evolution to many scientists. For example, Samuel Morse, the very learned author of *The American Geography* (1783), accepted contemporary estimates based on the Book of Genesis that just sixteen centuries passed from the "chaotic state" of the Earth's creation to Noah's time, and that the great mountain chains were the residue of free-floating debris that was deposited unevenly during the great deluge.

One of the earliest proponents of a non-scriptural explanation for the earth's evolution was American cartographer Lewis Evans, whose journal was first published in 1776. Evans had investigated a bank of shells near London, Maryland that was being fossilized by stages in three levels comprised of loose sand, sandy clay, and hard clay solidifying into rock; he hypothesized that a similar cycle of petrification had produced the different strata of rock, containing seashells and other fossils of water life, that he had seen high above sea level in the mountains. Evans was unaware of how drastic changes in the oceans' depth could explain the presence of aquatic life at those elevations, but he correctly assumed that mammoth geologic formations such as mountain ranges and river gorges could not have been formed within a chronology based on a literal reading of the Book of Genesis. Although not a geologist, Evans had devised a strikingly modern theory about how sedimentation occurred on the Earth's surface.

The most comprehensive geological study of the Revolutionary era was written by Johann David Schoepf. Schoepf first saw America as a doctor in a Hessian regiment. After returning in 1784 to spend eight months of field work between New York and South Carolina, had published his *Geology of Eastern North America* in 1787 at Erlangen, Germany. Schoepf improved upon earlier delineations of the boundary between the Atlantic coastal plain and piedmont, recognized that the Allegheny Plateau was a vast highland plain rather than a true range of mountains, and mapped the main belts of bedrock underlying the soil. Schoepf's exemplary research appeared only in German and was little known to scientists in the United States.

It was Samuel Latham Mitchill who emerged as the father of American geology in 1797 when he published his *Sketch of the Mineralogical and Geological History of the State of New York*. This seminal work divided the country's terrain into granitic, sandstone, calcareous, and alluvial regions based upon their rock formations, and then described their relations to each other. Mitchill's work had particular value because his familiarity with European research on geology allowed him to avoid explanations that had been discredited and to appreciate the significance of many natural phenomena that Americans had long misunderstood. It was Mitchill who provided an American model that could be followed to produce extensive and well-organized accounts of the geology of the United States. Although none of the research done in the United States ranked with the scholarship of European geologists and mineralogists by 1800, Mitchill had lain the foundation for his compatriots to make useful contribution in these disciplines.

Inventions

When the colonial period ended, the technology and economy of Anglo-America was rude, crude, and inefficient. Water-power provided the only source of energy for driving machinery. Ships depended entirely on wind or oars for propulsion. Farming and manufacturing remained so heavily labor-intensive that neither could achieve any significant gains in productivity. Within the short span of a quarter-century, however, a handful of Yankee inventors inaugurated a new era by devising machines and technical processes that made possible the advent of steam-powered transport, the Industrial Revolution, and the mechanization of agriculture.

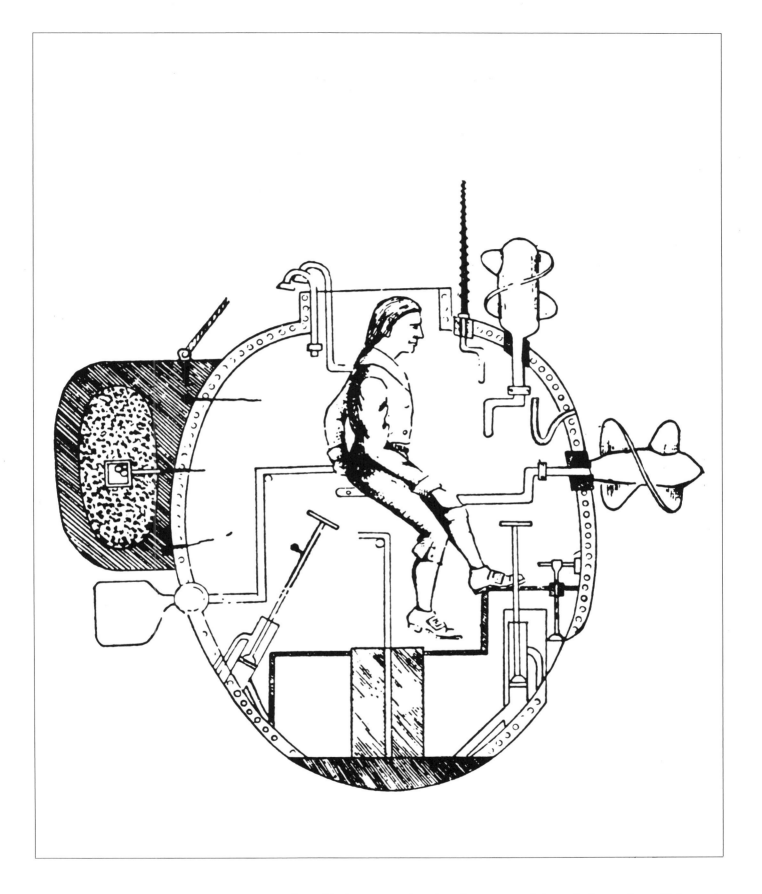

David Bushnell, a Connecticut Yankee, designed and built the world's first operational combat submarine. Named the *Turtle,* this vessel resembled a wooden shell and was large enough for a single crewman to submerge it by cranking a propeller on top and then guide it by another propeller to his front. (Courtesy Library of Congress)

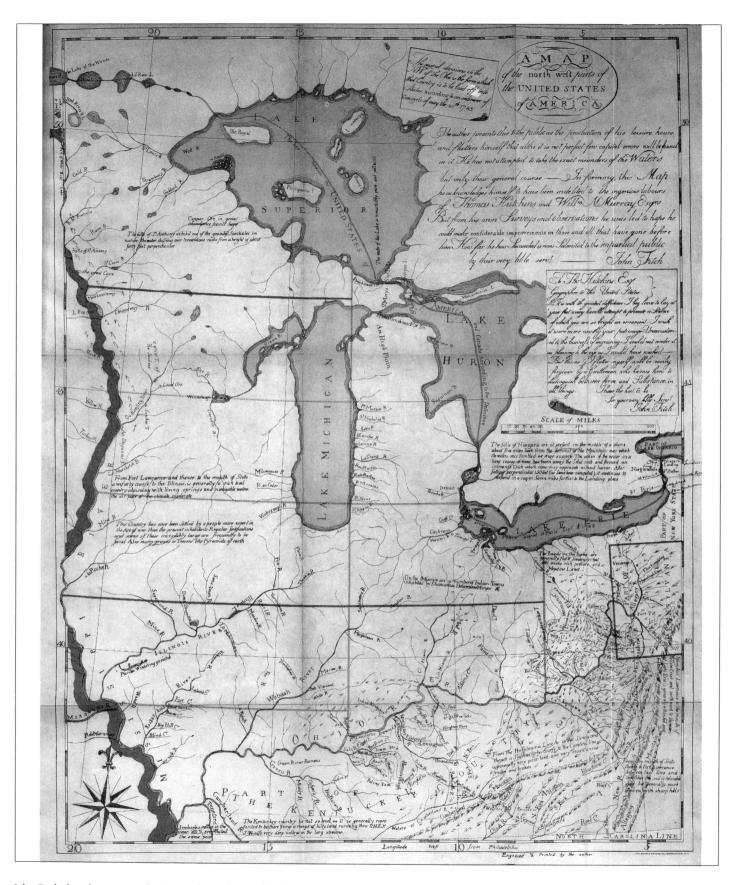

John Fitch, best known as a developer of steamboat technology, published this map of the Northwest Territory in 1785. Fitch based his work on an earlier map by Thomas Hutchins—which was superior in quality to Fitch's copy. Fitch's depiction of the Great Lakes, and to a lesser extent the Ohio River, demonstrates that cartographic accuracy still eluded early America's mapmakers. (Courtesy Geography and Map Division, Library of Congress)

A notable innovation signaled the start of a revolution in waterborne transport. In 1776, a young Yale man named David Bushnell built the world's first combat submarine, the *Turtle*. Measuring 7.5 feet long and 6 feet tall, the *Turtle* held a single crewman who cranked the first screw propeller known to be used in navigation. Sergeant Ezra Lee conducted its only attack, on the British warship *Eagle* in New York Harbor, but he was unable to complete his mission because the *Turtle* lacked sufficient mass to provide the necessary pressure for Lee to screw a bomb to the *Eagle*'s hull. Bushnell then abandoned submarine warfare and created floating mines that sank several enemy ships.

Another historic—and premature—leap forward came in 1787 when Connecticut-born John Fitch launched the world's first successful trial of a full-sized, steam-powered boat, the *Perseverance,* at Philadelphia. In August, with Fitch at the helm, the 45-foot ship and

its 7-ton engine reached speeds up to 4 miles per hour on the Delaware River. Fitch later operated the boat commercially between Philadelphia and Trenton, but his venture went bankrupt. Depressed by financial failure, Fitch later killed himself with an overdose of opium pills at Bardstown, Kentucky, in 1798. Less than a decade afterward, Robert Fulton built the first commercially successful steamboat on the Hudson River.

Although the application of steam power to manufacturing would not develop until much later, American inventors pioneered other techniques that greatly improved industrial efficiency. Between 1777 and 1785, Oliver Evans devised machinery to operate the world's first fully automated mechanical mill, in this instance for grinding flour. Evans went on to experiment with applying steam power to manufacturing, and by 1787 he had produced America's earliest noncondensing, high-pressure steam engine. Starting in 1798, Eli Whit-

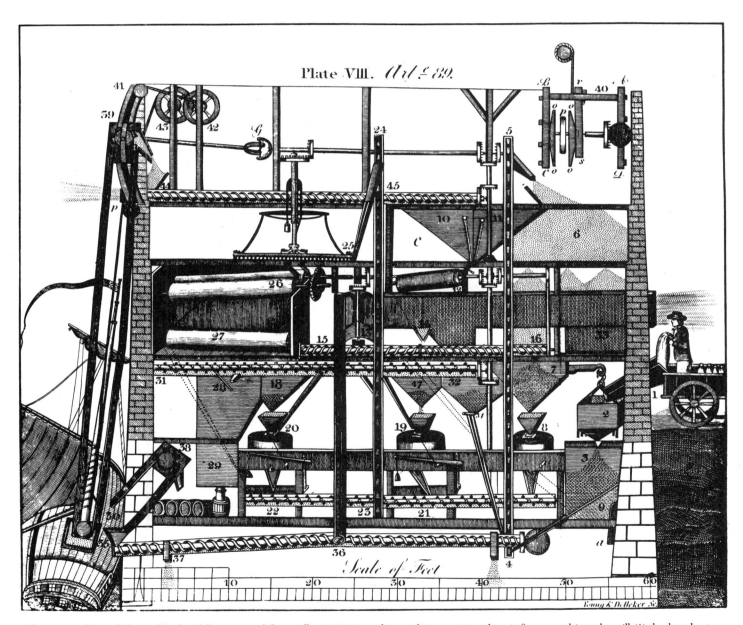

Oliver Evans designed the world's first fully automated flour mill in 1785. According to this engraving, wheat is first poured into the mill (1); bucket elevators (39, 24, 5) carry the grain and flour vertically; screw devices carry flour horizontally (37, 21, 31, 15, 45); and the automatic hopper boy (to spread and dry the meal) is shown at 25. (Courtesy Library of Congress)

TABLE 14.1 SIGNIFICANT INVENTIONS DEVELOPED IN UNITED STATES, 1775–1799

Year	Inventor	Location	Invention
1799	Elikim Spooner	. . .	Seeding machine
1798	Eli Whitney	Conn.	Jig to guide tools in making interchangeable parts
1797	Charles Newbold	N.J.	Cast-iron plow
1793	Thomas Jefferson	Va.	Improved mold-board plow
1793	Eli Whitney	Ga.	Cotton gin
1790	Jacob Perkins	Mass.	Nail-making machine
1790	Samuel Hopkins	Vt.	Potash-making process[a]
1787	John Fitch	Pa.	Steamboat
1787	Oliver Evans	Pa.	Noncondensing, high-pressure steam engine
1787	Oliver Evans	Pa.	Wool-card manufacturer
1785	Oliver Evans	Pa.	Fully automated flour mill
1783	Benjamin Franklin	Pa.	Bifocal spectacles
1783	John Stevens	N.J.	Multitibular boiler
1775	David Bushnell	N.Y.	Submarine

[a] First patent issued by U.S., Apr. 10, 1790.
Source: Richard B. Morris, ed., *Encyclopedia of American History* (1961 ed.), 565.

ney made the earliest attempts to raise factory productivity by manufacturing interchangeable parts at his Connecticut gunworks.

The first major application of mechanical technology in farming was also owed to Eli Whitney's genius. In 1793, while residing on a Georgia plantation, he perfected a cleverly simple machine that pulled cotton fiber with a wire-toothed cylinder through a fine iron grid that was too narrow for the seeds to follow. This cotton gin suddenly made large-scale cotton cultivation profitable and revolutionized Southern agriculture.

TABLE 14.2 PATENTS ISSUED FOR INVENTIONS IN UNITED STATES, 1790–1800

Year	Patents	Year	Patents
1800	41	1794	22
1799	44	1793	20
1798	28	1792	11
1797	51	1791	33
1796	44	1790	3
1795	12	1790–1800	309

Source: Bureau of the Census, *Historical Statistics of the United States: Colonial Times to 1957* (1961), 608.

John Fitch, Oliver Evans, and Eli Whitney all experienced great difficulty in preventing others from pirating their ideas. This situation improved after the United States began issuing patents on inventions on April 10, 1790, although patentees still faced problems in enforcing their rights to royalties. From 1790 to 1861, patents conveyed exclusive rights for 14 years and could not be renewed. The only ground for denying a patent was lack of novelty until 1836, when the government began making applicants demonstrate that their inventions were both original and had useful purposes.

By 1800, American inventors had made several key discoveries that would have profound economic ramifications during the next century. They had begun to harness steam power for water transport and industrial output. They had experimented with mass production

of interchangeable parts and designed the earliest prototype of an automated factory. They had introduced the first significant labor-saving machinery into agriculture. Under the sponsorship of the U.S. Patent Office, Americans had begun to unleash a flood of inventions that would revolutionize industry and transportation.

Scientific Exhibitions

Prior to the Revolutionary era, the few museums in the thirteen colonies had been little more than modest collections of natural history and scientific instruments at several libraries in Newport, Rhode Island; Philadelphia; Charles Town, South Carolina; and Harvard College at Cambridge, Massachusetts. Such exhibitions usually consisted of motley collections of curiosities assembled absentmindedly and shown in glass cabinets. Only after 1770 did museums evolve into separate institutions designed for disseminating scientific knowledge to a broad public audience. In 1774 at Philadelphia, Abraham Chovet opened a short-lived waxworks depicting the human body's internal structure at various ages and the effects of disease on organs. In 1782, at Philadelphia, Pierre du Simitière founded his American Museum, which housed an eclectic assortment of coins, illustrations, archaeological artifacts, fossils, and freakish animals preserved in alcohol.

When the American Museum closed in 1784, Charles Willson Peale bought most of its natural-history collections. Peale used them as the foundation for the first museum worthy of that name at Philadelphia in 1784. He lured paying customers with the promise of seeing a "collection of preserved beasts, birds, fish, reptiles, insects, fossils, minerals, [and] petrifications." Peale acquired many other specimens, including one of Benjamin Franklin's pet cats (a French Angora). Peale later added a mastodon skeleton that he had personally excavated in New York, and he gave the first showing of materials from the Lewis and Clark expedition.

Peale's exhibits proved financially remunerative—partly because he catered to the public's taste for showmanship and freaks—and his success inspired others to follow his example. In the spring of 1790, Robert Leslie opened a museum of technology that displayed models of manufacturing machines, such as Oliver Evans's fully automated flour mill; he operated the venture successfully until 1793, when he embarked on an extended business trip to England. Gardner Baker initiated another pioneer museum at New York in 1789. This institution, the American Museum of the Tammany Society, exhibited items concerning both natural history and technology, such as a guillotine and wax figure of a beheaded victim, an air gun, a model of a horse-drawn threshing machine, accidents of birth such as a two-headed lamb, and a large assortment of stuffed and live birds, animals, and reptiles; it remained open under a succession of owners until P. T. Barnum bought it in 1853.

Proposals to found a national scientific museum arose as early as 1788, when the *Pennsylvania Gazette* printed an anonymous essay advocating government support for a national university, a science museum, and a botanical garden. The United States took a small step in this direction before 1800 by creating a public display of patent models at the capital, often referred to as the American Museum of [Scientific] Arts. This American Museum became the forerunner of, and ultimate inspiration for, the Smithsonian Institution when it was founded in 1858.

CHAPTER 15 Architecture

Two architectural traditions coexisted within Revolutionary America. The best known of these two was the high style, which was the predominant form of design used for public buildings and elegant mansions. The other tradition was that of folk housing, which expressed itself in varied regional and ethnic patterns. Both styles evolved in subtle ways during the late eighteenth century. Formal architecture self-consciously adopted classical motifs associated with the Roman Republic in a fashion now termed Late Georgian or Early Federal. Folk housing gradually borrowed features characteristic of the Georgian style to provide more symmetry in both exterior design and interior use of space.

Post-Revolutionary architecture remained fundamentally similar to the Georgian style of the colonial era, which had originated in England and appeared in America after 1740. The Georgian tradition expressed balance and order through a building's structural outline and the relationship of windows to doors; its archetypal design imposed a sense of visual harmony through the use of proportion and spacing. Because its length, width, and height were roughly equal, the classic Georgian house resembled a cube. Its squared dimensions facilitated the symmetrical division of interior space into eight rooms

This classic Georgian home was built about 1773 for William Corbit, along Appquinimink Creek, near Odessa, Delaware. Although modified by twentieth-century restoration, it remains essentially the same as when it was completed before the Revolution. (Courtesy National Images of North American Living, Research and Archival Center, Washington)

of equal size: two rooms wide, two rooms deep, and two stories high. By spacing an identical number of windows on each side of a central doorway, the building's face reinforced the sense of equilibrium created by the building's cubelike dimensions. A four-sided roof rising to a platform best accentuated the sense of squared proportions and was preferred to gabled covering.

A huge gap separated the refined world of formal architecture from folk housing. Of 576,616 residences inspected for a special federal tax assessment in 1798, the most elegant dwelling recorded was a three-story mansion in Salem, Massachusetts that held 15 rooms in its 8,757 square feet; its valuation exceeded $30,000. The typical American family occupied a one-story home with less than 500 square feet that had been divided into two or three rooms (not counting a loft used for sleeping and storage), which was made of wood frame and worth about $135. If housing for whites was rudimentary, the quarters allocated to slaves were truly crude. Slaves were the only class of Americans ordinarily found living in one-room log cabins, which rarely exceeded 12 feet square (less than a third the size of most white residences).

Although cramped by modern standards, the average eighteenth-century house suited the basic needs of an agricultural population. Farmers and their children considered the "out-of-doors" to be their natural habitat, and they became hardened to seasonal changes through long exposure to the elements. Farm wives also spent most of their hours outside the house managing their vegetable patch or tending to barnyard animals and poultry, besides doing a majority of their food preparation, washing, and needlework in the open air. Early Americans viewed the confined quarters of their dark and musty cabins primarily as a place to sleep and a temporary refuge from inclement weather. Only as American society urbanized would the assumption take hold that it was normal to spend extended periods of time indoors when good weather prevailed outside.

Eighteenth-century folk housing provided very little individual space for family members, but early Americans seem to have assumed that privacy was best sought outside the house rather than indoors. Prior to 1800, the population devised simple, unspoken routines to lead modest lives in the absence of rigid physical privacy. Modesty dictated that husband and wife have some secluded space—invariably a separate room—but other family members felt entirely comfortable sleeping together in a common bed. Modesty also dictated that each sex bathe separately and give the other regular opportunities to make complete changes of clothes. Travelers' accounts indicate that while the spectrum of family behavior may have ranged from prim to earthy, the great majority led decorous lives.

The absence of private spheres and segregated social spaces in folk housing created an eclectic, spontaneous, and hospitable environment. When thrown together at evening or during bad weather, family members learned how to relax while sharing a confined space with several other people and how to concentrate on an individual task within a group of people carrying on multiple activities. Since all rooms within a typical house opened directly upon one another, and family members routinely tramped through them on various errands, occupants of any room instinctively readied themselves to be interrupted by unexpected visitors. Because the entrance of most homes led directly to their hall—the bosom of any family, where its members most commonly gathered—children grew accustomed to having unannounced outsiders suddenly barge into their living space. These circumstances nourished social customs that encouraged informality and hospitable behavior toward strangers, who might appear without warning and yet be immediately invited to warm themselves at the family hearth.

Unlike the high style of building, which derived from a single architectural tradition, folk housing exhibited much variety. The overall trend in popular construction was nevertheless toward more

uniformity in design. Dutch and Swedish styles of home building went out of vogue and did not survive as viable traditions into the nineteenth century. By the late eighteenth century, three major styles of regional architecture existed within the United States: the hall-and-parlor, the most common house in the South and lower Delaware Valley; the saltbox, a uniquely New England design; and German Colonial, unique to the area from Lancaster, Pennsylvania to Virginia's Shenandoah Valley. All three traditions increasingly imitated the Georgian sense of balanced proportions, and they also broke with custom by changing the allocation of interior space.

The Hall-and-Parlor

The hall-and-parlor was the basic structure that predominated from southern New Jersey through Georgia. Most of these dwellings rose just one story high, but they were capped by a high, narrow roof that allowed the addition of a half-story loft for sleeping; in rare cases, the loft became a small room with the addition of gabled windows into the roof. The typical hall-and-parlor had modest dimensions. A tax assessment of St. Mary's County, Maryland, where this style overwhelmingly predominated, found that about half of all homes were no larger than 24 by 16 feet in 1798.

Traditional hall-and-parlor homes divided internal space into two rooms. The hall functioned as the family gathering place for meals, sleeping, indoor crafts, and conviviality. The parlor, or conversation room, was usually a third of the hall's size; it often served as the parental bedchamber, a place to display the family's best possessions, and a retreat for private discussions. Outside doors gave entrance to the hall, not to the more private parlor. Southern families made do with one chimney that warmed the hall, where most social interaction took place, but in northern locales there was often a second chimney to heat the parlor. Although never part of the original design, butteries, bottleries, and kitchen sheds might appear as appendages for storage or cooking space.

The influence of Georgian architecture gradually modified hall-and-parlor design. Carpenters ceased placing the front entrance off center and positioned it squarely at the house's middle; they likewise took care to set windows symmetrically in relation to the door. Internal space also came to be balanced to a formal scale, so that parlor and hall were drawn to equal dimensions. Hall-and-parlor dwellings thus began to reflect Georgian ideals of balance and proportion, if only on a modest scale.

The use of interior space changed significantly after builders added an internal passageway behind the front door to buffer hall from parlor. This floorplan fostered a new sense of privacy in folk housing by allowing persons to reach any room in the house without passing through the others. By changing the dynamics of how people traveled through the house, the central entryway inhibited interaction between the hall, where family members congregated, and the parlor, which increasingly emerged as a special sphere reserved for the parents. The central passageway also erected a symbolic barrier against the outside. Whereas the hall's hospitality had customarily embraced strangers immediately upon crossing the front threshold,

This hall-and-parlor home exemplifies the scale of housing that sheltered most families from southern New Jersey through Georgia. Such buildings, with just two ground rooms and a loft serving as sleeping quarters, were the domestic environment in which most parents raised seven or eight children. The loft was made into a bedroom with windows after 1800, and the shed was likewise appended at a later time. (Historic American Buildings Survey [Virginia], courtesy Library of Congress.)

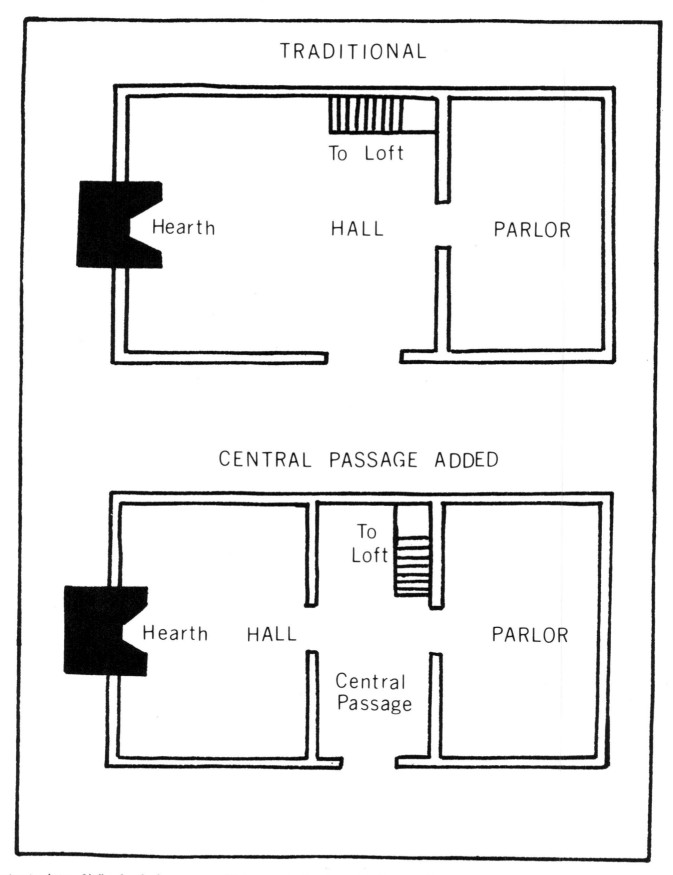

TRADITIONAL

To Loft

Hearth   HALL   PARLOR

CENTRAL PASSAGE ADDED

To Loft

Hearth   HALL   PARLOR

Central
Passage

The interior design of hall-and-parlor homes was modified during the Georgian period. Carpenters began constructing a central walled passageway behind the front door that separated the hall from the parlor, rather than having the front entrance open directly into the hall. This development marked the start of a trend toward creating domestic space that was more individualized and private. (Courtesy of author)

guests henceforth entered a transition area where the inhabitants performed a ceremony of formal admission, rather than volunteering the spontaneous welcome formerly given to visitors. The addition of a simple passageway sowed unintended consequences by offering family members more private space and emphasizing the social distance between the household and the outside community.

The Saltbox

The saltbox was a distinctive New England modification of the basic hall-and-parlor ground plan. Unlike Southerners, who built their chimneys into a side wall, New Englanders put their fireplace in the building's center to radiate heat more efficiently during winter. The saltbox differed from hall-and-parlor construction by the addition of an enclosed lean-to shelter along the back wall. A lean-to represented the easiest way to enlarge living space; it normally included a small bedroom for the parents, a kitchen, and a buttery

or bottlery. The lean-to's extra ceiling space became an extension of the house loft and afforded a sleeping area for farm hands or children. The lean-to's most important advantage was to insulate the central hall with a pocket of air during New England's harsh winters; it also functioned as a summer kitchen that kept house temperatures lower during warm months than if meals had been cooked over the hearth.

The saltbox fell out of fashion during the late eighteenth century because its lopsided roof clashed with Georgian notions of balance and proportion. In its place emerged a modified design that might be termed Yankee, or New England, Federal. The Yankee house featured a conventional gabled roof resting on four walls of equal height. Instead of attaching a lean-to shed against the rear, however, the hall and parlor were shortened to allow a kitchen and pantry to be set inside the back wall. The floorplan remained identical to the saltbox's, and consequently provided the same advantages of energy conservation, but the exterior presented a symmetrical image that

This saltbox, dating from around 1760, shows the usual scale of New England folk housing, which generally rose just one and a half stories. The half-story was originally a loft without windows, but later generations have modified it into regular living quarters and added windows. The door and window trimmings remain in the simple style of the eighteenth century. (Courtesy National Images of North American Living, Research and Archival Center, Washington)

As the saltbox fell out of favor because of its asymmetrical lines, New Englanders increasingly built farmhouses influenced by Georgian conventions, like this home in Wethersfield, Connecticut. The Yankee, or New England, Federal style resulted in homes that were usually rectangular rather than cubic in dimensions, and that dispensed with the saltbox's elongated rear roof; such buildings nevertheless retained the saltbox's unbalanced floorplan instead of laying out rooms of equal dimensions in Georgian style. (Courtesy National Images of North American Living, Research and Archival Center, Washington)

was reinforced by a balanced and regular placement of windows surrounding the door. Originally one story, the Yankee house eventually expanded into a rectangular dwelling two rooms deep and two stories high. The Yankee house was a classic compromise between folk and formal architecture: functional and traditional in its use of interior space, but entirely compatible with current fashion in its outward appearance.

German Colonial and German Georgian

During the fifty years between 1720 and the Revolution, German colonists established an architectural style borrowed from peasant housing of the Rhine Valley. The early Germans borrowed techniques of log construction from Swedes living along the Delaware River, but by the late eighteenth century they did most of their building in limestone or brick. German folk housing resembled English style in placing a door off center and setting windows without regard to symmetry; it primarily differed from English in the allocation of interior space. The basic German ground plan had a single chimney, centrally positioned, and three rooms. Slightly more than half the floor space fell within the kitchen, which fronted an enormous hearth and was roughly analogous to an Anglo-American hall

(except that the family did not eat there). Children might sleep around the kitchen hearth or in the loft. Germans divided the remaining area into a small parental bedroom and a parlor, which served as a room for dining, showing off the family's best property, and discussing business with visitors.

After the Revolution, German architecture became substantially anglicized. Germans acquired a taste for the Georgian style and abandoned aspects of their Old World architecture that appeared asymmetrical or otherwise unsophisticated. A new style rapidly emerged in central Pennsylvania and western Maryland known as German Georgian. At its grandest, this budding tradition expressed the classic Georgian formula for exterior balance: a building whose dimensions were more cubic than rectangular, with doors centrally positioned and windows placed at regular intervals to create the sense of mathematical balance. German Georgian nevertheless had a distinctly different appearance from conventional Georgian: it always utilized a gabled roof, instead of the more symmetrical four-sided type; it favored brick construction over stone or wood frame; and it incorporated two gable-end chimneys in place of a central fireplace. Aside from substituting the central hearth with two wall chimneys, the German Georgian home retained its character as a folk structure by laying out rooms according to the three-room pattern of Rhine Valley peasant dwellings. By combining elements of high architecture

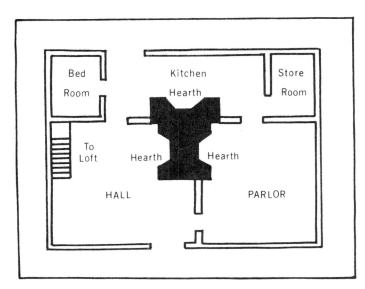

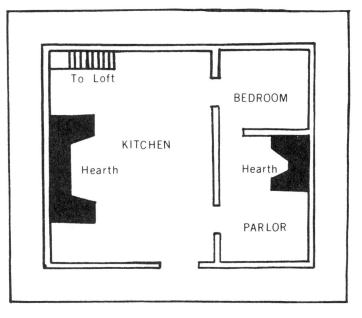

Floorplan of saltbox construction. The saltbox was constructed in stages. The basic hall-and-parlor design was built first—often modified by a hearth placed to provide central heating; a lean-to appendage was then added to accommodate special rooms such as a buttery, a kitchen, or sleeping quarters for servants and hired laborers. (Courtesy of author)

Floorplan of German Colonial housing. Despite their symmetrical Georgian exteriors, early German Colonial ground plans retained the imbalanced, three-room division that was typical of folk housing in the Rhine Valley. This mixing of styles between vernacular and high architecture died out after 1800, when a Georgian, four-room floorplan became the standard design used for interior space. (Courtesy of author)

German Georgian was the only style of American folk homes that designed farmhouses to appear cubic in dimensions rather than rectangular. The interior design was a traditional three-room plan brought over from the Rhine valley but modified to replace the central hearth with two gable-ended chimneys. This Emmaus, Pennsylvania, house has two full stories, but the one and a half-story structure partially hidden behind it is probably more representative of vernacular housing in the late 1700s. (Courtesy Schwenkfelder Library, Pennsburg, Pennsylvania)

with their ancestral culture, the German stock dotted the landscape with houses that gave visible testimony to their economic success and hard-won place in Anglo-American society but still preserved part of their ethnic heritage.

The subtle transformation of exterior design and floorplans symbolized important social changes underway in the Revolutionary era. By expressing a desire for housing that resembled upper-class homes, in style if not in scale, ordinary Americans had started to replace traditional, and often wonderfully idiosyncratic, folk dwellings with styles set by the elite's architectural fashions. New spatial divisions within the home also anticipated the nineteenth century's subdivision of living space into separate rooms that privatized domestic life. The full implications of these new attitudes would only become apparent during the late nineteenth century, when folk architecture would wither away as a viable tradition and nearly all housing would be designed according to published plans.

CHAPTER 16 Holidays and Calendars

Holidays

No regularly established legal holidays existed during the late eighteenth century (save for July 4 in a handful of states). Except for the Southern custom of reserving Christmas week for relaxation, feasting, and tippling, Americans kept few religious feasts, especially in the northern states where the predominantly Calvinist majority scorned holy days as a relic of Roman Catholicism. In most of the countryside, however, it was customary to treat the county court's monthly meetings, known as court days, as an excuse for a communal gathering. Court days took on a festive air as neighbors socialized and peddlers hawked their wares, and merrymaking often continued well after dark. The annual summer muster of militia, at which all enrolled members drilled and presented their equipment for inspection, always produced a huge collective frolic once the troops were dismissed.

Early America's closest equivalent to legal holidays were the periodic days of thanksgiving that various governments proclaimed in appreciation for presumed acts of divine providence. The first instance when a thanksgiving celebration occurred simultaneously in all thirteen states came during the Revolutionary War after the decisive American victory at Saratoga, New York, in 1777. Congress approved a resolution by Samuel Adams designating December 18 as a day of "Thanksgiving and praise" to be observed with prayers and banquets. The festivities commemorating the Battle of Saratoga marked the last time during the war that a thanksgiving was held simultaneously throughout the nation. Congress's other thanksgiving proclamations elicited only partial cooperation from the states, and consequently the Revolution ended without the establishment of any thanksgiving service as a national holiday.

George Washington proclaimed the next national celebration of thanksgiving when he designated Thursday, November 26, 1789, as a day of rejoicing that the Constitution's ratification had created "a form of government that would make for safety and happiness." Washington proclaimed another Thanksgiving Day in 1795, after which no president declared another national day of celebration until 1815. John Jay attempted to have New York set aside a fixed date for Thanksgiving's observance in 1795, but the legislature ignored his suggestion. Thanksgiving survived as a local custom, most commonly in New England, that usually occurred in early December, and it only became a national holiday during the Civil War.

The Fourth of July was the only secular holiday universally celebrated through the United States for most of the country's first century. John McRae's engraving shows Americans in 1776 reacting to news of independence by hoisting a liberty-pole festooned with flags, while another group cuts down a tavern sign emblazoned with a figure of George III. (Courtesy Library of Congress)

Americans almost universally agreed that national independence merited annual remembrance, but they showed some initial confusion over when to do so. The Continental Congress had voted to sever all legal connections with Great Britain on July 2, which marked the country's first day as a sovereign nation. It was this date that John Adams described as most proper for celebration. "It ought to be solemnized," Adams wrote, "with pomp and parade, with shows, games, sports, guns, bells, bonfires, and illuminations, from one end of this continent to the other, from this time forward." The country's first anniversary of independence accordingly took place in 1777. The Congress at Philadelphia held a formal dinner, at which entertainment was furnished by a band of captured Hessian mercenaries, and each soldier in the Continental Army enjoyed an extra gill of rum.

Rather than honoring the specific legal act of separation, the custom quickly developed of dating independence to July 4. It was on July 4 that Congress adopted Thomas Jefferson's extended list of grievances against George III as a preamble to the resolution ending British authority. Jefferson's "Declaration" had no legal bearing on independence, nor on any other matter, but its ringing indictment of tyranny caught the public imagination. Many citizens seem to have assumed that Congress voted for Jefferson's preamble simultaneously with independence, and July 4 became the preferred date on which to celebrate freedom from British rule. Massachusetts passed the earliest law recognizing that date as a holiday in 1781. By law or custom, other states followed suit and July 4 assumed the status of the country's chief patriotic holiday.

Commemoration of George Washington's birthday briefly rivaled Independence Day's popularity. The first public ceremony honoring him took place at Valley Forge, Pennsylvania on February 11, 1778, when an artillery unit serenaded their commander-in-chief in person. Washington had been born while the British Empire used the Julian Calendar, and his birth had originally been recorded as February 11; but when Britain adopted the Gregorian Calendar, all people born from 1700 to 1752 were supposed to adjust their birthdates by adding eleven days. Washington nevertheless did not revise his birthdate to February 22 until late in life, and confusion inevitably developed about which day should be celebrated in his memory. The first public ceremony to observe Washington's birthday on February 22 took place in 1783 at New York. By the time he was elected president, it had become the convention to ascribe his birth to February 22.

In 1781, the French army at Newport, Rhode Island, honored Washington with a parade on his birthday. The first civilian community to declare Washington's birthday a holiday was Richmond, Virginia, in 1782. The next year, there were festivities held on both the eleventh and twenty-second in New York City; Cambridge, Massachusetts; and Talbot County, Maryland. Celebrations of Washington's birthday became customary during his presidency, and they normally took the form of a parade followed by a banquet or ball.

Celebrations of Washington's birthday attracted criticism as inappropriate for a democratic society, but the practice continued after he left office in 1797. (His successor, John Adams, seems to have thought that his own birthday should have then replaced Washington's as a holiday.) Washington's death in 1799 inspired Congress to resolve that he be eulogized throughout the entire United States on February 22, 1800, the first time his birthday was proclaimed a national holiday. Memorialization of the first president's birthdate thereafter attracted little attention until 1832, the centennial of his birth, after which special observations of his birthday became rooted as a national tradition.

The three-hundredth anniversary of Columbus's discovery of America led to the first celebration of this event in the United States. The Tammany Society held a dinner in honor of the event on October 12, 1792, and Baltimore, Maryland dedicated the country's first monument to the explorer. The tricentennial inspired Americans to name their capital district after the explorer, and to adopt Columbia as a synonym for their country, but no more celebrations of October 12 are known to have been held until the four-hundredth anniversary of 1892, and it would not become a national holiday until 1937.

Observance of St. Patrick's Day developed into a regular custom in many communities during the Revolutionary era. On March 17, 1763, British troops at Ft. Pitt, Pennsylvania, relieved the tedium of frontier garrison duty by celebrating the day. Large numbers of Irish soldiers served in both the Continental and British armies, and both insisted upon honoring their patron saint. The Volunteers of Ireland, a Tory regiment fighting for George III, conducted New York's first St. Patrick's Day parade in 1777. Irish redcoats organized Philadelphia's earliest public parade for the feast in 1778, even as the Continental Army was enjoying the day with an extra issue of grog at Valley Forge. During and after the war, chapters of the Friendly Sons of St. Patrick and the Ancient Order of Hibernians sprang up in most of the major seaports, where they held banquets each March 17 and drank to their homeland with toasts such as "May the enemies of Ireland . . . be tormented with itching, without benefit of scratching." These scattered observances spread and became traditional during the early nineteenth century, until St. Patrick's Day festivities became a yearly event in most cities.

Not surprisingly, given the Revolution's outcome, April 23 ceased to be celebrated as the day of St. George, England's patron saint. The custom of holding banquets or parties on St. David's Day (March 1) by the Welsh and St. Andrew's Day (November 30) by Scots also became casualties of the Revolution, although neither feast died out entirely until the early nineteenth century. Since Germans and Dutch had never remembered their national origins on any religious feast days, celebrations of ethnic identity had virtually passed out of existence by 1800, except among the Irish.

Perpetual Calendars

The following perpetual calendar can be used to determine the exact day of the week upon which any event occurred between 1763 and 1800 according to the Gregorian calendar. The Gregorian calendar was originally created in 1582 as a reform of the Julian calendar. It was officially adopted by England and its colonies in 1752 and is still used today. To find the exact day of the week for any given month of any year between 1763 and 1800, one must first locate the appropriate Dominical letter in table 16.1 for the year under consideration. Find the year in the leviation section and match it with the horizontally corresponding letter for the correct century. Two letters are listed for leap years. In leap years the first letter listed is to be used for January and February, the second for the remainder of the year.

Once the Dominical letter for the year desired is found, use the key to figure out the corresponding day of the week. First consult the top half of the key and pick the month desired from the left portion and then follow the line horizontally to the right to match up with the appropriate Dominical letter. That location of the Dominical letter aligns vertically with the column in the bottom half of the key needed to find the correct day of the week.

To find the exact day of the week, pick the numerical day desired found in the leviation bottom section of the key and follow its line horizontally to match vertically with the Dominical letter located above. This day is the exact day of the week for the month and year being considered.

The date of Christmas in 1776 is an instructive example. According to table 16.1, 1776 was a leap year. Since Christmas falls in

December, the correct Dominical letter is the second letter listed for that year: "F." In the top section of the key, pick the horizontal line containing the month December and follow it to the letter "F." Then from the bottom section of the key, pick the horizontal line containing the number 25 and follow it until the day of the week matches vertically with the column containing the Dominical letter "F" above. The exact day of Christmas in 1776 was a Wednesday.

TABLE 16.1 DOMINICAL LETTER—GREGORIAN CALENDAR

Year of Century				Century	
				1700	1800
00				C	E
01	29	57	85	B	D
02	30	58	86	A	C
03	31	59	87	G	B
04	32	60	88	F E	A G
05	33	61	89	D	F
06	34	62	90	C	E
07	35	63	91	B	D
08	36	64	92	A G	C B
09	37	65	93	F	A
10	38	66	94	E	G
11	39	67	95	D	F
12	40	68	96	C B	E D
13	41	69	97	A	C
14	42	70	98	G	B
15	43	71	99	F	A
16	44	72		E D	G F
17	45	73		C	E
18	46	74		B	D
19	47	75		A	C
20	48	76		G F	B A
21	49	77		E	G
22	50	78		D	F
23	51	79		C	E
24	52	80		B A	D C
25	53	81		G	B
26	54	82		F	A
27	55	83		E	G
28	56	84		D C	F E

Note: In leap years the first letter relates to January and February, the second to the remainder of the year.

KEY

Month	Dominical Letter						
January, October	A	B	C	D	E	F	G
February, March, November	D	E	F	G	A	B	C
April, July	G	A	B	C	D	E	F
May	B	C	D	E	F	G	A
June	E	F	G	A	B	C	D
August	C	D	E	F	G	A	B
September, December	F	G	A	B	C	D	E

Day of Month					Day of Week						
1	8	15	22	29	Sun.	Sat.	Fri.	Thur.	Wed.	Tues.	Mon.
2	9	16	23	30	Mon.	Sun.	Sat.	Fri.	Thur.	Wed.	Tues.
3	10	17	24	31	Tues.	Mon.	Sun.	Sat.	Fri.	Thur.	Wed.
4	11	18	25		Wed.	Tues.	Mon.	Sun.	Sat.	Fri.	Thur.
5	12	19	26		Thur.	Wed.	Tues.	Mon.	Sun.	Sat.	Fri.
6	13	20	27		Fri.	Thur.	Wed.	Tues.	Mon.	Sun.	Sat.
7	14	21	28		Sat.	Fri.	Thur.	Wed.	Tues.	Mon.	Sun.

Source: Explanatory Supplement to the Astronomical Ephemesis and the American Ephemesis and Nautical Almanac. London: Her Majesty's Stationary Office, 1961, 419, 427.

CHAPTER 17 Popular Life and Recreations

At the core of popular culture in the eighteenth century stood the family. The family played such a central role because of the exceptionally isolated quality of rural life in early America. In 1800, the nation's center of population lay in the rolling hills just west of Baltimore, Maryland. The average number of people per square mile in that region was only twenty, which meant that on average just three families occupied a square mile. Within a circle encompassing a radius of one and a half miles—a comfortable hour's walk down dirt roads or across fenced pastures—any of those three households could count on having no more than two dozen other families as its "neighbors," about the same as would now line the sides of a typical suburban cul-de-sac. Most farmers, furthermore, would have found it awkward to spare the two hours needed for such a round-trip out of their workday, and so would rarely travel as far as a mile and a half unless they were upon special business or it was the Sabbath. (Traveling on horseback was not necessarily quicker. An Englishman named J. F. D. Smyth, who traversed Virginia in 1772, wryly noted that "a man will frequently go five miles to catch a horse, to ride only one mile afterwards.") Under these circumstances, family members primarily interacted with each other, or with near relatives such as uncles, aunts, or cousins. Forming a household thus loomed as the most basic decision that would shape the character of a person's social life from that point forward.

In an age when divorce was virtually unheard of, marriage was an irrevocable decision for all practical purposes. No other event, save for those that brought individuals face-to-face with death, remained more deeply embedded in peoples' minds. When it came time for him to testify in behalf of his mother's claim to a pension as the widow of a Revolutionary soldier in 1842, Bartlett Harlow, Jr., found it natural to digress and tell the officiating magistrate in Madison County, Kentucky that "during his father's lifetime he has often heard his father speak of his marriage to his mother. That he was married before the close of the Revolutionary War, and about coming home in his regimentals [i.e., uniform] and his mother's conduct at his appearance etc." The image of the conquering hero being showered with his future bride's kisses in old Virginia had remained a vivid part of that family's lore for over sixty years.

In the case of this particular family, marriage had sealed the infatuation of an impetuous sixteen-year-old girl named Lucy Thacker for a battle-hardened veteran twelve years her senior. Such unions commonly occurred in the late eighteenth century, when men delayed marriage well into their twenties to save money for farm tools and livestock, and young women sought older men with sufficient property to afford raising children. The typical age at marriage seems to have been between seventeen to twenty for brides and twenty-two and twenty-seven for grooms.

Lucy Thacker and Bartlett Harlow, Sr., evidently married out of romantic attraction in 1781, a practice that had become common by that date, but was far from universal. Equally conventional was the traditional European custom of selecting a first or second cousin as one's spouse, or finding a mate from among the relations of a brother- or sister-in-law. A study of marriage among Scotch-Irish Presbyterians in Lancaster County, Pennsylvania, by Russell M. Reid found that at least 22% of marriages joined cousins between 1725 and 1799. Many members of that congregation migrated en masse to the Virginia frontier, and then to Kentucky, but in each successive generation approximately one-quarter of marriages was between blood relations, even though the local population was large enough to allow every individual to find unrelated spouses. Another study of Prince George's County, Maryland, whose population was predominantly English or Welsh in descent, also found that over a quarter of all marriages connected blood relatives between 1760 and 1790, while one of every eight linked in-laws or persons with some other affinal relationship.

Most courtship probably occurred during social visits to the woman's home by the man on Saturday evening or after church on Sunday. The few other chances for rural couples to socialize primarily came at seasonal festivals such as Christmas week (in the South, at least) or harvest frolics. Chaperons were rare in America. During the seventeenth century, conventional morality had dictated that couples refrain from sexual contact until marriage. Couples routinely met this expectation, for about 92% of first children born through 1680 arrived nine months or more after their parents's marriage. After 1760, premarital intercourse became much more common. The number of first children delivered nine or more months after marriage had declined to 77.5% by the period 1721–1760, and it sank to 67.0% during the period 1761–1800.

TABLE 17.1 KINSHIP TIES IN MARRIAGES OF PRINCE GEORGE'S COUNTY, MD., 1760–1790

Marriage Between Blood Relatives		Marriage Between In-Laws or Other Affinal Relatives	
Between first cousins	15%	Between brother-in-law and sister-in-law	4%
Between second cousins	6%	Between step-sibling and sibling's cousin	2%
Between more remote blood relations	7%	Between more remote affinal relatives	7%
Total Related	28%	Total Related	13%
Total Marriages Between Relatives		41%	
Total Marriages Between Non-Relatives		58%	

Source: Allan J. Kulikoff, *Tobacco and Slaves: The Development of Southern Cultures in the Chesapeake, 1680–1800* (1986), 254.

Although the rise in premarital conceptions must have dismayed the clergy, and mortified large numbers of grandparents, it was not an especially drastic departure from traditional European behavior. Seventeenth-century Americans—at least those in New England—had themselves broken with European practices by setting strict rules that proscribed making love until after marriage. The usual custom in Europe was that sex should be delayed during courtship, but was permissible (although not entirely respectable) once a couple had publicly announced their betrothal. By engaging more frequently in premarital intercourse, Revolutionary Americans were not becoming morally lax, but rather were resuming practices more representative of European folk attitudes about sexual relations.

Americans were certainly coming to accept a wider range of sexual freedom, but only when a commitment had already been made to marriage. Transgressions against this unwritten code carried a stigma that lingered interminably and sometimes descended to the next generation. When Thomas Ballard of Albermarle County, Virginia (a neighbor of Bartlett Harlow and Lucy Thacker) wrote his will in 1779, he pointedly—and needlessly—reminded all the heirs to whom it would be read that his girl Frances had borne an illegitimate child named Rachel in 1754, a quarter-century earlier. Ballard left that granddaughter a bequest, but once again had held up her base origins for family censure. About four years after Ballard's will was probated and read, his granddaughter moved to the wilds of Kentucky with her husband, Gabriel Mullins, and it is extremely tempting to imagine Rachel's eager anticipation of a new life where no one would know she was her mother's "natural" child, even if that new home swarmed with Indians and wolves.

Marriage was supposed to be forever, but many Americans of the eighteenth century learned the hard way that those who wed in haste often repent at leisure. Every Protestant church in Anglo-America actively discouraged divorce, although every one permitted it in extreme cases, but common law permitted marriages to be annulled by government statutes. It was during the late 1700s that legislative divorces began increasing and a more permissive attitude about divorce emerged.

The number of requests for annulments rose sharply after 1764. In Massachusetts, half of all divorce petitions from 1692 to 1786 arrived after 1764, and a third came after 1774. Pennsylvania approved 104 divorces between 1786 and 1801, compared to just 13 during 1766–1785. In most cases, adultery drove either party to request the marriage's dissolution—for marriages without love lead inevitably to love without marriage. Much of the increase after 1774 came because more women filed for divorce, and it would seem that wives were becoming less tolerant of unfaithful husbands and more aggressive in ending unsatisfactory unions. In the long run, this development marked the beginning of a gradual revolution in American attitudes toward marriage that would result in several states liberalizing their divorce statutes in the early 1800s.

As of 1800, however, recourse to breaking a household remained unusual. Massachusetts granted a record number of divorces between 1765 and 1786, yet the actual number of families involved was equal to only one of every 387 households in the state as of 1790. In Pennsylvania, all divorces awarded between 1786 and 1801 amounted to just one in every 710 of the state's households as of 1790.

The typical person's social life largely centered around family events. Most family gatherings were informal visits paid to express congratulations or commiseration at some unexpected news, or impromptu reunions spent enjoying the company of long-absent kin back to tell about adventures in the military or about new farms cleared from distant frontiers. It was furthermore in homes, rather than in churches, that most individuals conducted their most important family celebrations: funerals and weddings.

Funerals were often austere. In densely populated New England, church bells might identify the dead by tolling nine times for a man, six for a woman, and three for children, and then chiming his or her age. In the middle-Atlantic and Southern countryside, news passed by word of mouth about an imminent burial. By the 1760s, a rising standard of living allowed families to bury their deceased in coffins, rather than by wrapping them in shrouds as was commonly done until the early eighteenth century, but most people went to rest in rude boxes hastily built the night before by a close male

TABLE 17.2 PERCENT OF FIRST BABIES BORN LESS THAN NINE MONTHS AFTER PARENTS' WEDDING, 1760–1800

Community and Period	Number of Months Born After Parents' Marriage			
	Under 6 Months	Under 8.5 Months	Under 9 Months	After 9 Months
Hingham, Mass.				
1761–1780	19.0%	33.5%	36.5%	63.5%
1781–1800	21.0%	32.8%	39.1%	60.9%
Watertown, Mass.				
1761–1780	15.2%	24.1%	29.4%	70.6%
1781–1800	15.3%	26.1%	32.5%	67.5%
Dedham, Mass.				
1760–1770	19.2%	30.1%	32.9%	67.1%
Hollis, N.H.				
1761–1780	13.1%	26.2%	29.8%	70.2%
1781–1800	10.5%	31.6%	35.1%	64.9%
Gloucester Co., Va.				
1761–1770	12.1%	22.7%	24.2%	75.8%
1771–1780	12.7%	25.4%	30.1%	69.9%
Coventry, Conn.				
1771–1800	. . .	. . .	25.0%	75.0%
Mansfield, Conn.	. . .	. . .	20.6%	79.4%
Bristol, R.I.	. . .	. . .	44.0%	56.0%
Average, 1761–1800	16.7%	27.2%	33.0%	67.0%

Source: Daniel S. Smith and Michael S. Hindus, "Premarital Pregnancy in America, 1640–1971: An Overview and Interpretation," Journal of Interdisciplinary History V (1975), 561–65.

TABLE 17.3 DIVORCE PETITIONS FILED AND GRANTED IN PENNSYLVANIA AND MASSACHUSETTS, 1765–1801

	Number of Petitions Filed	Number of Petitions Granted	Filed by Husband	Filed by Wife
Pa.				
1786–1801	. . .	104	40	64
1775–1785	35	11	23	12
1766–1774	6	2	5	1
Mass.				
1775–1786	86	61	53	33
1765–1774	46	24	29	17

Source: Nancy F. Cott, "Divorce and the Changing Status of Women in Eighteenth-Century Massachusetts," William and Mary Quarterly XXXIII (1976), 592. Thomas R. Meehan, " 'Not Made Out of Levity,' Evolution of Divorce in Early Pennsylvania," Pennsylvania Magazine of History and Biography XCII (1968), 441–55.

relative. Mourners viewed the dead in the house's parlor and shared whiskey with the survivors. If the corpse stayed above ground overnight, children and visitors slept alongside it in the same room. Prominent families might persuade ministers to lead prayers over the coffin on their farms, but average people seldom went to earth with a clergyman's blessing. Burial took place on family property (rarely in churchyards) after a formal procession. Graves received temporary wooden tablets that soon disintegrated, not stone markers. When an unrelated family bought the land, they eventually built over or plowed under any preexisting gravesites.

Weddings likewise occurred most often on a family's farm rather than at a church, even when the bride lived reasonably close to a chapel. Most marriages took place in wintertime from November through February. In much of rural America, the wedding day began with a good-humored procession of the groom's party to the wife's home, where the ceremony would take place at noon. Neighbors and friends often played pranks such as tying grapevines across the path or staging a mock ambush by firing off a volley of guns loaded with blanks. If the bride's virginity was doubted, the party would find poles festooned with horns along the way, and the groom would likely receive a pair during the banquet or dancing. About a mile from the house, the mounted men of the party would be organized into a horse race known as the run for the bottle, in which they would tear across the most difficult terrain to reach a whiskey jug on the bride's doorstep. The winner would return with the whiskey, give a dram to the groom and everyone accompanying him, and receive compliments on his horsemanship and daring.

The wedding preceded a large feast where merrymaking and humor regaled the guests. Dancing started after dinner. Jigs usually dominated the entertainment, with men competing to cut one another out for the privilege of winning the most desirable partners. The music and festivities usually continued through sunrise, and it was considered bad form to fall asleep before then. Two or three hours before midnight, the bride's friends stole her off to bed and her husband soon joined her. Throughout the night they were brought food and drink, which they were obliged to sample. When the fiddler needed a rest from playing, guests gathered outside the newlyweds' window to serenade them with a shivaree of ribald suggestions and songs. The celebrations often continued for another day at the groom's house, where the feasting and dancing continued.

Women enjoyed few chances to socialize outside the home aside from religious services, and even then, regular church attendance was difficult during winter and in many rural areas south of New England. Women sometimes organized quilting bees, where they worked on a collective project or simply conversed while sewing by themselves. Most farm wives, however, rarely mixed with non-relatives except at harvest frolics following autumn reaping, when neighbors feasted until dusk and then danced well past midnight.

The distinguishing characteristic of eighteenth-century dancing was that men and women did not primarily join as partners, but as members of a group—in contredanses—or as individuals, in jigs. (Not until after the European waltz entered the United States in the 1820s would Americans start to redefine dancing as an activity for autonomous couples.) In contredanses, participants performed repetitive steps in predetermined patterns while moving up, down, or around fellow dancers arranged in lines or circles. Contredanse required all involved to synchronize their actions and, in effect, submerged every couple into a unit of the larger group.

Between contredanses, many individuals engaged in competitive displays of zestful dancing called jigs. During a jig, the company would form a circle and cheer while the boldest fellows competed for the attention of unmarried girls by attempting to cut out one another through robust displays of imaginative movements. A variation of the jig pitted married couples against one another in tests of endurance during which each tried to dance the other, and any subsequent challengers, into exhaustion. Once in 1764, the chief justice of New Jersey capped an evening of vigorous contredanses by outlasting six couples who challenged him and his mistress in jigs—and then collapsed dead of a heart attack.

Unlike women, whose chances for social mingling were highly restricted, men gathered in large numbers every few months to participate and observe court proceedings, vote at elections, or train as militia. These events provided the main venue for males to engage in games, gambling, fighting, and drinking at local taverns. So noted were such events for frivolity, which often lasted well after dark, that it is tempting to attribute turnouts for these governmental functions less to civic responsibility than to a collective longing by semi-isolated farmers for male diversions.

Travelers and other observers did not commonly mention the playing of team sports. Cudgels, a popular British game using a ball and clubs that often pitted town teams against each other, was known to Americans but seems to have declined in popularity over the early eighteenth century. Although many whites had witnessed the Indian game of lacrosse, in which a ball carried with pouched rackets is fought over between two goals, they never adopted the sport. In most of rural America, the sparsely populated countryside provided few chances for young men to practice ball games or build a tradition of towns competing against one another.

The only collective sport popular in late-eighteenth-century America was fox hunting. Wealthy Philadelphians formed the country's earliest fox-chasing society, the Gloucester Fox Hunting Club, on October 29, 1766. The club soon became controversial because its chases frequently left farmers with trampled crops and fits of profanity. Elite organizations like the Gloucester Club refined the sport by adopting many of the ceremonial rituals held before and after hunts by English aristocrats. Riding to the hounds was the gentry's prime outdoor pastime, and it became nearly an obsession for some individuals. George Washington sometimes brought his hounds along while riding to inspect his estate, and he unhesitatingly followed them if they spotted a prey. During 1769, Washington attended church on fifteen days, but he hunted foxes on forty-nine.

Most sports entailed individual rather than team competition. Since they were easy to organize and required no special dexterity, running contests were the most universal sport. Races often came after militia musters, with each company's champion sprinting for personal reputation or to win prizes contributed by the officers.

Proving one's prowess with weapons served as another common outlet for competition. Throwing knives or tomahawks at targets was a popular diversion whenever crowds gathered at courthouses. Marksmanship was the most admired of all martial skills. Shooting matches attracted large crowds and undoubtedly ranked as the eighteenth century's most observed spectator sport. Large meets sometimes offered a butchered hog as prize, but more usually the winner got a jug of liquor and sometimes nothing more than the right to retrieve all the lead left in the target. Some of the best riflemen even played to the crowd by making trick shots from awkward positions when their opponents had hit wide of the mark. Daniel Boone, for example, enjoyed firing his winning rounds while holding his rifle with just one arm, after which he would stroll past the losers, pat them on their shoulders, and announce that "they couldn't shoot up to Boone."

Wrestling matches were common because they could be arranged in short order. Young men in many communities established pecking orders based on how many fellows each could throw from a circle. A wrestling champion enjoyed high prestige if he made good a claim to stand among his neighbors as "the big buck of this lick," and—

Howard Pyle's sketch of a Kentucky wedding shows the groom and bride leading out for the Virginia Reel while a slave does the honors as fiddler. Wedding guests usually danced until the fiddler was exhausted, and then adjourned to enliven the newlyweds' imagination with a bawdy shivaree. (Howard Pyle Collection, courtesy Delaware Art Museum, Wilmington, Delaware)

as among deer—his status carried connotations of having first choice at courting attractive women.

Travelers often commented on the readiness of Anglo-Americans to box one another but also indicated that a thin line separated sport from mayhem. The closest that boxing came to legitimate recreation as the manly art of self-defense was in New England. Yankees condemned other Americans who fought with no holds barred. A Connecticut soldier, Pvt. James Plumb Martin, recalled Yankees referring to Southerners as "men with one eye (alluding to their practice of gouging.)" It would seem that New Englanders fought in arranged matches—of the bare-knuckled variety—under customary rules that forbade the use of teeth, fingernails, and kicking.

Below New England, many Americans viewed the chance to pummel one another with genuine relish. Private Martin once described an encounter between two Irish soldiers, evidently from Pennsylvania, who interrupted a perfectly enjoyable conversation over grog when the first man offered, "Faith, Jammy, will you take a box," and his companion answered "Aye, and thank ye, too." They went outside into the cold December air, stripped to the waist, and flailed at one another until—as Martin remembered—they "made the claret, as they called the blood, flow plentifully." Satisfied with their mutual battering, they returned to their whiskey, "bloody as butchers, to drink friends again, where no friendship had been lost."

Anglo-Southerners boxed with less restraint than any Americans. Fights often resulted when patrons of a tavern allowed boisterous bantering to cross the line that marked insult, such as by failing to follow an angry rejoinder of "You lie, sir," with an acceptable disclaimer like "I mean under a mistake." Challenges also followed the careless use of fighting words, such as calling someone a buckskin, lubber, roughneck, or Scotchman, or by forgetting to wipe a bottle's mouth when passing the table's whiskey to another.

When private grievances necessitated a public fight (and nearly all fighting seems to have been public), the bystanders formed a circle to witness whatever rules of engagement the combatants agreed on and prevent any violations of them. Because southern custom accepted kicking, biting, and gouging eyes as legitimate, there were few reasons for bystanders to intervene short of the use of concealed weapons. Such fights often ended with more wrestling than boxing, as each man tried to immobilize the other and force his opponent to cry out "King's cruse" before his eye was scooped out or his ear bitten away. Failure to yield in reasonable time led to permanent disfigurement. Although travelers' accounts certainly exaggerated stories of gouging in the South, it is clear that a small number of one-eyed men offered mute, gruesome testimony that laws against the practice went unenforced.

Fox hunting was an upper-class sport enjoyed by the Anglo-American gentry. This anonymous folk painting depicts the increasing amount of ceremony that Americans imitated from English example. While the master of hounds addresses the dogs and horsemen with calls of "oyez, oyez," a slave in livery prepares to blow a bugle announcing the hunt's formal start. (Anonymous, *Start of the Hunt*. Gift of Edgar William and Bernice Chrysler Garbisch, c. 1993, National Gallery of Art, Washington)

Cards and dice were widespread and attracted little censure as a form of legitimate recreation. The absence of controversy concerning table games reflected the general perception that most of them involved small purses and were played as a ritual part of hospitality or holidays. As late as 1800, the United States had yet to develop a subculture of professional gamesters, and even its largest cities lacked public houses functioning mainly as gambling institutions. Not until the 1800s, when "card sharps" and gambling halls became a more visible part of American society, would table gaming receive serious criticism as a threat to public morals.

Horse racing likewise retained much of its amateur quality throughout rural America and was a frequent occurrence at court days or militia musters. The predominant form of this sport was the quarter race, which matched two riders over a straight course measuring a quarter-mile. These contests generally permitted the mounts to bump or jostle one another and sometimes degenerated into wild affrays in which each rider tried to unsaddle his opponent. Quarter racing was popular, not only because it gave an excuse to make bets, but also because it frequently afforded the spectacle of a mounted free-for-all at breakneck speed.

A more formal and exclusive style of racing gradually became the preferred style of betting for the upper class. By the 1760s, the gentry were importing English thoroughbreds to compete during a restricted season at circular tracks near New York City, Charles Town, and Williamsburg. The Continental Congress ordered horse racing suspended in 1774, but the gentlemen of the turf ignored its edict. In 1779, while yet under severe pressure from Indians (and even before they had built a licensed academy to educate their children), Kentucky planters built their first circular racetrack. By 1793, the trustees of Lexington, Kentucky, had to prohibit horse racing in the city streets as a menace to pedestrians.

Horse racing did not recover from wartime disruption in New York until the mid-1790s. In Philadelphia, where the city fathers had long banned the sport, so many horsemen began galloping against one another on Sassafras Street that it was renamed Race Street; by 1788 a stud farm had appeared on the city's outskirts to sire foals by English thoroughbreds, including Messenger, the first trotting horse seen in America. Richmond, Virginia emerged as the postwar center for racing, with four tracks nearby at Newmarket, Tree Hill, Fairfield, and Broad Rock. By 1789, Virginia breeders had purchased several noted champion thoroughbreds from England, such as Shark, who earned a record 16,057 guineas by winning 19 of his 29 races before being retired and sold to a Fredericksburg planter.

Cockfighting seems not to have become a common entertainment in the thirteen colonies until the 1720s, when isolated combats began to be arranged following court days or militia musters. Originally an event for whites of average means, in which slaves and free blacks also participated, this blood sport became a popular diversion for both sexes of the southern gentry, who wagered large purses on the outcomes. Interest in cockfighting became so keen, that when news spread by word of mouth about an impromptu match between two noted victors, it was not unusual for several hundred enthusiasts to journey up to forty miles for the event. Contests matching champion fighters from rival counties became customary at fixed times of the year, such as Easter and Pentecost. On occasion, tournaments were held that organized up to sixty game cocks into "mains" (or sides) and awarded prize money according to which main had killed the greatest number of opponents in each day's battles. Such contests sometimes became major social occasions, at which wives and children joined their husbands in cheering on the bloody combatants and then retired to formal balls for an evening of dancing and mirth.

Lotteries provided another outlet for the gambling impulse. Early lotteries were unsophisticated raffles in which agents subscribed a set number of tickets and then drew winners after they sold the entire lot. Payouts were unusually high, sometime 85% of proceeds, and tickets had to be refunded if sales were insufficient to cover the advertised prizes. Every colony but Maryland and North Carolina required that each lottery be licensed by a special statute regulating its operation to protect buyers from fraud.

Lotteries primarily originated in New England, and Rhode Island spawned the greatest number. Of the 176 raffles licensed between 1763 and 1789, 78 (44%) originated in Rhode Island. Most lottery sponsors were churches, schools, debtors hoping to raise cash demanded by their creditors, or entrepreneurs seeking to finance toll bridges, turnpikes, or swamp clearance. Numerous cities and counties used drawings as a way of financing wharf expansion, bridge repairs, or road improvements. During the Revolution, five states and the Continental Congress resorted to them as an alternative to higher military taxes, but they flooded the country with so many tickets that the state drawings took exceptionally long to complete and Congress's grand lottery fizzled out for lack of subscriptions by 1779. The country's first major experiment in financing government by lottery sales had failed.

Lotteries remained infrequent until after 1790. In only six of twenty-seven years from 1763 to 1789 did more than nine drawings occur in all the states. Excluding the wartime lotteries of 1776–1780, only £5,500 worth of subscriptions could be purchased in a typical year after 1763. Issued at that rate, the supply of tickets gave just one free family in twenty-five the option of buying a ticket worth four shillings (about $1.00) around 1790.

Although some religious groups, especially the Quakers, frowned on gambling by raffles, lotteries evoked little condemnation by American religious or political leaders. The sole opposition to them came from the British government, which enjoyed a monopoly over lotteries in England and sold tickets worth at least £600,000 in lieu of taxes during the 1760s. In 1769, all royal governors received orders forbidding them from authorizing any colonial lotteries without first seeking approval from London. Exempted from this prohibition were the charter colonies of Connecticut and Rhode Island, and proprietary Maryland, whose legislation did not require approval by royal authorities.

Lotteries generated excitement across the complete spectrum of early American society. The *Columbian Centinel* reported on April 28, 1790 that when "the Ladies found the [Massachusetts] government had established a Lottery to ease the taxes of the people, they generally became adventurers, and it is pleasing to find . . . *their* sex sharing the First *Capital Prize*." The Salem, Massachusetts *Gazette* reported on May 10, 1791, that the top prize of $2,000 in the Massachusetts lottery went to four African Americans from Rhode Island. Lotteries had few detractors before 1800. Because they were infrequent and funded socially worthy projects, most people viewed them as being more akin to charitable gifts than to gambling.

No national pastime was more ubiquitous in Revolutionary America than imbibing alcoholic substances. Southern gentlemen assumed that hospitality obliged them to offer their guests enough liquor to get drunk. When Filippo Mazzei, an Italian writer who traveled widely through Virginia, asked for water to accompany supper at a plantation in 1774, his host became so confused that he asked Mazzei to select another drink. Northerners were just as capable of quaffing on a heroic scale. New York governor George Clinton once honored a French ambassador with a dinner at which the 120 guests downed 135 bottles of Madeira, 36 bottles of port, 60 bottles of English beer, and 30 large cups of rum punch.

By tradition, the cocktail originated as the Revolution began. Around 1776, at a tavern in Elmsford, New York, that festooned rooster feathers on a wall as interior decorations, barmaid Betsy Flanagan put plumes in the grog of her favorite customers. Her patrons then started calling for "cocktails" in all their mixed drinks.

In the midst of a life-and-death struggle for independence, Americans made distilled spirits their ally against the British. Each Continental soldier drank a daily ration of four ounces (a gill) of rum or whiskey, plus double allowances whenever victories or holidays merited celebration, and so was fortified by nearly a gallon of spirits per month. Alcohol occasionally proved a more tempting target than the British, such as at the Battle of Eutaw Springs, South Carolina, in 1781, when American forces interrupted their attack on a British encampment to confiscate the enemy's liquor supply. They became too inebriated to hold their ground when the redcoats counterattacked to reclaim their stock of spirits.

There were some legitimate reasons for imbibing rum, the country's most popular alcoholic beverage. Rum furnished an inexpensive supply of calories to fishermen, lumberjacks, or any laborers working through cold winter weather. At 147 calories per ounce, it allowed men to do strenuous physical work outdoors while remaining warm and avoiding excess loss of body weight. Cider likewise helped provide several vitamins needed for a balanced diet, especially in winter when fresh fruit was unavailable.

The average American aged fifteen or older consumed about 40 gallons of cider, wine, or distilled spirits per year. Because few women or slaves drank great amounts of liquor, the typical adult white male must have ingested about 50 gallons every year, or about a gallon per week. Two-thirds of this amount was taken as hard cider, whose alcoholic content averaged about 10%, but nearly all the rest was distilled molasses or grain of 90 proof. The annual intake of absolute alcohol exceeded six gallons during most of the period from 1770 to 1800. (In 1978, per capita intake of absolute alcohol equaled only 2.82 gallons among drinking-age Americans.)

By the late eighteenth century, Americans were drinking far more whiskey, rum, or bourbon than had previously been the case. Consumption of distilled spirits had almost doubled in the preceding century, from 3.8 gallons per adult in 1710 to 7.2 gallons in 1800. The use of cider, however, crested at 34 gallons per adult in the 1790s and dropped to about 30 gallons by 1805.

The earliest American temperance society formed at Litchfield, Connecticut, in 1789 to discourage drinking from planting to harvest time, but it was short-lived. Only Quakers and Methodists insisted that their members avoid liquors distilled from grains or molasses (although not necessarily wine or cider). Drinking was otherwise common among all races, sexes, and ages except the very young— and even then many parents thought that giving alcohol to children in small amounts would benefit their health and stamina.

Despite the rise in alcoholic consumption, public drunkenness remained infrequent. This anomaly resulted in part from so many adults acquiring such a high tolerance for liquor that they could disguise the outward appearance of inebriation. The general absence of conspicuous drunkenness primarily derived from the manner in which people used spirits. Americans used drink as a dietary supplement by rationing its intake during the day, and few people engaged in excessive binges except for weddings, holiday feasts, special entertainments, or other celebrations. John Adams, for example, began each morning with a pint of hard cider, and yet prided himself on being a foe of excessive drinking. Artisans and farmers customarily enjoyed a dram of liquor during morning and afternoon breaks from work. Custom also dictated that alcohol be taken during meals to aid digestion and before retiring to bed as a relaxant. Americans remained nominally sober by sipping small amounts of spirits throughout the day, but by 1800 their total intake was approaching the highest level of alcoholic usage ever seen in the United States.

By the 1790s, new customs were recasting Americans into a breed quite different from New England's stolid Puritan forebears or

TABLE 17.4 LEGALLY LICENSED LOTTERIES HELD IN UNITED STATES, 1763–1789

Year	Number	(Value)	Distribution by Colony or State
1789	14	(£19,800)	1 R.I. (£400); 2 Mass. (£11,000); 2 Conn. (?); 2 Vt. (£350); 1 N.J. (?); 2 Pa. (£1,400); 4 Va. (£6,650).
1788	5	(£3,850)	1 R.I. (£2,100); 2 Mass. (£1,750); 2 Vt. (?).
1787	8	(£5,000)	3 R.I. (£1,700); 1 N.H. (£1,800); 1 Del. (?); 1 Va. (£500); 2 N.C. (£1,000).
1786	9	(£2,255)	2 R.I. (£555); 1 Mass. (?); 1 N.H. (£200); 2 N.J. (?); 2 Va. (£800); 1 N.C. (£700).
1785	13	(£6,215)	5 R.I. (£515); 1 Mass. (£600); 1 Conn. (?); 2 N.H. (£1,900); 2 Pa. (?); 1 Va. (£2,700); 1 Ga. (£500).
1784	14	(£12,585)	4 R.I. (£1,520); 2 Mass. (£1,300); 1 Conn. (£1,000); 1 N.H. (£1,000); 1 Pa. (£5,915); 1 Va. (£1,000); 2 N.C. (£500); 1 S.C. (?); 1 Ga. (£350).
1783	12	(£9,780)	3 R.I. (£530); 5 Mass. (£7,900); 3 Conn. (£1,150); 1 Vt. (£200).
1782	5	(£3,900)	1 R.I. (?); 3 Mass. (£3,900); 1 Va. (?).
1781	4	(£3,150)	1 Mass. (£200); 1 Conn. (£250); 1 N.H. (?); 1 N.Y. (£2,700).
1780	8	(£59,800)	2 R.I. (£9,900); 2 Mass. (£48,600); 3 Conn. (£1,400); 1 N.Y. (?).
1779	6	(£104,500)	2 R.I. (£2,900); 3 Mass. (£99,500); 1 Vt. (£2,100).
1778	5	(£109,680)	1 R.I. (£300); 1 Conn. (£1,500); 1 N.H. (£280); 1 Mass. (£105,600); 1 N.Y. (£2,000).
1777	1	(?)	1 Va. (?).
1776	1	(£141,550)	1 Continental Congress (£141,550).
1775	. . .	. . .	. . .
1774	13	(£15,340)	10 R.I. (£2,940); 1 Conn. (£400); 1 N.Y. (£12,000); 1 Del. (?).
1773	6	(£1,848)	3 R.I. (£570); 3 Conn. (£1,278).
1772	17	(£4,282)	13 R.I. (£1,295); 3 Conn. (£1,937); 1 N.J. (£1,050).
1771	1	(£220)	1 R.I. (£220).
1770	2	(£100)	2 R.I. (£100).
1769	5	(£6,257)	3 R.I. (£1,470); 2 Pa. (£4,787).
1768	4	(£6,320)	2 R.I. (£70); 1 N.H. (£1,000); 1 Pa. (£5,250).
1767	6	(£4,375)	3 R.I. (£2,875); 1 N.H. (?); 1 Pa. (£500); 1 Md. (£1,000).
1766	2	(?)	1 N.H. (?): 1 West Fla. (?).
1765	3	(£6,704)	1 Mass. (£3,200); 1 N.J. (£500); 1 Pa. (£3,004).
1764	3	(£536)	3 R.I. (£536).
1763	9	(£13,050)	7 R.I. (£9,750); 1 Mass. (£300); 1 N.Y. (£3,000).

Note: Certain amounts reported in Spanish dollars were reduced to pound equivalents at a rate of £1 (proclamation) to $7.10.
Source: John S. Ezell, *Fortune's Merry Wheel: The Lottery in America* (1960), 55, 64, 65, 71.

Early American attitudes toward drinking encouraged the custom of beginning the day with a shot of alcohol. It was not unusual for pillars of the community to take a "morning horn" by measuring out a good slug of rum into a hollowed cow's horn and quaffing it down before leaving their home. (*Harper's Magazine*, March 1881)

TABLE 17.5   ESTIMATED CONSUMPTION OF ALCOHOLIC BEVERAGES AND ABSOLUTE ALCOHOL (IN GALLONS) BY PERSONS OVER AGE 15 IN UNITED STATES, 1770–1800

	Wine[a]		Spirits[b]		Cider, Beer[c]		Total	
	Gal. of Drink	Gal. of Alcohol	Gal. of Drink	Gal. of Alcohol	Gal. of Drink	Gal. of Alcohol	Gal. of Drink	Gal. of Alcohol
1800	.6	.1	7.2	3.3	32.0	3.2	39.8	6.6
1795	.6	.1	5.9	2.7	34.0	3.4	40.5	6.2
1790	.6	.1	5.1	2.3	34.0	3.4	39.7	5.8
1785	.6	.1	5.7	2.6	34.0	3.4	40.3	6.1
1770	.2	.05	7.0	3.2	34.0	3.4	41.2	6.6

[a]18% alcohol.
[b]45% alcohol.
[c]10% alcohol.
Source: W. J. Rorabaugh, *The Alcoholic Republic: An American Tradition* (1979), 233.

the plodding Chesapeake tobacco farmers who had been trapped in dire poverty for several generations before 1720. This new type of chap came into his own on the frontier, where fewer restraints limited his behavior. Andrew Jackson once summarized the essence of these frontiersmen when he remarked, with obvious approval, that he had never met a Kentuckian without a rifle, a pack of cards, and a jug of whiskey.

CHAPTER 18 Crime and Violence

Hector St. John de Crèvecoeur, a Frenchman long a resident in Anglo-America, wrote in 1782 that a European traveling through the United States would be struck that "he seldom hears of punishments and executions." At the same time that Americans could read this statement, however, the prominent New Yorker John Jay was helping organize his state's Society for the Suppression of Vice and Immorality. The different reactions of Crèvecoeur and Jay probably tell more about their social expectations than social reality. To Crèvecoeur, who grew up in Europe—where widespread poverty caused numerous behavioral problems—the United States was remarkably free of lawless troublemakers. To Jay, who grew up in New York and took America's prosperity for granted, *any* criminal activity in his country was far too much. Historians have never provided a comparative perspective in which the dimensions of crime in the late eighteenth century could be evaluated. Despite the ambiguity surrounding this topic, it seems reasonable to conclude that the problems of crime and violence were generally less frequent and less serious than they have become two centuries later.

Almost three-quarters of all people convicted of crimes in New York before 1775 had committed one of the following six offenses: breaking the peace or violating public order (22.8%), personal violence (21.5%), theft (15.3%), contempt of authority (7.0%), corruption by public officials (4.1%), and prostitution (2.5%). Only about half of all indictments resulted in convictions. New York did not build a penitentiary to restrain perpetrators of the most serious crimes until after the Revolution. The records of admittances to this institution indicate that the most common offenses were larceny, and that violent crimes such as armed robbery, battery, and criminal assault on women were not major problems.

The criminal element included a disproportionate share of ethnic or racial minorities that occupied a marginal place in American society. Of the 693 convicts incarcerated at the New York Penitentiary

Long-term incarceration, rather than fines or corporal punishment, increasingly came to be seen as the most appropriate manner of dealing with malefactors by the 1790s. Philadelphia's Walnut Street Penitentiary, pictured here, was the first prison constructed with individual cells when built in 1790. (I. N. Phelps Stokes Collection, Miriam & Ira Wallach Div. of Arts, Prints and Photographs. Courtesy The New York Public Library. Astor, Lenox and Tilden Foundations.)

TABLE 18.1 OFFENSES OF CONVICTS ENTERING NEW YORK STATE PRISON, 1797–1801

Offense	Number	Percentage
Petit Larceny (under $12.50)	277	40.0%
Grand Larceny (over $12.50)	260	37.5%
Forgery	66	9.5%
Burglary	34	4.9%
Assault and battery	20	2.9%
Horse theft	15	2.2%
Arson	5	.7%
Manslaughter	4	.6%
Perjury	3	.4%
Receiving stolen goods	2	.3%
Highway robbery	1	.1%
Stealing from a church	1	.1%
Swindling	1	.1%
Bigamy	1	.1%
Rape	1	.1%
Sodomy	1	.1%
Total	693	100.0%

Source: D. B. Warden, *A Statistical, Political, and Historical Account of the United States of North America*, 3 vols. (1819), III, 475.

TABLE 18.2 BACKGROUNDS OF CRIMINALS CONVICTED AT PHILADELPHIA MAYOR'S COURT, 1794–1800

	1794	1795	1796	1797	1798	1799	1800
Repeat Offenders	. . .	3.6%	2.8%	15.6%	5.4%	14.7%	10.8%
Men	56.3%	76.8%	69.0%	71.1%	78.6%	67.6%	70.3%
Women	43.7%	23.2%	31.0%	28.9%	21.6%	32.4%	29.7%
Whites	50.0%	67.9%	71.8%	75.6%	75.0%	66.2%	62.2%
Blacks	50.0%	32.1%	28.2%	24.4%	25.0%	33.8%	37.8%
Born Ireland	25.0%	27.9%	38.9%	39.4%	36.7%	28.8%	25.0%
Born Elsewhere in Europe	43.8%	34.9%	31.5%	21.2%	16.3%	26.9%	25.0%
Born United States	31.2%	37.2%	29.6%	39.4%	47.0%	44.2%	50.0%
Born Pa.	. . .	9.3%	7.4%	3.0%	6.1%	7.7%	8.3%
Born Philadelphia	12.5%	2.3%	5.6%	6.1%	8.2%	3.9%	8.3%
Pardoned	62.5%	37.5%	21.1%	22.2%	3.6%	2.9%	10.8%
Total Number	16	56	71	45	56	68	37

Source: John K. Alexander, *Render Them Submissive: Responses to Poverty in Philadelphia, 1760–1800* (1980), 180.

from 1797 to 1801, 42% (290) were immigrants born in Europe. Immigrants composed 60% of all people convicted by the Mayor's Court in Philadelphia from 1794 to 1800. Although only 11% of whites in Philadelphia were of Irish background in 1800, 32% of all convicts punished by the Mayor's Court during those six years had been born in Ireland. Natives of Pennsylvania made up only 12% of those found guilty by this tribunal, and those born in Philadelphia comprised just 6% of the total. Although blacks equaled only 4% of all Philadelphians in 1800, they made up 32% of those sentenced by its Mayor's Court. Immigrants and nonwhites were more likely to be poor, and they faced a greater likelihood of becoming involved in theft or of seeing violence as an appropriate response for the gnawing sense of frustration produced by social prejudice.

It is extremely ironic that the group most predisposed to illegal activity, convicts sentenced by British courts to be sold as servants in the colonies, seem to have committed relatively few offenses after being transported. From 1763 to 1775, approximately 12,000 British convicts arrived in the colonies to labor seven years for whoever would purchase them. Americans continually expressed apprehension at the prospect of runaway convicts terrorizing the countryside with crime sprees, but few such episodes occurred. Many convicts did

escape, but most immediately took ship for Britain. The great majority of those who served out their seven-year sentences likewise seem to have returned home. Convict laborers did little to contribute to the crime rate, not necessarily because they had become rehabilitated, but because American society was uncongenial to their methods of criminal behavior. Most convict laborers had been sentenced for theft and had operated in a society with a criminal infrastructure designed to distribute stolen goods efficiently. The colonies lacked a similar criminal network for selling stolen property, and it was rare for families to have substantial amounts of cash at home that might be discovered, so thieves, pickpockets, and burglars soon discovered that America was not the land of opportunity for them. Honest work, ironically, was much easier than a life of crime.

To deter criminal behavior, early Americans relied on simple, direct, and highly visible punishments. Few prisons existed for long-term incarceration because taxpayers wanted to avoid the cost of maintaining malefactors for extended periods. Jails primarily existed to hold dangerous felons before trial, not as a place of punishment afterward. Although debtors were often kept behind bars for long periods as a means of compelling them to sell off property to satisfy their creditors, they were generally forced to have their families carry meals to them or bring provisions for the jailor to prepare.

In place of jail sentences, Revolutionary society exacted retribution for crime through fines for the majority of offenses, which were

TABLE 18.3 CRIMES AND BACKGROUNDS OF INMATES AT PHILADELPHIA JAIL, 1793

Residences of inmates (27 men and 10 women)

	Philadelphia City	Philadelphia County	Huntingdon County	Franklin County	Berks County	Delaware County	Washington County
Burlgary	1	. . .	. . .	2	. . .	. . .	2
Felony	12	4	1	2	3	. . .	. . .
Deceit	1	. . .	. . .	. . .	. . .	1	. . .
Forgery	2	. . .	. . .	. . .	. . .	. . .	. . .
Horse theft	. . .	2	. . .	. . .	2	. . .	. . .
Highway robbery	. . .	1	. . .	. . .	. . .	. . .	. . .
Receiving stolen goods	. . .	1	. . .	. . .	. . .	. . .	. . .
Total	16	8	1	4	5	1	2

Source: William Bradford, *An Enquiry How Far the Punishment of Death is Necessary in Pennsylvania* (1793), 108.

minor or nonviolent. For more serious violations, courts literally exacted blood through corporal punishments. Almost as dreadful as the pain of physical correction was the prospect of public humiliation, since punishments were inflicted at community centers and often attracted large crowds. A strong indication of the deterrent power of such spectacles is given by the following verses, which appeared in a Massachusetts handbill announcing the punishment of three men for counterfeiting in 1767.

A few lines on
Magnus Mode, Richard Hodges & J. Newington Clark.
Who are Sentenc'd to stand one Hour in the
PILLORY AT CHARLESTOWN;
To have one of their EARS cut off,
and to be Whipped 20 Stripes at the public Whipping Post,
for making and passing Counterfeit DOLLARS, etc.

BEHOLD the villains rais'd on high!
(The *Post* they've got attracts the eye:)
Both Jews and Gentiles all appear
To see them stand exalted here;
Both rich and poor, both young and old,
The dirty slut, the common scold,
What multitudes do them surround,
Many as bad as can be found.
And so encrease their sad disgrace,
Throw rotten eggs into their face,
And pelt them sore with dirt and stones,
Nay, if they could wou'd break their bones.
Their malice to such height arise,
Who knows but they'll put out their eyes:
But pray consider what you do
While thus expos'd to public view.
Justice has often done its part,
And made the guilty rebels smart;
But they went on did still rebel,
And seem'd to storm the gates of hell.
To no good counsel would they hear;
But now each one must loose an EAR,
And they although against their will
Are forc'd to chew the bitter pill;
And this day brings the villains hence
To suffer for their late offence;
They on th' Pillory stand in view:
A warning fire to me and you!
The drunkards song, the harlots scorn,
Reproach of some as yet unborn.
But now the Post they're forc'd to hug,
But loath to take that nauseous drug
Which brings the blood from out their veins,
And marks their back with purple stains.
From their disgrace, now warning take,
And never do your ruin make
By stealing, or unlawful ways;
(If you would live out all your days)
But keep secure from Theft and Pride;
Strive to have virtue on your side.
Despise the harlot's flattering airs,
And hate her ways, avoid her stares;
Keep clear from Sin of every kind,
And then you'll have true peace of Mind.

The only major crime wave in eighteenth-century America struck the frontier of South Carolina in the mid-1760s. The newly settled area was devastated in the Cherokee Indian War of 1760–1761, which brutalized many young men, threw a large portion of the population into poverty, and disrupted law enforcement. Outlaw bands almost immediately began to be formed by homeless residents, runaway slaves, and ex-soldiers who were either too violent or restless to lead a peaceful life. Establishing large camps in the wilderness, these gangs engaged in a wanton spree of robbery, torture, gang rape, and murder. By 1766, the outlaws reigned virtually supreme in the area and had established an extensive horse-stealing enterprise with fencing connections in neighboring colonies.

Lacking an adequate system of local law enforcement, in 1767 desperate settlers organized posses of Regulators, which were the country's earliest vigilantes. Destroying the banditti required a two-year, para-military campaign. Having driven out the gangs, the Regulators began rounding up nonviolent, but disreputable, residents such as vagrants, petty thieves, and prostitutes, who were flogged or ordered out of the area after drum-head trials. Although the Regulators managed to break the back of an insidious crime wave and restore order out of social chaos, they became increasingly arbitrary and sometimes inflicted sentences that smacked of sadism. Alarmed over their excesses, the legislature instituted a system of courts and law officers that could keep order on the frontier in 1769, whereupon the Regulators disbanded.

South Carolina's Regulators established the model for later organizations of vigilantes (a term that did not come into use until the California Gold Rush). An American tradition had begun, and it reappeared several times west of the Appalachians wherever sparsely settled communities lacked effective law enforcement. Most of the subsequent regulator organizations were short-lived movements begun in response to the depredations of a few hard-core criminals such as the Harpe brothers, Big Micajah and Little Wiley.

The Harpes were the most ruthless and purposeless serial killers to run amok in early America. The sons of a Scottish Tory in North Carolina, they came to Tennessee in 1795 and committed their first crime, the robbery of a Methodist minister. Still young in the ways of vice, they not only told the victim their names but also neglected to kill him. After their description became known (they were always exceptionally unkempt, ragged, and filthy), they began to kill every lone traveler they robbed; eventually they killed almost everyone they met.

Arrested for horse stealing at Knoxville, they escaped and headed for Kentucky. Presently they killed a guest at a Tennessee tavern, next a peddler on the Wilderness Road, and then three men in short order in Kentucky, for a total of five murders in as many weeks. By this time, Micajah and Wiley had collected a harem of three women, who had all become pregnant by them, although none of the women could say by which brother. Jailed again at Danville, Kentucky, the brothers bored through a log wall and escaped while still shackled. They fled west to the Ohio River and killed another three men on their way.

Joining a group of river pirates at Cave-in-Rock, on the Illinois shore, they plundered passing flatboats, exterminated entire families, and occasionally amused themselves by torturing victims to death. They later meandered back through Tennessee and Kentucky masquerading as itinerant preachers, and during this jaunt they murdered a minimum of eleven men, one woman, and a baby. Hunted down by a posse of Regulators, they were overtaken in west Kentucky; Wiley escaped into the forest, but Micajah was shot and decapitated while yet alive. His head was left spiked on a post. Wiley fled to New Orleans, where he lived peacefully until 1803, when he was recognized by a Kentuckian, tried, and executed. So ended the most brutal interstate crime spree in early America.

The Revolutionary era witnessed numerous instances of crowd actions and collective intimidation. The majority happened in the dozen years preceding independence. Contrary to British propa-

TABLE 18.4 CROWD DISTURBANCES AND REGULATOR MOVEMENTS, 1764–1799

Year	Location	Event
1799	New York, N.Y.	Brothel Riot
1799	Bethleham, Pa.	Fries's Anti-tax Disturbances
1798	Western Ky.	Regulator Anti-Criminal Movement
1798	Knoxville, Tenn.	Regulator Anti-Criminal Movement
1794	Western Pa.	Whiskey Rebellion
1793	Russellville, Ky.	Regulator Anti-Criminal Movement
1790s	Green River, Ky.	Regulator Anti-Criminal Movement
1790s	Barren River, Ky.	Regulator Anti-Criminal Movement
1788	New York, N.Y.	Graverobbers Riot
1786	Western Mass.	Debtors forcibly close courts
1775	Ga.	Anti-Customs disturbance
1775	Sassafrass-Bohemia, Md.	Anti-Customs disturbance
1774	Newport, R.I.	Anti-Customs disturbance
1774	East Greenwich, R.I.	Intimidation of Royal supporters
1774	Providence, R.I.	Disturbance over licensing rules
1773	Boston, Mass.	Boston Tea Party
1772	near Providence, R.I.	Customs schooner *Gaspee* burned
1771	R.I.	Anti-Customs disturbance
1771	Providence, R.I.	Violence against customs tidesman
1771	Boston, Mass.	Brothel dispossessed
1771–1768	Western N.C.	Regulator Anti-Corruption Movement
1770–1774	Vt.	Dispossessions and other violence against N.H. grants
1770	Newark, N.J.	Anti-proprietary arson and protests
1770	Boston, Mass.	Boston Massacre
1770	New York, N.Y.	Liberty pole violence
1770	Philadelphia, Pa.	Anti-Customs disturbance
1770	R.I.	Anti-Customs disturbance
1769–1770	Monmouth Co., N.J.	Anti-Lawyer disturbances
Late 1760s	New York, N.Y.	Anti-Adulterer disturbances
Late 1760s	Providence, R.I.	Anti-Adulterer disturbances
Late 1760s	Newport, R.I.	Anti-Adulterer disturbances
1769	Philadelphia, Pa.	Anti-Customs disturbance
1769	Newport, R.I.	Anti-Customs disturbance
1769	New London, Conn.	Anti-Customs disturbance
1769	New Haven, Conn.	Anti-Customs disturbance
1767–1769	S.C. backcountry	Regulator (Vigilante) Movement
1768	Norfolk, Va.	Smallpox disturbance
1768	Boston, Mass.	Sloop *Liberty* violence
1767	Norfolk, Va.	Anti-impressment violence
1766	Norfolk, Va.	Anti-Customs disturbance
1766	New Haven, Conn.	Anti-Customs disturbance
1766	Falmouth, Maine	Anti-Customs disturbance
1766	New London, Conn.	Violence to Rogerene Church members
1766	Hudson Valley, N.Y.	Anti-rent disturbances
1765	Mass., R.I., Md.	Stamp Act violence
1765	Newport, R.I.	Anti-impressment violence
1765	Mecklenburg Co., N.C.	Violence against land surveyors
1765	Cumberland Co., Pa.	Violence toward Indian traders
1764	Newport, R.I.	Anti-Customs disturbance
1764	Dighton, Mass.	Anti-Customs disturbance
1764	Newport, R.I.	Anti-impressment violence
1764	New York, N.Y.	Soldiers riot
1764	New York, N.Y.	Anti-impressment violence
1764	Philadelphia, Pa.	Threatened riot by Paxton Boys
1763	Lancaster, Pa.	Mob violence toward Christian Indians

Source: Richard M. Brown, "Violence and the American Revolution," in Stephen G. Kurtz and James H. Hutson, eds., *Essays on the American Revolution* (1973), 119–120, and Richard M. Brown, "The American Vigilante Tradition," in Hugh D. Graham and Ted R. Gurr, eds., *The History of Violence in America* (1969), 218–26.

ganda, and to the general impression that has taken hold since then, the leaders who opposed unconstitutional British measures strongly disapproved of violence as a tactic to advance American interests. The preferred tactics for resisting British policies were trade boycotts and legislative enactments, both of which were entirely pacific.

As a general rule, leaders of the American resistance only resorted to forcible measures when peaceful methods were no longer feasible. Their most spectacular instance of destruction, the Boston Tea Party, only resulted at the last possible moment, after the Massachusetts governor had rejected several proposals that would have allowed the tea to be returned to England undamaged. American leaders discountenanced any terroristic assaults or ambushes on British soldiers, royal officials, or their supporters. During the entire period from the Stamp Act until British troops fired upon Massachusetts militia at Lexington, no British troops or civilian officers died as a result of the protests against violations of American rights. The only fatalities of these years were shot by redcoats at the Boston Massacre in 1770. Americans orchestrated mass demonstrations to express popular disgust with British policies, and the participants often behaved with a vehemence shocking to British observers, but they rarely failed to take precautions that would keep the crowd from committing physical assaults or committing unconscionable property damage.

What violence did occur was usually a spontaneous or unforeseen response to a perceived provocation by British officials. In all but a few cases, assaults on British officials involved abuses of authority by the Customs Service. The years after 1767 witnessed an epidemic of "customs racketeering" in which officials used numerous technical infractions of trade regulations to confiscate the cargoes of merchants who were guilty of nothing more than inadvertently violating minor provisions of a very complex set of rules. At least eight major riots against revenue collectors occurred for such reasons; all had their roots in exasperation with corrupt bureaucrats, not in political dissatisfaction. Even the Boston Massacre stemmed from this source of unease, for the redcoats found themselves beset by a riotous crowd because they were stationed as a guard to protect the local customs house from the townspeople's wrath.

CHAPTER 19 A Documentary Sampler of Revolutionary American Life

The everyday lives of Americans in the late eighteenth century were primarily influenced not by politics or constitutional change, but by military campaigns during the Revolution and the frontier's rapid expansion. Residents in every section of the United States witnessed large-scale military operations from 1775 to 1783. Many families suffered substantial losses of property when the army's foragers appropriated their livestock or crops in exchange for promissory receipts that in many cases were paid in wildly inflated Continental dollars. Well over half of all free adult males under age 45 performed active duty in the military. Every tenth soldier died in uniform, and most Americans experienced the death of at least one nephew or cousin. Second only to the war as a collective historical experience was frontier migration. By 1800, perhaps one-third of all American families lived on farms hacked out of raw wilderness since 1763—most of them in the huge tracts of virgin forest that remained unsettled east of the Appalachian crest from Maine to Georgia—and pioneers were flooding into the Ohio Valley. The following documents provide first-hand statements of four people whose lives were molded by frontier expansion and the Revolutionary conflict: an Irish immigrant woman adopted by Indians, a New England Continental soldier, a runaway slave, and a child raised on a wilderness farm.

Dickewamis: The "White Woman" of the Seneca

In April 1758, Shawnee Indians captured fifteen-year-old Mary Jemison and sold her to Senecas at Ft. Duquesne. Her adoptive Seneca family named her Dickewamis and treated her so warmly that she refused to return to white society. Unlike most Seneca, who left upstate New York for Ontario during the Revolution, Dickewamis stayed in the Genesee Valley; she established title to more than 30 square miles, rented land to white tenants, and lived to be ninety.

Source: James E. Seaver, ed., *A Narrative of the Life of Mrs. Mary Jemison* (1961 ed. of 1824 imprint), 27, 32–33, 36, 38, 40, 42, 44–47, 52–53, 66, 72–73, 82–85, 103, 105, 112–113, 152.

Excepting my birth, nothing remarkable occurred to my parents on their passage [from Ireland], and they were safely landed at Philadelphia. My father being fond of rural life, and having been bred to agricultural pursuits, soon left the city, and removed his family to the then frontier settlements of Pennsylvania. Breakfast was not yet ready [in April 1758], when we were alarmed by the discharge of a number of guns. On opening the door, a man and horse lay dead near the house, having just been shot by the Indians.

The party that took us consisted of six Indians and four Frenchmen, who immediately commenced plundering. Having taken as much provision as they could carry, they set out with their prisoners in great haste. Whenever the little children cried for water, the Indians would make them drink urine or go thirsty. Towards evening we arrived at the border of a dark and dismal swamp. As soon as I had finished my supper, an Indian took off my shoes and stockings and put a pair of moccasins on

my feet. During this time, the Indians stripped the shoes and stockings from the little boy that belonged to the woman who was taken with us, and put moccasins on his feet. An Indian took the little boy and myself by the hand, to lead us off from the company.

I felt a kind of horror, anxiety, and dread. Early the next morning the Indians and Frenchmen that we had left the night before, came to us; but our friends were left behind. They took from their baggage a number of scalps. Having put the scalps, yet wet and bloody, upon the hoops, and stretched them to their full extent, they then held them to the fire till they were partly dried and then with their knives commenced scraping off the flesh. Those scalps I knew at the time must have been from our family by the color of the hair. My mother's hair was red; and I could easily distinguish my father's and the children's from each other.

We came in sight of Fort Pitt (as it is now called), where we halted. I was now left alone in the fort. But it was not long before I was in some measure relieved by the appearance of two pleasant looking squaws of the Seneca tribe, who came and examined me. After a few minutes absence they returned with my former [Shawnee] masters, who gave me to them to dispose as they pleased.

At night we arrived at a small Seneca Indian town. All the Squaws in the town came to see me. I was soon surrounded by them, and they immediately set up a most dismal howling, crying bitterly and wringing their hands in all the agonies of grief for a deceased relative. In the course of that ceremony, from mourning they became serene, joy sparked in their countenances, and they seemed to rejoice over me as over a long lost child. I was made welcome amongst them as a sister to the two Squaws before mention, and was called Dickewamis . . . pretty girl. I was ever considered and treated by them as a real sister.

The first summer of our living at Wiishto, a party of Delaware Indians came up the [Ohio] River. Not long after the Delawares came to live with us, at Wiishto, my sisters told me that I must go and live with one of them, whose name was She-nin-jee. I went; and Sheninjee and I were married. His good nature, generosity, tenderness, and friendship towards me, soon gained my affection. We lived happily together till the time of our final separation, which happened two or three years after our marriage. He was taken sick and died at Wiishto. When my son Thomas [by Sheninjee] was three or four years old, I was married to an Indian, whose name was Hiokatoo, by whom I had four daughters and two sons.

No people can live more happy than the Indians did in times of peace, before the introduction of spiritous liquors amongst them. Their lives were a continual round of pleasures. Their wants were few, and easily satisfied; and their cares were only for to-day. The moral character of the Indians was uncontaminated. Their fidelity was perfect, and became proverbial; they were strictly honest; and chastity was held in high veneration.

Our Indians lived quietly and peaceably at home, till a little before the breaking out of the Revolutionary War. Upon this, the Chiefs concluded a treaty with the British Commissioners, in which they agreed to take up arms against the rebels. For four or five years we sustained no loss in the war, except the few who had been killed in distant battles. In the fall of 1779, a large and powerful army of the rebels, under the command of General Sullivan, was making rapid progress towards our settlement. Sullivan and his army arrived at Genesee River, where they destroyed every article of the food that they could lay their hands on. They burnt our houses, killed what few cattle and horses they could find, destroyed our fruit trees, and left nothing but the bare soil.

I immediately resolved to take my children and look out for myself, without delay, and the same night arrived on the Gardow Flats [N.Y.]. Two negroes, who had run away from their masters sometime before, were the only inhabitants of those flats. As they were in want of help to secure their crop, I hired to them to husk corn till the whole was harvested. I have laughed a thousand times to myself when I have thought of the old negro, who hired me, who fearing that I should get taken or injured by the Indians, stood by me constantly when I was husking, with a loaded gun in his hand. I husked enough for them, to gain for myself, twenty-five bushels of shelled corn. This considerable supply made my family comfortable for samp and cakes through the succeeding winter. The snow fell about five feet deep, so much so that almost all the game upon which the Indians depended for subsistence, perished, and reduced them almost to a state of starvation.

The negroes continued on my flats two or three years after this. I lived undisturbed, without hearing a word on the subject of my land, till the great council was held at Big Tree in 1797 . . . securing to me the title to all the land I had described. My flats were extremely fertile; but needed more labor than my daughters and myself were able to perform, to produce a sufficient quantity of grain. In order that we might live more easy, Mr. Parrish, with the consent of the chiefs, gave me liberty to lease or let my land out to white people to till on shares.

In the month of November 1811, my husband Hiokatoo, died at the advanced age of one hundred and three years. During the term of nearly fifty years that I lived with him, I received, according to Indian customs, all the kindness and attention that was my due as his wife. He uniformly treated me with tenderness, and never offered an insult, yet, as a warrior, his cruelties to his enemies were unparalleled. I have been the mother of eight children; three of whom are now [in 1824] living, and I have thirty-nine grand children and fourteen great grand children.

Joseph Plumb Martin: Continental Veteran

Joseph Plumb Martin, a minister's son, was born in 1760 at Becket, Massachusetts, but was raised mainly on his grandfather's farm at Ashford, Connecticut. He joined the Continental Army when just sixteen and fought most of the war with the Eighth Connecticut Regiment. In 1784, Martin settled in Prospect, Maine, where he married and raised five children and died at age eighty-nine.

Source: George F. Scheer, ed., *Private Yankee Doodle: Being A Narrative of Some of the Adventures, Dangers and Sufferings of a Revolutionary Soldier* (1962 ed. of 1830 imprint), 15–16, 22, 33–37, 43–45, 103–05, 114–15, 135–38, 280–81.

In the month of June [1776], orders came out for enlisting men. I one evening went off with a full determination to enlist. I went with several others of the company on board a sloop bound to New York. Americans were invincible in my opinion.

I remained in New York two or three months. We had a chain of sentinals quite up the [East] river [on September 14]. At interval of every half hour, they passed the watchword to each other, "All is well," I heard the British on board their shipping answer, "We will alter your tune before tomorrow night." And they were as good as their word for once. As soon as it was fairly light, we saw their boats coming out of a cove on the Long Island side of the water, filled with British soldiers, until they appeared like a large clover field in full bloom. And now was coming on the famous Kip's Bay affair . . . when all of a sudden there came such a peal of thunder from the British shipping that I thought my head would go with the sound. I made a frog's leap for the ditch and lay as still as I possibly could and began to consider which part of my carcass was to go first. We kept the lines till they were almost leveled upon us, when our officers, seeing we could make no resistance and no orders coming from any superior officer and that we must soon be entirely exposed to the rake of their guns, gave the order to leave the lines.

The grapeshot and language flew merrily, which served to quicken our motions. I found myself in company with one who was a neighbor of mine when at home and one other man belonging to our regiment. Where the rest of them were I knew not. We went into a house by the highway in which were two women and some small children, all crying most bitterly. We asked the women if they had any spirits in the house. They placed a case bottle of rum upon the table and bid us help ourselves. We each drank a glass and bidding them good-by betook ourselves to the highway again.

The demons of fear and disorder seemed to take full possession of all and everything that day. Several of the British came so near me that I could see the buttons on their clothes. We had eight or ten of our regiment killed in the action. When we came off the field we brought away a man who had been shot dead. Just as we had laid him in the grave as decent a posture as existing circumstances would admit, there came from the house towards the grave two young ladies. Upon arriving at the head of the grave, they stopped and with their arms around each other's neck stooped forward and looked into it, and with a sweet pensiveness of countenance which might have warmed the heart of a misogynist, asked if we were going to put the earth on his naked face. Being answered in the affirmative, one of them took a fine white gauze handkerchief from her neck and desired that it might be spread upon his face, tears at the same time flowing down their cheeks. Worthy young ladies!

We arrived at the Valley Forge [on December 18, 1777]. I lay here two nights and one day and had not a morsel of anything to eat all the time, save half of a small pumpkin. I was warned to be ready for a two days command. Here we understood that our destiny was to go into the country on a foraging expedition, which was nothing more or less than to procure provisions from the inhabitants for the men in the army and forage for the poor perishing cattle belonging to it, at the point of the bayonet.

We marched till night when we halted and took up our quarters at a large farmhouse. One of the men proposed to the landlady to sell her a shirt for some sauce. She very readily took the shirt, which was worth a dollar at least. By the time it was eatable, the family had gone to rest. We saw where the woman went into the cellar, and she having left us a candle, we took it into our heads that a little good cider would not make our supper relish any worse; so some of the men took the water pail and drew it full of excellent cider, which did not fail to raise our spirits considerably. Before we lay down the man who sold the shirt, having observed that the landlady had flung it into a closet, took a notion to repossess it again. We marched off early in the morning before the people of the house were stirring, consequently did not know the woman's chagrin at having been over-reached by the soldiers.

I happened to be at a farmer's house with one or two of the wagon masters. The man of the house was from home and the old lady rather crabbed; she knew our business and was therefore inclined to be *rather* unsociable. There was a little Negro boy belonging to the house, about five or six years of age, who, the whole time I was there, sat upon a stool in the chimney corner; indeed, he looked as if he had sat there ever since he was born. One of the wagon masters said to the landlady one day, "Mother,

Pictured here is Howard Pyle's conception of George Washington giving Baron von Steuben his first look at the Continentals camped at Valley Forge, Pennsylvania. It was in huts like these that Pvt. James Martin endured the winter at Valley Forge with his ragged Connecticut Regiment. (Howard Pyle Collection, courtesy Delaware Art Museum, Wilmington, Delaware)

is that your son that sits in the corner?" "My son!" said she. "Why, don't you see he is a Negro?" "A Negro? Is he?" said the man. "Why I really thought he was your son, only that he had sat there until he was smoke-dried."

Several of our party went to a tavern in the neighborhood. We here gambled a little for some liquor by throwing a small dart or stick, armed at one end with a pin, at a mark on the ceiling of the room. I found that the landlord and I bore the same name, and upon further discourse I found that he had a son about my age, whose given name was the same as mine. This was taken prisoner at Fort Lee, on the Hudson River, in the year 1776, and died on his way home. These good people were almost willing to persuade themselves that I was their son. The landlord used to fill my canteen with whiskey or peach or cider brandy to enable me, as he said, to climb the Welch mountains [of Pennsylvania]. I often wished afterwards that I could find more namesakes.

[In 1778] I was transferred to the Light Infantry. It was a motley group—Yankees, Irishmen, Buckskins and what not. The regiment that I belonged to was made up about half New Englanders and the remainder were chiefly Pennsylvanians. Consequently, there was not much cordiality subsisting between us, for, to tell the sober truth, I had in those days as lief have been incorporated with a tribe of western Indians as with any of the southern troops, especially of those which consisted mostly, as the Pennsylvanians did, of foreigners. To make matters worse, I was often, when on duty, the only Yankee that happened to be on the same tour for several days together. "The bloody Yankee," or "the d----d Yankee," was the mildest epithets that they would bestow upon me.

There was an Irishman belonging to our Infantry, who after an affray [with Hessian cavalry] was over, seeing a wounded man belonging to the enemy lying in the road and unable to help himself, took pity on him, as he was in danger of being trodden upon by the horses, and having shouldered him was staggering off with his load. While crossing a small worn-out bridge over a very muddy brook, he happened to jostle the poor fellow more than usual, who cried out, "Good rebel, don't hurt poor Hushman." "Who do you call a rebel, you scoundrel?" said the Irishman, and tossed him off his shoulders as unceremoniously as though he had been a log.

[In January 1780, at Morristown, New Jersey] Martial law was very strict against firing muskets in camp. Nothing could, therefore, raise the officers' "lofty ideals" sooner, or more, than to fire in camp. Finding they were watched by the officers, they got an old gun barrel which they placed in a hut that was unfinished. This they loaded a third part full and putting a slow match to it, would then escape to their own huts, when the old barrel would speak for itself, with a voice that would be heard. The officers would then muster out, and some running and scolding would ensue; but none knew who made the noise, or where it came from. The farce was carried on the greater part of the night; but at length the officers getting tired of running so often to catch Mr. Nobody, without finding him, that they gave up the chase, and the men seeing they could no longer gull the officers, gave up the business.

Time thus passed to the nineteenth of April [1783], when we had general orders read which satisfied the most skeptical, that the war was over. We had lived together as a family of brothers for several years, setting aside some little family squabbles, like most other families, had shared with each other the hardships, dangers, and sufferings incident to a soldier's life; had sympathized with each other in trouble and sickness; had assisted in

bearing each other's burdens or strove to make them lighter by council and advice; had endeavored to conceal each other's faults or make them appear in as good a light as they would bear. In short, the soldiers, each in his own particular circle of acquaintance, were as strict a band of brotherhood as Masons. I doubt there was a corps in the army that parted with more regret than ours did, the New Englanders in particular. Ah! it was a serious time.

Jehu Grant: African-American Revolutionary Teamster

Jehu Grant ran away from a Tory master of Narragansett, Rhode Island, in August 1777 and enlisted for eighteen months as a wagoner in the Continental Army. He served ten months before his master located him and reclaimed him as a fugitive slave. He later became free, settled in Milton, Connecticut, and in 1832 filed a pension claim, which was rejected because he had joined the army illegally under the wrongful pretenses of being free. In the following letter of 1836, Grant defended his right to a pension in a heartfelt evocation of the hopes engendered among African-Americans by the Revolution's political ideals. His appeal went unheeded, however, for he never received a pension and died in penury.

Source: John C. Dann, ed., *The Revolution Remembered: Eyewitness Accounts of the War for Independence* (1980), 27–28.

To J. L. Edwards
Commissioner of Pensions
Washington

Your servant begs leave to state that he forwarded to the War Department a declaration founded on the Pension Act of June 1832 praying to be allowed a pension (if his memory serves him) for ten months' service in the American Army of the Revolutionary War. That he enlisted as a soldier but was put to the service of a teamster in the summer and a waiter in the winter. In April 1832 I received a writing from Your Honor, informing me that my "services while a fugitive from my master's service was not embraced in said Act," and that my "papers were placed on file." In my said declaration, I just mentioned the cause of leaving my master, as may be seen by a reference thereunto, and I now pray that I may be permitted to express my feelings more fully on that part of my said declaration.

I was then grown to manhood, in the full vigor and strength of life, and heard much about the cruel and arbitrary things done by the British. Their ships lay within a few miles of my master's house, which stood near the shore, and I was confident that my master traded with them, and I suffered much from fear that I should be sent aboard a ship of war. This I disliked. But when I saw liberty poles and the people all engaged for the support of freedom, I could not but like and be pleased with such thing (God forgive me if I sinned in so feeling). And living on the borders of Rhode Island, where whole companies of colored people enlisted, it added to my fears and dread of being sold to the British. These considerations induced me to enlist into the American Army, where I served faithfully about ten months, when my master found me and took me home. Had I been taught to read or understand the precepts of the Gospel, "Servants obey your masters," I might have done otherwise, notwithstanding the songs of liberty that saluted my ear, thrilled though my heart. But feeling conscious that I have since compensated my master for the injury he sustained by my enlisting, and that God has forgiven me for so doing, and that I served my country faithfully, and that they having enjoyed the benefits of my service to an equal degree for the length of time I served with those generally who are receiving the liberalities of the government, I cannot but feel it becoming me to pray Your Honor to review my declaration on file.

A few years after the war, Joshua Swan, Esq., of Stonington [Conn.] purchased me of my master and agreed that after I had served him a length of time named faithfully, I should be free. I served to his satisfaction and so obtained my freedom. He moved into the town of Milton [Conn.], where I now reside, about [1788]. After my time expired with Esq. Swan, I married a wife. We have raised six children. Five are still living. I must be upward of eighty years of age and have been blind for many years, and, not withstanding the aid I received from the honest industry of my children, we are still very needy and in part are supported from the benevolence of our friends. With these statements, . . . I humbly set my claim upon the well-known liberality of government.

his
Jehu   X   Grant
mark

Daniel Drake: A Frontier Farm Boy

Daniel Drake was born in 1785 at Plainfield, New Jersey, and taken to Mays Lick, Kentucky, at age three. Drake spent his early life absorbed in farm work on his parents' homestead. Pioneer life entailed many privations for young Daniel, but in many respects his annual regimen of work closely resembled that of most farm children in the United States. Although Drake obtained virtually no formal education, a Cincinnati doctor agreed to train him as an apprentice in 1800; he earned an M.D. degree from the University of Pennsylvania in 1818 and became perhaps the most respected physician in the Ohio Valley prior to his death at Cincinnati in 1852.

Source: Emmet F. Horine, ed., *Pioneer Life in Kentucky, 1785–1800 by Daniel Drake, M.D.* (1948 ed. of 1870 imprint), 6, 15, 24–27, 48–52, 74–75, 78–79, 108, 179–180.

Mays Lick, Kentucky, was a colony of East Jersey people, amounting in the aggregate to 52 souls. The immigrants from other states were almost entirely Virginians and Marylanders. The Jersey people were generally without slaves, partly from principle, and partly from the want of means. Most of the settlers from Virginia and Maryland brought slaves with them, though the number in each family was small—often one only.

Now fancy yourself a log cabin of the size and form of a dining room—one story high—without a window—with door opening to the south—with a half-finished wooden chimney—with a roof on one side only—without any upper or lower floor . . . and you will have the picture which constitutes *my first memory*. When older & locomotive enough to totter over the doorsill and get out on the grass, as I was sitting there one day, a mad dog came along. I looked at the mad animal, and he thought it prudent to pass me by, and attack a small herd of cattle, several of which died from his bite!

For the next 6 years [after 1788] my father continued to reside at the same place, in the same original log cabin, which in due course acquired a roof, a puncheon floor below and a clap board floor above, and a small window without glass, and a chimney. The rifle, *indispensable* both for hunting & defense, lay on two pegs driven into one of the logs. In the morning the first duty was to ascend a ladder which always stood, leaning behind the door, to the loft and look through the cracks for Indians lest they might have planted themselves near the door, to rush in when the strong crossbar should be removed, and the heavy latch raised.

About [1790] the Indians attacked a body of travelers, encamped a mile from our village on the road to Washington. They were sitting quietly around their camp fire, when the Indians shot among them, and killed a man whose remains I remember to have seen brought, the next day, into the village on a rude litter. The heroic presence of mind of a woman saved the party. She broke open a chest in one of the wagons with an axe, got at the ammunition, gave it to the men and called upon them to fight. This, with the extinction of their Camp fires, led the Indians to retreat.

In or about the year 1791, my aunt Lydia Shotwell was married. A number of Father's acquaintances in and around Washington were invited. They came armed, and while assembled in the house, report was brought that the Indians, about 5 miles up the road toward Lexington, had attacked a wagon. All the armed men mounted their horses & galloped off in a style so picturesque that I shall never forget it. The alarm proved to be false.

The first and greatest labour after father had thus domiciled his little family, was to clear sufficient land for a crop the following year, which was, of course, to consist of corn and a few garden vegetables. It was two or three years before his fields grew to any great extent. The soil, however, was highly productive and the autumn of 1789 would have brought forth a sufficient abundance but that on the night of the last day of August there came so severe a frost as to kill the unripe corn, and almost break the hearts of those who had watched its growth from day to day in joyous anticipation.

There was no fear of famine. Deer were numerous and wild turkies numberless. The latter were often so fat that in falling from the tree when shot their skins would burst.

Nothing is equal to Indian corn for the settlers of a new and isolated spot. In the new soil, corn, with moderate cultivation, yielded from 60 to 80 bushels to the acre. Every domestic animal fed and flourished on it—the horse, the cow, the sheep, the hog and the dog who, as wheat bread came into use, would not eat it. Several things in its cultivation can be done by small boys, and from my 8th year, I participated in them. When the field was cross furrowed, the furrows being about 4 feet apart, dropping the corn was a simple task, and father, following with the hoe, would cover it.

As soon as the young corn began to "come up" two most acute and active animals began to pull it up. These were crows and squirrels. It was my special function to repel these aggressions. My means of defense were very harmless and may almost be summed up in the word, *noise*. Old Lion [his dog], however, was a faithful ally and I made a *show* of resistance with clubs and stones. When I was about 11 years old, father purchased me a little old shot gun, and I circum-perambulated the little field with the eye of a hunter—and the self-importance of a sentinel on the ramparts of a fortress.

This same good old Lion and myself were boon companions and co-workers. When the hogs got into the corn field he would labour till the last was lugged out. If mother wanted a chicken he would run it down and hold, without biting it, under his paws. When I went into the woods he would "tree" squirrels for me; & when I was out after dark he kept by my side, and taking one of my wrists in his mouth would run with me till I got out of breath.

From the age of 8 to 15 I had much care of our stock; for boys can do that kind of work. The cows & sheep had to be hunted up in the woods, & driven home at night, one of each dignified with a bell. On hearing a cow bell in the woods, you can always tell whether the animal is feeding or walking. When our sheep laid out in the woods, they were often destroyed by the wolves, which still infested that country when I left it for the study of medicine [i.e., 1800].

Father and mother were early risers, and I was drilled into the same habit before I was 10 years old. In winter we were generally up before the dawn of day. After making a fire, the first thing was feeding and foddering the horses, hogs, sheep & cattle. Corn husks, blades & tops had to be distributed, & times without number, I have done this by the light of the moon reflected on the snow. This done at an earlier hour than common, old Lion and I sometimes took a little hunt in the woods. Among the pleasant recollections of those mornings are the red birds, robins and snow birds, which made their appearance to pick up the scattering grains of corn where the cattle had been fed. I well remember my anxiety to get some fresh salt to throw on their tails. I often made conical lattice traps, and set them; but . . . my captures were not numerous.

Breakfast over, my function was to provide the "sauce" for dinner. In winter, to open the potato or turnip "hole," and wash what I took out—in spring, to go into the fields and collect the "greens;" in summer and autumn, to explore the "truck patch," or our little garden; and from among the weeds dig or pull whatever might be in season. If I afterward went to the field, my culinary labours ceased till night. If not, they continued through the day, and consisted of participation in all that was going on—now tending the "child"—now hunting eggs to boil—now making up the fire—now sweeping the hearth, and putting things to rights—now cleaning the old iron candle stick—now looking at the sill of the front door, to see by the shadow of its cheeks, whether it was time I should put the potatoes in—now twisting a fork in the meat to know if it were nearly done & now "fetching" a pail of fresh water, that father might wash his hands and take a drink.

The time *has* been (*perhaps* should be still), when I looked back upon the years thus spent as *lost*. Lost as it respects my destiny in life—lost as to distinction in my profession. I was preserved from many temptations, and practically taught self-denial because indulgence, beyond certain narrow limits, was so much out of the question as not to be thought of. I was taught to practice economy, and to think of money as a thing not to be expended on luxuries, but to be used for useful ends. I was taught the value of time, by having more to do day after day than could be well accomplished. But better than all these, I . . . received an early moral training, to which I owe, perhaps, more of my humble success in life, than to any other influence.

Bibliography

Bibliographies of works about Revolutionary America include David L. Ammerman and Philip D. Morgan, eds., *Books About Early America: 2001 Titles* (Williamsburg, Va., 1989); Ronald M. Gephart, ed., *Revolutionary America, 1763–1789: A Bibliography,* 2 vols. (Washington, 1984); Dwight L. Smith, ed., *Era of the American Revolution: A Bibliography* (Santa Barbara, 1975); and Lawrence H. Gipson, *A Bibliographical Guide to the History of the British Empire, 1748–1776* (New York, 1968). Major reference sources on the period include Lester J. Cappon, ed., *Atlas of Early American History: The Revolutionary Era, 1760–1790* (Princeton, 1976) and Mark Mayo Boatner, *Encyclopedia of the American Revolution* (New York, 1966); Jack P. Greene and Jack R. Pole, *The Blackwell Encyclopedia of the American Revolution* (Cambridge, Mass., and Oxford, Eng., 1991); and John Mack Faragher, *The Encyclopedia of Colonial and Revolutionary America* (New York, 1990). Congress published the premier collection of source materials on the Revolutionary era as its *American State Papers: Documents, Legislative and Executive,* 38 vols. (Washington, 1832–1861), which is divided into classes, among which are Indian Affairs (Class II), Finance (Class III), Commerce and Navigation (Class IV), Military Affairs (Class V), and Miscellaneous (Class X).

A complete listing of late-eighteenth-century climatic records is given in James M. Havens, "An Annotated Bibliography of Meteorological Observations in the United States, 1715–1818," published as the U.S. Weather Bureau's *Key to Meteorological Records Documentation,* No. 5.11 (Washington, 1958). The most complete collections of temperature and precipitation records are in Charles A. Schott, ed., *Tabulation of Resulting Mean Temperatures from Observations Extending Over a Series of Years, . . . for Stations in North America* (Washington, 1874) and the work of Helmut E. Landsberg as published in H. H. Lamb, *Climate: Present, Past, and Future,* 2 vols. (London, 1977), II: 577, 625, 626. The most comprehensive study of historical geography to 1800 is Donald W. Meinig's *The Shaping of America: A Geographical Perspective on Five Hundred Years of History,* I, *Atlantic America, 1492–1800* (New Haven, 1986). The best examinations of environmental change are Michael Williams, *Americans and their Forests: A Historical Geography* (Cambridge, Eng., 1989), and Stephen J. Pyne, *Fire in America: A Cultural History of Woodland and Rural Fire* (Princeton, 1982). The best compilation of natural disasters is Jay R. Nash, *Darkest Hours: A Narrative Encyclopedia of Worldwide Disasters from Ancient Times to the Present* (Chicago, 1976).

The outstanding reference series on Native Americans is the Smithsonian Institution's *Handbook of North American Indians,* under the general editorship of William C. Sturtevant. Of the volumes that have so far appeared in print, the most relevant for the Revolutionary period are Vol. IV, Wilcomb E. Washburn, ed., *History of Indian-White Relations* (Washington, 1988), and XV, Bruce G. Trigger, ed., *Northeast* (Washington, 1978). Significant works by other authors include Helen Hornbeck Tanner, ed., *Atlas of Great Lakes Indian History* (Chicago, 1987), Gregory E. Dowd, *A Spirited Resistance: The North American Indian Struggle for Unity, 1745–1815* (Baltimore, 1992), James H. O'Donnell, III, *Southern Indians in the American Revolution* (Knoxville, 1973), and Francis P. Prucha, *American Indian Policy in the Formative Years: The Indian Trade and Intercourse Acts, 1780–1834* (Cambridge, Mass., 1962).

The best introduction to early American economic history is Edwin J. Perkins, *The Economy of Colonial America,* 2d ed. (New York, 1988). The most comprehensive survey is John J. McCusker and Russell R. Menard, *The Economy of British America, 1607–1789* (Chapel Hill, 1985); besides its detailed examination of different economic topics, this book concludes with seventy-seven pages of bibliography that list every significant book and journal article concerning the pre-1790 economy. Valuable quantitative information is provided in two monographs coauthored by James F. Shepherd and Gary M. Walton: *Shipping, Maritime Trade, and the Economic Development of Colonial North America* (Cambridge, Eng., 1972) and *The Economic Rise of Early America* (New York, 1979).

An overview of population studies during the Revolutionary era can be found in Jim Potter, "Demographic Development and Family Structure," in Jack P. Greene and Jack R. Pole, eds., *Colonial British America: Essays in the New History of the Early Modern Era* (Baltimore, 1984), 123–156, in which the author expands upon his earlier essay, "The Growth of Population in America, 1780–1860" in D. V. Glass and D. E. C. Eversley, *Population in History* (London, 1965), 631–688. The best compilations of censuses and other population statistics are Bureau of the Census, *A Century of Population Growth: From the First Census of the United States to the Twelfth, 1790–1900* (Washington, 1909), and Evarts B. Greene and Virginia D. Harrington, *American Population Before the Federal Census of 1790* (New York, 1932). Statistical examinations of how late-eighteenth-century immigration and the slave trade changed the population's ethnic mix include Bernard Bailyn, *Voyagers to the West: A Passage in the Peopling of America on the Eve of the Revolution* (New York, 1986); Thomas L. Purvis, "The European Ancestry of the United States Population, 1790," *William and Mary Quarterly* LXI (1984), 85–101; and Roger Anstey, "The Volume of the North American Slave-Carrying Trade from Africa, 1761–1810," *Revue Française d'Histoire d'Outre-Mer* LXII (1975), 47–66.

The best works on Revolutionary-era medicine and health include Whitfield J. Bell, Jr., *The Colonial Physician and Other Essays* (New York, 1975); James H. Cassedy, *Medicine in America: A Short History* (Baltimore, 1991); John Duffy, *Epidemics in Colonial America* (Baton Rouge, 1953); J. Worth Estes, *Hall Jackson and the Purple Foxglove: Medical Practice and Research in Revolutionary America, 1760–1820* (Hanover, N.H., 1979); Martin Kaufman, *American Medical Education: The Formative Years, 1765–1910* (Westport, Conn.; 1976); Morris H. Saffron, *Surgeon to Washington: Dr. John Cochran* (New York, 1977); and Richard H. Shyrock, *Medicine and Society in America, 1660–1860* (New York, 1969).

An overview of the main themes in early American religious history can be found in David D. Hall's "Religion and Society: Problems and Reconsiderations" in Jack P. Green and Jack R. Pole, *Colonial British America: Essays in the New History of the Early Modern Era* (Baltimore, 1984), 317–344. An invaluable source of information on the distribution and local concentrations of various denominations is Edwin S. Gaustad, *Historical Atlas of Religion in America,* 2d ed. (New York, 1976). Additional information on the major denominations can be found in Sydney E. Ahlstrom, *A Religious History of the American People,* 2 vols. (New Haven, 1972).

The most important synthesis of urban history—and a major source of quantitative information on Boston, Philadelphia, and New York during the Revolutionary period—is Gary B. Nash, *The Urban Crucible: Social Change, Political Consciousness, and the Origins of the American Revolution* (Cambridge, Mass., 1979). After Nash, the only other comparable examination of late-eighteenth-century seaports is Carl Bridenbaugh, *Cities in Revolt: Urban Life in America, 1743–1776* (New York, 1955).

The most systematic study of early American education can be found in Lawrence A. Cremin's magisterial *American Education,* I, *The Colonial Experience, 1607–1783* (New York, 1970) and II, *The National Experience, 1783–1876* (New York, 1980). Regarding college education, see David W. Robson, *Educating Republicans: The College in the*

Era of the American Revolution, 1750–1800 (Westport, Conn., 1985), and Walter C. Eells, *Baccalaureate Degrees Conferred by American Colleges in the Seventeeth and Eighteenth Centuries,* U.S. Office of Education Circular No. 528 (May 1958). Works on libraries include Jesse H. Shera, *Foundations of the Public Library: The Origins of the Public Library Movement in New England, 1629–1855* (Chicago, 1949); Louis Shores, *Origins of the American College Library* (New York, 1966); and Josephine Metcalf Smith, *A Chronology of Librarianship* (Metuchen, N.J., 1968).

The premier book on early American arts and letters is Kenneth Silverman's superb *Cultural History of the American Revolution: Painting, Music, Literature, and the Theatre in the Colonies and the United States from the Treaty of Paris to the Inauguration of George Washington, 1763–1789* (New York, 1976), which includes an extensive bibliography of secondary and primary source materials. The best study of literature subsequent to Silverman's work is Cathy N. Davidson, *Revolution and the Word: The Rise of the Novel in America* (New York, 1986). Comprehensive listings of newspapers and magazines, including details on their publication histories, are provided in Clarence S. Brigham, *History and Bibliography of American Newspapers, 1690–1820,* 2 vols. (Worcester, Mass., 1947); Edward C. Lathem, *Chronological Tables of American Newspapers, 1690–1820* (Barre, Mass., 1972); and Frank L. Mott, *A History of American Magazines, 1741–1850* (Cambridge, Mass., 1957). An overview of current scholarship on publishing is David D. Hall and John B. Hench, eds., *Needs and Opportunities in the History of the Book: America, 1639–1876* (Worcester, Mass., 1987).

Starting points for the examination of late-eighteenth-century science are Whitfield J. Bell, Jr., *Early American Science: Needs and Opportunities for Study* (Chapel Hill, 1955), and Brooke Hindle, *Technology in Early America: Needs and Opportunities for Study* (Chapel Hill, 1966). Useful books on this topic are Silvio A. Bedini, *Thinkers and Tinkers: Early American Men of Science* (New York, 1975); John C. Greene, *American Science in the Age of Jefferson* (Ames, Iowa, 1984); and Brooke Hindle, *The Pursuit of Science in Revolutionary America, 1735–1789* (Chapel Hill, 1956).

The best introduction to architecture and material culture in the Revolutionary era is Henry Glassie, *Pattern in the Material Folk Culture of the Eastern United States* (Philadelphia, 1968). Other valuable studies include Henry Glassie, *Folk Housing in Middle Virginia: A Structural Analysis of Historic Artifacts* (Knoxville, 1975); Brooke Hindle, ed., *Material Culture of the Wooden Age* (Tarrytown, N.Y., 1981); Jack Larkin, *The Reshaping of Everyday LIfe, 1790–1840* (New York, 1988); and Barbara Clark Smith, *After the Revolution: The Smithsonian History of Everyday Life in the Eighteenth Century* (New York, 1985).

It has always been difficult to recover the lives of everyday people from the past. Few contemporary Americans realize that the U.S. government has preserved information regarding every fourth man who came to adulthoood during the Revolutionary decades (more than 80,000 individuals) in its pension files for military service. John C. Dann has edited the most colorful and dramatic pension declarations in his volume *The Revolution Remembered: Eyewitness Accounts of the War for Independence* (Chicago, 1980). Dann's volume provides the best single source for reconstructing the experience of living through the Revolution. A listing of other travelers' accounts, journals, and diaries kept by individuals during the late eighteenth century can be found in David L. Ammerman and Philip D. Morgan, eds., *Books About Early America: 2001 Titles* (Williamsburg, Va., 1989), 108–110.

APPENDIX: LIST OF TABLES

Index

This index is arranged alphabetically letter by letter. Page numbers in *italic* indicate illustrations or captions.
Page numbers followed by *t* indicate tables; by *m* indicate maps; by *n* indicate notes; and by *b* indicate biographical profiles.

imports 103
East Kingston, N.H.
  census: 1773 127*t*; 1790 131*t*
East Manchester, Conn.
  glassmaking 88*t*
Easton, Mass.
  census: 1776 135*t*; 1790 139*t*
Easton, Md.
  U.S. Circuit Court 225
Easton, N.Y.
  census: 1790 152*t*
East Sudbury, Mass.
  census: 1776 135*t*; 1790 137*t*
East Town, N.H.
  census: 1773 127*t*
East Windsor, Conn.
  census: 1774 144*t*
eating *see* diet
Eaton, N.H.
  census: 1790 131*t*
economic depressions 33, 37, 111
economy
  agriculture: dairies 40, 42–44; exports 37, 44–63; impact of Revolution 37; gross acreage 42; gross output 42; labor utilization 42, 45–46, 48, 63; land utilization 38–40, 41*m*; yields 41
  American Revolution impact 37
  animal husbandry: cattle 42–44; fodder 40; horses 50–51; mules 51; pork 52–53; sheep 55
  communications 118
  currency: colonial and state 37, 105–107; Continental 104–105; exchange rates 37, 107; U.S. coinage 107
  depression of 1780s 33, 37, 111
  expansionary periods 111
  farms 37–42; animal husbandry 42–44, 50–53, 55; crops *see specific crop (e.g., tobacco)*; gross output 42; labor yields 42, 44–46, 48, 63; land utilization 39–40, 41*m*; marketing overhead 41; size (by colony) 38, 40; tools 40, 112
  finance: banking 32, 108; insurance 31, 108–109; stock exchange 34, 109–111
  forestry products: deforestation 4; lumber 71–74; naval stores 74–77; potash 34, 77–78
  fur trade: beaver and peltries: exports 78–79; organization 78; deerskins: exports 80; organization 79–80; prices 79
  incomes: national income (gross national output) 42, 111; per capita 111; wages 96–98

labor: occupations 95–96; unfree 120–122; wages 96–98; yields 42, 45–46, 48, 63, 86
  manufacturing and business: distilling 81–82; firearms 88–89; glass 87–88; home construction 89; iron 84–87; paper making 89–90; pottery 90; shipbuilding 82–84; shoemaking 90–91; sugar refining 92; textiles 29, 34, 92–93
  maritime industries: fisheries 63–67; merchant marine 68–70; shipping earnings 68–70; whaling 64–67
  mining: coal 94–95; copper 93–94; lead 95
  price indexes 116–117*t*
  trade: balance of 99, 103; exports 44–67, 72–82, 86–87, 91, 94, 99–104
  transportation 118–119
  wealth: aggregate nation 113; poverty 114–115; property ownership 112–114
Eddy, Me.
  census: 1790 140*t*
Eddyville, Ky.
  census: 1800 175*t*
Eden, Robert 245
Edenton, N.C.
  census: 1790 167*t*; 1800 170*t*
  family sizes 180
  shipwreck 5*t*
Edgartown, Mass.
  census: 1776 135*t*; 1790 139*t*
Edgecomb, Me.
  census: 1776 136*t*; 1790 140*t*
Edgecombe County, N.C.
  census: 1786 167*t*; 1790 167*t*; 1800 170*t*
Edgefield County, S.C.
  census: 1790 172*t*; 1800 173*t*
Edinburgh, Scotland
  rank in British Empire 253
Edinburgh, University of 188, 195–196
education 269–275
  academies: curriculum 270; number chartered 271; origin 270
  John Adams on 273
  co-education 271
  colleges: campus plan 272; degrees awarded 195–196, 272*t*, 273*t*; denominational origins 271; faculties 271–272; institutions founded 217; state endowed 269, 271–272
  female 271
  grammar schools: curriculum 269–270; decline of 270
  instructional techniques 269
  Thomas Jefferson on 173
  literacy 274–275
  pre-collegiate 269–271
  regional variations 269

school-age population 269*n*
schoolmasters 270
school terms 269
student-teacher ratios 269
teacher income 96*t*
Edwards, John 257
Edwin and Angelina (1796) 287*t*
Eel River Indians
  treaties 22
Effingham, N.H.
  census: 1773 addenda 129*n*; 1790 131*t*
Effingham County, Ga.
  census: 1790 173*t*; 1800 173*t*
Egremont, Mass.
  census: 1776 136*t*; 1790 139*t*
Elbert, Samuel 244
Elbert County, Ga.
  census: 1800 173*t*
election days 311
elections
  congressional 215–217
  county 211
  legislative (state) 211
  presidential: returns 218; voter participation 215
  qualifications: of candidates 213; of voters 211–212
  voter eligible 213
  voter turnout 213–215
Electoral College 34
  elects Washington 34
  returns 218
  tie vote 36
  voter participation 215
electrical experiments 219
Elements (Euclid) 274
elephants 35
Eliot, John 285*t*
Elizabeth City County, Va.
  census: 1790 163*t*; 1800 164*t*
  student-teacher ratio 269
  taxables (1782–89) 162*t*
Elizabethtown, Ky.
  census: 1800 175*t*
Elizabeth-Town, N.J.
  magazines published 278
elk
  depletion of 4
  exports 79
Elk Ridge Landing, Md.
  potteries 90*t*
Ellery, William 250
Ellicott, Andrew 292
Ellicott, George 263
Ellington, Conn.
  census: 1790 149*t*
Ellsworth, N.H.
  census: 1773 addenda 129*n*
Ellsworth, Oliver 225*t*, 233*t*, 243
Elmira, N.Y. 31
Elmore, Vt.
  census: 1790 132*t*
Elmsford, N.Y.
  cocktails 314–315
emigration *see* immigration
Emmaus, Pa.
  folk housing 303

Empress of China (ship) 33
Encyclopaedia Britannica (1796) 280
Enfield, Conn.
  census: 1774 144*t*; 1790 149*t*
Enfield, N.H.
  census: 1790 130*t*
Engel, Jacob 201
England
  exports to 100–101*t*
  immigration 120*t*, 180*t*, 182*t*
  imports 100*t*, 102*t*
  literacy 274
  newspaper subscription rates 277, 277*t*
  schools 269
  soldiers height 187*t*
  taxation per capita 230, 231*t*
England, Church of *see* Anglican Church; Protestant Episcopal Church
English-Americans
  ethnic holidays 306
  family intermarriage 309
  immigration 120*t*, 180*t*, 182*t*
  indentured servants 120*t*
  urban population percentage: Baltimore 255*t*; Boston 255*t*; New York 258*t*; Philadelphia 261*t*
  white population percentage 182*t*
Ephrata, Pa.
  potteries 90*t*
epidemics 15, 34, 189, 191*t*
epilepsy 190
Episcopal Church *see* Anglican Church; Protestant Episcopal Church
E Pluribus Unum (One From Many) (coin motto) 33
Epping, N.H.
  census: 1773 127*t*; 1790 131*t*
Epsom, N.H.
  census: 1773 127*t*; 1790 131*t*
Erie County, Pa.
  census: 1800 159*t*
Erie Harbor, Pa. 249
erosion 4
Errol, N.H.
  census: 1790 130*t*
Erwin, N.Y.
  census: 1790 152*t*
erysipelas 192
Essex, Vt.
  census: 1790 132*t*
Essex County, Mass.
  census: 1776 135*t*; 1790 137*t*; 1800 142*t*
  livestock 39, 43, 50, 52, 55
  papermills 90
Essex County, N.J.
  census: 1784 153*t*; 1790 154*t*; 1800 155*t*
Essex County, N.Y.
  census: 1800 153*t*
Essex County, Va.
  census: 1790 163*t*; 1800 164*t*
  taxables (1782–89) 162*t*
Essex County, Vt.
  census: 1800 134*t*
Estill's Station, Ky., battle of 20

ethnicity
  black population 184
  urban population: Baltimore
    255*t*; Boston 255*t*; New
    York 258–259; Philadelphia
    261*t*
  white population 182*t*
Euclid 274
Euripides 274
Europe
  distribution of wealth 114
  exports to 102*t*
  imports 103
European ancestry
  by city: Baltimore 255; New
    York 258–259; Philadelphia
    261
  by state 182
Eutaw Springs, S.C., battle of
  32, 264
  Francis Marion at 266*b*
  whiskey looting at 315
Eutropius 269
Evacuation Day holiday 258
Evangelical Church 200–201
evangelical churches *see specific church (e.g., Baptist
  Churches)*
Evangelical United Brethren
  200–201
Evans, Lewis 292
Evans, Oliver 295–296
Evans, Robert 40
exchange rates
  colonial currency: to sterling
    37; to U.S. dollars 37
  Spanish dollars 37
Exeter, N.H.
  census: 1773 127*t*; 1790 131*t*
  magazines published 278
  U.S. Circuit Court 225
Exeter, R.I.
  census: 1774 143*t*; 1790 143*t*;
    1800 148*t*
expansions (economic) 37, 111
exploration
  Bartram, John 6, 6*m*
  Bartram, William 6
  Boone, Boone 6–7
  Columbia River 7
  Cumberland Gap, Ky. 7
  by French 5
  Gist, Christopher 7
  Kentucky 6–7
  Portola, Gaspar de 7
  Robert Gray 7
  Walker, Thomas 7
  Wilderness Road 7
explosives industry 243
exports 44–67, 72–82, 86–87,
  91, 94, 98–99, 99*t*–104*t* *see also
  specific country (e.g., France)*
  1768–1772 99*t*, 101*t*
  1790–1800 101–102*t*
  major commodities 101*t*
  per capita 111*t*
  by region 99–100*t*
  by state 103*t*, 104*t*, 243–251
eye disease 190, 192

F

Fables (Aesop) 269
faculties (college) 271–272, 272*t*
Fairfax, Vt.
  census: 1790 132*t*
Fairfax County, Va.
  census: 1790 163*t*; 1800 164*t*
  taxables (1782–89) 162*t*
Fairfield, Conn.
  census: 1774 144*t*; 1790 149*t*;
    1800 150*t*
Fairfield, Me.
  census: 1790 140*t*
Fairfield County, Conn.
  farms 39
Fairfield County, S.C.
  census: 1790 171*t*; 1800 173*t*
Fair Haven, Vt.
  census: 1790 133*t*
Fairhaven, Vt.
  magazines published 278
Fairley, Vt.
  census: 1790 133*t*
Fallen Timbers, Battle of 8, 13,
  35, 244, 264
Falmouth, Ky.
  census: 1800 176*t*
Falmouth, Mass.
  census: 1776 135*t*
  whaling 65*t*
Falmouth, Me.
  census: 1776 136*t*; 1790 139*t*,
    140*t*
  customs protests 322*t*
  rank in state 245
families
  adolescent mortality 179
  and American Revolution
    179
  divorce 310, 310*t*
  fertility 179
  home behavior 298
  immigrant 182
  intermarriage within 309,
    309*t*
  marriage ages 179
  possessions 40, 112
  pre-marital conception 309,
    310*t*
  size 179, 180, 180*t*
  slave ownership 122
  social interaction 310
farmers
  average wealth 113*t*
  in Congress 220
  immigration 182
  income 40, 96; in
    Cheaspeake 96; in mid-At-
    lantic area 40, 96
  as indentured servants 120
  as laborers 96–98
  in U.S. Cabinet 219
  in workforce 95*t*
Farmer's Almanac 34
Farmer's Weekly Museum 279
Farmington, Conn.
  census: 1774 144*t*; 1790 149*t*
  library catalogue 275

farm laborers
  income 96–98; in New Eng-
    land 96–97; in New Jersey
    97; in New York 97; in
    Pennsylvania 96–97; in
    South 96
farms and farming 37–42 *see
  also* agriculture
  acreage: average 38*t*, 40*t*;
    yields 41*t*
  animal husbandry: cattle
    42–44; horses 50–51; mules
    51; pork 52–53; sheep 55
  barns 43, 50
  child labor 327–328
  crop rotation 40*t*
  crops *see* corn; cotton; flax;
    hemp; indigo; rice; silk; to-
    bacco; wheat
  field division 39–40, 41*m*
  gross output/product (1800)
    42*t*
  income from 40, 96–98
  labor *see* farm laborers
  livestock 38*t*
  rents 42*t*
  tenants 96
Fauquier, Francis 252
Fauquier County, Va.
  census: 1790 163*t*; 1800 164*t*
  taxables (1782–89) 162*t*
Fayette County, Ky.
  census: 1790 174*t*; 1800 175*t*
Fayette County, Pa.
  census: 1790 156*t*; 1800 159*t*
  taxpayers (1760–86) 155*t*
Fayetteville, N.C.
  census: 1790 167*t*; 1800 171*t*
  rank in state 248
federal employees
  salaries 98
Federalist papers 265
Federalist Party
  congressional leadership 221
  congressional strength
    222–224
  in mid-Atlantic politics 243,
    247–249
  in New England politics 243,
    246–247, 250, 251
  partisan press 280
  presidential elections 218
  in Southern politics 245, 248,
    250
federal judges
  salaries 98*t*
felons *see* criminals, British
female education *see* education
Fenner, Arthur 250
Ferdinand, Vt.
  census: 1790 133*t*
Ferrers, John 110
Ferrisburg, Vt.
  census: 1790 132*t*
fertility 179, 194
  diet and 186
fetal deaths 195*n*
fevers 190, 192

fiat money *see* colonial currency;
  Continental money; state currency
fiction
  best-sellers 283*t*
  female audience 279, 282
  first novel 282
  magazines 279
  novelists: Brackenridge, Hugh
    283*t*; Brown, William H. 282; Fos-
    ter, Hannah Webster 283, 283*t*;
    Rowson, Susanna Haswell 283,
    283*t*
  poets: Warren, Mercy Otis
    267–268*b*; Wheatley, Phillis 268*b*
Fielding, Henry 283
fighting 311
Fille de Chambre (1793) 283
finance
  banking 32, 108
  insurance 31, 108–109
  stock exchange 34, 109–111
Fincastle County, Va.
  census: 1800 166*t*
Fine Arts, American Academy of *see*
  American Academy of Fine Arts
Finland
  distribution of wealth 114*t*
Finley, James 35
firearms production 88–89
fire insurance 109
  Baltimore Insurance Fire-Com-
    pany 109
  policy certificate *109*
firewood
  price movements 117*t*
  woodland consumed to provide
    4, 4*t*
First Amendment
  religion and 198
  Statute for Religious Freedom and
    33
First Continental Congress *see* Continental Congress, First
First Pennsylvania Corporation 108
fish and fisheries 63–67 *see also specific fish (e.g., cod)*
  cod fleet: crewmen 65–66*t*; decline
    of 63, 65–66*t*; gross cargoes
    65–66*t*; home ports 65–66*t*; ton-
    nage 64, 65–66*t*, 69*t*; vessels
    65–66*t*
  dietary allowances 185*t*
  exports 63, 64*t*, 65*t*, 66*t*, 101*t*; de-
    cline of 63, 65–66*t*; France 101;
    markets for 63, 67*t*; from Massa-
    chusetts 245; from New Hamp-
    shire 247; value 65, 101*t*;
    volume 65–66*t*, 67*t*, 101*t*
  fishermen, wealth of 113*t*
  prices 63*t*
  Revolutionary War and 63
  value of catch 63
Fisher, William 261
fishermen 113*t*
Fishkill, N.Y.
  census: 1790 152*t*
fistula 190

state capital 211, 243
U.S. Circuit Court 225
Hartford, Ky.
census: 1800 176t
Hartford, Vt.
census: 1790 134t
Hartford County, Conn.
census: 1774 144t; 1790 149t;
1800 150t
farms 39
papermills 90
Hartland, Conn.
census: 1774 146t
Hartley, Thomas 19
Hart's Location, N.H.
census: 1790 130t
Harvard, Mass.
census: 1776 135t; 1790 138t
Harvard College (Mass.)
ceases ranking students'
status 28
degrees awarded 272t
and John Adams 263b
and John Hancock 265b
and John Winthrop 289
library collection 276, 276t
medical education 196
physics instruction 291
state support and 271
Harvard University see Harvard College
Harwich, Mass.
census: 1776 135t; 1790 139t
Harwinton, Conn.
census: 1774 146t; 1790 149t
Hasell, James 248
Hasenclever, Peter 84
Hatfield, Mass.
census: 1776 136t; 1790 137t
hatters 95–96
Haverhill, Mass.
census: 1776 135t; 1790 137t
distilling 82t
Haverhill, N.H.
1790 130t
census: 1773 129t
Haverstraw, N.Y.
census: 1790 152t
Hawke, N.H.
census: 1773 127t; 1790 131t
Hawkins County, Tenn.
census: 1800 177t
Haycock, Pa.
potteries 90t
Haydn, Franz Joseph 287
Haynes, Lemuel 33
Hays, George 266
Hayward, William 245
hay yield 40t
Headquarters Secret Service 31
health boards 191
Heard, Stephen 244
Heath, Mass.
census: 1790 137t
Hebron, Conn.
census: 1774 144t; 1790 149t
Hebron, N.Y.
census: 1790 151t
Hecla Iron County, Pa. 87

Heidelberg, Pa.
glassmaking 87t
height (adult)
American-born soldiers 185,
187
diet and 185
European-born soldiers 185,
187
Helm, James 250
hemoptysis 192
hemorrhoids 192
hemp 49–50
annual output 42t
bounty 49
cordage 49
cultivation 49
exports 49–50t
gross acreage 42t
labor input 49
prices 41t, 49t
yield 49
Henderson, Ky.
census: 1800 175t
Henderson, Richard 7, 29
Henderson County, Ky.
census: 1800 175t
Henniker, N.H.
census: 1773 128t; 1790 131t
Henrico County, Va.
census: 1790 163t; 1800 165t
coal mining 94t
taxables (1782-87) 162t
Henry, John 110, 245
Henry, Patrick 27
Bill Establishing a Provision
for Teachers of the Christian
Religion 198
"give me liberty or give me
death" speech (Mar. 23,
1775) 29
Virginia governor 252t
Henry County, Ky.
census: 1800 175t
Henry County, Va.
census: 1790 163t; 1800 165t
taxables (1782-87) 162t
Henshaw, Joshua 255t
Herkimer, N.Y.
census: 1790 152t
Herkimer, Nicholas 19, 31
Herkimer County, N.Y.
census: 1800 153t
hernias 192
Herring Pond, Mass.
Indian population 24t
Herschel, William 289
Hertford County, N.C.
census: 1790 167t; 1800 170t
Hessian fly 60–61
Hessians 30–31, 180n, 251, 265,
267, 306
Heth Coal Pits 94
Hewitt, James 287t
Hibernians, Ancient Order of
see Ancient Order of Hibernians
Hicks, Whitehead 259
hides prices 117t
Higginson, Stephen 257t

Highgate, Vt.
census: 1790 132t
Highland (Scottish) troops 19,
27
highway improvements 118
highway robbery 320t
Hill, N.H.
census: 1773 addenda 129n
Hillhouse, James 221
Hillsborough, N.C.
census: 1800 169t
Hillsborough, N.H.
census: 1773 128t
Hillsborough County, N.H.
census: 1773 128t; 1790 130t,
131t; 1800 132t
Hillsdale, N.Y.
census: 1790 152t
Hinde, Thomas 283
Hinesburgh, Vt.
census: 1790 132t
Hingham, Mass.
census: 1776 135t; 1790 138t
family formation 179
fishing fleet 65t
pre-marital conception in 310
Hinsdale, N.H.
census: 1773 128t; 1790 130t
Hinsdale, Vt.
census: 1790 134t
Hiokatoo 323–324
Hiram, Me.
census: 1790 141t
historical geography 5–12
exploration 5–7; Columbia
River 7; Cumberland Gap,
Ky. 7; Daniel Boone 6–7; by
French 5; Gaspar de Portola
7; Gist, Christopher 7; John
Bartram 6; Kentucky 6–7;
Robert Gray 7; San Francisco Bay 7; Thomas
Walker 7; Wilderness Road
7; William Bartram 6m
frontier expansion 7–10;
Boone, Daniel 6–8, 28–29,
263b; Fallen Timbers, Battle
of 8, 13, 35; founding of
new communities 8t; Georgia 8, 13; Indiana 8, 35; Indian land cessions 7–8, 13,
22–23, 35; Indian resistance
7–8, 13, 19–20, 27, 29, 34–35;
Kentucky 7–8, 13, 28–29,
244; Lord Dunmore's War
7, 13, 29; Mississippi 8;
New England 7–8; Ohio 8,
13, 33, 35; Ohio Valley 7–8,
13, 35; Pennsylvania 7; Pontiac's War (1763–66) 7, 13,
15, 19, 27; Proclamation of
1763 (Oct.7, 1763) 7, 13, 27;
Tennessee 7–8, 28–29, 251;
Virginia 7
population density 10–12,
12m; in England 11; in Germany 11; in Ireland 11
territorial organization 8–10

Historical Narrative and Topographical Description of Louisiana and West-Florida (292) 292
History of Constantius and Pulchrea, The (1795) 283
History of the Heathen Gods 269
History of the Rise, Progress, and Termination of the American Revolution (1805) 268
Hitchcock, Enos 271
Hobart, John S. 285t
Hobkirk's Hill, S.C., battle of 32, 264
Hodges, Richard 321
hogs see pork; swine
hogshead staves see staves
Holden, Mass.
census: 1790 138t
Holderness, N.H.
census: 1773 addenda 129n
holidays 305–306
Holland, Mass.
census: 1790 137t
Hollis, N.H.
census: 1773 128t; 1790 131t
pre-marital conception in 310
Holliston, Mass.
census: 1776 135t; 1790 137t
Holmes, John B. 257
holy day celebrations 305
home construction 89
housing starts 89t
New York City 258t
Philadelphia 261t
value of new homes 89t
home furnishings 113
Homer 274
hoop (barrel) exports 73–74
Hoosick, N.Y.
census: 1790 152t
Hopewell, Pa. ironworks 86
Hopkins, Esek 30, 242
Hopkins, Samuel 34, 296
Hopkins, Stephen 250t
Hopkins Grant, Vt.
census: 1790 133t
Hopkinson, Francis 287t
Hopkinton, Mass.
census: 1776 135t; 1790 137t
Hopkinton, R.I.
census: 1774 143t; 1790 143t; 1800
148t
Hopkintown, N.H.
census: 1773 128t; 1790 131t
hops
output 42t
price 40t
Horace 270
horn of alcohol 316
horse racing 314
horses 50–51
average owned 38t
breeding laws 50
breeds: Conestoga 50; Morgan 50
exports 50t, 51t; by state 50t
fodder 40t
prices 40t, 50t
as status symbol 309
theft of 320t
horse theft 320t

prices 85*t*, 116*t*
ironmaking 84–87, *87*
  coke smelting 85, 94
  freight charges 85*t*
  fuel costs 86*t*
  gross output 86*t*
  ironworks 86*t*
  labor: costs 85*t*; productivity 85*t*, 86*t*
  in New Jersey 247
  in Pennsylvania 249
  woodland consumption for 4, 4*t*
Iroquois Indians *see also* Cayuga; Mohawk; Oneida; Onondaga; Seneca; Tuscarora Indians
  land cessions 7, 13, 22
  population 24*t*
  Revolutionary War 19–20, 31
  as storm victims 5*t*
  warfare 19, 31
  warriors 25*t*
Irwin, Jared 244
Isleborough, Me.
  census: 1790 140*t*
Isle Mott, Vt.
  census: 1790 132*t*
Isle of Wight County, Va.
  census: 1790 163*t*; 1800 165*t*
  taxables (1782–89) 162*t*
Islip, N.Y.
  census: 1790 151*t*
Italian colonists 28
Italy
  exports to 102*t*
  immigration 28
  imports 103
  merchant marine 70
Izard, Ralph 221*t*, 250*t*

J

Jack, Samuel 19
Jackson, Andrew 251*t*, 317
Jackson, Hall 192
Jackson, James 244
Jackson County, Ga.
  census: 1800 173*t*
Jaffry, N.H.
  census: 1773 128*t*; 1790 130*t*
jails *see* prisons
Jamaica, N.Y.
  census: 1790 151*t*
Jamaica, Vt.
  census: 1790 134*t*
Jamaica cod *see* cod
James City County, Va.
  census: 1790 163*t*; 1800 165*t*
  taxables (1782–89) 162*t*
James River Valley, Va.
  coal mining 94
Jamestown, R.I.
  census: 1774 142*t*; 1790 143*t*; 1800 148*t*
Japan
  first U.S. ship to 36
jaundice 190, 192
Jay, John 224
  ambassador 233*t*

on crime 319
New York chief justice 248*t*
New York governor 248*t*
New York Society for Promoting Useful Knowledge 285*t*
president of Congress 221*t*
secretary of state 219*t*
Thanksgiving Day proclamation 305
U.S. chief justice 225*t*, 248*t*
Jay's Treaty (1795) 13, 33, 37, 233*t*
  diplomatic consequences 35, 68–69
  economic consequences 35, 68–69, 99, 253
  terms 35
Jefferson, Thomas
  ambassador 233*t*
  American Philosophical Society 285*t*
  Declaration of Independence 30, *265*, 266, 306
  on education 273
  Federalist Papers 36, 114, 306
  Library of Congress 276
  meteorological notes 1
  Notes on the State of Virginia 266
  on novels 281
  plow patented 296*t*
  on poverty 114
  presidency 36, 252, 266
  profile 266*b*
  public education proposal 269
  secretary of state 219, 266*b*
  Statute for Religious Freedom 33, 199
  vice-presidency 219, 266*b*
  Virginia governor 252*t*, 266*b*
Jefferson County, Ga.
  census: 1800 173*t*
Jefferson County, Ky.
  census: 1790 174*t*; 1800 175*t*
Jefferson County, Ohio
  census: 1800 178*t*
Jefferson County, Tenn.
  census: 1800 177*t*
Jeffersonian Democracy 266
Jeffry, James 109
Jemison, Mary (Dickewamis) 323–324
Jemison, Thomas 323
Jenner, Edward 192
Jerico, Vt.
  census: 1790 132*t*
Jerusalem, N.Y.
  census: 1790 152*t*
Jessamine County, Ky.
  census: 1800 175*t*
Jewish Americans *see also* Judaism
  notable individuals 29, 205, 267
  religious history 295
jig 311
John Hancock (slang) 265

Johnson, Sir William 14–15, 27
Johnson, Thomas 225*t*, 245
Johnson, Vt.
  census: 1790 132*t*
Johnson glassworks 88
Johnson's Gore, Vt.
  census: 1790 134*t*
John St. Methodist Church (New York) *200*, *201*
Johnston, R.I.
  census: 1774 143*t*; 1790 143*t*; 1800 148*t*
Johnston, Samuel 248
Johnston County, N.C.
  census: 1790 168*t*; 1800 170*t*
joiners
  incomes 97*t*
  in workforce 96*t*
Jones, Isaac 262
Jones, John 188
Jones, John Paul
  battle of Whitehaven 31
  Bonhomme Richard versus *Serapis* 31
  famous quotation 31
Jones, Thomas 257
Jones, Willie 248
Jonesboro, Tenn. 251*t*
Jonesboro, Tenn., battle of 20
Jones County, N.C.
  census: 1790 168*t*; 1800 170*t*
Jones Plantation, Me.
  census: 1776 136*t*; 1790 140*t*
journalism 277–280
  magazines 278–279; cities published 278*t*; growth of 278; subject matter 279
  newspapers: circulation 277; expansion 277, 280*t*; news coverage 279; political dimension 279; timeliness 279
journeymen shoemakers 97*t*
Judaism
  historical sketch 267
  number of synagogues 198, 202
  population 197, 205
judges, U.S.
  salaries 98*t*
Judicial Department, U.S. 224–225
Judiciary Act 34
Julian Calendar 306

K

Kanawha County, Va.
  census: 1800 166*t*
Kanawha Valley, Va.
  lead mining 95
Kaskaskia, Ill.
  census: 1792 178*t*; 1800 178*t*
  earthquake 5*t*
  Revolutionary War 244, 263
Kaskaskia Indians
  treaties 22
  warriors 25*t*
Keene, N.H.
  census: 1773 128*t*; 1790 130*t*

Kennebec County, Me.
  census: 1800 142*t*
Kennebec Valley, Me.
  naval stores industry 74
Kensington, N.H.
  census: 1773 127*t*; 1790 131*t*
Kent, Conn.
  census: 1774 146*t*; 1790 149*t*
Kent County, Del.
  census: 1774–84 160*t*; 1790 160*t*; 1800 160*t*
Kent County, Md.
  census: 1782 161*t*; 1790 161*t*; 1800 162*t*
  tobacco prices 60
  wheat prices 60
Kent County, R.I.
  census: 1790 143*t*; 1800 148*t*
Kentucky
  agriculture 37, 49, 58
  congressional representation: apportionment 222*t*; party affiliation 222–224*t*; turnover 215–217*t*
  economy: bourbon 82; iron production 85
  elections: congressional turnover 215–217*t*; for presidential electors 215*t*; presidential returns 218*t*; voter eligiblity 212–213*t*; voter participation 213*t*
  exploration 6–7, 28, 263
  government: constitutional change 209*t*; purchase of 7, 29; statehood 8, 9*t*, 34, 244; Virginia jurisdiction 251
  historical sketch 244
  legislature: constitutents per member 210*t*; qualifications 213*t*; size 210*t*; term 210*t*; turnover 211*t*
  militia 19–20, 244
  natural disasters 5*t*
  newspapers 280*t*
  officeholders 209–210*t*; chief justices 244; governors 244; how selected 209*t*; qualifications 213*t*
  population: censuses 174*t*–175*t*; density 10–11*t*, 12*m*
  regulator movements 322*t*
  residents characterized 317
  Revolutionary War 19–20*t*
  settlement of 8, 29, 174; area surveyed 12*t*; counties/towns founded in 8*t*
  wildlife depletion 4
Kentucky Gazette 277, 279
Kentucky Militia
  in Indian wars 19–20, 244
  in Revolution 244
Kentucky Resolutions 36, 244, 266*b*
Kersage Gore, N.H.
  census: 1790 131*t*
Kershaw County, S.C.
  census: 1800 173*t*
Kickapoo Indians
  location 15*m*, 24*t*
  population 24*t*
  treaties 22
  warfare 20

McIntosh, Lachlan 244*t*
McIntosh County, Ga.
  census: 1800 173*t*
McKean, Thomas
  Delaware governor 243*t*
  president of Congress 221*t*
McKinley, John 243
Meacham, Joseph 202
meals *see* diet
measles 189, 191–192
meat
  caloric value 187*n*
  consumption: annual 187*t*;
    average daily 185
  dietary allowances 185*t*
  price movements 117*t*
Mecklenburg County, N.C.
  anti-surveyor violence 322*t*
  census: 1790 168*t*; 1800 169*t*
Mecklenburg County, Va.
  census: 1790 163*t*; 1800 165*t*
  taxables (1782–89) 162*t*
Medfield, Mass.
  census: 1776 135*t*; 1790 138*t*
Medford, Mass.
  census: 1776 135*t*; 1790 138*t*
  distilling 82*t*
medical education 195–196
medical journals 196
Medical Repository 196
medicine
  diseases 189–191
  education 195–196
  health boards 191
  hospitals 188–189
  inoculations 192
  mental illness 189
  theory 187
  therapy 187–188
  wartime 192–194
Meduncook, Me.
  census: 1776 136*t*; 1790 140*t*
Medway, Mass.
  census: 1776 135*t*; 1790 138*t*
melancholy 190
Memoirs of the Bloomsgrove Family (1790) 271
Mendon, Mass.
  census: 1776 135*t*; 1790 138*t*
Mennonites 198*t*, 200–201
Menominee Indians 24*t*
mental asylums 189
mental illness 115, 189
Mercer County, Ky.
  census: 1790 174*t*; 1800 175*t*
Mercer County, Pa.
  census: 1800 159*t*
merchandizers 95–96
merchant marine 68–70
  American built 84*t*
  in coastal trade 69*t*
  foreign competition 68–69
  foreign discrimination 33, 68
  foreign ownership 69*t*
  from Massachusetts 245
  neutral status 69–70
  shipping earnings 68, 69*t*, 70*t*
  smuggling 68

tonnage 69*t*, 70*t*; from Baltimore 255; from Boston 255;
  from Charleston 257; in
  fisheries 65–66*t*, 69*t*; in foreign trade 69*t*; Newport,
  R.I. 260; from New York
  259; Philadelphia 261
  U.S. preferential duties 68
  vessels: average size 68;
    number 68; as privateers
    34, 68, 242; seizures: in
    1790s 69, 70*t*; in Revolution
    68; tonnage 69*t*, 70*t*
merchants
  average wealth 113*t*
  in Congress 220*t*
  immigration 180*t*
  in workforce 95*t*, 96*t*
merchant's clerk 96*t*
Meredith, N.H.
  census: 1773 127*t*; 1790 131*t*
Merrimac, N.H.
  census: 1773 128*t*; 1790 131*t*
Mesquakie Indians *see* Fox Indians
Messenger (horse) 314
Messiah (oratorio) 287
metalworkers 95*t*, 96*t*
Metamorphoses (Ovid) 269
meteorological observations
  see climate
Methodist Episcopal Church
  denominational college 201,
    271
  firsts: bishop 201; black missionary 35; church (1768)
    200
  historical sketch 201
  membership 197, 201
  number of churches 197–198*t*
  schism *see* Republican Methodist Church
  temperance and 315
Methuen, Mass.
  census: 1776 135*t*; 1790 137*t*
Miami Indians *see also* Little
Turtle
  historical sketch 14
  location 15*m*, 24*t*
  population 24*t*
  treaties 22
  warfare 8, 19–20
  warriors 25*t*
Michigan
  copper deposits 93
  Pontiac's War 19
  Revolutionary War 32
Michikinikwa *see* Little Turtle
Mid-Atlantic region
  aggregate wealth 113
  gross economic output 111
Middleboro, Mass.
  census: 1776 135*t*; 1790 138*t*
Middlebury, Vt.
  census: 1790 132*t*
Middlebury College (Vt.)
  charter 271*t*
  first class 271

Middlefield, Mass.
  census: 1790 137*t*
Middlesex, Vt.
  census: 1790 132*t*
Middlesex County, Conn.
  census: 1790 149*t*; 1800 150*t*
  farms 39
Middlesex County, Mass.
  census: 1776 135*t*; 1790 137*t*;
    1800 142*t*
  farms 39
  papermills 90
Middlesex County, N.J.
  census: 1784 153*t*; 1790 154*t*;
    1800 155*t*
  papermills 90
Middlesex County, Va.
  census: 1790 163*t*; 1800 165*t*
  taxables (1782–89) 162*t*
Middlesex Gore, Mass.
  census: 1790 138*t*
Middleton, Mass.
  census: 1776 135*t*; 1790 137*t*
Middleton, N.H.
  census: 1790 131*t*
Middleton, Henry 221
Middletown, Conn.
  census: 1774 144*t*; 1790 149*t*
  diphtheria epidemic 191
  distilling 82*t*
  lead mining 95
Middletown, N.Y.
  census: 1790 151*t*
Middletown, R.I.
  census: 1774 143*t*; 1790 143*t*;
    1800 148*t*
Middletown, Vt.
  census: 1790 133*t*
Midway, Vt.
  census: 1790 133*t*
Mifflin, Thomas 221*t*, 249
Mifflin County, Pa.
  census: 1790 157*t*; 1800 159*t*
Mikveh Israel Synagogue
  (Philadelphia) 205
Miles, Samuel 261
Milford, Conn.
  census: 1774 144*t*; 1790 149*t*
Milford, Mass.
  census: 1790 138*t*
military contributions (state)
  Continentals raised 234–240
  financial costs 228
  militia on campaign 234–240
  privateers commissioned 242
military draft 234
militia
  deployed with Continental
    Army 234–240
milk
  consumption 187*t*
  dietary allowances 185*t*
Mill Creek Meeting House
  (Va.) *203*
Milledgeville, Ga.
  state capital 211
Miller, Lewis (folk artist)
  paintings 124, 186, 206

millers
  fees for grinding 187*n*
  in workforce 95*t*
Millersburg, Ky.
  census: 1800 175*t*
Millfield, N.H.
  census: 1790 130*t*
"Millions for defense, but not one
  cent for tribute" (Harper, Apr. 3,
  1798) 36
mills, automated 295, *295*
Milton, Mass.
  census: 1776 135*t*; 1790 138*t*
Milton, Vt.
  census: 1790 132*t*
Minden, Vt.
  census: 1790 132*t*
Minehead, Vt.
  census: 1790 133*t*
mines *see* mining
mine warfare *see* Bushnell, David
Mingo Indians 16
  location 15*m*, 24*t*
  Lord Dunmore's War 19
  population 24*t*
  treaties 21*t*
  warriors 25*t*
mining
  coal 94–95
  copper 93–94
  lead 95
Minisink, N.Y.
  census: 1790 152*t*
ministers
  income (Virginia) 96*t*
mink pelt exports 79
Mint, U.S.
  coins issued 107
  opens 105
Missiaga Indians *see* Chippewa
Mississippi
  counties founded in 8*t*
  exploration 6*m*
  Indians 18
  population: censuses 176*t*
  territorial history 9, 36, 244
Missouri 14, 27
Mitchell, Samuel L. 196
Mitchill, Samuel Latham 291, 292
Mode, Magnus 321
Modern Chivalry (1792) 283
Mohawk, N.Y.
  census: 1790 152*t*
Mohawk Indians
  Christianity 14
  historical sketch 14
  land cessions 7, 22*t*
  location 15*m*, 24*t*
  population 24*t*
  treaties 22*t*
  warfare 19*t*
  warriors 25*t*
Mohawk Valley Indian raid 19
Mohegan Indians 24*t*
molasses
  consumption 187*t*
  dietary allowances 185*t*
  price movements 116*t*
  for rum 81

New York Society for the Promotion of Arts, Agriculture, and Economy 92
New York Society for the Suppression of Vice and Immorality 319
New York Stock Exchange Board 34, 109
New York Suspending Act (July 2, 1767) 28
Nicholas, Samuel
  Marine Corps commandant 242, 249
Nicholas County, Ky.
  census: 1800 175t
Nicholasville, Ky.
  census: 1800 175t
Nicholson Glassworks 88
Nigeria, slaves from 183t
Niles, Jeremiah 250
Nobleborough, Me.
  census: 1790 140t
Nockamixon, Pa.
  potteries 90t
Nomenclator 269
Nomenclature of the New Chemistry (1794) 291
noncommissioned officer, U.S. Army
  salary 98t
non-condensing steam engine 295
nonimportation agreement (1765) 27
nonimportation agreement (1767) 28, 258
nonimportation agreement (1774) see Continental Association
Norfolk, Conn.
  census: 1774 146t
Norfolk, Va.
  census: 1800 165t
  crowd disturbances 322t
  distilling 82t
  epidemics: yellow fever 191
  family sizes 180
  population 253t
  rank in state 251
Norfolk County, Mass.
  census: 1800 142t
  farms 39
Norfolk County, Va.
  census: 1790 163t; 1800 165t
  taxables (1782–89) 162t
Norridgewock, Me.
  census: 1790 140t
North, Lord 28, 32
Northampton, Mass.
  census: 1776 136t; 1790 137t
  diphtheria epidemic 191
  magazines published 278
Northampton, N.C.
  census: 1786 167t
Northampton, N.H.
  census: 1790 131t
Northampton County, N.C.
  census: 1790 167t; 1800 170t

Northampton County, Pa.
  census: 1790 158t; 1800 159t
  livestock 39, 43, 50, 52, 55
  taxpayers (1760–86) 155t
Northampton County, Va.
  census: 1790 163t; 1800 165t
Northborough, Mass.
  census: 1776 135t; 1790 138t
Northbridge, Mass.
  census: 1776 135t; 1790 139t
North Carolina
  American Revolution 21, 30
  average male height 187
  banking 108
  congressional representation: apportionment 222t; party affiliation 222–224t; turnover 215–217t
  elections: congressional turnover 215–217t; legislative turnover 211t; for presidential electors 215t; presidential returns 218t; voter eligiblity 212–213t; voter participation 214–215
  finances: debts federalized 229t; war expenses 228t
  forestry 73–74
  government: capital relocated 211t; constitutional change 209t; U.S. Constitution ratified 210t
  historical sketch 248
  hurricane 5t
  legislature: constituents per member 210t; qualifications 213t; size 210t; terms 210t; turnover 211t
  lotteries 315t
  military: wartime contributions: Continentals raised 234–240t; financial costs 228t; militia on campaign 234–240t
  newspapers 280t
  officeholders: chief justices 248; governors 248; how selected 209t; qualifications 213t; terms 209–210t
  population: censuses 167t–170t; density 11t, 12m
  regulators 322t
  religion: churches, by type 198; disestablishment 198
  servant imports 120t
  settlement of: area settled 12t; cedes western lands 9t; counties founded in 8t; western lands 9t, 33
  slave imports 183
  state university 269, 271
  taxation: revenues collected 231t; systems of 232t; taxes per capita 231t
  U.S. Constitution and 33–34
North Carolina Gazette 279t
North Castle, N.Y.
  census: 1790 152t

Northeast, N.Y.
  census: 1790 152t
Northfield, Mass.
  census: 1776 136t; 1790 137t
Northfield, N.H.
  census: 1790 131t
Northfield, N.Y.
  census: 1790 151t
Northfield, Vt.
  census: 1790 133t
North Hampton, N.H.
  census: 1773 127t
North Haven, Conn.
  1790 cesus 149t
North Hempstead, N.Y.
  census: 1790 151t
North Hero, Vt.
  census: 1790 132t
North Kingstown, R.I.
  census: 1774 142t; 1790 143t; 1800 148t
North Providence, R.I.
  census: 1774 143t; 1790 143t; 1800 148t
North Salem, N.Y.
  census: 1790 152t
Northumberland, N.H.
  census: 1773 129t; 1790 130t
Northumberland County, Pa.
  census: 1790 158t; 1800 159t
  taxpayers (1760–86) 155t
Northumberland County, Va.
  census: 1790 163t; 1800 165t
  taxables (1782–89) 162t
Northwest Ordinance (1787) 9–10, 33
Northwest Territory
  census: 1792 178t; 1800 178t
  Land Ordinance of 1785 33
Northwood, N.H.
  census: 1773 127t; 1790 131t
North Yarmouth, Me.
  census: 1776 136t; 1790 140t
Norton, Mass.
  census: 1776 135t; 1790 139t
Norwalk, Conn. 108
  census: 1774 144t; 1790 149t
  potteries 90t
Norway
  distribution of wealth 114
  exports to 102t
  imports 103
Norwich, Conn.
  census: 1774 144t
  distilling 82t
  library catalogue 275
  population 253t
  potteries 90t
  ranking in state 243
Norwich, England
  rank in British Empire 253
Norwich, Mass.
  census: 1776 136t; 1790 137t
Norwich, Vt.
  census: 1790 134t
Notes on the State of Virginia 266
Nottingham, N.H.
  census: 1773 127t; 1790 131t

Nottingham West, N.H.
  census: 1773 128t; 1790 131t
Nottoway County, Va.
  census: 1800 165t
Nottoway Indians 24t
Nova Scotia 94
novels
  authors (U.S.): Brackenridge, Hugh 283t; Brown, William H. 282; Foster, Hannah Webster 283, 283t; Rowson, Susanna Haswell 283, 283t
  best-sellers 283t
  female audience 282
  market for 282
  reprinted British 281
  Thomas Jefferson on 281
nullification 36
Number 1, Me.
  census: 1776 136t
Number 2, Me.
  census: 1776 136t
Number 4, Me.
  census: 1776 136t
Number 5, Mass.
  census: 1776 136t
Number 6, Me.
  census: 1776 136t
Number 7, Mass.
  census: 1776 136t
nutrition see diet

O
Oakham, Mass.
  census: 1776 135t; 1790 139t
oatmeal
  dietary allowances 185t
oat yield 41–42t
occupations 95–96 see also specific profession
  artisans: percent of workforce 95t, 96t
  incomes 96–97, 96t, 97t, 98t
  non-agricultural workers: percent of workforce 95t, 96t
  occupational structure 95–96
  structure of workforce 95–96
oceanic trade
  balance of 68, 99t, 103t
  exports 44–67, 72–82, 86–87, 91, 94, 99t–104t
  imports 99t–103t
officeholders
  how chosen 209–210t
  listed: chief justices (state) 243–252; Continental Congress presidents 221; governors 243–252; mayors 255, 257, 259, 261; presidents pro tempore 221; speakers of U.S. House 221; U.S. presidents 219; U.S. Supreme Court 225
  qualifications 213t
  terms of office 209t
Ogle, Benjamin 245
Oglethorpe County, Ga.
  census: 1800 173t
O'Hara glassworks, James 88

Wright, Patience 247, 284
Wrightstown, Pa.
  potteries 90t
Wyandot (Huron) Indians
  historical sketch 17
  location 15m, 24t
  population 24t
  treaties 21, 22
  warfare 19–20
  warriors 25t
Wyoming Valley, Pa. 9t
  massacre 19
Wythe County, Va.
  census: 1800 166t

X
Xenophon 273
XYZ Affair 36

Y
Yale College (Conn.)
  degrees awarded 272, 272t
  faculty 271
  library collection 276t
  medical education 196
Yale University see Yale College
Yankee Federal architecture 301–302, 302
yardarms 74
Yarmouth, Mass.
  census: 1776 135t; 1790 139t
  fishing fleet 65t
Yates, Robert 248
yellow fever 34, 191, 259, 261
yeoman-farmers 95t

Yonkers, N.Y.
  census: 1790 152t
York, Me.
  census: 1776 136t; 1790 141t
York, N.Y.
  census: 1790 152t
York, Pa.
  census: 1790 158t
  cuisine 186
  national capital 210
  occupational structure 96
  rank in state 249
  U.S. Circuit Court 225
York County, Me.
  census: 1776 136t; 1790 141t; 1800 142t
York County, Pa.
  census: 1790 158t; 1800 159t

taxpayers (1760–86) 155t
York County, S.C.
  census: 1790 171t; 1800 173t
York County, Va.
  census: 1790 164t; 1800 165t
Yorktown, Va., surrender at 32, 32, 209, 251, 268

Z
Zach, Franz von 289
Zoar Plantation, Mass.
  census: 1790 139t
zoology
  Bartram, William 6, 291
  Mitchill, Samuel L. 291
Zuntz, Alexander 110